World Security

CHALLENGES FOR A NEW CENTURY

SECOND EDITION

*A Project of the Five College Program
in Peace and World Security Studies*

Michael T. Klare

HAMPSHIRE COLLEGE

Daniel C. Thomas

CORNELL UNIVERSITY

ST. MARTIN'S PRESS
NEW YORK

Senior editor: Don Reisman
Manager, publishing services: Emily Berleth
Project management: Omega Publishing Services, Inc.
Art director: Sheree Goodman
Cover design: Glen Ruga/Visual Communications

For information, write:
St. Martin's Press, Inc.
175 Fifth Avenue
New York, NY 10010

ISBN: 0-312-08584-2 (paper)
       0-312-10265-8 (cloth)

Acknowledgments

It is a violation of the law to reproduce these selections by any means whatsoever without the written permission of the copyright holder.

An earlier version of Jessica Tuchman Mathews's chapter, "The Environment and International Security," appeared in *Foreign Affairs,* Spring 1989, Volume 68, Issue 2. Copyright 1989 by the Council on Foreign Affairs, Inc.

Portions of Thomas Homer-Dixon's chapter, "Environmental Scarcity and Intergroup Conflict," originally appeared in Thomas F. Homer-Dixon's "On the Threshold: Environmental Changes as Causes of Acute Conflict," *International Security,* Volume 16, Number 2 (Fall 1991), pp. 76–116. Reprinted by permission of the MIT Press.

Preface

We began work on the first edition of *World Security* in 1989, when it first became evident that the world was entering a period of systemic transformation. Our goal then was to provide college students and general readers with an introduction to what we believed would be the critical world security problems of the 1990s. Fortunately, we were able to revise the manuscript in late 1990, enabling us to refer to such key developments as the fall of the Berlin Wall and the onset of the Persian Gulf conflict. Nevertheless, earth-shattering events have continued to occur at breathtaking speed, and so, even as the first edition began to appear in bookstores, we knew that we would want to start work on a new edition—one that would be better positioned to analyze the sweeping changes of the post–Cold War era. This book is the result of that endeavor.

In preparing the second edition of *World Security,* we sought to go beyond a mere updating of the essays in the first edition—we sought to illuminate the emerging contours of the post–Cold War world and to consider how the global changes now under way will affect world security in the twenty-first century. Thus, we decided to delete some essays from the first edition on topics that we no longer consider crucial (for example, the U.S.-Soviet military competition in space), and to add new chapters on themes that now appear more pressing (such as regional conflict, violence against women, and global demographic change). The result, then, is an entirely new book—one that should remain salient for years to come.

Although the book is composed of a series of separate essays by different authors, it is designed as a comprehensive overview of the world security *problematique* of the 1990s. Thus, we begin with four essays (those by Seyom Brown, Daniel Nelson, Terry Karl and Philippe Schmitter, and Michael McFaul) on the broad political and social contours of the emerging international system. We then cover what we see as the critical world security issues of the post–Cold War era: nuclear proliferation, conventional arms trafficking, ethnic and regional conflict, Third World militarism, international human rights, violence against women, environmental degradation, demographic change, persistent underdevelopment, and world hunger.

In discussing these perils, each author was asked to provide a status report on the problem as it exists today, to speculate on the likely evolution of the problem in the years ahead, and to offer concrete suggestions for how these problems might be resolved or ameliorated by the international community. Not all of the resulting essays fit this model exactly, but they all provide the reader with a rigorous introduction to one of the critical world security issues of the post–Cold War era.

All of our authors naturally harbor their own views on the status of these various issues, and on how they can best be addressed; all of us, however, share a belief in the need for *global solutions* to what we see as *global problems*. This insistence on a globalist approach to the solution of international problems is encapsulated in the term *world security*, meaning the safety and well-being of all the world's nations and peoples. While we recognize that many people will continue to look to the nation-state to provide security against global perils, we believe that such nation-level efforts will not succeed unless supplemented by cooperative action at the international level. For this reason, we conclude the book with a discussion by Robert Johansen on the types of norms, treaties, and institutions that will be needed to devise and implement a cooperative agenda for the pursuit of world security in the twenty-first century.

By looking forward to the next century, we also hope to stimulate readers to devise new and innovative solutions to world problems. As suggested by the book's subtitle, "Challenges for a New Century," we expect that all of the perils addressed in this book will persist in some form well into the twenty-first century. We thus see a need both for the continuous improvement of remedies already at our disposal and for the development of new solutions. Some of this work can be done by the leaders and scholars of today, but much will of necessity be passed on to the leaders and scholars of tomorrow. It is our fervent hope that the student readers of this book will be ready to accept this challenge when they assume positions of responsibility in the years ahead.

At every stage in the production of this book, we relied on the advice and assistance of others—far more than we can thank properly here. Most important, of course, are the twenty-two individuals who wrote or coauthored the essays that appear in the book. All of these people are very busy, with multiple demands on their time, and we are truly grateful that they agreed to contribute an essay to this volume. We are confident that their efforts will be rewarded through the constructive impact of this book on its readers.

Next, we wish to express our appreciation for the advice and assistance provided by our colleagues and coworkers at the Five Colleges. Particular recognition is due to the Steering Committee of the Five College Program in Peace and World Security Studies (PAWSS), under whose auspices this volume was produced: Pavel Machala, William Taubman, and Ronald Tiersky of Amherst College; Elizabeth Hartmann and Allan Krass of Hampshire College; Asoka Bondarage and Vincent Ferraro of Mount Holyoke College; Deborah Lubar, Thomas Riddell, and Susan Peterson of Smith College; and James Der Derian, Eric Einhorn, George Levinger, and Mary Wilson of the University of Massachusetts. Special thanks are also due to Adi Bemak and Linda Harris of the PAWSS staff, and to Lorna Peterson and her colleagues at the Five College Center. Without the help and guidance of these people, we could never have completed a project as complex and demanding as this volume.

Daniel Thomas also wishes to acknowledge the helpful suggestions of his colleagues at Cornell University's Peace Studies Program and Stanford University's Center for International Security and Arms Control, where he resided during the editing of this book.

As with the first edition, we received outstanding cooperation from the fine people at St. Martin's Press, and we wish to acknowledge their support. For offering comments to St. Martin's about the book in its various stages of development, we wish to thank Simon Duke, Pennsylvania State University; Roger Hamburg, Indiana University—South Bend; Bradley S. Klein, Trinity College; Philip A. Schrodt, The University of Kansas; and Mohamed M. Wader, Portland State University.

Finally, and most important, we wish to thank our editor, Don Reisman, and his associate, Frances Jones, for their critical role in bringing this project to fruition.

Michael T. Klare and Daniel C. Thomas
Amherst, Mass.

Contents

Introduction: Thinking about World Security

Three and one-half years after the fall of the Berlin Wall, the new security challenges of the post–Cold War era are gradually coming into focus. As Warren Christopher remarked upon his appointment as secretary of state, the United States and the world face a diverse, and often unfamiliar, set of security concerns:

> While the risk of nuclear threat has diminished, the new era has produced a new set of dangers—ethnic and religious conflicts threaten to ignite widespread hostilities in Central and Eastern Europe. Weapons of mass destruction may reach the hands of untested and unstable powers, and new threats spring from old rivalries in the Middle East, in Europe, and in Asia. At the same time, we face a world where borders matter less and less, a world that demands we join with other nations to face challenges that range from overpopulation to AIDS, to the very destruction of our planet's life support system.[1]

Other recent surveys of the global security environment, including the declaration of the United Nation's first-ever summit of the heads of the member states of the Security Council, have identified a similar range of global problems.[2]

In order to respond appropriately to these new security challenges, we must do more than add new issues to the global agenda: we must change how we *think* about the nature and pursuit of security. Fortunately, this reconceptualization is already underway: citizens and policymakers alike are beginning to question whether traditional concepts of national interests and national security are appropriate to the political, economic, technological, and environmental challenges of the twenty-first century.

This book is designed to contribute to this discussion by introducing the concept of "world security" and the global agenda that springs from it. Our purpose in articulating a *world security* concept is not to suggest that citizens or policymakers should (or will) cease to be concerned about the security of their own country. We do hope, however, to stimulate a fundamental rethinking of the nature and the goals of human security, involving a recognition of the need to link national security to the well-being of the world at large. Other contributors to this volume may not accept every proposition advanced in this essay, and they often differ with one

1

another on key points of policy. Taken together, however, their essays provide a comprehensive introduction to "world security" thinking.

In this essay, we draw an especially sharp distinction between the concept of "national security" and that of "world security." Before discussing these individual concepts, however, we must clarify the nature of security concepts in general. Such concepts are neither causal theories—that is, theories that seek to explain particular outcomes in terms of particular causes—nor statements of fact. Although they rely on theoretical premises, and reflect observations of empirical facts, such concepts function as general organizing principles that policymakers and citizens rely upon to evaluate global trends. As such, a concept of security—whether national or world—cannot be disproven; it can only be adopted or rejected depending upon its analytical usefulness and its consistency with one's own normative or theoretical inclinations.

Moreover, the fact that two people profess adherence to a particular security concept does not necessarily mean that they will always agree on what course of action is appropriate in dealing with a specific challenge. Rather, a security concept provides a *framework* in which particular issues can be considered, and particular outcomes debated; it cannot, however, determine the outcome of any policy debate or the appropriate response to a given problem.

This having been said, we can proceed to a comparison of the national security and world security concepts. This comparison will focus in particular on the two concepts' different assumptions about the nature of international politics, the sources of insecurity, the role of unilateral versus cooperative remedies, and the ultimate standards by which security is assessed.

Starting at a theoretical level, the national security concept is heavily influenced by "Realist" theories of international relations—theories that emphasize the absence of world government and the relative distribution of power among states as the primary determinants of state behavior.[3] According to the Realists, international cooperation is impeded by states' need to prioritize self-interest when it conflicts with a larger collective interest. Second, foreign military attack is seen as posing a constant and overriding threat to the physical survival of states and their populations. Third, the security of national societies is considered to be segregatable, and thus achievable by unilateral means; in other words, one state may be secure while its neighbors or rivals are insecure. As a result, a state's security is thought to reflect the balance of power among rival states, and it is assumed therefore that the surest method for a state to achieve security in this context is to maximize its unilateral military capabilities. Effective management of the balance of power, including the ability to threaten the use of military force, is thus the hallmark of national security strategy.[4]

To the extent that security analysts have attempted to incorporate other issues, such as economics or the environment, under the rubric of "national security," they have generally had to depart from these core assumptions.[5]

Such departures are required because, when dealing with issues such as ozone depletion or resource degradation, attempts to maximize one's own welfare without regard for others tends to impede rather than to facilitate the pursuit of appropriate solutions. The resulting interest in nurturing "positive-sum" political dynamics—that is, behavior that is intended to result in gain to many parties—represents less a modification of the traditional concept of national security than tentative steps toward an alternative security approach.

In the final years of the Cold War era, as the imminent threat of nuclear war receded and new issues come to the fore, some independent scholars and political figures began to articulate aspects of what we call here the "world security" paradigm. Particularly noteworthy were international commission reports on the global political economy chaired by former German Chancellor Willy Brandt,[6] on the global arms race chaired by former Swedish Prime Minister Olof Palme,[7] and on the global environment chaired by Norwegian Prime Minister Gro Bruntland.[8] At the same time, grassroots movements from around the world added their voices to the mounting dissatisfaction with the national security paradigm and the policy priorities it engendered.[9]

As implied above, the world security concept is inspired by recognition of a range of new perils that transcend national borders and exceed the reactive capabilities of nation-states. It is informed theoretically by a range of theories that emphasize the growth of global interdependence and the possibility of international cooperation.[10] These theories view world politics not as a historically frozen realm of power-hungry states, but rather as a dynamic process of interaction among individuals, groups, states, and international institutions, all of which are capable of adapting their sense of self-interest in response to new information and changing circumstances.

Continuing competition between states may be likely, as the Realists suggest, but adaptation and cooperation in pursuit of joint gains *are* possible. This process is evident, for example, in the concerted international response to the depletion of ozone in the global atmosphere. The theoretical challenge, then, is to provide evidence for a reconceptualization of human security interests and to identify the political and institutional mechanisms that permit expanded cooperation.

The first departure of world security from the national security concept is the recognition that security is often interdependent, and thus not sustainable through unilateral means. In fact, measures taken by one state in pursuit of its own security interests often decrease the security of others.[11] For instance, the buildup of nuclear weapons—however justified by principles of "deterrence"—is inevitably viewed as threatening by rival states, leading them to adopt reciprocal measures that in turn appear threatening to the first state. Instead of interpreting this "security dilemma" as an obstacle to cooperation, however, the world security perspective sees it as the reason to develop adaptive strategies, such as arms reduction and the defensive restructuring of forces, aimed at promoting a more fundamental common-ality of interests.[12]

This commonality of interests is even more evident in nonmilitary areas—and especially in the economic and environmental areas—where adverse trends in one state quickly spill across national boundaries. From the nuclear fallout that encircled the globe after the Chernobyl meltdown in 1986 to the global warming that increasingly threatens the earth's ecosys-tem, and from the destabilization of national currencies induced by trans-national capital flows to the global recession that follows depressed demand in major markets, the most serious challenges to security in today's world are not contained within the boundaries of individual states.

Interdependence does not automatically abolish competitive politics among states—in some cases it may even increase competition—but the intermingling of our fates limits the options available to policymakers and provides real incentives for cooperation in the pursuit of security. As Presi-dent Bill Clinton suggested in his 1993 Inaugural Address: "There is no longer division between what is foreign and what is domestic—the world economy, the world environment, the world AIDS crisis, the world arms race—they affect us all."[13] In this context, as the Brandt, Palme, and Brunt-land Commissions first argued, the surest route to security for one nation is pursuing security for all nations.

As we have seen, the world security concept is also distinguished by the belief that security involves more than protection against military attack. Indeed, for the nations of the industrialized "North," the risk of such attack has greatly diminished due to the existence of vast nuclear arsenals, the interconnectedness of economies and societies, and the relative robustness of regional institutions.[14] On the other hand, ecological, economic, and demographic trends pose serious challenges to these countries. And even in the less-developed "South," where the threat of armed conflict remains sig-nificant, nonmilitary trends pose equal or greater threats to people's secu-rity. In most cases, states are proving less and less capable of meeting these diverse challenges.

We thus conclude that human security cannot be measured by compar-ing states' relative preparation for war. Instead, the world security approach assesses existing security conditions and proposed remedies in terms of such criteria as the promotion of human rights and the protection of the global environment.[15] States sometimes promote and sometimes deny these values, but national sovereignty is not assumed to be a reliable surrogate or guar-antee of security. When human rights and the environment are protected, people's lives and identities are likely to be secure; where they are not pro-tected, people are not secure, regardless of the military capacity of the state under which they live.

As indicated, every contributor to this volume does not necessarily share this understanding of the world security paradigm. Taken together, however, the collection of essays reflects the range of issues and the globalist approach that we have associated with the world security perspective.

The first two chapters in the volume explore some of these larger themes of human security and international politics in general terms.

In "World Interests and the Changing Dimensions of Security," Seyom Brown explores the widening gap between the structures of governance inherited from the Cold War era and the challenges we face in the world of today. Brown identifies a set of "world interests" as a basis for assessing policy alternatives, and concludes with suggestions for institutional measures that the international community could take to increase accountability among member states.

Daniel Nelson's essay, "Great Powers and World Peace," addresses the problems created by relying on the military capacities of states as the principal basis of world order. He also identifies the negative regional consequences that could follow from a more assertive international role for the German and Japanese militaries, and calls instead for the great powers to develop collective mechanisms for conflict prevention.

The next two chapters address processes of democratization whose outcome will shape the character of world politics and the likelihood of international cooperation well into the next century.

Terry Karl and Philippe Schmitter begin their essay on "Democratization around the Globe" by placing the collapse of communism in Eastern Europe in the context of the global struggle for democratization seen worldwide since the mid-1970s. They discuss the serious problems involved in consolidating the new democracies of Latin America, Asia, Africa, and Eastern Europe, and consider the international implications—including intensified intergroup tension and the destabilization of borders—that often accompany a lessening of repression.

Michael McFaul explores the processes, problems, and implications of democratization in Russia. In particular, he discusses the difficulty of attempting to consolidate political democracy while privatizing and revitalizing a stalled economy. He then identifies several possible outcomes of the present struggle in Russia, and considers their implications for Russia's relations with the other former Soviet republics, with the West, and with the world at large.

The next three chapters address security threats arising from the global abundance of armaments, both nuclear and conventional.

In "The Second Nuclear Era," Allan Krass considers one of the most significant and dangerous legacies of the Cold War: the existence of tens of thousands of nuclear weapons in the stockpiles of the United States and the successor states of the Soviet Union. He begins by questioning the logic for maintaining such weapons in U.S. arsenals, and argues for a substantial reduction in their number. Krass also examines the immense technical problems that must be overcome in dealing with all of the nuclear weapons that are slated for destruction (especially those in Russian hands).

Zachary Davis then addresses the problems arising from the spread of nuclear weapons to the Third World, and analyzes the effectiveness of the Nuclear Nonproliferation Treaty (NPT) in light of recent revelations concerning Iraq's secret weapons program. Davis also discusses the proliferation problems arising from the dissolution of the Soviet Union, and evaluates the various measures being considered for reinforcement of the existing nonproliferation regime.

In "Adding Fuel to the Fires," Michael Klare examines the international trade in nonnuclear, "conventional" weapons. He argues that such trafficking is likely to increase in the post–Cold War era, thereby intensifying local arms races and increasing the destructiveness and duration of regional wars. Klare concludes with a discussion of proposals for international control of the arms trade.

These three essays are followed by six chapters on problems of war, militarization, international peacekeeping, and human rights.

In "Regional Conflicts in the Post–Cold War Era," Louis Kriesberg analyzes the nature and dynamics of regional wars, and discusses the various strategies that have been developed to prevent, control, and resolve such conflicts. While insisting that prevention is the best response to this problem, he shows that a variety of creative peacemaking techniques have been devised in recent years to resolve existing conflicts with a minimum of bloodshed.

Donald Horowitz then examines one of the most widespread, and often intractable, sources of political disintegration and violence in the contemporary world: ethnic conflict. Ranging broadly over many cases, he argues that ethnic and nationalist conflicts have very diverse causes, take many different forms, and thus pose a very significant challenge to the international community.

In the post–Cold War world, the United Nations is increasingly called upon to prevent or resolve regional conflicts of all sorts. Margaret Karns and Karen Mingst's essay on international peacekeeping shows how the world body has adapted itself to changing demands and opportunities over time, but argues that its effectiveness depends upon the political and financial capital that the leading states alone can provide. Continued innovation and expansion of the UN's peacemaking capabilities is possible, they conclude, but will require unprecedented political support.

In the next chapter, Nicole Ball analyzes the historical roots and distinctive character of militarization in the Third World. She shows that the growth of Third World military forces is rarely a response to external military threats but more often a product of internal political considerations (particularly the efforts of ruling elites to preserve their power and prerogatives in the face of popular discontent). Ball concludes with a discussion of various methods for promoting the demilitarization of Third World societies.

Closely related to problems of militarization and democratization is that of the protection of human rights. In "International Human Rights after the

Cold War," Jack Donnelly traces the evolution of international concern about human rights since 1945 and identifies the most pressing human rights issues of the present era. He discusses the spread of rights-protective regimes in recent years, but warns that the present wave of democratization is unleashing passions often incompatible with the protection of human rights.

In "Global Violence against Women," Charlotte Bunch and Roxanna Carrillo argue that traditional concepts of human rights fail to acknowledge the degree to which women around the world are subjected to violence and discrimination solely on the basis of their gender. Showing that patterns of gender violence and exploitation are entrenched everywhere, they argue for the expansion of human rights concepts that would include greater protection for women against—and thereby allow for greater participation by women in—the process of development.

The next five chapters focus on related problems of the environment, population growth, underdevelopment, and world hunger.

In "The Environment and International Security," Jessica Mathews argues that existing concepts of national and international security must be modified in light of the growing evidence of severe environmental threats to human survival. She shows that a combination of population growth, resource depletion, and human-induced changes in the global ecosphere could combine in catastrophic fashion. Only by developing common, multilateral responses to these problems, Mathews argues, can world leaders successfully avert such disasters.

Thomas Homer-Dixon carries this analysis further in his discussion of the relationship between environmental decline and intergroup conflict. By examining a number of illustrative case studies, he shows that environmental decline is already affecting world security by degrading the habitability of certain areas and forcing the people who live there to migrate to other areas—often provoking conflict in the process.

A related set of problems is considered by Dennis Pirages in his essay "Demographic Change and Ecological Insecurity." Arguing that population growth and persistent poverty in resource-poor areas of the Third World are fueling increased migration to already overpopulated cities in the South and to unwelcoming states in the North, Pirages suggests that demographic pressures are likely to prove a major source of intergroup conflict in the decades ahead.

Vincent Ferraro and Melissa Rosser address the Third World debt crisis—another problem that affects the living conditions of hundreds of millions of people worldwide, yet defies solution by individual states. After evaluating the origins of the Third World's massive debt, Ferraro and Rosser explain how this debt is breeding instability in Third World states and hindering economic expansion in the world at large. The only economically and politically viable solution, they conclude, is one that takes account of the welfare of weak Third World states and their populations.

Finally, in his chapter on world hunger, Joseph Collins shows how many of the developments noted earlier—environmental decline, persistent under-development, undemocratic political systems, and population growth—are combining to deprive adequate foodstuffs to the hundreds of millions of humans who are suffering from hunger and malnutrition. Collins argues that hunger can be overcome if political and economic power is distributed more equitably and thus poor people are better able to command the resources needed for their survival.

The book concludes with a chapter on international institution-building by Robert Johansen. Suggesting that existing international institutions are inadequate for overcoming the various world security perils described in the previous chapters, Johansen provides a blueprint for new and strengthened institutions. Johansen also lays out a new international "code of conduct" that must be honored if we are to avert perpetual warfare and ecological disaster in the twenty-first century.

Articulating the outlines of a "world security" perspective is only the start. However much one may hope for a solution to any given problem, the world's peoples will not soon be organized under a single political authority, nor share a homogenized universal culture. If they are to have any hope of success, proposed remedies to global problems must address the potential for conflict that is inherent in a pluralistic world system.

The essays that follow illustrate the urgency of a new approach to global problems, outline some of the possible courses of action, and assess the difficulties that will be encountered en route. Taken together, they should help students and scholars to begin thinking in terms of world security, and give policymakers at the national and international levels a new perspective on the challenges we face in preparing for the twenty-first century.

Notes

1. As quoted in *The New York Times,* December 23, 1992, pg. A10.
2. For the text of the UN summit declaration, see *The New York Times,* February 1, 1992. See also Paul Kennedy, *Preparing for the Twenty-first Century* (New York: Random House, 1993).
3. On contemporary realist thought, see Kenneth N. Waltz, *Theory of International Politics* (Reading, MA: Addison-Wesley, 1979); Robert O. Keohane, ed., *Neorealism and Its Critics* (New York: Columbia University Press, 1986).
4. See Donald M. Snow, *National Security: Enduring Problems in a Changing Defense Environment,* 2d ed., (New York: St. Martin's Press, 1991).
5. See Richard H. Ullman, "Redefining Security," *International Security* 8:1, Summer 1983.
6. Independent Commission on International Development Issues, Willy Brandt, chairman, *North-South: A Programme for Survival* (Cambridge, MA: MIT Press, 1980).
7. Independent Commission on Disarmament and Security Issues, Olof Palme, chairman, *Common Security: A Blueprint for Survival* (New York: Simon & Schuster, 1982).
8. World Commission on Environment and Development, Gro Harlem Bruntland, chairman, *Our Common Future* (New York: Oxford University Press, 1987).
9. For an analysis of the content and significance of these grassroots positions, see R. B. J. Walker, *One World, Many Worlds* (Boulder, CO: Lynne Reinner Publishers, 1988).

10. See, for example, Emanuel Adler and Beverly Crawford, eds., *Progress in Postwar International Relations* (New York: Columbia University Press, 1991); Robert O. Keohane and Joseph P. Nye, eds., *Transnational Relations and World Politics* (Cambridge, MA: Harvard University Press, 1972); Keohane and Nye, *Power and Interdependence,* 2nd ed., (Glencoe, IL: Scott, Foresman Publishers, 1987); Keohane, "Neoliberal Institutionalism: A Perspective on World Politics," in *International Institutions and State Power: Essays in International Relations Theory* (Boulder, CO: Westview Press, 1989); Stephen D. Krasner, ed., *International Regimes* (Ithaca, NY: Cornell University Press, 1983); James R. Rosenau, *Turbulence in World Politics: A Theory of Continuity and Change* (Princeton, NJ: Princeton University Press, 1990); and Oran R. Young, *International Cooperation: Building Regimes for Natural Resources and the Environment* (Ithaca, NY: Cornell University Press, 1989).

11. For discussion of how the "security dilemma" hinders cooperation, see John Herz, "Idealist Internationalism and the Security Dilemma," *World Politics* 2, January 1950; and Robert Jervis, "Cooperation under the Security Dilemma," *World Politics* 30:2, January 1978.

12. See Richard Smoke and Andrei Kortunov, eds., *Mutual Security: A New Approach to Soviet-American Relations* (New York: St. Martin's Press, 1991); and Richard Ned Lebow and Janice Gross Stein, "Beyond Deterrence," *Journal of Social Issues* 43:4, 1987.

13. Quoted in *The Washington Post,* January 21, 1993, p. A26.

14. See James Goldgeier and Michael McFaul, "A Tale of Two Worlds: Core and Periphery in the Post-Cold War Era," *International Organization* 46:2, Spring 1992.

15. For an earlier articulation of this position, see Robert C. Johansen, *The National Interest and the Human Interest: An Analysis of U.S. Foreign Policy* (Princeton, NJ: Princeton University Press, 1980).

1 / World Interests and the Changing Dimensions of Security

SEYOM BROWN

This essay offers a conceptual framework for understanding and responding to the expanding range of security issues featured in the following chapters. I find that the so-called "realist" view of international relations does not provide such a framework, since it fails to adequately comprehend the incongruence that has developed between the anarchic structure of the nation-state system and the increasing interdependence of the world's peoples.[1] I argue that policies and institutions for relieving the threatening incongruities need to be informed by a concept of *world interests* that will provide a basis for reconciling or arbitrating among conflicting national, transnational, and subnational interests, and that will legitimize giving priority to the needs of humankind as a whole.

THE INADEQUACY OF "REALISM"[2]

The major contribution of the "realists" has been their virtually exclusive focus on nation-states (meaning, for the most part, national governments) as both agents and objects of the most significant occurrences in world politics. There has been considerable justification for this focus, since in a world polity structured basically as an anarchic system of nation-states, individuals and peoples must rely ultimately on the power and authority of the national government in whose jurisdiction they reside to secure their basic needs and amenities. The "realists," accordingly, deem it appropriate that national statespersons in every country are obligated first and foremost to do all they can to serve "the national interest"—the safety and well-being of the nation as a whole.

But the narrowly focused "realist" lens fails to illuminate many of the momentous developments occurring within, above, and across the jurisdictions of the nation-states and that, as shown below and in the following chapters, are creating dangerous incongruities in world politics and society. The peaceable and just amelioration of these incongruities will require enhancement of the authority of norms and institutions to which the nation-states themselves must be held accountable—a development considered infeasible, to the extent it is addressed at all, in most contemporary "realist" treatises on international relations.

Another contribution of the "realists" has been their persistent attention to the international distribution of coercive power, especially military capabilities and resources, but also other resources that can be used coercively. Citing as the essence of political wisdom Thucydides's account of the Athenian warning to the Melians that the strong can have their way with the weak, contemporary "realists" confidently invoke the historical record in support of the proposition that force is ultima ratio of international relations. Presumably, no nation can reliably secure its existence and well-being unless it can fend off or overwhelm the coercive capabilities of its rivals—if not by itself, then in combination with the capabilities of its allies. As Hans Morgenthau taught, in the anarchic world polity, rational statecraft requires the pursuit of the national interest defined in terms of power. Foreign policy, from this perspective, is essentially national security policy, which in turn is predominantly military policy (that is, about the threat and use of force); and international relations analysts and theorists are doing their job when they give heavy emphasis to military balances of power and alliance relationships.

To be sure, attention to the distribution of coercive power among countries is a necessary aspect of statecraft in the anarchic world polity, and those concerned with national or world security ignore this dimension of international relations at their peril. Necessary yes; sufficient no. For while war continues to be available as an ultimate arbiter of international disputes, most of the issues over which peoples must deal with each another across national borders in this age of burgeoning interdependence (import barriers and export subsidies; rules for the investment, transfer, and exchange of money; interest rates; regulations on international transportation and communication; migration; the use of transborder and global ecologies) are best handled—and usually handled—at levels of bargaining far removed from the exchange of threats of military action.

There may well be the temptation for those dissatisfied with bargaining outcomes in the normal arenas to "up the ante" to threats of violence; particularly if the dissatisfied parties have access to powerful military or paramilitary forces. But this is precisely the problem with a model of international relations that attributes negotiating outcomes largely to the distribution of coercive capabilities, and that is morally neutral with respect to crossing the threshold between nonviolent bargaining and the use of force. The "realist" model, to the extent that it influences the way officials and policy analysts view their options, tends to be self-confirming, in that it perpetuates a picture of an international system in which it is futile to attempt to substantially reduce the reliance on military power.

But is this model of the way the world works truly *realistic*? Does it provide a conceptual framework that can assist contemporary statespersons and citizens in making policy choices that are rational (let alone morally tenable) in the sense of servicing their basic interests and values?

Perhaps the "realist" model did essentially correspond to the reality of world politics during most of the three centuries preceding World War II.

The dominant statecraft then operated on the premise that the most intensive patterns of human interaction would take place *within* territorially demarcated countries. Each of these presumably sovereign states would control interpersonal and intergroup behavior within its jurisdiction to provide at least the minimum personal and institutional security necessary for the performance of basic societal functions: the protection of persons and property from physical attack; the enforcement of laws and contracts; the orderly exchange of goods and services; the husbanding of resources essential to the healthy survival of the population; and the maintenance of the society's cultural, moral, and legal norms, including the rights and obligations of individuals and standards of distributive justice. Interstate and transborder interactions would be relatively sparse and could be managed, for the most part, by diplomacy, or by war when conflict was unresolvable by peaceful bargaining. Most countries would be willing to take their chances in this anarchic world polity when it came to handling international relations, in preference to subordinating the sovereignty of their territorial unit to "supranational" governing bodies purporting to act on behalf of some larger inchoate international community.

The contemporary world system, however, departs considerably from the traditional picture of sovereign nation-states warily interacting with each other only at the margins of their existence. As will be argued below, and as other chapters in this book show in greater detail, the separate nation-states have become ever-more impotent in dealing on their own (that is, mainly through *national* laws and *national* institutions) with material and political realities that are increasingly threatening the safety and well-being of their citizens.

At best, the "realist" model, while continuing to generate elegant theoretical discourse, has become largely irrelevant to policy analysis because of its failure to comprehend some of the most serious predicaments of contemporary society.[3] At worst, the effort to conduct statecraft-as-usual in terms of this model can jeopardize the healthy survival of the human species. It has become an anachronistic, if not counterproductive, frame of reference for individuals as well as for collectivities, since the attempt to secure the power of the nation-state of which one is a citizen is no longer, in many areas of one's life, a sufficient, or even the best, means for protecting or advancing one's interests and basic values.

THE INCONGRUENCE OF SOCIETY AND GOVERNANCE IN THE NATION-STATE SYSTEM[4]

The "realist" model, in short, diverts our attention from the most profound structural problem of contemporary world society: the widening gap between (a) the emergent realities of material interdependence and patterns of interaction among peoples and (b) the inherited legal/political structure of the nation-state system. This incongruence is creating dangerous instabilities along at least five interrelated dimensions of civil society: the peace and public order dimension, the commercial dimension, the ecological dimension, the cultural dimension, and the human rights dimension. Political systems owe their viability and legitimacy to their effectiveness in servicing the public order, commercial, ecological, cultural, and human rights needs of communities. Where a society's highest agencies of governance—the national governments, in the case of world society—neither adequately control, represent, nor are accountable to the most active human groupings in these fields, the society's political system is in crisis and the values of civil society are insecure.

The Crisis in World Public Order

Many of the post–Cold War headline-grabbing events—violent secessionist and self-determination movements; xenophobic attacks against refugee and immigrant groups in Western Europe; contraband in nuclear, chemical, and biological weaponry; criminal activities of transnational drug syndicates; international terrorism—are symptoms of the incongruence of society and governance in the international system. Autonomous national enclaves of security and order, isolated from the "chaos" of the world at large, are becoming unviable. Affluence, cultural homogeneity, and powerful national armies and navies are no longer sufficient bases for sustaining barriers against one's country being penetrated, if not engulfed, by hostile or unwanted people, substances, or ideas that can disturb the domestic peace.[5]

Human society cannot return to the simpler political configurations for assuring public order that prevailed before the twentieth-century revolutions in transportation and communication technology. Efforts to restore national border controls against waves of migrants escaping from political persecution or economic destitution, for example, are not only very expensive but also demand levels of policing contrary to the open-society traditions of most of the advanced industrial democracies. Nor can the growing transboundary contraband in weapons, drugs, and other harmful substances be effectively suppressed simply by tightening surveillance by customs officials at standard points of entry. An unprecedented degree of multilateral cooperation (and trust) between policing agencies at operational levels is required for apprehending the deftly evasive and transnational criminal syndicates, themselves utilizing highly sophisticated communications systems and countersurveillance technologies.

Political terrorism, too, is facilitated by the new technologies for rapid international movement of people, materials, and messages and by the fact that much of this movement, at the commercial and governmental levels, is exposed and vulnerable, while secret terrorist networks have the luxury of stealth and surprise, sometimes aided clandestinely by paramilitary and spy agencies of disaffected states. Counterterrorism, even when engaged in the relatively narrow mission of meeting force and brutality with counterforce, is unlikely to be very effective against such transnational networks if it is conducted, for the most part, unilaterally through national agencies.

Meanwhile, new technologies of warfare have been overwhelming and rendering dysfunctional even the traditional alliance and power-balancing processes of the nation-state system—the system's principal means of protecting relatively weak and small countries from attack and bullying by more powerful adversaries. When going to war can place the national community at high risk of virtually total destruction (which can happen readily today, even with "conventional" weapons), an intolerable strain is put on alliance relationships. Publics and parliaments begin to question whether any foreign interests, save perhaps those deemed essential to the defense of the homeland itself, are worth the destruction of the entire national community. Countries lacking sufficient military force of their own to deter provocations from a great power armed with awesome destructive capabilities are no longer able to count on allies to redress the imbalance of power. Formal "mutual security" pacts are suspected of being hollow commitments, unlikely to be honored at moments of truth. Even before the end of the Cold War, NATO and the Warsaw Pact, under the impact of Mutual Assured Destruction capabilities of the superpowers, were experiencing this profound crisis of credibility; only the demise of the U.S.-Soviet rivalry mooted the need for a fundamental reappraisal of the strategic worth of these alliances.

Could an enhancement of the collective security features of the United Nations ameliorate those aspects of the world public-order crisis that result from a declining credibility of great-power deterrent threats? Not unless there were a collateral change in the constitutive national sovereignty norms of the nation-state system—norms that remain deeply imbedded in the United Nations Charter. For as long as the military forces that can be deployed under direct command and control of the United Nations organization will be clearly inferior to the military forces remaining under the sovereign control of national governments who might be adversaries in future international conflicts, the actual implementation of United Nations collective security decisions will continue to fall to particular militarily well-endowed countries; and these countries will still have to generate national decisions that incur the prospect of terrible war costs, including having to absorb retaliatory strikes on their homelands from the aggressor states. The contemplation of such costs and risks are still likely to prompt the militarily capable guardians of world order to work against true UN collective security responses in particular cases, and certainly against giving any UN agencies standing authority to *order* members' forces into action.

The role of the United Nations in response to Iraq's 1990 invasion of Kuwait might seem to contradict this pessimistic assessment. But the functioning of the world organization in the 1990–91 Gulf war, like the UN action in Korea forty years earlier, was an anomaly—brought on by circumstances unlikely to recur. The aggressor, Iraq, had no allies among the permanent members of the UN Security Council in 1990 who might be willing to oppose the Bush administration's desire to obtain international legitimacy for its plans to remove Iraq from Kuwait by force. The Bush administration had convinced itself and a majority of the American public that allowing Saddam Hussein to keep control of Kuwait would put a Hitler-like aggressor in a position to control the economically and strategically crucial energy resources of the Middle East. Moreover, the ensuing military action against Iraq, as happened in Korea in 1950, was not really a "collective security" operation; it was, by design of the Bush administration, undertaken by only a handful of countries acting in the mode of a traditional ad hoc military coalition, and mobilized and directed by the coalition leader, the United States.

In short, the world is still operating basically under a national self-help, military power-balancing mode of enforcing minimum global order, while the threats to community and individual security are becoming increasingly transnational. Ultimately, weakly armed states may still have to rely on the old type of alliance commitments to secure themselves against powerful aggressors, while most people know (like the child who shouted "the emperor has no clothes") such commitments, given the society-devastating effects of modern war, are becoming less and less credible.

Transnational Economy versus National Polity

The ability of individuals and communities to secure what they value for themselves and their posterity is also jeopardized by the growing incongruence between the world's most dynamic contemporary economic relationships and its traditional political structure (the nation-state system and its legal norms of national sovereignty and noninterference by foreigners in a country's domestic affairs).

Government agencies, commercial enterprises, political movements, and criminal syndicates in possession of (or able to use) advanced transportation and communication systems can leapfrog many of the controls on the movements of people, goods, and information across international borders, by which countries traditionally have attempted to retain sovereignty over their national economies. More than ever before, in fields crucial to the functioning of a country's system and the well-being of its people, investors and producers and buyers and sellers are thickly linked in networks of interdependence with their customers or suppliers in other countries. In some fields the interdependencies give rise to collusion across national borders, with transnational interests conspiring, as it were, in price, supply, and market-sharing arrangements and to bring pressure on their respective national governments.

Decisions of giant multinational/multiproduct firms to invest in new plants here or there, to build roads and seaports, or to pull up stakes for a more congenial locale, can drastically affect (positively and negatively) the life chances of people the world over. Constituting a family of firms located in different countries, and joined together by a head office usually located in one of the advanced industrial countries, many multinational corporations have greater impact on the world economy than do some of the important nation-states.

The emergent breed of powerful transnational entrepreneurs comprises more than producers and marketers of goods and services. The movers and shakers also include banks, investment houses, and money brokers engaged in the global distribution of capital, the lifeblood of every country's economy. The most effective entrepreneurs in this money arena often operate through multiple partnerships, and have financial ties to and strategic information on all the world's major money markets and to firms in numerous countries—"enterprise webs," Robert Reich calls them—that enable them to obtain early information on changes in demand for products and services and contemplated shifts in interest rates or currency values.[6] These transnational enterprise webs frequently transfer huge financial investments in and out of countries to take advantage of demand shifts and in anticipation of currency devaluations or upward revaluations by particular countries. The tremendous amounts of money circulating around these networks of currency speculators now changes national hands so fast that the whole thrust of a country's domestic policy can be overthrown, literally overnight, by nongovernmental financial transactions.

By comparison, the national official agencies operating in the fields of commerce and banking are sluggish and lack spans of control congruent with the global scope of operation of the most dynamic transnationals. The ascendancy of the new breed of globally active transnational entrepreneurs is generating new insecurities among other groups. Some have ample reason to worry. When a country's policies for regulating national markets can be avoided or overwhelmed by transnational buyers, sellers, and investors, the national polity is eroded at its very essence: the capacity to sustain, within the country's jurisdiction, national standards of health and safety, orderly commerce, social justice, and the integrity of the national culture.

Mismatch between Ecology and Polity

It is now common knowledge that nature-altering technologies employed by humans in their pursuit of economic and political security are jeopardizing ecological conditions required for the sustenance of healthy human life on the planet. Yet human society has been dangerously slow, if not baffled, when it comes to developing political/legal instruments to effectively counter even the most serious and widely recognized ecological threats—cancer-producing sun rays flooding through the depleted ozone layer, and excessive global warming from the thickening of greenhouse gases in the atmosphere.

This new security predicament results to a large extent from the lack of sufficient correspondence between the basic political structure of world society (built on the foundation of autonomous nation-states) and the structure of the natural environment (which is unavoidably transnational in many of its dimensions). Originally formed in part to harness an area's natural ecologies, many of the world's territorially specific political jurisdictions are not at all congruent with dimensions of the ecologies now being perturbed.

Some of the most tangible and immediately visible disturbances are against natural ecologies that, while transnational in scope, are still local and regional. And many of these, as forecast in Chapter 15 by Thomas Homer-Dixon and Chapter 16 by Dennis Pirages, will be exacerbated over the coming decades as population growth and industrialization strain and deplete essential environmental resources. The resulting conflicts over access to and control of scarce resources are likely to be of the kind that historically have been least susceptible to noncoercive diplomatic resolution in the anarchic world polity.

To the traditional war-provoking disputes over rights to navigate, fish, or divert the waters of rivers, lakes, or seas used in common by various countries we now have added conflicts over the pouring of effluents in such bodies of water that can degrade their value for other users. Similarly, the growing awareness of how the injection of industrial by-products into the planet's other highly mobile medium—the atmosphere—can severely injure agricultural productivity, as well as cause life-threatening human illness in neighboring populations, has multiplied the opportunities for nations to get angry against one another. In addition, transborder injuries caused by mega-accidents, such as nuclear power-plant meltdowns and oil-tanker spills, further expose the inadequacy of the existing political/legal order to handle the interdependencies and mutual vulnerabilities of peoples across national lines.

Nations without States

Humans characteristically seek to secure not only their physical survival, health, and material possessions, but also a way of life—meaning, a set of beliefs about good and bad behavior, folkways, language and art forms, and religious views about their place in the universe. This typically translates into membership in a national community with others committed to essentially the same way of life, usually as a result of similar ancestral ties and historical experiences. National communities located within states whose territorial boundaries are essentially congruent with them tend to have a better chance of securing their way of life than do national communities that are minorities in states run by other national communities. Understandably, most nations would prefer to have states of their own; and throughout history, wars have been initiated by nations attempting to realize this goal against states within which they feel unjustly subordinated.

A stable world polity, in theory, would be one in which most large nations lived within their own states. Conversely, a system of presumably sovereign states characterized by a high degree of incongruence between state boundaries and the location of major nationality groups would be inherently unstable. If true, this augurs poorly for the stability of the contemporary world polity, given the wide dispersal of nationality groups across state boundaries—political demarcations that, more often than not, have been drawn by powerful multinational states for reasons of their military and economic security, largely indifferent to the desires of the peoples affected. Indeed, the notion of a stable nation-state system has turned out to be an oxymoron—and an increasingly dangerous one, conducive to neither individual security, national security, nor world security, especially given the wide dispersal of weapons of mass destruction.

Human Rights versus State Sovereignty

The efforts of many people around the world to secure for themselves and their families what are widely claimed be their fundamental human rights— "life, liberty, and the pursuit of happiness [variously defined]"—and, in some places, certain minimum levels of economic welfare, often contradict the foundational norms of the nation-state system: the sovereignty of each country and the prohibition against intervention by foreigners in a country's internal affairs. On the one hand, we have the insistence that every human being, simply by virtue of being human, has certain basic rights vis-à-vis all other humans and that governments are created to secure these rights—in other words, all human beings are "naturally" endowed with rights, but governments and other collectivities possess merely artificial and recallable powers. On the other hand, we have the prevailing state-centric view that a stable and durable community is at least the necessary context for, if not the source of, individual human rights, and that, therefore, the existing governing institutions of the recognized national states must be respected as agencies of public order and justice and also as the legitimate authorities for arbitrating among competing human rights claims.

The debate is more than abstract and philosophical. In the years ahead, as has happened many times in history (from the French Revolution in 1789 to Tiananmen Square in 1989), the tensions between the champions of elementary human rights and the defenders of the prerogatives of established states can ignite lethal confrontations that, before they run their course, can destroy the most basic security of the individuals and communities that are drawn into the fray.

THE CONCEPT OF WORLD INTERESTS[7]

An enhancement of norms and institutions that express the interests of *world* society is essential if the growing incongruities between the inherited state-sovereignty system and the expanding interdependence of peoples are to be rectified. We can conceive of the norm-building and institution-building process as the contemporary counterpart of the process that began in earnest some three hundred years ago to rectify the incongruence between the medieval feudal polity and the emerging patterns of nationwide commerce and cultural identity. Just as in the previous era when the time had come to give national interests primacy over the interests of manor and town, so in the contemporary era the time has come to give certain world interests primacy over various national, local, and special interests.

The challenge to contemporary political theorists is to elaborate an appropriate concept of such world interests—a concept capable of commanding wide assent among the world's peoples—that can provide a basis for controlling and arbitrating the conflicts among lesser interests (national, subnational, and transnational) that otherwise threaten to undermine the security of us all.

The conceptual framework should lay out assumptions about what is good (or bad) for the world as a whole. Just as much of the foreign and domestic policy discourse within countries assumes that there are "national interests" (meaning conditions that are desirable for the whole country viewed as an entity), there is ample reason to consider as "world interests" those conditions that are desirable for the entire planet Earth viewed as an entity.

This is not to say that everyone will agree on which interests deserve to be placed in the category of world interests that must be secured (there are, after all, continuing debates in most countries over what interests ought to be considered national interests[8]); nor will there be universal agreement on their definition, let alone on policies for implementing them. What is claimed here, as a minimum, is that there *are* world interests that have high value in their own right; that such interests, in addition to national and special interests, need to be taken into account in evaluating and managing the behavior of states and other actors in world society; and that the question of what ought to be the priority world interests is crucially important to debate.

My candidates for the highest-value world interests are listed below, rank ordered. Those that I rank highest, I contend, would also command the widest support among the world's peoples. Those lower on my list are likely to be more controversial—all the more reason, then, to present them for domestic and international debate.

1. *Survival of the human species.* Few would contest that this should be the cardinal world interest, since humankind's survival is the necessary condition for the realization of every other value (except, perhaps, salvation in the afterlife). "Survival" should be taken to mean "in a reasonably healthy condition of body and mind," so that at least the reproduction of healthy offspring can be sustained across generations.

This world interest cannot be taken for granted, however. Modern weapons of war powerful enough to negate it are deployed around the globe; and there are no reliable guarantees against their use in a world polity where force continues to be the ultima ratio of who gets what, when, and how, and in which war is still widely regarded as "a continuation of politics by other means."

The survival of the species is also placed at risk by nature-altering agricultural and industrial processes capable of severely disturbing the natural balances of the earth's biosphere that sustain human life. The life-threatening activities are undertaken by national agencies, corporations, or other special entities in the service of their particular interests, usually with no hostile intent whatsoever to others, but also with little or no reference to larger community interests. Even "external" ecological effects that are not always immediately evident or calculable can, through cumulative increments, eventually degrade or reduce the value of the entire human population's life-sustaining resources.

It is now becoming widely understood (as demonstrated by the Rio Earth Summit of 1992) that a more active assertion of this overriding world interest—through processes and institutions that compel taking it into account when more particularistic decisions are made—is needed to prevent irreversible catastrophes.

2. *Reduction in the amount of killing and other extremely brutal treatment of human beings.* Human society in most places has evolved to the point where killing and torture of one's fellows *within* the national community are generally regarded as evil and are discouraged through stringent legal penalties (except during periods of revolution or civil war), unless they can be justified by the necessity of preventing at least as great an evil (usually also killing or torture). A universal extension of the imperative of reducing physical violence to include actions that would inflict death and pain on people with whom one has no ethnic or other primordial bonds would represent a further stage in the evolution of humankind.

It is questionable, however, whether most of the world's peoples are ready to embrace the minimization-of-violence ethic a priori—as a self-evident good requiring no other justification. The existence of cauldrons of interethnic and communal violence on virtually every continent is testimony to the fact that many groups and individuals continue to give higher priority to other values ("give me liberty or give me death").

Efforts to make the reduction of violence anywhere a high-priority world interest (and to give it clout in the form of well-funded and equipped world conflict-resolution and peacekeeping institutions) must rely mainly on the consequentialist argument that violence tends to feed upon itself, drawing increasing numbers of people into its contagious vortex, particularly in the contemporary world where instruments of violence with wide ranges and radii of lethal effects have fallen into many hands.

This world interest is the primary rationale for increasing the deployment in the post–Cold War era of United Nations peacekeeping (and "peace*making*") units into situations of intense local conflict, such as the former Yugoslavia, Cambodia, and Mozambique. It also underlies the revival of serious attempts to create a standing UN police force.[9] And it is a central assumption of the analysis in the chapters by Louis Kriesberg and by Margaret Karns and Karen Mingst.

3. *Provision of conditions for healthy subsistence to all people.* The elevation of this objective to the level of a world interest emanates from the fundamental ethical premise that the most basic human right is the right to live one's naturally given life (the sine qua non of all other rights)—a right that can be negated not only by physical violence but also by the denial of the requisites for human survival: uncontaminated and adequate water, food, and air; shelter against climatic extremes; and protection against disease.[10]

Basic utilitarian security considerations can also be invoked on behalf of this world interest. Some of the most lethal diseases that feed on poverty (AIDS, for example) cannot be readily quarantined, and therefore extreme poverty anywhere threatens the well-being of even those who would confine themselves to enclaves of affluence. It is also in the interest of the affluent to make good-faith efforts to ameliorate the suffering of the desperately poor, lest the latter become so alienated and angry at those better off that they organize revolutionary movements and wars to forcibly rectify the maldistribution of resources and wealth. Moreover, a situation of chronic political alienation and instability in the poor countries, even if confined primarily to the Third World, can threaten the economic security of the more-affluent countries and communities. Major manufacturing and marketing sectors of the economies of the United States, Japan, and the European Community are crucially dependent upon stable commercial relationships with a wide array of developing countries. U.S. trade with developing countries is about one-third of total U.S. trade; and, according to a World Resources Institute study, over a million U.S. workers lost their jobs in the 1980s due to the failure of economic growth in debt-ridden Third World countries. Third World poverty also has been enlarging the flow of job-seeking migrants and their families into the advanced industrial countries, producing in turn a wave of ugly nationalistic and xenophobic backlashes, particularly in Western Europe, among middle-class workers fearful of losing their jobs.

Finally, countries convulsed and consumed by the misery of their desperately impoverished populations are unlikely to be willing partners in the international cooperative projects required to sustain the world's essential ecological systems.

4. *Protection of citizen rights.* This world interest embraces the exercise by individuals of the standard civil, political, and economic rights—in addition to survival and basic subsistence—now claimed by persons all around the world simply by virtue of being human. To elevate the protection of such citizen rights to a world interest, even though ranked fourth, is to take issue with the traditional normative basis of the nation-state system that puts a higher value on the sovereign autonomy of the recognized nation-states than on the rights of individuals vis-à-vis one another or

vis-à-vis governments. It also thereby challenges the associated rule against interference by outsiders in the domestic affairs of countries.

Even though moral philosophers continue to debate whether the rights of individuals ought to take precedence over the imperatives of community, the universalization of the claim to basic participatory citizenship is now an unavoidable fact of life. Global security, national security, and individual security require that national governments and international agencies be responsive to this claim, for a major source of violence within countries and international military interventions in the contemporary world is the failure by governing elites to base their policies on the uncoerced consent of the governed. The particular means for assuring that governments are accountable to their citizenry will, of course, vary from country to country, but governments and ruling elites ignore this requirement for durable domestic peace at their peril, and ultimately to the peril of a peaceful world order.

5. *Preservation of cultural diversity.* Lower on this list, but nonetheless a world interest deserving of great respect, is the right of peoples to practice and experiment with different ways of life and societal organization. It is in the interest of humankind as a whole that this basic right not be sacrificed in the pursuit of what some might see as the security imperative of a centralized and unitary world state or the moral imperative of a totally open, borderless world society.

The human species—only recently evolved, and still evolving as nature and human volition select the traits worth preserving—has yet to find *the* form of polity most conducive to the realization of basic human needs and wants. This argues for maintaining considerable political pluralism and decentralization in the world system; then, even if those in control of particular states repress the minorities in their midst, the repressed minorities have the possibility of migrating to another state where they will be better treated, or perhaps even constitute the majority culture. Decentralization of the polity in the service of cultural pluralism remains not only a stimulus to creativity but also a crucial safety valve for world society, allowing for the deflation of dangerously combustible domestic situations that otherwise could lead a full-scale civil war and international intervention on behalf of the warring parties.

6. *Preservation of the planet's basic natural ecologies and environment.* In addition to the self-evident world interest in protecting those biospheric conditions required for the sustenance of human life on earth, there is good reason for humans to respect, if not stand in awe of, nature's givens. We are still very primitive in our understandings of the connections in the universe—what causes what, both concretely and transcendentally in space and time—and therefore ought to be highly reluctant to cause changes in the natural order (or disorder).

The objective, accordingly, should be to preserve as much of the basic natural environment as possible without crucially sacrificing other, higher priority, world interests; and vice versa, to serve the other world interests while minimizing any probable damage to important natural conditions of the known universe.

7. *Enhancement of accountability.* These world-interest imperatives are likely to remain largely unrealized statements of principle unless authority to facilitate their implementation is lodged in appropriate agencies. This returns us to the central structural deficiency of the nation-state system: the incongruence between its dominant institutions of governance and many of the most dynamic interactions of peoples. Even with widespread assent on the substance of what the world interest demands in a particular field, the lack of public accountability by states or private actors for harms they inflict on people across national borders means that the traditional business-as-usual avoidance of responsibility for the well-being of humankind will persist, and the "realist" prognosis will be vindicated.

Being a necessary means for giving flesh and blood to the concept of world interests, international accountability itself deserves to be championed as a high-priority world interest. Such accountability, as pointed out by Robert Johansen in Chapter 19, needs to be elaborated in "horizontal" (transborder) and "vertical" (democratic representation) dimensions. Consistent with Johansen's recommendations, I offer the following principle for determining the appropriate locus and functions of institutions along both of these dimensions: *Those who can or do substantially affect the security or well-being of others (especially by inflicting harm) are assumed to be accountable to those they can or do affect.*

Morally appropriate and politically feasible accountability arrangements will inevitably range across a wide spectrum of configurations—from ad hoc meetings between those who can affect one another (meetings in which information and/or threats are exchanged and/or behavioral adjustments are negotiated, after which the parties go home) to permanently sitting decision-making institutions. The configuration of such institutional arrangements will also vary with respect to the *degree* of accountability members are willing to accept, ranging from the most minimal of obligations to keep the affected or potentially affected informed of what is being (or will be) done to them, to enforceable agreements not to act without the approval of the affected parties.

Fortunately, we need not start from totally unprepared ground in attempting to build such accountability relationships into the world system. Rudimentary accountability relationships already exist in the fields of arms control, international commerce, environmental management, international transportation and communications, and human rights—serving as a scaffolding, as it were, on which more elaborate structures can be built to meet emerging needs. Although progress has been slow, the countries of the European Community, by fits and starts, but nonetheless inexorably, have been leading the way in constructing such accountability regimes congruent with their thickening day-to-day interactions—both interstate and intersectoral.

Nor is the academic discipline of international relations entirely fallow with respect to what Johansen and I call accountability. A considerable amount of fruitful empirical and conceptual work during the past two decades has been devoted to understanding the proliferation of global and regional "regimes" for coordinating trade, monetary affairs, banking, communications, and transportation, and the management of the commons (oceans and seas, rivers, the atmosphere, and outer space). Concentrated mainly among scholars in the subfield of international political economy, however, the analysis of regime formation and maintenance, with a few notable exceptions, has not significantly engaged the energies of scholars whose province has been "security affairs" as traditionally defined.[11] But in the words of a song by the troubadour Bob Dylan, "The times, they are a'changin.'"

THE EXPANSION OF SECURITY

The field of "security studies," having come of age in the United States in the late 1940s at the start of the Cold War, relegated international organizations, international law, and universal collective security to the back burner. For nearly four decades, most foreign policy officials and scholars, to the extent that they did concern themselves with world security, tended to regard what was good for the security of the United States as good for the world. If there *were* world interests, they were derivative of national interests—the conceit of "nationalistic universalism" that enlightened "realists" like Hans Morgenthau warned against.

But as the incongruities of the state-centric system of world politics have become increasingly evident to officials, laypersons, and scholars alike, the need for a broader and deeper basis for securing the safety and well-being of peoples has begun to be more widely recognized.

The chapters in this book are part of the current of scholarship and writing—rapidly becoming mainstream—that has been expanding the definition of security. This thinking challenges the notion that the pursuit of the country's national interests, as narrowly defined by the "realists," is essentially the only obligation of the statesperson, and that such putative world interests as may exist are in any case best serviced as a by-product of statespersons rationally pursuing their national interests.[12] The post-"realist" analysis shows that more often than not the opposite is true: The securing of world interests of the kind outlined above is the necessary condition for maintaining many of the national and special interests that continue to be highly valued.

The broadening of views about *whose* interests are to be secured is complimented by an enlargement of the definition of *what* interests are the legitimate domain of world security policy. My outline of world interests reflects this growing awareness that whatever the scope of the polity—city, province, country, the entire planet—the fundamental human interests that deserve to be accommodated and reliably secured include not only physical safety and minimum public order, but also economic subsistence and basic health of the population (which implies a sustainable ecological environment), individual civic and property rights, and opportunities for cultural and religious communities to develop their own ways of life.

World security policy thus breaks out of the confines of "geopolitics" and its focus on military balances of power, alliance relationships, and traditional "collective security" measures. Its expanded definition encompasses economics as well as politics, cultural as well as material values, ethical altruism as well as amoral self-interest, and nongovernmental actors as well as states.

Those who choose to work in this field—in the arenas of either policy or scholarship—must be prepared, more than their predecessors, to deal with the complexities of world society.

Notes

1. I use quotation marks around the terms "realist" and "realism" throughout this essay to remind the reader that those adhering to this school of thought are simply making a *claim* of realism, which, according to my lights, is not sufficiently merited.

2. The most influential recent exposition of international relations "realism" is Kenneth N. Waltz's *Theory of International Politics* (Reading, MA: Addison-Wesley, 1979). Waltz attributes the behavioral characteristics of states to the anarchic structure of the international system, and for that reason calls his theory "structural realism." Waltz's progenitor (often called the father of modern "realism") was Hans J. Morgenthau, whose seminal treatise, *Politics Among Nations: The Struggle for Power and Peace* (New York: Knopf, 1954), also gave determinative weight to international anarchy; but Morgenthau, like the philosopher Thomas Hobbes, located the source of the anarchic world polity in the human animal's "lust for power." Domestically suppressed in the modern nation-state, this power drive, Morgenthau taught, was projected into the international arena where, given the holocaust potential of modern weapons, it would lead to the destruction of the human species unless (again echoing Hobbes) it could be disciplined by a centralized world government—a development that presumed the prior development of a genuine world community (which Morgenthau considered highly unlikely). For an analysis of the larger corpus of "realism," of which Waltz and Morgenthau are only partial expressions, see Michael Joseph Smith, *Realist Thought from Weber to Kissinger* (Baton Rouge: Louisiana State University Press, 1986).

3. A similar (but considerably more detailed) criticism of the "realist's" failure to capture the complexity of contemporary world politics is provided in James Rosenau's *Turbulence in World Politics: A Theory of Change and Continuity* (Princeton: Princeton University Press, 1990). See especially his chapter 2: "Justifying Jailbreaks: The Limits of Contemporary Concepts and Methods."

4. This section draws on chapter 7 of my *International Relations in a Changing Global System: Toward a Theory of the World Polity* (Boulder, CO: Westview Press, 1992), pp. 115–127.

5. For an analysis of the expanded range of international and transnational public-order problems characteristic of the post–Cold War era, particularly the increasing salience of "North-South" (rich vs. poor) issues, see Donald M. Snow, *Distant Thunder: Third World Conflict and the New International Order* (New York: St. Martin's Press, 1993).

6. Robert B. Reich, *The Work of Nations: Preparing Ourselves for 21st-Century Capitalism* (New York: Knopf, 1991), pp. 87–135.

7. This section draws on chapter 8 of my *International Relations in a Changing Global System*, pp. 131–138.

8. An excellent discussion of the problem of achieving agreement in the U.S. policy community on the nature of the country's national interests is provided by Alexander L. George and Robert O. Keohane, "The Concept of National Interests: Uses and Limitations," in Alexander L. George, *Presidential Decisionmaking in Foreign Policy: The Effective Use of Information and Advice* (Boulder: Westview Press, 1980), pp. 217–237.

9. See Boutros Boutros-Ghali, *An Agenda for Peace: Preventive Diplomacy, Peacemaking and Peace-keeping* (New York: United Nations, 1992).

10. The argument that subsistence is a basic human right equal to the right to life itself is made persuasively by Henry Shue, *Basic Rights: Subsistence, Affluence, and U.S. Foreign Policy* (Princeton: Princeton University Press, 1980).

11. The "regime" literature in the field of international political economy is well represented in Stephen D. Krasner, ed., *International Regimes* (Ithaca: Cornell University Press, 1983). Concerns about ecological management are also generating important studies on the development and operation of international regimes, such as Peter M. Haas, *Saving the Mediterranean: The Politics of International Environmental Cooperation* (New York: Columbia University Press, 1990); and Oran R. Young, *International Cooperation: Building Regimes for Natural Resources and the Environment* (Ithaca: Cornell University Press, 1989). Mainline "security affairs" specialists who have contributed prominently to the "regime" literature include Robert Jervis, the contributor of an essay on "Security Regimes" to the Krasner volume; Joseph Nye, co-author with Robert Keohane (a leading international political economy theorist) of *Power and Interdependence: World Politics in Transition* (Boston: Little, Brown, 1977); and Robert M. Axelrod, whose *The Evolution of Cooperation* (New York: Basic Books, 1984) applies game-theoretic analysis to the explanation of how enemies can learn to escape from mutually destructive patterns of behavior and regularize patterns of cooperation.

12. A foreshadowing of how mainstream international relations thinking would soon be moving is found in Stanley Hoffmann's *Duties Beyond Borders: On the Limits and Possibilities of Ethical International Politics* (Syracuse: Syracuse University Press, 1981).

2 / Great Powers and World Peace

DANIEL N. NELSON

INTRODUCTION

As the millennium draws to a close, and we reflect on its final century, peace and prosperity seem everywhere fragile and imperiled. This was not what we expected. After "winning" the Cold War, Americans thought for a moment that a "new world order" and a "Europe whole and free" were at hand. Nothing could have been further from the truth.

Instead, components of what we had known for two generations—a bipolar distribution of power and hegemonic alliance systems that housed Soviet and American allies—have receded or evaporated. And, as argued below, other elements of the way in which an international system has operated, such as the centrality of the nation-state and the military-industrial foundations of power, are being called into question.

At certain cusps of history, new and old paradigms clash, as humans engaged in social, political, and economic policy-making struggle to understand the new environment. Few grandiose theories offer day-to-day guidance. But we all know intuitively when, as Joseph Nye wrote, the tectonic plates have shifted[1]—when a fundamental transformation of world affairs has occurred. The demise of European Stalinist regimes, the end of the Warsaw Pact, the dissolution of the USSR coupled with the reunification of Germany, and the diplomatic end of the Cold War together constituted such a tectonic movement.

Such a movement was not, however, a stark shift. Many of the trends and processes evident in Europe and on other continents before 1989 remain present and powerful today. The proliferation of advanced weapons, ecological deterioration, debt and underdevelopment, overpopulation and migration, and public disenchantment with political authority—these and many other issues form a transnational backdrop and undercurrent to any seemingly national or regional event. And, some of the principal actors on the global stage prior to 1989 have now inherited roles that have been expanded or changed due less to their own efforts than others' collapse.

In this chapter, I pose dramatic questions for which there are no dramatic answers. Can states formed in the eighteenth and nineteenth centuries, with power derived from twentieth century sources, confront and manage threats to peace and prosperity in the twenty-first century? Are the principal nation-states at the end of this century, notably the United States, Japan, and Germany, *able* and *willing* to assume the task of building a new global order through which to obtain the benefits of security? Or should we be looking elsewhere, beyond states and their power, to other guarantees of our twenty-first century peace and prosperity?

At the heart of these questions are two critiques of a security-through-resources equation and of the assumption that security is always of, by, and for the state. Such a focus on the capacities of states errs, I will argue, both by failing to see an alternative strategy towards security *and* by ignoring evidence of states' decreasing abilities to perform essential functions autonomously.

My answers to these issues of grand scale are at best partial. While we must offer a fundamental reassessment of security, the proposals that scholarship can derive for today's policymakers are necessarily modest. My aim is less to plot an entire sojourn towards a twenty-first century global order, than to suggest the direction in which such an order may lie and the first plausible steps in that direction.

But, in the end, an unequivocal melancholy penetrates the millennium's close. During this thousand years, humankind has created states, industries, sciences, and literatures, but we have yet to find ways to prevent the mass suffering engendered by warfare and political violence. Cognizant of such "reality" in the world, proponents of one school nod sagely, arguing that Hobbes was not much off the mark, and that power is the only fungible asset in world affairs when deployed wisely in the pursuit of national interests. More than anything else, it is in response to this knee-jerk "political realism" (realpolitik) that this chapter is directed.

As we confront the full force of our own frustration that a Cold War victory was incomplete, and as we grapple with dangerous post-euphoric transitions, it will be far too easy to seek security in the ". . . threat, use and control of military force"—i.e., an outlook that ". . . fits comfortably within a realist paradigm."[2]

But to stay the course—to continue to be guided by such a realist paradigm—places us all in terrible jeopardy. If we focus on military power, military threats, the likelihood and character of war, and statecraft that attends these matters,[3] then great powers—much like a century ago—will be the only actors that count in the latest production of war and peace.

As Barbara Tuchman noted in her popular history-on-a-grand-scale, *March to Folly,* "woodenheadedness"—staying the course, rigidly maintaining policies nothwithstanding clear evidence that change was required—has been a trait common to leaders and policymakers over the millennia.[4] By rejecting a transformed vision of security, and by adhering to principal states as bearers of our peace and prosperity, we risk similar folly.

STATES, POWER, AND PEACE

A Hobbesian vision of mankind's natural condition portrayed an environment so brutish that reason dictated cooperative action and a common investment in joint political structures.[5] The state and its power were the only route by which to avoid the calamity of man's incivility. "Covenants without the sword are but words," said Hobbes, ". . . and of no strength to secure a man at all."

The state and its power as the sine qua non of peace have been central to an unchallenged principle of world affairs since Westphalia in 1648 and, arguably, much earlier. While the nature of political and state power has long been debated,[6] the equation of the state, power, and security has been axiomatic for decision makers throughout the past five centuries. The "raw power of the state", and specifically its ability to mobilize and project power ". . . through such . . . organs as the military, the militia, the police, the bureaucracy and the judiciary" were central to the belief that only the state could provide security.[7]

Power as the fundamental commodity of international relations, national interests as the guiding principles of policymakers, a balance of power as the means by which to pursue such interests without war, and states as the only significant actors in this grand drama are tenets of *political realism*.

Realists see peace and stability as the ". . . result [of] the operation of a balance of power propelled by self interest."[8] The precise denotation of a balance of power has been thoroughly debated among post–World War II realist theorists—in the first postwar generation by such scholars as Morgenthau, Haas, Kaplan, Claude, and Rosecrance.[9] A consistent feature of these debates, however, has been to define peace, itself, only in terms of distributions of power.

Raymond Aron, for example, wrote of several "types of peace" defined by the distribution of power in each—equilibrium, hegemony, and empire.[10] Of these, the next century's peace in Europe would seem plausible, in a realist's eyes, only through equilibrium.[11] Soviet hegemony that constrained ethnic schisms on its Western periphery is no more, and the Moscow-dominated empire has (at least for the foreseeable future) broken apart, unleashing numerous irredentist conflicts.

In a realpolitik vision, then, the fabric of peace hangs everywhere on the thread of a power equilibrium more than it has for generations. And, outside the Pacific Rim and the Euro-Atlantic regions, where some semblance of stable multilateral or bilateral arrangements remain, volatile issues and unequal power can erupt quickly. In the so-called "Third World," and sub-regions of Central, South, and Southwest Asia, West Africa, the Horn, etc., creating and maintaining power equilibriums will be daunting tasks.

Daunting as it may be, however, realists maintain that only an interlocking grid of balances will avoid interstate warfare or limit the spread of civil wars beyond one country. Whether in the Middle East, Asia, Africa or Latin America, a lifting of superpower rivalry connotes to realists a heightened need to maintain an equilibrium of power—presumably by manipulating economic assistance and arms transfers, while injecting one's own forces if necessary to assert the role of larger, wealthier nation-states in maintaining balances.

"Balance of power" theorists see the end of post–World War II bipolarity as a return to an environment where conflict is always possible, and the components of power are always present. Without the "tight bipolarity" of the Cold War, realists expect that nation-states will return to a general struggle for power, defined primarily in military terms, as they pursue national interests. For the moment, the United States retains a military force superior to any conceivable adversary and demonstrates a capability to project that force globally. But American preponderance will neither go unchallenged nor will it last at the level seen from the late 1980s into the mid 1990s.

Thus, arms and influence, used in the pursuit of great-power interests, have once again been identified by realists as the only means by which to balance forces around the world and, thereby, avert war.

These arguments and assumptions, however, are spurious. If principal states of the late twentieth century make policy based on realists' outlook, opportunities to avoid wars and abate conflicts will be missed.

MOVING BEYOND NEOREALISM

The Changing State of States

A state's raw power no longer translates directly into tools relevant to challenges of the twenty-first century, and security defined in military terms is no more a guarantor of peace and prosperity. From below and inside, weak states on all continents are being weakened further. The demise of multinational states in Europe's eastern half—the Soviet Union, Yugoslavia and Czechoslovakia—is mirrored by the growing sectarian upheavals in India, Canada, and thus far to a lesser degree, by the divisive movements within Italy. Nations and regionalism resurgent are powerful factors in this process. Although we were lulled into the convenient and reassuring notion that the legal and constitutional confines of the state could provide one element of international order, the fragility of many nation-states has been all too apparent at the century's end. Nations and nationalism,[12] far from being subsumed or tamed by twentieth-century states, have emerged from an imposed latency to become a ferment that threatens not only single states but entire regions.

Further, within-state limits on the ability of states to act autonomously in world affairs are increasingly evident in foreign policy-making. Peace, human rights and antinuclear activists, and environmental or defense-industry advocates all have domestic (or global) constituencies that far outweigh any calculus based on national well-being. The idea of the state as an autonomous, unitary and rational actor is thus out of sync with the landscape of policy-making.[13]

From above and outside, even the largest and most wealthy states are being buffeted by strong gusts of interdependence and integration—obligations by treaty or de facto arrangements that signal that the firewall of sovereignty has been breached. Pushed less by public demand than by the sheer inability of individual states to address or resolve critical socioeconomic or political problems, leaders have set aside long-cherished notions of autonomous action and protectionism to join in *Maastricht*, commit themselves to global environmental standards at Rio, and open their markets to free competition via NAFTA, the Andean Free Trade Area, and other endeavors.

Even those realists for whom power remains the core concept in understanding the international environment acknowledge that the concentration of power evident during the Cold War—a tight bipolarity—is no more. The resulting "diffusion of power" reduces America's ability to go it alone as a hegemon among friends, particularly vis-à-vis Japan.[14]

Macro-political trends, created and accelerated by globalized communications, mass movements of people, the spread of weapons of mass destruction and ecological peril, and the dependence of people's well-being on international commerce have all chipped away at the state's supremacy in matters of peace and prosperity.

States' Cooperation in Flux

Even venerable Cold War institutions composed of many large developed states, multilateral in the sense of being cooperative, albeit not collective, have been busy recoding and recalibrating their operations to survive into the next century. An alliance for common defense, NATO, is edging toward an eastern expansion via the "halfway house" for former Warsaw Pact states called the North Atlantic Cooperation Council (NACC). Were additional states admitted (at first, perhaps, Poland, Hungary, or the Czech Republic), that action would accelerate NATO's metamorphosis into an organization that has neither a single state as its nemesis nor a single hegemon as its guiding hand and benefactor. An implicit and incremental move away from state-focused security, however, may be too little, too late.

Meanwhile Bretton Woods institutions (the World Bank and the International Monetary Fund) have become key actors in the creation of market economies—far afield from their original intention. IMF, meant to oversee the management of the world's currency exchange rates when they were fixed, has since stepped into many of the World Bank's original roles of promoting economic recovery and development.

States and organizations of, by, and for states are challenged by a multitude of factors, especially the increasing presence of non-state actors and transnational processes. "The structural capacity of the state to continue to 'hold the ring' of social, economic and political development in the twenty-first century . . . is not self-evident, but problematic."[15]

To insist, by default if not by purpose, that states use power to ensure security places far too much on the shaky capacities and dubious intentions of those guided by so-called realism. Even when acting cooperatively, presumably prompted by shared interests, groups of states are far more likely to cohere when they share a common enemy than when they share common values.[16]

States and the Creation of Conflict and Threat

Beyond the question of whether it is a wise bet to depend on state power to provide requisite conditions for peace and prosperity, lies a yet more devastating indictment—namely, that the modern state is an inherently conflict-*creating* institution. Rather than an organization by which preexisting conflict is resolved, the roles of the modern state involve far more than sorting out "who gets what, when and how." States today engage in many cooperative tasks that, rather than reconciling conflict, create conflict that then requires follow-on conflict management or resolution.[17]

States are their own worst enemy, in a sense, adding to the reservoir of issues from which society seeks protection. Alternatively, one might say that state's keep themselves in business. At the least, realists' faith in the supremacy of the state and its power as bulwarks of world peace is subject to many questions.

By the early 1980s, as the Reagan administration resolutely pushed an American military expansion, scholarly debate began in earnest about broadening the definition of security.[18] Ironically, there was never much discussion about the parallel and equally significant *narrowing* of state power. Yet, neither a broadened concept of security nor constraints on state power would have existed without the other.

Put succinctly, states were creating more new threats than they could meet alone or cooperatively; arms and influence, as utilized by great or "super" powers, were generating crises and peril, not maintaining regional or global balances of power. Great power military interventions in the "Third World" had done little or nothing to augment the well-being of political systems or populations, regardless of whether the case in point was Vietnam or Afghanistan, Angola or Nicaragua.

Further, each increment in a major state's military industry or armed might in response to perceived threats always *engenders* heightened threat to any potential adversary. This "security dilemma" has been observed by many scholars, but warrants emphasis here. Henry Kissinger is one who saw this paradox almost four decades ago, writing that any one state's efforts to gain "absolute security" will lead to other states' perception of absolute insecurity.[19]

Raising capacities as a path toward security, rather than abating the threats against which capacities would be arrayed, is thus an inefficient route to peace and prosperity. A capacity-intensive strategy costs more in terms of human and socioeconomic resources and provides the impetus for what the press and public knew as the arms race.

Further, by providing blank checks to armed forces and military industries, a security-as-capacities strategy obviates civilian control of the national security agenda while draining talent, investment, and innovation from the population's well-being. In the extreme, the Soviet communist regime devoted an enormous proportion of national wealth to a huge military, well-endowed with offensive armaments. The consequences were grievous, bleeding the best people, ideas, and material from the economy and society as a whole, thereby creating a significant drag on an already inefficient system and ultimately contributing to the demise of a communist party regime.[20]

Perhaps most devastating is the damage that can be done to prospects for the maturation of emerging democracies. One of the little noted, yet all-too-obvious benefits about George Washington's parting maxim—to avoid "entangling alliances"—was the ability of the fledgling United States to avoid large standing armies. With the great advantage of geographic insulation, the United States democracy could abide by the Washingtonian principle without really trying, and thus endure periods of great weakness and internal chaos without substantial conflict with major foreign powers.

Rethinking Military Roles

The ephemeral role of the state in providing security and the illusory link between power and security are two twenty-first century realities for which the United States and other states with global roles must now prepare. Already, American military commanders are reading the tea leaves, beginning to assess their role in an environment where large, capable armed forces per se are no longer the apotheosis of security.

Although senior American commanders still express their duties and force planning in terms of missions serving the national interest, and are not soon going to stray far from realist orthodoxy, one sees and hears "new thinking." A greater role in peacetime, with heavy emphasis on ". . . nation-building activities, . . . disaster relief, and humanitarian assistance . . . ," is understood as a proper endeavor for U.S. forces, particularly when combined with more-traditional global roles in security assistance and training programs. A military that provides "both swords and plowshares" is being acknowledged because the raw power at their disposal does less today to ensure our well-being than at any time in the last half century.[21]

This unavoidable post–Cold War conclusion does not mean that today's admirals, generals, and defense industry CEOs are sanguine about force cutbacks and order cancellations. Yet, the strategy of abating threats, rather than the costly and often destabilizing strategy of enlarging capacities, requires a different voice from the military, and that voice is beginning to be heard.

As forward-looking as these views might seem, however, the projection of influence, power, and force is still understood as the core of national security policy.[22] When push comes to shove, such new thinking has not been sufficiently strong or pervasive to dislodge the well-worn axioms of realpolitik. The state's power, used in pursuit of national interests, is still considered the only sure way to security.

IMPLICATIONS FOR GREAT POWERS

And what are the consequences of such thinking on principal states of the late twentieth century? To the degree that the United States and its erstwhile Cold War allies insist on a capacity-centered security strategy, with states and alliances for common defense as core actors in the pursuit of influence, power, and force-projection capacities, the end of rigid bipolar confrontation is likely to yield more numerous and more intense threats from within states, while non-state external threats also multiply.

By relying once again on states and their alliances, we place upon the "great powers," that is, those with the largest reservoir of socioeconomic or military resources, the "burden" of international security. With such an enlarged burden, the security dilemma mentioned above will be quickly apparent and deepened. And, none of the capacities that states and alliances produce will be able to do much against threats of mass migration, the breakdown of civil order so severe that economies collapse and starvation ensues, or ecological calamity.

To encourage and demand that Japan or Germany "share the burden" is a graphic display of the woodenheadedness inherent in national security policy beholden to state power. Were both states to leap over constitutional impediments to a more forceful global role—impediments we once advocated and wrote into constitutions and basic laws—threat perceptions in their regions will grow and promote reciprocal efforts to enlarge capacities by Japan's or Germany's neighbors.

Even more ominous is the contribution that an enlarged regional or global military role might make to nationalism and demagoguery in Germany, Japan, or any number of other sizeable states.

For more than forty years, Germany's division and Japan's reliance on the U.S. defense relationship, combined with constitutional provisions in both countries that prohibited the deployment of armed forces beyond their borders (and, in Japan, Article 9 of the Constitution, which supposedly bars the country from maintaining land, sea, or air forces), provided reassurance to friends and neighbors. The continuation of parliamentary democracies in both countries, membership in alliance systems with other democracies, the presence of sizeable American forces on Japanese and German soil, and the Japanese and Germans' apparent disinterest in playing any greater international role all reinforced confidence.[23]

This reassurance notwithstanding, the economic success of Toyota, Hitachi, Matsushita, Nissan, Toshiba, and so forth, gradually altered American perceptions of Japan—heightening both respect for products and friction because of a mammoth imbalance in the bilateral trade. American threats of retaliatory protectionism (via such laws as "Super 301") added to wide cultural differences and memories of World War II, and fueled negative sentiments and acrimonious language that became common by the early 1980s.[24] At the same time, complaints became audible from the American side that Tokyo was not shouldering its proper "burden" for its own defense, and numerous Japanese politicians were quoted as having uttered disparaging remarks about U.S. ethnic diversity.[25]

It takes little imagination to see that a more well-armed Japan, acting regionally or globally, would not be universally applauded. Indeed, as a Diet member asked me in 1986, when I raised with him the issue of Japan's defense burden, "Do you Americans really wish to see once again a strong Japanese fleet and a capacity to project power throughout Asia and the Pacific? Are Americans actually comfortable with this image?"[26] As the world's greatest investor and aid donor, the largest force in financial markets, and the strongest player in world trade, Japan's entry into military expansion beyond its already sophisticated conventional military forces would be discomfiting to the United States, to Japan's neighbors, and indeed to many Japanese. Were Tokyo to inaugurate a more active security role in East Asia or beyond, in concert with greater foreign policy independence, mixed with ". . . more than faint signs of contempt for others, including Americans," gains for worldwide peace and prosperity would quickly fade as the security dilemma went into high gear.[27]

By late 1992, the Japanese government had finally succeeded in overcoming domestic opposition to the deployment of peacekeeping forces to Cambodia, although the Diet (with a coalition of Socialist, Komeito, and Liberal Democratic party deputies) had restricted the activities of those 600 troops to nonconflict regions. Less than half a year later, however, powerful LDP faction leader and foreign minister, Michio Watanabe, began to build a consensus for a much larger and less constrained Japanese military role. Japanese Self-Defense Forces, heretofore confined narrowly to the business of defending the country's shores and airspace, would (in Watanabe's view) "[f]rom now on . . . maintain global peace and order under the leadership of the United Nations."[28] Watanabe may not succeed entirely in the near term, but his effort is only one step in a logical regression toward a renewed military and political place commensurate with Japan's immense industrial, financial, and technological resources.

Ironically, this reassertion of Japan's regional and world role is precisely that which has been sought by American and European advocates of political realism. For years, U.S. politicians, policymakers, and scholars have criticized Tokyo for not holding up its part of the defense burden, and have advocated purchases of U.S.-made weapons for that purpose. And now, with Japanese peacekeeping forces being deployed and American AWAC planes being purchased, the larger implications for the next century may begin to be clear—a Pacific Rim destabilized as Japan, China, and other states compete in a dangerous game of capacity expansion, fueling the security dilemma's spiral of threat and counterthreat.

A reunited Germany, already possessing a powerful military relative to its neighbors and an economy substantially larger than any other European Community member, is the other Cold War "winner." But rather like Japan, Germany's assertiveness after reunification has been met with nervous smiles. Issues began to mount in 1991–1992, about which the CDU government of Chancellor Helmut Kohl took positions decidedly at odds with the best judgments or best interests of EC or NATO members.

The Germans' 1991 insistence that Slovenia, Croatia, and other states emerging from the former Yugoslavia be recognized was criticized at the time by the United States and by European allies who were upset by Kohls's unilateralism. And in 1992, heated debate and arguments were audible within NATO's corridors concerning the German/French EuroCorps and its ties to NATO versus WEU (Western European Union). Additional resentment was created by German decisions to restrict asylum/immigration and to maintain high interest rates, because of Germans' strong fear of inflation, but thereby curtailing growth while endangering Western currencies.

TOWARDS "DE-STATIZED" SECURITY

After the shift of "tectonic plates" undergirding international relations, the United States has made assiduous efforts to retain all of the comfortable Cold War structures in which American interests held sway. Such a cautious approach has been evident through a process of incremental adjustment—for example, by adding an appendage to NATO, such as NACC (North Atlantic Cooperation Council) at the December 1991 Rome summit,[29] or by talking about a wider humanitarian role for a downsized military that retains the same structure (i.e., the "Base Force Concept" endorsed by former Secretary of Defense Richard Cheney). This tendency is not necessarily a consequence of intra-U.S. politics, for it is not at all clear that Democrats would have acted in significantly different ways in 1989–91 than did a Republican administration. But it is clear that American leaders thus far have rejected any diminution of their prerogatives beyond recognizing resource constraints that necessitate cooperative, "multilateral," or "coalitional" endeavors, such as the war against Iraq in 1991.

International relations are decidedly more global and interwoven at the end of the twentieth century than in the second decade of the nineteenth, yet we continue to imbue balance of power with magical properties, and states with rationality to identify and act upon intangible national interests. To continue humankind's reliance on a condominium of wealthy, populous states—modern versions of what Henry Kissinger found so appealing in the outcome of the Vienna peace conference after the Napoleonic Wars—will provide no security guarantee as we enter the next millennium.

Together with the other two principal objectives/goals of the post–Cold War period—free government and free-market economies—security is an unlikely product of states acting alone or in cooperation with one another. It was people in Leipzig and Timisoara who overthrew communist regimes, not NATO's tanks; *individual* entrepreneurs are recreating free-market economies, not the World Bank and IMF. The sole consequence of encouraging states, particularly the states that already exhibit components of strength, to heighten their influence, power, or ability to employ force—even in the innocuous name of peacekeeping—will be to create more of a threat to others.

Encouraging Japan to share burdens emphasizes Tokyo's role qua state on behalf of its national interests in a region and world that will be threatened by those interests and strength. Pushing Germany toward a role that involves more regional or global assertiveness, merely in the name of sharing burden, will not be understood or accepted by Russia or smaller victims of Germany's prior episodes of expansionism. Led by large and wealthy states, the pursuit of security through balance-of-power prescriptions, seeking everywhere to mend balances with infusions of arms, displays of influence or power, or ultimately the use of force, will condemn us to replays of tragedies that we know too well. The debacle of American support for the Iraqi regime of Saddam Hussein during the 1980s, virtually until the day his tanks rolled into Kuwait, is but the most recent and costly among a long series of efforts to balance power gone awry.

No one can deny the need for capacities to balance threats, an equation that is the operational heart of security. But capacities do not equal power conceived in primarily military terms. Capacities are derived from the strength and resources found in consensual societies, growing economies, legitimate polities, *and* (but not only) effective militaries. Further, security is not only capacities of states or groups of states alone, but also the ability to abate threats without the threat or use of force. For the next century, our security strategy must look much more to the latter domain, one in which we can and must "de-statize" security.

In this alternative construction of international security, the military interventions of powerful nation-states, no longer sufficient or necessary for peace and stability, and often damaging to both ends, would be supplanted by an interlocking web of regional collective security arrangements. Abating threats through such collective architectures, rather than building capacities of states and their alliances to defeat threats, represents a strategic shift comparable to and parallel with the "tectonic shift" that Nye sensed but could not accept. It does not deny the presence of force or the right of self-defense in the international arena, but stresses ways to preclude a resort to force rather than a continuum leading to and threatening the use of force.

Collective security begins with the premise that threats may arise from within, not externally, and that avoidance of peril is at least as critical as countering threats with capacities. Collective security arrangements are bound to *include*, not exclude, potential sources of concern for the peace, stability, and well-being of all participants. Non-offensive defense strategies of members, studies of conflict reduction by joint academic/policy centers, mediation via crisis resolution organs, collective and binding economic sanctions for punitive responses, and ready peacekeeping forces to separate disputants—these and other measures are all part of collective, non-state efforts to avoid resort to military capacities. States' proprietary armed forces and alliances for common defense (e.g., NATO) can exist shoulder-to-shoulder with collective security endeavors, functionally dividing the quite different tasks of deterring or defeating aggression from outside versus defusing tensions or derailing preparations for confrontation that may otherwise lead to hostilities.

How can such an alternative to a balance of power world order be generated? Critical determinants are (1) the inauguration of a "test-bed" Euro-Atlantic organization as a follow-on to the Conference on Security and Cooperation in Europe (CSCE), (2) the continued cooperation of the United States and other major states in zones of regional conflict, and (3) the financial and material support of the richer developed countries (especially Japan and Germany). Japan's and Germany's role in building such collective architectures will be far more beneficial to security than would "sharing burden" of the old kind.

From now into the next decade, the construction of regional collective security organizations should have high priority, with Europe's endeavors providing an initial framework for examination in other locales. Institutionalizing CSCE in the reluctant and modest ways to which the United States agreed, and for which the November 1990 Paris CSCE summit gave its approval, is inadequate. The small secretariat in Prague and the minimal responsibilities in other domains (election monitoring and a center for conflict resolution) provide neither an opportunity to assess the potential of collective security nor an experimental base on which other regions can draw.

American, Russian, German, Japanese, and policymakers in other large or advanced nation-states must strive to see beyond national security to global security.[30] Their cooperation to limit disputes and conflicts around the world, because of the capacities they possess in military, economic, and political contexts, will have greater consequences for threat abatement than any effort solely within the Third World. The United States retains military might, clearly able to project force in various regions much more readily than any other state. Nevertheless, as was demonstrated by U.S. requests for other states to pay for much of the U.S. commitment of forces against Iraq, the large-scale military deployment of U.S. armed forces in combat roles is far more costly than can be absorbed (without grievous economic consequences) by the United States itself. Thus, the economic role of Japan and Germany become critical components of any endeavor to establish alternative security architectures. After the Cold War, Washington can be the first to agree that regional conflicts are no longer grounds for confrontation; other countries need to join in the search for global security by contributing heavily to the costs of creating institutions, processes, and peacekeeping units in South and Southeast Asia, Africa, Latin America, and the Middle East.

Parallel notions to encourage the demilitarization of security may include tying aid to cuts in military expenditures (an idea raised by former Secretary of Defense and World Bank President Robert McNamara).[31] Debt-for-demilitarization swaps could also be negotiated, exchanging outstanding debts for the value of weapons destroyed and defense industrial plants rendered unable to produce armaments. These innovative approaches are not isolated solutions to regional security; yet, these incentives to disarm may be important components of new security architectures in various parts of the world.

Where ought these regional security organs direct their attention? The answers are painfully evident—to bring cease-fires and negotiated settlements to civil wars and insurgencies. Implicit to this charge is the reference of disputes to mediation, and the monitoring and extension of human rights and democratic processes—tasks undertaken not in a manner of neocolonial oversight from Europe or North America, but rather by acts of regional organs of collective security.

How ought all of this begin? Permanent members of the UN Security Council, which should soon include Japan and Germany, should act as cosponsors to convene regional Helsinki processes with many of the initial goals seen in Europe. Especially important in early stages would be activities in the domains of human rights and confidence and security-building measures (CSBMs). In regions such as Southeast Asia, where ASEAN has already shown signs of pushing ahead in these arenas, institutionalization of the process, to include a secretariat, assembly, and specialized commissions in security and human rights fields, could be undertaken.

Funding this multifaceted process cannot be seen as intraregional alone. Most areas in which conflict is most likely are unable to generate sufficient resources to underwrite initial infrastructure development for a new security architecture. The G-7 countries should, therefore, inaugurate a "Fund for Regional Security" from which nascent regional organizations could draw in order to establish collective security organs, with initial grants for short-term assistance.

But these notions about specific steps are less important in the near term than recognizing broader principles to guide a post–Cold War search for security. An end to superpower rivalry need not connote a revitalized global power struggle, with peace everywhere hanging on a precarious balance of power. Capacities built on armed strength might yield implicit threats to others, undercutting the delicate ratio from which security results.

Alternative strategic visions that guide collective security can be implemented, although we cannot expect weak-capacity states caught in a threat-

[handwritten annotation: assumption that "great states" are perfect and will work for the betterment of the global community as a whole — complete opposite of capitalist ideology]

rich environment to take these steps alone. The so-called great powers have that clear responsibility—to lead in the construction of post-hegemonic global security.

[handwritten annotation: "realism: he with the most guns wins— so why not he with most guns" just take over? who's gonna stop him?]

CONCLUSION

States, national interests, military power—the actors, ends, and means that are written indelibly into realist descriptions and prescriptions of world politics—are once again au courant. It looks and feels like Saddam was stopped by America's projection of power, that Milosevic will understand nothing less, and that a little policing by the sole remaining superpower may have salutary consequences. The larger lessons about peace and prosperity in the twenty-first century, though, are quite different.

First, the more states are invested with the responsibility of maintaining a dynamic balance between threats and capacities, the more that irrational calculus based on national interests leads to expanding militaries and weapons' sophistication. Second, efforts by one state to find absolute security through enhancing power threatens others and leads to a destabilizing competition. Third, great powers' efforts to redress regional imbalances through arms sales, technology transfers, or more direct intervention invariably provides only short-term relief at great cost to long-term prospects for peace and stability. Fourth, readjusting or redistributing a perceived "burden" of defense among large and strong states fuels the fires of a security dilemma, risking fearful and negative responses to what at first seems perfectly palatable among great powers.

The rationale for setting a new course well away from our previous reliance on state power is multifaceted and compelling. Our need is nothing less than a strategic shift toward the other side of the security equation as great as the realignments of global politics at the close of the twentieth century. By investing in non-state, *collective* mechanisms for threat abatement, we will create robust partners for states and alliances in today's quest for post-hegemonic security.

Were all of these points accepted as unequivocal, states would nevertheless remain core actors. But their conflict-creating role can be constrained, and their impedance to threat abatement can be reduced. Learning these lessons, in short, can enable states to join in endeavors that diminish reliance on power used in pursuit of national interests—a reliance that denudes the international system of tools appropriate to mitigate new, global threats.

Notes

1. Joseph Nye, "American Strategy after Bipolarity," *International Affairs*, Vol. 66, No. 3 (1990), p. 513.

2. This definition of security studies by Stephen M. Walt, "The Renaissance of Security Studies," *International Studies Quarterly*, Vol. 35 (1991), p. 212, is shared by many others in

academe and reflects, as well, an assumption that underpins many policymakers' understanding of security.

3. Ibid, p. 213.

4. Barbara Tuchman, *The March of Folly* (New York: Knopf, 1984).

5. Aside from re-reading Thomas Hobbes's seventeenth century work, *The Leviathan* (Oxford: Clarendon, 1965), among the most useful commentaries on Hobbesian philosophy remain Sterling Lamprecht, "Hobbes and Hobbism," *American Political Science Review,* Vol. 34 (1940), pp. 4–37, or Howard Warrender, *The Political Philosophy of Thomas Hobbes* (Oxford: Oxford University Press, 1957).

6. A useful summary is provided by John M. Rothgeb, Jr., *Defining Power: Influence and Force in the Contemporary International System* (New York: St. Martin's, 1993), pp. 18–22 and his citations to seminal works by Dahl, Nye, Wolfers, Knorr, Lasswell, and others.

7. See L. S. Stavrianos, *Lifelines from Our Past* (Armonk, NY: M. E. Sharpe, 1989), p. 77.

8. This succinct summary of realists' thoughts on peace and stability is offered by Charles W. Kegley and Eugene R. Wittkopf, *American Foreign Policy: Pattern and Process,* 3rd ed. (New York: St. Martin's, 1987), p. 76.

9. See, for example, Hans Morgenthau and Kenneth Thompson, *Politics Among Nations,* 6th ed. (New York: Alfred A. Knopf, 1985), pp. 187–197; Ernst B. Haas, "The Balance of Power: Prescription, Concept or Propaganda?," *World Politics* Vol. 5, No. 3 (Fall, 1953), pp. 442–477; Morton Kaplan, *System and Process in International Politics* (New York: Wiley, 1957); Inis Claude, *Power in International Relations* (New York: Random House, 1962); and Richard Rosecrance, *Action and Reaction in World Politics* (Boston: Little, Brown, 1963).

10. Raymond Aron, *Peace and War* (New York: Praeger, 1970), p. 151.

11. The importance of a power equilibrium within a balance-of-power system, particularly as a result of states joining in alliances, has been the subject of historical and empirical research over more than a century. Manus I. Midlarsky cites, for example, a work by G. F. Leckie, *An Historical Research into the Nature of the Balance of Power in Europe* (London: Taylor and Hessey) that dates from 1817. See Midlarsky's *The Disintegration of Political Systems* (Columbia, SC: University of South Carolina Press, 1986), p. 57. Dina Zinnes has undertaken formal theoretical analyses of equilibriums within balance of power theories. See, for example, her "An Analytical Study of the Balance of Power Theories," *Journal of Peace Research,* Vol. 4, No. 4 (1967), pp. 270–288.

12. Still the best summary of nationalism and its effect on states is Alfred Coban, *The Nation State and National Self-Determination* (New York: Crowell, 1969).

13. An interesting foray into the web of domestic influences on foreign policy formulation is David Skidmore and Valerie M. Hudson, eds., *The Limits of State Autonomy* (Boulder: Westview, 1992).

14. This is the perspective of one noted commentator, William P. Bundy, in "The 1950s versus the 1990s," in Edward K. Hamilton, ed., *America's Global Interests* (New York: Norton, 1989), pp. 33–81, especially pp. 62–63.

15. On the nature of the state and its metamorphosis, see Philip G. Cerny, *The Changing Architecture of Politics: Structure, Agency and the Future of the State* (London: Sage, 1990), pp. 113–144 and passim.

16. This was a point made long ago by Thucydides in *The Pelloponesian Wars* and underscored by contemporary authors such as George Liska, *Nations in Alliance* (Baltimore: Johns Hopkins University Press, 1968). Cooperative actions of states, involving a locus of decision making *within* each member state, rather than investing such authority in joint bodies that are charged with maintaining a collective good, not national interests, fall far short of collective regional security.

17. This intriguing perspective and insight is that of Charles E. Lindbloom, *Inquiry and Change* (New Haven: Yale University Press, 1990), pp. 48–50.

18. Among the earliest, and still the best, of these intellectual considerations are Richard H. Ullmann, "Redefining Security," *International Security,* Vol. 8, No. 1 (Summer, 1983), pp. 129–153, and Barry Buzan, *Peoples, States and Fear: The National Security Problem in International Relations* (Chapel Hill: University of North Carolina Press, 1983).

19. *A World Restored: The Politics of Conservatism in a Revolutionary Age* (Boston: Houghton Mifflin, 1957), pp. 144–145.

20. For empirical assessments of the trade-offs and costs incurred in the USSR and its Warsaw Pact allies during the 1960s, 1970s and 1980s, see Daniel N. Nelson, "Power at What Cost: The Burden of Military Effort in the WTO," *Journal of Soviet Military Studies,* Vol. 2, No. 3 (September, 1989), pp. 317–345.

21. See, for example, Admiral Paul David Miller, USN (Commander, U.S. Atlantic Command and NATO's Supreme Commander, Atlantic), "Both Swords and Plowshares: Military Roles in the 1990s," manuscript (November, 1992).

22. Miller, op. cit., pp. 25–26.

23. Japanese "introversion" and the lack of any aspiration to play a superpower role, through the early 1970s, is discussed by Akio Watanabe, "Japanese Public Opinion and Foreign Affairs, 1964–1973," in Robert A. Scalipino, ed., *The Foreign Policy of Modern Japan* (Berkeley: University of California Press, 1977), pp. 119–122.

24. A good account of the onset of U.S.-Japan antagonism, pushed by the trade issue, was David MacEachron, "The United States and Japan: The Bilateral Potential," *Foreign Affairs* (Winter 1982–1983).

25. For example, *Report on Allied Contributions to the Common Defense,* a report submitted to Congress by Secretary of Defense Caspar Weinberger (July 21, 1982).

26. Author's interview, Tokyo, August 2, 1986.

27. These quotes are from William P. Bundy, op. cit.

28. See a report on Watanabe's initiative by David E. Sanger, "Japanese Discuss Widened Military," *The New York Times* (January 10, 1993), p. A7.

29. My critical assessment of U.S. and European resistance to alternatives to NATO-first policies was "NATO—Means But No Ends," *Bulletin of the Atomic Scientists,* Vol. 48, No. 1 (January/February, 1992), pp. 10–11.

30. See the introduction in this volume, plus Michael Intriligator, "Global Security," paper presented at the Conference on Conversion and De-Militarization of Security, co-sponsored by IMEMO and the Council on Economic Priorities, Moscow, November 10–14, 1990.

31. See a report by Stephen Fidler, "McNamara Calls for Aid to be Linked to Cuts in Arms Spending," *Financial Times* (27 April, 1991).

3 / Democratization around the Globe: Opportunities and Risks

TERRY LYNN KARL and PHILIPPE C. SCHMITTER

On April 25, 1974, a conspiracy of young military officers over-threw the authoritarian regime that had been ruling Portugal for forty years. At the time, no one imagined that this isolated and unexpected event would be followed in relatively short order by the demise of over *forty* other autoc-racies. This wave of democratization spread first to the neighboring, semi-peripheral, Southern European countries of the First World, and later to almost the entire continent of Latin America.[1] In the mid-1980s, it reached Asia, beginning with "people power" in the Philippines, then extending to South Korea, Taiwan, Thailand, and even to some elites in China.[2] Surpris-ing as these regime changes were to most of the actors involved and to all of the academics observing them, they pale in comparison to the shock pro-duced by the sudden collapse of Soviet-style regimes during 1989–1990. This event resounded dramatically in Africa, where by 1991 eight countries could be considered democratic.[3]

Communism's "grand failure" also led to triumphalist claims of the "un-abashed victory of economic and political liberalism."[4] Indeed, the end of the Cold War, the collapse of the Soviet Empire, and the virtual elimination of a viable alternative to capitalist development sparked extraordinarily hope-ful prescriptions regarding the prospects for democracy in the future. But are such prescriptions warranted? And what are the implications of this democratic sweep for the international system?

In this chapter, we will first explore the dynamics of the "wave" of regime transformations that has engulfed the world since 1974 and then discuss the differences in its impact upon world regions. We pay particular attention to the peculiarities of Eastern Europe, where democratization is inextricably linked to the collapse of the planned economy. Finally, we ask some ques-tions about the prospects for the eventual consolidation of these experiments with democracy and the risks and opportunities that they pose for the inter-national system.

A GLOBAL WAVE OF DEMOCRATIZATION?

We are currently witnessing the fourth historical wave of democratization.[5] The first wave, often marked by the introduction of universal suffrage (initially limited to white male property-owners) in the United States in the late 1820s, lasted until the so-called "Springtime of Freedom" that engulfed Europe in 1848–49 and then receded quickly, leaving relatively few democracies in its wake. The second corresponded to World War I and its aftermath, although this too met with a reverse wave initiated by Mussolini's termination of Italy's fragile democracy. The third took place during World War II and its aftermath, and eventually included countries as diverse as West Germany, Italy, Austria, Japan, South Korea, Brazil, and Costa Rica.

The second and third waves had a more lasting impact on the global distribution of political regimes, especially the latter, which triggered a veritable avalanche of decolonization. Not all of these ex-British, French, Dutch, Belgian, U.S., and Japanese colonies in Africa, Asia, the Caribbean, and the Pacific remained democratic for a long time, but a few did: India, Jamaica, Trinidad and Tobago, Malta, Botswana, the Gambia, Malaysia, and Sri Lanka. Yet here, too, democratization was followed by a reverse wave. Most of the newly independent Third World countries descended into various forms of single-party and personal autocracy during the 1960s, an authoritarian trend that was dramatically intensified in Latin America as first Peru, then Brazil, Bolivia, Argentina, Ecuador, and finally the long-standing democracies of Uruguay and Chile fell under military rule. The global swing away from democracy also swept Asia (especially South Korea, Indonesia, and the Philippines), the Mediterranean (Greece and Turkey), and Africa, where the largest proliferation of authoritarian governments occurred.[6]

Compared to these previous waves, the fourth one is distinctive in two respects:

1. It is not the result of a cataclysmic exogenous event, that is, worldwide or regional warfare. While this wave was produced in part by common causes affecting many countries, there is no single event of the scope and scale of World War I or World War II that provoked democratization. Instead, a variety of factors, ranging from the numerous economic and military failures of authoritarian rulers to the changing policies of external actors like the Catholic Church, the European Community, the former Soviet Union, and the United States, have played significant roles in bringing about these new transitions.[7]

2. It has been much more global in its reach. It began in Southern Europe, spread to Latin America, affected some Asian countries, and literally swept through Eastern Europe. Even Africa, often considered too poor to produce democracies, is currently experiencing its effects. Moreover, from Mongolia to Mali, Madagascar to Mexico—in countries that are experimenting with liberalization rather than full-blown democratization—important changes are still in the offing. Only the Arab countries of North Africa and the Middle East seem to have remained immune, although some democratic momentum has occurred in Algeria, Tunisia, and Jordan. As a consequence, the fourth wave has affected far more countries and been more thorough in its regional impact than its predecessors. Some parts of the

world that were previously almost uniformly autocratic are now almost equally democratic.

Diffusion is the most obvious hypothesis for explaining these differences. Where diffusion occurs, the successful example of one country's transition establishes it as a "model" to imitate. Once a given region is sufficiently saturated with this mode of political domination, pressure will mount to compel the remaining autocracies to conform to the newly established norm. Democratic "contagion" of this sort occurred in past waves, but it was confined to the exchanges between countries that were geographically proximate and culturally comparable. Researchers once found empirical proof of its presence by tracking the spread of political innovation from nearby units to those farther away. Such tests are no longer adequate in light of the global development of "complex communicative interdependence." Today people from China to Chile simultaneously are exposed to pictures of "people power" in the Philippines, and democratization can "leapfrog" from Southern Europe to Latin America without first affecting nearby North Africa or Eastern Europe. With the spread of television and communications satellites in the 1970s and short-wave radios and fax machines in the 1980s, authoritarian governments have found it increasingly difficult to control the information available to their subjects. Global communications networks not only demonstrate to people in one country that autocrats can be successfully removed in another; they often show just how it can be done!

Diffusion is thus a particularly appealing explanation for the contemporary wave of democratization. It does not illuminate why a wave a democratization may start in the first place, but it helps to understand how and why it may spread. Because modern systems of communication are not spatially bound and may not even be culturally confined, their new reach suggests the likelihood that the relevance of the international context will increase steadily with each successive instance of successful regime change. Those coming later in the wave will be more influenced by those that preceded them. Whether later transitions can be expected to learn from mistakes made earlier is perhaps less predictable, but there may be an advantage to "delayed democratization"—just as it has been argued that "late economic development" occasionally had its advantages. There is already some evidence to support this supposition. Spaniards were profoundly affected by the end of forty-five years of Portuguese dictatorship prior to the death of Franco, and democratizers there shaped their strategies accordingly. The Spanish transition, in turn, was very influential in Latin America, especially Argentina and Chile. Today, democrats in Eastern Europe eagerly seek lessons from these prior transitions that might be applicable in their own very different context.

Such diffusion does not rely upon the development and spread of communications alone. Particular to the fourth wave of democratization is another phenomenon that has fostered this demonstration effect and that may have less to do with contagion than with what could be called consent.

Each successive case of democratization has contributed more and more to the development of formal nongovernmental organizations and informal informational networks devoted to the promotion of human rights, protection of minorities, monitoring of elections, provision of economic advice, and fostering of exchanges among academics and intellectuals—all intended to promote further democratization. In the initial cases of Portugal, Greece, and Spain, this sort of an international infrastructure hardly existed. Indeed, some of the key lessons were learned from these experiences and subsequently applied elsewhere. By now, there exists an extraordinary variety of international parties, associations, foundations, religious and social movements, networks, and firms ready to share practical advice on "how to" democratize or to intervene either to promote or to protect democracy.

Their efficacy is enhanced by regional and international organizations that have been revitalized with the end of the Cold War and that have adopted democratic promotion as a means of keeping the peace. Nowhere is this more notable than in Nicaragua and El Salvador, where for the first time the United Nations, backed by a thick network of democratic contacts, has presided over demilitarization and fair elections, mediated human rights disputes, and negotiated peace agreements.[8] This suggests a second hypothesis: the international context surrounding democratization may have shifted from a primary reliance on public, bilateral intergovernmental channels of influence "downward," on the one hand, toward an increased involvement of private, nongovernmental organizations, and "upwards," on the other hand, toward a greater role for international organizations. If so, it may be the concrete activity of these agents of consent, rather than the abstract process of contagion, that accounts for the "global reach" of regime change and the fact that so few regressions to autocracy have thus far occurred.

Yet, even if the world has become a sort of global village in which democratic norms, practices, and experiences are more widely shared, the argument for "contagion" is especially persuasive within specific regional contexts. In Latin America, for example, the unexpected (and highly controlled) transition in Paraguay seems to have been influenced by the fact that the country was surrounded by nascent democracies, although Chile under Pinochet held out successfully against such pressures for a period during the 1980s. Shortly after the Catholic Church played a major role in the downfall of the Marcos regime in the Philippines in 1986, Cardinal Kim called for democracy in South Korea, and it is probable that events in these two countries subsequently influenced the push toward liberalization in China, Burma, and Taiwan.

Eastern Europe provides the best possible case for contagion, even though the initial impetus for regime change was given by an exogenous event, that is, the shift in Soviet foreign and defense policy towards the region. No one can question the accelerating flow of messages and images that went from Poland to Hungary to East Germany to Czechoslovakia to

Romania to Bulgaria and, eventually, to Albania, or the impact that successive declarations of national independence had upon the member republics of the Soviet Union. Indeed, the experiences of Eastern Europe, and to a lesser extent Central America, suggest that the lessons of contagion and the mechanisms of consent seem to function better at the regional, rather than the binational or global, level.[9]

ONE ROAD TO DEMOCRACY OR A CONTRAST BETWEEN CONTINENTS?

Global democratization—whatever its extent (or, as we shall see, its durability)—has been a very diverse process. There is no "standard" context in which autocracies become politically vulnerable, nor is there a single "modal" way of removing autocrats from office. The early democratizations of the fourth wave were the result of a variety of factors: an unwinnable colonial war, a military defeat in Cyprus, and the death of Franco precipitated transitions respectively in Portugal, Greece, and Spain. Once they occurred, however, the changes in these "leaders" helped to stimulate and shape events elsewhere. Subsequent democratizations have been at least indirectly interconnected, and one can find a substantial amount of overlap between each of the world regions. Still, it is possible to distinguish four contrasts between the regime changes that have occurred in Southern and Eastern Europe, South and Central America, Asia and, most recently, in Africa in: (1) their respective points of departure; (2) their modes of transition from autocratic rule; (3) the significance of external actors for triggering and guiding the events; and (4) the variety and sequencing of their transformative processes.

The Points of Departure

The classical contention that differences in level of development, literacy, urbanization, and so forth could explain the emergence of democratization has not stood up well during the fourth wave of democratization. While it is true that most of the societies involved were in the "middle-range" on most of these aggregate indicators, only three, Spain, South Korea, and Taiwan, were close to being full members of the exclusive club of advanced industrial countries. The others were strung out across a broad spectrum ranging from the relatively industrialized and highly literate ex-Communist systems of Czechoslovakia, Hungary, and Poland to such relatively impoverished and illiterate capitalist systems as Bolivia, Paraguay, Honduras, Peru, Benin, and Pakistan—with a large group of countries lying somewhere in between on one or another of the development indicators: for example, Brazil, Uruguay, Chile, Argentina, Portugal, Greece, Turkey, Romania, Bulgaria, Estonia, Latvia, Georgia, and Lithuania. If democratization should occur in one of the real "outlyers" in the development process, (e.g., Haiti, Albania, Mongolia, Mali, the Congo, Namibia, and Ethiopia), then a whole generation of theorizing about economic development as its major precondition will have to be rejected!

Points of departure may also be distinguished by the nature of the previous autocracy. These regimes have come in a great variety of types: from civilian to military, personal to institutional, and authoritarian to totalitarian. Under the pressure of the contemporary wave, all possible permutations of these types have collapsed. Romania was "civilian/personal/totalitarian"; Brazil was "military/institutional/authoritarian." As we shall see, there is some reason to suspect that the mode of transition may be related to these distinctions. In Romania, where power was concentrated in one individual, Ceaucescu was overthrown violently within a very short time; in contrast, the Brazilian generals presided over a peaceful and long, drawn out, regime change largely under their control.

Policymakers and scholars generally assume that the starkest contrast should be between "the East" and "the South," that is, between communist/totalitarianism and capitalist/authoritarianism systems, given the extreme differences in their modern histories. In fact, most of these Eastern political systems had long since degenerated into some form of authoritarian rule, not that far removed from the ways in which their Southern brethren were governed. Romania and Albania were obvious exceptions, although their high degree of personalization of power suggests a possible analogy with such cases of "sultanism" as Somoza's Nicaragua, Trujillo's Dominican Republic, Stroessner's Paraguay, or Mobutu's Zaire. What did remain a distinctive attribute of the East, however, was the monopolistic fusion of political and economic power into a party-state apparatus, the so-called *nomenklatura*, which (with the exception of Cuba and possibly Mexico) has had little parallel in the autocracies of Latin America, Asia, and Africa.

But what is most striking between the East and the South are the differences in point of departure in socio-occupational structure as the result of so many years of policies in the East designed to compress class and sectoral distinctions, equalize material rewards and, of course, eliminate the diversity of property relations under communism. Except where a "second economy" had emerged earlier and prospered commercially (e.g., Hungary), Eastern social systems seem very "amorphous" in their social structure, and it is difficult to imagine how the parties and interest associations that are so characteristic of all types of "Western" democracy could emerge, stabilize their respective publics, and contribute to the general consolidation of the regime. While the greater equality of the East puts these countries at a certain advantage when compared to the highly inequitable countries of Latin America, it is simultaneously a great disadvantage. Without more substantial and more stable class and sectoral differences, the politics of these neo-democracies are likely to be driven by other, much less tractable, cleavages, especially ethnicity or religious identity. In this sense Eastern Europe resembles Africa, where ethnic and other conflicts based upon identity have generally predominated.

The Modes of Transition

Regime changes are "produced" by actors who choose strategies that lead from one kind of regime to another. They are constrained in the choices available to them by their point of departure, that is, their prevailing social, economic, and political structures, and by the tremendous uncertainty that characterizes any regime change. The interaction of their strategies may often result in outcomes that no one initially preferred. But the identity of these political actors and the concrete strategies they collectively choose combine to define which type of transition will occur in a particular country.

Different modes of transition are depicted in Figure 3.1.[10] Simplifying a very complex choice on the horizontal axis, *strategies of transition* can vary along a continuum that runs from unilateral recourse to force to multilateral

Figure 3.1 / Modes of Transition: The Distribution of Recent Cases

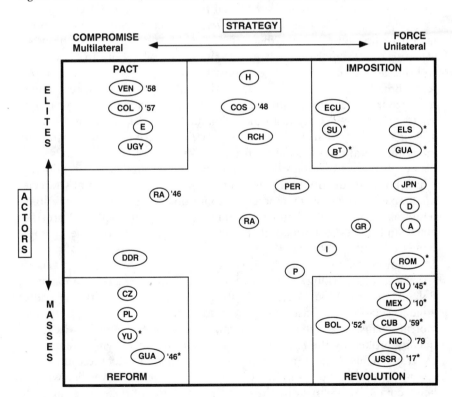

*These countries either did not then become or have not yet become democracies.

willingness to compromise. In short, transitions can be "ordered" or they can be bargained. In between lies a muddled and ambiguous zone of action in which mutual threats are exchanged, acts of physical intimidation and coercion may be committed, and substantial mobilizations of support may occur. The vertical axis distinguishes between cases in which most, if not all, of the impetus for change comes "from below," that is, from actors in subordinate or excluded positions in the social, economic, and political order of the ancien régime, and those in which elite actors "from above," that is, from within the dominant institutions of authoritarian rule, social prestige, and/or economic exploitation, play the leading role in moving the system toward some form of democracy. Again, it is important to note that the range of variation cannot be collapsed into a neat dichotomy, thus the diagram leaves room for a "messy" intermediate category in which elites and nonelites mingle and compete for the direction of the transition. Actors coming "from outside" may intervene directly and significantly on either axis—encouraging compromise or force, on the one hand, and mass activity or elite actions, on the other. As the democratization of Japan and Germany illustrate, they can play an especially significant role when they have defeated the previous authoritarian regime in international warfare!

From the four "extreme" corners of the plot in Figure 3.1 emerge four ideal types of regime transition: (1) *pact*, when elites agree upon a multilateral compromise among themselves (e.g., Spain, Uruguay, Colombia, Venezuela); (2) *imposition*, when elites use force unilaterally and effectively to bring about a regime change against the resistance of some incumbents (e.g., Brazil, Ecuador, Turkey, Soviet Union); (3) *reform*, when masses mobilize from below and impose a compromised outcome without resorting to violence (e.g., Czechoslovakia, Poland, Yugoslavia, and Guatemala in 1946); and (4) *revolution*, when masses rise up in arms and defeat the previous authoritarian rulers militarily (e.g., Nicaragua). In the capacious space between the four extremes lie presumably a large number of situations in which both the identity of the relevant actors and the selection of strategies are "mixed." Violence is tempered by compromise before it becomes dominant; masses are aroused and active, but still under the control of previous elites; and domestic actors and strategies are significant, but the outcome hinges critically on what foreign occupiers or intervenors do.

Countries seldom fit neatly into boxes, so it is not always easy to classify specific cases according to the coordinates of Figure 3.1. Take, for example, Poland's transition. It began in 1980 in the *reform* box with the rise of Solidarnosc—a mass-based movement advocating regime change by nonviolent means. This "phase" ended with a *pact* in 1981, which was subsequently broken by the *imposition* of a military regime—whose temporary effect was to abort the transition process altogether. In 1989 these autocratic rulers chose, under pressure from two successive strike waves but without being compelled to do so by the organized violence of their adversaries, to enter into "roundtable" negotiations that subsequently produced another *pact*, which in turn lead to restricted elections in June that brought to power a mass-based *reform* government. Since its transition began and ended in the *reform* box, and since it was conditioned all along by the presence of a mass movement, we place Poland there—in effect, ignoring the tortuous path by which it left and returned.[11]

Portugal is another hard case to classify. It began its 1974 transition suddenly and unexpectedly by imposition—a coup d'état launched by junior military officers in the context of impending military defeat in Guinea-Bissau. Virtually overnight, the successful seizure of power triggered a mass response that first pushed the process in a reformist direction and, then, in the spring and summer of 1975, seemed to be leading toward a revolutionary outcome. The defeat of radical military elements in November prevented that and for some time the Portuguese polity remained suspended between reform and imposition (efforts to negotiate pacts failed), until the elections of 1987 and consequent changes in the constitution placed the country at last on the road to consolidation.[12]

Other countries show similar "mixed" modes of transition. Chile was firmly (and protractedly) entrenched in the imposition mode until General Pinochet misjudged his capacity to win a key plebiscite in 1988. Subsequently, its revived civilian politicians opted for a pacted transition based on a "grand alliance" of all opposition parties. Hungary is a somewhat similar case in which the initial impetus came from within the dominant party, but these elites lost control and were forced to "roundtable" with opposition groups who, themselves, aroused little popular support. The German Democratic Republic would have been a standard case of reform from below were it not for the substantial interference of elites from the neighboring Federal Republic at key moments in its transition. Similarly, Romania may have first undergone an accelerated regime change under revolutionary conditions of violence and mass involvement, but the (unclear) role of the Soviet Union and the subsequent recuperation of the *nomenklatura* and military apparatus resemble the imposition mode.[13]

One major East-South difference that seems to emerge, irrespective of the mode of transition, is the extent of collapse of the previous regime. Not only were the Eastern European regime changes less "preannounced" and the opposition forces less "pre-prepared" to rule than in the South, but once new governments were formed the role of previous power-holders declined much more precipitously and significantly than it has elsewhere. There were a few exceptions where rebaptized (and possibly reformed) communists managed to do well in the initial "founding elections" and to hold on as a group to key executive positions, but even then they often proved incapable of governing effectively and were displaced in relatively short order, vide Albania, Bulgaria, and Estonia. By our calculation, only in Romania, Mongolia, Ukraine, Azerbaijan, Lithuania, and Serbia are previous communists continuing to play a significant role, either as a party governing alone or a party in alliance with others.

This contrasts with Southern Europe and Latin America, where neo-democracies were often governed initially by centrist or rightist parties that had important elements (and persons) from the previous regime in their ranks, and where "traditional" powers such as the armed forces or the police retained very significant power to intervene in policy-making and affect the choice of institutions. Spain, Brazil, and Chile may be the most extreme cases, but almost everywhere the transition takes place in the shadow—if not under the auspices—of the ancien régime. This is also the case in Africa, where the armed forces remain a "veto" force even when they have withdrawn from direct rule. In contrast, given the virtual abdication of their previous rulers, Eastern Europeans could harbor the (momentary) illusion of a tabula rasa upon which to build new rules and practices, rather than behave as if they had to cautiously wend their way through a "living museum" of powerful actors from the past.

The Role of External Actors

One of the more confident generalizations of the early literature on democratization emphasized the much greater importance of domestic forces and calculations, as opposed to foreign influences, in determining the nature and timing of regime transition. It was hinted, however, that the latter might play a more significant role, subsequently, in the consolidation phase.[14] This observation, which was based on the experiences of Southern Europe and South America, does not fit either Eastern Europe or Central America. Without a previously announced and credible shift in the foreign and security policies of the Soviet Union, and a less dramatic though equally telling change in U.S. policy toward its neighbors, neither the timing nor the occurrence of regime change would be easily explicable in these two regions.

Moreover, there is much more evidence of "contagion" within these two regions, that is, of events in one country accelerating a response in its neighbors. Unlike Southern Europe, South America, and Asia, where democratization did not substantially alter long-standing commercial relations or international alliances, the regime changes in Eastern Europe triggered a major collapse in intraregional trade and the dissolution of the Warsaw Pact. Into this vacuum moved an extraordinary variety of Western advisors and promoters—binational and multilateral. In Central America as well, external actors have imposed political "conditionality" upon the process of consolidation, linking specific rewards explicitly to the meeting of specific norms, or even to the selection of specific institutions.[15]

The Sequence of Transformations

All of the above differences pale in importance before the sequence of transformations, in our opinion. In none of the Southern European, South

American, or African cases did the regime change from autocracy to democracy occur alone, in complete isolation from other much-needed military, social, and economic transformations. Except in Central America and Eastern Europe, it was usually possible to deal with these variegated demands sequentially; that is, a change in the polity did not immediately call into question the economic model or the existence of the military. In some especially favored cases, major structural changes had already been accomplished under the previous autocracies. For example, most of these transitions "inherited" acceptable national identities and boundaries—even if the degree of local or regional autonomy remained contested. In a few, the military had already been largely subordinated to civilian control (e.g., Spain under Franco), or the economy had undergone substantial restructuring to make it more internationally competitive (e.g., Chile under Pinochet).

In Eastern Europe, by contrast, not only are such major transformations all on the agenda for collective action and choice, but very little authoritative capacity exists for asserting priorities among them. This *simultaneity* means that there is a great deal more to do than in the South, and it seems as if it must be done at once. Many decisions have to be made in the same time frame, and their uncontrolled interactions tend to produce unanticipated (and usually unwanted) effects. Even within a given issue area, the absence of historical precedents makes it difficult to assert theoretically what should come first: holding elections or forming a provisional government? drafting a national constitution or encouraging local autonomy? releasing prices or controlling budget deficits? privatizing state industries or allowing collective bargaining? creating a capital market or sustaining a realistic exchange rate?, and the list could continue indefinitely.

Even if "transition theory" can offer a few generic insights strictly within the political domain, these risk being quite irrelevant given simultaneous—rather than sequential—demands for changes in major economic, social, cultural/national, and military institutions. For example, one knows in the abstract that the formation of provisional governments can be a bad thing, especially before the configuration of national party systems is evident, but what if (as seems to have been the case in Czechoslovakia) it is necessary to head off a polarized conflict among nationalities? In retrospect, it seems to have been a crucial error for Gorbachev to have convoked (or tolerated) elections at the level of republics *before* holding a national election that would have legitimated his own position and, with it, the All-Union framework of territorial authority, but this was presumably necessitated by the correlation of forces within the Communist party and the military at the time.

One thing is becoming abundantly clear—and this was observed already in the classic article of Dankwert Rustow that lies at the origin of much of today's work on transition:[16] that without some prior consensus on overarching national identity and boundaries little or nothing can be accomplished to move the system out of the protracted uncertainty of democratic transition into the relative calm (and even boredom) of consolidation. This places the former Soviet Union and Yugoslavia in a radically different sequence, and it is not inconceivable that all of their "successor republics" will be paralyzed by a similar imperative. It also bodes ill for Africa, where borders drawn by colonizers are likely to be contested in the future regardless of the firm intentions of African governments to the contrary.

A VARYING RANGE OF OUTCOMES?

Different modes of transition from authoritarian rule do not necessarily lead to democracy. Indeed, *consolidated democracy* is only one possible outcome. Democracy can be defined in generic terms as "a system of governance in which rulers are held accountable for their actions in the public realm by citizens, acting indirectly through the competition and cooperation of their representative."[17] For this arrangement to work, certain procedural norms must be met,[18] including: (1) control over decisions by elected officials; (2) regular and fair elections; (3) adult suffrage; (4) widespread eligibility to run for office; (5) rights to free expression, speech, and petition; (6) access to alternative sources of information; (7) rights to form/join associations and parties; and (8) civilian control over the military. Where these procedural norms exist and are respected through regularized and fair "rules of the game" based on political competition, consolidated democracies can be found.

But some of these procedural norms can also be found in a context in which actors may not have been successful in producing a stable and legitimate form of governance, that is, in establishing a type of democracy that is appropriate for and accepted by a given population. Thus, a second possible outcome is *unconsolidated democracy*. Another way of putting the point is that democracy, in its most generic sense, may persist after the demise of autocracy, but not be consolidated into a specific and reliable set of rules or institutions. Some countries (Argentina is most frequently cited, but Botswana is another case) may be "condemned" for the foreseeable future to remain democratic only because no feasible alternative mode of domination is (presently) available. Elections are held; associations are tolerated; rights may even be respected to some extent; the procedural minima are met with some degree of regularity, but the *ensemble* of rules and institutions do not jell into regular, acceptable and predictable patterns that can reproduce themselves over time and command the allegiance of citizens. "Democracy" is not replaced by something else—say, the old form of autocratic rule—it just persists by reacting in ad hoc and ad hominem ways to successive problems. Under these circumstances, there is no underlying agreement to govern the relationship between parties, organized interests, and ethnic or religious groups.

A third possible outcome of transition is the formation of a *hybrid regime*, that is, a polity which cannot meet the procedural minima of democracy but also does not return to the status quo ante. These have been referred to as *dictablandas*, authoritarian regimes that recognize some rights and protection for the individual but do not permit political competition, and *democraduras*, regimes which often severely restrict popular participation but do allow a degree of political competition.[19] They have become increasingly common, especially in Central America and Africa, as authoritarian rulers seek to introduce democratic mechanisms into their polities in order to assuage international forces encouraging democratization. El Salvador, where elections since 1982 have been held in the context of the systematic violation of political and human rights, is one such *democradura*, although it may cross the threshold to democracy if UN-negotiated peace accords guarantee a different context for the 1994 elections. The Ivory Coast and Gabon are others. Hybrid regimes are unlikely to provide a stable political solution after transition, and thus may be more usefully viewed as an interim stage before a return to full authoritarianism or progress toward democracy.

Finally, a fourth possible outcome of transition is *regression to authoritarian rule*. Statistical data from the prior three waves of democratization suggest that this may be the most probable result. Indeed, each earlier wave was followed by a reverse wave of authoritarian rule that eliminated many (but not all) of the previous transitions to democracy. In 1990, at the height of transitions, roughly 45 percent of all independent countries were democratic, the same percentage as in 1922.[20] Still, each wave of democratizations has left more democracies in place, and there have been relatively few regressions to date. Haiti, Peru, Thailand, and Nigeria are the most evident cases of regression, while the very start of a transition has been blocked in Burma and China and stalled in Algeria. For whatever reason, democratic waves seem to last approximately two decades, so the extent of regression may not be known until the end of the 1990s—a factor that makes the recent military coup attempts in democratic Venezuela especially troubling.

Even where some form of democracy does result from the demise of authoritarian rule, new democracies face distinctive problems related to both the timing and nature of their transitions. On the one hand, political democracy in the contemporary period may be rooted in a fundamental paradox: the modes of transition that appear to enhance initial survivability may preclude the democratic self-transformation of the economy or polity further down the road. Transitions are highly uncertain moments; for democracies to emerge from them, actors must often limit uncertainty by entering into bargains that protect the privileges of those who formerly supported authoritarian rule. In Chile, for example, democratizers had to accept a constitution imposed by the Pinochet regime that contained blatantly antidemocratic provisions, including a guarantee for the military of 10 percent of all copper revenues over and above its normal budget. Cruelly, these bargains, while permitting democracies to persist in the short run, may constrain their potential for resolving the problems of poverty and inequality that continue to plague them. They may be especially costly during the present time of economic hardship, when virtually all new democracies are coping with crises in growth, employment, foreign-exchange earnings, debt repayment, and so forth.

Such trade-offs are especially evident in elite-dominated processes of democratization, which are unilaterally imposed by authoritarians in power. Pacted and reform democracies, whatever their defects, have been honed through compromise between at least two powerful contending actors, thus their institutions tend to be more flexible when faced with future bargaining over substantive issues and/or demands for the revision of existing rules. In Uruguay, for example, while the agreed-upon rules made it very difficult to challenge agreements between the military and the political parties on the issue of amnesty for crimes committed during authoritarian rule, the left opposition, excluded from this accord, was nevertheless able to force the convocation of a plebiscite on this major issue—which it subsequently lost. It is difficult to imagine that anything similar could occur in Brazil. Because the Brazilian armed forces exerted almost complete control over the timing and content of the transition, they never curtailed their own prerogatives nor fully agreed to the principle of civilian control and they have not been compelled to adopt institutional rules reflecting the need for compromise.

It is reasonable to hypothesize that what occurs in the phase of transition or early consolidation may involve a significant trade-off between some form of political democracy, on the one hand, and equity, on the other. The contrast between the cases of Uruguay and Brazil suggests the reasoning behind this hypothesis: where transitions are unilaterally imposed by armed forces who are not compelled to enter into compromises, they threaten to evolve into civilian governments controlled by authoritarian elements who are unlikely to push for greater participation, accountability, or equity for the majority of their citizens. Paradoxically, in other words, the heritage left by what some would call "successful" authoritarian experiences, that is, those characterized by relatively moderate levels of repression and economic success that has left the military establishment relatively intact, may prove to be the major obstacle to future democratic self-transformation.[21] This same danger exists, albeit to a lesser extent, in civilian-directed unilaterally imposed transitions, for example, Mexico under Salinas, because the institutional rules are likely to be systematically rigged to favor incumbents and to permit less scope for contestation.

Thus, even though the emergence of new and stable democracies is by far the most desirable of the four outcomes sketched above, they confront significant problems in their struggle to consolidate rather than collapse. They must establish new constitutional and electoral systems; abolish authoritarian bastions, like death squads or secret police; establish a professional pattern of civil-military relations and a reduced role for the military; cope

with torturers; design forums for interaction between business, government, and labor; and contain ethnic or regional conflict—all in the context of economic hardship. In some cases, as Eastern Europe so painfully demonstrates, the mere fact of democratization, that is, the promise of free expression for the first time, unleashes pent-up forces previously suppressed by coercion that threaten the stability of both states and regimes. These democracies guarantee a greater respect for law and human dignity when compared to their authoritarian predecessors, but they may be unable to carry out substantive reforms that address the lot of their poorest or most oppressed citizens.

NEW REWARDS AND RISKS FOR THE INTERNATIONAL SYSTEM?

We now return to our initial questions: What are the prospects for consolidating the regime changes of this fourth wave of democratization? And what implications will these changes have for the international system as a whole?

One can point to some optimistic features of the present context. According to Freedom House, which has been surveying the progress of human and political rights since the early 1970s, more people live under freedom than ever before.[22] Although democracies can abuse individual and collective freedoms, especially those of ethnic minorities, they tend to respect rights much more predictably and extensively than their authoritarian counterparts. To the extent that they are consolidated, they also provide regular channels for the expression of dissent and offer reliable mechanisms for peacefully changing their government leaders and policies.

Moreover, the proliferation of popularly accountable government has direct implications for peace and security. One of the few "laws" of international relations that seems to hold invariably is that democracies do not go to war with other democracies. Autocracies have frequently fought each other as well as democracies; and democracies have invaded authoritarian regimes, even small ones where the national security threat is questionable at best—vide the recent cases of the United States in Grenada and Panama—but a world or a region populated by consolidated democracies is definitely likely to be less insecure and violent. Its member states will still have international conflicts, but where two democracies are concerned, they are much more likely to resort to compromise, mediation, and adjudication in resolving them.[23]

There is also reason to believe that the fourth wave may be followed by less regressions to authoritarian rule than the past three. To no small degree, this can be attributed to the steady growth of international nongovernmental organizations (NGOs) that provide services for neodemocracies and

monitor their performance in elections and human rights, as well as mobilize support for them when threatened by military coups, rigged elections, or arbitrary government action. Complementing this development of an embryonic "transnational civil society" is the strengthening of the role of international, intergovernmental organizations (IGOs), either at the global level in the United Nations and its specialized agencies or at the regional level through such entities as the European Community, the Organization of American States, or the Association of Southeast Asian Nations. The "political conditionality" they have imposed, along with the material support they have mobilized or the collective sanctions they have applied, has not always been sufficient to prevent regression to autocracy and violence—witness the sad cases of Burma, Haiti, and Bosnia-Herzegovina; but they have led to some important successes in Nicaragua, El Salvador, and Namibia. There is little question that the growing strength of these transnational forces makes it more difficult for authoritarian rulers to anoint themselves as self-appointed "saviors of the fatherland."

But there are also good reasons to avoid the triumphalism of those who believe that the demise of communism and the exhaustion of utopian ideologies heralds the definitive victory for democratization. All previous waves of regime change eventually receded—and it simply may be too early to tell how many polities will be dragged back to autocracy this time. Certainly the fact that most neodemocracies are simultaneously having to cope with declining economic performance, accelerating inflation rates, heavy external indebtedness, severe fiscal crises, insistent demands for industrial restructuring to meet increased international competition, and persistent capital flight is not making their task easier. Although citizens in new democracies thus far have responded to these strains of economic austerity and adjustment by focusing their discontent on specific governments rather than on the notion of democracy itself, it is uncertain how long they can "punishment vote" parties out of office or remove corrupt officials from their positions before the regime itself is questioned.

Indeed, there are growing signs of what the Spaniards have called *desencanto* (disenchantment) with democracy itself. The perception that democratization can increase corruption, that professional politicians have arrogated disproportionate salaries and perquisites to themselves, that policies imposing burdens on privileged groups do not get applied, that such entrenched powers as the military have protected and even increased their share of the public budget, that crime has increased, that arbitrary violations of human rights by police forces persist, that the tax burden is unfairly distributed or collected, that unsavory nationals or even foreigners are reaping too many of the benefits from policies of privatization and deregulation—some or all of these complaints have emerged with regularity in nascent democracies. They have been taken up by opportunistic demagogues or populists who promise that the "temporary" use of exceptional powers and suspension of civil and human rights will right all these wrongs

and return the polity to a "better" democracy. The recent attempted coups in Venezuela, or Peruvian President Fujimori's suspension of the legislature in 1992, his subsequent rule by decree and eventual convocation of a controlled election to draft a new (and, presumably, more authoritarian) constitution, may well be harbingers of future developments.

But these problems of economic suffering and political disappointment pale when compared to those of cultural conflict. One frequent characteristic of autocracies is their tendency to suppress or manipulate ethnolinguistic minorities. The nascent democracies that succeed them inherit these accumulated resentments and provide the discriminated groups with the freedom to openly express their demands. In Southern Europe and Latin America, where national borders were relatively secure before the transition, demands by subnational groups have met with repression and violence, but conflicts have remained relatively confined, if no less brutal. In Eastern Europe and Africa, where historical resentments run deep and existing borders often divide rather than unite nations, mobilization along ethnolinguistic lines is especially explosive and threatens to overwhelm the usual bases of social cleavage: class, status, generation, gender, and so forth, which underlie stable party and interest-group systems. The sad fact is that democracy depends on the *prior* existence of a legitimate political unit—and this can only be accomplished by complex and often lengthy historical processes. There is no democratic way of deciding what the physical and cultural boundaries of that unit should be. Slogans such as the self-determination of peoples, and devices such as plebiscites or referenda, simply beg the question of who is eligible to vote and whether the majority can legitimately impose its will on the minority.

The contemporary international system will be deeply affected by this fourth wave of democratization, but not in a single or predictable way. What is certain is that multilateral organizations and transnational forces will be called upon to deal with more and more issues, including many that were previously regarded as lying exclusively under the jurisdiction of national states. Traditional notions of sovereignty will be increasingly questioned as international actors monitor domestic elections, verify human-rights conditions, and demobilize national armies. Whether such organizations will slide down a "slippery slope" toward operational overload, or can find ways to successfully circumscribe their involvements, remains to be seen.[24]

At the same time, long-established democracies like the United States will be pushed to decide whether or not to make the promotion and sustenance of democracy a central foreign policy goal. In this debate, detractors will point to the poor performance record of the past, especially in Latin America, while proponents will put their faith in "political conditionality," aimed at linking the provision of international aid to the fulfillment of specific democratic objectives within and between states.[25] Sanctions may be more frequently applied to those who dramatically and systematically

violate widespread norms of human rights. The fact that democratic practices and respect for fundamental rights stands as an explicit requirement
for membership in the European Community, that the United States has
begun to explore the prospect of making democratization a condition for
assistance, and that financial and technological aid is increasingly available
from autonomous democratic organizations, creates new incentives to sustain the fourth wave. Yet, it also carries the danger that big-power faith in
political engineering seeks to impose a uniform political model that ignores
the broad variations in local circumstances among countries. What ultimately will determine the efficacy of these external incentives depends as
much upon the sensitive recognition by "conditioners" that democracies
come in diverse types, by various routes, from different points of departure,
and under different constraints, as it does upon the actions taken by authoritarians reluctant to reform.

Notes

1. For a discussion of the initial sweep of democratization across Southern Europe and
Latin America, see the four-volume study by Guillermo O'Donnell, Philippe C. Schmitter, and
Laurence Whitehead, eds., *Transitions from Authoritarian Rule* (Baltimore: Johns Hopkins
University Press, 1986).

2. For a discussion of democratization in Asia, see Larry Diamond, Juan J. Linz, and
Seymour Martin Lipset, eds., *Democracy in Developing Countries: Asia* (Boulder, CO: Lynne
Rienner Publishers, 1989).

3. These are Benin, Botswana, Cape Verde, Gambia, Mauritius, Namibia, Sao Tome and
Principe, and Zambia. By 1992, Mali had joined these ranks, and important negotiations
toward democracy were occurring in South Africa as well. See Larry J. Diamond, "International and Domestic Factors in Africa's Trend Toward Democracy," (Stanford: Hoover
Institution, Working Papers in International Studies, 1992).

4. See Zbigniew Brzezinski, *The Grand Failure: The Birth and Death of Communism in
the Twentieth Century* (New York: Charles Scribner's Sons, 1989) and Francis Fukuyama,
"The End of History?" *The National Interest*, 16 (Summer 1989), p. 3.

5. Samuel Huntington contends that this is actually the third wave of democratization,
with the first one lasting almost one hundred years, from 1828–1926. This seems excessively
long, especially because, by our criteria, a wave involves interactive and interdependent choices
across national boundaries within a more compressed period of time. Hence, below we
distinguish an earlier wave in the first part of the nineteenth century from the wave that
surrounded World War I. See his *The Third Wave: Democratization in the Late Twentieth
Century* (Norman and London: University of Oklahoma Press, 1991).

6. By some counts, one-third of the globe's democracies had fallen under authoritarian
rule by the mid-1970s. See Juan Linz and Alfred Stepan, "Political Crafting of Democratic
Consolidation or Destruction: European and South American Comparisons," in Robert A.
Pastor, ed., *Democracy in the Americas: Stopping the Pendulum* (New York: Holmes and
Meier, 1989), p. 47.

7. This observation lends weight to the contention that no single factor is adequate to
explain the emergence of new democracies. On this point, see Terry Lynn Karl, "Dilemmas of
Democratization in Latin America," *Comparative Politics*, Vol. 23, No.1 (October 1990).

8. In Nicaragua, the UN monitored internal elections for the first time and oversaw the
demobilization of the contras. It subsequently expanded its role in El Salvador from electoral
supervision and peacekeeping to actual peacemaking. For a discussion of its role in this latter
country, see Terry Karl, "El Salvador's Negotiated Revolution," *Foreign Affairs*, Vol. 7, No.2
(Spring 1992). For an excellent discussion of the changing role of the United Nations and the
challenges facing it, see Ernst B. Haas, "Collective Conflict Management: Evidence for a New
World Order?" in Thomas G. Weiss, ed., *Collective Security in a Changed World* (Providence,

RI: Brown University, World Peace Foundation and the Thomas J. Watson Institute for International Studies and World Peace, 1992).

9. Extraregional powers seem to have learned this lesson. Most of the U.S. intervention in the delicate early years of the Portuguese transition was channelled through friendly European powers, just as much of the American aid for Eastern Europe is slated to pass thorough the European Bank for Reconstruction and Development.

10. This depiction of different modes of democratic transition originally appeared in Terry Lynn Karl, "Dilemmas of Democratization in Latin America," op.cit.

11. For a detailed discussion of these later events, see Marjorie Castle, "A Successfully Failed Pact? The Polish Roundtable of 1989," Ph.D. dissertation (Stanford University, 1993).

12. See Philippe C. Schmitter, "Liberation by *Golpe*: Retrospective Thoughts about the Demise of Authoritarian Rule in Portugal," *Armed Forces and Society*, Vol. 2, No. 1 (Fall 1975). ʳ

13. Cf. Michel Castex, *Un mensonge gros comme le siècle: Roumanie, histoire d'une manipulation* (Paris: Albin Michel, 1990); also "Enigmas of a Revolution," *The Economist* (January 6, 1990).

14. For the initial observation, see Guillermo O'Donnell and Philippe C. Schmitter, *Transitions from Authoritarian Rule: Tentative Conclusions about Uncertain Democracies* (Baltimore: Johns Hopkins Press, 1986), pp. 17–21. It should be noted that the cases upon which this generalization was based did not include those of Central America. In that subregion, external influence and intromission has been (and continues to be) much more significant. For a criticism with regard to Southern Europe, see Geoffrey Pridham, ed., *Encouraging Democracy: The International Context of Regime Transition in Southern Europe* (Leicester: Leicester University Press, 1991).

15. The changing international context for democratization is discussed at greater length in Philippe C. Schmitter, "The International Context for Contemporary Democratization: Constraints and Opportunities upon the Choice of National Institutions and Policies," paper presented at the East-South Systems Tranformation (ESST) Conference, 4–7 January 1992, Toledo.

16. Dankwart Rustow, "Transitions to Democracy," *Comparative Politics*, 2 (1970), pp. 337–363.

17. For a more detailed explication of this definition, see Philippe C. Schmitter and Terry Karl, "What Democracy is . . . and is not," *Journal of Democracy*, Vol. 2, No. 3 (Summer 1991), pp. 75–88.

18. These have been explored most thoroughly in the work of Robert Dahl, especially, in his *Dilemmas of Pluralist Democracy* (New Haven: Yale University Press, 1982). In the above-cited article by Schmitter and Karl, two additional criteria for assessing the existence of democracy have been added to Dahl's original seven.

19. Guillermo O'Donnell and Philippe C. Schmitter, op.cit.

20. Huntington, op.cit., p. 25.

21. The notion that especially "successful" authoritarian regimes paradoxically may pose important obstacles for democratization can be found in Anita Isaacs, "Dancing with the People: The Politics of Military Rule in Ecuador, 1972–1979," Ph.D. thesis, Oxford University (1986) and Guillermo O'Donnell, "Challenges to Democratization in Brazil," *World Policy Journal*, Vol. V, No. 2, (Spring 1988), pp. 281–300.

22. Cf. Freedom House, *Freedom in the World: Political Rights and Civil Liberties, 1990–1991* (New York: Freedom House, 1991) and previous editions. For a more general discussion of the problem of measuring democracy and its change over time, see the articles in the special number of *Studies in Comparative International Development*, Vol. 25 (1990) by Alex Inkeles, "Introduction: On Measuring Democracy," pp. 6–14 and R. D. Gastil, "The Comparative Survey of Freedom: Experiences and Suggestions," pp. 25–50.

23. See Michael W. Doyle, "Liberalism and World Politics," *American Political Science Review*, 80 (December 1986) and Bruce Russett, "Politics and Alternative Security: Towards a More Democratic Therefore More Peaceful World," in Burns H. Weston, ed., *Alternative Security: Living Without Nuclear Deterrence* (Boulder, CO: Westview Press, 1990).

24. Ernest Haas warns that if these organizations try to address all of these tasks simultaneously, they invite failure. See his "Beware the Slippery Slope: Notes Towards the Definition of Justifiable Intervention," prepared for the Committee on International Security Studies of the American Academy of Arts and Sciences, January 5, 1993.

25. In summing up the record of the United States in Latin America, Abraham Lowenthal warns that efforts to promote democracy "have rarely been successful, and then only in a narrow range of circumstances." See "The United States and Latin American Democracy: Learning from History," in his edited volume, *Exporting Democracy: The United States and Latin America* (Baltimore: Johns Hopkins Press, 1991). For a proponent's view, see Larry Diamond, "Promoting Democracy," *Foreign Policy*, No. 87 (Summer 1992).

4 / The Dynamics of Revolutionary Change in Russia and the Former Soviet Union

MICHAEL McFAUL

For the last forty years, the international system was dominated by two superpowers anchoring two antagonistic political and socioeconomic subsystems. Conflict between the United States and the Soviet Union and their respective transnational socioeconomic systems—capitalism versus communism—constituted the defining characteristic of the international system for the first four decades after World War II.[1]

In 1991, one pole within this bipolar system collapsed. For the first time in the history of the modern world, the balance of power within the international system changed without a major war.[2] How? Why did communism collapse in the Soviet Union and Eastern Europe? What will emerge in its wake? What are the implications for the international system?

This chapter seeks to provide at least preliminary answers to these questions by understanding change in the former Soviet Union and Eastern Europe as revolutions, comparable to other great political and socioeconomic transformations in history. After defining revolution and outlining a model of revolution as a framework for understanding change in the USSR, we then review the period of reform begun by Gorbachev that unleashed the current revolutionary situation in Russia and the former Soviet Union. We next explore the dynamics of democratization (or lack thereof) in Russia after the collapse of the Soviet Union in August 1991; examine the creation of a capitalist economy in Russia since the August coup; and discuss the foreign policy implications of domestic change for Russian relations both with the "near abroad" (the other states of the former Soviet Union) and the Western world. We conclude the chapter with outlines of possible scenarios for the future.

ANTICOMMUNIST REVOLUTIONS

Revolutions are rare and distinct moments in history characterized by "a sweeping, fundamental change in political organization, social structure, economic property control and the predominant myth of social order, thus indicating a major break in the continuity of development."[3] This definition emphasizes the *simultaneity* of radical change in both the polity and socio-economic structure, distinguishing revolutions from situations in which the polity and/or government changes without altering the organizing principles of the socioeconomic structure, or historical developments when the socio-economic structure changes without altering the basic organization of the polity.[4]

Change in the former Soviet Union approximates this definition of revolution in two key respects. First, the old Soviet polity, consisting of a state subordinated to the Communist party of the Soviet Union, has been destroyed. In the vacuum, the newly evolving Russian state (and some of the other states, to varying degrees, that have emerged from the former Soviet Union) seeks to institute democratically elected parliaments and executives, a separation of power between the legislature and the executive, an independent judiciary, and a multiparty system. Second, the old Soviet command-economy, in which virtually all production and distribution was controlled by the party-state, has also collapsed. In its place, Russia's new leaders (and to varying degrees, leaders in other former Soviet republics) seek to create an economy based on private property, free prices, and market forces.

The simultaneous creation of a democracy and market economy in place of a dictatorship and command economy is a revolutionary undertaking currently being attempted in Russia and most of the former communist world. *Commitment to a revolutionary agenda, however, does not guarantee a revolutionary outcome.*[5] Russian leaders aspire to make revolutionary changes, but neither Russia nor any other former Soviet republic has yet succeeded in achieving a revolutionary outcome. The institutionalization of democracy and capitalism in the former Soviet Union is impeded by the sources of the revolutionary ideology, the method of revolutionary change, and the unintended consequences of the revolutionary project. First, "democracy" and the "market" were ideologies of opposition adopted by anti-communist revolutionaries to mobilize resistance to the Soviet system. Like other ideologies of opposition, these concepts were imported (and, to a certain extent, resurrected from Russia's past) to mobilize anticommunist sentiment. Only after seizing state power were Russia's revolutionaries compelled to add content to these ideologies of opposition. Second, unlike most other great social revolutions, Russia's revolutionaries have not used force (yet) to destroy the ancien régime. While Louis XVI was beheaded, and the Russian peasants were brutally collectivized, the new Russian regime has sought revolutionary transformation through peaceful, co-optive means. This peaceful strategy for accomplishing revolutionary ends allows individuals, social groups, and even institutions formed under the old system to continue to exist. It remains uncertain whether this peaceful strategy can produce revolutionary outcomes.

Finally, the destruction of the communist ancien régime also catalyzed the decolonization of the Soviet empire and rethinking of ethnic identities. With the implosion of the Soviet economic and state system, diverse states and ethnic groups have emerged with different and often conflicting strategies for developing new polities and economies. National self-determination, suppressed by the Soviet state and now unleashed with the collapse of the Soviet state, may alter, impede, or stall altogether the creation of democracy and capitalism in the former Soviet Union.

REFORMING THE UNREFORMABLE SOVIET REGIME, 1985–1991

Upon becoming General Secretary of the Communist Party of the Soviet Union (CPSU) in 1985, Mikhail Gorbachev began to temper the party-state monopoly on the Soviet polity and economy. During the twenty years of stagnation under Brezhnev, the Soviet economy had ground to a halt. While Brezhnev attained nuclear parity with the United States during the 1970s, the Soviet economy lagged far behind Western standards with no signs of "catching up." Moreover, the new American military buildup under Ronald Reagan in the 1980s, and the threat of a new technological race with the announcement of the Strategic Defense Initiative in 1983, threatened to further squeeze the Soviet economy. Most of the Soviet Union's best material and human resources were already devoted to the military-industrial complex. The Soviet economy could not afford even greater expenditures devoted to the military.

Gorbachev began to respond innovatively to the Soviet crisis with a two-pronged strategy. Internationally, Gorbachev sought to relieve external pressure on the Soviet system by engaging the West, and the United States in particular, in a new relationship. Gorbachev's "new political thinking" renounced class struggle as the defining element of international politics and, instead, proposed a new Soviet commitment to "universal human values" as the cornerstone of a new world order.[6] Soviet withdrawals from Afghanistan, Angola, and, eventually, even Eastern Europe, demonstrated Gorbachev's resolve to create a new basis of relations between the East and West.[7]

Domestically, after a year of tinkering with old tactics of *uskorenie* (acceleration) and greater discipline, Gorbachev realized that revitalization of the system required radical action, not minor adjustment.[8] Different from his Chinese counterparts, Gorbachev believed that economic reform could only be achieved if the political system was reorganized first. Gorbachev's agenda, however, neither aspired to create a democratic political system nor a capitalist economy. Gorbachev's liberalization of political processes aimed to stimulate restructuring and renewal of the Soviet socialist system.[9] *Glasnost* (openness) and democratization were means for stimulating *perestroika* (restructuring). In prompting grass-roots political activity by these liberalizing policies, Gorbachev hoped to create an alliance for change, between reformers at the top of the party and "the people" from below, against the entrenched party bureaucrats who opposed reform.

By reforming the ancien régime, however, Gorbachev unleashed revolutionary forces ultimately bent on destroying the old order. After decades of repression, independent political association flourished in the late 1980s, first as clubs, then as fronts and movements, and ultimately as independent political parties.[10] Initially, these groups in Russia were devoid of any obvious political content, focused instead on cultural renewal, urban remodeling, environmental issues, or scientific questions.[11] Gradually, however, politicized committees or factions crystallized within these organizations. When politicized members from these informal social groups began to interact with each other, overt political associations coalesced.

Elections, first in 1989 for the USSR Congress of People's Deputies and again in 1990 for the Russian Congress of People's Deputies, catalyzed independent political activity.[12] Gorbachev hoped to use these elections to transfer political authority from the Communist Party of the Soviet Union to these legislative organs. Gorbachev, however, always believed that he and his reformist wing *within* the CPSU could maintain political control over these soviets.[13] The 1989 election served this purpose; many conservative officials from the Communist party were not elected to the USSR Congress, while Gorbachev's allies within the CPSU assumed complete control of the Soviet parliament. By 1990, however, public exploration of the Communist party's sordid past, combined with growing discontent with Gorbachev's slow pace of economic reform, produced new campaign themes of anticommunism, anti-status quo, and even anti-Gorbachev during the spring 1990 elections for the Russian Congress of People's Deputies. This common ideology of opposition helped to create the "Democratic Russia" bloc, a coalition of candidates running against the old order. This organization, stretched across the entire Russian Republic, uniting almost all non-Communist and non-Fascist political clubs, groups, and associations. While elections in the provinces yielded soviets still dominated by Communist party apparatchiks, Democratic Russia did win clear majorities in the Moscow and Leningrad city soviets, as well as a near majority in the Russian Congress of People's Deputies.[14] Concomitantly, elections in other republics in 1990, especially in the Baltic republics of Estonia, Latvia, and Lithuania, activated anti-Soviet and pro-independence movements.

By the fall of 1990, politics in Moscow had become polarized between the Soviet "center" and the Russian republic (as well as the Baltic republics), each claiming sovereign authority over the same territory.[15] This polarization eradicated centrist policies or compromising tactics; Gorbachev turned increasingly toward hard-liners for support, while Boris Yeltsin, the newly elected Chairman of the Russian Supreme Soviet, and Democratic Russia became more radical in their demands for democracy, the market, and Russian independence. Especially after the invasion of Lithuania and Latvia in January 1991, Baltic leaders made similar demands for independence from the Soviet regime. This highly volatile condition ended in August 1991, when a coup attempt by conservatives within the Soviet state failed miserably. The failed coup exposed the weakness of the Soviet "center" and the ruling Communist Party of the Soviet Union, leading ultimately to the dissolution of the Soviet Union in December 1991, and the creation of independent states out of the former Soviet republics.

POSTCOMMUNIST DEMOCRATIZATION

Dividing State Power between the Executive, the Legislature, and the Judiciary

When the Soviet state and the Communist party still existed, anticommunist forces such as Boris Yeltsin and Democratic Russia could pledge their support to democracy and the market without any obligation to realize these revolutionary ideas. After the collapse of the USSR, these slogans of opposition had to be translated into government policy. As stated above, the unfamiliar source of these concepts, the intransigence of the ancien régime, and the countervailing forces unleashed by the devolution of Soviet state power have impeded the consolidation of a democratic government and the creation of a market economy.

The Executive

Elected as President of Russia in June 1991, Boris Yeltsin attempted to fill the political vacuum created by the implosion of the USSR after the August 1991 coup by strengthening the independent executive branch of government. Before Gorbachev, Soviet government organs had been subordinated to Communist party control. Soviets, government councils assigned de jure legislative, executive, and judicial power under Lenin, enjoyed virtually no de facto power during the CPSU reign; they only rubber-stamped decisions approved by the CPSU ruling bodies. Gorbachev's reforms had accorded these soviets some marginal legislative power, but never equipped these councils with the means to execute their decisions. The Russian Congress of People's Deputies, the highest soviet in the Russian Republic, created the office of an executive president, elected directly by the people, as a step toward dividing power and executing government (not Communist party) decisions. When the Soviet state collapsed, Yeltsin saw his executive office as the only legitimate political power capable of governing.

Yeltsin's strategy for enhancing executive power, however, was, for the most part, undemocratic. In the heady weeks immediately after the coup, Yeltsin asked for and received from the Russian Congress of People's Deputies the power to rule by decree. Soon thereafter, Yeltsin appointed heads of administration and presidential representatives at lower levels of government to execute his presidential directives. Instead of seeking reform of the system of soviets, Yeltsin hoped to bypass these remnants of the ancien régime by ruling by decree. True to their revolutionary mandate, Russia's new political leaders were seeking to undermine the old Soviet political system. Whether the system replacing it was democratic or not, however, was difficult to discern.

The Soviet Backlash

After initial passivity, growing concern over the form and structure of the executive branch prompted major challenges against Yeltsin's executive rule during both the Sixth Congress of People's Deputies in April 1992, and the Seventh Congress in December 1992. Elections for seats in the Congress of People's Deputies had produced a parliament roughly split between "communists" and "democrats" in 1990.[16] This dichotomy collapsed, however, after the August putsch, when the common enemy uniting the democratic pole disappeared. Disarray among the people's deputies formerly supporting Yeltsin, coupled with appointment of "democratic" deputies in the executive branch, altered the balance of forces within the Congress. Under the new leadership of Ruslan Khasbulatov, the Russian Congress eventually coalesced into Yeltsin's principal foe. Because a new constitution had not been approved, the Congress of People's Deputies began to reclaim its authority embodied in the 1977 Soviet Constitution as the highest state organ. By the end of the first year of Russian independence, the Congress successfully had removed Yeltsin's prime minister, Yegor Gaidar, retracted the president's power to rule by decree, and threatened to reduce the office of the executive to its previous ceremonial status.

The Constitutional Court

After the coup, the Congress of People's Deputies and the Russian president worked together to create a third branch of government, the Constitutional Court. In the absence of a new constitution, the Russian parliament appointed the first court, though Yeltsin and his allies lobbied hard for several of their candidates. The Court's first few decisions demonstrated both the potential and the feebleness of this third force. The Court succeeded, for instance, in striking down a presidential decision to merge the Russian Ministry of the Interior and the KGB, and managed to make an apolitical ruling regarding the highly politicized trial of the Communist Party of the Soviet Union.[17] The Court failed, however, to enforce its decision about the constitutionality of a referendum on independence in Tatarstan. Again, the autonomous power of the Court as a third government branch was demonstrated during the highly volatile standoff between President Yeltsin and Chairman of the Congress of People's Deputies Ruslan Khasbulatov in December 1992, at which Valery Zorkin, the chairman of the Court, negotiated the compromise. Two months later, however, Zorkin abandoned his neutral stance in this conflict, which suggests that the institutionalization of an independent court system will be a difficult and long process during Russia's revolutionary transition.

The Federation

The difficulties of establishing a division of power between the executive, legislative, and judicial branches of power have been compounded by the ambiguous definition of state boundaries both between newly independent states that emerged from the former Soviet Union and between autonomous republics within the Russian Federation. Border disputes between Russia and other post-Soviet states already have sparked civil strife in the Caucuses, and threaten to precipitate war between Russia and Ukraine, and Russia and Moldova. Additionally, the treatment of ethnic Russians now suddenly living "abroad" throughout the other newly independent states has fueled hostility and even raised the specter of interstate war between these new sovereigns.

Within Russia's borders, self-determination, one of the very issues that mobilized Russia's anticommunist movement in 1990–91 and spawned the new Russian state in December 1991, now threatens to partition Russia itself. The devolution of power that eventually destroyed the Soviet Union has continued, unabated, to stimulate independence movements in several non-Russian autonomous republics as well as a handful of ethnically Russian oblasts tired of Moscow domination.

The growing significance of these independence movements—particularly in Tatarstan and Chechen-Ingushetiya—stems as much from Moscow's vastly weakened central authority as it does from the appeal of independence in these regions, as such. Again, the absence of a new constitution has allowed continued drift between different levels of government power. Yeltsin negotiated a new federation treaty with most of Russia's autonomous republics, but continued disagreements between the new center and the new periphery continue to threaten the territorial integrity of the Russian Federation.

A Multiparty System?

As already noted, the simplified poles of "communist" and "democrat" evaporated after August 1991, allowing Russia's postcommunist politics to develop along new trajectories. Some parties and social movements that were very active during liberalized communism now play no role in the postcommunist era, while other parties and social groups born prematurely in the communist era are now emerging as real forces. Still others have emerged to meet the specific conditions of a communist society in transition. All these political movements are highly volatile, with fragile social bases and constantly changing alliances and political orientations. These ambiguities surrounding Russia's unfolding civil society have complicated and inhibited the formation and consolidation of a multiparty system in post-communist Russia.

After much reshuffling, three main political blocs have coalesced since the August coup. Though weakened by splits and attrition, Democratic Russia regrouped to become the most militant advocate of revolutionary political and economic change. Regarding political reform, Democratic Russia supported the dissolution of the Soviet Union and the creation of a new Russian Federation. Democratic Russia also has pushed for the abandonment of the system of soviets and the adoption instead of a new Russian constitution based on the division of power between the executive, legislative, and judicial power. Regarding economic reform, Democratic Russia has promoted massive and rapid privatization, demonopolization, a tight money supply, and the extraction of the state from the economy more generally. In Western political parlance, Democratic Russia's platform would be neoconservative; in Russia's postcommunist ideological spectrum, Democratic Russia's ideas are revolutionary.

Democratic Russia's major strength during the communist era is its major weakness in the postcommunist period. From its creation in October 1990, Democratic Russia was a grass-roots anticommunist political movement that relied on demonstrations, strikes, and other mass actions. While effective in opposition, these tactics have been inappropriate for the postcommunist task of building a new state and economy. Today, Russia needs competent bankers and civil servants, not rally organizers. Second, Democratic Russia does not have a social base. The group claims to defend the interests of the middle class in a country where no middle class exists. Third, Yeltsin did not turn to Democratic Russia to staff his government or mobilize support for his reforms during the first year of his presidency. Consequently, Democratic Russia has struggled to find its political niche in postcommunist Russia.

The second major political force, and first political coalition to emerge after the coup, is Civic Union (*Grazhdanskii Soyuz*). Initially, this coalition formed in June 1992 as an alliance between three parties: (1) the Democratic Party of Russia, headed by Nikolai Travkin; (2) the People's Party for a Free Russia, headed by Vice President Alexander Rutskoi; and (3) Union of "Renewal," the political arm of the Union of Industrialists and Entrepreneurs, headed by Arkady Volsky. In forging this alliance, Civic Union claimed to represent a centrist and pragmatic alternative to the radical, liberal Democratic Russia.

Regarding economic policy, Civic Union has declared its support for the general *objective* of creating a market economy based on private property. Civic Union, however, disagrees with the *strategy* employed for achieving this end by Yeltsin's first government. In particular, Civic Union has pushed to: (1) slow down the pace of privatization; (2) increase credits to large state factories; (3) accompany these credits with indexed wages and prices (to stimulate demand); and (4) disregard the recommendations of the International Monetary Fund (IMF) and World Bank (i.e., increase the export of raw materials and decrease industrial production), which Civic Union considers a set of guidelines for turning Russia into a Third World country.

In addition to economic reform, the second major unifying concept for the Civic Union coalition concerns the collapse of Soviet and Russian state power. Unlike Democratic Russia, Civic Union leaders lamented the collapse of the Soviet Union. As state power continued to devolve in 1992, Civic Union leaders protested that under no circumstances should autonomous republics be allowed to leave the Russia Federation. Civic Union also has supported a more assertive Russian foreign policy, both toward the "near abroad" where Russian minorities live and the West.

During the first year of Russian independence, Civic Union has been better situated to realize its objectives than Democratic Russia. First, regarding tactics, Civic Union has functioned more as a lobby than as a political party or mass movement. With major representation in both the Congress of People's Deputies and the executive branch, Civic Union has access to government decision-makers that Democratic Russia lacks. Second, Civic Union has sought to represent classes and social groups constructed during the Soviet era. Because little has changed yet in Russia's postcommunist socioeconomic structure, these identities constitute a solid and formidable social base for Civic Union.[18] Industrial directors constitute the most important social group that Civic Union professes to represent. Because Arkady Volsky is both the chairman of the Union of Industrialists and Entrepreneurs and a leader of Civic Union, this political coalition claims to enjoy the support of this very powerful and highly respected class. Civic Union also has courted support with workers and workers' organizations. In seeking to protect Russian factories from bankruptcy or hostile buyout, Civic Union claims to represent the interests of workers as well as managers. The Federation of Independent Trade Unions (FNPR), the former official association of Soviet trade unions, has joined Civic Union as an observer, while several independent workers' councils have pledged their support for the "centrist" bloc. Former Communist party functionaries form a third constituency that Civic Union has courted. After the collapse of communism and the ban of the CPSU, these apparatchiks had nowhere to turn. The People's Party for a Free Russia (Rutskoi's party) seized this moment to actively recruit this social group.[19] Finally, Civic Union has played on General Rutskoi's charismatic appeal to enlist support from professional military officers. In claiming to represent these concrete social forces, Civic Union has successfully lobbied Yeltsin to alter the course of his reforms. It remains to be seen whether the influence of these "centrist" forces impedes the fulfillment of a true revolutionary outcome, or whether Civic Union evolves to become the pragmatic executors of a genuinely transformative agenda.

The "Red-Brown" Coalition

The third major force to solidify after the coup has been the nationalist-communists. For the first year after the August coup, communist and nationalist forces floundered in the new political situation. Popular fanatics led almost weekly demonstrations to protest the collapse of the Soviet state and economy, but militant opposition to the Yeltsin government was unorganized and dispersed. In October 1992, however, several smaller nationalist and communist organizations joined together to form the Front for National Salvation.[20]

This alliance between nationalists and communists has been an uneasy one. When compelled to spell out their economic or political programs, neocommunists and nationalist organizations aspire to create very different societies. Nationalists have advocated the creation of a *nationalist* market (i.e., protected from Western competition or ownership), while communists seek to maintain state ownership over the means of production. These differences, however, have been eclipsed by two unifying principles: hatred of Yeltsin and all other Westernizing liberals, and a nostalgia for the past.[21] Order, stability, and the achievement of Russian greatness are the Front's most important objectives. All other objectives, including democracy and a market economy, can be sacrificed for these more important ends.

This coalition has not yet developed a significant social base. Aside from pensioners and anarchic youth, few social classes openly have identified with the Front or affiliated organizations. The future of this coalition therefore depends on the success of political and economic reform. If monthly inflation rates remain near 50 percent and Russians and Tatars begin killing each other, the Front's pledges to create an authoritarian state to correct these evils of "liberalism" will resonate with an increasing segment of Russian society.

Russia has only just begun to take the *initial* steps toward institutionalizing a democratic political system. Russia has neither approved a new constitution with a clear delineation of power between executive, legislative, and judiciary, nor constructed a postcommunist federal system, nor conducted a founding election based on political parties. At the same time, political institutions from the ancien régime, such as the system of soviets, the imperial federation, and even the Communist party, still exist. The revolutionary transformation of the Soviet political system into a democratic polity is still a goal, not an outcome.[22]

RUSSIA'S ECONOMIC REVOLUTION: IRREVERSIBLE OR YET TO BEGIN?

Economic transformation, even more than the promise of democratic governance, became the critical component of Boris Yeltsin's revolutionary challenge to the Soviet ancien régime. Even before the collapse of the Soviet Union, Yeltsin (as chairman of the Russian Supreme Soviet) promoted the creation of a market economy based on private property as a means to challenge Gorbachev's more cautious adherence to market socialism. Whether

Yeltsin personally understood or believed in the principles of capitalism, the rhetoric of market reform provided a revolutionary alternative to the failing Soviet economy.

After the collapse of the Soviet Union, Yeltsin's rhetoric became government policy. After initial hesitation, Yeltsin appointed a team of young economic advisors, headed by Yegor Gaidar, to implement a radical-reform strategy. Gaidar and his associates were devout believers in neoliberal, monetarist economics—a revolutionary doctrine in the context of the Russian command-economy they sought to change. When Gaidar's team launched their economic program in January 1992, they aimed not simply to reform the old, but to destroy it. In the wake of this destruction, they believed that the invisible hand of the market would create a new and prosperous economic system. In their view, destruction of a seventy-year entrenched command-economy could only be accomplished by "shock therapy," that is, rapid and radical economic change.[23]

Though highly disputed, Gaidar sequenced his shock-therapy program in the following way; price liberalization first, financial stabilization second, followed immediately by massive privatization. Beginning in January 1991, the state stopped setting prices for most non-basic commodities, while at the same time opening Russia's borders to imports of consumer goods. As prices skyrocketed, shortages of consumer goods endemic to the Soviet planning-system disappeared. Everything from prime rib to M&M's could now be purchased in Russian shops.

Yeltsin's economic team hoped to offset the inflationary pressures of price liberalization by drastically decreasing the government deficit through a combination of cuts in government spending (including, first and foremost, the elimination of subsidies to state enterprises), taxes on new profits, and strict control of the money supply. This tight monetary policy, in turn, would create the proper environment to stabilize the value of the ruble against hard currencies, a condition considered necessary for attracting vitally needed foreign investment. To attain ruble convertibility, Gaidar hoped for international financial assistance from the International Monetary Fund, including most importantly, a $5 billion stabilization fund, similar to the $1 billion fund established for the Polish zloty.

Privatization constituted the third component of the Gaidar reform package, to be executed in parallel to price liberalization and macroeconomic stabilization. Because the Soviet state owned virtually everything under communism, Gaidar's proposal for rapid and massive privatization of most of Russia's productive and trade operations constituted the largest transfer of property rights ever undertaken by a single government. For small properties such as stores, restaurants, and cottage industries, the Russian government sought to use auctions as a means to sell assets to individual owners. For larger properties, Yeltsin declared that state enterprises first must be incorporated as joint stock companies. After this reorganization at the enterprise level, the workers' collective (consisting of both management and labor) had to choose between three different strategies for privatization. Enterprises involved in the production of vital military wares or strategic resources initially were exempted from the privatization program.

The options for privatizing large state enterprises offered the management and workers a significant advantage in acquiring control of their enterprise. However, because of the long-standing paternalistic relationship between the directors and the workers at Soviet factories, this privatization program allowed directors to gain de facto control over the enterprises they manage. As a means to introduce outside market discipline on these directors, the Russian government demanded that these newly incorporated joint stock companies be open and that their shares be traded publicly. To provide outside stockholders, Gaidar's team created the voucher system. Under this program, every Russian citizen was issued a voucher or privatization check with a face value of 10,000 rubles. Citizens could pledge this voucher toward the purchase of shares of a given enterprise, entrust this voucher to an investment fund, or sell it for cash. By issuing everyone a voucher, Yeltsin's government hoped to create widespread interest in the privatization process.

The context within which Gaidar's revolutionary program was launched ensured that shock therapy was bound to fail. Recognizing this situation, Gaidar predicted that he would be in office only a few months. His goal was to launch economic reform, not carry it out.

Gaidar was right; shock therapy became extremely unpopular among most Russian citizens. Consumer goods appeared in shops, but at prices the vast majority could not afford. Moreover, inflation diminished already meager incomes to extremely meager. Meanwhile, the rewards of ownership through privatization remained unrealized; few believed that their vouchers would translate into real ownership, causing the trading price for the voucher to fall to less than 3,000 rubles by the end of 1992. Nor did faith in the ruble take hold. At the beginning of 1992, the ruble-dollar exchange rate hovered around 90: 1. By February 1993, the rate had fallen to 660: 1. Finally, gross domestic product and industrial production in particular fell dramatically during the first year of shock therapy. Factory managers predicted massive bankruptcies if the state did not intervene. In their view, Gaidar's plan was all shock and no therapy.

In December 1992, at the Seventh Congress of Peoples Deputies, the young economic theoretician, Gaidar, was replaced as prime minister by Victor Chernomyrdin, an experienced industrial manager who had worked for several decades in the Soviet system. The first phase of Russia's economic revolution had ended.

Several major obstacles—some inherent to the transition from socialism to capitalism, others created by the particular exigencies of Russia's post-communist political situation—derailed Gaidar's program. First, regarding price liberalization, Gaidar and his government lifted state controls on prices without first dismantling state monopolies. The result was not market prices, but monopoly prices that fueled inflation.

Second, Gaidar's monetarist focus on zero deficits and a convertible currency neglected the financial needs of Russia's state enterprises. If economic efficiency is the objective, many of Russia's state enterprises must either be restructured (and, first and foremost, downsized) or shut down. Not all Russian factory directors, however, shared the government's commitment to economic efficiency. Fearful of bankruptcy and unaccustomed to competition, these directors instead lobbied for state orders and subsidies to sustain their operations. Had Gaidar and his team enjoyed complete control of the government, many of these directors seeking state support would have been rejected. The legacies of the all-powerful soviets, however, placed many economic levers out of the hands of the president and prime minister. Most importantly, the Supreme Soviet, and not the executive branch, controlled the Russian Central Bank. In June 1992, the Russian parliament appointed a new head of the bank, Victor Gerashenko, who immediately issued millions in new credits to flailing state enterprises. This action fueled inflation and undermined international and domestic confidence in the government's macroeconomic stabilization plan, which in turn stalled plans for converting the ruble. This flood of government credits also removed the specter of bankruptcy for many inefficient state enterprises and raised expectations for future state interventions to save Russian industry.

Third, as a consequence of inflation, growth in small private businesses virtually stalled during the first year of shock therapy. Because capital for small entrepreneurs is often represented in hard-cash earnings, inflation devastates their profits and subsequently their investment prospects. While small businesses (called cooperatives) accounted for much of the dynamism in the Soviet economy in the late 1980s, this sector of the economy was being squeezed by inflation in 1991.

In place of production, trade of natural resources, speculation on both commodities and hard currencies, and mafia operations exploded as the most profitable ventures in postcommunist Russia. None of the profits earned in these transactions, however, were being reinvested into the Russian economy. The result was stagflation: the deadly combination of inflation, verging on a hyperinflation rate of 50 percent per month, and declining production rates.

By the end of 1992, the mass privatization program remained the one surviving component of the Gaidar reform package. Successful auctions had removed thousands of shops and small enterprises from the state budget while, at the same time, creating new owners of private property. The heart of the Soviet economy, the military-industrial complex, still remains firmly entrenched within the state and resistant to market forces. This military-industrial complex is not merely a sector of the Russian economy, it is the largest and most productive core of the former Soviet economy. During the collapse of the Soviet Union, some military plants (aircraft factories, telecommunications firms, or computer companies) seized the opportunity of state collapse to escape the military-industrial complex, convert to civilian production, and privatize spontaneously. The vast majority of military enterprises, however, cannot make this conversion so easily. Instead, they have sought to remain within the state-controlled military-industrial complex and to continue to produce arms and other military products for both internal consumption and export. The challenge of privatizing these plants, institutes, and design bureaus will continue to burden Russia's economic reform process for the foreseeable future.

The economic program drafted by Gaidar and supported by Yeltsin sought to dismantle the Soviet command-economy and replace it with a system based on market forces and private property. This goal was revolutionary. It remains to be seen whether the strategy adopted by the Gaidar team will succeed eventually in realizing this revolutionary objective. The restoration of the Soviet command-economy is highly unlikely, but the kind of market system likely to emerge will bear only slight resemblance to the blueprint Gaidar's team of neoliberal economists originally envisioned.

FOREIGN POLICY

Yeltsin looked to the Western democracies and their capitalist economies as models to be emulated in the construction of Russia's new economic and political system. Like many Western governments, Yeltsin welcomed the collapse of the bipolar system and eagerly embraced, at least initially, a new international order dominated by one set of principles regarding economic and political organization. According to initial calculations by the Russian government after the collapse of the Soviet Union, the faster Russia entered this new international system, the more likely democratic and market reforms would succeed.

Given this initial orientation, Yeltsin and his liberal foreign minister, Andrei Kozyrev, placed friendly relations with the West—and the United States in particular—as Russia's highest foreign policy priority. Though the United States and other West European governments had virtually ignored Russia's anticommunist democratic movement during Gorbachev's reign, Yeltsin consciously overlooked this and courted Western favor after the collapse of the USSR. In return for tacitly accepting American hegemony in world affairs, Yeltsin hoped to receive Western financial assistance and, subsequently, private-capital investment. Gaidar's strategy for macroeconomic stabilization, in fact, hinged on infusions of financial credit from the International Monetary Fund and the World Bank. To coordinate conditionalities of international financial institutions with Russian state actions, Gaidar even invited Western consultants to work in and with his government.

After a brief honeymoon, Russia's romance with the West has already begun to sour. The greatest impediment to effective cooperation with the West has been a set of false expectations about the benefits of revolutionary victory. Once they defeated communism, many Russians expected to enjoy overnight Western standards of living. Instead, most Russians have been frustrated with the minimal fruits of nascent capitalism or democracy. Life was better and easier under Brezhnev.

These disappointed expectations have been compounded by the form, amount, and speed of Western assistance. Great fanfare surrounded both the forty-seven-nation conference on aid to the former Soviet republics hosted by the United States in January 1992, and the April pledge of $24 billion. Only a fraction of these funds, however, has been delivered.

Russian leaders also have become increasingly unhappy with the type of economic assistance. Rather than focus on macroeconomic issues, such as the convertibility of the ruble, or humanitarian assistance, such as food and medicine, Russian critics have argued that greater attention should be placed on helping to rebuild Russia's infrastructure and provide technical assistance, that is, the "know-how" of capitalism. Even the form of assistance to Russia has been degrading: "Made in America" labels on food packages disturb proud Russian citizens. Many Russian leaders have criticized American aid programs, in particular, as self-serving and political, more important for the voters of New York than for the Russian people. As already noted, critics of Western aid programs have suggested that the United States and its allies have a comprehensive strategy for reducing Russia to a Third World country.

Disappointment with the West has been accompanied by new foreign policy challenges with Russia's new neighbors, the independent states of the former Soviet Union. First, threats to Russian minority populations now living in the "near abroad" have soured relations between Russia and the Baltic states, Moldova, Ukraine, and, to a lesser extent, Uzbekistan. Second, territorial disputes between Russia and Ukraine, and Russia and Moldova, have raised the specter of military conflict. Third, Russian military forces already have been engaged in civil wars in Tadjikistan, Georgia, and Moldova, and interstate conflict between Armenia and Azerbaijan. The security regime that will replace the former communist world has not yet emerged.

The combination of disappointment and suspicion with the West and new international threats closer to home has kindled new discussion about the definition of Russian national interests. In a replay of the Slavophile-Westernizer debates of the nineteenth century, Russian nationalists have assaulted the Western orientation of Yeltsin and Kozyrev as a threat to Russia's great-power status and a betrayal of Russia's historical Eurasian orientation. Instead of pleading for Western acceptance from a position of weakness, these "Eurasianists" have argued that Russia should seek to expand its influence in the Balkans, the Middle East, South Asia, and the Far East.

This debate has not been decided, and probably never will be won by one side or the other. Even under the same foreign policy team, however, Russia already has amended its once-unequivocal support for Western positions regarding sanctions against Serbia, renewed bombing of Iraq, or the sale of arms to third parties. Continued failure of market and democratic reforms at home is likely to fuel greater Russian hostility toward the West.

FUTURE SCENARIOS

Russia's revolutionary project of creating simultaneously a democratic polity and a market economy, while at the same time managing the breakup of the Soviet empire, has only just begun. Moreover, because Russia's revolutionaries have used peaceful methods to carry out their transformative agenda, the process will encounter sustained resistance in the best of circumstances. In the worst of circumstances, the revolutionary project may grind to a halt altogether. In midstream of the greatest political and economic transformation of this century, predictions about future developments in Russia, and the former Soviet Union more generally, are still premature. The start of economic and political reform after the Soviet collapse, however, suggests three possible scenarios.

The Consolidation of Democracy and the Triumph of Liberal Capitalism

Russia's initial flirtation with democratic procedures for deciding political outcomes bears little resemblance to similar contestations in Western democracies. Yet, feuding branches of government and competing social forces have not resorted to violence to settle their differences. While minimalist, this level of pluralism is already greater than at any other time in Russian history.[24]

Likewise, on the economic front, price liberalization has compelled Russian citizens to become discriminating consumers and self-promoting entrepreneurs. Similarly, privatization has begun to monetize transactions between enterprises, while also introducing concepts of competitiveness, efficiency, and profits at the enterprise level. These are radical departures from practices under the Soviet system.

The maturation of these seeds of democracy and the market will require some minimalist level of political consensus, both between the executive and legislative branches of government and between the radical democrats of Democratic Russia and the more conservative Civic Union. Agreement between these political forces about the basic kind of democracy and market Russia aims to create would obstruct nondemocratic and nonmarket challengers. One could even imagine the emergence of a two-party system that would overshadow the more radical challengers from both left and right. A relatively stable center also would help to quell calls for independence in the autonomous republics and Siberia.

This scenario would result in greater integration of Russia into the international capitalist system. Domestic stability would encourage foreign investment and support a compradorial capitalist class. Of course, even under the best of circumstances, the wealth of outsiders will threaten indige-nous entrepreneurs, and thereby create an inevitable tension between these two sectors of the economy. Moreover, the mafia—already a dominant force in the Russia economy today—will also be threatened by foreign competi-tion. The key to regulating this competition will be the creation and consoli-dation of legal institutions. A capitalist-friendly legal structure will have the best chance to evolve if some level of consensus prevails among Russia's dominant political forces.

Political stability followed by economic integration with the West will establish Russia as *the* regional power in Central Asia, and as one of the important regional powers in Eastern Europe and the Far East. If this sce-nario unfolds, it is unlikely that Russia will reemerge as a world superpower for the foreseeable future. Democratic and capitalist consolidation at home, however, will make Russia a natural ally for the United States and the West in this region of the world. Working with (or on behalf of) the Western powers, a Russian democracy once again could assume responsibility for policing interstate conflicts in areas of the former Soviet Union. Russian interventions in Nagorno-Karabakh, Georgia, and the Tadjik-Iranian bor-der already have established this precedent.

One-Party State Capitalism

The initial difficulties encountered in creating both a democratic polity and a market economy suggest that the first scenario may be most ideal, but the least likely. The conservative swing of the political pendulum already por-tends a different kind of transition for Russia than witnessed in East Central Europe.[25] If liberal "market reform" generates hyperinflation, falling indus-trial productivity, bankruptcy, and unemployment, while "democratic re-form" paralyzes effective central governance and foments independence movements in the republics, advocates of order and stability will gain in-creasing popularity. In this scenario, the liberal wing of Russia's political spectrum (Democratic Russia) will collapse altogether, Civic Union will as-sume center stage, and all major political debates will take place between Civic Union "centrists" and proponents of even greater order and stability, the Front for National Salvation.

If this scenario unfolds and Civic Union becomes the dominant political force, the central Russian state will assume a greater role in economic and political affairs. To protect Russian enterprises from total collapse, the state will impose greater restrictions on foreign investment and imports while, at the same time, providing increased credits and financial support to Russian industry. Rather than rushing to wean large industrial enterprises from the state budget, the state will seek to enhance and expand greater cooperation between the state and the "private" sector. Russia's vast internal market will be reserved for Russian manufacturers, and only opened after *national* industrialists are ready to compete with foreign firms.

Regarding political reform, this Russian state will move to arrest the devolution of power. If necessary, secessionist movements will be quelled by force, while independent regional governors will be replaced with more loyal representatives of Moscow. Other parties will be allowed to operate, but serious challenges to the "centrist" ruling coalition will either be co-opted or harassed. When necessary, civil liberties and political rights will be suspended in the name of order and stability. In this scenario, Russia's polity will more closely resemble Mexico's one-party system than West European multiparty democracies.

Relations between Russia and the West under this scenario would include elements of conflict and friction. Tired of American arrogance in international affairs, this Russian state would declare its own Monroe Doctrine for the Caucuses and Central Asia, and warn Western powers that Eastern Europe (meaning, now, Ukraine, Belarus, and maybe the Baltics), the Balkans, and the Far East are Russian spheres of interest. Because the international struggle between capitalism and communism has ended, the rivalry between the United States and Russia experienced during the Cold War will never return. However, conflicting definitions of national interests regarding Serbia, Iraq, or Ukraine will fuel tensions between Russia and the West.

Fascist Dictatorship and the Collapse of the Russian Federation

If Russia's economy collapses entirely and ethnic conflicts within the federation escalate into civil wars, pleas for moderation, caution, or "centrism" will fall on deaf ears. Just as Gorbachev unsuccessfully tried to carve out a center position in conditions of revolutionary crisis, an acute acceleration of economic and political chaos could mobilize militant political forces on both the left and the right. If this scenario unfolds, lines of political struggle will be drawn starkly, between those for democracy and the market, and those against.

This polarization could precipitate a replay of the Soviet collapse. A climaxing conflict between these opposing forces, such as a coup attempt or successful coup, could trigger a rejection of central authority altogether from the republics and other independent-minded regions, just as the Soviet republics used the window of opportunity of the August coup attempt to assert their independence. If such a coup attempt failed, the liberal victors in Moscow would have difficulty legitimizing a campaign to recentralize power. If the coup succeeded, Moscow's new fascist government would deploy military force to reconstruct the Russian state, including attempts to seize territories in neighboring republics where large concentrations of Russians live. Quite obviously, this situation would result in prolonged civil war within Russia accompanied by several inter-states conflicts on Russia's borders.

Under this scenario, Russia becomes a vast Yugoslavia with nuclear weapons. The presence of nuclear weapons, coupled with the still vast military potential of Russia (and to a lesser extent, Ukraine) makes this civil war, or series of civil wars, a security threat for every neighboring country and even the United States. If this scenario unfolds, Russia's old communists will be joined by the Western states in longing for the nonrevolutionary stability of the Cold War era.

CONCLUSION

The collapse of the Soviet Union has challenged the way in which both American policymakers and academics must think about world security. According to traditional realist conceptions of international relations, questions of security are decided *between* states; stability within the international system is measured according to the balance of power between these states.[26] Change in this balance of power occurs only after a major war.[27]

The international security arrangements that emerged after World War II—the bipolar system balanced between the United States and the Soviet Union—are now undergoing change without a major war. Rather, the catalyst for change in the international system originated from revolutionary processes unleased within one state, the Soviet Union. This suggests that not all issues of security are between states; rather, events *within* states can influence both the security of that state and international security arrangements more generally. Changes in the internal balance of power within a given state can effect changes within the international balance of power within the international system. Revolution, in addition to war, can precipitate major shifts in the international system.

This dynamic interplay between domestic and international presents a different menu of policy options for Western decision-makers seeking to defend their states' interests. First, state-to-state relations is only one, limited dimension of foreign policy, especially when the Russian state (along with all others in the region) is weak and volatile. Western governments must supplement these state interactions with policies and programs that affect internal developments. Specifically, the best defense of Western interests in the former Soviet Union is the promotion of democracy and capitalism.[28]

Democracy and capitalism are foreign ideas in Russia and the former Soviet Union, making their promotion difficult and dangerous. Too little intervention on the part of foreigners will signal neglect, but too much intervention will be chastised as interference. The vast size of Russia, the enormity of the task of transformation, and the limited available resources from the West mean that outside impact on democratic and market development will be minimal, even under the best of circumstances.

Given these constraints, Western efforts should focus on technical assistance—that is, the transfer of knowledge and know-how—about democratic market institutions. Regarding economic reform, technical assistance can provide valuable information and technology that will help Russia implement its own reforms. Western governments do not have financial resources to rebuild Russia's economy. If, however, the proper political and economic institutions were consolidated in Russia, private capital might be attracted to invest. Regarding political reform, technical assistance programs can help substitute for a historical experience with democracy, without appearing too interventionary by those Russian nationalists wary of Western intentions.

The United States and its allies spent trillions of dollars to contain and defeat communism; they must now direct at least a fraction of these expenditures to build a new democratic polity and market economy in its place. As briefly described above, the implications of failing to consolidate a democratic, market-oriented state will be grave for both Russia and the world.

Notes

1. For analyses of U.S.-Soviet relations during this period, see Walter LaFeber, *America, Russia, and the Cold War: 1945–1980*, 4th ed. (New York: John Wiley & Sons, 1980); Raymond Gartoff, *Detente and Confrontation* (Washington: Brookings Institution, 1985); Alexander George, Philip Farley, and Alexander Dallin, eds., *U.S.-Soviet Security Cooperation* (Oxford: Oxford University Press, 1988); and Adam Ulam, *Expansion and Coexistence: The History of Soviet Foreign Policy, 1917–1973* (New York: Praeger, 1974). For a set of theoretical discussions about the nature of this socialist-states system, see Christopher Chase-Dunn, ed., *Socialist States in the World-System* (Beverly Hills: Sage Publications, 1982); and Immanuel Wallerstein, "The Rise and Future Demise of the World Capitalist System: Concepts for Comparative Analysis," *Comparative Studies in Society and History*, Vol. 16, No. 4 (September 1974), pp. 387–415.

2. What international system will emerge in the wake of the Soviet collapse remains uncertain. For two opposing views, see John Mersheimer, "Back to the Future: Instability in Europe After the Cold War," *International Security*, Vol. 15 (Summer 1990), pp. 5–55; and James Goldgeier and Michael McFaul, "A Tale of Two Worlds: Core and Periphery in the Post–Cold War Era, *International Organization*, Vol. 46, No. 2 (Spring 1992), pp. 467–492.

3. Sigmund Neumann, "The International Civil War," *World Politics*, Vol. 1, No. 1 (April 1949), pp. 333–334. The term *revolution* is problematic; laden with normative assumptions. Most scholars of revolutions, including Marxists, political-conflicts theorists, and functionalists, subsume this basic description within their definitions of revolution. Disagreements arise when other features, such as class conflict, violence, or individual relative deprivation, are added to the definition. For discussions of the different definitions of revolutions, see Peter Calvert, *Revolution and Counter-Revolution* (Minneapolis: University of Minnesota Press, 1990); Mark Hagopian, *The Phenomenon of Revolution* (New York: Dodd, Mead & Co., 1974); Chalmers Johnson, *Revolutionary Change* (Stanford: Stanford University Press, 1982); Theda Skocpol, *States and Social Revolutions: A Comparative Analysis of France, Russia, and China* (Cambridge: Cambridge University Press, 1979), chapter 1; Charles Tilly, "Revolutions and Collective Violence," in Fred Greenstein and Nelson Polsby, ed., *Handbook on Political Science*, III (Reading, MA: Addison Wesley), pp. 483–555; and two very useful survey articles, Lawrence Stone, "Theories of Revolution," *World Politics*, Vol. 18, No. 2 (January 1966) pp. 159–176, and Jack Goldstone, "Theories of Revolution: The Third Generation," *World Politics*, Vol. 32, No. 3 (April 1980), pp. 425–453.

4. Transitions from authoritarian rule in Latin America and southern Europe have been concerned with changing the political system without tampering with the basic form of private rights (capitalism) or the basic proprietors of those properties. See Guillermo O'Donnell and Philippe Schmitter, *Transitions from Authoritarian Rule: Tentative Conclusions*, Vol. 4 (Baltimore, MD: Johns Hopkins University Press, 1986), p. 69.

5. On the important distinction between revolutionary situations and revolutionary outcomes, see Charles Tilly, *From Mobilization to Revolution* (Reading, MA: Addison-Wesley, 1978), pp. 189–200; Chalmers Johnson, *Revolutionary Change* (Stanford: Stanford University

Press, 1982), chapter 4; and Samuel Huntington, *Political Order and Changing Societies* (New Haven: Yale University Press, 1968), p. 268. Structural theorists of revolutions, such as Theda Skocpol or, much earlier, Karl Marx, would not accept this kind of contingency. See Skocpol, *States and Social Revolutions*, p. 5.

6. See Mikhail Gorbachev, *Perestroika: New Thinking for Our Country and the World* (New York: Harper & Row, 1987).

7. On Gorbachev's foreign policy, see Coit Blacker, *Hostage to Revolution: Gorbachev and Soviet Security Policy, 1985–1991* (New York: Council on Foreign Relations, 1993); Allen Lynch, *Gorbachev's International Outlook: Intellectual Origins and Political Consequences* (New York: Institute for East-West Security Studies, 1989); and Dan Oberdorfer, *The Turn: From Cold War to a New Era* (New York: Poseidon, 1991).

8. For assessments of Gorbachev's political reform agenda, see Archie Brown, "Perestroika and the Political System," in Tsuyoshi Hasegawa and Alex Pravda, eds., *Perestroika: Soviet Domestic and Foreign Polices* (London: Royal Institute of International Affairs, 1990); Jerry Hough, "Gorbachev's Endgame," *World Policy Journal* (Fall 1990); and George Breslauer, "Evaluating Gorbachev as Leader," *Soviet Economy*, Vol. 5, No. 4 (October-December 1989). For assessments of Gorbachev's economic reforms, see Ed Hewitt, *Reforming the Soviet Economy: Equality versus Efficiency* (Washington: The Brookings Institution, 1988) and Anders Aslund, *Gorbachev's Struggle for Economic Reform* (London: Pinter Publishers, 1989).

9. Guillermo O'Donnell and Philippe Schmitter refer to such reforms as "liberalized authoritarianism." See O'Donnell and Schmitter, *Transitions from Authoritarian Rule*, p. 9.

10. On this period, see Michael McFaul and Sergei Markov, *The Troubled Birth of Russian Democracy* (Stanford, CA: Hoover Institution Press, 1993); Michael McFaul, "Russia's Emerging Political Parties," *Journal of Democracy*, Vol. 3, No. 1 (January 1992); Judith Seditas and Jim Butterfield, *Perestroika from Below: Social Movements in the Soviet Union* (Boulder, CO: Westview Press, 1991); Vera Tolz, *The USSR's Emerging Party System* (New York: Praeger, 1990); and Vladimir Brovkin, "Revolution from Below: Informal Political Associations in Russia, 1988–1989," *Soviet Studies*, Vol. 42, No. 2 (June 1990), p. 233–258.

11. Given the degree of penetration of the Soviet state and the Communist party into all aspects of society, seemingly apolitical issues were actually packed with political meaning for those participating. Because the party had tried to control all forms of social association, be it a science club or chess association, any form of independent social activity constituted an implicit protest against the state-party structures.

12. See Michael Urban, *More Power to the Soviets* (Aldershot: Edward Elgar, 1990).

13. A soviet, literally "council," is the Russian equivalent of the legislative branch of government. At the federal level, the Russian parliament has two parts: the 1,000-member Russian Congress of People's Deputies, which meets twice a year to take major decisions, and the smaller (200 members) Supreme Soviet, which convenes on a regular basis throughout the year. At the local level, the city soviet would be the equivalent of an American city council. These are not exact equivalents. As discussed in detail below, soviets in Russia, in addition to their legislative functions, also exercise powers commonly associated with the executive and judicial branches of government in the United States.

14. For a detailed study of the Moscow election, see Timothy Colton, "The Politics of Democratization: The Moscow Election of 1990," *Soviet Economy*, Vol. 6, No. 4 (October-December 1990), pp. 285–344.

15. This situation was called the wars of laws, as the Soviet and Russian parliament purposely produced contradictory legislation as a means of gaining control of the state.

16. The label "democrat" in Russia's contemporary discourse does not refer necessarily to one who adheres to the democratic process. Rather, the term refers to those who oppose the Soviet system. In many contexts, the label has pejorative connotations.

17. Immediately after the coup, Yeltsin banned the Communist Party of the Soviet Union. The party responded by taking Yeltsin to court, claiming that his decree was unconstitutional. Yeltsin then responded by arguing that the CPSU was a criminal organization. After reviewing the entire history of the party, the Court ruled that the CPSU historically was an unconstitutional group, but the CPSU that existed by the time of the August coup was not. The Court also ruled that the party had no direct role in the coup. Therefore the ban on the party was lifted.

18. Optimistic estimates claim that 10 percent of the Russian work force is employed in the private sector.

19. Before the August coup, this party was a liberal faction *within* the Communist Party of Soviet Union. During the coup attempt, this group then formally quit the CPSU and formed the People's Party for a Free Russia.

20. Several days later, Yeltsin banned this organization as anticonstitutional, but the group continues to function.

21. To which past Russia or the Soviet Union should return is heatedly debated. *Edinstvo*, for instance, would like to return to the Stalinist era, while the Russian Communist Workers Party has romanticized the Soviet era under Lenin. Meanwhile, groups such as Victor Aksiuchits's Christian Democrats and Mikhail Astafiev's Cadets regard prerevolutionary Russia as the golden era. These assorted organizations wince at each other's ideological platforms. However, the level of their disdain for the current Russian government has been sufficient to eclipse these tedious issues of whether Russia should return to communism or feudalism.

22. Though most references in this section have been to the Russian state, the same argument could be made for emerging polities in all of the former Soviet republics. Space limitations, however, do not permit a comprehensive discussion of all the newly independent states.

23. See Anders Aslund, *Post-Communist Economic Revolutions: How Big a Bang?* (Washington: Center for Strategic International Studies, 1992).

24. For an optimistic assessment of the prospects for Russian democracy, see Nina Belyaeva, "Russian Democracy: Crisis as Progress," *The Washington Quarterly*, Spring 1993, pp. 5–17.

25. For elaboration of the comparison, see Michael McFaul, *Post-Communist Politics: Democratic Prospects in Russia and Eastern Europe* (Washington: Center for Strategic and International Studies, 1993).

26. Kenneth Waltz, *Theory of International Politics* (Reading, MA: Addison-Wesley, 1979). For a critical discussion of Waltz, see Robert Keohane, ed., *Neorealism and Its Critics* (New York: Columbia University Press, 1986).

27. Robert Gilpin, *War and Change in World Politics* (Cambridge: Cambridge University Press, 1981).

28. Democracies rarely fight each other. See Immanuel Kant, *Perpetual Peace* (1796; reprint, Los Angeles: U.S. Library Association, 1932); and Michael Doyle, "Liberalism and World Politics," *American Political Science Review*, Vol. 80 (December 1986), pp. 1151–69.

5 / The Second Nuclear Era: Nuclear Weapons in a Transformed World

ALLAN S. KRASS

INTRODUCTION

The world's first nuclear explosion took place on July 16, 1945, and as this is written there appears to be a real possibility that its last one could take place sometime around July 16, 1995. In 1992, the United States Congress declared a moratorium on nuclear testing until July 1, 1993, and Russia, France, and Great Britain observed similar moratoria during this period. The same legislation allowed only fifteen more low-yield nuclear tests before requiring a complete end to U.S. testing in 1996, as long as other states do not resume testing. There has been some speculation that the Clinton administration may end the U.S. testing moratorium to allow some, or all, of the fifteen nuclear tests to be performed, and it is unclear what effect such a decision might have on other states' testing policies. Still, no one has challenged the legal obligation of the United States to cease all testing by 1996, and it seems unlikely that such a challenge would be successful. For the first time in the nuclear age a comprehensive nuclear test ban seems clearly within reach.

There is, of course, much more to the "nuclear age" than nuclear testing, so even if testing should stop in the near future it will not be the end of our problems with nuclear weapons; we can never go back to the state of innocence that existed before nuclear fission was discovered. But an end to nuclear explosions would signal an important change in attitudes toward nuclear weapons and in the role they play in both world politics and national military strategies. The purpose of this chapter is to explore these changes and to raise a number of urgent questions and problems that will have to be addressed as we enter the "second nuclear era."

WHERE HAVE WE BEEN?

It was the Prussian strategist Carl von Clausewitz who said that "War is merely the continuation of policy by other means. The political object is the goal, war is the means of reaching it, and means can never be considered in isolation from their purpose." [1] In other words, war is a political instrument, weapons have both military and political purposes, and a rational military policy must reconcile and integrate these purposes. From their inception, nuclear weapons have resisted all attempts at such an integration. The political significance of nuclear weapons has been divorced from their military utility to a degree not shared by any other weapon in history.

The political importance of nuclear weapons was apparent from the moment that nuclear fission was discovered in Germany in the winter of 1938. Europe was descending toward war, and the discovery that made nuclear weapons possible was made in the country primarily responsible for that descent. To the scientists who understood the implications of nuclear fission it seemed clear that German physicists would try to make a bomb and that the United States and Great Britain had no alternative but to press forward as fast as possible toward the same goal.[2] Political leaders, especially U.S. President Franklin D. Roosevelt and British Prime Minister Winston Churchill, were receptive to these arguments, not only because of their fear of Adolf Hitler and Nazi Germany, but because they could appreciate the political advantages of controlling such a powerful force in the postwar world.

While the political significance of nuclear weapons was clear, their military significance was vague and has remained so to this day. Two nuclear bombs were used at Hiroshima and Nagasaki to end the war in the Pacific, but their actual contribution to ending that war has been a matter of intense debate ever since. Even if one accepts that the bombings brought the war to an end sooner than it would have ended without them, this still begs the important question of whether there might have been other ways to end the war without obliterating two cities and incinerating or irradiating hundreds of thousands of civilians. Many analysts have argued that the use of the bombs could have been avoided, or at least delayed, if more flexible and imaginative approaches to a Japanese surrender had been attempted.[3]

As it happened, the question was simply not asked by those responsible for dropping the bombs. To the extent that it was thought about at all, it was assumed that when atomic bombs were ready they would be used in the war. With a few notable exceptions, no one seriously challenged this assumption when the weapons became available in the summer of 1945. The moral, psychological, and military foundation for the use of atomic bombs had been laid by the extensive firebombing of German and Japanese cities during the war, and the atomic bomb fit naturally into this tradition.[4]

The political purpose of the bombs has also remained controversial. President Truman and his military and civilian advisors maintained that the primary purpose of the nuclear attacks was to save American and Japanese lives by ending the war as quickly as possible. Others have argued that U.S. leaders saw the bombings more as a political message to Josef Stalin and the Soviet Union than as a necessary weapon against Japan.[5] The historian Barton Bernstein has spent many years following the debate between these two schools, and his most recent comments are worth quoting at some length:

In analyzing the 1945 use of the atomic bombs, analysts risk serious error if they frame their conceptions and phrase their questions in the following distorting terms: How could American leaders have overcome their moral scruples and purposely committed this *obviously horrible* act of intentionally killing well over 100,000 Japanese, mostly non-combatants? What were the hidden ulterior motives that overwhelmed those scruples? In looking for such motives and emphasizing such scruples, these analysts err by imposing their own values on the American leaders of 1945. In doing so, analysts fail to understand those men in their own time, and greatly misunderstand the evolution of attitudes, the growth of national hatreds, and the practice of virtually total war that made the bombing of Hiroshima and Nagasaki relatively easy for American leaders at the time. . . . To understand that world of 1945 does not mean morally acceding, in 1991, to its values. But careful historical analysis does require understanding that 1945 world, and not confusing our *wishes* for different decisions back then with the *reasons* for the decision leading to the use of the atomic bomb.[6]

This analysis is important for two reasons: it not only puts the events of 1945 into their appropriate moral, political, and military context, but it also emphasizes that that context has changed in the ensuing forty-seven years. What appeared a militarily appropriate, morally justifiable, and politically acceptable use of nuclear weapons to many people at the end of World War II, would be seen today by a similar if not greater number as militarily pointless, politically self-defeating, and morally abhorrent. Consequently, arguments about the military value of atomic bombs in World War II have little relevance to the question of the military utility of nuclear weapons today.

With the advent of the Cold War and the rise to nuclear status of Britain, France, and China, it became apparent that the political significance of nuclear weapons was far more important in driving national security policy than their potential military uses. President Harry Truman never apologized for, or even seriously questioned, his decision to bomb Hiroshima and Nagasaki, but he also made clear in his private and public writings that he had no desire to use these weapons again if it could possibly be avoided. President Dwight D. Eisenhower came to office determined to overcome the inhibitions against the use of nuclear weapons on the battlefield, and his administration was responsible for the development and deployment of thousands of tactical nuclear weapons all over the world. Yet, whenever serious questions arose in his administration about the actual use of such weapons—for example in Korea in 1953, or the Quemoy and Matsu crises in 1954–55 and 1958, or to help the French in Vietnam during the siege of Dien Bien Phu in 1954—Eisenhower rejected them with little hesitation.[7]

The nuclear war plans of the Truman and Eisenhower administrations were nothing more than all-out attacks designed to explode most of the U.S. arsenal over the Soviet Union and its allies in as short a time after the beginning of hostilities as possible. The military objective was graphically described by one U.S. officer who envisioned the Soviet Union being reduced to "a smoking, radiating ruin at the end of two hours."[8] Military planners saw no way to tailor nuclear strikes to less than total war, and since total nuclear war was too destructive to have any rational political purpose, nuclear weapons were in effect militarily useless. Their chief purpose was political: to deter Soviet aggression against the U.S. and Western Europe, and to demonstrate U.S. resolve to defend its interests anywhere the Soviets chose to challenge them.

Because nuclear weapons were political and symbolic, rather than military and functional, there were no logical bounds on their numbers and no functional constraints on their power. The early hydrogen weapons (first tested in 1952) were too powerful, even for most large cities, and the so-called "tactical" weapons intended for use on European battlefields were too numerous and powerful to allow for rational military use in a densely populated industrialized region. Nevertheless, for the first twenty years after World War II both the numbers of nuclear weapons on both sides and their explosive power grew astronomically. Weapons proliferated in the tens of thousands, and explosive yields (as measured in tons of TNT), went from the tens of kilotons of early fission weapons to the tens of megatons of fusion weapons or hydrogen bombs. By 1966, the United States had over 30,000 nuclear weapons in its stockpile.[9]

It was John F. Kennedy's Secretary of Defense, Robert S. McNamara, who first challenged the notion that the nuclear arms race should be open-ended, and it was in the Office of Systems Analysis in McNamara's Pentagon that the question "How Much Is Enough?" was first asked in a serious way.[10] The answer was the doctrine of "mutual assured destruction," in which stable deterrence would be achieved by each side maintaining the capability to destroy a sizable fraction of the other's population and industrial base, even if subjected to a surprise nuclear attack. The new doctrine, which took as its premise the permanent mutual vulnerability of the two superpowers, was derisively labeled "MAD" by critics, who argued that Soviet planners were less concerned about suffering heavy losses than Americans, and that unless the United States maintained a significant advantage it could be subjected to nuclear blackmail by an adventurous or desperate Soviet leader.

McNamara's struggle to gain control over the accumulation of nuclear weapons was only partially successful. While the stockpile leveled off and began slowly to decline after reaching its peak of 32,000 warheads in 1967, this did not represent a commitment by the U.S. government to MAD. Instead, it represented a shift in emphasis from quantitative superiority over the Soviet Union to qualitative superiority. The goal would now be to improve the accuracy, reliability, flexibility, and survivability of weapons, giving the arsenal a more sophisticated and potent war fighting capability, even as its absolute numbers declined.

Along with the new weapons came new doctrines and strategies for their use in war. The idea that the most powerful weapon ever developed should remain militarily useless was anathema to many strategic planners, and

McNamara himself tried to find ways to make nuclear weapons more usable. It was McNamara's "wizards of Armageddon"[11] who began to introduce greater flexibility, allowing options short of all-out attack into U.S. nuclear war planning. This effort was carried on by the Nixon, Carter, and Reagan administrations under Secretaries of Defense James Schlesinger, Harold Brown, and Caspar Weinberger. Terms like limited nuclear options, escalation dominance, and countervailing strategy—all variations on the theme of usable, rational, winnable nuclear combat—became fashionable among nuclear planners. In contrast with the Truman and Eisenhower years, nuclear war plans came to encompass a spectrum of possibilities, from small "demonstration" strikes to ward off an attack by Soviet forces in Europe all the way to preemptive "decapitation" strikes aimed at annihilating and immobilizing the Soviet political and military leadership in general nuclear war.[12]

On the Soviet side, it was Josef Stalin who first appreciated the political significance of nuclear weapons. In fact, Stalin was so little interested in the military relevance of these weapons that he refused to allow his military officers even to study and debate their impact on military strategy.[13] Only after his death in 1953 did articles begin to appear in Soviet military journals about the strategic implications of nuclear weapons for military operations, and the ensuing debate turned out to be at least as fuzzy and inconclusive as its counterpart in the United States. American analysts who have studied Soviet nuclear doctrine have come up with widely differing interpretations. Some have seen planning for preemptive strikes, and a Soviet belief that nuclear war was a rational implement of policy.[14] Others have seen an essentially defensive Soviet doctrine of deterrence quite similar to mutual assured destruction.[15] With the opening of Soviet society in the past several years, one might have hoped for a clarification of the "real" Soviet nuclear strategy. So far, however, no such clarification has been forthcoming, and Soviet strategists seem as perplexed as their American colleagues about the proper role of nuclear weapons in military planning.[16]

For the British, French, and Chinese the decision to acquire nuclear weapons was based on a combination of political, psychological, and military rationales. In the case of Britain and France, the first two were predominant. The military justification for independent British and French nuclear forces was always weak, given the U.S. nuclear guarantee to NATO, although President DeGaulle of France did question the credibility of that guarantee as part of his argument for a French nuclear arsenal. Still, the British and French arsenals have served little purpose other than to endow their possessors with membership in the prestigious nuclear club. For China, nuclear weapons had a more meaningful military role in its confrontation with Soviet forces deployed on its northern border. But the original motivation for Chinese weapons was more political, arising out of their determination to prevent future U.S. nuclear blackmail like that attempted in the Korean War and the Quemoy-Matsu crises of the 1950s. Whatever their motivations, British, French, and Chinese arsenals have remained relatively small compared to the superpowers, small enough so that their lack of a coherent military rationale could be overlooked.

By the 1980s, U.S. nuclear strategy had evolved to a high art, but the logic of nuclear war could never escape the basic truth that had dictated the Truman and Eisenhower strategies. In strictly military terms, nuclear weapons give a massive advantage to the side that strikes preemptively and decisively against the other side's offensive systems and command structure in the opening moments of a war. But the "advantage" can never be big enough to avoid the risk of massive retaliation with weapons that survive the first strike. So, while it makes no military sense to pull one's punches in a nuclear war, it also makes no sense to throw any punches at all. No rational decision-maker has ever found, nor is any ever likely to find, a political objective for which such an outcome makes sense. Nuclear weapons have put an end to Clausewitz: nuclear war cannot be an instrument of policy, at least against a nuclear-armed opponent. Even major conventional war between nuclear-armed states is out of the question given the risks of escalation to nuclear war.

So the more that nuclear strategy changed, the more it remained the same; there was no escape from MAD. The best one can say about nuclear weapons is that they can prevent war by making the risks too high for both sides. It is not the numbers of weapons or even their detailed characteristics that matter; it is their mere existence that imposes caution and prudence on national leaders in times of tension. Deterrence is not so much a "strategy" as it is a fact of life. In this sense, and for most people *only* in this sense, nuclear weapons can be seen as having played a positive role in world politics during the Cold War. Whether they were really necessary for this role, or whether the role might have been fulfilled with far fewer weapons and at much lower cost, are questions that will be argued for many years to come.

To carry the analysis one step further, let us accept the hypothesis that the possession of nuclear weapons by the United States and the Soviet Union had a stabilizing effect on their adversarial relationship and made war between them less likely. We no sooner accept such a hypothesis than we find ourselves in serious difficulty with another fundamental assumption of the nuclear age, that is, that the proliferation of nuclear weapons to other states is dangerous and destabilizing. The problem is obvious but surprisingly seldom acknowledged by advocates of nuclear deterrence. If the possession of nuclear arsenals by the United States and the Soviet Union is believed to have stabilized their relationship and helped to prevent war between them, then why shouldn't the possession of nuclear weapons by India and Pakistan, or by Israel and Iraq, or by Brazil and Argentina, or by North Korea and South Korea also stabilize *their* relationships and help to prevent war between *them*. In short, how can the nuclear-weapon states take the position that what, for them, has been stabilizing and beneficial will, in the hands of others, necessarily be destabilizing and harmful?[17]

The traditional answer to this question has been that the possession of nuclear deterrents by the two superpowers and the de facto division of the world into two major alliance systems provided all necessary stability, and that proliferation of nuclear weapons to other states only eroded it. In the heyday of strategic theory this was called the "nth country problem." That is, stable deterrence could be expected to prevail between any two actors by the mathematical techniques of game theory, but third, fourth, fifth, and more players made the stability equations insoluble—and, therefore, the world unpredictable. But we should not take this argument too seriously. The leaders of the United States and the Soviet Union certainly did not understand the mathematics of game theory, and there were far less abstract reasons for their opposition to nuclear proliferation. As long as nuclear weapons were controlled by two dominant superpowers surrounded by coteries of militarily dependent "allies," sheltered under their respective nuclear "umbrellas," the superpowers were in control. As far as the superpowers were concerned that was how it should be, and one did not need a mathematician to understand that.

But however mathematically elegant and politically satisfying the Cold War world may have been, it is now a thing of the past. Instead of a single, bipolar confrontation dominating world politics, we are moving into a world characterized by a growing number of regional confrontations, some bipolar and others multipolar. Should nuclear deterrence be relied on to stabilize these regional rivalries, or can world stability be best maintained by eliminating all nuclear arsenals? Even more to the point, can the present situation, embodied in the Nuclear Nonproliferation Treaty (NPT), in which five countries are legitimately entitled to nuclear deterrents while all others are not, be preserved indefinitely?

These are critical questions, and they will be very much on the agenda as the NPT comes up for renewal in 1995. But to address them seriously here would take us well beyond the focus of this chapter, which is the future of nuclear weapons policy in the present nuclear-weapon states. (See Chapter 6 for a full discussion of nuclear proliferation.)

ISSUES FOR THE 1990s

How Many Nuclear Weapons? What Kinds? What for?

A remarkable thing happened in 1987: the United States and the Soviet Union began to collaborate on nuclear disarmament. In the three years from June 1, 1987, to May 31, 1990, the two states eliminated all of their intermediate nuclear-armed missiles under the Intermediate Nuclear Forces (INF) Treaty and implemented a system of information exchanges, notifications, and on-site inspections that literally shifted the nuclear arms race into reverse. The Bush administration, dealing first with Mikhail Gorbachev of the Soviet Union and then with Boris Yeltsin of Russia, accelerated this trend, and by 1992 a rapid succession of bilateral agreements and mutual unilateral declarations had reduced the prospective nuclear arsenals of each country to around 4,000 by 2003, including both tactical and strategic weapons (see Tables 5.1 and 5.2). Assuming that these agreements are honored, this will take the U.S. stockpile back to the size it had been in 1956 and the Russian arsenal back to that of the early 1960s.

If all of these cuts are implemented, the combined U.S. and Russian nuclear stockpiles will drop from more than 50,000 weapons in 1992 to about 8,000 in the early twenty-first century. This means that at least 42,000 nuclear weapons will have to be dismantled in the next ten years, and this task poses its own set of problems, to which we will return shortly. But first we should stop and ask an obvious question: why stop at 8,000? Instead of 4,000 on each side, why not have 2,000, or 400, or 100? Is there a military doctrine that rationalizes any of these goals? If so, does that doctrine also specify what kinds of weapons the United States should have and how they should be used for deterrence or warfighting?

As now planned, the U.S. strategic nuclear arsenal in 2003 will consist of 500 warheads deployed on land-based ICBMs, about 1,700 warheads on submarine-launched ballistic missiles (SLBMs), and about 1,300 weapons on long-range bombers.[18] To this should be added the several hundred "tactical" weapons the United States plans to keep for delivery by other types of aircraft. The vast majority of these warheads were designed to attack Soviet missile silos, command bunkers, submarine bases, airfields, and major industrial complexes, and have nuclear yields in the hundreds of kilotons (ten to twenty-five times as powerful as the Hiroshima bomb). Such

Table 5.1 / Strategic Weapons Inventories

	1990		Post-START I		Post-START II	
	USA	RUSSIA	USA	RUSSIA	USA	RUSSIA
ICBMs	2,450	6,612	1,400	3,153	500	504
SLBMs	5,760	2,804	3,456	1,744	1,728	1,744
Bombers	4,436	1,596	3,700	1,266	1,272	752
Total	12,646	11,012	8,556	6,163	3,500	3,000

Strategic nuclear weapons are those that can be delivered by either the United States or Russia onto the territory of the other. This table shows inventories of warheads on the three strategic delivery systems as they existed in 1990, and as they will exist after the reductions mandated by the START I Treaty, and the further reductions agreed to in January 1993 when START II was signed. As this chapter goes to press, the START I Treaty has not yet been ratified by all parties, and START II cannot be ratified and implemented until this is accomplished. It is important to note that approximately 3,250 of the warheads listed under Russia in the table are actually located in Ukraine, Belarus, or Kazakhstan. (See *Arms Control Today,* Jan/Feb 1992, p. 25.)
Source: Data from *Arms Control Today,* July/August 1992, p. 35.

Table 5.2 / Cuts in Tactical Nuclear Weapons

	U.S. cuts	Russian cuts
Ground-based	2,150	up to 10,000
Sea-based	approx. 2,175	up to 2,000
Air-based	approx. 700	unspecified
Total	approx. 5,025	up to 12,000

Tactical nuclear weapons include all warheads not classified as strategic. They include ground-launched battlefield weapons, such as artillery shells and short-range missiles; naval nuclear weapons, such as cruise missiles, anti-submarine weapons, and bombs on naval aircraft; and bombs and missiles on land-based aircraft. All of the reductions given in the table were declared unilaterally by President Bush in September 1991 and January 1992, and Presidents Gorbachev and Yeltsin in October 1991 and January 1992 respectively.
Source: Data from Comparison of U.S. and Russian Nuclear Cuts, Arms Control Association Fact Sheet, March 6, 1992.

weapons are not designed for use against Third World countries or on the conventional battlefield. It is unclear, therefore, what purpose they will serve if the actual military challenges faced by U.S. forces are to be mid- or low-intensity conflicts in many possible locations around the globe. It is thus appropriate to ask why these particular weapons are being kept, or why they shouldn't be replaced by different types that are better suited to cope with the threats we expect to face in the coming years.

It is difficult to discuss the size and composition of the future U.S. nuclear arsenal in the present state of world politics. It is not at all clear that the agreements already discussed will actually be implemented, and, even if they are, the process is likely to take at least a decade. During that decade many things could happen that could either retard or accelerate the disarmament process and alter attitudes toward nuclear deterrence and the utility of nuclear weapons. All that can be done at this point is to outline a few proposals that span the range of possibilities.

The conventional wisdom is that the United States will have to retain an arsenal of 3,000–5,000 strategic nuclear weapons for the foreseeable future.[19] But the rationale for such an arsenal remains the admittedly remote prospect of nuclear war with Russia, and it is only this contingency that can produce a list of as many as 1,000 military targets for nuclear strikes.[20] All other potential adversaries can presumably be deterred by a far smaller arsenal. But for these adversaries, the types of strategic nuclear weapons the United States now has and is likely to retain into the next century seem singularly inappropriate.

There have been a number of proposals for much smaller arsenals. For example, the Union of Concerned Scientists (UCS) has suggested 1,000 weapons as an appropriate goal,[21] and former Secretary of Defense McNamara has gone even further, urging "a return, in so far as practicable, to a non-nuclear world."[22] McNamara's proposal has the advantage of being able to avoid any discussion of nuclear targeting, but this cannot be said for the UCS suggestion. Nevertheless, the UCS analysts, in keeping with the traditional approach to "minimal deterrence," say nothing about what targets the 1,000 weapons would be aimed at, and under what conditions they might actually be used. This is an example of the disjunction between political and military considerations that has characterized discussions of nuclear weapons from the beginning.

One place where a serious effort has been made to reconcile nuclear strategy with post–Cold War military policy is the U.S. nuclear weapons laboratories at Livermore, Calif., and Los Alamos, N.M. In the fall of 1991, several analysts from these labs published articles examining the question of how nuclear weapons could continue to serve U.S. foreign policy goals after the disappearance (or at least drastic reduction) of the Soviet/Russian threat. The theme of the articles was stated most clearly by Thomas Ramos, then a special advisor to the secretary of defense and a former project leader at Livermore. According to Ramos, "For a nuclear deterrent to be credible, an adversary must believe that use of the weapons is plausible. For that reason, it is important to identify scenarios in which nuclear weapons might be used."[23] It was in this spirit that two Los Alamos analysts proposed a major restructuring of the U.S. nuclear arsenal to meet "threats from diverse regions in the world," especially from "tyrants" or "despots" who might threaten preemptive attacks against U.S. forces deployed near their countries.[24]

One of the lessons taught by the Persian Gulf war, according to these analysts, is that the United States could not credibly deter Saddam Hussein with threats of nuclear attack, because "the destructive power of available nuclear weapons is so great that the peace-loving societies of the world, including our own, might perceive such use as disproportionate to the attack that provoked it." Their answer to this dilemma is to develop a new class of "small" nuclear weapons: "micronukes" with explosive yields of only 10 tons of TNT for use against buried bunkers, "mininukes" with yields of 100 tons for defense against ballistic missile attacks, and "tinynukes" with yields of 1,000 tons (1 kiloton) for use against tank and troop formations sent by the "despot" to attack U.S. forces before they are deployed at full strength.

It would be easy to ridicule this proposal for its tendentious use of words like "tyrant" and "despot" and its choice of "cute" nicknames for the weapons.[25] But such ridicule would miss the point of what is, in fact, a serious attempt to develop a military rationale for nuclear weapons in the post–Cold War world. The argument that U.S. weapons are too powerful for rational military use is certainly valid. When their possible use in the Persian Gulf war was suggested, CIA Director William Webster found the prospect "appalling," and there is no evidence that nuclear attacks were seriously considered by the Bush administration.[26] But if U.S. nuclear weapons were smaller and more discriminating, their use might not appear so appalling. If properly used against strictly military targets, they would not necessarily violate the "principle of proportionality" that forms the basis of just war theory.[27]

But the political and strategic implications of the proposal are far more serious than the authors suggest. If the United States were to pursue a new generation of nuclear weapons with the intention of making them usable in wars against smaller states, it would amount to a re-legitimation of nuclear weapons and a major new incentive for proliferation. It would require a reversal of the congressionally mandated phaseout of nuclear testing, and major investments in rebuilding the nuclear weapon production complex that was shut down in 1988 for environmental and safety reasons. It would jeopardize the renewal of the NPT when it expires in 1995, and reactivate quiescent antinuclear movements in Europe and the United States.

For all these reasons it is highly unlikely that the United States will proceed with development of mininukes. But that leaves us with the original question: how many of our current weapons should we keep, and for what purpose? For deterrence? If so, of whom? Suppose the Russians, French, British, and Chinese are willing to agree to much smaller numbers, even to zero? Would the United States still require nuclear weapons in order to deter nuclear use by Third World states? Is it even necessary to threaten nuclear retaliation to deter a small state from using nuclear weapons? Or does what happened to Iraq in the Persian Gulf war show that the threat of retaliation with modern conventional weapons is just as effective and, because it is actually usable, a far more credible deterrent than nuclear weapons?

These questions cannot be answered definitively, but they do suggest that a serious reevaluation of the role of nuclear weapons in military and foreign policy is needed. Most of the world's nuclear arsenals are products of the Cold War, and now that that struggle is over, it is not sufficient to say that nuclear weapons should be retained simply because they are there. Reduction of the U.S. arsenal by at least 90 percent is possible, assuming the necessary cooperation of other nuclear-weapon states, and even deeper reductions should be possible once these are achieved. Nor should the possibility of total nuclear disarmament be dismissed out of hand. It is a truism that the knowledge on which nuclear weapons are based cannot be lost. Verification of a total nuclear weapons ban would be difficult and expensive, and still would not guarantee that nuclear weapons would never return. Nevertheless, the potential benefits of a world without nuclear weapons make it worthwhile to explore seriously the technical and political feasibility of a worldwide ban on their production, testing, and deployment.

Problems of Nuclear Disarmament

Whether the United States and Russia reduce to 8,000 nuclear weapons or to zero, or to some number in between, most of the same problems will have to be solved. How will weapons be dismantled in a safe and environmentally responsible way? What will happen to the fissile materials that could be used to produce other nuclear weapons at some future time? How will nuclear disarmament be verified, and how much will verification cost? How will the nuclear weapons production complexes of the nuclear-weapon states be reconfigured to prepare for the demands of smaller nuclear arsenals? How will the environmental damage created by past nuclear operations be repaired?

For all of the recent progress in nuclear arms reduction, it is remarkable that no provision has been made for the verified dismantlement of nuclear warheads. Several kinds of missiles were destroyed under the INF Treaty, and many hundreds of delivery systems will be retired under the START agreements and by unilateral actions, but there is nothing in any of these agreements that specifies what will happen to the actual warheads. In principle, each side could simply put all of its warheads into storage and, at some time in the future, put them back on new delivery systems. Unless effective controls are established over the dismantlement of warheads and the disposal of the uranium and plutonium they contain, no one will ever be certain that this material has been properly disposed of.[28]

The need for such controls was made clear by the Senate in its ratification vote for the START Treaty. It attached the so-called Biden Condition, a nonbinding request that in future negotiations with Russia the president "seek an appropriate arrangement" for monitoring weapon stockpiles and fissile material production facilities.[29] Such an arrangement will be difficult to achieve, but more for political than technical reasons. If American observers are to be able to monitor Russian weapons disposal, then Russians will want to do it for American weapons as well. Out of professed concern for military and industrial secrets, the U.S. government has so far refused to permit this, demanding instead that Americans supervise Russian warhead dismantlement without reciprocity; it is hardly surprising that the Russians have found this unacceptable.

Added to these difficulties are problems with the former Soviet republics. Russia has reportedly repatriated all of its tactical nuclear weapons from Eastern Europe and the republics, but large numbers of strategic weapons remain deployed in Belarus, Kazakhstan, and Ukraine (see notes to Table 5.1). These states have signed the protocols to the START Treaty and have agreed in principle to join the NPT as nonnuclear-weapon states, but the details of these agreements remain to be worked out. Meanwhile, Ukraine and Russia have a number of outstanding disputes over boundaries, military assets, and other problems, and the temptation for Ukraine to employ the nuclear weapons on its territory as bargaining chips is always present.[30]

Verification of the START Treaty and a number of other major arms control agreements has also been made more complicated by the breakup of the Soviet Union, and thus the entire question of arms control verification is likely to be reexamined in light of changing world politics. The START Treaty mandates the elimination of missiles, submarines, and bombers deployed at dozens of bases on the territories of the United States and former

Soviet Union. Where the INF Treaty employed five kinds of on-site inspection, START will employ twelve; and where the cost of implementing the INF inspections was in the tens of millions of dollars per year, the corresponding costs for START will be measured in hundreds of millions.[31]

These costs must be added to those of verifying all of the other agreements that have been reached in the past few years, including, among others, the Conventional Forces in Europe (CFE) Treaty and the Chemical Weapons Convention (CWC). The U.S. Congressional Budget Office estimates one-time costs to the United States alone of verifying all these agreements at $645 million to $3 billion, with additional costs of $200 to $660 million per year for an indefinite number of years into the future. These estimates do not include the costs of monitoring a possible comprehensive nuclear test ban, or the substantially greater support required by the International Atomic Energy Agency (IAEA) if it is to implement a more effective safeguards program against nuclear weapon proliferation.

In the heyday of the arms race it could be argued that, however great the cost of verification, it would still be only a fraction of the cost of an open-ended arms competition. That remains true, but now that the arms race is coming to an end and political attention is turning toward stagnant domestic economies and the increasing costs of education and health care, the prospect of spending up to a billion dollars a year for verification of arms control agreements takes on a different aspect. In addition, Russia's economic problems make it unlikely that it can afford to carry out its full allocation of inspections under these treaties, or provide adequate support for foreign inspections of its own facilities. It has already required aid from the West to help it dismantle its nuclear weapons and destroy its chemical weapon stockpile, and it will undoubtedly require more aid if it is to allow inspections of its nuclear facilities under any future expansion of IAEA safeguards. Just how this need for financial aid can or will be reconciled with Russian demands for equal treatment under arms reduction treaties remains to be seen. The already mentioned dispute over asymmetric inspections of warhead dismantlement may be a harbinger of similar disputes in the future.

Intimately connected with the warhead dismantlement problem is the question of what to do with the hundreds of tons of uranium-235 and plutonium that will be removed from them. In principle, these materials could be used to produce electricity in nuclear reactors. In practice, however, this will not be so easy. Almost all operating nuclear reactors use U-235 as fuel, but it is in much more dilute form than the highly "enriched" bomb-grade uranium used in bombs. The latter can be diluted for use in reactors by mixing it with natural uranium, but this would multiply the amount of fuel produced by a factor of twenty-five or thirty, and there is already a glut of reactor-grade uranium on world markets because of stagnation in the nuclear power industry. Dismantlement of more than 80 percent of U.S. and Soviet nuclear weapons over the next ten years will add at least 1,000 tons of nearly pure U-235 to world supplies, enough to run the entire U.S. nuclear power industry for more than ten years.[32] It will be the United States that will gain control of most of this material, since Russia has agreed to sell 500 tons of its own weapon-grade uranium to the United States over the next twenty years.[33] (U.S. intelligence had originally estimated 500 tons as the full Soviet stockpile, but public remarks by President Yeltsin have suggested that they have considerably more, possibly more than 1,000 tons.[34])

If the problems with uranium are difficult, those with plutonium are mind-boggling. Plutonium can also be burned in nuclear reactors, but because uranium has become so cheap and plentiful there has been little incentive to build reactors that can handle plutonium, which is a more hazardous and costly material to employ. Plutonium is produced in all operating nuclear reactors, but extracting it from the intensely radioactive spent fuel is expensive and environmentally risky. For this reason, only France, Britain, and Japan have made large investments in civilian plutonium recovery, and even these countries have yet to build the reactors that can burn the plutonium to make electricity.[35] In these circumstances, the prospect of a new generation of nuclear reactors being built to burn up the uranium and plutonium liberated from weapons is remote, to say the least.

All that can be done with this dangerous material today is to put it into storage for the indefinite future. The storage sites will have to be constantly monitored, which could be done either bilaterally by the United States and Russia or under IAEA safeguards. Either way, it will not be cheap. Russia has already said it will need new facilities to store its plutonium, and the United States will probably have to subsidize them. The United States may also need more storage space if it turns out that all of the plutonium cores from dismantled U.S. weapons cannot be stored safely in existing facilities at the Pantex Plant near Amarillo, Texas.[36] The IAEA is already greatly overextended in monitoring the Nonproliferation Treaty, and will need greater financial support whether or not it takes the responsibility for monitoring U.S. and Russian plutonium.

Finally, there remains the need to clean up and restructure the nuclear weapons production establishments of the United States, Russia, and other states. Fifty years of nuclear research, development, testing, production, deployment, and retirement has left a staggering legacy of environmental pollution, waste accumulation, and public-health concerns that will take decades and hundreds of billions of dollars to deal with, if indeed they can be dealt with satisfactorily at all.

The U.S. nuclear weapons complex has been effectively shut down since 1988, when, in the wake of the Chernobyl accident, a number of critical facilities were discovered to have serious health, safety, and environmental problems.[37] Plutonium production at Hanford, Wash., was terminated, as was tritium production at Savannah River, S.C., and plutonium component fabrication at Rocky Flats, Colo. In May 1992, the Department of Energy

(DOE) announced that it had abandoned its plans to reopen Rocky Flats, and later that year the DOE also cancelled a multibillion dollar project to build a new tritium production reactor. By sometime in 1990 or 1991, the United States had ended all production of nuclear weapons.[38]

If the United States wants to resume the manufacture of nuclear weapons it will have to construct several new facilities at a cost of many tens of billions of dollars.[39] At the same time, the DOE bears the responsibility for cleaning up the environment at dozens of former weapons facilities, encompassing thousands of sites where hazardous wastes—both chemical and nuclear—have been dumped or buried during the past fifty years. Many of these sites contain unknown quantities of unknown materials that have migrated unknown distances into the surrounding land and created unknown health and environmental impacts. Just to inventory, characterize, and prioritize these threats will take at least a decade and cost billions of dollars. To clean them up—if this is even possible in all cases—will take a generation or more, and cost hundreds of billions of dollars more.[40]

The drunken nuclear binge that has taken up most of the second half of the twentieth century is over. It is now the morning after, and the party goers face the necessity of both sobering up and cleaning up. The costs of monitoring disarmament and repairing the environment are going to dominate the nuclear picture for the foreseeable future, and place real constraints on any state that may entertain dreams of restarting the arms race. These costs will also play a key role in determining how many nuclear weapons are to be retained in national arsenals, and what new facilities, if any, will be required to develop, manufacture, and maintain them. These mundane concerns will bring the debate over the future of nuclear deterrence down from the abstract strategizing of professors and military theorists to the practical politics of setting economic and social priorities in a highly competitive and interdependent world.

Strategic Defense

Intimately connected to the debate over nuclear deterrence and the utility of nuclear weapons is the question of whether it is feasible or desirable to defend the country against nuclear attack. This debate is as old as nuclear weapons themselves, and while it has waxed and waned in the media and domestic politics, it has remained a preoccupation, some would say obsession, with scientists, strategists, and military planners. With the advent of the Clinton administration, the debate has moved away from the intensely ideological form it took during the Reagan and Bush years; even though President Clinton has abandoned the more exotic space-based aspects of Reagan's "Star Wars" program, the concept of ballistic missile defense is far from dead. Research and development budgets of $3–4 billion per year are still very much a part of Clinton's defense program, and Secretary of Defense Aspin and several of the Senate's most influential voices in military affairs have endorsed a strong commitment to the development of ground-based ballistic missile defenses.

To many of the original atomic scientists it was axiomatic that no defense against nuclear attack was possible. In World War II, using conventional bombs, it required hundreds of aircraft and tens of thousands of bombs to devastate a city. However, Hiroshima and Nagasaki were each destroyed by a single aircraft dropping one bomb. No affordable air defense system can be certain of protecting a city attacked by only a dozen aircraft carrying atomic bombs. With the advent of intercontinental ballistic missiles, the infeasibility of meaningful defense of cities became even more apparent. Incoming ICBM warheads travel at speeds of 17,000 miles per hour, and even if some way could be found to intercept a single warhead, it was inconceivable that dozens of warheads, capable of evasive maneuvers and accompanied by hundreds of decoys, could be stopped with 100 percent effectiveness.

In the twenty years following World War II, improvements were made in rocket engines, guidance systems, radars, infrared sensors, communications, data processing, nuclear and nonnuclear kill mechanisms, and in many other fields. By the middle of the 1960s, some U.S. and Soviet scientists believed that an effective defense against ballistic missile attack might be feasible, and both sides began the development and deployment of such systems in the latter part of the decade. The Soviets deployed an antiballistic missile (ABM) system around Moscow—a system that is still there and that was extensively modernized in the 1970s and 1980s. In the United States, the Johnson and Nixon administrations attempted to deploy an ABM system, but their efforts were frustrated by anti-ABM scientists and activists, and by the antimilitary atmosphere created by the Vietnam War. The U.S. ABM program was terminated when President Nixon and Soviet Premier Brezhnev signed the ABM Treaty in 1972, banning all future efforts to create a nationwide defense against ballistic missile attacks.

The ABM Treaty did not mean that the two sides had given up on the *feasibility* of ballistic missile defense; it was signed because many people on both sides had become convinced of the *undesirability* of such defenses. The treaty was premised on McNamara's concept of stable deterrence through mutual assured destruction: each side depended for its security on its assured ability to respond with devastating force to an attack by the other, so if one side improved its defenses the other would have to respond by increasing its offensive deployments. Therefore, a prohibition on strategic defenses was an essential prerequisite for achieving major reductions in offensive weapons.

Not everyone was convinced by these arguments. A powerful group of conservative analysts, scientists, and politicians accused proponents of the MAD doctrine and the ABM Treaty of yielding the traditional right of the United States to self-defense, and of entrusting its survival to the good faith and judgment of communist leaders in the Kremlin. From this point of view,

MAD and the ABM Treaty were the height of liberal self-delusion, and, as the 1970s wore on and American politics swung to the right, the treaty came under increasingly vigorous attack.

The anti-MAD, anti-arms control philosophy ascended to power in 1981 with the inauguration of President Ronald Reagan. In his famous "Star Wars" speech of March 23, 1983, Reagan denounced mutual assured destruction as unworthy of a great nation and asked why the same scientists who had gotten us into this terrifying stalemate couldn't turn their efforts to defense and find a way to "render nuclear weapons impotent and obsolete." We have since learned that Reagan acted impulsively in making this statement, and that he surprised many of his advisors as well as the scientific and technical community. His belief that defense against nuclear attack might be feasible was based on scientific advice that was, at best, incompetent and, at worst, self-interested and dishonest.[41] He needed no advice to convince himself that SDI was desirable; he had been a long-time foe of MAD, nuclear arms control, and the ABM Treaty, and he saw SDI as a way to kill all three birds with one stone.

In the ensuing years, the SDI program has spent more than $25 billion and stimulated research and development on a wide variety of exotic military technologies. There are some who argue, not altogether convincingly, that it helped to persuade Mikhail Gorbachev that further pursuit of the nuclear arms race was pointless.[42] But it did not succeed in producing a workable defense against ballistic missile attacks, nor did it kill the ABM Treaty (which remains an effective barrier to the ambitions of the more extreme proponents of ballistic missile defense). Still, the idea of defense against ballistic missile attack refuses to die, and the apparent success of the U.S. Patriot system against Iraqi missiles in the Persian Gulf war caused a number of previously skeptical people—particularly the influential Chairman of the Senate Armed Services Committee, Sam Nunn of Georgia—to reevaluate their position on strategic defense. Despite later exposure of Pentagon distortions of the Patriot record,[43] Congress directed the Pentagon to work toward deployment of a limited ABM system called Global Protection Against Limited Strikes (GPALS), designed to protect the continental United States against accidental launches of ballistic missiles or attacks by hostile smaller states.

The new leadership in Russia has taken a very different attitude toward strategic defense from that of the old Soviet government. In 1992, President Boris Yeltsin of Russia endorsed continued research and development on ABM systems in collaboration with the United States. The commitment amounts to little more than words at this time, but it is nonetheless significant because it was made at the same summit meeting in which the two sides agreed to make much deeper cuts in their offensive arsenals. This suggests that the traditional assumption that defenses must be prevented if offenses are to be reduced is no longer valid, and that defensive deployments and offensive reductions can proceed together. President Bush's Secretary of

Defense, Dick Cheney, certainly thought that this was what the agreements meant. But others argued that the Russians had not renounced the old assumptions. Then Secretary of State James Baker commented that "if we had said we're walking away from the ABM Treaty just pure and simple . . . I don't think we would have gotten this arms reduction agreement." [44]

Baker was certainly correct. A complete rejection of the ABM Treaty would have been taken by Russian negotiators as a repudiation of the entire arms control regime that had been so painstakingly erected by two generations of U.S. and Soviet leaders. Conservatives in the former Soviet Union would have used such a repudiation to support their arguments that the United States still cannot be trusted. But Cheney also had a point. The traditional relationship between limiting ballistic missile defenses and reducing offensive arsenals was premised on a continuing relationship of hostility and nuclear deterrence between the United States and the USSR. That relationship has changed, so it is necessary to reexamine the logical connection between strategic defense and offensive arms control.

It is true that GPALS, in its presently envisioned form, would pose no threat to the Russian or American deterrents, and if the two countries collaborate and deploy it together, there is no logical reason why both couldn't continue to reduce their offensive arsenals to much lower numbers. But this rosy scenario is hardly a realistic possibility, if for no other reason than the cost of such a system. It will run into the tens or hundreds of billions of dollars, and it is obvious that Russia cannot afford such lavish investments in "insurance" against highly improbable attacks. If the defensive system is to be shared, the United States will have to pay most of the bill.

Therefore, it is highly unlikely that the collaboration will ever be consummated, and so, if the United States continues with its own development and deployment, this will inevitably raise anxieties—not only in Russia, but in any state that sees itself as a potential rival of the United States. Hence, the essence of the strategic argument against SDI remains valid: if the United States maintains an offensive arsenal of several thousand warheads and develops a workable defense against limited strikes, this can still look like a "first strike capability" to any state, including Russia, that lacks its own defense and has some reason to distrust U.S. intentions. Even a limited defense requires widespread deployments of early warning systems and development of virtually all of the components of a more militarily significant territorial defense; the potential for "breakout" into full-scale deployment will therefore accompany the deployment of any ABM system, no matter how limited its initial mission.

Strategic arguments are important, but far more immediate are the domestic economic and political arguments against a commitment to ballistic missile defense. Faced with chronic recession, steadily rising national debt, and substantially reduced military budgets, the United States must ask if is it worth the money and technical resources that such a program would require, especially given the improbable nature of the attacks against which it is supposed to defend. SDI may have seemed to some like a good idea in

1983, but the revolutionary developments in world politics that have occurred since its announcement have placed it in an entirely different strategic and economic context. Still, the Clinton administration appears reluctant to abandon the idea completely. Despite the shelving of Ronald Reagan's utopian "peace shield," and the abolishing of its bureaucratic embodiment, the Strategic Defense Initiative Office (SDIO), Mr. Clinton and his military and scientific advisors have not given up on ballistic missile defense. Indeed, the commitment to some kind of ground-based system seems stronger than ever, and who can say what brilliant new idea for space-based weapons might once again turn the heads of this or a future administration?

CONCLUSION

During the long years when the nuclear arms race seemed destined to go on forever, it was easy to avoid thinking about the practical problems and costs of nuclear disarmament. Most of the intellectual and political effort went into trying to stop the nuclear buildup. The details of how nuclear weapons would be disposed of, how much it would cost, what we would do with the excess fissile materials, and how we would clean up the mess we made in producing them, seemed almost a luxury to have to worry about; far less dramatic and frightening than preventing nuclear war. Now we must think about these problems, and we must think about them urgently and rationally. Priorities must be set, long-term financial and bureaucratic commitments made, new scientific knowledge and technical capabilities developed, and new political institutions and relationships created.

All of these demands have come upon us with breathtaking suddenness, and the modes of thinking and acting that evolved during the Cold War are not easily altered. But unless they are, the world could find itself in at least as much trouble as it was before: awash in uranium and plutonium with their potential to accelerate nuclear proliferation, unable to account for hundreds or thousands of nuclear warheads and delivery systems in the hands of potentially unstable states, and entangled in bitter domestic disputes over weapons and facilities that have lost their military rationale but persist because of bureaucratic momentum or local political interests. These problems are certainly not unique to the United States, but as the world's leading nuclear power, and as the one superpower still commanding significant economic resources, the United States has no choice but to assume leadership. It promises to be one of the greatest challenges we have faced as a nation.

Notes

1. Carl von Clausewitz, *On War* (Princeton, NJ: Princeton University Press, 1976), p. 87.
2. For an excellent account of the politics and physics of the first atomic bomb, see Richard Rhodes, *The Making of the Atomic Bomb* (New York: Simon and Schuster, 1986).
3. Rufus E. Miles, Jr., "Hiroshima: The Strange Myth of Half a Million American Lives Saved," *International Security* (Autumn 1985), pp. 121–140.

4. Ronald Schaffer, *Wings of Judgment: American Bombing in World War II* (New York: Oxford, 1985) and McGeorge Bundy, *Danger and Survival: Choices About the Bomb in the First Fifty Years* (New York: Random House, 1988).

5. See, for example, Gar Alperovitz, *Atomic Diplomacy: Hiroshima & Potsdam* (New York: Penguin Books, 1985) and Martin J. Sherwin, *A World Destroyed* (New York: Alfred A. Knopf, 1975).

6. Barton J. Bernstein, "Marshall, Truman, and the Decision to Drop the Bomb," *International Security* (Winter 1991/92), pp. 214–221.

7. Bundy, op. cit., chapter 6.

8. David A. Rosenberg, "A Smoking, Radiating Ruin at the End of Two Hours," *International Security* (Winter 1981/82).

9. Thomas B. Cochran, William M. Arkin, and Milton M. Hoenig, *Nuclear Weapons Databook, Volume I, U.S. Nuclear Forces and Capabilities* (Cambridge, MA: Ballinger, 1984).

10. Alain C. Enthoven and K. Wayne Smith, *How Much Is Enough?* (New York: Harper & Row, 1971).

11. Fred Kaplan, *The Wizards of Armageddon* (New York: Simon and Schuster, 1983).

12. Lawrence Freedman, *The Evolution of Nuclear Strategy* (New York: St. Martin's Press, 1989).

13. H. S. Dinerstein, *War and the Soviet Union* (New York: Frederick A. Praeger, 1962).

14. On Soviet warfighting, see Richard Pipes, "Why the Soviet Union Thinks It Could Fight and Win a Nuclear War," *Commentary* (July 1977), pp. 21–34.

15. On Soviet deterrence, see Raymond L. Garthoff, *Deterrence and the Revolution in Soviet Military Doctrine* (Washington: Brookings, 1990).

16. For a revealing study of the confusion in the minds of both U.S. and Soviet nuclear strategists, see Steven Kull, *Minds At War: Nuclear Reality and the Inner Conflicts of Defense Policymakers* (New York: Basic Books, 1988).

17. A similar argument has been advanced by Kenneth Waltz in "The Spread of Nuclear Weapons: More May Be Better," International Institute for Strategic Studies, Adelphi Papers no. 171, Autumn 1981.

18. "Past and Projected Strategic Nuclear Arsenals," *Arms Control Today* (July/August 1992), pp. 35–36.

19. Michèle A. Flournoy, ed., *Nuclear Weapons After the Cold War: Guidelines for U.S. Policy* (New York: Harper Collins, 1993), see note 17, p. 148.

20. Ibid., chapter 3.

21. Jonathan Dean and Kurt Gottfried, "A Program for World Nuclear Security," Union of Concerned Scientists, Cambridge, MA, February 1992.

22. Robert S. McNamara, "The Changing Nature of Global Security and Its Impact on South Asia," Address to the Indian Defense Policy Forum, New Delhi, reprinted by Washington Council on Nonproliferation, Washington, DC, November 20, 1992.

23. Thomas F. Ramos, "The Future of Theater Nuclear Forces," *Strategic Review* (Fall 1991), pp. 41–47.

24. Thomas W. Dowler and Joseph S. Howard, Jr., "Countering the Threat of the Well-armed Tyrant: A Modest Proposal for Small Nuclear Weapons," *Strategic Review* (Fall 1991), pp. 34–40.

25. For an insightful analysis of this practice among predominantly male strategic analysts, see Carol Cohn, "Slick'ems, Glick'ems, Christmas Trees, and Cookie Cutters: Nuclear Language and How We Learned to Pat the Bomb," *Bulletin of the Atomic Scientists* (June 1987), pp. 17–24.

26. Flournoy, op. cit., p. 45.

27. Michael Walzer, *Just and Unjust Wars* (New York: Basic Books, 1977).

28. The problems of warhead dismantlement and fissile material production monitoring are analyzed in Frank von Hippel, "Ending the production of fissile materials for weapons; Verifying the dismantlement of nuclear warheads: The technical basis for action," Federation of American Scientists, Washington, DC, June 1991.

29. John F. Cushman, Jr., "Senate Endorses Pact to Reduce Strategic Arms," *New York Times* (October 2, 1992), p. A1.

30. "Ukraine Says it May Sell Nuclear Arms to Highest Bidder," *Boston Globe* (November 6, 1992), p. 10; Serge Schmemann, "Ukraine Asks Aid for Its Arms Curb," *New York Times* (November 13, 1992), p. A10.

31. All cost estimates are from Congressional Budget Office, *U.S. Costs of Verification and Compliance Under Pending Arms Treaties,* Washington, DC, September 1990.

32. von Hippel, op. cit., p. 39.

33. "U.S. to Buy Uranium from Russian Bombs," *Arms Control Today* (September 1992), p. 34.

34. NRDC Policy Brief: Disclosure of Vast Russian Nuclear Stockpile, Washington, DC, September 11, 1992.

35. William Walker and Frans Berkhout, "Japan's Plutonium Problem—And Europe's," *Arms Control Today* (September 1992), pp. 3–10.

36. Robert S. Norris and William M. Arkin, "Nuclear Notebook: Pantex Lays Nukes to Rest," *Bulletin of the Atomic Scientists* (October 1992), pp. 48–49.

37. For an overview of the problems of the weapons complex, see Peter Gray, ed., "Facing Reality: The Future of the U.S. Nuclear Weapons Complex," Nuclear Safety Campaign, Seattle, WA, May 1992.

38. Thomas W. Lippman, "New Strategic Era Sees Transformation of U.S. Nuclear Arms Establishment," *Washington Post* (May 11, 1992), p. 1.

39. Nuclear Weapons Complex Reconfiguration Study, U.S. Department of Energy, DOE/DP-0083, Washington, DC, January 1991.

40. U.S. Congress, Office of Technology Assessment, Complex Cleanup: The Environmental Legacy of Nuclear Weapons Production, OTA-O-484, Washington, DC, February 1991.

41. William J. Broad, *Teller's War: The Top-Secret Story Behind the Star Wars Deception* (New York: Simon & Schuster, 1992).

42. For the argument that SDI helped make the Soviets more reasonable, see John Lewis Gaddis, "How Relevant Was U.S. Strategy in Winning the Cold War?" Strategic Studies Institute, U.S. Army War College, Carlisle Barracks, PA, March 17, 1992. For an alternative interpretation of the role of SDI in the U.S.-Soviet rapprochement, see Allan S. Krass, "The People, the Debt, and Mikhail," *Bulletin of the Atomic Scientists* (November 1991), pp. 12–17.

43. John Conyers, Jr., "The Patriot Myth: Caveat Emptor," *Arms Control Today* (November 1992), pp. 3–10.

44. The Cheney and Baker quotes and much of the following analysis are from Matthew Bunn, "The ABM Talks: The More Things Change . . . ," *Arms Control Today* (September 1992), pp. 15–23.

6 / Nuclear Proliferation and Nonproliferation Policy in the 1990s

ZACHARY S. DAVIS

After the Cold War, the potential use of nuclear weapons continues to pose one of the greatest immediate dangers to world security. The likelihood of a nuclear war between the United States and the former Soviet Union drastically decreased as relations between Washington and Moscow improved during the late 1980s and early 1990s. The rapid demise of the Soviet Union hastened negotiations on deep reductions in both superpower nuclear arsenals. (See Chapter 5.) However, while the United States and Russia begin to retire large portions of their nuclear forces, other countries retain an interest in joining the nuclear weapons club. Stopping the spread, or "proliferation," of nuclear weapons thus remains a top priority for world security.

What are the dangers associated with nuclear proliferation? Even "small" or relatively unsophisticated nuclear weapons constructed with fifty-year-old technology can inflict massive death and destruction. The bombs that destroyed Hiroshima and Nagasaki in 1945 were small, crude weapons by today's standards.[1] As more nations acquire nuclear weapons, the likelihood of their use may increase. Nuclear weapons could be fired accidentally, change possession due to unexpected changes of government, or fall into the hands of terrorist or subnational groups. Political turmoil is not uncommon in a number of nuclear-capable countries. Actual or threatened use of nuclear weapons could escalate conflicts and perhaps incite the use of chemical or other weapons of mass destruction to counteract nuclear threats. Moreover, ballistic missiles extend the reach of these threats. As wars escalate, more nations could become involved. Such "worst-case" scenarios might cause some nations to reconsider previous decisions not to arm themselves with nuclear weapons.

For these reasons, there has been a strong international consensus against the spread of nuclear weapons. Efforts to block proliferation can claim many notable successes. Indeed, many people expected in the early nuclear era that more nations would try to acquire nuclear weapons. So far, there are only five acknowledged nuclear weapons states: China, France, Great Britain, Russia, and the United States. However, several other countries (India, Israel, Pakistan) have some undeclared nuclear weapons capabilities and are considered to be de facto nuclear weapons states. Some other nations have recently abandoned their nuclear weapons programs. Thus, South Africa was widely believed to have a secret nuclear program until it signed the

Nuclear Nonproliferation Treaty (NPT) in 1991 and opened its nuclear facilities to international inspection. Argentina and Brazil, both of which had secret nuclear weapons programs, also pledged not to build nuclear weapons and agreed to open their nuclear installations to inspection.

Despite these successes, other countries have demonstrated an interest in developing a nuclear weapons option. Iraq, which had signed the NPT, had a secret nuclear program that was close to producing its first nuclear bomb before it was exposed after the 1991 Persian Gulf conflict. North Korea, which signed the NPT in 1985 but delayed inspections until 1992, is widely suspected of having a clandestine nuclear weapons project. Countries such as Iran, Algeria, Syria, and perhaps some of the newly independent nations of the former Soviet Union, maintain an ambiguous posture regarding the possible military uses of their nuclear technology programs. It is possible that a decision by these or other countries to develop nuclear weapons could cause neighboring countries to reconsider their decisions to sign the NPT and remain nonnuclear weapons states. Against a backdrop of post–Cold War regional conflicts, uncertainty about the nuclear intentions of certain countries and the continued growth of arsenals of chemical weapons, missiles, and advanced conventional weapons may persuade some governments to keep their nuclear options open.

These trends could signal hard times for international efforts to block the spread of nuclear weapons. Conversely, the end of the Cold War generated new hope and opportunities to strengthen the international consensus against nuclear proliferation. The NPT, which is the centerpiece of the nonproliferation "regime," is due for a twenty-five-year review conference in 1995. At this conference the members of the treaty must decide whether to extend the treaty in its present form or amend it. Responding to revelations about Iraq's secret nuclear program and concern about the proliferation dangers associated with the breakup of the Soviet Union, many countries have renewed their interest in improving international nuclear inspections and tightening controls on exports of nuclear and nuclear-related technology. However, the original international consensus on the benefits of nonproliferation was formed largely as a result of superpower influence on less powerful nations. The United States and the Soviet Union cooperated throughout the Cold War to prevent all but a few nations from acquiring nuclear weapons; now that superpower influence has waned in a more multipolar world, it may prove more difficult to sustain the international consensus against proliferation.

PROLIFERATION VS. NONPROLIFERATION POLICY

The United States developed its nuclear weapons during World War II under the tightest possible secrecy. After the war, some U.S. officials believed that it was possible to maintain the American monopoly on nuclear weapons by continuing to shroud the atomic bomb program—known as the Manhattan Project—in secrecy. Many Manhattan Project scientists objected to this view; they thought it was inevitable that other countries, especially the Soviet Union, would soon develop their own nuclear weapons. To prevent the spread of such weapons, some U.S. scientists and policymakers favored putting all uses of nuclear technology under the control of the United Nations.

A proposal based on this idea for international control of atomic energy became official U.S. policy in 1946. The Baruch Plan, named after the U.S. negotiator who presented the proposal to the United Nations, called for all nations to turn over all nuclear materials, including weapons, to a special UN agency. The United Nations would oversee the peaceful and military applications of nuclear technology. However, the plan was probably doomed to fail because it would have required the Soviets to surrender their nuclear program before the United States would give up its nuclear weapons. The Baruch Plan also contained an unspecific threat of punishment against violators.[2] Moscow rejected the plan.

With hopes for international control of atomic energy dashed, the United States resorted to a policy of secrecy and denial. This did not prevent the Soviet Union from testing its first nuclear weapon in 1949, nor did it discourage other nations from pursuing nuclear research and development. While the United States could guard its knowledge of the industrial processes used by the Manhattan Project to build nuclear bombs, knowledge of nuclear physics was impossible to control.

Atoms for Peace and War

The United States changed its nuclear policy in the early 1950s in connection with President Eisenhower's 1953 "Atoms for Peace" proposal. The proposal was intended to promote transfers of peaceful nuclear energy technology from technologically advanced nations to developing nations in exchange for commitments from recipient countries not to use the civilian nuclear technology they acquired in this fashion for military uses. Another part of the proposal would have created an international "atom bank" for civilian nuclear materials that could be used by participating nations. In 1954, Congress amended the Atomic Energy Act to establish guidelines for nuclear cooperation that enabled U.S. companies to pursue international markets for nuclear commerce. As part of this "nuclear bargain," nuclear reactors and fuel were widely disseminated, subject to assurances that they would not be used to make nuclear weapons. These assurances were to be verified by a new UN-affiliated organization, the International Atomic Energy Agency (IAEA), which was established in 1957. The IAEA set up a system of "safeguards" that included inspections of nuclear facilities and materials and other accounting procedures to detect diversions.

Atoms for Peace combined self-interest in helping U.S. companies to export nuclear technology, idealism about nuclear energy's potential for improving economic conditions in developing countries, and a pragmatic approach toward nonproliferation policy. In retrospect, Atoms for Peace overestimated the economic benefits of nuclear energy and underestimated the proliferation risks of disseminating nuclear technology.[3] However, the basic "nuclear bargain" established the framework for international nuclear cooperation that remains at the heart of the nuclear nonproliferation regime. And the IAEA safeguards system has evolved and expanded to require more intrusive inspections on a wider range of nuclear activities.[4]

Some proliferation was probably inevitable. Great Britain acquired knowledge about nuclear weapons as a participant in the Manhattan Project and detonated its first nuclear bomb in 1953, despite being excluded from the U.S. nuclear program in 1946. France tested its first bomb in 1960. In both nations, nuclear programs were motivated by doubts about the reliability of U.S. security guarantees and a desire for prestige and influence in the postwar world.[5] The United States restored nuclear weapons cooperation with Britain in 1958, but rejected French President de Gaulle's insistence on equal treatment. The Soviet Union initially offered nuclear assistance to China, but suspended its aid as relations between Moscow and Beijing turned sour in the late 1950s. China became the fifth declared nuclear-weapon state in 1964.[6] India tested what it called a "peaceful nuclear explosion" in 1974, but has not tested since. No other nation has openly crossed the nuclear threshold by testing a nuclear device.[7]

The Nuclear Nonproliferation Treaty

The centerpiece of international efforts to stop the spread of nuclear weapons is the Nuclear Nonproliferation Treaty. The treaty was negotiated during the 1960s, when the United States and the Soviet Union began to acknowledge their shared interests in preventing more nations from acquiring nuclear weapons. Proliferation, they realized, could reduce their influence with nuclear-armed countries and, in addition, could invite dangerous nuclear confrontations in regional hotspots around the world. After the first twenty years of experience with U.S.-Soviet nuclear deterrence, policymakers from both superpower countries eventually reached agreement on a common policy to prevent other nations from seeking security in nuclear weapons.

The NPT entered into force in 1970 with a twenty-five-year term. When the first term ends in 1995, NPT members will hold a review conference to decide whether to renew the treaty and on what terms. They may extend the treaty indefinitely or for a shorter period, such as five years.[8] The NPT's central provisions (Articles I and II) contain pledges by the nuclear powers (defined as countries having exploded a nuclear device prior to 1967) not to transfer nuclear explosive devices to any nonnuclear weapon state, and by the nonnuclear weapon states not to acquire such devices. Nonnuclear states agree to accept IAEA safeguards on all of their nuclear facilities (so-called full-scope safeguards), rather than just on particular imported items as required under the Atoms for Peace inspection arrangements.

Two other key provisions of the NPT, both subjects of perennial controversy, are Article IV, pledging support for international cooperation in peaceful nuclear energy, and Article VI, promising "good faith" efforts toward arms control and disarmament by the nuclear weapon states. Some Third World NPT member countries have complained that nuclear assistance has been in short supply, and that the nuclear weapon states have ignored their commitments to reduce their own armaments. In particular, continued nuclear testing by the weapon states came to symbolize the discriminatory nature of the NPT. Some nations have threatened not to extend the treaty when it comes up for review in 1995, or to extend it on a temporary basis, unless the nuclear weapon states negotiate a comprehensive test ban agreement.[9] Recently, there has been some movement toward a test ban. In 1992, Russian President Boris Yeltsin declared a one-year moratorium on testing; later that year, the U.S. Congress passed (and President Bush signed) a law that limits future U.S. tests to fifteen before they are ended in 1996.[10] France also agreed to a testing moratorium in 1992, and Great Britain depends on the United States for all its testing, thus leaving China with the only active testing program. It remains to be seen whether this apparent progress toward a test ban will lead to a test ban treaty. Such a treaty, combined with deep reductions in the United States and Russian nuclear arsenals, may satisfy the arms control expectations of some NPT members and improve prospects for the renewal of the NPT in 1995.

The NPT helped to create an international norm of nonproliferation, in effect delegitimizing the acquisition of nuclear weapons by additional countries. With France and China finally joining the treaty in 1992, all of the declared nuclear weapon states are members. South Africa, which was widely considered to be a nuclear threshold state, also signed in 1991 and completed a safeguard inspection agreement with the IAEA. Following the disintegration of the Soviet Union, Russia inherited Moscow's NPT status as a nuclear weapon state. The other newly independent republics pledged to remove all nuclear weapons from their territory and to sign the NPT as nonweapon members, although Ukraine and Kazakhstan have wavered in their commitment to give up nuclear weapons on their territory. These additions bring NPT membership to nearly 160 countries.

Despite these developments, which help strengthen the norm of nonproliferation, some countries still refuse to join the NPT. India, a long-standing critic of the treaty, claims the right to keep its nuclear options open unless all nations disarm. Pakistan will not sign the treaty unless India does. Israel will not sign the treaty while its neighbors possess weapons of mass destruction. Argentina and Brazil have apparently forsworn nuclear weapons and made progress toward opening their nuclear programs to inspection, but have not signed the NPT. Still other countries have signed the NPT but have either violated it, such as in the case of Iraq's clandestine nuclear weapons program, or refused to comply with it, as in the case of North Korea, which signed in 1985 but delayed inspections until 1992, and then threatened to withdraw from the treaty in 1993. Signing the NPT does not guarantee that a country has no interest in nuclear weapons, or that it will not acquire one in the future.[11]

The Evolution of the Nonproliferation Regime

The NPT did not stop proliferation. Not long after the treaty entered into force in 1970, several developments in the mid-1970s indicated that the danger of proliferation was growing. First, in 1974, India detonated a nuclear explosive device, which it called a peaceful nuclear explosion, using plutonium from a reactor supplied by Canada under an early Atoms for Peace project. Second, France, West Germany, and other European countries emerged as challengers to United States domination of the nuclear export market by agreeing to supply a broad range of sensitive nuclear technologies—including those required to produce weapons-grade plutonium and uranium—to customers in the Third World.[12] Enrichment technology makes it possible to enrich the level of uranium-235 from 0.7 percent in widely available natural uranium to over 90 percent required for nuclear weapons; reprocessing technology is used to extract plutonium from uranium fuel that has been "burned" in nuclear reactors. Germany offered reprocessing and enrichment technology to Brazil as part of a multi-reactor sale; France agreed to supply reprocessing plants to Pakistan and South Korea; and Italy sold reprocessing technology to Iraq. Third, the oil crisis of the mid-1970s stimulated new interest in nuclear power, including the development of "breeder" reactors that could operate using recycled plutonium and would produce still more plutonium as a waste product. The prospect of energy independence held strong attraction for many nations. However, widespread use of plutonium as an energy resource would involve the transportation, storage, and handling of large quantities of nuclear materials that could be used in nuclear weapons.[13]

If these trends continued, and more countries developed nuclear weapons options based on civilian nuclear technology, the line between peaceful and military uses of nuclear energy would be increasingly blurred. Exports of advanced nuclear technology gave many countries the ability to produce enriched uranium and plutonium. With ready access to bomb-making materials, even a country that had signed the NPT could quickly make nuclear bombs; those that refused to sign the treaty were not obligated to obey its restrictions on weapons-related activities. During the 1970s, evidence of clandestine nuclear programs in India, Pakistan, Iraq, Israel, South Africa, and other countries underscored the weaknesses of international nonproliferation efforts.[14] In addition to India's "peaceful nuclear explosion" in 1974, Pakistan used legal and illegal means to import equipment to build a gas centrifuge uranium enrichment plant, and Iran and Iraq used oil income to buy reactors. And, in 1979, U.S. intelligence satellites detected a mysterious flash in the sky above the Indian Ocean, which was interpreted by many analysts to have been a joint Israeli-South African nuclear test.[15]

Growing recognition of the gaps in the nonproliferation regime prompted a U.S.-led effort to strengthen nonproliferation policies. The renewed effort included the formation by the leading Western countries of the Nuclear Suppliers Group (NSG), which established more stringent international standards to guide and control exports of nuclear technology. In addition, the Carter administration opposed exports of enrichment, reprocessessing, or breeder reactor technology. As an alternative to these technologies, the United States sought to assure clients who bought U.S. nuclear reactors that it would continue to be a reliable supplier of nuclear fuel and nuclear fuel services. Furthermore, the U.S. Congress passed the Nuclear Nonproliferation Act of 1978, which tightened the legal guidelines for nuclear cooperation with the United States,[16] and also passed several amendments to the Foreign Assistance Act that called for a cutoff of U.S. aid to countries that sold or received enrichment or reprocessessing technology without placing them under safeguards.[17]

Not all nuclear suppliers agreed with every aspect of the tougher nonproliferation restrictions on exports. Several Western European countries rejected the proposed abandonment of breeder reactor technology and continued to support the development of a plutonium fuel cycle. Japan also remained committed to using plutonium as an energy resource. France, which had not yet signed the NPT, maintained its right to sell reactors to countries such as Pakistan, which did not allow inspections of certain facilities widely suspected of housing its covert enrichment equipment. Germany continued to sell advanced nuclear technology to Brazil, Iran, and Iraq. The goal of the NSG was to harmonize the international nuclear export control policies of the major Western suppliers. But because of its informal, voluntary nature, the group lacked authority to enforce the new standards. One component of the tougher controls imposed by the Carter administration policy was removed in 1981 when the Reagan administration dropped United States opposition to the use of plutonium by certain allies.

The 1980s began with the first preemptory attack on a nuclear reactor. In June 1981, Israeli jets bombed Iraq's large Osirak reactor. The stated objective of the attack, which evoked considerable controversy, was to prevent the reactor from contributing to Iraq's suspected bomb project.[18] Critics of the attack condemned the preemptive bombing of a nuclear reactor as a dangerous precedent for future nonproliferation policy.[19] The bombed reactor, as it turned out, was not intended as the main thrust of Iraq's quest to build nuclear weapons, and the attack may have encouraged Saddam Hussein to take greater precautions to hide his clandestine bomb project. In 1986, new evidence came to light regarding Israel's own nuclear program when Mordechai Vanunu, a former technician at Israel's Dimona reactor complex, divulged details of Israel's clandestine bomb-making capability.[20]

Evidence also continued to accumulate regarding ongoing covert nuclear weapons programs in Argentina, Brazil, South Africa, India, Pakistan, and North Korea. Several other countries, including South Korea and Taiwan, appeared to be reassessing earlier decisions against keeping open a nuclear option.[21]

The continued advancement of nuclear proliferation in the 1980s outpaced the sometimes half-hearted attempts by nuclear suppliers to clamp down on the spread of nuclear technologies that could be used to build nuclear weapons. Whereas the nuclear suppliers initially focused on expanding export controls on uranium enrichment and plutonium reprocessing technology, many proliferators either discovered ways to evade controls (often by giving false information on export license applications) or focused their efforts on acquiring "dual-use" equipment that was not subject to nuclear controls, but could be used in their bomb-making operations. Dual-use goods include everything from computers to raw materials and machine tools that can give a determined proliferator the means necessary to build its own Manhattan Project. Instead of trying to import fissile material, or the equipment needed to produce it, proliferators could acquire the materials and tools needed to make enrichment or reprocessing equipment. Controls on nuclear goods and technology were ineffective against countries like Iraq, Israel, and Pakistan that operated sophisticated international procurement networks to acquire the resources necessary to build their own bomb-making facilities.[22]

Emerging New Suppliers

Efforts to control the spread of nuclear and nuclear-related, dual-use technology were further undermined by the emergence of a number of new suppliers. Following the pattern established earlier by Western suppliers, a few developing and newly industrialized nations acquired the expertise and the capability to manufacture nuclear equipment and to compete for a share of the world nuclear market. Argentina, Brazil, China, India, Taiwan, South Africa, and a few other countries added a new complication to the proliferation problem by offering a possible alternative source of nuclear technology to countries not willing to satisfy the restrictive export criteria of the more established nuclear exporters. A new pattern of cooperation developed between the emerging suppliers themselves, many of whom were already excluded from nuclear commerce with traditional suppliers who insisted on their acceptance of full-scope safeguards as a condition of supply.[23]

Throughout the 1980s, vertical proliferation (increases in the arsenals of the major nuclear weapons states) often eclipsed the unseen, or "opaque," advance of horizontal proliferation (the spread of nuclear weapons to more countries).[24] U.S. and Soviet preoccupation with Cold War tensions often obscured nonproliferation objectives and forced them to take a back seat to other foreign policy goals. However, at the close of the decade, nuclear developments in a number of countries forced a broader recognition of the influence of nuclear proliferation on regional and international politics.

REGIONAL NONPROLIFERATION PROBLEMS

In most cases, when proliferation occurs it reflects the underlying security considerations of particular nations. Security is a universal concern that is manifested differently according to national and regional conditions. The following is a summary of regional proliferation considerations.

South Asia

India and Pakistan stand at the brink of a nuclear arms race. Although neither country openly admits to having assembled complete nuclear bombs, there is convincing evidence that both could complete the necessary steps very quickly following a decision to do so. With a long history of conflict between them, and a number of outstanding disagreements that have periodically led to violence, the potential for nuclear conflict may be growing. A flare-up of a bitter ongoing conflict over the border province of Kashmir in 1990 emphasized this possibility. Both nations have disavowed any interest in nuclear weapons and claim only peaceful applications for their unsafeguarded nuclear programs. However, both countries admit to having developed the capability to build nuclear weapons and also assert their sovereign right to use whatever means necessary to defend themselves.

India has not tested another nuclear device since its original 1974 "peaceful nuclear explosion." It has, however, continued to produce quantities of plutonium from unsafeguarded reactors and reprocessing facilities at a rate sufficient for perhaps as many as two hundred bombs (or as few as sixty) by 1992.[25] Indian officials have confirmed that their country has the ability to make nuclear weapons, but steadfastly maintain that no decision has been reached to build a nuclear arsenal. Although Pakistan's nuclear program is a cause of concern, India views China—which has had nuclear weapons since 1964—as a much more serious threat to its security. India also possesses a variety of missiles and has tested a long-range nuclear-capable missile, the Agni, which could reach as far as Beijing. India has defeated Pakistan in previous wars and could probably do so again. Nevertheless, a Pakistani nuclear test would probably cause India's leaders to change their essentially ambivalent nuclear policy and deploy a nuclear arsenal.

Following India's 1974 test of a nuclear device, Pakistan made steady progress toward nuclear status. Using uranium centrifuge technology purloined from the West, Pakistan built an enrichment plant thought to be capable of producing enough enriched uranium for a few bombs per year. China reportedly supplied the Pakistanis with warhead design and testing data.[26] Pakistani officials confirmed in 1992 that Pakistan possesses "cores" for nuclear weapons; Senator Larry Pressler placed the number of bombs that could be assembled within a matter of hours at seven.[27] These statements confirmed that half-hearted attempts by Washington to persuade Pakistan not to produce weapons-grade enriched uranium had failed. Pakistan's plans for deploying or delivering nuclear arms in time of war remain largely unknown. Some nuclear analysts and members of the U.S. Congress suspect that Pakistan plans to employ American-supplied F-16 fighter aircraft as its primary delivery system, but could use other aircraft.[28] Pakistan has also received nuclear-capable ballistic-missile components and launchers from China.[29] Its nuclear weapons program is controlled by military leaders and has at times appeared to be out of reach of civilian leaders, especially former Prime Minister Benazir Bhutto, who opposed it.[30]

On the diplomatic front, Pakistan insists that it will sign the NPT if India does. It has repeatedly proposed regional nonproliferation arrangements that would make South Asia a nuclear weapons-free zone. New Delhi rejects the NPT because it is discriminatory, and refuses to participate in regional arrangements that would leave Pakistan's close ally, China, with nuclear weapons while India disarmed. India prefers a global approach to nuclear disarmament that would affect all nuclear weapon states equally. Despite the lack of progress on arms control, Pakistan and India signed an agreement in 1989 under which both sides pledged not to attack each other's nuclear installations. Such "confidence-building measures" have little direct impact on nuclear policies, but may, over time, contribute to a climate that is more favorable for negotiating substantive arms control agreements.

The nuclear standoff in South Asia reflects not only the bitter rivalry between the two nations, but also the failure of external pressures in support of nonproliferation objectives. For much of the past twenty years, nonproliferation came into direct competition with other superpower interests in the region. This was particularly acute with respect to the United States response to the Soviet Union's invasion of Afghanistan in 1979, after which Pakistan's strategic value as a conduit for aid to the anti-Soviet Afghan rebels was judged to outweigh the risk of Pakistan's advancing nuclear weapons program.

The U.S. cut off aid to Pakistan in 1979 (as required by the Foreign Assistance Act) in response to Islamabad's ongoing efforts to acquire uranium enrichment technology and its refusal to open all of its nuclear facilities to inspection. However, in 1981, Congress amended the law to allow the president to waive the required cutoff of assistance if the president determined that it was "in the national interests of the United States" to do so. President Reagan then restored assistance to Pakistan as part of a policy to support the Afghan rebels. In 1985, Congress added a new condition for the president; to waive the cutoff of aid to Pakistan, he must certify annually that "Pakistan does not possess a nuclear explosive device and that the proposed U.S. assistance program will reduce significantly the risk that Pakistan will possess a nuclear explosive device."[31] Presidents Bush and Reagan made the annual certifications despite growing evidence of Pakistan's advancing nuclear status. Finally, in 1990, President Bush did not make the certification and aid was cut off.[32]

There is hope for nuclear stability in South Asia. Some observers of nuclear developments in the region agree with Indian and Pakistani expressions of optimism that a stable nuclear deterrent relationship is evolving between the two countries. Other observers warn of the dangers that may be encountered by attempting to recreate the type of nuclear deterrence practiced by Washington and Moscow over the course of the Cold War and beyond. At best, a degree of stability might be derived from an arms race that is sure to cost both countries massive investments of scarce resources. At worst, deterrence modeled after the U.S.-Soviet experience could lead to nuclear crises, similar to the Cuban Missile Crisis, that would radically increase the risk of nuclear war.

The Middle East

The Middle East presents an extremely complex set of political relationships that form the backdrop for nuclear developments in the region. Only Israel is currently believed to have nuclear weapons; Iraq was probably within a few years of acquiring a nuclear capability before its nuclear program was destroyed in 1991 during Operation Desert Storm and dismantled by United Nations teams in its aftermath. Libya has expressed interest in nuclear weapons, but has not built the necessary equipment to launch its own nuclear program. Iran and Algeria have active civilian nuclear programs that could eventually give them the capability to develop a nuclear weapon, if they chose to do so. Syria renewed its interest in nuclear technology in 1991 when it ordered a small nuclear reactor from China. China also assisted Iran's nuclear program, and has discussed the possibility of helping to revive Egypt's abandoned plans for nuclear power.

The Middle East nuclear balance is further complicated by the proliferation of chemical, biological, and conventional weapons and ballistic missiles throughout the region. A number of nations justify their possession of chemical weapons—often called "the poor country's nuclear alternative"—as a counter to Israel's suspected nuclear arsenal. Egypt, Iran, Iraq, Israel, Libya, and Syria have produced chemical weapons. All of these nations signed the 1925 Geneva Protocol, which bans the use (but not the possession) of chemical weapons. Iraq, Libya, and Syria are among the nations thought to have developed biological weapons.[33] Several countries have developed or acquired ballistic missiles with ranges that would enable them to strike targets throughout the region. Egypt, Iran, Libya, Syria, and Yemen have Scud-B or modified Scud-type missiles capable of carrying a 1,000-kilogram payload for a distance of at least 300 kilometers. Iraq's Scud missiles were to be destroyed under the terms of the UN ceasefire agreement (Security Council Resolution 687), although the full extent of Iraq's missile inventory was not known, and some may remain. Israel and Saudi Arabia have missiles with significantly longer ranges and payloads that may give them a capability to strike targets beyond the Middle East.[34]

Israel developed nuclear weapons using technology acquired largely from France, which supplied a reactor during the 1960s. The reactor and its related reprocessing and enrichment facilities is located at Dimona, in the Negev Desert. Israel has some minor facilities under IAEA safeguards, but has not signed the NPT. Estimates of Israel's arsenal range from around 50 to 300 weapons, some of which may be hydrogen bombs.[35] Israel also possesses a nuclear-capable missile, named Jericho, with a 900-mile range. This combination would enable Israel to target sites inside the former Soviet Union. Israel maintains a scrupulously ambiguous posture regarding its nuclear strategy, Israeli officials stating only that "Israel will not be the first to introduce nuclear weapons" into the region. This ambiguous posture may provide a degree of diplomatic flexibility vis-à-vis Tel Aviv's Arab neighbors, and also may help to avoid open confrontation with the United States over nonproliferation policy. Most observers speculate that Israeli strategists view nuclear weapons as a deterrent that would only be used as a last resort, should the continued existence of their nation face an imminent threat.

Iraq was a charter member of the NPT when it entered into force in 1970. It used its oil wealth to buy nuclear technology in the 1970s, which it submitted for regular inspections by the IAEA. In addition to its declared nuclear facilities, however, Iraq operated a sophisticated international procurement network that it used to acquire a broad range of nuclear and nuclear-related goods, ranging from nuclear triggers to raw materials. With these imports, Iraq built its own Manhattan Project, complete with updated copies of fifty-year-old uranium enrichment equipment, called calutrons, that were used by the United States to build its first atomic bombs.[36] Iraq also had plans for a large centrifuge enrichment program, and experimented with small-scale plutonium separation. These activities were violations of Iraq's commitments under the NPT and its safeguard agreement with the IAEA.[37] Iraq also had nuclear weapon design information, equipment, and facilities, some of which may have been derived from U.S. sources.[38] Rather than seize safeguarded fuel from one of its small research reactors, Iraq apparently planned to build its bombs using highly enriched uranium produced from its secret calutrons and centrifuges. These may have been capable of producing enough material for two or three bombs per year by about the end of 1993.

Years of inspections of Iraq's known nuclear facilities and material did not detect convincing evidence of the full-blown, billion-dollar clandestine nuclear weapons project that was exposed after the 1991 Persian Gulf war.

However, some official and unofficial analysts tracked the advance of Iraq's covert nuclear program from its origins before the Israeli bombing of the Osirak reactor in 1981 through the UN inspections after the Gulf war.[39] While some specific aspects of the Iraqi bomb program may have come as a surprise, much was known. This fact highlights a familiar pattern in nonproliferation policy in which other foreign policy objectives, in this case supporting Iraq to prevent its defeat in its war with neighboring Iran, were judged by U.S. policymakers to be more important than stopping proliferation. American policy toward Iraq sought to bring Saddam Hussein "into the community of nations" by offering positive incentives such as loans, credits, and access to high-technology exports.[40] Iraq, like Pakistan, took the incentives but pressed ahead with its nuclear objectives.

Israel and Iraq outpaced other Middle Eastern nations in seeking nuclear capabilities. However, Iran, under the Shah, laid the foundation for an extensive nuclear power and technology infrastructure (despite Iran's rich oil and natural gas reserves). Many of Iran's nuclear facilities were damaged in the war with Iraq, or were allowed to decay during the Islamic revolution. More recently, Iran's clerical leadership appeared determined to revive their country's nuclear program in the early 1990s, when they sought nuclear assistance from China, Russia, India, Germany, and several other countries, and invited nuclear scientists who fled after the fall of the Shah to return home. Germany refused to repair the large reactors it originally built at Bushehr, but China and Russia agreed to provide extensive nuclear cooperation. In 1992, Moscow and Beijing both agreed to sell nuclear power reactors to Iran. Iranian government officials have fueled speculation about Iran's nuclear intentions by making statements about the need for Islamic states to acquire nuclear weapons to counter Israel's nuclear capability, while other Iranian officials have denied having any interest in nuclear weapons. Still, Iran has sufficient nuclear resources and expertise to build a nuclear technology infrastructure that will suffice to keep its nuclear options open. According to recent U.S. intelligence estimates, Iran could be capable of building nuclear weapons by the end of the decade.[41] Although it has signed the NPT and allows inspections of its nuclear facilities, the Iraq example illustrates the difficulties of finding and exposing clandestine nuclear activities if they exist.

Other countries lag even farther behind in nuclear capabilities, but could eventually catch up. Algeria advanced its nuclear technology base during the 1980s using a combination of Argentinean expertise and a secret reactor deal with China. The existence of the reactor deal was exposed in 1991, in spite of Chinese denials.[42] Syria also arranged to purchase a small reactor from China in 1991. The deal was delayed by the IAEA until Syria, an NPT state, completed the required safeguard agreement with the agency. While these kinds of purchases alone do not necessarily give a country nuclear weapons options, possession of nuclear technology can sometimes have symbolic importance for governments. Nuclear programs can be symbols of technological progress and sources of national pride, especially for developing nations. It is also possible that the uses of nuclear technology by a particular country can change as a result of political instability and changes of government. Peaceful nuclear programs can lay a foundation for the pursuit of nonpeaceful objectives.

For many years, the United Nations and the IAEA have passed annual resolutions supporting the establishment of a nuclear weapons-free zone (NWFZ) for the Middle East. Nearly all nations in the region, including Israel, have endorsed the concept, though there are wide differences on the terms for bringing it about. Arab states have suggested that support for such a zone be contingent on Israel's dismantling of its nuclear weapons and production facilities, but without reciprocal commitments for negotiations on chemical or conventional arms, and without recognition of Israel's right to exist—terms that are obviously unacceptable to Israel.

In 1991, President Bush announced a Middle East Arms Control Initiative, part of which called for states in the region to implement a verifiable ban on the production and acquisition of weapons-usable nuclear materials and called on states that have not done so to accede to the NPT.[43] The plan would place all nuclear facilities in the region under IAEA safeguards. This approach could represent a significant step toward eventual creation of a NWFZ. It is notable that the proposal would not require Israel to dismantle its undeclared nuclear capabilities as a precondition for negotiations, and it allowed linkage of chemical and conventional disarmament with nuclear disarmament. Realistically, negotiations on a NWFZ would have to be linked to regional peace and security arrangements that address a broad range of outstanding issues. Middle East peace negotiations began in the Bush administration and continued into the Clinton administration, but no breakthroughs in arms control are currently in sight.

Encouraging Signs in the Southern Hemisphere: South America and South Africa

Proliferation can be rolled back in some cases. Proliferation threats have diminished in South America and South Africa, mainly in connection with political changes that have taken place in three nuclear threshold states: Argentina, Brazil, and South Africa. In each case, unsafeguarded nuclear facilities—some thought to be associated with nuclear weapons—were brought under international safeguards.

In the 1980s, Argentina and Brazil demonstrated their mastery over nuclear reactor and uranium enrichment technologies. Much of the technology and training was supplied by West Germany. Nuclear weapons and ballistic missile programs prospered with the strong support of military leaders in both countries who valued their nuclear programs as sources of pride, income, and security. Weak civilian governments were unable or unwilling to control nuclear programs that risked involving Argentina and

Brazil in a nuclear arms race.[44] Argentina and Brazil also demonstrated their willingness to compete aggressively for a share of the world export market in nuclear and missile technology. Argentina cooperated with Egypt and Iraq to develop its Condor II missile, sold nuclear technology to Algeria, and, in 1992, agreed to sell nuclear technology to Iran until Washington insisted that the sale be cancelled. Brazil had prepared a nuclear test site in the Amazon, and developed a nuclear submarine program. Neither country was a member of the NPT, nor would either country sign the Treaty of Tlatelolco, which would establish a NWFZ for South America.

These trends toward proliferation were reversed. One important factor in the rollback of nuclear proliferation in South America was a shift toward democracy in Argentina and Brazil that empowered civilian leaders with the authority needed to change the direction of nuclear programs that had a history of close association with the military. Under civilian leadership, Argentina and Brazil moderated their nuclear rivalry. The presidents of the two countries signed a series of confidence-building measures, which led eventually to an agreement with the IAEA to allow inspections of all nuclear facilities in both countries. The leaders of both countries have pledged their intention to sign the Treaty of Tlatelolco, and there is hope that this process could eventually lead to signing of the NPT. However, this optimistic view is tempered by the possibility that political reforms could be reversed by a return to military rule, which could bring about a revival of dormant nuclear programs.[45]

A somewhat similar situation exists in South Africa, which was a nuclear weapon threshold state until it signed the NPT in 1991 and opened its nuclear facilities to inspection. South Africa's unsafeguarded enrichment facilities could have produced enough material for several tens of weapons; it conducted experiments related to weaponization and prepared a test range in the Kalahari Desert. In 1993, South African President de Klerk admitted that his country had built six nuclear devices, and was working on a seventh, when the program was scrapped in 1990. South Africa has had close military ties with Israel; there is also evidence of nuclear cooperation between South Africa and Israel. Many analysts believe that the mysterious flash detected by a U.S. satellite over the south Atlantic Ocean in 1979 was a joint South African-Israeli nuclear test.[46]

Since it joined the NPT, South Africa has been visited by IAEA inspectors on nearly 100 occasions to verify its initial inventory of declared materials.[47] Like Argentina and Brazil, South Africa's willingness to reverse course, by signing the NPT and opening its facilities for inspections, was probably related to the process of political development. The closing down of active nuclear weapons programs in these countries could provide a model for proliferation rollback of nuclear programs in other threshold nuclear states.[48] However, in the South American and South African cases, it is difficult to imagine how nuclear weapons could have been used to counter the main threats to the security of these nations in the first place.

Thus, their nuclear weapons programs were easier to give up because these countries did not depend on them for their security.

East Asia

North Korea's nuclear program presented the international community with its first test of will to enforce international nuclear nonproliferation policy in the post Iraq era. In 1991, top United States government officials labeled North Korea's nuclear program "the number one threat to security in East Asia."[49] North Korea received nuclear technology and training from the Soviet Union, but that was gradually cut off as the country became increasingly isolated, and much of its nuclear infrastructure was built and designed indigenously. North Korea signed the NPT in 1985, but delayed implementation of a safeguards agreement until 1992. Despite the government's repeated denials of having any interest in reprocessing, initial IAEA inspections confirmed the existence of a large, but incomplete, reprocessing facility at Yongbyon, a reactor capable of producing plutonium, and small quantities of plutonium that had been separated from spent reactor fuel.[50] These inspections also revealed discrepancies in North Korea's declaration of its past plutonium reprocessing activity. Guided by intelligence information provided by member countries, IAEA inspectors demanded access to two sites believed to house undeclared nuclear materials. North Korea refused, and in March 1993 began the three-month process of withdrawing from the NPT—the first country ever to do so. Denied access to the sites, the IAEA reported to the UN Security Council that it was unable to verify North Korea's compliance with the NPT. On June 11, 1993, North Korea cancelled its threatened withdrawal from the NPT, but a confrontation with the Security Council is likely over Pyongyang's refusal to open the sites.

Controversy about North Korea's nuclear ambitions coincide with a rise in diplomatic contacts between Pyongyang and the government of South Korea. During negotiations on reconciliation and eventual reunification of the two countries, both sides pledged not to operate reprocessing facilities in their respective countries; they also agreed to augment regular IAEA inspections with bilateral inspections, but were not able to reach agreement on the scope and intrusiveness of such inspections. If North Korea were to comply with its nonproliferation commitments, progress would be possible on a wide range of outstanding issues. However, continuing uncertainties about its nuclear activities block the reconciliation process with South Korea and bring increasing pressures from the international community.

One possible negative effect of North Korea's nuclear program is that it may cause other countries in the region, particularly South Korea (but possibly others), to reconsider their nuclear options. South Korea operates many nuclear power reactors and clearly has the technical capability to develop nuclear weapons, should it decide to do so. In the 1980s, Washington persuaded South Korea not to pursue a nuclear weapons option and to give up plans to build its own reprocessing facilities.[51] In 1992, the United States removed its tactical nuclear weapons from South Korea and began to withdraw some of its troops. Without the extended deterrent provided by United States nuclear weapons and troops, and if relations with North Korea deteriorate badly, South Korea may reevaluate its nuclear policies. On the other hand, if reunification is achieved, Seoul could inherit North Korea's nuclear program—a prospect that surely causes concern in Beijing and Tokyo.

Japan's nuclear program also affects the proliferation equation in East Asia. Although Japan's nonproliferation credentials are impeccable, it clearly could build nuclear weapons if it wanted to.[52] Japan has an extensive nuclear power industry and is building large-scale plutonium reprocessing facilities to extract plutonium from spent reactor fuel. Japan also has plans to develop a breeder reactor that would produce even more plutonium. This investment in nuclear technology contributes to a long-term goal of energy independence. However, critics question the need for Japan to build a plutonium economy when uranium fuel (for Japan's light water reactors) is abundant and cheap on the world market, and the economic, security, and environmental risks associated with large-scale use of plutonium are so high. While other countries have gradually abandoned the plutonium fuel cycle—mainly for economic reasons—Japan may be building a large stockpile of plutonium.

Japan currently has contracts with French and British firms to extract plutonium from spent fuel, which is then shipped by sea back to Japan. These shipments have become the focus of controversy, mainly because of fears that the plutonium boats could be attacked by terrorists (who would steal the plutonium to make bombs) or have an accident that would spill deadly plutonium into the seas.[53] Because some of the reactor fuel was originally sold to Japan by the United States (under the terms of a bilateral agreement for cooperation), the United States government has some influence over the arrangements for each shipment. So far, the United States Department of State has expressed satisfaction with the arrangements. Other governments, however, have restricted the passage of the shipments through their territorial waters, and members of the U.S. Congress have attempted to attach legislative conditions to the shipments. Japan's plutonium policy could strongly influence the future of nonproliferation in Asia.

POST–COLD WAR PROLIFERATION CHALLENGES: A NUCLEAR "YARD SALE" IN THE FORMER SOVIET UNION?

Regional proliferation dilemmas will continue to pose major challenges for nonproliferation in the 1990s. Several relatively new issues may further complicate international and national efforts to control the spread of nuclear weapons. These new challenges will test the will of the international community to strengthen and enforce the nonproliferation regime.

The demise of the Soviet government initially raised concerns about the possibility of a breakdown of the military command and control system that could lead to unauthorized possession or use of nuclear weapons. This was the so-called "loose nukes" issue.[54] Another aspect of the problem is that the resources of the Soviet nuclear weapons complex could "leak" out of the countries of the Commonwealth of Independent States (CIS) and contribute to the proliferation problem. Some radioactive materials have been smuggled out of Russia and were sold on the black market, but reports of entire warheads being sold to Iran were not confirmed. However, the ultimate fate of many tons of weapons-grade material in Russia—many tons more of which will be recovered from nuclear warheads that are retired and dismantled—creates a major new proliferation problem. (See Chapter 5.)

Russia inherited the Soviet Union's nonproliferation commitments along with most of its nuclear weapons. Under the START Treaty and its protocols, only Russia will remain a nuclear weapon state; all strategic nuclear weapons are to be removed from Ukraine, Kazakhstan, and Belarus. These countries agreed in protocols signed in May 1992 to join the NPT as non-weapon states, and to allow all nuclear weapons on their soil to be returned to Russia. Ukrainian officials have nevertheless continued to express reservations about giving up the nuclear weapons on their territory and about implementing the START Treaty. Ukraine wants additional security guarantees, and also wants a share of the profits from sales of uranium extracted from nuclear warheads that are dismantled under the terms of the treaty. The government of Kazakhstan voiced similar concerns. The United States offered $175 million to encourage Ukraine to ratify and implement the START Treaty, but the future of nuclear weapons in the new nations of the former Soviet Union remains uncertain.

Although some nuclear activities, such as uranium mining and nuclear power plants, are located outside Russia, nearly all of the critical nuclear weapons facilities, including the main nuclear laboratories, are in Russia. Thus, only Russia will retain a complete nuclear weapons production complex. The disintegration of the political, economic, industrial, and military institutions that shared responsibility for operating the weapons complex may result in a breakdown of nuclear policy, including confusion about who has authority for nuclear safety and nuclear export controls. Such a breakdown could create opportunities for people to acquire and sell nuclear resources to proliferators. Skilled scientists and fissile nuclear materials would probably be at the top of a proliferator's shopping list. Of course, proliferators may also be interested in buying complete nuclear warheads, but these may be more useful for retrieving the design information and fissile materials they contain than for actual military use.

Like the United States, the Soviet Union stored excess uranium and plutonium in temporary facilities, many of which pose grave environmental hazards as well as being attractive targets for proliferators. The Russian government has asked for and will receive American assistance to assure the security of its nuclear weapons and weapons materials. The ultimate disposition of Russian (and world) stockpiles of plutonium and, to a lesser extent, highly enriched uranium, has become a major proliferation dilemma.

PRESERVING AND STRENGTHENING THE NONPROLIFERATION REGIME

The nuclear nonproliferation regime has become increasingly interdependent with the regimes to control the spread of other weapons of mass destruction. A nation that cannot match an adversary's nonnuclear forces may view nuclear weapons as a way to deter an attack. The same may be true for other weapons of mass destruction that are cheaper and easier to make or buy. An increasing number of nations are able to build *and export* ballistic missiles capable of delivering nuclear or chemical warheads over long distances.[55] The proliferation of all types of unconventional weapons tends to reinforce pressures on nations to seek security by deploying their own weapons of mass destruction.[56] The result could be a pattern of regional arms races that ultimately reduces security for all. Preserving and strengthening the nuclear nonproliferation regime may be essential to the success of future efforts to control other weapons of mass destruction.[57]

A Comprehensive Nonproliferation Policy: Controlling the Spread of Missiles and Chemicals

In the 1980s, the United States initiated a coordinated international effort to control the spread of the most sophisticated missile technology by forming a suppliers control group called the Missile Technology Control Regime (MTCR). Another informal suppliers association, called the Australia Group, coordinates multilateral controls on chemicals that can be used for chemical weapons.[58] Both groups focus on controlling international sales of dual-use commodities that have legitimate uses in a wide range of industrial applications. For example, militarily useful missile technology often overlaps with items used in the civilian aerospace industry, especially space launch and satellite technology. Chemicals commonly used in agriculture can be used to make chemical weapons. Computers present a particularly difficult "dual-use" problem, because they can be used for a variety of scientific and industrial projects, including designing missiles and nuclear weapons. How can nonproliferation policy distinguish between legitimate civilian and military applications of technology?[59]

Export controls represent one aspect of a comprehensive approach to nonproliferation. Yet, overemphasis on technology denial has many weaknesses, not the least of which is that export controls can never be completely "leak proof." Experience has shown that resourceful proliferators can find ways to circumvent export controls. This was expertly demonstrated by Iraq's weapons procurement programs.[60] Not all countries are equally committed to stopping potentially dangerous exports, especially when very large sums of money in commercial trade are at stake. Very often in the past, when one country refused to sell to a suspicious buyer, another country gladly stepped in to make the deal. Export controls, if they are rigorously enforced, can mean lost contracts. But even if export controls are effective at both the national and multilateral level, more and more proliferators may be developing indigenous scientific and industrial capabilities that will enable them to build weapons without outside assistance. Thus, export controls address only one part of the proliferation dilemma.

The United States and other countries have sought to complement informal multilateral export control regimes such as the Nuclear Supplier's Group (NSG), the Missile Technology Control Regime, and the Australia Group, with international conventions that establish recognized norms of nonproliferation. Until recently, treaties for chemical and biological weapons outlawed only the use, not the possession, of such weapons.[61] By contrast, the NPT formally outlaws possession of nuclear weapons by non-weapon states and is reinforced by the IAEA safeguards inspection system. After years of negotiation, a global Chemical Weapons Convention with verification procedures was completed in 1992.[62] While some policy specialists argue that narrow, informal arrangements, such as NSG, MTCR, and the Australia Group, provide needed diplomatic flexibility to focus on particular proliferation problems, other experts favor more comprehensive, or universal, approaches to nonproliferation that apply to all countries and all types of weapons of mass destruction.

While formal international commitments probably add to the effectiveness of global nonproliferation efforts, they may be viewed as a necessary, but not sufficient, component of the nonproliferation regime. Like export controls, treaties may influence—but, alone, do not normally determine—a sovereign nation's decision to acquire weapons of mass destruction. A comprehensive nonproliferation strategy should combine unilateral and multilateral export controls, international agreements, and flexible diplomacy to preserve and strengthen the nuclear nonproliferation regime. But should the nuclear nonproliferation regime unravel, efforts to control other weapons of mass destruction seem doomed as well.

The Future of the NPT: The 1995 Review Conference

The NPT is the institutional heart of the nuclear nonproliferation regime. In 1995, its nearly 160 members will hold a conference to decide whether to extend the treaty indefinitely, for a fixed period, or not at all. If the members of the treaty are unable to resolve certain contentious issues, such as the desired linkage by some members between the NPT and a comprehensive test ban, the future of the NPT may be at risk. Countries (such as India) that view the NPT as fundamentally flawed (because it reinforces discrimination between nonnuclear weapon states and the five nuclear weapon states) argue that the treaty should be scrapped. While a few nonsigners of the treaty may encourage its demise, almost all nations continue to view the NPT as a useful instrument of nonproliferation policy. Thus, its extension is widely viewed as a critical test for preserving the nuclear nonproliferation regime. The accession of France, China, and South Africa to the treaty in 1991 and 1992 strengthened the NPT. However, suspicions about the activities and intentions of some NPT members may weaken support for the treaty. To assuage such concerns, IAEA inspections will have to provide members with greater confidence that outlawed nuclear activities will not go undetected or unpunished.[63]

International Safeguards, Inspections, and the IAEA

One way to increase confidence in commitments made by NPT states is to improve the international inspection system of the IAEA. The IAEA safeguards system was originally designed to account for nuclear material that was voluntarily identified by each member state. If a diversion is discovered, and cannot be explained, the IAEA can report the discrepancy to the UN Security Council. Each NPT state must negotiate a safeguards agreement with the agency, part of which includes an initial declaration of its nuclear materials and nuclear facilities. Periodic inspections confirm that declared materials have not disappeared. (Before the Persian Gulf war, the IAEA inspected Iraq's nuclear materials about twice a year.) The IAEA system was not originally designed for the purpose of investigating suspicions about possible undeclared nuclear materials or secret nuclear installations, such as those discovered in Iraq. Yet, this has turned out to be the major proliferation challenge. The IAEA's nonproliferation mission may, therefore, be changing in the direction of a more intrusive, more investigative, approach to inspection.

To prevent a repeat of Iraq, the IAEA has begun to implement reforms of its safeguards system intended to make civil nuclear programs more transparent, to make its inspections more intrusive, and to assure access to all relevant locations. Reforms being adopted include stricter enforcement of initial declaration requirements (in 1991–92, this proved especially important for North Korea and South Africa, both suspected of possessing some weapons-related items), and assertion of IAEA authority to conduct more investigative inspections on *all* nuclear sites and materials in nonweapon NPT states. To aid these tasks, the IAEA has called on its member states to provide specific intelligence information on suspicious nuclear activities in countries of concern.[64] However, at a time when the IAEA is being called on to inspect more facilities in more countries—including new inspection responsibilities in Iraq, South Africa, Argentina, Brazil, North Korea, and the newly independent nations of the former Soviet Union—the agency's budget remains frozen. As a United Nations-affiliated international organization, the IAEA is dependent on its members for political as well as financial support. The IAEA experienced budget shortfalls in 1991 and 1992 due mainly to the inability of Russia, with its continuing fiscal nightmare, and the new nations to pay their annual assessments to the agency. Thus, implementation of the proposed reforms may depend on the willingness of IAEA member countries to increase its budget.[65]

A Possible Role for the United Nations in Nonproliferation?

Until Operation Desert Storm exposed Iraq's nuclear program, the IAEA had never officially reported a diversion of nuclear material. According to the agency's governing statute, the director general of the IAEA can report safeguards violations to the UN Security Council, which must decide what to do about them. In the case of Iraq, the Security Council passed a series of resolutions that created a Special Commission to defang Iraq's nuclear, chemical, biological, and missile capabilities. Security Council Resolution 687, which ended the 1991 Gulf war, directed the Special Commission to work with the IAEA to investigate, verify, remove (or render harmless), and monitor Iraq's nuclear program. This direct linkage between the Security Council and the IAEA established a precedent that some analysts have interpreted to be a potent new international nonproliferation instrument that could be used to address other problem countries. They advocate making the Special Commission, or some similar group, a permanent nonproliferation institution. Others, however, argue that the joint UN-IAEA role in Iraq—a country defeated in war by an unusual international coalition—is a unique circumstance that probably could not be replicated. If Iraq had not invaded Kuwait, it seems likely that Saddam Hussein's nuclear program would have continued to advance as planned, without international intervention. The Security Council's response to North Korea's NPT violations will, therefore, strongly influence the future role of the UN in nonproliferation.

The UN Security Council has recognized nuclear proliferation to be a threat to international security.[66] A UN-affiliated agency, the IAEA, has been on the front line of nonproliferation since its creation in 1957. The IAEA's nonproliferation responsibilities have evolved, but not as quickly as the proliferation problem. Whether the Security Council will take decisive action to confront proliferation threats remains to be seen, although it does appear unlikely that the UN would take preventative military action against suspected proliferators. Areas where the potential is greatest for the United Nations to play a more active role in nonproliferation include expanding international safeguards and verification to accommodate vast quantities of fissile nuclear materials from retired nuclear weapons, addressing nuclear safety and environmental hazards, and addressing the root causes of proliferation.

CONCLUSION

Insecurity is the root cause of proliferation. Conventional and/or unconventional weapons provide nations with assurances of their survival. How can nations be persuaded that nuclear weapons do not increase their security? At a fundamental level, nonproliferation policy should offer alternative routes to security. But what are the alternatives?

Collective security alliances can help to control proliferation by extending security guarantees to their members. NATO, the defunct Warsaw Pact, and other superpower military alliances were able to provide security assurances to their members, reducing the motivation for countries such as East and West Germany, North and South Korea, Japan, and others to possess independent nuclear forces. (It did not work for France, China, or Israel.) Security alliances can offer a nation an alternative source of security by substituting an ally's weapons for its own. Historically, such guarantees of "extended nuclear deterrence" have not always seemed completely credible, especially if the guarantor would risk destruction of its own society by aiding an alliance partner. Would the United States *really* have launched a nuclear attack on the Soviet Union in response to Soviet aggression against West Germany? While military alliances may still offer countries an alternative to proliferation, "extended nuclear deterrence" may also become a Cold War relic.

In some cases, Washington and Moscow tried to prevent their allies from acquiring nuclear weapons by providing them with enough conventional firepower to satisfy their security needs. Yet this approach also has problems, as was demonstrated by the case of Pakistan, which received large quantities of conventional arms from Washington for the explicit purpose of capping its nuclear weapons program. Not only did Pakistan continue its nuclear program, it apparently incorporated U.S.-supplied F-16 aircraft into its nuclear delivery system. Conventional weapons do not always slake the thirst for nuclear capabilities.

When nonproliferation policies fail, how should other countries respond to a new nuclear power? The alternatives range from providing technical assistance to new members of the nuclear club to help them prevent nuclear accidents, to preemptive military actions against nuclear targets. Both of these alternatives could actually encourage proliferation. Military action proved largely unsatisfactory against Iraq's hidden nuclear facilities, and also raises the delicate political issue of which threshold nuclear states to bomb, and which to spare. Another response to proliferation is to develop defenses. Nuclear and missile proliferation has replaced the Soviet threat as the primary justification for continuing development and deployment of strategic defenses in the United States. Military options may be necessary as a last resort in extreme cases, but carry considerable risk of failure.

Arms control offers another alternative to proliferation. Verifiable agreements to hold armaments within limits can provide knowledge about an adversary's capabilities that may reduce pressures to proliferate. Various regional and bilateral security arrangements, such as NWFZs, test bans, and inspection agreements, can help to moderate or avoid arms races that may fuel proliferation. Confidence-building measures, such as exchange programs, partial inspections, and mutual declarations of intent, may also contribute to improved relations that may eventually lead to more substantive agreements or limitations. When these options are combined with multilateral technology denial strategies (export controls) and norm-building treaties like the NPT, the multilayered international nonproliferation regime presents a formidable obstacle to all but the most dedicated proliferators.

Notes

1. The gun-type bomb that destroyed Hiroshima produced an explosive force equivalent to between 10 to 15 kilotons of TNT. The implosion-type bomb dropped on Nagasaki produced an explosive force equivalent to about 17 kilotons of TNT. For comparison, each of the 192 warheads (24 missiles, each with 8 warheads) on a Trident missile submarine can produce the equivalent of 100 kilotons of explosive force; warheads deployed on the Minuteman III missile can produce over 300 kilotons. For information on nuclear weapons, see T. Cochran, W. Arkin, M. Hoenig, *Nuclear Weapons Databook, Volume I, U.S. Nuclear Forces and Capabilities*, (Cambridge, MA: Ballinger, 1984).

2. For a history of nuclear diplomacy after World War II, see Richard Hewlett and Oscar Anderson, *A History of the United States Atomic Energy Commission, The New World, 1939–1946* (University Park: Pennsylvania State University Press, 1962); and Gregg Herken, *The Winning Weapon*, (New York: Alfred Knopf, 1981).

3. On Atoms for Peace, see Richard Hewlett and Jack Holl, *Atoms for Peace and War, 1953–1961* (Berkeley: University of California Press, 1989).

4. See Lawrence Scheinman, *The International Atomic Energy Agency and World Nuclear Order* (Washington: Resources for the Future, 1987).

5. On the British and French bomb programs, see Margaret Gowing, *Britain and Atomic Energy, 1939–1945* (New York: St. Martin's Press, 1964); Gowing, *Independence and Deterrence: Britain and Atomic Energy, 1945–1952, volumes 1 and 2* (New York: Macmillan, 1974); and Wilfred Kohl, *French Nuclear Diplomacy* (Princeton: Princeton University Press, 1971).

6. See John Wilson Lewis and Xue Litai, *China Builds the Bomb* (Stanford, CA: Stanford University Press, 1988).

7. In 1979, U.S. intelligence detected a suspicious flash over the southern Atlantic Ocean. Some people believe it was a nuclear test, perhaps conducted jointly by two nuclear threshold states—Israel and South Africa. See Seymour Hersh, *The Sampson Option* (New York: Random House, 1991).

8. On the history of the NPT and prospects for its extension beyond 1995, see Joseph Pilat and Robert Pendley, eds., *Beyond 1995: The Future of the NPT Regime* (New York: Plenum Press, 1990); and John Simpson, ed., *Nuclear Nonproliferation: An Agenda for the 1990s* (Cambridge, U.K.: Cambridge University Press, 1987). Both books contain the text of the NPT and other relevant documents.

9. NPT review conferences occur every five years. A group of countries has used past review conferences to express their displeasure with the lack of progress on arms control by the

weapon states and to link the fate of the NPT to a comprehensive test ban treaty. The test ban issue was especially prominent during the last review conference in 1990. See William Epstein, "Conference A Qualified Success," and Leonard Spector and Jacqueline Smith, "Deadlock Damages Nonproliferation," both in *The Bulletin of the Atomic Scientists,* December 1990.

10. For the debate in the United States Senate on the proposed test ban legislation, see the *Congressional Record,* August 3, 1992, S11167-S11212. Also see the *Congressional Record* for September 24, 1992, H9420-H9424.

11. The treaty allows any nation to withdraw upon giving three months notice. See Leonard Weiss, "Tighten Up on Nuclear Cheaters," *The Bulletin of the Atomic Scientists,* May 1991.

12. Nuclear weapons can be made from two fissile materials, plutonium (Pu) and uranium-235 (U-235). Plutonium is created when natural uranium-238 is irradiated in a nuclear reactor. The Pu is extracted from the spent fuel by a chemical separation method, called reprocessing. Weapons-grade uranium is made by increasing the concentration of U-235 from the 0.7 percent in natural U-238 to over 90 percent using various isotope separation, or enrichment, methods. These include gaseous diffusion, centrifuge, laser, and electromagnetic.

13. There is some debate about the suitability of reactor grade plutonium for use in weapons. Weapons designers prefer nearly pure Pu 239. Reactor grade plutonium has a higher concentration of Pu 240, which can generate more harmful radioactivity and can cause nuclear reactions to advance too rapidly for efficient detonation. Nevertheless, the U.S. has tested a bomb using reactor grade plutonium and the IAEA considers it to be a weapon-usable material.

14. For a comprehensive analysis of nuclear weapons programs in these countries, see Leonard Spector, with Jacqueline Smith, *Nuclear Ambitions* (Boulder: Westview Press, 1990).

15. See note 7.

16. The tighter restrictions contained in the Nuclear Nonproliferation Act of 1978 included the acceptance of full-scope safeguards on all of the peaceful nuclear activities of any country that buys nuclear technology from the U.S. This requirement mandated the renegotiation of all U.S. bilateral agreements for nuclear cooperation. Some countries, including India, Pakistan, Iran, South Africa, and Brazil, did not accept the new standards for U.S. cooperation, and the agreements lapsed.

17. The Glenn-Symington amendment to the Foreign Assistance Act requires that U.S. assistance be cut to countries that acquire unsafeguarded nuclear enrichment or reprocessing technology. The law is focused primarily on Pakistan, which has received considerable sums of U.S. economic and military assistance, even while it was secretly building a nuclear bomb. Another amendment, called the Pressler amendment, placed a condition on continued U.S. aid to Pakistan that required the president to certify to the Congress that Pakistan does not possess a nuclear explosive device and that continued aid to Pakistan would advance U.S. nonproliferation objectives. Sponsors of the legislation, including Senators Glenn and Pressler, have expressed the view that Presidents Reagan and Bush supplied the required certifications despite information that Pakistan was indeed building a bomb.

18. On Israel's raid on Osirak, see Amos Perlmutter, Michael Handel, Uri Bar-Joseph, *Two Minutes Over Baghdad* (London: Vallentine, Mitchell and Co., 1982).

19. During the Iran-Iraq war, both sides targeted the other's nuclear reactors, although none of the reactors were operational when attacked and no nuclear materials were released as a result. The U.S. bombed Iraq's Tuwaitha nuclear research center during Operation Desert Storm. Subsequent inspections of the destroyed reactors confirmed that nuclear materials were contained within the immediate compound. On the subject of bombing nuclear reactors, see Bennett Ramberg, *Nuclear Power Plants as Weapons for the Enemy* (Berkeley: University of California Press, 1984).

20. For a full discussion of Israel's nuclear options, see Shai Feldman, *Israeli Nuclear Deterrence* (New York: Columbia University Press, 1982).

21. For a comprehensive review of nuclear proliferation in the 1980s, see Leonard Spector's books, *Nuclear Proliferation Today* (New York: Vintage Books, 1984); *The New Nuclear Nations* (New York: Vintage Books, 1985); *Going Nuclear* (Cambridge: Ballinger, 1987); and *The Undeclared Bomb* (Cambridge: Ballinger, 1988).

22. See David Albright and Mark Hibbs, "Iraq's Shop Till You Drop Nuclear Program," *The Bulletin of the Atomic Scientists,* April 1992; and Albright and Hibbs, "Pakistan's Bomb: Out of the Closet," *Bulletin of the Atomic Scientists,* July/August, 1992.

23. Rodney Jones, Cesare Merlini, Joseph Pilat, William Potter, *The Nuclear Suppliers and Nonproliferation* (Lexington: D.C. Heath and Co., 1985); and William Potter, ed., *International Nuclear Trade and Nonproliferation* (Lexington: Lexington Books, 1990).

24. On the concept of "opaque" proliferation, see Ben Frankel, ed., *Opaque Proliferation* (London: Frank Cass, 1991).

25. Spector, *Nuclear Ambitions*, p. 72.

26. On Pakistan's nuclear capability, see David Albright and Mark Hibbs, "Pakistan's Bomb: Out of the Closet," *Bulletin of the Atomic Scientists,* July/August, 1992, p. 38; and Spector, *Nuclear Ambitions,* chapter 7.

27. Senator Larry Pressler, interview on NBC Nightly News, December 1, 1992. Pressler said the Central Intelligence Agency described the Pakistani nuclear program to him. NBC also reported that Pakistan readied a nuclear weapon for delivery and loaded it on a C-130 transport plane during a period of tension brought about by Indian military exercises near the Pakistan border in 1990.

28. See note 27 and testimony of Senator John Glenn before the Senate Foreign Relations Committee, July 30, 1992.

29. R. Jeffrey Smith, "China Said to Sell Arms to Pakistan," *The Washington Post,* December 4, 1992, p. A10.

30. In an interview with NBC News, ousted Prime Minister Benazir Bhutto confirmed reports that she was informed about her government's nuclear weapons program from the United States ambassador in 1990. NBC News, December 1, 1992.

31. The original cut off is known as the Glenn-Symington amendment, section 669 of the Foreign Assistance Act of 1961. The certification requirement added in 1985 is known as the Pressler amendment, which added a new section to the Foreign Assistance Act of 1961. See note 13.

32. In 1992, however, Congress discovered that the State Department had interpreted the aid cutoff to include only direct military and economic assistance, and not commercial military sales. Thus, certain military sales, including spare parts for Pakistan's F-16s, continued. See the *Congressional Record*, March 19, 1992, S3950-3958 on the Bush administration's interpretation of the Pressler amendment.

33. For an analysis of weapons capabilities in the Middle East, see Geoffrey Kemp, *The Control of the Middle East Arms Race* (Washington: Carnegie Endowment for International Peace, 1991); Frank Barnaby, "Arms Control After the Gulf," *Conflict Studies,* April 1991; and Anthony Cordesman, *Weapons of Mass Destruction in the Middle East* (Washington: Brassey's, 1991).

34. For an analysis of missile proliferation and missile capabilities, see Janne Nolan, *Trappings of Power* (Washington: The Brookings Institution, 1991).

35. Estimates of the size of Israel's nuclear arsenal vary according to assumptions about the size and operating record of the Dimona reactor, which is presumed to be the source of Israel's nuclear weapon materials. On Israel's nuclear arsenal, see Frank Barnaby, *The Invisible Bomb: The Nuclear Arms Race in the Middle East* (London: I. B. Tauris & Co., 1989); Seymour Hersh, *The Sampson Option* (New York: Random House, 1991); Leonard Spector, *Nuclear Ambitions,* chapter 9; and Spector, "Threats in the Middle East," *Orbis,* Spring 1992, p. 181.

36. The Iraqi bomb scientists renamed their version of the calutron (short for "California magnetron") the "Baghdatron." On the original calutrons, see Richard Rhodes, *The Making of the Atomic Bomb* (New York: Simon and Schuster, 1986), p. 601. Iraq's use of calutrons is described in David Albright and Mark Hibbs, "Iraq's Nuclear Hide and Seek," *Bulletin of the Atomic Scientists*, September, 1991.

37. A good summary of the inspections of Iraq's nuclear program conducted by the IAEA under the authority of Security Council Resolution 687 is *IAEA Inspections and Iraq's Nuclear Capabilities* (Vienna: International Atomic Energy Agency, 1992).

38. Iraqi scientists attended a U.S. government-sponsored "conference on detonation," held in Portland, Oregon, in 1989. Weapons scientists from many countries met to exchange information and ideas directly relevant to nuclear weapons. See Hearings of the Subcommittee on Oversight and Investigations of the Committee on Energy and Commerce, House of Representatives, "Failed Efforts to Curtail Iraq's Nuclear Weapons Program," April 24, 1991 (Washington: Government Printing Office, 1992).

39. Analysts who were writing about Iraq's nuclear program in the early 1980s include Leonard Spector, *Nuclear Proliferation Today* (New York: Vintage Books, 1984); Steve

Weissman and Herbert Krosney, *The Islamic Bomb* (New York: Times Books, 1981); and Jed Snyder, "The Road to Osiraq: Baghdad's Quest for the Bomb," *The Middle East Journal*, Autumn 1983.

40. An investigation of U.S. policy toward Iraq by the House Committee on Banking, Finance, and Urban Policy exposed many details of the attempt to use U.S. government credits and loans to lure Saddam Hussein into a more constructive relationship with the West. See Elaine Sciolino, "Iraq Policy Still Bedevils Bush as Congress Asks: Were Crimes Committed?" *The New York Times*, August 9, 1992, p. 18.

41. Testimony of Director of Central Intelligence Robert Gates before the Senate Governmental Affairs Committee, January 15, 1992.

42. As of 1992, Algeria had not signed the NPT, but did agree to submit the reactor to IAEA safeguards. See Vipin Gupta, "Algeria's Nuclear Ambitions," *International Defense Review*, April 1992.

43. See "Bush Unveils Long-Awaited Middle Eastern Arms Control Plan," *Arms Control Today*, June 1991, p. 27; and James Leonard, "Steps Toward a Middle East Free of Nuclear Weapons," *Arms Control Today*, April 1991, p. 10.

44. On Argentina's and Brazil's nuclear programs, see John Redick, *Argentina and Brazil: An Evolving Nuclear Relationship*, Programme for Promoting Nuclear Nonproliferation, Occasional Paper No. 7, (Southampton: Programme for Promoting Nuclear Nonproliferation, 1990); and Leonard Spector, *Nuclear Ambitions*, part IV, Latin America.

45. Paul Leventhal and Sharon Tanzer, eds., *Averting a Latin American Nuclear Arms Race* (New York: St. Martin's Press, 1992).

46. On South African nuclear cooperation with Israel, see Spector, *Nuclear Ambitions*, p. 283; Frank Barnaby, *The Invisible Bomb* (London: I. B. Tauris Ltd., 1989) pp. 16–20; and note 7 on the mysterious 1979 flash.

47. Leonard Spector has raised the issue of remaining uncertainty about the nuclear capabilities of near-nuclear weapon states, such as South Africa, who join the NPT as nonnuclear members. See Leonard Spector, "Repentant Nuclear Proliferants," *Foreign Policy*, Fall 1992, p. 21.

48. It also suggests that it may be easier to implement rollback in a country with an undeclared capability than in a recognized nuclear weapons state.

49. The quote is from Secretary of State James Baker during a trip to South Korea in November 1991. Secretary of Defense Dick Cheney made similar statements in a visit the following week. See "North Korea Shifts Stance on Inspection," *The Washington Post*, November 27, 1991, p. A19; and "Background Materials on North Korea and Nuclear Nonproliferation," by the Arms Control Association, Washington, D.C., June 1992.

50. David Albright and Mark Hibbs, "North Korea's Plutonium Puzzle," *Bulletin of the Atomic Scientists*, November 1992; "North Korea Seen Closer to A-Bomb," *The Washington Post*, February 7, 1992, p. A1; and Joseph Bermudez, "North Korea's Nuclear Programme," *Jane's Intelligence Review*, September 1991, p. 404.

51. For background on South Korea's nuclear program, see Joe Yager, ed., *Nonproliferation and U.S. Foreign Policy* (Washington: The Brookings Institution, 1980), chapter 3. For an overview of perspectives on South Korea's nonproliferation policy, see *The Korean Journal of Defense Analysis*, volume IV, Summer 1992.

52. Japan had a nuclear weapon program during World War II, but its experimental equipment was destroyed by U.S. occupation forces. See Richard Rhodes, *The Making of the Atomic Bomb*, pp. 457, 580.

53. The plutonium is shipped in a specially fitted cargo ship with an armed escort ship provided by Japan's maritime agency. See William Walker, "Japan's Plutonium Problem—and Europe's," *Arms Control Today*, September 1992, pp. 3–10.

54. See *Arms Control Today*, Special Issue on Nuclear Weapons in the Former Soviet Union, January/February 1992, volume 22, number 1; and Curt Campbell, Charles Zracket, *Soviet Nuclear Fission* (Cambridge: Center for International Affairs, Harvard University, 1991).

55. See Janne Nolan, *Trappings of Power*.

56. On the relationship between unconventional threats, see Aspen Strategy Group, *New Threats: Responding to the Proliferation of Nuclear, Chemical, and Delivery Capabilities in the Third World* (Lanham: University Press of America, 1990).

57. Another view holds that the spread of nuclear weapons can increase national and international security by creating stable deterrence relationships similar to the deterrence that characterized U.S.-Soviet relations throughout the Cold War. See Kenneth Waltz, *The Spread of Nuclear Weapons: More May Be Better*, Adelphi Papers no. 171, (London: International Institute for Strategic Studies, 1981).

58. For a review of nonproliferation regimes, see Zachary Davis, *Nonproliferation Regimes: Policies to Control the Spread of Nuclear, Chemical and Biological Weapons and Missiles* (Washington: Congressional Research Service, 1993); and Aspen Strategy Group, *New Threats*.

59. For policy analysis of the U.S. export control system, see National Academy of Sciences, *Finding Common Ground: U.S. Export Controls in a Changed Global Environment* (Washington: National Academy Press, 1991).

60. On Iraq's procurement networks, see Albright and Hibbs, "Iraq's Shop Till You Drop Nuclear Program" (note 22); Kenneth Katzman, *Iraq's Campaign to Acquire and Develop High Technology* (Washington: Congressional Research Service, 1992); and Kenneth Timmerman, *The Death Lobby: How the West Armed Iraq* (New York: Houghton Mifflin, 1991).

61. The Geneva Protocol of 1925 prohibits the *use in war* of asphyxiating or poisonous gases and liquids, and all bacteriological methods of warfare. The 1975 Convention on the Prohibition of the Development and Stockpiling of Biological and Toxin Weapons and on Their Destruction commits signatories to destroy all stocks of biological weapons and pledge not to transfer such weapons to other countries. Neither treaty has verification provisions.

62. See the story by Michael Gordon, "Negotiators Agree on Accord to Ban Chemical Weapons," *The New York Times*, September 2, 1992. For analysis of the chemical weapons convention, see Brad Roberts, *Chemical Disarmament and International Security*, Adelphi Papers no. 267 (London: International Institute of Strategic Studies, Spring 1992).

63. For discussion, see George Bunn, Charles Van Doren, and David Fischer, *Options and Opportunities: The NPT Extension Conference of 1995*, Programme for Promoting Nuclear Nonproliferation, Mountbatten Centre for International Studies (Southampton: Programme for Promoting Nuclear Nonproliferation, 1991).

64. This proposed reform has encountered resistance from some countries, who suspect most of the intelligence provided to IAEA would come from Western intelligence agencies. Some Third World countries fear that Western intelligence agencies would select certain developing countries, such as Iran and Iraq, for scrutiny, while ignoring others, such as Israel. There has also been concern that sensitive intelligence information cannot be properly protected by an international organization.

65. The director general of the IAEA, Hans Blix, has regularly complained to the agency's member nations about inadequate funding for IAEA programs, including the safeguards program. IAEA has been held by its members to a zero-growth policy since 1984.

66. United Nations Security Council Declaration on Disarmament, Arms Control and Weapons of Mass Destruction, January 31, 1992.

7 / Adding Fuel to the Fires: The Conventional Arms Trade in the 1990s

MICHAEL T. KLARE

The Persian Gulf conflict of 1991 and subsequent revelations concerning Iraq's clandestine military programs have attracted unprecedented international attention to the problem of weapons proliferation. Much of this attention has been focused on issues arising from the proliferation of *unconventional* arms—that is, nuclear, chemical, and biological (NCB) weapons. But the Gulf war has also directed considerable attention to problems arising from the spread of *conventional* arms—the tanks, planes, ships, guns, and missiles used by regular combat forces. Unlike NCB weapons, conventional arms can be readily purchased on the international market—a circumstance that has led to a massive flow of munitions from the arms-producing nations to their customers in many regions. Because this flow is stimulating arms races and fueling conflicts around the world, it is essential that we learn more about the conventional weapons trade and consider how it might be brought under effective international control.[1]

When we speak of the conventional arms traffic, we are normally referring to the transfer from one country to another of weapon systems, ammunition, and support equipment (radar sets, radios, jeeps, helicopters, and so forth). Such transfers are typically conducted on a commercial basis, entailing the sale of arms for cash or credit, but are sometimes provided gratis through military assistance channels. In addition to these overt, state-sanctioned transfers of arms there is also a significant black-market trade in guns to insurgents, separatist groups, and other paramilitary formations. All told, the global arms trade averages somewhere in the vicinity of $40–50 billion per year.[2]

Although the industrialized nations account for a significant portion of global arms imports, the largest share is consumed by the less-developed countries (LDCs). According to the U.S. Arms Control and Disarmament Agency (ACDA), the LDCs were the recipients of approximately 75 percent of all arms traded on the international market in the 1980s.[3] There are, however, significant regional variations in arms imports by the LDCs. Not surprisingly, the major market for arms is to be found in the Middle East, where a potent combination of vast oil wealth and intense regional antagonisms has generated an insatiable demand for modern weaponry. According to the ACDA, Middle Eastern countries jointly imported $203 billion worth of arms in the 1980s, or nearly half of all arms acquired by the developing countries in those years.[4] Large arms markets have also emerged in other conflict-prone areas, including South Asia, East Asia, and sub-Saharan Africa.

Despite this correlation between high levels of arms imports and areas of chronic tension, control of the conventional arms traffic has been a relatively minor international concern until fairly recently. For most of the post–World War II era, arms sales were considered a legitimate form of international trade, or, in the case of the superpowers, as a necessary adjunct to East-West competition in the Third World. Following the Iraqi invasion of Kuwait, however, the international community became much more concerned about conventional arms trafficking. The fact that Saddam Hussein had been able to accumulate such a massive military arsenal—5,500 tanks, 3,700 heavy artillery pieces, 7,500 armored personnel carriers, 700 combat planes, and so on[5]—led many world leaders to regret their earlier failure to control the arms trade. Thus, when the Gulf conflict was over, these leaders pledged to impose new constraints on the global arms traffic.

Although the United States had not been one of the major suppliers of arms to Iraq, American leaders took the lead in proposing new restraints on conventional arms transfers. At the very height of the Persian Gulf conflict, Secretary of State James Baker declared that arms transfer restraint would be a major U.S. priority after the war had been concluded. "The time has come," he told the House Foreign Affairs Committee on February 6, 1991, "to try to change the destructive pattern of military competition and proliferation in [the Middle East] and to reduce the arms flow into an area that is already over-militarized."[6] President Bush also addressed the need for arms transfer restraint, saying on March 1, 1991, that he hoped that "out of all this there will be less proliferation of all different types of weapons, not just unconventional weapons."[7]

In accordance with these views, the Bush administration invited leaders of the other major supplier nations to join with Washington in devising a system of multilateral controls on the conventional arms trade. On July 7–8, 1991, representatives of the five permanent members (P-5) of the UN Security Council—the United States, the Soviet Union, Great Britain, France, and China—met in Paris to begin work on such a system.[8]

Three months later, on October 18, 1991, representatives of the P-5 countries met again to address the issue of arms transfer restraint, this time in London. After two days of discussion, the five adopted a set of draft guidelines to govern their exports of conventional weapons. These guidelines obliged the signatories to consult with one another regarding major military sales, and to avoid transfers that would be likely to "prolong or aggravate an existing armed conflict," or that could be used for any purpose save "the legitimate defense and security needs of the recipient state."[9]

In yet another initiative to curb the arms trade, the United Nations voted on December 9, 1991, to establish a voluntary "register" of arms imports and exports. The register, which began functioning in early 1993, is designed to prevent dangerous arms buildups in conflict-prone areas by providing early warning of any sharp increases in arms deliveries to aspiring local powers.[10] This effort, and the adoption of the P-5 guidelines, suggested that the world community was moving toward the creation of an arms transfer control regime, similar to the existing nonproliferation regimes covering nuclear, chemical, and biological weapons.[11]

Unfortunately, subsequent developments quickly put the lie to such presumptions. In the months following adoption of the P-5 guidelines, the United States announced billions of dollars' worth of new arms transfers to Israel, Kuwait, Saudi Arabia, and Turkey—an unparalleled selling spree that was viewed by the other major military suppliers as bestowing carte blanche on their own marketing activities.[12] And when President Bush announced a $6 billion sale of 150 F-16 fighters to Taiwan in September 1992—a move interpreted by many observers as an election-year ploy to demonstrate his concern over rising unemployment in the aerospace industry[13]—China pulled out of the P-5 talks, and all progress toward an arms transfer control regime ground to a halt.

As 1992 drew to a close, it appeared that global arms sales were headed toward record levels. In addition to the F-16 sale to Taiwan, the United States announced a $9 billion sale of F-15 fighters to Saudi Arabia and a $4 billion sale of 256 M-1A2 tanks to Kuwait.[14] At about the same time, Russia announced the sale of three submarines and 96 late-model MiG fighters to Iran, plus several dozen Su-27 fighters and other weapons to China.[15] With the other arms suppliers also announcing major new transactions, virtually all restraint had disappeared from the weapons trade; except for the continuing embargo on Iraq and a cash shortage in many Third World areas, no barriers stood in the way of prospective arms buyers in conflict-prone areas.

The world's failure to establish new constraints on conventional arms transfers will have far-reaching consequences. In several areas—particularly the Middle East and East Asia—we will see reinvigorated arms races at higher levels of lethality and sophistication. Such rivalries have periodically ignited armed conflicts in the past, and are likely to do so again in the future. The growing traffic in conventional arms will also make it easier for insurgents and separatist groups to siphon off some of this hardware into their own arsenals—thus prolonging the ethnic and sectarian conflicts that are now plaguing many areas of the world.

In order to appreciate the scale and impact of the conventional arms traffic, it is necessary to understand in greater detail how this trade operates. A greater understanding of the dynamics of the arms trade will also help us to develop control mechanisms when (and if) the world community is prepared to move in this direction.

A PRIMER ON THE ARMS TRADE

The international weapons traffic as we know it today is a composite of a vast number of individual transactions between particular suppliers and recipients. In 1989, for instance, the ACDA found that a total of 120 countries each imported at least $5 million worth of munitions.[16] These interactions varied from the sale of a few items, worth perhaps several tens of thousands of dollars, to major transactions involving the transfer of billions of dollars' worth of advanced military systems.

Each of the individual transactions that constitute the weapons trade entails a bilateral *arms transfer relationship* of some sort: a two-way exchange in which the supplier provides military equipment to the recipient in return for cash, credit, barter goods (e.g., oil or agricultural products), or political/military services (e.g., participation in military alliances or support for the supplier's positions at the United Nations). Depending on the strength of the motives involved and the extent of recipient resources, these relationships can be relatively brief and shallow or can develop into long-lasting associations, involving multiple transfers of major weapons systems.

Like all other international relationships, the bilateral linkages that make up the arms trade are to some degree shaped and influenced by developments in the international system as a whole. In periods of high international polarization, such as that which prevailed during much of the Cold War era, recipients tend to align with one polar supplier or the other, depending on their geopolitical situation and their ideological preferences. (Hence, the Eastern European countries procured most of their arms from the Soviet Union during this period, while the Latin American countries procured most of their arms from the United States.) Similarly, in times of diminished polarization—such as that which prevails today—recipients tend to be more eclectic in their buying patterns, seeking arms from several major suppliers. The status of the global economy also has an impact on the dynamics of the arms flow: periods of prolonged recession tend to produce a decline in arms imports, while periods of growth are usually accompanied by an increase in military orders.

In studying the arms trade, therefore, we must pay close attention to developments in the international system that might bear upon the direction and magnitude of the arms flow.[17] Indeed, an awareness of changes in the international system is particularly crucial now, as the world undergoes a profound transformation in the aftermath of the Cold War's demise. The collapse of the Soviet Union, and the resulting disappearance of the bipolar system, has produced a significant rearrangement in North-South arms transfer relationships, with many former clients of the USSR turning to suppliers in the West. The Persian Gulf conflict of 1991 has also had a significant impact on the global arms flow, with the United States emerging as the supplier of choice for countries that seek high-tech weapons of the sort used with such devastating effect in Operation Desert Storm. As we shall see, these and related developments are systematically reshaping the basic features of the global arms traffic.

In examining these changes, it is useful to think in terms of four key parameters of the arms trade: (1) the *motives* for arms transfers; (2) the principal *suppliers* of arms; (3) the buyers or *recipients* of arms; and (4) the specific *commodities* being sold. These four factors are continually interacting with one another and with broad global developments to determine the scale, character, and direction of the global arms flow.

Motives

As in any transfer of goods from one party to another, arms transfers entail both a "push" and a "pull"—the *push* being those motives that impel the major military suppliers to provide the instruments of war to another country, and the *pull* factor being those motives that impel the recipient to obtain arms from a foreign supplier.[18]

The supplier is usually motivated to export arms by economic or political/military considerations, or by some combination of both. The *economic motives* for arms sales begin with purely commercial incentives: the receipt of cash or barter goods from the prospective buyer. In addition, export sales can also be used to help subsidize the design and production of a weapon intended for domestic military use, and/or to extend the life of a product line that is scheduled for closure (thus threatening the livelihood of workers and managers at the plant involved).

The *political/military motives* for arms exports can include a desire to enhance an ally's defenses against internal or external attack (thus descreasing the likelihood that the supplier will someday be obliged to come to the defense of its ally), a desire for increased influence over the policies and behavior of the recipient, and the development of common logistical systems. Arms transfers can also be used as a "diplomatic tool," to signal support for the government of the recipient country, or to repay that government for some service rendered to the supplier (for example, the servicing of ships or aircraft belonging to the supplier, or the establishment of an electronic listening post).

The recipient is usually motivated to import weapons by powerful security considerations. Nations that face a military threat of some sort (whether internal or external), and that are incapable of producing sufficient arms on their own, will normally seek military equipment from external suppliers if they have the funds (or the political capital) with which to procure such hardware. Recipients will also seek arms from a particular supplier in the hope that this will entail (or be seen as entailing) a security guaranty of some sort, thus discouraging aggression by hostile powers.

Other motives of a political nature may also play a role in the decision to acquire arms. Thus, it is not uncommon for newly independent (or newly affluent) Third World nations to make conspicuous purchases of certain types of sophisticated weapons—typically, a squadron or two of modern jet fighters—in order to serve as symbols of national pride and modernity, or to compensate for similar moves on the part of a traditional rival or enemy.

These motives tend to be relatively stable over time, reflecting the durability of basic economic and security considerations. Like all other aspects of the arms trade, however, these motivational factors have been affected by the changes now taking place in the international system. In particular, we are seeing a shift in the relative weight accorded by suppliers to the motives for military exports, with economic motives gaining much greater saliency. Thus, for Russia and the other successor states to the USSR, the quest for hard currencies with which to prop up their ailing economies has replaced virtually all security considerations as the prime motive for arms sales. Similarly, for the United States and the major European suppliers, a sharp decline in domestic military spending (occasioned by the end of the Cold War) has generated strong pressures for increased foreign sales, in order to prevent the closure of military production lines no longer needed for domestic consumption.[19]

Suppliers

Although many countries now produce and export at least some types of arms, a relatively small number of countries supply most of the major weapons sold on the international market. According to the ACDA, five nations—the United States, the Soviet Union, France, Great Britain, and China—supplied three-quarters of the total value of all arms transferred on the international market between 1985 and 1989.[20] These five countries are "full service" suppliers, providing a wide range of aircraft, ships, missiles, armored vehicles, and artillery, along with small arms and other basic combat systems. Among these countries, moreover, there is a distinctive hierarchy, with the United States and the USSR (until 1991) each supplying several times the amount provided by the others.[21]

The dominant position in the arms trade occupied by the United States and the Soviet Union during the Cold War era was a product of two key factors: first, their possession of a massive military-industrial complex capable of producing vast numbers of weapons of every type; and second, their willingness to use arms transfers as a mechanism for promoting diplomatic and military ties with emerging powers in the developing world.[22] Between 1975 and 1990 alone (after which virtually all Soviet military exports were converted to a cash-only basis), the two superpowers together supplied an estimated $325 billion worth of arms and ammunition to Third World countries.[23]

In addition to the superpowers and the other major producers named above, there are a number of "second tier" suppliers that specialize in the sale of certain types of weapons (for example, naval weapons in the case of Holland), or that produce a range of low- and medium-technology weapons for the Third World market. Included in this category are several long-industrialized nations of Europe (notably Austria, Belgium, Czechoslovakia, Germany, Italy, the Netherlands, Spain, Sweden, and Switzerland) along with a number of newly industrialized states of the Third World (notably Brazil, Israel, Singapore, and South Korea). Although their annual sales rarely match those of the major producers, these countries have captured a significant share, or "niche," of the world arms market, and no doubt will seek to expand their market share in the years ahead.[24]

Although all of these countries—including both first- and second-tier suppliers—are likely to remain significant factors in the arms trade for years to come, several recent developments have affected their relative competitive position. Most significant, the breakup of the Soviet Union into fifteen separate states has shattered the industrial infrastructure of the former USSR, scattering military plants among several of the new nations and undermining their productive capability. Russia emerged with the largest share of these plants, and will no doubt remain a major supplier of conventional arms, but will not soon be able to duplicate the annual sales tallies of the former Soviet state.[25]

The Persian Gulf war of 1991 has also had a significant impact on the dynamics of the arms trade, in that it demonstrated the potent effectiveness of high-tech conventional weapons and established the United States as the leading supplier of such hardware. In the wake of the Gulf conflict, U.S. producers have been deluged with requests for such systems as the Patriot air-defense missile, the F-15 and F-16 fighters, and the M-1A2 tank. Sales of these and other high-tech weapons pushed U.S. arms exports to record levels in 1992, and assured a steady demand for follow-on systems and services in the years ahead.[26] The growing emphasis on high-tech weapons will also benefit the more advanced European producers, especially France, Britain, and Germany, while penalizing such suppliers as Russia, China, and Brazil, which lag behind the major Western suppliers in the development of sophisticated munitions.

The lineup (and nature) of the major arms suppliers is also likely to be affected by economic conditions in Europe, where the decline in Cold War spending and the move toward a unified European market has threatened the continued viability of many national munitions companies. In order to survive in a more severe economic climate, many of these companies are seeking alliances or mergers with similar firms in other countries—thus producing multinational arms combines like Eurocopter, Euromissile, and Panavia.[27] As the number of these firms grow, and as they establish links with companies in Asia and elsewhere, it may be that the emerging category of "multinational producers" will surpass many of the individual states now on the list of major military suppliers.

Finally, when discussing the topic of suppliers, it is important to note that there is a substantial trade in black-market weapons, involving the covert transfer of munitions to terrorists, guerrillas, and separatist forces, and to such "pariah states" as Iraq, Libya, North Korea, and South Africa. These forces and countries are not able to acquire arms from the established arms suppliers, and so must rely for their military needs on covert, illicit sources. Such suppliers include legitimate traders who have been tempted by bribes or inflated profits to conceal a number of illegal sales among their regular, licit transactions, along with professional smugglers who transport guns along with other contraband.[28] Because the demand for black-market arms is likely to remain strong (given the recent proliferation of insurgent and ethnic conflicts), these black-market suppliers are likely to remain a significant (if largely unnoticed) factor in the arms trade.

Recipients

While the production of arms is largely concentrated in the industrial "North," the principal recipients of imported arms are to be found in the nonindustrial "South." According to the ACDA, three-fourths of all arms transferred across international boundaries in 1985–89 (when measured in dollars) were acquired by Third World countries.[29] Within this category, moreover, certain regions account for a disproportionate share of the arms flow: the Middle East, with but 3.5 percent of the world's population, accounted for 33 percent of total world arms imports and 43 percent of LDC imports. Other regions with a large share of Third World arms imports were South Asia and the Far East.[30]

The data on arms transfers also suggests that a relative handful of nations are responsible for a very large proportion of the total arms traffic. Just fifteen countries—Afghanistan, Angola, Cuba, Egypt, Ethiopia, India, Iran, Iraq, Israel, Libya, Saudi Arabia, Syria, Taiwan, Turkey, and Vietnam— accounted for 72 percent of all Third World arms imports in the 1985–89 period.[31] Analysis of this list suggests that the major Third World importers tend to have several features in common: most are either oil producers (Iran, Iraq, Libya, Saudi Arabia) or major recipients of superpower aid (Afghanistan, Angola, Cuba, Ethiopia, and Vietnam in the case of the USSR; Egypt, Israel, Taiwan, and Turkey in the case of the USA); all, moreover, have been engaged in internal or interstate conflicts over the past few years. This combination of means (the cash or credit to buy arms) and motive (a sense of danger) propelled these nations to the top of the list of major importers in the 1980s.

For many of these countries, the prevailing conditions of the 1990s are such that they are likely to remain on the list of major arms recipients. With the continuing tensions in the Middle East, we can expect Egypt, Iran, Israel, Saudi Arabia, Syria, and Turkey to remain on the list. (Iraq, now subjected to an arms embargo imposed by the United Nations in 1990, will inevitably drop off.) India and Taiwan are also likely to continue as major recipients in the 1990s, barring a major improvement in their relations with Pakistan and China, respectively.

As we move further into the 1990s, however, it is likely that we will see the disappearance of several of the major recipients in the 1980s. In general, these shifts will reflect changes in the status of their relative means and requirements. For some, the question of means will be paramount. With the Soviet Union no longer in existence and its successor states in no condition to supply arms on a charitable basis, such long-term Soviet allies as Afghanistan, Angola, Cuba, Ethiopia, and Vietnam will probably drop off the list of major recipients altogether.

But just as we are likely to see the disappearance from this list of some major recipients, we are also likely to see the appearance there of some newly prominent Third World buyers. Again, means and motives will be the key determinants of these changes. Thus, new entrants to this list are likely to include Kuwait and the United Arab Emirates—both of which are major oil producers that have increased their arms spending in the wake of the Persian Gulf conflict. Pakistan, which faces a military buildup in both India to its east and Iran to its west, is also likely to increase its arms spending in the years ahead.

Aside from the Middle East and South Asia, the area that is likely to experience the largest gains in military procurement in the 1990s is East Asia. Here too, the combination of means and motives is critical: the Pacific Rim area harbors some of the world's most vigorous economies (notably those in China, Japan, Malaysia, Singapore, South Korea, Taiwan, and Thailand) as well as some of its most intractible disputes (e.g., those between China and Taiwan, North Korea and South Korea, Thailand and Vietnam). And while the 1990s have brought an increase in trade between these countries, all continue to harbor suspicions about the long-range intentions of their more powerful neighbors and thus have placed great stress on the modernization of their military capabilities. It is likely, therefore, that South Korea, Singapore, and Thailand will join Taiwan on the list of major arms recipients in the later 1990s.[32]

Also likely to emerge as major recipients in the later 1990s are some of the Third World countries that now face major ethnic or insurgent conflicts in their own or adjacent territories. Among those that may be included in this group are Algeria, Burma, Indonesia, Morocco, Peru, Sri Lanka, and Sudan. Although the purchasing power of these countries will be limited by domestic economic conditions and the relative availability of foreign aid, they are likely to seek large supplies of counterinsurgency weapons and mobility gear (helicopters, transport planes, and so on) in the years ahead.

Commodities

Finally, in completing our assessment of key parameters, it is useful to examine the commodities carried by the international arms flow. Normally, arms transfer activities are measured in *dollar* terms, this being the most convenient indicator of relative trade patterns. Such data are useful for comparing the level of imports and exports by any given country from one year to the next, but do not tell us very much about the particular commodities involved. And since we are speaking here of the implements of war, it is essential that we look beyond the dollar value of arms transfers to consider the actual products being traded.

As now configured, the international arms trade encompasses a broad range of weapons and military systems, ranging from small arms to tanks, aircraft, and warships. Also included are *combat-support systems* (i.e., communications devices, radar systems, transport vehicles, and the like) and *technology* (i.e., blueprints, machine tools, and specialized materials used in the production of arms). Significant sales in all of these categories can usually be found in the global arms flow at any given time, but the relative popularity of any particular type often varies in response to changing international conditions.

At the beginning of the 1980s, the major Third World buyers exhibited a strong preference for the acquisition of major frontline systems: heavy tanks, supersonic jet fighters, and large warships. Having lacked such systems before, these buyers were eager to modernize all components of their military forces at the same time. Thus, between 1980 and 1983 alone, Third World countries acquired 7,889 tanks and self-propelled guns (SPGs), 2,258 supersonic combat aircraft, 83 major surface warships, and 1,300 helicopters.[33] Because "big ticket" items of this sort are the costliest items sold on the international arms market, large multiple sales of such products in the early 1980s pushed the annual tally of military exports to unprecedented heights.

By the end of the decade, however, the demand for major combat systems of this sort had begun to decline. Deliveries of supersonic combat aircraft in the 1987–90 period dropped by 23 percent from the 1983–86 figure, while deliveries of tanks and SPGs fell by 30 percent.[34] With fewer big-ticket items being sold, the total value of LDC arms imports also dropped during this period—from an average of $47 billion per year in the mid-1980s to $41 billion in 1988 and $35 billion in 1989.[35] Several factors accounted for this decline in big-ticket orders. Most important, the global recession of the late 1980s produced a severe fiscal crisis in many Third World countries, forcing them to scale back their spending on imported goods of all types. At the same time, the rising cost of frontline systems— driven by the incorporation of ever more sophisticated technology—forced many buyers to reduce the quantities of arms being purchased.

Although purchases of major combat systems declined in the late 1980s, observers of the arms trade noted a significant increase in the procurement of "upgrade kits" for existing military hardware. Such kits, consisting of advanced propulsion, fire-control, and armament systems, are designed to increase the life cycle and effectiveness of older-model tanks, aircraft, and warships. For a relatively modest investment, the recipients of such kits can greatly enhance the overall capacity of their existing military arsenals.[36]

With the onset of the 1990s, several new trends began to emerge. By far the most significant of these new trends was the explosion in demand for high-tech conventional weapons of the sort used by the United States to cripple Iraqi forces in the Persian Gulf conflict of 1991. Such weapons—notably precision-guided bombs and missiles, multi-role strike aircraft, and all-weather reconnaissance systems—are widely perceived as providing U.S. forces with an extraordinary military advantage. "The exploitation of these new technologies," Secretary of Defense Dick Cheney said in 1991, "will change warfare as significantly as did the advent of tanks, airplanes, and aircraft carriers."[37] With this in mind, the leaders of many Third World countries seek to acquire such technologies for their own forces, mainly through the purchase of sophisticated arms from the United States and from the more advanced European producers.[38]

The impact of the Persian Gulf conflict on the buying patterns of Third World recipients is most evident in the Middle East and East Asia. Saudi Arabia, which has spent more than any other Third World country on imported weapons in the 1990s, has shown a distinct preference for advanced U.S. arms of the types used against Iraq, including F-15 multi-role fighters, Patriot anti-missile missiles, Maverick air-to-ground missiles, and Hellfire antitank missiles. Similar items have been ordered (although in smaller quantities) by the governments of Egypt, Israel, Kuwait, and the United Arab Emirates.[39] High-tech weapons of this sort are also being acquired by China, Japan, South Korea, and Taiwan, all of which are now engaged in the modernization of their military forces.[40]

Developments in the Pacific Rim area spotlight another significant feature of the contemporary arms flow: a desire on the part of many rapidly developing Third World countries to acquire technology for the domestic manufacture of modern arms. Rather than remain dependent indefinitely on foreign sources of military hardware, many of the these countries aim to become self-sufficient in the production of basic combat gear. The establishment of modern military industries is also seen by some Third World countries (Brazil and Indonesia, for instance) as a means of spurring high-tech economic development. For these, and other, reasons, many Third World buyers now insist that any purchase by them of imported weaponry be accompanied by a substantial transfer of military technology.[41]

Finally, the character of the arms flow is likely to be influenced by the growing incidence of insurgency, ethnic warfare, and other forms of "low-intensity conflict." These conflicts rarely provoke major battles of the sort witnessed in the 1991 Persian Gulf conflict, but often entail continuing violence of the sort seen in Afghanistan, Angola, Burma, El Salvador, Lebanon, Somalia, and the former Yugoslavia. To sustain these conflicts, many Third World governments have ordered vast quantities of small arms, light artillery, and other basic weapons. And while sales of such hardware contribute relatively little *in dollar terms* to the total value of military sales, they do represent an important and growing segment of the global arms traffic.

TRENDS AND CONSEQUENCES

As we have seen, the arms traffic has been significantly affected by the systemic transformations of the late 1980s and early 1990s, particularly the collapse of the Soviet Union and the U.S. victory in Operation Desert Storm. These developments have affected the relative vigor of the various motives for arms transfers, and caused some shifts in the rank order of major suppliers and recipients. Despite these changes, however, the weapons trade remains lively and lucrative, with new suppliers and recipients eager to replace those that have moderated their arms transfer activities.

As noted earlier, the declining demand for major combat systems in the mid- to late-1980s produced a drop in the annual value of Third World military imports. This decline continued into the early 1990s, as worldwide economic conditions mitigated against any upturn in weapons orders. However, in 1992, the tempo of international arms trafficking began to pick up speed again. Major purchases by China, Iran, Kuwait, Saudi Arabia, Taiwan, the UAE, and other big spenders added billions of dollars to the year's total trade figures, and hinted of many lucrative follow-up orders to come.

It thus appears that the arms trade is on the verge of a new expansionary cycle, similar to those of the mid-1970s and the early 1980s. Adding credence to this assessment are a number of disturbing trends: (1) the reinvigoration of the Middle East arms race; (2) the emergence of a major new arms race in the Pacific Rim area; (3) and the growing intensity of ethnic, tribal, and national conflicts. Each of these trends is discussed briefly below.

1. *The reinvigoration of the Middle East arms race.* After booming in the 1970s and early 1980s, the Middle East arms race slowed in the late 1980s as the Iran-Iraq war drew to a close and the global economic recession cut into the military budgets of regional powers. According to the ACDA, total imports into the region dropped from an average of $22.6 billion per year in 1981–87 to $16.3 billion in 1988 and $12.1 billion in 1989 (in constant 1989 dollars).[42] In the aftermath of the Persian Gulf conflict, however, military orders began to pick up again, reaching new heights in 1991 and 1992. Saudi Arabia alone ordered $25.7 billion worth of U.S. equipment in 1990–92, and Kuwait ordered an estimated $6.8 billion worth.[43] Egypt, Israel, Turkey, and the UAE also placed major orders for U.S. equipment, and Iran and Syria placed multibillion-dollar orders for Soviet/Russian weapons.[44]

As noted earlier, the Bush administration made control of the Middle East arms trade a major diplomatic priority in the immediate post-Gulf war period. However, arms control considerations soon lost out to the powerful motives underlying the arms trade, and Washington went back into the business of supplying arms to allies and clients in the region.[45] At the same time, other major suppliers, including Russia and China, also sought to benefit from the surge in regional arms spending. The result has been a renewed arms race in the area, with each major recipient citing the military purchases of its rivals as justification for still further acquisitions of its own.[46]

2. *The emergence of a major new arms race in the Far East.* Unlike other regions of the Third World, the Pacific Rim area in Asia did not experience a drop in military expenditures in the late 1980s. With national incomes rising as a result of aggressive trade policies, the countries of this region have had more funds available for military purposes and many of them have used these funds to acquire sophisticated weapons. According to the ACDA, combined arms imports by the East Asian nations rose from an average of $6.1 billion per year in 1981–86 to $7.1 billion in 1987–89 (in constant 1989 dollars),[47] and recent arms purchases by China, Japan, South Korea, and Taiwan are certain to boost this figure to much higher levels in the years ahead.

To some extent, these increases in military spending are prompted by the desire of the newly industrialized Pacific Rim countries to replace older equipment with modern weapons of the sort fielded by the major Western powers. But these countries are also engaged in a number of major political and territorial disputes (between North Korea and South Korea, China and Taiwan, Thailand and Vietnam, and so on), and the growing tempo of arms procurement in the area seems to reflect a desire by the nations involved to expand their arsenals lest any of these disputes erupt in armed warfare. The decline in U.S. and Soviet influence in the area has also led the Southeast Asia nations to fear the growing might of China, and for China to worry about a resurgent Japan. Given these concerns, it appears likely that the Pacific Rim will generate an increasing demand for arms in the later 1990s.[48]

3. *The intensification of ethnic, tribal, and national conflicts.* Wherever we look in the world today, we see determined groups of people that are struggling for greater political and economic autonomy, or for the establishment of their own nation-state. As noted by Professor Myron Weiner of the Massachusetts Institute of Technology, "'Peoples'—however they define themselves by race, religion, language, tribe, or shared history—want new political institutions or new relationships within existing institutions."[49] And because existing states are generally loath to grant such demands, many of these groups have taken up arms to press their claims. The resulting violence takes the form of separatist and nationalist conflicts (as seen in the struggles of the Croats and Slovenes in Yugoslavia, the Palestinians in the West Bank and Gaza, the Kurds of Iraq and Turkey, and the Tamils of Sri Lanka), or interethnic strife within existing multinational societies (as in Bosnia, Moldava, and the Sudan).[50]

Although these conflicts do not generally entail the use of heavy military equipment, like tanks and planes, they do generate an enormous demand for small arms, grenades, mortars, and other light infantry weapons. Any governments that participate in such conflicts can acquire these weapons on the international market (unless blocked by an arms embargo); all others, however, must obtain their arms from black-market suppliers. This is clearly evident in the former Yugoslavia, where all participants in the current fighting must rely on black-market sources for their supplies of arms and ammunition.[51] Because the world is likely to experience more such conflicts in the years ahead, we can expect a flourishing trade in black-market arms.

If these trends persist, we are likely to witness a steady increase in the flow of arms and ammunition to areas of conflict in the years ahead. Global economic conditions will, of course, affect the size and speed of this increase, with any major upturn or downturn in economic activity tending to produce a parallel shift in the tempo of arms exports. Even without a major improvement in the global economy, however, it is likely that many prominent recipients in the Middle East, the Far East, and elsewhere will continue to modernize their forces and to build up their stockpiles of war-making materiel. As a result, many Third World countries will possess the capacity to conduct wars of great intensity, duration, and reach.

Of course, no one can predict that the growing availability of modern weapons will lead to an increase in the frequency of regional conflicts. It is evident, however, that there is a high correlation between the growing diffusion of war-making materiel and the increased tempo of global violence: as the global flow of arms has expanded, there has been a corresponding increase in the number of major conflicts under way at any given time, and the duration of these conflicts seems to be growing.[52] The recent history of the Middle East suggests, moreover, that an increase in the flow of arms will aggravate regional tensions and could prompt one country or another to launch a preemptive war.[53] As suggested by then Senator William Proxmire in 1979, supplying arms to the Middle East may not be "like throwing a lighted match into a gasoline tank, but it is like adding more gasoline to a tank that has exploded in flaming destruction over and over in the past few years."[54]

Once armed combat has erupted, moreover, the increased availability of modern arms made it easier for belligerents to conduct wars of great duration and destructiveness. The Iran-Iraq war, for instance, lasted eight years, consumed $55 billion worth of imported arms and ammunition, and resulted in the death or injury of an estimated 1.25 million people.[55] Similarly, the conflict in Afghanistan has produced as many as 500,000 deaths over the past ten years, and resulted in the virtual annihilation (through constant bombing and rocket attacks) of many provincial towns and villages. In the former Yugoslavia, the fighting between rival states and ethnic groups had killed an estimated 100,000 people by the end of 1992, and the death toll keeps rising. And continued fighting in Somalia resulted in the death, through starvation, of hundreds of thousands of civilians prior to the intervention of U.S. forces in December 1992.[56]

Arms transfers have also contributed to the escalatory potential of regional wars by increasing the destructive capacity of imported munitions. During the Iran-Iraq war, for instance, both sides acquired missiles and other weapons that enabled them to engage in a variety of escalatory moves.

Thus, to disrupt the oil exports of their respective enemy (exports that generated funds for the purchase of arms), both belligerents fired missiles at ships and loading facilities located far from the front lines of battle—often hitting vessels belonging to neutral countries (including the United States) in the process. Both sides, moreover, used chemical weapons in combat and fired ballistic missiles at the cities of their opponent.[57]

A significant risk of nuclear escalation also developed during the 1990–91 standoff between India and Pakistan over the crisis in Kashmir. When Pakistani-backed Moslem insurgents in Indian-controlled Kashmir threatened to overwhelm local security forces, prompting a massive deployment of Indian troops, both sides put their armed forces on high alert and prepared for the possible use of nuclear weapons. "When [India and Pakistan] were running up to the possibility of war," CIA analyst Gordon Oehler revealed in 1992, "there was a real possibility that if it did go to war, it would be nuclear."[58] The risk of nuclear escalation also arose during the Persian Gulf conflict of 1991, when Iraq fired ballistic missiles at Israel; had any of these missiles carried chemical weapons, it is conceivable that Israel would have retaliated with nuclear weapons.

Nor are Israeli-Iraqi or Indian-Pakistani clashes the only encounters that could trigger a nuclear exchange. A future war between Israel and Syria could result in an Israeli nuclear attack, if Israel faced catastrophic defeat on the battlefield, or if Syria were to fire chemically armed ballistic missiles at Israeli territory.[59] There are, in addition, other clusters of potential belligerents that are equipped with large numbers of conventional weapons as well as nuclear and/or chemical munitions. So long as these nations are prepared to fight a major nonnuclear conflict with one another, there will always be a risk that a major defeat at the *conventional* level will prompt the loser to consider escalation to the *unconventional* level.

Given this danger, it is apparent that there is a close relationship between efforts to prevent the outbreak of regional nuclear conflict and the control of conventional arms trafficking. So long as prospective belligerents in areas of chronic tension are able to build up large stockpiles of conventional arms, other nations in the area will be predisposed to acquire (or, if they have them already, to retain) weapons of mass destruction as a hedge against catastrophic defeat. Thus, to reduce the risk of nuclear war, it is essential to constrain the flow of conventional weapons. At the same time, such constraint is sorely needed to reduce the frequency and intensity of *nonnuclear* conflicts in the years ahead.

POLICY PRESCRIPTIONS

Despite widespread recognition of the perils associated with uncontrolled arms exports, the world community does not at this point appear ready to impose tight restraints on conventional arms trafficking. The presumed advantages of such sales—and particularly their perceived economic benefits—outweigh the impulse to regulate arms exports in the interests of global stability. As time goes on, however, the hazards of such neglect will become increasingly evident, and hopefully this will prompt world leaders to adopt new controls on the global arms traffic.

Leadership in developing such controls should come from the United States, now the world's paramount arms exporter. The need for such leadership was acknowledged by Bill Clinton during the 1992 presidential campaign and reiterated after the election. "I expect to review our arms sales policy and to take it up with the other major arms sellers of the world as part of a long-term effort to reduce the proliferation of weapons of destruction in the hands of people who might use them in very destructive ways," he declared on November 19, 1992.[60] It is likely, therefore, that Clinton will announce a number of new initiatives in this field, including an attempt to revive the multilateral arms control effort begun by the P-5 powers in 1991.

Once a consensus develops on the need for conventional arms transfer control, what sort of controls should the world community impose on the conventional arms traffic? The complexity of this trade makes it unlikely that any single treaty or agreement—such as the Nuclear Nonproliferation Treaty (NPT)—can effectively curb all facets of the arms trade.[61] Instead, it will be necessary to construct an integrated *arms transfer control regime* composed of several disparate measures.[62] Many of the components of such a system now exist in embryonic form, but will have to be further developed. These components are: transparency; supply-side restraints; regional agreements; and economic conversion.

Transparency

The first step in imposing greater international control over the weapons trade is to promote greater "transparency" in the reporting of arms transfers—that is, the declaration by states of their arms imports and exports. Such openness will counteract the tendency of nations to over-arm in response to hazy or incomplete information regarding their rivals' arms acquisitions (a tendency that often leads to excessive purchases of one's own in order to compensate for "worst-case" assumptions regarding an enemy's capabilities). Transparency can also serve as an "early warning system" to alert the world community to excessive military buildups by potential belligerents.[63]

In line with these views, the UN General Assembly voted on December 9, 1991, to establish an international "register" of conventional arms transfers. When fully functioning, the register will collect and publish data on the arms imports and exports of all member nations.[64] Although voluntary, many nations have agreed to cooperate with the UN register and it is hoped that other countries will join as experience is gained in its operation.[65] Proponents of the plan hope that it will also be used as the basis for future arms export control systems, such as those discussed below.

Supply-side Restraints

Although the technology to produce arms has been widely diffused over the past few decades, a handful of nations continue to dominate the trade in high-technology armaments. It is possible, therefore, to establish supply-side restraints, or "supplier cartels," to curb the trade in conventional arms. Such measures have generally failed in the past because of nonparticipation by the Soviet Union and China; now that Russia and China appear willing to cooperate in such measures—witness the successful UN arms embargo on Iraq—it is possible to conceive of supplier agreements that include all of the major military suppliers. This, indeed, is the basis for the arms control talks initiated by the P-5 powers in July 1991.

Under the draft guidelines adopted by the P-5 countries in London on October 18, 1991, the five major suppliers are obliged to consult with one another regarding pending sales of major military systems to areas of conflict, and to avoid sales that would contribute to instability in these regions.[66] This is not a treaty, however, and enforcement of the guidelines is left to the states involved—and, as we have seen, the United States and the other major suppliers have interpreted the guidelines in such a way as to permit virtually all of the sales that they have sought to make.

Assuming, however, that the P-5 states will someday be inclined to adopt more sweeping and enforceable agreements, what sort of measures would be most desirable? The goal of such restraints should not be to cut off the flow of arms entirely (as that would be exceedingly difficult to enforce), but rather to significantly *constrict* the arms flow to areas of tension by setting a ceiling on the annual volume (in dollar terms) of arms exports by any given supplier to a region, and to prohibit the delivery of certain types of high-tech weapons (say, deep-penetration bombers, submarines, and cruise missiles) whose introduction would have a destabilizing effect.[67]

Regional Arms Control Agreements (by Recipients)

Ultimately, any effort to curb the flow of arms into an area will require the cooperation of recipients, as no supplier-based control system can ever be made 100 percent effective—the technology to produce conventional arms is now so widespread, and prospective suppliers will encounter too many incentives to cheat. Supplier cartels are also resented by many Third World leaders because of their association with imperial systems of control. Thus, any system for arms control within a region must rely as much on multilateral *recipient restraints* as on supplier restraint—with the latter used as a stimulus for the former, or as a substitute when recipient restraint does not appear likely.[68]

The region that is receiving most attention in this regard is the Middle East. A regional arms control agreement in this area could take several forms: restrictions on the acquisition of certain types of high-technology weaponry; annual ceilings on imports of particular categories of basic combat systems (tanks, bombers, artillery pieces, and so on); limits on technology transfers for domestic arms production; and the establishment of "tank-free zones" or "artillery-free zones" along contested borders and in areas of particular tension. Following the example of the Conference on Security and Cooperation in Europe (CSCE), such agreements should also include liberal provision for confidence- and security-building measures, such as exchanges of military observers or an "open skies" agreement permitting surveillance of military units by unarmed aircraft, as well as regular consultation on matters of regional peace and security.[69]

Economic Conversion

Finally, to overcome resistance in the arms industry (and in surrounding communities) to new international controls on the weapons trade, it is essential to encourage and assist these firms to *convert* their operations from military to civilian production. Such assistance can take the form of government grants for community-based conversion planning efforts, for job retraining, and for research on new products and technologies. Low-cost loans can also be provided for the acquisition of new tools and raw materials. If assisted in this way, plants that are now locked into endless arms production can manufacture products for which there is civilian demand.[70]

In the United States, conversion assistance should be provided by the federal government, as provided for in recently enacted bills. At the international level, a special fund should be set up through the World Bank and/or other lending institutions to finance conversion efforts in poorer countries. Such instruments are especially needed in Eastern Europe and the former Soviet Union, where there is strong support for conversion but a dire shortage of funds with which to carry out such efforts.[71]

None of these measures, by themselves, can eliminate the dangers associated with uncontrolled arms transfers. Joined together in a comprehensive arms transfer control regime, however, they would screen out many of the most destabilizing transfers and reduce the overall flow of war-making materiel. The design and implementation of such measures must, therefore, be seen as a major international priority in the years ahead.

Of course, a conventional arms transfer control regime will not eliminate all of the military violence now threatening the international community. Other initiatives, including regional peace agreements, tension-reducing efforts, and international peacekeeping operations, will be needed to reduce the incidence and intensity of warfare in the 1990s. (For discussion of such measures, see Chapter 19.) But a concerted effort to curtail the international trade in armaments could help reduce the risk of war and inhibit the escalation of those conflicts that do occur.

Notes

1. The author first attempted such an analysis in "Deadly Convergence: The Perils of the Arms Trade," *World Policy Journal*, vol. 6, no. 1 (Winter 1988–89), pp. 141–168. See also Klare, "Who's Arming Who? The Arms Trade in the 1990s," *Technology Review*, May-June 1990, pp. 42–50.

2. For data on the annual value of international arms transfers, see U.S. Arms Control and Disarmament Agency, *World Military Expenditures and Arms Transfers 1990* (Washington: U.S. Government Printing Office, 1991). (Hereinafter cited as ACDA, *WME&AT-1990*.) Similar data, accompanied by a list of recent arms deliveries, is provided in Stockholm International Peace Research Institute, *SIPRI Yearbook 1992, World Armaments and Disarmament* (Oxford: Oxford University Press, 1992). (Hereinafter cited as SIPRI, *SIPRI Yearbook 1992*.)

For background on the basic mechanics of the arms trade, see Michael T. Klare, *American Arms Supermarket* (Austin: University of Texas Press, 1984), chaps. 1, 2, 10; Edward J. Laurance, *The International Arms Trade* (New York: Lexington Books, 1992); and Andrew Pierre, *The Global Politics of Arms Sales* (Princeton: Princeton University Press, 1982).

3. ACDA, *WME&AT-1990*, p. 89.

4. Ibid., p. 91. (In constant 1989 dollars.)

5. For a complete inventory of Iraqi arms holdings prior to the Persian Gulf conflict of 1991, see International Institute of Strategic Studies, *The Military Balance 1990–1991* (London: Brassey's, 1990), pp. 105–106.

6. Opening Statement by Secretary of State James Baker before the House Foreign Affairs Committee, Washington, D.C., February 6, 1991 (mimeo).

7. From Bush's comments at White House press conference, March 1, 1991, as transcribed in *The New York Times*, March 2, 1991, p. A5.

8. "Statement of the Five Issued After the Meeting on Arms Transfers and Non-Proliferation," Paris, July 9, 1991, *Department of State Dispatch*, July 15, 1991, p. 508.

9. "Communique of the Five Countries—London, October 18, 1991," as reproduced in ACDA, *WME&AT-1990*, pp. 24–24B.

10. For discussion of the UN register and text of the enacting resolution, see *SIPRI Yearbook 1992*, pp. 299–301, 305–307.

11. For discussion, see *SIPRI Yearbook 1992*, pp. 291–305.

12. For discussion, see Lee Feinstein, "Arms R Us," *The Bulletin of the Atomic Scientists*, November 1992, pp. 8–10; William D. Hartung, "Curbing the Arms Trade: From Rhetoric to Restraint," *World Policy Journal*, vol. 9, no. 2 (Spring 1992), pp. 225–229; and David C. Morrison, "To Arms!" *National Journal*, January 2, 1993, pp. 14–20.

13. On the F-16 sale to Taiwan, see John Lancaster, "Military Moves with Political Overtones," *The Washington Post*, September 3, 1992, p. A1; and Gerald F. Seib, "Bush Is Likely to Sell F-16s to Taiwan," *The Wall Street Journal*, September 2, 1992, p. A1.

14. See Andrew Rosenthal, "Bush Plans Sale of 72 F-15 Planes to Saudi Arabia," *The New York Times*, September 12, 1992, p. A1; and Eric Schmitt, "Kuwaitis Will Buy Tanks Made in U.S.," *The New York Times*, October 13, 1992, p. A1.

15. See "Iran/Russia Wrap Up $2 Billion Arms Deal," *Flight International*, July 21, 1992, p. 13; Michael R. Gordon, "Moscow is Selling Weapons to China, U.S. Officials Say," *The New York Times*, October 18, 1992, p. A1; and Jim Mann, "China Seeks Russian Weapons," *Los Angeles Times*, July 12, 1992, p. A1.

16. ACDA, *WME&AT-1990*, pp. 94–130.

17. For further discussion of the systemic determinants of international arms trafficking, see Keith Krause, "The Political Economy of the International Arms Transfer System," *International Journal*, vol. 45 (Summer 1990), pp. 687–722; and Laurance, *The International Arms Trade*, chaps. 3, 6, 7.

18. For further discussion of the motives for arms sales, see Klare, *American Arms Supermarket*, chaps. 2, 3; Keith Krause, *Arms and the State: Patterns of Military Production and Trade* (Cambridge: Cambridge University Press, 1992), chaps. 5, 6, 8; and Pierre, *The Global Politics of Arms Sales*, parts 2, 3.

19. For discussion, see Bruce Stokes, "Export or Die," *National Journal*, January 2, 1993, pp. 8–13; Morrison, "To Arms!"; and *SIPRI Yearbook 1992*, pp. 275–283.

20. ACDA, *WME&AT-1990*, p. 131.

21. For further discussion of the structure of the arms market, see Krause, *Arms and the State*, chap. 4; and Laurance, *The International Arms Trade*, chaps. 5, 6. For an annual summary of the arms trade activities of the major suppliers, see the "arms trade register" in the *SIPRI Yearbook*.

22. For discussion, see Klare, *American Arms Supermarket*, chaps. 3, 10; Krause, *Arms and the State*, chap. 5; Laurance, *The International Arms Trade*, chaps. 5, 6; and Pierre, *The Global Politics of Arms Sales*, pp. 45–82.

23. Richard F. Grimmett, *Trends in Conventional Arms Transfers to the Third World by Major Supplier, 1983–1990* (Washington: Congressional Research Service of the Library of Congress, 1991) p. 45, and previous editions. (Hereinafter cited as Grimmett, *Conventional Arms Transfers 83–90*.)

24. For discussion of the second-tier producers, see Krause, *Arms and the State*, chaps. 6, 7. For data on the annual value of these countries' arms exports, see ACDA, *WME&AT-1990*, pp. 94–130; for an indication of their product range, see the "arms trade register" in *SIPRI Yearbook 1992*, pp. 315–352, and earlier editions.

25. For discussion, see Peter Almquist and Edwin Bacon, "Arms Exports in a Post-Soviet Market," *Arms Control Today*, July/August 1992, pp. 12–17; and *SIPRI Yearbook 1992*, pp. 279–281, 380–390.

26. For discussion, see *SIPRI Yearbook 1992*, pp. 275–279, 283–286.

27. For discussion, see U.S. Congress, Office of Technology Assessment, *Global Arms Trade* (Washington: U.S. Government Printing Office, 1991), chap. 4. (Hereinafter cited as OTA, *Global Arms Trade*.) See also *SIPRI Yearbook 1991*, pp. 331–344.

28. For discussion of the black-market arms traffic, see Michael T. Klare, "Secret Operatives, Clandestine Trades: The Thriving Black Market for Weapons," *Bulletin of the Atomic Scientists*, April 1988, pp. 16–24; Edward J. Laurance, "The New Gunrunning," *Orbis*, vol. 33, no. 2 (Spring 1989), pp. 225–237; and *SIPRI Yearbook 1988*, pp. 190–195.

29. ACDA, *WME&AT-1990*, p. 131.

30. Ibid., pp. 131–134.

31. Ibid.

32. For annual tallies of arms imports by these countries, see ACDA, *WME&AT-1990*, Table II. For discussion, see Steven Erlanger, "Rush for Resources Impels a New Asia Arms Race," *The New York Times*, May 6, 1990, p. A18; and R. Jeffrey Smith, "E. Asian Nations Intensify Arms-Buying from West," *The Washington Post*, March 9, 1992, p. A1.

33. Grimmett, *Conventional Arms Transfers 80–87*, p. 65.

34. Grimmett, *Conventional Arms Transfers 83–90*, p. 74.

35. ACDA, *WME&AT-90*, p. 89.

36. For discussion and examples, see Gerald M. Steinberg, "Recycled Weapons," *Technology Review*, April 1985, pp. 28–38; and *SIPRI Yearbook 1991*, pp. 225–227.

37. U.S. Department of Defense, *Conduct of the Persian Gulf Conflict*, An Interim Report to Congress (Washington, 1991), p. I-6.

38. For discussion, see *SIPRI Yearbook 1992*, pp. 283–286.

39. See "New World Orders: U.S. Arms Transfers to the Middle East," *Arms Control Today*, September 1992, pp. 36–37.

40. For data on the arms programs of these countries, see their entries in recent editions of *Jane's All the World's Aircraft, Jane's Fighting Ships*, and *Jane's Weapons Systems*.

41. For discussion, see Michael Brzoska and Thomas Ohlson, eds., *Arms Production in the Third World* (London and Philadelphia: Taylor and Francis, 1986); Klare, *American Arms Supermarket*, chap. 8; and OTA, *Global Arms Trade*, chaps. 7–11.

42. ACDA, *WME&AT-1990*, p. 91.

43. "New World Orders," pp. 36–37. Figure for Kuwait includes a $4 billion order for M-1A2 tanks announced in October 1992.

44. See Richard Ellis, "Syria Goes on £2bn Shopping Spree for Arms," *London Sunday Times*, May 5, 1991, p. 14; "Iran/Russia Wrap Up Arms Deal"; and "New World Orders."

45. For discussion, see Jackson Diehl, "Strategic Plans Giving Way to Mideast Arms Flow," *The Washington Post*, October 4, 1992, p. A24.

46. For discussion of arms race dynamics in the Middle East, see U.S. Congress, Congressional Budget Office, *Limiting Conventional Arms Exports to the Middle East*

(Washington, 1992), chap. 2. (Hereinafter cited as CBO, *Limiting Conventional Arms Exports*.) See also Geoffrey Kemp, *The Control of the Middle East Arms Race* (Washington: Carnegie Endowment for International Peace, 1991), chaps. 2, 4, 5.

47. ACDA, *WME&AT-1990*, p. 90.

48. For discussion, see Erlanger, "Rush for Resources"; Gordon, "E. Asian Nations"; and P. Lewis Young, "Southeast Asian Nations See No Sign of 'Peace Dividend,'" *Armed Forces Journal*, February 1992, pp. 30–34.

49. Myron Weiner, "Peoples and States in a New Ethnic Order?" *Third World Quarterly*, vol. 13, no. 2 (1992), p. 318.

50. Ibid., pp. 317–333.

51. See, for example, Blaine Harden, "Croatians Seek High-Tech Arms on World's Black Market," *The Washington Post*, August 6, 1991, p. 38; Edith M. Lederer, "Arms Reach Factions Despite Embargo," *The Philadelphia Inquirer*, August 11, 1992, p. 12; and Peter Maass, "East Bloc's Cold War Arsenals Are Arming Ethnics," *The Washington Post*, July 8, 1991, p. A14.

52. For an annual survey of major armed conflicts, see the *SIPRI Yearbook*.

53. For discussion, see Kemp, *Middle East Arms Race*, pp. 101–109.

54. From text of Senate speech, *Congressional Record*, May 14, 1979, p. S5726.

55. See "High Costs of the Persian Gulf War," in ACDA, *WME&AT-1988*, pp. 21–23.

56. *SIPRI Yearbook 1992*, pp. 424–456.

57. For discussion of the Iran-Iraq war and its various escalatory phases, see Anthony H. Cordesman and Abraham R. Wagner, *The Lessons of Modern War Volume II: The Iran-Iraq War* (Boulder: Westview Press, 1990).

58. Quoted in *The Washington Times*, October 31, 1992, p. 6.

59. For discussion, see Kemp, *Middle East Arms Race*.

60. Quoted in *The Washington Post*, November 20, 1992, p. A20.

61. For a discussion and assessment of past efforts to control the arms trade, see Pierre, *The Global Politics of Arms Sales*, pp. 281–290.

62. The author first proposed a system of this sort in "Gaining Control: Building a Comprehensive Arms Restraint System," *Arms Control Today*, June 1991, pp. 9–13.

63. See United Nations, General Assembly, *Study on Ways and Means of Promoting Transparency in International Transfers of Conventional Arms*, UN Report A/46/301 (New York, 1991), pp. 36–40, 44–46.

64. Paul E. Lewis, "U.N. Passes Voluntary Register to Curb Arms Sales," *The New York Times*, December 10, 1991, p. A11. The register plan is spelled out in UN General Assembly Resolution 46/36 of December 9, 1991, and its accompanying Annex. For texts, see *SIPRI Yearbook 1992*, pp. 305–307.

65. For discussion, see documents cited in note 66 and *SIPRI Yearbook 1992*, pp. 299–301.

66. For text of P-5 guidelines, see ACDA, *WME&AT-1990*, pp. 24–24B.

67. For further discussion of supplier restraints, see CBO, *Limiting Conventional Arms Exports*, chaps. 4, 5; and Janne E. Nolan, "The Global Arms Market After the Gulf War: Prospects for Control," *The Washington Quarterly*, Spring 1991, pp. 126–131.

68. For further discussion of recipient-based restraints, see Nolan, "Global Arms Market," pp. 131–132.

69. For discussion of such measures and of the obstacles standing in the way of such agreements, see Kemp, *Middle East Arms Race*, pp. 119–146.

70. For discussion, see Hartung, "Curbing the Arms Trade," pp. 240–241.

71. Ibid., pp. 242–243.

8 / Regional Conflicts in the Post–Cold War Era: Causes, Dynamics, and Modes of Resolution

LOUIS KRIESBERG

In the post–Cold War world, regional conflicts are rightfully receiving a great deal of international attention. They constitute a major issue confronting all peoples, and they exacerbate nearly every other problem humankind confronts. Enhancing the world's capacity to prevent and resolve such conflicts with a minimum of violence is therefore of the utmost concern.

In this chapter, we will first consider the definition, costs, and causes of regional conflicts, and then proceed to a discussion of the trends affecting the likelihood of regional conflicts in the years ahead. The remainder of the chapter will focus on the amelioration of such conflicts, discussed in terms of various peacemaking activities and the many types of peacemakers.

DEFINITIONS

All international conflicts have a regional base, but also have some links to countries or other large-scale actors from outside the region. The term "regional conflicts" refers most broadly to wars waged in a restricted area in the world, involving one or more states of that area. During the Cold War, the term was often used to designate major violent conflicts that did not involve the superpowers in a significant way. But the term also has been used in other senses.[1]

Some observers regard local-based conflicts, even if involving major global powers, as regional conflicts. Thus, even the wars between North and South Korea and between North and South Vietnam might be regarded as regional conflicts, despite the extent of United States and Chinese/Soviet support for the adversaries. For other analysts, however, wars involving extraregional powers as much as did those in Korea and Vietnam are regarded as "proxy wars" for the great powers. Whether to regard the 1950–53 war between the two Koreas, or the 1967 war between Israel and Egypt, Syria, and Jordan as regional wars or proxy wars is partly an ideological matter, serving to justify one or another policy by states external to the region.

In any case, many interstate conflicts are essentially local. They are based, for example, on border disputes or on the efforts of a regional power

155

to extend its dominance over neighboring countries. The Iraq-Iran war of 1980–87 is illustrative; it erupted after the Shah fled Iran in 1979, and Iraq then attacked the apparently weakened Iran in an effort to regain the territory and dominance it had yielded when Iran was more powerful.

Many other local conflicts involve subnational actors as well as state actors; thus, an embattled ethnic group in one country may be supported by the government of a neighboring country. For example, in 1974–75 the Kurds in Iraq were aided by the Iranian government in their struggle against the Iraqi government. With the intervention of neighboring states, these ethnically related struggles often become regional conflicts. Purely internal conflicts, whether class-based revolutions or ethnic-based secessionist movements, will not be treated as regional conflicts here.

Extraregional involvement takes various forms and is carried out by many kinds of actors. Thus, transnational religious or ethnic organizations may lend support to those who share their identity and are viewed as oppressed in the countries where they live. Multinational corporations based in large, industrialized countries may seek support from their home governments to protect and advance their interests when they make investments or negotiate purchases in a small developing country.

External involvement may also entail the actions of great power governments, through the selling of arms, the training of combatants, the dispatch of advisers, or the provision of intelligence information; it may also entail the sending of armed units to join a war or to aid a guerrilla force. Such intervention has frequently been undertaken by major powers, such as the United States, the former Soviet Union, and France; it may also be done by small powers, such as Cuba, which sent troops to help defend Angola's government against South Africa-backed UNITA guerrillas in 1975–90, and to fight for Ethiopia against Somalia in 1977–78.[2] The nature of involvement by governments and other large-scale actors from outside a region often changes during the course of a conflict, making the conflict more or less of a regional one.

COSTS

Most of the interstate wars fought since the end of World War II have been regional ones, with greater or lesser involvement by the superpowers. The fighting and dying has largely been in Third World countries, whether or not the intervening parties were from other parts of the world.

The losses in these wars have been severe, whether from bombing, shelling, and shooting, or from starvation and illness flowing from the social dislocation of warfare. It is estimated that over 22 million persons died between 1945 and 1990 in war and war-related events.[3] Of these, about 6 million persons died in regional interstate conflicts; some 14 million died as a result of civil wars, large-scale civil disorders, and wars of independence;

and over 2 million died from violence arising from governmental suppression of opposition forces.

The distinction between internal wars and regional wars, as indicated earlier, is not sharp. Sometimes extreme domestic oppression results in external intervention, as when Vietnamese military forces invaded Cambodia to oust the government controlled by the Khmer Rouge. Often, one or more sides in a civil war or a war of national liberation against colonial powers receive military aid from external powers, and armed units from neighboring countries may enter the fighting. This was the case with India's engagement in Bangladesh's secession from Pakistan in 1971, and with the U.S. and South African governments' involvement in the Angolan civil wars of 1961–75 and 1975–90. Over 4.7 million persons died between 1945 and 1990 in civil wars and large-scale civil disorders in which external intervention, in the form of military engagement, was significant; these also may be regarded as regional wars, broadly defined.

The preparation for war, and the reliance on military means of defense, is itself very destructive to the economic and political well-being of citizens, particularly in countries with economically low standards of living and those lacking strong and stable political systems that allow for popular participation. Some of these countries, especially those in war-threatened regions, devote very large proportions of their Gross National Product (GNP) to military expenditures. Thus, while Western European countries devoted around 3 to 4 percent of their GNP to military expenditures in the late 1980s, Iraq devoted 30 percent, Iran 21 percent, Israel 16 percent, Saudi Arabia 22 percent, Angola 20 percent, and Libya 12 percent.[4]

CAUSES

Regional conflicts arise from a wide variety of causes—some pertaining to the relationship between regional governments or other major actors, some arising from domestic conditions within one or more of the adversary countries, and some having to do with the place of the regional powers in the larger international context. Any particular conflict is the outcome of a mixture of these sources. If we are to develop effective strategies to prevent and resolve these wars, we must gain an appreciation of both the immediate and the deeper causes of violent hostilities.

The causes usually discussed in reference to a particular war or conflict typically stress the ostensible *issues* in dispute—that is, what the adversaries themselves say is in contention. However, the underlying conditions that shape the issues in dispute, as well as the partisans' characterization of these issues, bear significantly on the prospects for settlement and on the choice of conflict-resolution strategies. Often, therefore, our analysis must go deeper than the stated issues in contention when devising an effective strategy to promote enduring peace.

The relations *between* countries are often a primary source of regional conflicts. Thus, border disputes, rivalries for regional dominance, and disputes over water rights are common causes of conflicts. In addition, conditions *within* one or more of the adversary countries may be the primary source of regional conflict. Hence, internal political developments may lead to expansionist policies. Finally, the *international context* is another source, especially insofar as external powers are likely to intervene in support of one country in its claims against a neighboring country. With the end of the Cold War, analysts now stress the local conditions of a conflict more than in the past, when nearly every contest was viewed as a proxy struggle between East and West.

Relations between Adversaries

Wars tend to be fought between neighboring countries. Although neighbors tend to share interests and to have similar cultures, they are also likely to have competing claims for land and other resources, for control over people with shared ethnicity, and for relative dominance in their region. Such grounds for conflict are often generated by the shared feeling among the people of one country that a neighboring nation has oppressed and humiliated them, has denied them their rights, and has killed their kin.

Many regional conflicts persist for very long periods. For generation after generation, youth are raised with the belief that they live next to, and someday may have to fight, deadly enemies. War and large-scale violence may erupt and then halt, only to explode again and again. The experience of past wars, of defeats, and also of victories are the bases for judging present relations. Past humiliations and injustices may seem to cry out for revenge, while previous victories provide a basis for renewed claims of greatness.

More often than not, regional interstate conflicts are sparked by disagreements over which country can rightfully claim sovereignty over particular pieces of land. In a world where territory is divided into parcels, with each state claiming exclusive and total rights over its parcel and denying all other states any rights in that space, conflicts are inevitable. This is so because ethnic and religious affiliations, linguistic communities, past borders, and political ideologies do not correspond to current borders; one government or another can always justify calls for "correcting" existing borders in order to bring about "justice."

For example, India and Pakistan have contested control of Kashmir since their independence from British rule in 1947. This dispute has been manifested in several wars—in 1947–48, 1965, and 1971—and in periodic cross-border skirmishes. Although the Kashmiris are predominantly Muslim, their ruler before independence was a Hindu prince. At the time of independence, the ruler did not join either predominantly Muslim Pakistan or predominantly Hindu India.[5] However, when Pakistani Pathan tribesmen entered Kashmir in October 1947 to assist their coreligionists, then rising in rebellion, Kashmir's ruler requested India to come to its help; India was reluctant to do so until Kashmir joined India, and so the Kashmiri government "acceded" to India. Indian troops then intervened, and fighting went on until a cease-fire was agreed upon in January 1949, with India controlling the largest portion of Kashmir. In the years since, the dispute between India and Pakistan over the status of Kashmir has embittered relations between them, and in recent years Kashmiri nationalists have also challenged Indian rule. The status of Kashmir was to be resolved by a popular referendum, but one has never been held; numerous efforts at resolving the conflict have been attempted, without success.

Conflicts over territorial issues are generally exacerbated when they are viewed by opponents as arising from mutually exclusive claims made in the name of ethnicity. When a government, acting in the name of one people, seeks exclusive dominion over a contested piece of land, the expulsion of another people, or even their killing, may seem permissible or even desirable. Some of the most bitter struggles are conducted by two groups that both insist that a given piece of land is vital to them, and assert their exclusive control over it. The bloodshed and atrocities that such struggles can produce are painfully evident in the breakup of Yugoslavia.

Ethnic, religious, and regional differences within a state may take the form of secessionist efforts, through which one group seeks independence from a country dominated by another group. In such cases, a neighboring country may come to the assistance of the breakaway forces, thus igniting an interstate regional war. This happened, for example, when the Bengalis of East Pakistan attempted to secede from West Pakistan in 1971, and were aided in these efforts by Indian military intervention. As a result of that war, East Pakistan became the independent state of Bangladesh.

Ethnic differences are not inherently the basis for violent conflicts. When ethnic identify is joined with nationalist ideology, however, violent conflict is often the result. Nationalist ideology that asserts that a particular group of people should have its own territory and state is likely to generate conflicts whenever neighboring peoples make incompatible claims for the same territory. The land of Palestine, for instance, is claimed both by Jews—some of whom believe the land was given to them as a people by God, and others who lay claim to the land because their ancestors lived there thousands of years ago—and by Palestinian Arabs who live there, or whose parents lived there for many generations. Zionism, the Jewish national liberation movement, and Palestinian nationalist movements have confronted each other for over 100 years, producing frequent bloodshed.[6]

The drive for regional dominance often combines with issues of territory and ethnic solidarity. In virtually every area of the world, there has been persistent rivalry among neighboring countries as to which one would be the dominant power, able to exercise hegemony over the entire region. This, too, has been a factor in the struggles between Iran and Iraq, and between India and Pakistan.

Domestic Factors

Many conditions *within* one or more neighboring countries are conducive to regional conflicts. New revolutionary governments sometimes seek to extend their ideas by "liberating" other peoples from reactionary regimes. Similarly, countries recently swept by new religious doctrines (or the revival of old doctrines) may seek to spread the good news of their religious revelations to neighboring territories. Neighboring countries may also fear such activity on the part of a government, and thus may try to subvert a regime that proclaims such convictions; this has been a factor in the continuing conflict between North and South Korea.

Subnational groups within a state may have particular concerns that bring their government into intense conflict with neighboring countries. For example, an ethnic group may be concerned about the plight of their compatriots in another country and urge support for them—even at the risk of a severe conflict with the government of that other country. This impulse was exploited most notoriously by Nazi Germany through its claims to protect ethnic Germans in Czechoslovakia and Poland, leading to the outbreak of World War II. More recently, right-wing nationalistic forces in Russia have been pressuring the Yeltsin government to take more vigorous action on behalf of Russian minorities now experiencing discrimination in some of the former republics of the USSR.

Political, economic, military, and other institutions within a country may make it more or less likely that that country will engage in conduct that precipitates a regional war. Countries ruled by military elites are likely to expend resources on the military, justifying those expenditures on the basis of likely threats from other countries or of forthcoming efforts to rectify past injustices. When one or a few individuals or families dominate a government and a country, they may so identify themselves with the state that the search for personal glory, or the response to personal slights, are manifested in state actions.[7]

Extraregional Intervention

Some governments have the resources and the desire to project their power and influence to parts of the world far distant from their base territory. This was true of the European colonial powers, some of which continue to exercise influence in their former colonies by providing arms or military assistance to the governments of these newly independent countries.

Superpower competition during the Cold War was a major reason for long-distance intervention, helping to escalate and perpetuate many regional conflicts. The conflict between Israel and its neighboring Arab states is illustrative. Soviet support for Egypt (from the mid-1950s to the mid-1980s) helped sustain Arab beliefs that they would one day triumph, and so would not need to reach an accommodation with the Israeli government in the interim. Likewise, U.S. support of Israel assured the Israelis that they could hold out indefinitely, and thus need not accept unpalatable terms of peace. The resulting military rivalry between the Arabs and the Israelis produced several short but intense wars in 1956, 1967, 1973, and 1982.[8]

Clearly, there are many reasons that a conflict between neighboring countries will erupt, escalate into violence, and persist—often lasting longer than the ostensible goals would seem to warrant. Actual regional conflicts generally have multiple causes, combining many of the factors cited above.

TRENDS AND PROSPECTS FOR REGIONAL CONFLICTS

The recent attention accorded to regional conflicts follows naturally from the end of the Cold War and the shift in focus to other international security concerns. At the same time, it is also possible that the end of the Cold War has affected the nature and magnitude of regional conflicts. And we need to consider what other factors have affected the incidence and ferocity of regional conflicts in recent years.

The End of the Cold War

Although the Cold War is over, the world continues to live with its many legacies. Among these are economies distorted by immense military expenditures—in some cases, ruinously large. In addition, even with the disappearance of U.S.-Soviet rivalry in a country or a region, powerful military organizations and large amounts of superpower-supplied munitions have been left behind.

Consider, for instance, the recent history of Somalia. This territory had been divided and ruled by France, Britain, and Italy, finally achieving independence in 1960. The new government pursued an irredentist policy, seeking to incorporate portions of Ethiopia and Kenya where ethnic Somalis lived. Following a coup in 1969, a military government led by Major General Muhammad Siad Barre turned to the Soviet Union for assistance. The Soviets aided Barre until the Ethiopian government was seized by a Marxist military group in 1974 and Moscow began to provide aid to Ethiopia; the United States then began to provide military assistance to Somalia and to use the former Soviet military bases located there. Somalia thus became a highly militarized society, and fighting among hostile clans produced great bloodshed, while destroying the country's food distribution system.[9]

In some ways, the Cold War's demise has diminished the intensity of regional conflicts because the ability of belligerents to get outside assistance is reduced. With the Soviets no longer providing aid to one side in a conflict, the U.S. government sees less reason for aiding the opposing side; both sides thus have reduced prospects of obtaining external aid, and are more likely therefore to settle their dispute. Recent peace agreements in Central America, the Horn of Africa, and Southern Africa are illustrative of this process.[10]

On the other hand, the end of the Cold War and the dissolution of the Soviet Union have fostered the outbreak of new regional conflicts. This is because the disintegration of the USSR has led to the establishment of many new countries in the territory of the former Soviet Union. These new countries were born with many possible matters of contention among them, including border disputes and ethnically based grievances. The most conspicuous of these, perhaps, is the bloody contest between Armenia and Azerbaijan for control of the disputed territory of Nagorno-Karabakh. Furthermore, their leaders are inexperienced in international diplomacy and in managing conflicts without domination and coercion. In addition, the loss of Soviet control over Eastern Europe and the global uncertainties created by the end of the Cold War open up what appears to be opportunities for expansionism by ambitious local leaders.

Although reducing the worldwide need for weapons, the end of the Cold War has left many arms-producing countries with weapons stockpiles that are seen as a potential source of much-needed money, and with military production lines that governments are reluctant to close for fear of throwing people out of work. As a result, these countries continue to promote arms exports, often selling their products at bargain rates. The availability of such material intensifies regional conflicts and makes them more difficult to resolve. (See Chapter 7.)

Popular Participation

In the last 200 years, more and more segments of the world's population have fought for, and won, the right to participate in the decision making about their own governance. The role of elected representatives in making and implementing laws has increased in many countries of the world. Furthermore, the effective right to engage in the electoral process has expanded in many countries to include persons without property, women, and disenfranchised minority groups.

This trend toward fundamental democratization undermines the legitimacy of autocratic and authoritarian regimes. Such regimes may therefore become the targets of internal challenge and attack. In such circumstances, they may seem vulnerable to attacks from neighbors, or they themselves may seek and even create foreign enemies in order to justify internal repression, thereby improving their chance of surviving.

In the short-term, this trend toward democratization is a source of instability and regional conflict. There are reasons to believe, however, that in the long-run democratization will make for greater stability and peace. A clear research finding is that although democratic societies are no less likely than nondemocratic societies to be involved in wars, they do not fight wars with each other.[11]

Weapons Technology and Diffusion

Advances in military technology have greatly increased the destructive capability of modern weapons; moreover, many potent weapons are relatively cheap and easily transported. As a result, insurgent and separatist groups can arm themselves relatively easily and with devastating firepower. This capacity to carry on protracted armed struggles seems to hold out the promise of winning goals that, in earlier times, appeared unattainable by small groups of this kind.

The spread of arms-making technologies to emerging Third World powers is also contributing to the intensity of regional conflicts. Many developing countries now produce basic infantry gear, and a dozen or so produce tanks, aircraft, and missiles. As these capabilities spread, it is easier for belligerents to acquire the weapons needed to sustain a protracted regional conflict, thus making the settlement of disputes or the termination of war much more difficult. The proliferation of nuclear weapons looms as a further ominous threat in regional conflicts. (See Chapter 6 on nuclear proliferation and Chapter 7 on the spread of conventional military technologies.)

Rapid Change

The world is undergoing profound, multiple changes at an extraordinary rate. This is a consequence particularly of the cumulative effects of technological innovations. The means of production are changing in scale, form, and mobility in unprecedented ways. These changes are displacing traditional workers in societies throughout the world, as factories, and even whole industries in some areas, are unable to compete.

Furthermore, the speed and ease of movement of persons, goods, and symbols is increasing at an ever-more-rapid rate. While liberating for many persons, this ease of movement is generating a flow of immigrants and refugees who produce additional labor competition. To this is added the transforming impact of new ideas and forms of expression that seem to contradict or undermine traditional ways.

The high rate of change in the world is a destabilizing phenomenon. Old ways appear increasingly inappropriate to the new conditions, with a consequent loss of legitimacy for them and their advocates. Moreover, some people feel disoriented and adrift under such circumstances, and wish to reject the new patterns of thought and conduct. This makes them vulnerable to appeals by leaders who would rally them in solidarity against an enemy who may be blamed for their woes.[12]

Growing Interdependence

The world is becomingly increasingly integrated. What happens in one place is difficult to isolate from the rest of the world. This is true for environmental issues, population changes, and technological innovation. The globalization of the world economy is intensifying, reaching into new areas that, until recently, were relatively isolated from the larger world. The vulnerability of each segment of the world to global economic disorder is therefore increased, as is the sense that one's ability to control one's own fate at the local level is greatly diminished.

Many aspects of these new circumstances, and of the brisk tempo of global change, produce new issues of contention—for example, over environmental degradation, human rights, population pressures, and adaptation to large-scale immigration. New issues are relatively difficult to settle amicably because the procedures and mechanisms for doing so are less developed than is the case for older, more familiar problems.

All of these developments constitute underlying sources of conflict, some of which generate disorder within societies and/or changes in the established relations between neighboring states. This results, in some cases, in the outbreak of violent regional struggles.

AMELIORATING REGIONAL CONFLICTS

Since regional conflicts have manifold sources, there can be no single way of preventing or limiting them. Rather, there are many partial solutions. Those who seek to ameliorate regional conflicts must be familiar both with the characteristics of such conflicts and the various ways in which they can be prevented or controlled.

A careful analysis of the conflicts to be controlled is essential to any effective policy. In particular, this means taking into account the particular *stage* of the conflict. After all, the timing of efforts at peacemaking is critical for their effectiveness. Some methods are appropriate to the prevention of escalation, while others become pertinent only when the conflict appears to have become stalemated.[13]

We also must take into account the nature of the peacemaking that is sought. The goal may be simply to end large-scale killing; or it may be to establish a lasting peace with cooperative endeavors and mutual reconciliation. Some peacemaking methods may be effective for ending the fighting, but not for building an enduring peace (and vice versa).

The policy objectives of the belligerents must also be clarified. Limiting or ending the violence may be an important goal, but it is rarely the only one for government leaders or the popular forces involved. They may seek freedom or justice, and be willing to risk more deaths to achieve them. Only by addressing these goals forthrightly can a peacemaking effort expect to succeed.

For the balance of this chapter, we will first discuss a variety of means by which regional conflicts can be contained and constructively resolved. Some are more appropriate for one stage of a conflict than others, or for the attainment of one goal rather than another. After examining these various approaches, we will examine the kinds of organizations and persons who perform peacemaking activities of these types.

Prevention

Prevention covers a wide range of activities, some of which are relatively long-term. It can include forms of socialization that endow people with enough sense of self-worth and other attributes that they are at least partially resistant to inflammatory appeals that denigrate other peoples. Prevention also includes education that promotes understanding of other peoples and that eschews the indoctrination of hatreds and traditional grievances. Education can also include training in a wide array of constructive techniques for resolving intergroup conflict without violence. Finally, long-term prevention includes the development of democratic political structures, as there is strong evidence that democratic societies tend to avoid going to war with one another.

Prevention can be accomplished in more immediate ways, as well. For example, it may be possible to construct superordinate goals between traditional adversaries. That is, the leaders in neighboring countries may come to believe that they have goals that can best be achieved by cooperative effort. Such beliefs can arise from the generation of common projects that promise mutual gain, as, for example, in the development of joint river projects that would provide both parties with water for irrigation and energy for electricity.

Furthermore, social, economic, and organizational linkages that unite countries in a region tend to inhibit the eruption of conflicts. Neighboring countries that form security communities, within which war is not expected and generally absent, tend to be highly integrated, with constant movement of people between them.[14]

Limiting Escalation

Even if conflicts erupt, they need not escalate to the point of large-scale violence. Many institutional arrangements and practices can impede the escalation of a conflict. Thus, conflicts may be inhibited from escalation through the creation of regional institutions that provide mechanisms for settling disputes at an early stage. In addition, regional arms control agreements may limit the types of weapons that may be deployed in the area, thus limiting the intensity of the conflict.[15] For example, the Treaty of Tlatelolco, signed in 1967, bans nuclear weapons from Latin America. A country may also adopt a military strategy that is clearly defensive in nature and does not threaten attack, thus reducing insecurities in neighboring countries and removing the justification for a threatening buildup of their military forces.

Individual countries can also help limit escalation by conducting effective diplomacy and by avoiding steps that will provoke a massive and irreversible hostile response from their adversaries. An important example is the Cuban Missile Crisis of 1962, in which a nuclear war was averted by President John F. Kennedy's decision to impose a naval quarantine on Cuba (rather than to initiate a military attack), and to provide the Soviets with a (relatively painless) way to back away from confrontation with the United States.

Finally, there is evidence that contending governments can interact in such a fashion as to move toward cooperative (or at least nonantagonistic) relations.[16] Variations of the strategy of Graduated Reciprocation in Tension-reduction (GRIT) seem to be particularly effective for this purpose. In the GRIT approach, one party to a conflict makes unilateral cooperative moves, inviting reciprocation by the other side, but sustaining them even if not immediately reciprocated (in the hope of producing a long-term reduction in hostilities). A somewhat similar strategy is the so-called tit-for-tat approach, wherein one side undertakes a conciliatory move, but, after that, reciprocates the behavior of the other side, taking a further conciliatory action when the other side does, or an equivalent confrontational action (at about the same level of severity) if the other side acts confrontationally.

De-escalation

Once a conflict has erupted into large-scale violence, the task of halting it and moving toward mutually acceptable agreements is fraught with difficulty. The conventional wisdom holds that once a war has broken out, it is fought until one side is victorious and imposes its will on the defeated. Actually, this is relatively rare; more often, even when one side is dominant, the outcome is not totally one-sided. Sometimes the outcome is ambiguous, with both sides losing much and gaining only a little, or nothing at all.

We will consider here how movement toward a negotiated resolution, with some benefit for both sides, can occur. One approach is for international organizations to intervene in a bid to stop the fighting. The United Nations has performed this assignment several times, and, with the end of the Cold War, such intervention is likely to be more frequent. As a result of UN resolutions and/or mediation, a cease-fire may be ordered by the belligerents and peacekeeping forces deployed to monitor the cease-fire.

The Middle East has experienced many deployments of UN peacekeeping forces. In fact, the first such operation was that conducted by the United Nations Truce Supervision Organization (UNTSO), established in June 1948 to supervise the cease-fire in Israel/Palestine. UNTSO continues to function in the Middle East; its observers serve on the cease-fire lines as "go-betweens" who can help prevent isolated incidents from escalating into large-scale conflicts. Four other UN peacekeeping operations related to the Israeli-Arab conflict have been established, and two of them continue to function: the United Nations Disengagement Observer Force (UNDOF), established in June 1974 on the Syrian Golan Heights, and the United Nations Interim Force in Lebanon (UNIFIL), established in March 1978. (See Chapter 10 on UN peacekeeping activities.)

For effective peacemaking to occur, the adversaries involved need to change their calculations about war, recognizing that they can benefit from settling their conflict (and have much to lose by not doing so). This change in thinking is often a result of belligerents finding themselves in a hurting, debilitating stalemate, wherein neither side believes that it can defeat the other and yet finds that preventing its own defeat is very costly.[17]

In addition to a debilitating stalemate, it is necessary to reformulate the conflict so that a mutually acceptable outcome is considered attainable. Such a reframing of the conflict can arise from changed external circumstances, such as the emergence of a new common threat. It can also arise through the efforts of intermediaries, or through changes within one or both of the adversary countries. Pressure from peace organizations, opposition parties, factions within the dominant leadership, and the mass media can all provide new options and changed priorities.

Negotiation

At some stage in the conflict, the antagonistic parties may seek to reduce the fighting or to settle some of the matters in dispute. This is often done through explicit negotiations among representatives of the opposing parties. Such negotiations may be directed at ending a military engagement or a war, at settling particular issues in dispute, or at devising plans for cooperation on a specific project. Limited confidence-building measures (CBMs) may be agreed upon initially, leading to more substantial agreements as trust between the parties grows.

Negotiations may be conducted in face-to-face meetings between the adversaries, without the presence of intermediaries. However, such negotiations—particularly among highly antagonistic adversaries—are often aided by the involvement of intermediaries. Such persons or organizations may play a formal role as mediators or facilitators, or act informally and alongside the explicit formal negotiations.

Mediators come in many forms.[18] Some are representatives of powerful countries, with access to many resources that can be used in encouraging and enforcing a settlement; these are mediators with muscle. Other mediators are representatives of regional or global institutions. Still others are drawn from private entities, such as religious and humanitarian organizations.

Mediation includes a wide variety of services that can help adversaries in reaching an agreement and in implementing and sustaining an agreement once it has been made. Such services include transmitting messages between parties who will not meet with each other, providing resources that compensate for losses or risks being accepted, providing face-saving justifications for the acceptance of particular terms of settlements, and proposing new solutions (including those suggested privately to the mediator by representatives of one of the adversaries, since it may be more acceptable to everyone if it is first proposed formally by the mediator).

Resolution

A conflict settlement imposed by war may simply be the prelude to another struggle or war. This is particularly true when the settlement humiliates one party, creating the basis for a brutal new contest as shame and anger fuel efforts by the loser to regain its honor. An example is the Versailles Treaty ending World War I, which was viewed by the defeated Germans as unjustifiably harsh and humiliating. On the other hand, some settlements lead to additional agreements and, ultimately, to lasting peace. Certain types of actions and structures can contribute significantly to constructing an enduring and cooperative relationship.

One major contribution to the building of a cooperative relationship is the adoption of an equitable solution to a specific problem—a solution that satisfies the concerns and the interests of the various parties to the conflict. For example, one party may give highest priority to its claim to sovereignty over a particular piece of territory, while its neighbor gives highest priority to ensuring security from attacks that might be launched from bases in that territory. In this situation, both sides may gain what is most important to each by awarding sovereignty to the country that most prizes such possession, but establishing strict limits on the numbers and types of military forces that can be stationed there (as was done in regard to the Sinai in the 1979 Egyptian-Israeli Peace Treaty).

Another form of assistance to cooperative relations is the development of institutions that provide mechanisms for solving common problems and settling disputes at an early stage of a conflict. An important example of such an institution is the Conference on Security and Cooperation in Europe (CSCE), established by the 1975 Helsinki Accords. From the outset, the CSCE included both the NATO and the Warsaw Pact countries as well as the neutral countries of Europe; it legitimated the borders of Eastern Europe that were established after the defeat of Nazi Germany, provided for CBMs and other mechanisms to increase a sense of mutual security among the member countries, and established the right of member governments to insist that no member country violate the human rights of its citizens.

Overcoming enmities and achieving reconciliation are profoundly emotional endeavors. Each recognition by one side of the hurts and anguish the other party has suffered by its actions is a step toward reconciliation. This may include apologies, trials of those charged with committing atrocities, or simply acknowledgment of past harms done. The failure to openly acknowledge past troubles makes it more, rather than less, difficult to leave them in the past.

Recent developments in the former Yugoslavia underscore this point. During World War II, many atrocities were committed by various groups in Yugoslavia, for example, by the Croatian Ustazi organization (the allies of the German Nazis) against Serbs. After the war, many persons accused of committing atrocities were put on trial. The accusations, however, were phrased in terms of class struggle, and not in terms of ethnic animosities, because President Tito sought to avoid a fresh outbreak of ethnic tensions. But Tito's efforts to avoid such antagonisms by obscuring the ethnic dimensions of these events did not fully succeed, as the current fighting in the former Yugoslavia, aggravated by the desire of many Serbs to wreak their revenge on Croatians for the events of World War II, shows.

On the other hand, the post–World War II relationship between France and Germany illustrates the possibility of a *successful* reconciliation, and the ways to go about it. After generations of enmity, and after devastating wars fought to regain both territories and honor that had been lost in previous military struggles, war has become unthinkable between France and Germany. This is the result both of fortuitous circumstances and of thoughtful, step-by-step actions by French and German leaders. First, the emergence, soon after the war's end, of a common enemy—that is, the Soviet Union—and of common economic problems provided the basis for cooperative projects. Second, those projects entailed establishing institutions that offered mutual benefits to all parties and set in motion further steps toward integration. For example, the European Coal and Steel Community (ECSC), established in 1952, was a forerunner of the European Economic Community. The way in which the ECSC was organized fostered social, occupational, and political ties across the boundaries of the member states.[19] West Germany's assumption of responsibility for the horrors of Nazism also facilitated reconciliation. Furthermore, the immense disasters of World War II encouraged a larger European identity and a rejection of narrow nationalism. This happened to some extent after World War I as well, but those sentiments were not sufficient; after World War II, the fostering of the new identity and integration among former enemies was pursued by specific social, political, and economic institutions.

The experience in Europe has contributed to fresh thinking about how seemingly irreconcilable antagonisms can be overcome to everyone's satisfaction. This involves new concepts, such as ideas of shared sovereignty, of humanitarian intervention, of common security, and of autonomy.[20] New institutions have been developed that embody such new thinking, as demonstrated in the creation of the European Community and CSCE.

PEACEMAKERS

Peacemaking activities are conducted by many agencies, organizations, and individuals. These include official as well as nonofficial actors. Such actors can include people and organizations based outside the region of conflict as well as within the region, whether in regional organizations or in one of the adversary countries.

Extraregional Actors

Groups and organizations from outside the region can, and do, play important peacemaking roles. These include international governmental organizations, most especially the United Nations. The Office of the Secretary-

General of the United Nations has provided important mediating services over the past few decades, helping to end the civil war in Angola, the war between Iraq and Iran, and the insurgent struggle in Cambodia, and to negotiate the withdrawal of Soviet military forces from Afghanistan.[21]

In addition, individual governments have often acted as mediators. For example, the U.S. government played a key intermediary role in the negotiations that produced the 1979 Egyptian-Israeli Peace Treaty, while the Soviet government assisted the Pakistani and Indian governments in concluding the Tashkent Agreement of 1966.

International nongovernmental organizations, such as religious bodies, can also serve as intermediaries in settling regional conflicts. Thus, when Argentina and Chile were on the verge of war in 1978 over three barren islands in the Beagle Channel (a narrow passageway at the southern tip of South America), Pope John Paul II intervened and the two parties agreed to submit the matter to mediation by the Vatican. The Papal mediation effort went on for years without reaching an agreement, but, meanwhile, helped to prevent an outbreak of open warfare. Later, when domestic conditions changed—particularly with the return of Argentina to democracy—an agreement was reached under which Chile received the three islands, and Argentina retained most of the maritime rights in the region.[22]

In the Middle East, the U.S. government has been a major mediator for many years. For example, following the 1973 October War between Israel and its Arab neighbors, Secretary of State Henry Kissinger energetically mediated an agreement between Egypt and Israel for a disengagement of military forces in the Sinai, an agreement between Israel and Syria for a separation of military forces on the Golan Heights, and a second agreement between Israel and Egypt for a further Israeli withdrawal from parts of the Sinai.[23]

The U.S. government's mediation efforts in the Middle East took another course after Jimmy Carter assumed the presidency in 1977.[24] Determined to go beyond Kissinger's step-by-step peacemaking in the Middle East, Carter sought to hold a peace conference that would conclude a comprehensive peace for the Arab-Israeli conflict. Convinced that the conference would fail even if it were held, President Anwar Sadat of Egypt made a unilateral move to break what he thought were the psychological barriers to peace: in November 1977 he traveled to Jerusalem, in effect recognizing the legitimacy of the State of Israel. But despite the wild enthusiasm in Israel at this gesture, the subsequent bilateral negotiations between the Israeli and Egyptian governments failed to make much headway. At this point, President Carter invited a small Egyptian delegation led by President Sadat, and a small Israeli delegation led by Prime Minister Menachem Begin, to a secluded meeting at Camp David.

The initial meetings at Camp David produced such great tensions between Sadat and Begin that they were unable to negotiate directly; instead, the American delegation met separately with each side. The Americans drafted and redrafted agreements, asking each side to approve or to make comments and suggest changes of each version. After more than twenty drafts, and a deadline set by President Carter, two agreements were signed. It took twelve days of hectic work, from September 6 to 17, 1978, for the delegations to negotiate and sign two important accords: "The Framework of Peace in the Middle East," and "The Framework for the Conclusion of a Peace Treaty between Egypt and Israel."

The U.S. mediators served many functions at the Camp David meetings. For example, their relationship with each side provided each with justifications for accepting agreements that otherwise might have been regarded by their respective constituencies as concessions to an enemy. Furthermore, they sometimes presented certain ideas as their own, allowing both sides to accept them as being the work of the mediator (although the idea may originally have been suggested to the mediator by one of the negotiating parties). The U.S. government also served as a guarantor of the agreements, and offered various resources (including increased aid payments) to compensate each side for some of the costs and risks assumed by signing the agreements.

Regional Actors

Regional organizations, as well as global ones, provide mediation and other peacemaking services. These include the Organization of American States (OAS), the Organization of African Unity (OAU), and the Arab League. Although, between 1945 and 1981, fewer cases of conflict were handled by regional organizations than by the United Nations (80 compared to 123), the proportion of successful outcomes was slightly larger for the regional organizations than for the UN, perhaps because they dealt with somewhat less difficult cases.[25]

Governments may also work together at the regional level in conducting ad hoc multilateral mediation. For example, a complex set of revolutionary struggles and associated regional and extraregional interventions in Central America were largely settled by the Esquipulas Agreement of 1987 and subsequent negotiations. The particular set of conflicts dealt with in this process were the U.S.-backed contra campaign to overthrow the Sandinista-led government of Nicaragua, the Nicaraguan-supported revolutionary challenge to the government of El Salvador, and the long-standing civil war in Guatemala.

The movement toward settlement of the Central American conflicts began in the early 1980s, with mediation efforts undertaken by the governments of four neighboring countries: Mexico, Panama, Colombia, and Venezuela. When this effort faltered, largely due to a lack of U.S. support, a new attempt was initiated in 1986 at a meeting of the presidents of the five Central American countries in Esquipulas, Guatemala. The accord reached in 1987 has been called the "Arias Plan," after the President of Costa Rica,

Oscar Arias Sanchez, who was awarded the Nobel Peace Prize for his efforts in reaching this agreement.

The complex set of interlocking conflicts in Central America made it difficult to settle any one of them in isolation from the others. The solution, ultimately, was to settle them jointly. The accord was based on a formula with three components: (1) end violent conflicts with cease-fires, amnesties, negotiated demilitarization, and the prohibition of insurgents' use of neighboring territories; (2) promote democratization, human and civil rights, and civilian control; and (3) foster regional economic integration.[26] The agreements were implemented simultaneously, according to a fixed time schedule, and in public. A regional Commission for Verification and Support was established, as well as a National Commission of Reconciliation in each country. In this context, elections were held in Nicaragua in 1990, resulting in the defeat of the Sandinista government.

In addition to such official actors, many nongovernmental actors can, and do, play roles in mitigating regional conflicts. For example, private organizations or ad hoc meetings may provide channels for citizen exchanges that help to alleviate regional conflicts. Hence, elite or sub-elite groups from adversary countries may participate in problem-solving workshops in which the conflict is analyzed and possible remedies are discussed with the assistance of academics or other facilitators who are not from the adversary countries.[27]

Domestic Actors

Persons and groups within one of the adversary countries may try to influence the relations between their country and an opposing country through unofficial bilateral efforts. They may strive to foster shared interests with their counterparts in other countries, they may promote citizen exchanges to overcome the negative stereotype of the "enemy," and they may provide unofficial and informal channels and communication.

Groups or individuals in one of the countries engaged in a regional conflict who desire to reduce the level of that conflict may seek to influence their government to act in a more conciliatory way toward its adversary. They may organize peace demonstrations or social movements. In 1978, for example, a group of Israeli military reservists, academics, and students formed the Peace Now movement to pressure the Israeli government, then led by Prime Minister Begin, to be more responsive to initiatives from the Egyptian government following the breakdown in the peace process sparked by President Sadat's visit to Jerusalem in November 1977.[28]

Many other kinds of efforts are undertaken within many societies to reduce the likelihood that regional conflicts will erupt or escalate. Even efforts at educating students about their neighboring countries, so as to better appreciate their perspectives and history, can contribute to the long-term enhancement of cooperative relations. Similarly, education about ways of handling conflicts, so as to improve the likelihood of conducting them non-violently, and with the prospect of mutual benefit, can contribute to that end.

CONCLUSION

Threats of war abound. It is easy to point to terrible wars and violence among neighbors. It might seem that wars are best prevented by preparing for war; indeed, mutual threats may seem to be the hardheaded way to avoid wars. But the costs of such mutual threats are very high, and they too often do not deter, but rather provoke, an escalating cycle of threats and challenges, culminating in armed conflict.

We have seen, however, that more enduring and mutually beneficial resolutions of regional conflicts are possible. Some of these benefits can be fostered by global institutions, such as the United Nations and its specialized agencies. The end of the Cold War certainly opens up new opportunities for effective global institutions. Indeed, the United States' own interests may be better served by working through such institutions than by assuming the burden of unilateral intervention.

Regional institutions often provide particularly useful ways to maximize mutual benefits, as well as to reduce the chance of conflict escalation. Such institutions can foster economic development in general, or specific economic, cultural, or social projects. Through such efforts, some regions that have known wars in the past have become areas or peace, including Scandinavia, Western Europe, and North America.

That vision can encourage us all to consider not only how to avoid mutual destruction, but also how to promote the common welfare. Within whatever society we live, and whatever our official or unofficial role may be, we can contribute to the alleviation of regional conflicts.

Notes

I wish to thank Pat Coy, Michael Klare, Naeem Inayatullah, Stuart Thorson, and Saadia Touval for their comments on this chapter.

1. For discussions of regional conflicts, see, for example, Francis M. Deng and I. William Zartman, eds., *Conflict Resolution in Africa* (Washington: The Brookings Institution, 1991); I. William Zartman, ed., "Resolving Regional Conflicts: International Perspectives," special issue of *The Annals,* vol. 518 (November 1991); and Larry W. Bowman and Ian Clark, eds., *The Indian Ocean in Global Politics* (Boulder, CO: Westview Press, 1981.)

2. Jorge I. Dominguez, "Pipsqueak Power: The Centrality and Anomaly of Cuba," in Thomas G. Weiss and James G. Blight, eds., *The Suffering Grass: Superpowers and Regional Conflict in Southern Africa and the Caribbean* (Boulder, CO: Lynne Rienner, 1992), pp. 57–58.

3. Ruth Leger Sivard, *World Military and Social Expenditures, 1991* (Washington: World Priorities, Inc., 1991).

4. Ibid.

5. See Stanley Wolpert, *A New History of India,* 3rd ed. (New York and Oxford: Oxford University Press, 1989); U.S. Department of State, Bureau of Public Affairs, Office of the Historian, "The United States and the Kashmir Dispute, 1947–1990," in *Dialogues on Conflict Resolution: Bridging Theory and Practice* (Washington: U.S. Institute of Peace, 1992).

6. Charles D. Smith, *Palestine and the Arab-Israeli Conflict* (New York: St. Martin's Press, 1988).

7. Raoul Naroll, Vern L. Bullough, and Frada Naroll, *Military Deterrence in History* (Albany: State University of New York Press, 1974).

8. See Nadav Safran, *From War to War* (New York: Pegasus, 1969); and Fred J. Khouri, *The Arab-Israeli Dilemma*, 3rd ed. (Syracuse, NY: Syracuse University Press, 1985).

9. Edward R. F. Sheehan, "In the Heart of Somalia," *The New York Review of Books*, January 14, 1993, pp. 38–43.

10. Weiss and Blight, *The Suffering Grass.*

11. See Jack S. Levy, "The Causes of War: A Review of Theories and Evidence," in Philip E. Tetlock, et. al., eds., *Behavior, Society, and Nuclear War,* vol. 1 (New York and Oxford: Oxford University Press, 1989), pp. 209–313; and special issue of *Journal of Peace Research*, vol. 29, no. 4 (November 1992).

12. Samuel Huntington, *Political Order in Changing Society* (New Haven: Yale University Press, 1968).

13. See Louis Kriesberg, *International Conflict Resolution: The U.S.-USSR and Middle East Cases* (New Haven: Yale University Press, 1992); and Louis Kriesberg and Stuart J. Thorson, eds., *Timing the De-Escalation of International Conflict* (Syracuse, NY: Syracuse University Press, 1991).

14. Karl W. Deutsch, et. al., *Political Community and the North Atlantic Area* (Princeton: Princeton University Press, 1957).

15. Elise Boulding, "The Zone of Peace Concept in Current Practice: Review and Evaluation," in Robert H. Bruce, ed., *Prospects for Peace: Changes in the Indian Ocean Region*, Indian Ocean Centre for Peace Studies, Perth, Australia, and the Australian Institute of International Affairs, Canberra, 1991, pp. 75–106.

16. Joshua S. Goldstein and John R. Freeman, *Three-Way Street* (Chicago: University of Chicago Press, 1990).

17. Saadia Touval and I. William Zartman, eds., *International Mediation in Theory and Practice* (Boulder, CO: Westview Press, 1985).

18. See C. R. Mitchell and K. Webb, eds., *New Approaches to International Mediation* (Westport, CT: Greenwood Press, 1988); Paul Wehr and John Paul Lederach, "Mediating Conflict in Central America," *Journal of Peace Research*, vol. 28 (February 1991), pp. 85–98; and Louis Kriesberg, "Formal and Quasi-Mediators in International Disputes: An Exploratory Analysis," *Journal of Peace Research*, vol. 28 (February 1991), pp. 19–28.

19. Ernst B. Haas, *The Uniting of Europe* (Stanford: Stanford University Press, 1958).

20. Carolyn M. Stephenson, "The Need for Alternative Forms of Security: Crises and Opportunities," *Alternatives*, vol. 13 (1988), pp. 55–76.

21. For background on these UN activities, see United Nations, *The Blue Helmets: A Review of United Nations Peacekeeping*, 2nd ed. (New York: United Nations, 1990).

22. Thomas Princen, "International Mediation—The View from the Vatican," *Negotiation Journal*, vol. 3 (October 1987), pp. 347–366.

23. Jeffrey Z. Rubin, ed., *Dynamics of Third Party Intervention: Kissinger in the Middle East* (New York: Praeger, 1991).

24. See William B. Quandt, *Camp David* (Washington: Brookings Institution, 1986); Saadia Touval, *The Peace Brokers* (Princeton: Princeton University Press, 1982).

25. Ernst B. Haas, "Regime Decay: Conflict Management and International Organizations, 1945–1981," *International Organization*, vol. 37 (Spring 1983) pp. 189–256.

26. See P. Terrence Hofmann, "Negotiating Peace in Central America, *Negotiation Journal*, vol. 4 (October 1988) pp. 361–380; and Wehr and Lederach, "Mediating Conflict in Central America."

27. See Herbert C. Kelman, "The Problem-Solving Workshop in Conflict Resolution," in A. L. Merrit, ed., *Communication in International Politics* (Champaign: University of Illinois Press, 1972), pp. 168–204; and Ronald J. Fisher and Loraleigh Keashly, "The Potential Complementarity of Mediation and Consultation within a Contingency Model of Third Party Intervention," *Journal of Peace Research*, vol. 28 (February 1991), pp. 29–42.

28. Khouri, *The Arab-Israeli Dilemma*, p. 403.

9 / Ethnic and Nationalist Conflict

DONALD L. HOROWITZ

From Montreal to Mombasa, from the Karen areas of Burma to the Basque country of Spain, a new wave of ethnic sentiment seems to have been sweeping across the continents in the last twenty-five years. All of this seems to have come to a head with the disintegration of Yugoslavia and Somalia, forcing the realization that very few countries in the world are inhabited by a single ethnic group. Many are severely divided among groups that differ from each other in language, religion, color or appearance, regional affiliation, or some other attribute of origin. Such groups have been advancing political claims that have brought them into conflict with neighboring ethnic groups.

These conflicts are frequently accompanied by human rights abuses, often of a particularly brutal sort. They also have the potential for escalating into warfare that can produce famine and other forms of suffering, as well as major negative effects on development (destroyed infrastructure, diversion of governmental resources, and the like). If warfare does break out, that is typically because one or both sides of the conflict have attracted international support, but the international consequences do not necessarily end there. What begins as an internal conflict can become a very dangerous international one.

ETHNICITY: UBIQUITOUS, OFTEN DANGEROUS

The most severe manifestation of ethnic conflict has, of course, been violence: from riots to terrorism to wars of secession to international warfare. There are, however, many other examples of the pervasive force of ethnicity in daily political life in all regions of the world.

To gauge the formidable ability of ethnic affiliations to permeate public life, consider a few illustrations, drawn from many countries and many spheres of social and political activity.

The census, thought in stable, more or less homogeneous countries to be a dreary demographic exercise, is a bone of contention in many others. In Iraq, Nigeria, Lebanon, Kenya, and Pakistan, among others, the census has long been a delicate political issue, because the apportionment of legislative seats, revenue, and other public goods among various ethnic groups depends on what the census results show. Sometimes no census at all can be conducted for this reason. Lebanon has had no census since 1932. Sometimes the wording of the census questions is disputed. Very often the results are contested, especially if they show, as they did in Kenya in 1981, that the population of one ethnic group has increased dramatically, to the apparent disadvantage of others.

Occasionally, the census triggers warfare. In Assam, a state in northeast India, census results showing small changes in the proportion of Bengalis to Assamese in the 1970s paved the way for a violent reaction to an increase in Bengali names on electoral rolls later in the decade. Thousands died as a result. The census can become a life-or-death matter in an ethnically divided society.

The question of indigenousness is often a delicate one as well, and immigrant status can continue for generations. In France and Britain, North Africans and Asians, respectively, are referred to as "immigrants," even if they and their parents were born in the country. In Sri Lanka, Sinhalese are inclined to think that they are entitled to priority in the country, over Sri Lankan Tamils. Malays are called *Bumiputera*, a term meaning "sons of the soil."

Policy follows such conceptions. Indonesia and Kenya have adopted plans to promote indigenous ownership of businesses controlled by immigrant groups. Britain has tightened its immigration laws, Switzerland has held a referendum on foreign workers, and Uganda has expelled nearly all of its Asian population. Like a number of other countries, Malaysia has adopted far-reaching programs to redress economic imbalances between ethnic groups, defined in terms of indigenous Malays and immigrant Chinese and Indians. Targets for share ownership, employment, and education have been set up and enforced.[1]

In many countries, an array of organizations having no formal connection to ethnicity are in fact monoethnic. This applies to clubs, sports teams, cooperative societies, chambers of commerce, trade unions, political parties, and even revolutionary insurgencies. In Northern Ireland, people speak, only half in jest, of Catholic beers and Protestant beers, which are drunk in Catholic pubs and Protestant pubs. In Fiji, there are two teachers' unions, one Fijian and one Indian. In Angola, the government was dominated by one ethnic group; the guerrillas fighting it, by another. This is the common pattern in such warfare all over Asia and Africa.

Political parties based essentially on ethnic groups may seem strange phenomena to those accustomed to the broadly aggregative parties of Great Britain and the United States. Nevertheless, this is a very common propensity in divided societies, because the parties, reflecting what are seen to be incompatible group claims, cannot bridge the gap created by those claims. Ethnically based parties are, however, very dangerous to political stability, because they open the possibility that a party representing only one group can gain power and exclude from power or influence any group that supports a different party. Where this happens, it tends to pave the way for violence. Some military coups have reflected the grievances of those ethnic groups that are better represented in the army than in the civilian government. Where groups are territorially separate, exclusion from power may stimulate the growth of secessionist movements. In country after country, wherever one group gains control of the apparatus of the state, the legitimacy of government is contested.

In divided societies around the world, regional and ethnic disparities in wealth and in the distribution of government resources have become major political issues. But ethnic conflict does not merely involve disputes over material goods. Disputes over seemingly symbolic issues, such as recognition of one or another language as the official language or one design or another in a national flag, are, if anything, more severe.

There is, in ethnic conflict, an irreducible element of intergroup competition for an official declaration of relative group worth, and there is also an inescapable dimension of intergroup antipathy. Rationalist and materialist explanations for ethnic conflict have had great difficulty coming to grips with the struggle of ethnic groups for symbols that acknowledge group prestige and group legitimacy.

The element of antipathy is well illustrated by ethnic riots, in which members of one group set out to kill members of another. There have been hundreds of such riots in the last decade alone, ranging from the Azeri killings of Armenians in the Soviet Union in 1989 to the Sinhalese killings of Tamils in Sri Lanka in 1983 to the Krahn killings of Mano and Gio in Liberia in 1990. In such riots, hundreds, sometimes thousands, of victims die. The manner in which they are killed typically involves burning, hacking, or spearing, rather than shooting. Atrocities and mutilations are common. But such an episode does not involve random violence. Rather, victims are carefully chosen by ethnic affiliation, and the victimized group is generally one against which there is considerable animosity.

Given the widespread character of ethnic conflict, efforts to reduce it are common. (However, since many governments are dominated by some groups, at the expense of others, the policies of a good many governments exacerbate rather than mitigate ethnic tensions.) Belgium and Spain have adopted regional autonomy plans to counter conflict and secessionist sentiment. In Canada, there are recurrent proposals to readjust the federal relationship with Quebec, against the ebb and flow of separatism among the province's French-speaking majority. Czechoslovakia was long a binational and federal state, joining Czechs and Slovaks, but that did not prevent an upsurge of Slovak separatism. A regional autonomy plan in the Sudan was essentially repealed in 1983. This repeal resulted in a new and deadly round of armed insurrection—the latest of several, beginning in 1955. Burma, a most heterogeneous state that could certainly benefit from regional autonomy, has had no such program. Instead, the central government has been at war with ethnic groups, such as the Karen, steadily since independence in 1948.

Although different political systems handle ethnic problems differ- ently—or not at all—the existence of the problems is not confined to any region or any system, democratic or undemocratic.[2] Western Europe and North America, sometimes thought to have "outgrown" ethnic differences, are, like Asian and African states, experiencing a revival of ethnic conscious- ness. Latin America, with more muted ethnic problems, nevertheless has produced a number of militant Indian movements and experienced some racial tensions in countries, such as Brazil, that formerly had economies based on slavery. Eastern Europe has long been an area of ethnic tension and continues to be today. The movement toward democracy has created nu- merous opportunities for the expression of ethnic aspirations and antipa- thies. In Rumania, there has been violence in the Transylvanian region, inhabited by Hungarians as well as Rumanians. Several years ago, Bulgaria expelled thousands of Turks. The Soviet Union dissolved into its component republics, many of which were in turn divided between groups that threat- ened to divide the republics again: Moldavians, Slavs, and Gagauz in Mol- dova; Georgians, Ossetians, and Abkhazians in Georgia; and Kazakhs and Russians in Kazakhstan.[3] Yugoslavia has experienced serious conflict be- tween Serbs and Albanians in Kosovo, and Slovenia, Croatia, and Bosnia all chose to secede, leaving a truncated federation of Serbia and Montenegro and producing brutal warfare in Bosnia. The next decades will see continued strife between groups attempting to dominate existing units or trying to secede from them. On a world scale, there is every prospect of asymmetry: an international system consisting, on the one hand, of a number of large and powerful states, mainly in the West and in East Asia, and, on the other, of a large number of smaller states that are the product of ethnic fission.

THE ROOTS OF ETHNIC CONFLICT

To say that ethnic conflict is ubiquitous is not to explain its sources. What are the roots of ethnic conflict? And why does it seem to ebb and flow?

In accounting for the origins of ethnic sentiment, it is important to recognize its dual character. Ethnicity has meant conflict and violence, but it has also meant kinship and community. Without ethnic nationalism, after all, most of the modern states of Western Europe would not have come into being.

The depth of ethnic loyalties suggests that they respond to some rather basic needs. In times of rapid change, ethnic ties can provide a basis for interpersonal trust and affection when people move from the families that customarily meet these needs. When political systems seem new, alien, or remote, ethnic affinities between the leaders and the led can provide assurance that the interests of group members are being protected, attach- ing people to political institutions that would otherwise have dubious legitimacy.

No doubt, in a great many countries, these functions have not only been performed but overperformed. Some groups have been given so much security as to make others restless. Ethnic allocations that convince one group of a regime's benign intentions have served to persuade others of its unfairness. Nevertheless, it is necessary to bear in mind the functions ethnic ties serve, as well as the dangers they pose. Keeping ethnicity within manageable bounds may be a desirable goal; suppressing ethnic ties altogether may not.

In seeking the explanation for a phenomenon as intense and widespread as ethnic conflict is in the world today, it is natural to suppose that many forces, at many different levels, have contributed to its growth. This, indeed, turns out to be true.

At the broadest level, international currents provide an environment that is or is not favorable to the advancement of ethnic claims. Ethnic tensions tend to be submerged in times of world war, only to reemerge afterward. When states are at war, domestic differences tend to be suppressed for the sake of the greater effort. There are exceptions, of course. Ethnic tensions grew in Yugoslavia and in Burma during World War II, as armed groups fought each other. But, by and large, the periods after the First and Second World Wars were times for the revival of ethnic sentiment. The policy of President Woodrow Wilson, after World War I, favoring the "self-determination of nations," added to the postwar ethnic upsurge, and not just in Europe. Among others, the Kurdish movement in Iraq can be traced to this period. Following World War II, the Cold War impeded for a time the emergence of ethnic tensions in Eastern and Western Europe. But as the sense of immediate external danger abated, ethnic demands were increasingly heard.

Something comparable occurred in the new states of Asia and Africa. The nationalist movements that sought independence from the colonial powers from the 1940s onward were not always wholly representative of all the ethnic groups in their territories. Some groups that were not so well represented attempted to slow down the pace of the march toward independence. But, overall, until the anticolonial movements attained independence, ethnic differences tended to be muted.

Following independence, however, the context and the issues changed. No longer was the struggle against external powers paramount; no longer was colonial domination the issue. With independence secured, the question was who within the new state would control it.

As this issue began to emerge, the independence of Asia and Africa was being felt in Europe and America. The grant of independence to the former Belgian territories in Africa (Zaire, Rwanda, and Burundi) helped stimulate the ethnic movement among Flemings in Belgium itself. If, they said, tiny Burundi can have an autonomous political life, why should we be deprived of the same privilege? The emancipation of Africa, of course, had an impact on African Americans, and it probably made the system of racial segregation seem anomalous to many other Americans. In Canada, some French-speaking Quebeckers also cited African independence as a precedent for their own.

International conditions and foreign examples create a setting that makes ethnic demands seem timely and realistic, but such influences cannot create a conflict where one does not exist. The existence of ethnic conflict depends instead on a tangled skein of objective and subjective conditions—the relative position of groups and how they feel about that position.

Broadly speaking, two types of ethnic relationship can be distinguished. In the first, there is fairly complete subordination of one group by another. In the second, there may be inequalities of wealth, status, and prestige, but not complete subordination.

On a global scale, ethnic subordination is clearly in decline. The spread of egalitarian values has helped undermine caste untouchability in India and apartheid in South Africa, just as it undermined racial segregation in the United States South.[4] The two movements that qualify as genuine revolutions in postcolonial Africa—in Rwanda and Zanzibar—were both violent reactions to ethnic subordination. Where subordination continues, there are further struggles ahead. But there is a widely shared feeling that subordination based on ethnic criteria is illegitimate. This illegitimacy accounts for the strength of the movements against subordination.

Ethnic conflict does not, however, always derive from clear-cut superior-subordinate relations. On a world scale, conflicts between ethnic groups, neither of which has been subordinated, are far more common and likely to prove enduring than those that derive from a desire to escape the stigma and deprivation of inferior status. Here nationalist aspirations and uncertainty about relative group position, where two or more groups are located in a single state, spur antagonism. In such conflicts, it is often difficult to tell who has the advantage. Is it the educated Ibo or the more populous Hausa? The politically influential Malays or the economically well-off Chinese? The Basques who are powerful in commerce or the Castilians who control the state bureaucracy?

Not only is it difficult, in such cases, to make judgments about the justice of group claims; it is also sometimes difficult to sort out the exact claims being made. Still, there are some patterns.

Consider, for example, the role of immigration. As indicated earlier, in many countries, groups that claim to be indigenous have asserted their entitlement to priority over immigrants. (Never mind that most such "indigenous" groups were preceded by others, now usually identified as "aboriginal.") What is sometimes not immediately clear is that the "immigrants" may have come many centuries ago. The Turks have been on Cyprus since about 1581, but the Greeks have been there longer. The Scots and English who migrated to Northern Ireland and now form the nucleus of the Protestant population there arrived in the seventeenth century. The Ceylon Tamils came to Sri Lanka from India, on the average, perhaps a thousand years ago. In each case, there are lingering notions of priority based on earlier occupation.

Geography, as well as history, figures in ethnic psychology. Groups that have a strong position in domestic politics sometimes act the part of the weak and oppressed, often because they are looking beyond their borders to the ethnic balance of power in their region. Southern Sudanese do not wish to be merged into the Arab world. Some Québecois fear being swamped in an Anglophone North America, just as Ulster Protestants entertain comparable fears about the Catholics in the Irish Republic. The Sinhalese of Sri Lanka look apprehensively at the large Tamil population in South India, and the Maronites of Lebanon are uneasy about the large Muslim majorities in neighboring countries. The potential intrusion of international forces complicates domestic ethnic politics.[5]

Some ethnic conflicts are contemporary manifestations of ancient problems that never were resolved. Others stem from entirely new contacts between groups that had no prior experience with each other. This is particularly true in the new states, where independence has often brought peoples into competitive contact. It is also true in Northern Europe, where Turks, Italians, and Yugoslavs have come to work in recent decades. Still other conflicts result, paradoxically, from the reaction of ethnic groups to their previously successful assimilation in the majority culture. A number of powerful separatist movements—those of the Basques and the Kurds, for example—were begun by professionals or intellectuals who had either lost the use of their mother tongue or had become deeply concerned about the group's general loss of cultural distinctiveness.[6]

A common source of conflict is the competition of educated elites for secure, rewarding jobs in the state bureaucracy. Many disputes over language policy are related to this competition. If one language is given official status, then bureaucrats will have to be proficient in it. This puts speakers of the nonofficial language at a disadvantage.

Yet disputes over official languages and religions also involve people with no conceivable interest in civil service jobs. They seem to be emotionally committed, because the status of a language denotes the status of the group that speaks it. One of the objects of ethnic conflict seems to be official confirmation of group status. In the modern world, where nearly everything is politicized, the state's stamp of approval has both momentary and psychological value.

THE INTERNATIONAL SECURITY IMPLICATIONS OF ETHNIC CONFLICT

The present resurgence of ethnicity has not yet run its course. The claims of some groups continue to provide an example for others. A Canadian commission appointed in the 1960s to study bilingualism and biculturalism (French and English) ended by endorsing bilingualism and *multiculturalism*. It was not possible to recognize only two cultures. In Spain, other groups have followed the lead of the Basques and Catalans in demanding autonomy. Spanish-speaking Americans, American Indians, and a variety of Americans of Central European origin have emulated African Americans in organizing to improve their lot. The same has been true virtually everywhere. Ethiopia, which for years contended only with a secessionist movement in Eritrea— indeed, a movement supported by only one part of the Eritrean popula- tion—ended up fighting several ethnic civil wars simultaneously.

Whether the worldwide upsurge in ethnic conflict will produce a healthy period of modest self-assertion and adjustment of group interests or dan- gerous instability and upheaval depends on both international and domestic forces. Their interplay is a complex matter.

The most common threats to state borders are secessionist movements and irredentist movements (to annex territory populated by ethnic kins- men). Although irredentism has been a recurrent fear of those concerned with international stability, the fear is misplaced. Irredentism has not been a serious threat in most areas so far and probably will not become one, because most states that are potential annexationists are themselves multi- ethnic. Embarking upon such international adventures jeopardizes ethnic balances at home.[7] There are prominent exceptions, but they are few. More- over, given a choice between annexing one's region to an adjoining state and seceding to create an independent state out of such a region, most politicians would prefer to control an independent state.[8]

Secession is therefore a wholly different matter. There are dozens of secessionist movements around the world, and there will surely be more. Secessionist movements arise because of domestic grievances, but they gen- erally cannot succeed without either international help or the consent of central governments. So far, with a few exceptions, neither sufficient help nor central consent has been forthcoming. Nevertheless, in some regions, restraints on international involvement in ethnic disputes may be declining, while in others the Soviet example of more or less peaceful separation may make divorce by mutual consent somewhat more likely. If some states feel freer than they have felt to support the claims of ethnic groups across bor- ders and other central governments permit the exit of separatist regions, the extraordinary boundary stability of the post–World War II period may be at an end. Perhaps this is what the dissolution of the Soviet Union, the fragmen- tation of Yugoslavia, and the secession of Eritrea, taken together, signify.[9]

The motives that induce foreign states to provide aid to secessionists are various. They begin with the global interests of major powers. The United States and the Soviet Union were on the side of the central government in the war of the attempted Biafran secession, but France supported the Ibo se- cessionists. The United States and China were allied with Pakistan at the time of the Bangladesh secession, but the USSR was aligned with India, which supported the Bengali secessionists.

If global power balances can play a role, it stands to reason that regional and local balances can play an even bigger role. This is assuredly the case, as the support of Ethiopia and the Sudan for secessionists in each other's territory attests. Beyond this, a desire for a specific quid pro quo motivates many assisting states. Iran supported a Kurdish separatist insurgency in Iraq in order to secure Iraqi concessions about a disputed waterway. Malaysia was hospitable to Moro secessionists in the Philippines in order to induce the Philippine government to abandon its territorial claim on the Malaysian state of Sabah. Support for armed separatists seems an inexpensive way to pursue the interests of a state.

To such national interests must be added the powerful force of ethnic affinity. Arab states have supported kindred Muslim separatists in Eritrea. The Ugandan regime of Idi Amin aided southern Sudanese in the early 1970s; the southerners were related to a number of ethnic groups in the north of Uganda. Where transborder ethnic affinities exist, there is considerable potential for separatism to flourish. Even if the neighboring state is wary of supplying the insurgents, it may find itself embarrassed in domestic politics if it attempts to deny them sanctuary.

Nevertheless, there are some important limits to the external assistance most secessionists can expect to receive. The international interests of neighboring states, even those that foment or assist the secession, can prove to be surprisingly ephemeral. If the central government of the threatened state is prepared to offer a quid pro quo to the state assisting the separatists, the assistance may end precipitously. This is what the Kurds in Iraq discovered when Iraq offered to settle its waterway dispute with Iran in 1975. The Kurdish insurgency simply collapsed.

Moreover, the central government of a state threatened with separatist warfare has other weapons. If the state assisting the secessionists has other enemies, they may come to the aid of the threatened state. If the state assisting the secessionists has potential separatists of its own, the threatened state may assist them in turn, until some modus vivendi is worked out. Separatist warfare typically takes a long time to achieve results. During that time, there are many ways in which assisting states can be induced to forbear from further assistance. Many states will meddle for a while in a secessionist insurgency. Few will stay with assistance to a successful conclusion. That is an important reason why most separatists fail to achieve independence.

In fact, many states can be deterred from assisting separatists in neighboring countries in the first place. With its large, discontented Kurdish minority, Turkey has refrained from aiding Kurdish separatism even in states with which it did not have particularly good relations. Changing patterns of alliance and interest, the consummation of an agreement on an unrelated matter, and the fear of either retaliation or demonstration effects at home are all forces that point to restraint.

On the other hand, the conjunction of ethnic affinity and strong regional rivalry can produce a dangerous propensity to intervention. Until Slovenia made its exit from Yugoslavia in 1991, the one successful case of forcible secession in the postwar world was Bangladesh.[10] Seceding from Pakistan,

Bangladesh obtained its independence through the intervention of the Indian army. That intervention had triple roots. First of all, for India, it accomplished something, cleanly and quickly, that two previous wars with Pakistan had not accomplished: a change in the balance of power between regional rivals. Second, it responded to the aspirations of the well-situated Bengalis in India to aid their cousins across the border. Third, by quickly establishing an independent Bangladesh, the intervention thwarted any possible attempt to create instead a Bengali irredenta that might join Bangladesh to India, thereby upsetting ethnic and religious balances within India—or, worse, any attempt to create a movement for an independent pan-Bengali state that would detach Bengali areas from both India and Pakistan. So the threat of irredentism abetted a secessionist outcome.

There are equivalent possibilities now in Pakistan. The Pakistanis have encouraged Sikh separatism in India. Like the Sikhs, most Pakistanis speak Punjabi, and so they can claim—and perhaps feel—an affinity across the border.[11] Perhaps more dangerous are Pakistani efforts directed at the predominantly Muslim state of Kashmir. Detaching Kashmir from India might also affect the Indo-Pakistani balance of power, and it would satisfy Muslim sensibilities in Pakistan as well. Cases like Kashmir are very dangerous. Since Kashmir borders, not merely Pakistan and India, but Pakistan's ally, China, there is a serious chance of escalation into international warfare.

Moreover, while restraints that generally reduce the chance of irredentism probably apply in the Kashmir case, that may ultimately heighten the disintegrative impact of Kashmir on Pakistan. If, as seems likely, most Kashmiris prefer independence to union with Pakistan,[12] why, then, should Sindhis or Baluch not prefer their own independence to remaining in Pakistan? The example of Kashmiri nationalism threatens the pan-Muslim basis of the Pakistani state. Put more generally, multiethnic states that engage seriously even in fruitless irredentas jeopardize their own cohesion.

On the other hand, the threat of irredentism may actually inhibit secession across the irredentist border. After the fall of the communist regime in Hungary, the Hungarian government dissociated itself from the treaties that fixed its territorial boundaries, thus raising the specter that Hungary might attempt to retrieve Hungarians in Rumania, in the Yugoslav region of Voyvodina, and in the Slovak Republic of Czechoslovakia. This prospect was a prominent but ultimately insufficient force in preventing the ascendance of separatism among Slovaks, some of whom feared that an independent Slovakia might be unable to prevent Hungary from seizing its southern tier.[13]

To be sure, in many parts of the world, international conditions may facilitate retrieval efforts like those of Pakistan in Kashmir or Hungary in Slovakia. With the end of the Cold War, the rivalry of superpowers does not color all regional events. For secession, this cuts both ways. Every secessionist movement does not present opportunities for gains by a superpower. To that extent, external support will probably decline. On the other hand, neighboring states, unrestrained by major world powers, may become freer,

for their own various motives, to assist secessionists. By the same token, the Yugoslav example may suggest declining international tolerance for the repression of secessionists; new international norms may be developing on this subject. If so, there will be more opportunities for low-level warfare in support of separatist objectives. Certainly, the international community seems more disposed to tolerate secessions that alter national boundaries than it has been at any time since World War II.

This does not necessarily mean that there will be many more irredentas or secessions that actually succeed through warfare. The restraints on irredentas remain intact. It is significant that the Pakistani irredenta has increasingly become a Kashmiri secessionist movement and that the Hungarians are not keen to retrieve the Hungarian population of Rumania if that requires, as it would, a substantial accession of Rumanian population as well. The restraints on irredentism affect calculations on both sides of the border that irredentists seek to change. The restraints on secession may be reduced somewhat by the consensual disintegration of the Soviet Union and the international recognition achieved by Slovenia, Croatia, and Bosnia. Yet, most secessionist movements will not be able to attain independence from central governments determined to resist them unless the movements enjoy a generous measure of sustained external support.

Of course, separatist sentiment, with its roots in all of the elements considered earlier, usually seems unaffected by the generally dim prospects of success. Consequently, there are likely to be many, low-level secessionist insurgencies, some of which, like those in Burma and the Sudan, may endure for decades. They and military campaigns mounted against them can take an enormous toll in destroying lives and the productive capacity of whole countries, as the Sudanese and Ethiopian cases, among many others, illustrate. Yet few are likely to succeed through warfare.

What is still not known, however, is how many can succeed through consent. Until now, the modern territorial state, extremely jealous of its sovereignty, has rarely been willing to permit secessionists to withdraw peacefully. One reason has been that such states almost never have just one potential secessionist movement within their borders. As a result, if they permit one region to secede, they fear the demonstration effect on other separatists, and they suspect there will be no stopping, short of disintegration of the state. The Soviet case is conspicuous by its exceptional character. There, ethnic separatists achieved by consent, or by the sheer collapse of central authority, what few of them could have achieved by warfare. If that were all there were to it, the Soviet example would provide enormous impetus for secessions around the world. But the rapid onset of second-generation ethnic problems within Georgia, Ukraine, Kazakhstan, Estonia, Tajikistan, and Moldova, not to mention the warfare between Armenia and Azerbaijan, seems likely to temper the force of the example by bringing home to putative secessionists the further conflicts that await them if they achieve independence.

The Soviet case underscores the direct relationship between the domestic and international sources of conflict and accommodation. Accommodation can take many forms; it does not necessarily imply a willingness to permit secession. But it has taken many countries a long time to recognize the need to come to grips with ethnic demands. Suppression and artificially generated "consensus" have been—and still are—more common. Nonetheless, some countries are putting their experience to work in constructive ways. For some states, one promising course is for groups to move somewhat apart without severing ties altogether. Regional autonomy schemes may make this possible. Another serious problem is the existence of political parties organized along ethnic lines, as they are in the most deeply divided societies. As indicated earlier, ethnically based parties are usually impediments to compromise. It is possible to foster the growth of multiethnic parties in democratic ways. Usually, this involves skillful constitutional engineering, with special attention to the electoral system and the apportionment of territory, particularly in federal systems.

Ethnicity, of course, poses great challenges to political creativity. The political leaders who are required to put in place the institutions of accommodation are, more often than not, subject to conflict-intensifying demands from within the groups they represent. If, despite these demands, conflict-management capabilities increase within states, there will be fewer dangers of international involvement in ethnic conflict.

Notes

1. For a recent comparative critique of such programs, see Thomas Sowell, *Preferential Policies: An International Perspective* (New York: Morrow, 1990). For the origins and effects of the Malaysian programs, see Donald L. Horowitz, "Cause and Consequence in Public Policy Theory: Ethnic Policy and System Transformation in Malaysia," *Policy Sciences*, Vol. 22, nos. 3–4 (November 1989), pp. 249–287. For some similar measures, based on indigenousness, see Myron Weiner, *Sons of the Soil: Migration and Ethnic Conflict in India* (Princeton: Princeton University Press, 1978).

2. For a sense of worldwide commonalities and variations, see Crawford Young, *The Politics of Cultural Pluralism* (Madison: University of Wisconsin Press, 1976).

3. On ethnicity in the former Soviet Union, see Alexander J. Motyl, ed., *Thinking Theoretically about Soviet Nationalities: History and Comparison in the Study of the USSR* (New York: Columbia University Press, 1992); Alexander J. Motyl, *Will the Non-Russians Rebel?* (Ithaca: Cornell University Press, 1987); Rasma Karklins, *Ethnic Relations in the USSR* (Boston: Allen & Unwin, 1986); and Geoffrey Wheeler, *Racial Problems in Soviet Muslim Asia* (London: Oxford University Press, 1962).

4. For a study of South Africa in comparative perspective, see Donald L. Horowitz, *A Democratic South Africa? Constitutional Engineering in a Divided Society* (Berkeley and Los Angeles: University of California Press, 1990).

5. See Astri Suhrke and Lela Garner Noble, eds., *Ethnic Conflict in International Relations* (New York: Praeger, 1977).

6. For the origins of separatist movements, see Donald L. Horowitz, *Ethnic Groups in Conflict* (Berkeley and Los Angeles: University of California Press, 1985), pp. 229–281.

7. For a more careful explanation of why irredentism is not a serious world problem, see ibid., pp. 281–288.

8. The logic of this calculation is more complex than I have depicted it here. I have expounded it in more detail in an essay, entitled "Irredentas and Secessions: Adjacent Phe-

nomena, Neglected Connections," in Naomi Chazan, ed., *Irredentism and International Politics* (Boulder, CO: Lynne Rienner, 1991), pp. 9–22.

9. See K. M. De Silva, *Ethnic Conflict, the Search for Peace, and the Development Process* (East Lansing: Michigan State University Center for Advanced Study of International Development, Distinguished Speaker Series, no. 11).

10. Singapore, often cited as a case of secession, was, in fact, expelled from Malaysia in 1965.

11. This is an extremely ironic turn of events. In 1947, when India and Pakistan were partitioned, there were horrendous reciprocal massacres of Sikhs and Muslims. See, e.g., Penderel Moon, *Divide and Quit* (Berkeley and Los Angeles: University of California Press, 1962).

12. See Ashutosh Varshney, "India, Pakistan, and Kashmir: Antinomies of Nationalism," *Asian Survey,* Vol. 31, no. 11 (November 1991), pp. 997–1019.

13. See Thomas S. Szayna, *The Military in a Postcommunist Czechoslovakia* (Santa Monica: RAND Corporation, 1992), pp. 37–38. I am also drawing on conversations in Bratislava, in May 1992.

10 / Maintaining International Peace and Security: UN Peacekeeping and Peacemaking

MARGARET P. KARNS AND KAREN A. MINGST

The award of the 1988 Nobel Peace Prize and the launching of thirteen new operations between 1988 and 1992 have given United Nations peacekeeping high visibility in this post–Cold War era. Recognizing its importance for future conflict management, the Security Council has stepped up efforts to increase the capacity of the United Nations for preventive diplomacy, peacekeeping, and peacemaking. With a body of precedent and experience developed over more than forty years, involving over 500,000 soldiers in more than twenty observer and peacekeeping operations, peacekeeping continues to evolve with new responsibilities for election monitoring, humanitarian assistance, and government operation. The heightened demands for a UN peacekeeping role in different parts of the world raise a number of important issues for the organization and its member states, including the financing and staffing of current and future operations, interventions to protect basic human rights, and peace*making* activities.

But what is peacekeeping? How does it relate to the UN Charter's provisions for a collective security system and to enforcement actions such as the Persian Gulf war? Where and how has it been used over the years? Why, with the Cold War over, is it being used so extensively? What factors contribute to successful peacekeeping efforts? And, how does peacekeeping relate to peacemaking? In this chapter, we examine how UN peacekeeping has developed and evolved over three time periods: during the Cold War, from 1945 to the mid-1980s; during the transition period, 1986–89; and during the post–Cold War period of the early 1990s. We then analyze the future ability of the United Nations to maintain peace and security in light of organizational constraints and changes in the international political system.

THE UN CHARTER AND THE MAINTENANCE OF INTERNATIONAL PEACE AND SECURITY

The founders of the United Nations, gathered at San Francisco in 1945, recognized that the organization they were establishing was not going to abolish war for all time. Yet, they believed it was "the best mechanism for maintaining international peace and security the statesmen assembled there could devise for the moment, and people generally would have been quite happy if the new instrument only *helped* in the prevention or regulation of war or in the settlement of disputes for a decade or two."[1]

Indeed, maintaining peace and security was and has been the most important function of the organization. But how the United Nations undertook this task has changed over time in ways never envisaged by the founders, and somewhat ironically, the provisions of the Charter itself, which lay largely unused during the forty years of the Cold War, have seen far more use since 1989 than at any previous time. Indeed, peacekeeping was developed in response to the inability of the United Nations to act as envisioned by the Charter.

The United Nations Charter in Article 2 (sections 3,4,5) obligates all members to settle disputes by peaceful means, to refrain from the threat or use of force, and to cooperate with UN-sponsored actions. The Security Council has primary responsibility for maintenance of international peace and security (Article 24), the authority to identify aggressors (Articles 39, 40), to decide what enforcement measures should be taken (Articles 41,42, 48,49), and to call on members to make military forces available, subject to special agreements (Articles 43–45). The council is composed of fifteen members, with five permanent members—the United States, Russia, France, Great Britain, and China—having veto power. More generally, under Article 34, "The Security Council may investigate any dispute, or any situation which might lead to international friction or give rise to a dispute, in order to determine whether the continuance of the dispute or situation is likely to endanger the maintenance of international peace and security."

The Security Council has actually used its enforcement powers in only five cases, three of them since 1990. The five include sanctions against Southern Rhodesia (now Zimbabwe) in 1966, an arms embargo against South Africa in 1977, the 1990 economic sanctions and subsequent military action against Iraq, an arms embargo against Yugoslavia in 1991, and an air and arms embargo against Libya in 1992. For the most part, the Security Council relied on the Charter's peaceful settlement mechanisms in responding to the many situations placed on its agenda over the years. The Charter provisions for earmarked military forces and for the Military Staff Committee have never been operationalized, but during the Gulf war, and with the increased demands for peacekeeping forces, they have drawn renewed attention.

Other UN organs also have responsibilities related to peace and security. The secretary-general is authorized to bring to the Security Council's attention any and all matters that threaten international peace and security (Article 99). Frequently, the secretary-general may be called upon (or seek) to play a formal or informal intermediary role between parties to a dispute. Article 7 gives the secretary-general broad responsibility for securing and upholding the principles and objectives of the organization. This, combined with Article 99, has been used as a legal basis for developing an international political role by the five successive secretaries-general.[2]

On the basis of the General Assembly's right to consider any matter within the purview of the Charter (Article 10), the Uniting for Peace resolution during the Korean War in 1950 established a precedent that has enabled the General Assembly to act when the Security Council was stymied by great power veto. The General Assembly also has the right to make inquiries and studies that might trigger further united action (Articles 13,14) and to be kept informed (Articles 10,11,12).

In the aftermath of World War II, two major trends—the breakdown of great power unity and decolonization—occurred. The first immediately challenged international peace and security and the ability of the United Nations to handle the ensuing problems. In contrast, the second, decolonization, was accomplished with relatively little threat to international peace and security, although later, regional conflicts would pose significant challenges to the organization.

Designers of the United Nations had assumed great power unity; indeed, effective functioning of the Security Council required the concurrence of the five permanent members. The veto assured that no collective measures could ever be instituted against the "Big Five."[3] Yet, with the deepening Cold War, concurrence was almost impossible to achieve. The sanctioning of UN forces to counter the North Korean invasion of South Korea in 1950 was made possible only by the temporary absence of the Soviet Union from the Security Council in protest against the UN's refusal to seat the newly established communist government of the People's Republic of China. Nonetheless, the procedural innovation that authorized continuance of those forces once the Soviet Union returned to its seat and exercised its veto—the Uniting for Peace resolution—provided the precedent for the General Assembly to assume responsibility for other issues of peace and security when the Security Council was deadlocked by the veto.

The Korean case came close to a collective security action. The UN provided a framework to legitimate U.S. efforts to defend the Republic of Korea and mobilize other states' assistance, with an American general designated as the UN commander, but taking orders directly from Washington.

The procedural innovation—Uniting for Peace—was subsequently used to deal with crises in Suez and Hungary (1956), in the Middle East (1958), and in the Congo (1960). In all, nine emergency special sessions of the Assembly have dealt with threats to international peace when the Security Council was deadlocked.

Peacekeeping was a second creative response to the breakdown of great power unity and the spread of East-West tensions to regional conflicts. First developed to provide observer groups for conflicts in Kashmir and Palestine in the late 1940s, peacekeeping was formally proposed by Canadian Secretary of State for External Affairs Lester B. Pearson at the height of the Suez Crisis in 1956 as a means for securing the withdrawal of British, French, and Israeli forces from Egypt, pending a political settlement. The innovative Uniting for Peace resolution, and the development of peacekeeping, demonstrate that the United Nations has not been a static organization with respect to its role in promoting and maintaining international peace and security.

THE EVOLUTION OF PEACEKEEPING: A TYPOLOGY OF ACTIVITIES

Peacekeeping has taken a number of different forms in the varied circumstances in which it has been applied. Since there is no provision for peacekeeping in the Charter, a set of customs, principles, and practices defying neat definition have emerged from experience.[4] These were drawn together for UNEF II in 1973 and have provided basic guidelines for all subsequent operations. Thus, the United Nations refers to peacekeeping as "an operation involving military personnel, but without enforcement powers, undertaken by the United Nations to help maintain or restore international peace and security in areas of conflict."[5] The International Peace Academy defines peacekeeping in similar fashion as "the prevention, containment, moderation, and termination of hostilities between or within states, through the medium of a peaceful third party intervention, organized and directed internationally, using multinational forces of soldiers, police, and civilians to restore and maintain peace."[6] Under-Secretary General for Peacekeeping Operations Marrack Goulding, in a 1991 speech, described peacekeeping as "United Nations field operations in which international personnel, civilian and/or military, are deployed with the consent of the parties and under United Nations command to help control and resolve actual or potential international conflicts or internal conflicts which have a clear international dimension."[7]

Inasmuch as the permanent UN military forces envisioned by the Charter were never created, peacekeeping operations have relied on ad hoc military (civilian or police) units, drawn almost exclusively from the armed forces of *nonpermanent* members of the Security Council (often small, neutral and nonaligned members). This pattern was particularly important during the Cold War era when peacekeeping often was used to prevent the escalation of regional conflicts, by keeping at bay the superpowers or, in the case of postcolonial problems, former colonial powers. The size of peacekeeping forces has varied widely, depending upon the scope of the operation and mandate. Small observer groups have numbered less than 100; major operations in the Congo in the early 1960s, and Cambodia and Yugoslavia in 1992–93, have required over 10,000 troops. Table 10.1 indicates the size of many UN peacekeeping operations. Countries that have contributed contingents to one or more operations range from Canada, India, Sweden, Norway, Fiji, Ghana, Brazil, and Argentina to Bangladesh, Senegal, Togo, and Nepal.[8]

Table 10.1 / A Guide to UN Peacekeeping Operations

Operation	Title	Location	Duration	Maximum Strength
UNTSO	UN Truce Supervision Organization	Egypt, Israel, Jordan, Syria, Lebanon	June 1948–Present	572 Military Observers
UNMOGIP	UN Military Observer Group in India and Pakistan	India, Pakistan	Jan. 1949–Present	102 Military Observers
UNEF I	First UN Emergency Force	Suez Canal, Sinai Peninsula	Nov. 1956–June 1967	3,378 Troops
ONUC	UN Operation in the Congo	Congo	June 1960–June 1964	19,828 Troops
UNFICYP	UN Peace-Keeping Force in Cyprus	Cyprus	March 1964–Present	6,411 Military Observers
UNEF II	Second UN Emergency Force	Suez Canal, Sinai Peninsula	Oct. 1973–July 1979	6,973 Troops
UNDOF	UN Disengagement Observer Force	Syrian Golan Heights	June 1974–Present	1,450 Military Observers
UNIFIL	UN Interim Force in Lebanon	Southern Lebanon	March 1978–Present	7,000 Military Observers
UNGOMAP	UN Good Offices Mission in Afghanistan and Pakistan	Afghanistan, Pakistan	May 1988–March 1990	50 Military Observers
UNIIMOG	UN Iran-Iraq Military Observer Group	Iran, Iraq	Aug. 1988–Feb. 1991	399 Military Observers
UNAVEM I	First UN Angola Verification Mission	Angola	Jan. 1989–June 1991	70 Military Observers
UNTAG	UN Transition Assistance Group	Namibia, Angola	April 1989–March 1990	7,500 Troops (authorized) with 4,493 (actual), 1,500 Civilian Police, and 2,000 Civilian Election Observers
ONUVEN	UN Observer Mission to Verify the Electoral Process in Nicaragua	Nicaragua	Aug. 1989–Feb. 1990	Civilian Election Observers
ONUCA	UN Observer Group in Central America	Costa Rica, El Salvador, Guatemala, Honduras, Nicaragua	Nov. 1989–July 1992	1,098 Military Observers

Table 10.1 (Continued) / A Guide to UN Peacekeeping Operations

Operation	Title	Location	Duration	Maximum Strength
UNIKOM	UN Iraq-Kuwait Observer Mission	Iraq-Kuwait	April 1991–Present	1,440 Military Observers and Troops
UNAVEM II	Second UN Angola Verification Mission	Angola	June 1991–Nov. 1992	350 Military Observers 90 Police Observers
ONUSAL	UN Observer Mission in El Salvador	El Salvador	July 1991–Present	135 Civilian and Military Staff
MINURSO	UN Mission for the Referendum in Western Sahara	Western Sahara	Sep. 1991–Present	375 Military Liaison Officers and Civilian Staff
UNAMIC	UN Advance Mission in Cambodia	Cambodia	Oct. 1991–Present	380 Military Liaison Officers and Civilian Staff
UNPROFOR	UN Protection Force	Yugoslavia	March 1992–Present	14,400 Troops
UNTAC	UN Transition Authority in Cambodia	Cambodia	March 1992–Present	Eventually 15,900 Troops, 3,600 Police Monitors, and 2,400 Civilian Administrators
UNOSOM	UN Operation in Somalia	Somalia	1992–Present	3,500 Troops Originally Eventually 28,000 Troops

Former Under-Secretary-General for Political Affairs Sir Brian Urquhart, widely regarded as the "father of peacekeeping," summarizes the political requirements for peacekeeping as follows:

- The consent of the parties involved in the conflict to the establishment of the operation, to its mandate, to its composition, and to its appointed commanding officer;
- the continuing and strong support of the operation by the mandating authority, the Security Council;
- a clear and practicable mandate;
- the nonuse of force except in the last resort in self-defense—self-defense, however, including resistance to attempts by forceful means to prevent the peacekeepers from discharging their duties;
- the willingness of troop-contributing countries to provide adequate numbers of capable military personnel and to accept the degree of risk which the mandate and the situation demand;

- (less often noted) the willingness of the member states, and especially the permanent members of the Security Council, to make available the necessary financial and logistical support.[9]

The advantages of the peacekeeping approach over collective security as envisioned in the UN Charter are numerous. Because peacekeeping requires the approval of the parties to the conflict, there is at least a nominal commitment to cooperate with the mandate of the forces. Troops are volunteered by member countries, so the commitment by most members is relatively small. No aggressor need be identified, so no one party to the conflict is singled out for blame. The precise form of peacekeeping, however, has varied and is becoming increasingly so. This is because operations are tailored to the requirements of individual conflicts and situations. As Weiss and Chopra note, "A typology of peacekeeping is thus largely determined by a typology of conflict."[10] To date, UN forces have been deployed to deal with interstate wars over territory, intrastate civil conflicts, conflicts over ethnic or social differences, territories/peoples demanding self-determination, the independence of new states, and outright invasions. Weiss and Chopra group peacekeeping activities in five categories: observation, separation of forces, law and order, use of limited force, and enforcement (technically beyond the scope of peacekeeping).[11] Humanitarian intervention is emerging as a combination of several of these activities.[12]

Observation encompasses a variety of traditional peacekeeping activities: (a) investigation of conflicts (for example, the UN Commission of Investigation, established in 1946 to examine the extent of involvement by the great powers in the Greek civil war); (b) armistice supervision (e.g., the 1948 United Nations Truce Supervision Organization to supervise the truce between the Israeli and Arab armies); (c) maintaining a ceasefire (such as, military observers sent under the UN Commission for India and Pakistan to verify the position of troops and monitor activities prohibited under terms of the cease-fire); and (d) cessation of fighting (the United Nations Iran-Iraq Military Observer Group of 1988, established to monitor cessation of fighting and withdrawal of forces). More recently, new activities have included: (e) verification of troop withdrawal (e.g., the UN Good Offices Mission in Afghanistan that oversaw the withdrawal of Soviet troops from that country); (f) observation of elections as occurred in Namibia, Nicaragua, and Haiti; (g) the verification of arms control and disarmament agreements (e.g., the Central American Esquipulas II agreement); (h) human rights observation (for example, the ONUSAL operation in El Salvador); and (i) reconnaissance (e.g., preliminary missions to Cambodia and Central America). Obviously, the range of UN activities covered under the category of observation is diverse. It is also "the least controversial range on the escalating spectrum of peacekeeping activities."[13]

Separation of forces involves interposing referees in a buffer zone between conflicting parties. It has been most extensively used in the Middle East, with the UN Emergency Force (UNEF II) between Israel and Egypt in the 1970s, the UN Disengagement Observer Force (UNDOF) between Israel and Syria from 1973 to the present, and the long-suffering force in southern Lebanon (UNIFIL) being prominent examples. (See Figure 10.1.)

Figure 10.1 / Second United Nations Emergency Force (UNEF II) Deployment as of July 1979

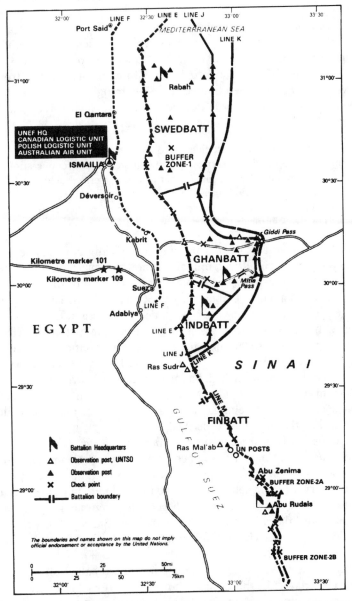

Source: United Nations, *The Blue Helmets: A Review of United Nations Peace-keeping,* Second Edition (United Nations, 1990), Map No. 3329.3 Rev. 1 (June 1990).

The third category of UN operations involve situations requiring moral authority and, sometimes, defensive actions to preserve *law and order,* often within a society. The United Nations Operation in the Congo (ONUC), established in 1960, is a telling example of peacekeeping being used to restore law and order in a civil war, as discussed below. Currently, UN forces in Cambodia (UNTAC), have taken on the complex tasks of civil administration and police, as well as observation, election supervision, and rehabilitation.

The principle that UN peacekeepers use military force only as a last resort and in self-defense was a response to the difficulties encountered in the Congo in 1961, when the Security Council authorized ONUC to use force to prevent civil war and to remove foreign mercenaries from that country. *Use of Force*—even limited force—is fraught with political and legal controversy: How much is limited force? Are such forces really used defensively? As Weiss and Chopra note, however:

> The end of the Cold War provides an opportunity to reevaluate many of the assumptions and standard practices governing international cooperation, including the use of force. The collegiality that has characterized deliberations by the Security Council since 1987 means eroding respect for shibboleths. . . . [and] as peacekeeping was a development of the restrictive Cold War atmosphere, it is likely to evolve significantly as great power tensions recede.[14]

Finally, *enforcement action,* although technically beyond the scope of peacekeeping, involves direct military action to ensure compliance with Security Council directives.[15] As noted earlier, the end of the Cold War has enabled the permanent members of the Security Council to cooperate in addressing regional conflicts and has opened a new era in UN activities, beginning with the Gulf war. New proposals to create a standing UN peace force anticipate the use of such forces both for traditional peacekeeping functions and for enforcement. And as explored below, it is anticipated that the latter will become a more prominent feature of world politics.

While this typology provides a useful overview of different UN activities subsumed under peacekeeping, in actuality most UN missions include at least several of the functions described above.

A new use of UN peacekeepers, *humanitarian aid* and *intervention,* is based on the notion that suffering people have an enforceable right to basic needs. The provision of food and medical supplies, and a secure environment necessary for their delivery, are fundamental human rights that may be guaranteed by UN peacekeepers. Such peacekeeping may keep supply lines open, and guard distribution centers, guaranteeing law and order, as in the case of Somalia, or providing safe havens, as established for the Iraqi Kurds in 1991.

Many of the tasks UN peacekeepers have been called on to undertake were never specified in the Charter, nor envisaged by the Founders. However, the broadening of UN functions in maintaining international peace and security shown in this typology of peacekeeping activities was a necessary institutional innovation if the UN was to play any role in this key aspect of world politics. We turn now to an examination of that evolution over three distinct periods: the Cold War era, the transition period from 1985 to 1989, and the post–Cold War era that began in 1990.

THE COLD WAR

During the Cold War era, UN peacekeeping forces were used most extensively in the Middle East and for conflicts arising out of the decolonization process, when the interests of neither the United States nor the Soviet Union were directly at stake. The Suez crisis of 1956 marked the first major example of their use. The General Assembly created the United Nations Emergency Force (UNEF I) following the British, French, and Israeli attack on Egypt for its nationalization of the Suez Canal and threat to close the canal to Israeli shipping. The UN troops separated the combatants, supervised the withdrawal of British, French, and Israeli forces, and thereafter patrolled the Sinai Peninsula and Gaza Strip.[16]

UNEF I was withdrawn at Egypt's request just before the Six-Day war in 1967. Only in 1973, following the Yom Kippur war, was UNEF II established to monitor that cease-fire and facilitate the disengagement of Egyptian and Israeli forces by supervising a buffer zone between the combatants. A separate force, the United Nations Disengagement Observer Force (UNDOF), supervised the disengagement of Syrian and Israeli forces on the Golan Heights and a similar buffer zone.

A fourth Middle East force, the United Nations Interim Force in Lebanon (UNIFIL), was established in 1978 following the Israeli invasion and occupation of southern Lebanon to monitor the withdrawal of Israeli forces and assist the government of Lebanon in reestablishing its authority in the area.

UNEF II was terminated in 1979 following the Camp David Accords, whose provisions have been monitored by a non-UN Multinational Force and Observers that includes one U.S. battalion. Both UNDOF and UNIFIL remain in place despite UNIFIL's inability to prevent repeated Israeli raids and the vulnerability of its members to attack and kidnapping by the various warring groups in southern Lebanon.

UN peacekeeping forces were also deployed in the former Belgian Congo (now Zaire) following its independence in 1960. The United Nations Operation in the Congo (ONUC) initially was designed to help the newly independent government establish law and order and to ensure the withdrawal of Belgian troops that had returned to the Congo when violence broke out. When the province of Katanga seceded, ONUC's mission expanded to restore the territorial integrity of the Congo and avert full-scale war. The controversial operation, which led the UN to the brink of bankruptcy because of disputes over payment for the force, ended in 1964.[17]

Another operation, the United Nations Force in Cyprus (UNFICYP), has been in existence since 1964 to provide a buffer zone between Greek and Turkish populations on the island of Cyprus. UNFICYP remained in place even during the Turkish invasion of 1974.

Evaluating the relative success of the traditional peacekeeping approach—the distinct innovation of the Cold War period—is not an easy task.[18] In several cases, armed hostilities were stopped, but permanent resolution of many disputes proved elusive. UNEF I averted war between the Arabs and Israelis for eleven years. UNEF II was one of many factors that facilitated the negotiation of the Israeli-Egyptian peace agreement at Camp David. ONUC succeeded in preventing the secession of Katanga province and, at a minimal level, helped restore order in the Congo. UNFICYP has averted overt hostilities between the Greek and Turkish communities in Cyprus, but could not prevent the coup d'état by Greek officers in 1974 or the subsequent Turkish invasion. UNDOF can take credit, at least in part, for the quietness of the Golan Heights since 1974.

Thus, the record of UN peacekeeping during the Cold War is a mixed one. For those whose definition of success is the peaceful settlement of conflicts, only UNEF II would be deemed successful. If success is defined in terms of ending armed hostilities and preventing their renewal at least for a period of time, then all the operations except UNIFIL could be deemed successful. Secretary-General Boutros Boutros-Ghali characterizes these thirteen pre-1988 Cold War peacekeeping operations as follows:

> . . . they were largely military in composition and their tasks were to monitor cease-fires, control buffer zones, investigate alleged arms flows, prevent a resumption of hostilities and so on. In other words, they were to maintain calm on the front lines and give time to the peacemakers to negotiate a settlement of the dispute which had led to conflict in the first place. Sometimes the peace-*makers* succeeded. More often they did not, which is why so many of the pre-1988 operations are still in the field.[19]

Cold War exigencies meant that the superpowers had to agree before action was taken. As a result, many important issues of peace and security, including the Vietnam conflict, never made it to the UN agenda. The innovation of peacekeeping, however, provided a valuable means to limit superpower involvement in regional conflicts (with their consent) and to cope with threats to peace and security posed by the emergence of new states, border conflicts among those states, and the intractable conflicts in the Middle East. As Weiss and Campbell note, the United Nations essentially had to "tiptoe around the Cold War" to play the role that it did.[20] In doing so, however, it developed a body of experience and practice in peacekeeping that has proven even more valuable in the transition period of the late 1980s and the post–Cold War era.

THE TRANSITION PERIOD—1985 TO 1989

The most striking feature of UN efforts to deal with threats to international peace and security in the late 1980s was the cooperation among the five permanent members of the Security Council in supporting not only peacekeeping but *peacemaking* in a series of long-standing regional conflicts. Never before in the forty years' of the UN's existence had there been such consensus. With the acquiescence of the nonpermanent members, and new collaboration between the Security Council and the secretary-general, UN peacekeepers chalked up a series of successes that led to the Nobel Peace Prize in 1988.

The single most important factor contributing to this development was the dramatic set of changes in Soviet foreign policy initiated by Mikhail Gorbachev. In early 1986, the Soviets began to pay close attention to the quiet efforts of Diego Cordovez, an assistant to Secretary-General Pérez de Cuéllar, to mediate the Afghan conflict and to find ways in which the UN could facilitate the withdrawal of Soviet forces. Somewhat later that same year, the Soviets announced their intention to pay their share of the expenses for the UN force in southern Lebanon, something they had specifically said in 1978 they would not do. These small signals took on more significance with the 1987 publication in *Pravda* of an article by Gorbachev expressing new Soviet interest in multilateral institutions and, especially, the UN for promoting peace and security.[21] To back up this verbal commitment, the Soviet Union announced that it would pay up financial arrears of $127 million, including assessments for UN peacekeeping forces it had long opposed. A second important factor that contributed to changing Soviet (and other permanent members') perceptions of the role the UN could play with respect to regional conflicts was the quiet diplomacy of then UN Secretary-General Pérez de Cuéllar and his aides. During the first half of the 1980s, the secretary-general and others patiently sustained discussions with Iran and Iraq over possible bases for ending their war, and with the various parties in Afghanistan over terms for Soviet withdrawal.[22]

The peacekeeping successes of the late 1980s also required a reversal in the attitude of the United States, which had become increasingly hostile to the UN and many of its specialized agencies under the Reagan administration.[23] In 1985, the U.S. Congress reduced U.S. contributions to the UN below the assessed amounts.[24] The United States was not the only country that was delinquent in its contributions, but when one country contributes 25 percent of the regular budget of an organization, failure to pay creates a financial crisis. By late 1987, however, there were signs that the Reagan administration's antagonism toward the UN was moderating. The alterations in Soviet attitude and reforms in the UN administrative and budgetary processes, as well as evidence of UN successes in conflict management, contributed to the changes.[25]

The attitudes of the two superpowers, then, were critical ingredients in facilitating UN efforts to end the war between Iran and Iraq, the Soviet presence in Afghanistan, the long stalemate over Namibia, and conflict in Central America. Successes in each of these regional-conflict arenas spurred unprecedented interest in the possibilities of UN peacekeeping.

Afghanistan

In 1988, the quiet efforts by UN mediator Diego Cordovez to find a way to facilitate Soviet withdrawal from Afghanistan paid off. Under pressure to devote more resources to domestic economic needs, and with counterinsurgency operations against Afghan *mujahedeen* threatening to prolong a costly presence indefinitely, Gorbachev agreed to withdraw Soviet troops from Afghanistan. As one author suggests, the United Nations in this case was "uniquely placed to resolve the stalemate in Afghanistan . . . [by serving] as a buffer between the United States and Soviet Union and conducting negotiations that were nominally between their Afghan and Pakistani proxies."[26] Fifty UN observers under the United Nations Good Offices Mission in Afghanistan and Pakistan (UNGOMAP), monitored and verified the withdrawal of over 100,000 Soviet troops, with a schedule for withdrawal and a map of withdrawal routes furnished by the Soviets, outposts at major border crossings and airports, and regular meetings with Afghan and Soviet military representatives. These innovations would have been impossible during the height of the Cold War. Yet, they illustrated the expanding possibilities for UN peacekeeping missions: in this case, the utility of a small number of UN soldiers observing the agreed departure of combat troops—"a face-saving device" that would prove to be a helpful component in other negotiated settlements, such as Angola in 1988.

Iran-Iraq War

In August 1988, with the passage of Security Council Resolution 598, Iran and Iraq agreed to a UN-supervised cease-fire. The resolution itself was the product of an extended effort by Secretary-General Pérez de Cuéllar, beginning in January 1987, to reconcile the views of the five members of the Security Council. Ten days later, the United States proposed the idea of a mandatory resolution ordering a cease-fire to the seven-year conflict and the withdrawal of forces. Any party not in compliance would be subject to an arms embargo. From February through April, the permanent members met in technical working groups and at the ambassadorial level to hammer out a comprehensive framework for ending the war. By July 1987, Resolution 598 was adopted, outlining a political position supported by the whole Security Council.

Although the war would continue for a year, the provisions were set for the deployment of United Nations Iran-Iraq Military Observer Group (UNIIMOG). Their function was to establish, with the participation of Iran and Iraq, the agreed upon cease-fire lines; to monitor compliance with the cease-fire; to investigate violations of the cease-fire; and to prevent any changes other than withdrawal of military forces to internationally recognized boundaries. Their task was completed in February 1991.

Angola and Namibia

Also in August 1988, an agreement on the withdrawal of Cuban and South African forces in Angola opened the way to the implementation of UN Security Council Resolution 435, which had been approved in September 1978, ten years earlier, to provide a framework for Namibia's independence. In the 1970s, the independence of Namibia, a former German colony administered by South Africa since the end of World War I, was the subject of intense efforts by five major Western powers, acting outside of but in close cooperation with the UN, to bring South Africa, the main liberation group in Namibia, SWAPO, and the so-called Front Line states in southern Africa to an agreement; their ad hoc efforts led to the agreement embodied in Security Council Resolution 435, but were unsuccessful in getting South Africa to undertake the next steps—implementation.[27]

By the end of the decade, lack of progress was blamed on the Soviet-backed Cuban presence in Angola that supported the Angolan government in the ongoing civil war in that country. The South Africans perceived that presence as a direct threat to their security and, after the Reagan administration took office, they gained support from the United States in that view. In 1981, U.S. Assistant Secretary of State for Africa Chester A. Crocker linked a Namibian settlement to removal of Soviet and Cuban troops. Efforts to make the complex linkages finally came to fruition in 1988; in February of that year, Cuba and Angola agreed to a withdrawal of Cuban troops as part of a regional peace settlement; in June, the United States and the Soviet Union jointly announced a target date for withdrawal of foreign forces from Angola and for Namibian independence. By December, the agreement for implementing Resolution 435 was in place and the UN moved to mount the two peacekeeping operations required: UNAVEM I and UNTAG.

As in Afghanistan, a small number of UN military observers provided a valuable component to the agreement between Cuba, Angola, and South Africa. Between January 1989 and June 1991, seventy soldiers monitored the withdrawal of Cuban troops from Angola.

By contrast, the UN Transition Assistance Group (UNTAG), deployed in April 1989, was not a traditional peacekeeping force. Its mandate, as noted earlier, included a diverse set of tasks, requiring military, police, and civilian personnel: to create conditions for an electoral campaign in Namibia; to secure repeal of discriminatory and restrictive legislation, release of political prisoners, and return of exiles; to conduct a free and fair election; to monitor the cease-fire and protect against infiltration of the Namibian/Angolan border; to monitor the conduct of the local police and the departure from Namibia of the South African Defence Force; and to monitor the confinement to bases of SWAPO forces. For almost one year, UNTAG, with personnel from 109 countries, played a vital role in creating conditions and supervising the process by which Namibia moved step-by-step from a cease-fire to independence. It was "an extremely political operation, in which the tasks of each element—civilian, police, military—were bonded together . . . with a view to achieving a structural change in society by means of a democratic process, in accordance with an agreed timetable."[28]

Another unique aspect of UNTAG, reflecting the importance the UN and the international community placed on the Namibian independence process, was the presence and role of the secretary-general's special representative in Namibia, Martti Ahtisaari. Each step had to be done to his satisfaction. Several subsequent peacekeeping operations have utilized this innovation to coordinate complex tasks and provide on-the-spot representation of the secretary-general's office.

Central America

The final peacekeeping operation of the transition period took place in Central America, where the United Nations Observer Group in Central America (ONUCA) played a key part in the peace process ending protracted conflicts in that region. ONUCA was complemented by ONUVEN, the UN Observer Mission charged with verifying the election process in Nicaragua, and subsequently by ONUSAL, an observer mission in El Salvador. Although only ONUCA fits the criteria of a traditional peacekeeping operation, the three together played an important part in assisting the parties concerned in controlling and resolving the conflicts in the region, thus illustrating the complexity of peacekeeping and, most definitely in this case, peace*making*.

Briefly, ONUVEN, consisting of civilian election observers, was deployed from August 1989 to February 1990 when the Nicaraguan elections took place under the scrutiny of the Organization of American States (OAS), nongovernmental organizations, as well as the United Nations. In November 1989, ONUCA deployed over a thousand military observers to verify the implementation of the Esquipulas II Agreement. With two successive expansions of its mandate, ONUCA was charged with ensuring the cessation of aid to insurrectionist forces, the nonuse of the territory of one state for attacks on others, and the disarmament of demobilized forces. Its work covered the territory of five Central American states, although most was concentrated in Nicaragua and Honduras, and was only completed in July 1992. Overlapping ONUCA and initiated in the post–Cold War era to monitor agreements concluded between the Government of El Salvador and the FMLN (Frente Farabundo Marti para la Liberacion Nacional), ONUSAL marks a new step for UN peacekeepers—monitoring and verifying human rights violations and making recommendations for their future elimination. We shall examine the significance of this innovation shortly.

Thus, the transition period of the late 1980s was marked by change in the two superpowers' attitudes toward the UN and the possibilities of UN peacekeeping. The United Nations itself, with the cooperation between the secretary-general and Security Council, devised a number of innovative arrangements beyond the scope of traditional peacekeeping—including verification of troop withdrawals by a superpower and the conduct and monitoring of elections. These developments made it possible to end a series of long-standing regional conflicts. Given the new significance of UN peacekeeping activities, the 1988 Nobel Peace Prize was awarded to UN peacekeeping forces in recognition of their "decisive contribution toward the initiation of actual peace negotiations."

THE POST–COLD WAR ERA

The fall of the Berlin Wall in November 1989, more than any other single event, signaled the advent of a new era in world politics. Within weeks, the communist-dominated governments of all the East-Central European countries had been toppled with the clear acquiescence of the Soviet Union. In 1990, General Secretary Gorbachev introduced changes ending the Soviet Communist party's constitutional monopoly on political power and proposed democratizing its internal procedures. But even within the Soviet Union, efforts to enact reforms could not keep pace with changes underway. By the winter of 1991, Gorbachev was ousted and the Union of Soviet Socialist Republics was rapidly being dismantled, to be replaced by a loose and highly uncertain Commonwealth of Independent States (CIS). Russia alone held the former Soviet Union's seat in the United Nations (with other republics admitted as new members); its president, Boris Yeltsin, declared communism dead. The Cold War was over. As Robert F. Ellsworth, director of the Atlantic Council of the U.S. stated, "The old paradigm of a world locked in a tension-filled Cold War is 'inoperative.'" "A new international system is being constructed, in fits and starts," said Ellsworth, "and the Europeans, the Americans and successor authority in the Soviet Union (the Russians?) must, in different ways, cooperate to plan and build it."[29]

Between 1988 and 1992, thirteen new UN peacekeeping operations were launched, eight of them after 1990. This was equal to the total number of operations for the previous forty years. Many observers predicted that the United Nations would become an even more important instrument to assuring international peace and security. But the road is not a smooth one. Demands for new peacekeeping roles have not been matched with new financial commitments by member states. And, the situations several of these peacekeeping operations face leave their outcomes uncertain.

The Gulf War

The first challenge to the post–Cold War order came with Iraq's invasion and annexation of Kuwait in August 1990. Unity among the five permanent members of the Security Council, including the Soviet Union, in spite of its long-standing relationship with Iraq, facilitated the passage of twelve successive resolutions, over four months, activating Chapter VII of the Charter. These included Resolution 678 (November 29, 1990), which authorized member states "to use all necessary means" to restore the status quo ante. The military operation launched under the umbrella of Resolution 678 was not a peacekeeping operation. Indeed, it did not qualify as a collective security action under Article 42 of the Charter, though it has been portrayed as such by many people. Weiss and Chopra describe the U.S.-led multinational coalition as "a type of 'sub-contract'. . . . acting on behalf of the organization." They note that unlike even the Korean situation in the early 1950s, UN flags and symbols were not used in the military action. Nor was the United States responsible to the authority of the UN through regular reporting and participation by UN personnel in decision making.[30] Only after the end of military action by the coalition was a UN peacekeeping force organized to monitor the demilitarized zone between Iraq and Kuwait. The unarmed UNIKOM force reports on violations (including minor incursions by soldiers and overflights by military aircraft) and investigates complaints. It is thus a fairly traditional peacekeeping operation.

Though the U.S.-led military action in the Gulf was widely regarded as exemplifying a new, stronger post–Cold War UN, that role, as distinct from the UNIKOM mission, came under critical scrutiny. Absent a direct link to the UN, as noted above, most UN members had no say in the operation. Even key economic powers, such as Germany and Japan, that were expected to contribute monetary resources for the collective action, were excluded from important decision-making meetings (a fact that fueled their interest in permanent membership on the Security Council). And the Southern states, while supporting the action, worried about precedents for UN interference in states' internal affairs and the diminution of national sovereignty when the UN supported construction of refugee havens for the Kurds in northern Iraq under the justification of humanitarianism. The Gulf war, thus, highlighted an important problem of the post–Cold War era. As Luck and Gati note, "The ambivalence of many states toward a stronger UN is now coupled with apprehension about a pax Americana, even a UN-centered one, without a Soviet counterweight."[31] Yet the Gulf war did leave a generally positive legacy for the UN in the minds of many people, especially Americans.

Since the conclusion of the Gulf war, the UN has launched six new peacekeeping operations—in Angola, El Salvador, Western Sahara, Cambodia (2), Yugoslavia, and Somalia. These post–Cold War efforts to respond to regional conflicts have required further innovations in traditional peacekeeping tasks. All are still underway as of this writing.

Other Regional Conflicts

The operations in Western Sahara (MINURSO), Angola (UNAVEM II), El Salvador (ONUSAL), and Somalia (UNOSOM) are all small in size, but distinctive in their requirements. MINURSO returns the UN to a decolonization role in the tiny northwest African territory that since the end of

Spanish colonial rule has been the object of dispute between Morocco, Mauritania, Algeria, and the liberation group, POLISARIO. UNAVEM II has extended and expanded the role of the UN in Angola in the peace process designed to end eighteen years of civil war.

As noted earlier, the UN's transition-period role in ending conflicts in Central America has extended into the post–Cold War period with the establishment of ONUSAL in El Salvador. This operation is truly path breaking in its human rights observation role. Military and police personnel, as well as civilian staff, investigate allegations of human rights violations and follow them up with competent state organs and with the FMLN. Their purpose is to establish the veracity of allegations and to monitor the actions taken to identify and punish perpetrators, as well as to deter future violations. The peacekeepers have also initiated a human rights education program and an information campaign. The military and police divisions supervise the separation and redeployment of government and insurgent forces, as well as the formation and training of a National Civil Police.

In 1991 and 1992, civil order totally collapsed in the east African country of Somalia as warring clans seized control of parts of the country and capital. Widespread death and destruction accompanied the fighting, forcing hundreds of thousands of civilians to flee and causing dire need for emergency humanitarian assistance. The absence of any central government and the resistance of some clan leaders to any UN or foreign presence, even to ensure delivery of food supplies, complicated, indeed endangered, UN peacekeepers. A small (500-man) contingent of Pakistani troops, sent to Somalia with a mandate to protect relief workers and food deliveries, proved totally inadequate. In December 1992, the Security Council authorized a large U.S.-led military/humanitarian intervention to secure ports and airfields, protect relief shipments and workers, and disarm Somali clansmen.

For many observers, however, the renewed popularity of UN peacekeeping faces its most severe tests in two post–Cold War undertakings: Yugoslavia and Cambodia. Both tax the resources of the UN, and the commitment of member states, by their very size and complexity. The Cambodian operation engages UN peacekeepers more deeply in a country's domestic affairs than in any previous case. The Yugoslavian situation enmeshes peacekeepers in multisided ethnic warfare, with a mandate (as of this writing) to ensure delivery of humanitarian assistance under conditions of continued fighting and to monitor the lines between Serbian and Croatian forces. Both could presage the kinds of challenges the UN might be asked to undertake elsewhere in the post–Cold War era. Both hold the possibility of massive failure, with attendant negative results for future multilateral efforts to maintain peace and security.

Cambodia

In October 1991, the Agreements on a Comprehensive Political Settlement of the Cambodia Conflict were signed in Paris. Cooperation between the

United States and the Soviet Union provided the impetus for China and Vietnam to support a cease-fire in Cambodia, demobilization of the armies, repatriation of 350,000 refugees, and elections by mid-1993. The four Cambodian parties accepted the framework of the settlement and agreed to form the Supreme National Council as the authority in Cambodia during the transition period. Security Council Resolution 718 (October 31, 1991) supported this agreement and requested that the secretary-general prepare a detailed plan of implementation.

Under the terms of agreement, the UN was given a central role in ensuring the accord's implementation, one that would give it effective responsibility for administering the country during an eighteen-month transition period. A small advance mission (UNAMIC) was to facilitate communication among the four Cambodian parties to maintain the cease-fire prior to deployment of the UN Transitional Authority (UNTAC) in March 1992. The seven distinct components of UNTAC's mandate are slated to engage up to 20,000 military and civilian personnel at the peak period. UNTAC will exercise direct control over Cambodia's defense, foreign affairs, finance, public security, and information administrative structures to ensure a neutral political environment prior to general elections. It is also to monitor the police, promote human rights, and organize the elections that will turn back authority to Cambodians themselves. The military component of UNTAC is charged with a variety of tasks associated with supervising the cease-fire, disarming, and demobilization of forces. UNTAC is also charged with repatriation and resettlement of refugees in cooperation with the Office of the United Nations High Commissioner for Refugees (UNHCR) and with rehabilitation of basic infrastructure and public utilities.

Never before have UN peacekeepers been asked to undertake such diverse and complex tasks. Keith Eirinberg suggests the importance of the scope of the UN commitment, "If the U.N. can't pull this off, they're certainly not going to have much success getting money for peacekeeping operations elsewhere."[32]

The problems, however, are formidable. The most critical is the refusal of the Khmer Rouge, the Maoist-inspired rebels under whose rule in the 1970s an estimated one million Cambodians perished, to put its soldiers under UN supervision, as mandated by the peace plan. Without the cooperation of all four parties—the Phnom Penh government originally installed after the Vietnamese invasion in 1978, the two non-Communist rebel groups, as well as the Khmer Rouge—the other stages of the settlement will be impossible to implement. The Khmer Rouge believes that it is not being treated as an equal in the peace process. In addition, it is playing on nationalistic sentiments of Cambodians who resent the continued presence of Vietnamese workers. Thus, the Cambodian peacekeeping (and peace*making*) undertaking, the culmination of decade-long negotiations by the secretary-general and others, is jeopardized by the hazards and animosities of domestic political rivalries.[33]

Yugoslavia

Yugoslavia provides another example of where multilateral peacekeeping efforts are confronted by stark domestic realities. The mandate of the UN peacekeepers is much more limited than in Cambodia, but the consequences of failure to halt fighting among former Yugoslavia's rival groups (*not* part of the UNPROFOR mandate) may nonetheless be far-reaching for other post–Cold War conflicts. The Yugoslav case illustrates why the key to successful peacekeeping in the past has been the readiness of the parties to cooperate.

The civil war in Yugoslavia was brought about by the Serbian leadership's attempts to maintain the country's unity in the face of strong separatist movements in Slovenia, Croatia, and Bosnia-Herzegovina. During 1991, the members of the European Community sought to negotiate cease-fires among the warring ethnic groups. This is consistent with Chapter VII of the UN Charter, which stipulates that regional organizations make every effort to resolve local disputes before referring them to the Security Council. EC mediation was successful in negotiating and in sending observers to guarantee the independence of Slovenia. However, with respect to the other republics, the Europeans could not agree on what their role should be, whether sanctions should be applied, how much force should be employed, and whether diplomatic recognition should be granted to the new republics (most notably Croatia).

Most of the EC effort was directed toward obtaining a cease-fire—but cease-fires were made and broken in rapid succession. On September 25, 1991, the UN Security Council, meeting at the ministerial level, unanimously adopted a resolution (713) expressing deep concern at the fighting and calling on all states to implement a "general and complete embargo on all deliveries of weapons and military equipment to Yugoslavia." The council invited the secretary-general to offer his assistance to the European Community and the CSCE states in restoring peace and promoting dialogue. The council's action led to the appointment of the secretary-general's personal envoy to Yugoslavia, former U.S. Secretary of State Cyrus Vance.

Vance was ultimately successful in securing agreement from all the Yugoslav parties on a cease-fire and establishment of a UN peacekeeping operation, and his efforts were endorsed by the Security Council (Resolution 721, November 27, 1991). Compliance with the cease-fire agreement, however, remained elusive. Indeed, UNPROFOR was authorized in February 1992, even though compliance of the parties was still uncertain. In his report, the secretary-general observed:

> The danger that a United Nations peace-keeping operation will fail because of lack of cooperation from the parties is less grievous than the danger that delay in its dispatch will lead to a breakdown of the cease-fire and to a new conflagration in Yugoslavia.[34]

The UN Protection Force for Yugoslavia was approved for an initial period of twelve months, with military and civilian personnel to be stationed in regions where Serbs and Croats were living in close proximity; however, both a cease-fire and a promise to control irregular troops were prerequisites. In March 1992, the UN dispatched over 14,000 peacekeepers to Yugoslavia, mostly to Croatia. The decision to target Croatia has been strongly criticized, for it allowed the Serbians to concentrate their efforts on Bosnia-Herzegovina, in particular the siege of its capital, Sarajevo. In May 1992, the Security Council imposed economic sanctions against the Serbian-dominated government of Yugoslavia (reduced to the territory of Serbia and Montenegro), reflecting the widespread Western view that Serbia's leader was largely to blame for the ethnic chaos. In June 1992, with public pressure building to provide humanitarian assistance to the people of Sarajevo at a minimum, the Security Council authorized the sending of peacekeepers to Sarajevo to reopen the airport and secure a truce to facilitate humanitarian relief efforts. UNPROFOR's restrictive mandate, however, precluded UN forces from intervening to halt the "ethnic cleansing" by Serbian regular and irregular forces that forced thousands of people, especially Bosnia's Muslims, to flee their homes—a gross violation of human rights reminiscent of World War II atrocities.

The international community's response to the Yugoslav crisis illustrates the thorny problems arising out of the civil wars and ethnic conflicts that have marked the early post–Cold War era in Central Europe and the former Soviet Union. Few states support direct military intervention, and mediators have been frustrated by divergent expectations of member states. Although UN peacekeeping forces are monitoring the Serbian/Croatian border and are attempting to ensure safe conditions for humanitarian relief efforts, there is much more that could be done. But UN forces can play only limited roles in the absence of commitment from the conflicting parties to a settlement. Such is the lesson of peacekeeping: its mandate and ultimately its success depend upon the consent of the parties to a conflict.

Thus far, in the post–Cold War period, the UN has been called on to provide more peacekeeping forces than in any previous four-year period. Those forces have also been required to play more expansive roles in a number of situations. As we have noted, these trends may be attributed to the new convergence in the interests of Security Council members, particularly the five permanent members, and to the expectations raised by several early successes. And, success has increased both demand and expectation. For example, the UN's role in organizing and monitoring elections in Nicaragua and Namibia led not only to provisions for those functions in the Cambodian operation, but to requests from more than a dozen countries for some type of electoral assistance as the trend toward democratization reached new parts of the world in the late 1980s and early 1990s. Those countries include Haiti, Cameroon, Ethiopia, Ghana, Zambia, Albania, Romania, and Guyana.

The UN's record of peacekeeping successes may well be tarnished, however, by the obstinacy of one or more parties in Angola, Western Sahara, Cambodia, and Yugoslavia. The latter two further illustrate the challenges ethnic conflict and civil disorder pose. It remains to be seen how successful the UN will be in new roles, such as human rights monitoring and promotion, election assistance, and civil administration.

The heavy demand for UN peacekeeping has also dramatically increased the financial resources and personnel required to support operations. Member states continue to be far quicker to approve new peacekeeping operations than to meet their financial commitments. Nonetheless, proposals to strengthen the capacity of the UN to support peacekeeping have proliferated. We examine some of these as part of our concluding assessment of the past and future value of UN peacekeeping.

THE PAST AND FUTURE OF UN PEACEKEEPING

The UN's experience with peacekeeping has highlighted a number of lessons that represent key issues for the future. These can be grouped roughly into five categories: consent of the parties to the conflict; political support of the Security Council and member states; operational mandate and the use of force; financial and logistical support; and command and coordination.

As Weiss and Chopra note, "For traditionalists, no requirement of peacekeeping is clearer than the consent of parties in conflict. . . . it is a political and operational imperative."[35] But opinions are changing on both the political and legal necessity of consent of the parties. The plight of Iraq's Kurds in Spring 1991, Sarajevo's besieged citizens, and Somalia's starving thousands in 1992 brought attention to justifications for humanitarian intervention without consent of the parties.[36] Strict adherence to a requirement for parties' consent will be problematic if the UN is to play any role in trying to manage or resolve conflicts involving insurgent ethnic groups and limited central government control.

The consensus among the permanent members of the Security Council that emerged in the late 1980s has been a critical variable in providing support for increased use of UN peacekeeping in very diverse circumstances. It also made possible the unique arrangements during the Gulf war and its aftermath. Such support is crucial for an operation's success and if peacekeeping is to be related to peacemaking. Clearly, if changes in Russia lead to the emergence of a new communist regime or a highly nationalistic one, then the post–Cold War consensus will be jeopardized.

An added dimension of political support involves expanding the role of the secretary-general and increased coordination between the Security Council and the secretary-general. The latter must be able to respond more quickly and flexibly to situations, assuming a more active role, identifying threats to peace, creating opportunities and an environment for negotiations, and ensuring that the United Nations does not become so closely identified with one party that it is unable to act impartially.

The operational mandates for peacekeeping operations are "authorizations for lawful action"[37] that UN-appointed commanders have to translate into practicable orders for the various military contingents and other personnel. Commanders prefer to have precise, clear mandates; diplomats, however, may prefer ambiguity, either because efforts to achieve clarity will lead to a breakdown in political support or because they wish to preserve leeway to influence future developments. For example, the observers charged with overseeing the Soviet withdrawal from Afghanistan (UNGOMAP) had a clear mandate to do just that, but not to report on violations of other provisions in the Geneva Accords. UN forces in Bosnia-Herzegovina have a mandate to facilitate relief efforts, but not to investigate charges of ethnic cleansing or to create safe havens for Moslem refugees. The ambiguous mandate for peacekeepers in northern and southern Iraq to protect Kurds and Shiites by enforcing a "no-fly zone" is another illustration of the challenges peacekeepers face when their operational mandate is not clear.

The issue of peacekeepers using force can be particularly difficult. Most peacekeeping troops have been authorized to use force only in self-defense. In Nicaragua, ONUCA was responsible for collecting and destroying weapons from the Nicaraguan resistance. Where future peacekeepers are expected to disarm local groups, they will need clear mandates to use force if they are challenged. And, when force is authorized, rules of engagement will be needed to ensure the use of force in a measured and restrained way.

Providing the necessary financial and logistical support for peacekeeping has long been a problem. Disputes over members' obligations led to a crisis for the organization in the early 1960s. An advisory opinion from the International Court of Justice on the issue in 1961 affirmed that peacekeeping expenses should be borne by all member states.[38] In fact, arrangements for financing vary. Observer missions are generally funded from assessed contributions. Peacekeeping operations have generally been funded through a modified version of the scale of assessments for the regular UN budget, which recognizes the primary responsibility of the permanent members of the Security Council for maintaining international peace and security. Thus, the latter account for 57 percent of the peacekeeping budget.[39] A few operations have been funded either by the parties themselves or through voluntary contributions. But, as has long been the case with regular budget assessments, member states large and small are frequently in arrears. And, as more peacekeeping operations are mounted, the financial strains increase. In 1987, the cost of peacekeeping was $233 million; in 1991, it had doubled to $421 million; and in 1992, it was projected at approximately $2.7 billion.[40]

An additional dimension of the funding problem is the need for ready capital to enable the UN to respond to a crisis immediately. The working capital fund has long since been exhausted. Only a small number of troop-contributing countries, such as Canada and the Nordic countries, can afford to sustain their troops in the field without reimbursement; for developing countries like Fiji, India, and Ghana, lack of repayment constitutes a further burden on their own peoples. And, the uncertainty of reimbursement has made some countries reluctant to contribute their troops. Under present conditions, it is necessary to solicit funds when a new operation is launched, which causes delays. Secretary-General Boutros-Ghali has proposed that a revolving capital fund be established to finance start-up costs; that member states pay immediately one-third of the estimated cost and pay on time other assessments; and that a reserve stock of commonly used equipment and supply items (such field kitchens, water-purification equipment, and tentage) be maintained.[41] Without the commitment of funds necessary for more extensive UN peacekeeping operations, statements of support for the UN are moot.

The issue of personnel for peacekeeping is more than just a funding issue, however. Historically, contingents have been drawn from middle and smaller powers, nonaligned and neutral countries being frequent contributors. As peacekeeping demands increase, however, more military units will be drawn from countries without UN peacekeeping experience. Only the Nordic countries have earmarked and trained personnel specifically for UN service. Proposals have long encouraged others to do likewise. In a 1992 report, the secretary-general called for a standing UN police force to enable the organization to respond quickly to crises with trained contingents.[42] France and the United States indicated that they would begin to train troops for peacekeeping operations.

The Gulf war placed substantial demands on coalition participants (incurring a cost ten times the annual outlay of the entire UN system) and generated pressures on Japan and newly united Germany, as "new" economic powers, to contribute to multilateral peacekeeping and enforcement. In 1992, the governments of both Germany and Japan undertook the necessary legislative and constitutional changes to enable them to contribute personnel to future UN operations.

In June 1992, after repeated delays and heated debate, a bill passed the Japanese Diet stipulating that up to 2,000 Japanese troops can be deployed for limited tasks—transport, medical care, construction, and restoring communications. Participation in such tasks as monitoring cease-fires and removing land mines requires a separate vote of approval. Japanese Prime Minister Kiichi Miyazawa noted, "As our economic strength has increased, so has our responsibility to the world."[43]

Having taken this historic step, the Japanese government committed a team to join the UN operation in Cambodia (UNTAC), with a proviso calling for their return should the cease-fire fail or should any parties not support Japan's participation. Despite the limitations, as one Japanese Foreign Ministry official put it, "The concept is in place."[44]

Germany, likewise in 1992, was moving to pass a constitutional amendment authorizing participation in UN peacekeeping operations. Even without its approval, however, a German field hospital was deployed to

Cambodia, and German helicopters were being flown and maintained by German military personnel supporting UN arms inspection teams. German Foreign Minister Klaus Kinkel noted, "As a reunited and sovereign country we must assume all the rights and obligations of a member of the United Nations to avoid any discrepancy between our verbal commitment to peace and human rights and our active involvement in their defense."[45]

The control and command of peacekeeping operations will be a critical issue the more UN peacekeepers are put in the field and the more expansive the responsibilities undertaken. To coordinate complex operations, such as those in Namibia, Cambodia, Central America, or Western Sahara, and to provide a direct link to the secretary-general, special representatives (of the secretary-general) have been sent to the field. The Gulf war (and proposals from the former Soviet Union) revived interest in the moribund Military Staff Committee. The committee, composed of the chiefs of staff of the five permanent Security Council members, was designed under the UN Charter to be the key to managing UN enforcement actions. It was never activated. With or without its revival, the UN needs a structure to coordinate the military aspects of increased numbers of peacekeeping operations. Other suggestions abound to strengthen the capacity of the UN to mount and support peacekeeping. These include the training of personnel, provision of logistical support and appropriate armaments, and greater use of high technology for surveillance (such as remote-piloted vehicles and satellite monitoring).[46]

Finally, we might ask what types of situations may give rise to new demands for UN peacekeeping in the future and how will the UN respond. It is already clear that the end of the Cold War has not ended regional conflicts. Many analysts of contemporary world politics predict increased violence within societies and between states as a result of the disintegration of the former Soviet Union and communist regimes in Central Europe, as well as a resurgence of ethnocentrism in many parts of the world. The UN in the past has largely averred dealing with issues of self-determination and secession beyond decolonization. It may well face new challenges in this respect. Before leaving office, former Secretary-General Javier Pérez de Cuéllar noted, "In dealing with incipient and existing regional disputes, we will need increasingly to understand the disparate nature of their origins."[47] He further stressed the importance of providing information-gathering tools for the UN to avert, as well as contain, conflicts on more than an ad hoc basis.

The issue is not just whether there will be conflicts and situations where UN peacekeeping could be effective, but whether there will be the political support to respond to such situations. In Spring 1992, Secretary-General Boutros-Ghali criticized Security Council members' preoccupation with events in Yugoslavia and failure to take proportionate interest in Somalia. Much as the end of the Cold War led to fears that international aid resources would be shifted from developing countries to Eastern Europe, there is a danger that conflicts in parts of Africa or elsewhere may be ignored. Furthermore, some states fear that the absence of a counterweight to the United

States, with the collapse of the Soviet Union, may mean that UN action will be equivalent to U.S. action. The Gulf war gave added credence to this fear. Finally, financial limitations and operational restrictions may lead members to curtail their support.

The United Nations will be challenged as never before to respond to diverse threats to international peace and security. Meeting those challenges requires efforts to strengthen preventive diplomacy, as well as the capacity of the organization to support increased numbers of peacekeeping operations performing complex tasks, and ensure the political support for peacemaking.

Notes

1. Charles Malik, *Man in the Struggle for Peace* (New York: Harper and Row, 1963), p. 124.
2. See Margaret P. Karns, "The Dynamics of Interaction between Domestic Politics and International Cooperation: The Role of IGOs as Intermediaries," paper presented at the Annual Meetings of the American Political Science Association, Washington, August 1991, pp. 23–36.
3. For discussion of the veto, see Inis L. Claude, Jr., *Swords into Plowshares,* 4th ed. (New York: Random House, 1984), chap. 8.
4. Some of the standard works that describe and trace the history of UN peacekeeping include: Indar Jit Rikhye, *The Theory and Practice of Peacekeeping* (London: Hurst, 1984); Jit Rikhye, Michael Harbottle, and Bjorn Egge, *The Thin Blue Line: International Peacekeeping and Its Future* (New Haven: Yale University Press, 1974); Larry L. Fabian, *Soldiers without Enemies: Preparing the United Nations for Peacekeeping* (Washington: The Brookings Institution, 1971); Alan James, *Peacekeeping in International Politics* (London: Macmillan, 1990); United Nations, *The Blue Helmets: A Review of United Nations Peacekeeping* (New York: UNDPI, 1990); Sir Brian Urquhart, *A Life in Peace and War* (New York: Harper and Row, 1987); and Henry Wiseman, ed., *Peacekeeping: Appraisals and Proposals* (New York: Pergamon Press, 1983).
5. *The Blue Helmets,* p. 4.
6. International Peace Academy, *Peacekeeper's Handbook* (New York: Pergamon Press, 1984), p. 22.
7. Marrack Goulding, "The Changing Role of the United Nations in Conflict Resolution and Peacekeeping," speech given at the Singapore Institute of Policy Studies, March 13, 1991, p. 9.
8. For a complete listing of contributors to peacekeeping operations, see *The Blue Helmets,* Appendix II, pp. 419–449.
9. Urquhart, *A Life in Peace and War,* p. 198.
10. Thomas G. Weiss and Jarat Chopra, *United Nations Peacekeeping: An ACUNS Teaching Text* (ACUNS, 1992), p. 8.
11. Ibid.
12. Ibid., pp. 47–48. See also Leon Gordenker and Thomas G. Weiss, eds., *Soldiers, Peacekeeping and Disasters* (London: Macmillan, 1991) for discussion of humanitarian relief efforts using soldiers.
13. Ibid.
14. Ibid., p. 23.
15. For a particularly good discussion of this point, see the articles on UN peacekeeping in the special issue of *Survival,* no. 3 (May/June 1990).
16. For a history of UNEF I, see Gabriella E. Rosner, *The United Nations Emergency Force* (New York: Columbia University Press, 1963).
17. For a history of ONUC, see Ernest W. Lefever, *Uncertain Mandate: Politics of the U.N. Congo Operation* (Baltimore: Johns Hopkins University Press, 1967).
18. For some systematic attempts to evaluate success, see Ernst B. Haas, "Regime Decay: Conflict Management and International Organizations, 1945–1981," *International Organization* 37:2 (Spring 1983), pp. 189–256; and Jonathan Wilkenfeld and Michael Brecher,

"International Crises, 1945–1975: The UN Dimension," *International Studies Quarterly* 28:1 (1984), pp. 45–68.

19. Address by the Secretary-General, "From Peace-Keeping to Peace-Building." Delivered at the Ninth Annual David M. Abshire Lecture. Washington, DC (13 May 1992), p. 4.

20. Thomas G. Weiss and Kurt M. Campbell, "The United Nations and Eastern Europe," *World Policy Journal* 7:3 (Summer 1990), p. 577.

21. M. S. Gorbachev, "Secure World," printed in *FBIS-SOV* (17 September 1987), p. 25.

22. On this quiet diplomacy, see *UN Observer,* 10:11 (November 1988), p. 11.

23. The "crisis of multilateralism" is discussed in Margaret P. Karns and Karen A. Mingst, eds., *The United States and Multilateral Institutions: Patterns of Changing Instrumentality and Influence* (Boston: Unwin Hyman, 1990), chapter 11 and in Margaret P. Karns and Karen A. Mingst, "The Past as Prologue: The United States and the Future of the UN System," in Gene M. Lyons, Chadwick R. Alger, and John E. Trent, eds., *The United Nations and the Policies of Member States* (forthcoming). See also Thomas L. Hughes, "The Twilight of Internationalism," *Foreign Policy* 61 (Winter 1985–86), pp. 25–48 and various replies to this article in *Foreign Policy* 65 (Winter 1986–87).

24. In 1985, the U.S. Congress passed the Kassebaum-Solomon amendment (P.L. 99–93) limiting payments of assessed contributions to the UN and its specialized agencies in excess of 20 percent of the total annual budget until the UN adopted changes in voting procedures to make voting proportionate to member state budget contributions.

25. The UN's Group of Eighteen recommended severe cuts in the top levels of UN staff and simplification of organizational procedures. For further discussion of the moderation in U.S. attitudes toward the UN in 1987–88, see Donald A. Puchala and Roger J. Coate, *The State of the United Nations, 1988* (ACUNS, 1988), p. 24.

26. Selig S. Harrison, "Inside the Afghan Talks," *Foreign Policy* 72 (Fall 1988), p. 34.

27. For an analysis of the Contact Group's efforts, see Margaret P. Karns "Ad Hoc Multilateral Diplomacy: The United States, The Contact Group, and Namibia," *International Organization* 41:1 (Winter 1987), pp. 93–123.

28. *The Blue Helmets,* p. 342.

29. Robert Ellsworth, "European Security in a New and Different World," Special Report, The Atlantic Council of the United States, II: 13 (November 5, 1991).

30. See Weiss and Chopra, *United Nations Peacekeeping,* pp. 28–30 for an analysis of the Gulf war.

31. Edward L. Luck and Tobi Trister Gati, "Where Collective Security," *The Washington Quarterly* (Spring 1992), p. 43.

32. Quoted in Robert S. Greenberger, "U.N. Peace Efforts Falter in Cambodia as Key Faction Withholds Cooperation," *Wall Street Journal* (July 13, 1992), p. A11.

33. William Branigin, "A Costly Way to Keep the Peace," *Washington Post National Weekly Edition* (December 7–13, 1992), pp. 9–19.

34. Report of the Secretary-General, (S/23592) 15 February 1992.

35. Weiss and Chopra, *United Nations Peacekeeping,* p. 31.

36. Ibid., p. 32. The discussion on pp. 32–36 regarding legal issues provides an excellent summary of the literature. For discussion of the bases for humanitarian intervention, see Jarat Chopra and Thomas G. Weiss, "Sovereignty Is No Longer Sacrosanct: Codifying Humanitarian Intervention," *Ethics and International Affairs,* vol. 6 (1992), pp. 95–117; and James A. R. Nafziger, "Self-Determination and Humanitarian Intervention in a Community of Power," *Denver Journal of International Law and Policy* 20:1 (Fall 1991), pp. 9–40.

37. Weiss and Chopra, *United Nations Peacekeeping,* p. 40.

38. *Certain Expenses of the United Nations Case, I.C.J. Reports* (1962).

39. Weiss and Chopra, *United Nations Peacekeeping,* p. 43.

40. Address by the Secretary-General, "From Peace-Keeping to Peace-Building," p. 11. Boutros-Ghali discusses various proposals for reform in peacekeeping financing arrangements.

41. UN Document A/44/605, pp. 19–20.

42. Report of the Secretary-General, "The Agenda for Peace" (S/24111) 17 June 1992. One of the interesting proposals in this report called upon members to finance their contributions for peacekeeping from their military budgets rather than foreign ministry budgets. This proposal has been made separately by UN supporters in the United States.

43. T. R. Reid, "Japan Takes a Step Toward Peace Force," *International Herald Tribune* (June 6–7, 1992), p. 1.

44. Quoted in David E. Sanger, "Japan's Parliament Votes to End Ban on Sending Troops Abroad," *The New York Times International* (June 16, 1992), p. 1, A15.

45. Paul Lewis, "Germany Asks Permanent U.N. Council Seat," *New York Times* (September 24, 1992), p. 1.

46. For a discussion of these possibilities, see Johan Jorgen Holst, "Enhancing Peacekeeping Operations," *Survival* 32:3 (May/June 1990), pp. 264–275.

47. United Nations General Assembly, Note by the Secretary-General, "Some Perspectives on the Work of the United Nations in the 1990s," (A/42/512), 2 September 1987, p. 3.

11 / Demilitarizing the Third World

NICOLE BALL

INTRODUCTION

The end of the Cold War and the disintegration of the Soviet Union have swept away the ideological constraints on post–World War II international relations, enabling global security issues to be examined in a more objective light. Previously, the East-West conflict led many policymakers in many countries to justify or tolerate high military budgets, war as a means of resolving disputes, large domestic arms industries, and politically active armed forces. Now, particularly in the wake of the Persian Gulf war, the serious disadvantages for all countries of governmental priorities skewed in favor of military interests (at the expense of the civilian sector) are increasingly evident.[1]

In the developing world, wars and conflicts have been responsible for some 40 million deaths since 1945. The proliferation of weapons of mass destruction, ballistic missiles, and sophisticated conventional weapons has not only given a growing number of countries the possibility of inflicting substantial damage on their opponents, but has also consumed vast sums that are desperately needed to redress social and economic inequities. Billions of dollars have also been devoted to housing, feeding, and compensating unnecessarily large armed forces in the poorest parts of the world, diverting valuable resources from productive development uses.[2]

Although it has long been evident that many Third World governments have accorded significantly greater priority to building up the military than to promoting economic and social development, the international aid and lending community—composed of bilateral donors, such as the United States, and multilateral lenders, such as the World Bank—largely ignored the trade-off between military spending and development during the Cold War period. In fact, the major powers—particularly the United States and (until 1990) the Soviet Union—often provided economic assistance to enable Third World governments to maintain their military budgets at levels that could not have been sustained using domestic resources only.

As the United States and the Soviet Union began to move toward increased cooperation in the late 1980s, the head of the International Monetary Fund (IMF), Michel Camdessus, and his counterpart at the World Bank, Barber Conable, began a discussion within the international lending community about the need for the developing nations to transfer money from their military budgets to development-related activities. In his address to the joint World Bank-International Monetary Fund annual meeting in 1989, Conable argued that, "It is important to place military spending decisions on the same footing as other fiscal decisions . . . and to explore ways to bring military spending into better balance with development priorities."[3]

A willingness on the part of the international lending community to address the issue of military expenditure is long overdue, given the large proportion of their budgets that many developing country governments allocate to their security forces. Indeed, the proportion of world military expenditure accounted for by these governments has grown substantially over the last four decades, from about 6 percent in 1955 to about 15 percent in 1989. At its height in the late 1970s and early 1980s, Third World military expenditure was some 20 percent of the world total.[4]

But the issue is not one of expenditure alone. There are at least two additional factors that need to be considered when determining how heavily militarized a country has become. The first is the degree to which the security forces play an active role in domestic politics, and the second is the extent to which the government pursues military rather than political solutions to both domestic and interstate disputes.

Looking at the first of these criteria, we find that most countries in the Third World can be said to have been highly militarized over the past forty years. Directly or indirectly, security forces have ruled approximately three-quarters of the nations in Africa, Asia, Latin America, and the Middle East since 1945, and the record of such governments in promoting popular participation in the decision-making process is poor. The record on seeking political rather than military solutions to problems is equally poor. Although precise figures are difficult to come by, there have been some 250 wars and conflicts in the Third World since the end of World War II. A portion of these have been exacerbated (if not actually caused) by the involvement of the great powers, particularly the two superpowers; nevertheless, pressures indigenous to the Third World underlie many of these conflicts.

This chapter will examine why so many governments in the Third World have given higher priority to the military sector than to development, and will consider if and how this trend can be reversed. It will begin by describing the major determinants of security expenditures in these countries, and then shift to the developmental implications of a politically active military. The chapter will conclude by discussing how countries in the developing world can take advantage of the new international climate to reorder their priorities, and by suggesting ways in which the international community can assist this process.

THE EXPANSION OF THIRD WORLD SECURITY SECTORS

The share and volume of Third World security expenditures have increased substantially over the last forty-five years, and these outlays have absorbed a significant proportion of the resources of certain states. There are, of course, several reasons for assuming that some natural growth in Third World military spending should have taken place since the end of World War II. First, as a result of the decolonization process, there are now three times as many independent nations in the Third World as there were in 1950. Second, many Third World countries, particularly those that did not have to fight to gain their freedom, had virtually no indigenous armed forces at independence. Hence, even if each newly independent country spent only a minimal amount on its security forces, Third World security sectors would have expanded over this period.

Aside from these historical factors, analysis suggests that the level and composition of security expenditure in a given country should be determined by an assessment of the likely security threats confronting the country and the most effective means of meeting these threats given the resources available to the government. In reality, however, other factors *unrelated to the security environment* often affect the allocation of resources to the security sector. These include domestic bureaucratic and budgetary factors, the political influence of the security forces themselves, and the role of the major powers.

External and Internal Conflict

In the industrial nations, armed forces exist primarily to protect against external aggression. Military spending and arms procurement are also closely linked to external conflicts in the developing world, and external security considerations are most often used to justify increases in security expenditure. The Third World countries with the largest defense establishments and the biggest military budgets tend to be those that are involved in conflicts with neighboring states. Until the breakup of Yugoslavia, virtually all of the interstate wars since 1945 had taken place in the developing world, although there were great power participants in a number of these conflicts. In 1989 (the last year for which data are available), major Third World spenders, such as Israel, Jordan, Libya, North Korea, Pakistan, Saudi Arabia, and Syria, devoted between 6.8 and 20 percent of their gross national product (GNP) to the military sector.[5]

The end of the Cold War, while certainly tending to reduce the intensity of some Third World disputes (for example, that between the two Koreas), has not moderated all such rivalries. China, for example, sought to underline its dominant position in Southeast Asia in 1992 by signing an agreement with a U.S. company to explore for oil in the waters surrounding the Spratly Islands in the South China Sea, thus sparking concern in neighboring countries, particularly Brunei, Malaysia, the Philippines, Taiwan, and Vietnam (all of which have laid claim to portions of the Spratlys).[6] Troubled by the withdrawal of U.S. and Soviet (now Russian) forces from the region, and worried about the growing military might of China and Japan, many states of the Pacific Rim have significantly increased their military spending in the past few years.

Although some developing countries do have genuine reasons for being concerned about the activities of their neighbors, the vast majority face few, if any, serious threats from abroad. Nevertheless, many of them allocate considerable resources to the security sector. Even those countries for which external threats have significantly diminished continue to allocate substantial sums to security forces. In Egypt, for instance, the armed forces continue to absorb about 22 percent of central government expenditure—approximately the same amount that was devoted to defense prior to the signing of the peace agreement with Israel in 1979.[7]

In many countries, the persistence of high levels of military spending reflects the fact that, when all is said and done, the principal task of the armed forces is to guarantee internal security. Actually, "internal security" is something of a misnomer, since the objective of such activity is rarely to make all citizens of a country equally secure. Rather, military support is frequently intended to enable a small group of elites—often including members of the military—to maintain power and enrich themselves at the expense of the vast majority of the population. In these cases, it is more accurate to speak of "regime security" or "elite security" than of "internal security." Under these conditions, conflicts among the different elites as they vie for power and privilege, and between the ruling elite and groups suffering from discrimination and/or repression, are inevitable.

When governments decline to seek political solutions to such conflicts, they require the assistance of the armed forces and/or paramilitary groups to maintain some semblance of order and to remain in power. For over thirty years, military-dominated governments in Burma have been fighting non-Burmese ethnic groups—the Shan, Karen, and Kachin—who oppose absorption into a political unit dominated by ethnic Burmese. The overwhelming disregard on the part of the Israeli government for the economic and political rights of Palestinians in the Occupied Territories gave rise in 1987 to the *intifada*—a popular revolt employing minimal force that has been answered by military force and significant Israeli violations of human rights. By seeking military solutions to political disputes such as these, governments both ensure that a substantial proportion of their budgets are allocated to the security sector and make it more likely that the armed forces will play a central role in the process of government itself.

It is not clear that the conditions that give rise to internal security problems have worsened in recent years. There are some analysts who look at the situation in places such as Israel, Kashmir, and Sri Lanka, and argue that ethnic and religious disputes are intensifying. In many cases, however, a diminished preoccupation with the East-West conflict has brought local conflicts and the domestic role of the armed forces into sharper relief. Most of the ethnic conflicts now under way in the Third World have been with us for twenty, thirty, or forty years, flaring up from time to time but never dying out because their root causes have never been addressed.

Domestic Bureaucratic and Budgetary Factors

The outer limits of all public expenditure are ultimately determined by the availability of resources. It is not only the existence of a series of unresolved regional and domestic conflicts that has caused countries in the Middle East and North Africa to lead the annual list of major Third World arms importers. The oil price increases of 1973–74 and 1979 greatly enriched the oil producers of the Middle East, enabling them to equip their forces with sizable amounts of sophisticated weaponry and to seek military solutions to outstanding conflicts.

Similarly, a lack of resources has not infrequently forced governments to reduce the size of their security forces or to reduce outlays on the security sector. Resources can become constrained for a variety of reasons. For developing countries during the 1980s, two of the more important constraints were a decline in the value of their major exports, leading to a reduction in export earnings, and ever-increasing debt burdens, brought on in part by indiscriminate lending during the 1970s. For example, the vastly increased revenues generated by income from oil enabled Nigerian governments to avoid demobilizing large portions of the armed forces after the war with Biafra, and to reverse a decline in the share of the federal budget allocated to military purposes in the mid-1970s; however, a glut in the international oil market and the effects of overambitious and ill-conceived development plans contributed to a decline in the size of the Nigerian armed forces and the defense budget in the late 1970s and early 1980s.

Once the broad parameters of resource availability are set, there is a tendency for inertia to set in. Macroeconomic surveys have found that two-thirds or more of the variance in security expenditure for any given year can be explained by the level of security expenditure in the previous year. This appears to be particularly true for operating (day-to-day) expenditure.[8] Intuitively, a close relationship between prior and current expenditure levels makes sense, because large portions of Third World security budgets are composed of operating costs. These will grow incrementally through pay or pension increases, or through normal price rises for such items as fuel, food, electricity, and office supplies. Barring rapid changes in the size of the security establishment, a large portion of a government's security budget will be predetermined by the need to keep troops paid, fed, clothed, and housed.

Despite this, the growth of security expenditure does not always occur in an orderly fashion. When military budgets jump appreciably from one year to the next, the reason is frequently bureaucratic-type expenditure requirements: inflation, larger than average salary and pension rises, equipment replacement, and so on. In Liberia in the early 1980s, following the overthrow of the Tolbert government and the imposition of military rule, the

Liberian armed forces awarded themselves substantial increases in pay, doubling military salaries. Since over half the Liberian security budget was allocated to salaries and wages, these increases were largely responsible for the two-fold rise of security spending—both as a share of GNP and as a share of the national budget—that occurred between 1980 and 1981.[9]

In many countries, the institutional objectives of the military establishment are frequently the single most important factor in determining security expenditure. In organizational terms, the security forces are concerned to maintain their share of government allocations, to ensure that their members—or at least the officer corps—are compensated as well as other comparable societal groups (such as civil servants and managers in the private sector), and to create as well-equipped a force as possible. The regular armed forces also seek to avoid being at a disadvantage in terms of pay and equipment to paramilitary security forces, and the different services within the regular forces may compete with one another for budgetary allocations; this often drives up total military outlays and the amount spent on imported weaponry.

As individuals, military officers seek to enhance their own status and wealth. This can be accomplished by ensuring that budgeted salaries are high, and that liberal health and education benefits are provided to their families. The personal status and wealth of military officers can also be enhanced by accepting rake-offs from overseas arms purchases, or by being in a position to funnel other kinds of military procurement and construction contracts to firms with which the officer in question (or a member of his family) has close ties. Often, corruption is the glue that holds together military-dominated governments, or the payoff that prevents challenges to the prevailing order by keeping officers busy lining their own pockets rather than plotting the overthrow of their superiors. There are few countries in the Third World where military corruption is not a problem, but it has reached major proportions in countries such as Indonesia and Thailand.[10]

The Role of External Powers

The participation of external powers in regional Third World conflicts is another factor that tends to result in high levels of military spending. During the Cold War, external powers often played an important role in the creation and exacerbation of conflict in the Third World: as colonial powers, as interventionary forces, as promoters of coups d'état, as providers of military assistance, and as arms sellers. Most frequently, it was the two superpowers and their allies that played this role, but governments of developing countries became increasingly active during the 1970s and 1980s. The post-1973 oil price increases were important factors in enabling countries such as Algeria, Iran, Iraq, Kuwait, Libya, Saudi Arabia, and the United Arab Emirates to send expeditionary forces to other Third World countries or to help friendly governments purchase sophisticated weapons. Cuba, India, Israel,

North Korea, Pakistan, and South Africa have also intervened in the affairs of other Third World countries.[11]

Indochina provides a tragic example of how a region can be transformed by external intervention, and how historic animosities can be given a new and deadly lease on life as a result. Enormous amounts of every imaginable kind of military and economic assistance were provided to the combatants in Vietnam, Laos, and Cambodia by their major power patrons between 1945 and 1975. The government in South Vietnam was essentially a creation of the United States, and U.S. economic and military assistance was essential to the survival of Ngo Dinh Diem and his successors. Eventually, U.S. troops were needed to keep the Saigon regime in power. Some 55,000 Americans died in this effort, and millions of Vietnamese, from both North and South, were killed, wounded, or lost in action.[12]

But peace did not return to Indochina in April 1975 when North Vietnamese troops entered Saigon (now Ho Chi Minh City) and the Khmer Rouge forces led by Pol Pot drove the Lon Nol government from Phnom Penh. New fighting broke out almost immediately as the new governments in Cambodia and South Vietnam contested border areas and offshore islands, and, by 1977, this conflict had escalated significantly. In addition, between 1975 and 1978, the Khmer Rouge government forcibly moved a large portion of the Cambodian population from the cities, where they had sought shelter from U.S. bombing during the Vietnam war, to rural areas, and killed anyone perceived to be an opponent of the regime. As a result, an estimated 1.5 million Cambodian civilians died during this period.

In December 1978, the Vietnamese government announced the creation of a new organization to liberate Cambodia and launched a full-scale invasion of the country. By the end of 1979, a pro-Vietnamese government had been installed in Phnom Penh, and some 200,000 Vietnamese troops occupied Cambodia for a decade. The withdrawal of Vietnamese troops, however, did not bring peace to Cambodia, as various domestic factions continued to vie for power. A peace agreement, known as the Comprehensive Settlement, was finally signed in Paris on October 23, 1991, by the Cambodian Supreme National Council (representing the four domestic parties) and the foreign ministers of eighteen countries. The United Nations was given the responsibility for disarming the various combatant groups and running the government during a transitional period; nonetheless, the timetable specified in the accords—and perhaps even the agreement itself—has been seriously compromised, as the Khmer Rouge have failed to demobilize their troops, hand over weapons, and completely end military operations.[13]

Unresolved regional conflicts, which frequently invite the intervention of external powers, have been a major factor in the increase in Third World military expenditures over the past forty years. However, for most of the countries of the Third World, the importance of external conflicts has been relatively minor. Instead, the imperatives of internal or regime security, bureaucratic factors such as budgetary inertia and the political role of the armed forces have contributed substantially to the growth in resources allocated to the security sector in the developing world.

THE MILITARY IN POLITICS

The security forces have played an important role in the political systems of a very large number of countries in Asia, Africa, the Middle East, and Latin America during the post–World War II period. It is not, however, only in this period that the armed forces in these regions have participated in politics. Military governments and rule by *caudillos* (military leaders who set themselves up as dictators) have been a central aspect of Latin American politics since the first South and Central American countries attained their independence in the early nineteenth century. The first military coup in Thailand, which established a pattern of government that endures to this day, occurred in 1932.

Despite this history of military involvement in politics in the Third World, the degree to which Third World security forces assumed a political role during the Cold War may seem surprising, given the stress that was placed by the United Nations and Western governments on decolonization and democratization. In reality, the major Western powers were more interested in the rhetoric of democracy and independence than in ensuring that functioning democracies were established.

As might be expected, Cold War considerations were largely responsible for this lack of commitment to democratic rule. In the late 1950s and during the 1960s, American social scientists and policymakers who sought to prevent the spread of communism in the Third World often argued that strong leadership and good organization were the keystone of both successful government and rapid modernization in Third World countries—attributes that they believed could be found in the leadership provided by the security forces. Nationalist (often left-wing) politicians who had inherited power from the departing colonial states were viewed by these analysts as "too weak" to withstand pressure from communist groups, which were invariably characterized as well-organized and highly purposeful. Eventually, civilian leaders might learn to "manage" the democratic process—that is, to control dissent and limit participation—but, in the interim, strong governments were needed to prevent communist groups from stepping into the "power vacuum" created by ineffective nationalist governments.[14] On this basis, the United States provided substantial military and economic assistance to right-wing military (or military-dominated) regimes in the 1950s, 1960s, and 1970s.

Interestingly, the Soviet Union also found ideological justifications for supporting Third World military governments during the Cold War. Prior to the mid-1960s, the official Soviet view had been that the armed forces in Third World countries were subordinate to, and always reflected the political orientation of, the ruling group, irrespective of whether that group were "bourgeois" or "socialist." However, following the 1966 ouster of the "socialist" Ghanaian leader Kwame Nkrumah by "reactionary" military officers, the Soviet line underwent a radical change. Third World armed forces began to be described as "the best-organized force in public life." Once military officers with a more progressive orientation began to take power in the Third World in the late 1960s and early 1970s, writers expressing the official Soviet line ceased to speak of creating (civilian) vanguard parties and started to discuss the benefits of military rule more openly.[15]

This assessment of the security forces as a central actor in domestic unity, economic development, and internal security of Third World countries strengthened the arguments of policymakers of both West and East who sought to channel more funds to the armed forces in the developing world. It was often argued, moreover, that such aid was beneficial economically and politically for the recipient. However, these predictions have, for the most part, not been borne out by reality.

Even relatively early on, in the mid-1960s, there were analysts who questioned whether the security forces were really models of efficiency, leadership, and moral authority.[16.] That such analyses appear to have been ignored by most U.S. administrations during the Cold War period makes them no less pertinent. Indeed, given the number of developing nations that have been ruled by military regimes during the last four decades, it is important to understand the strengths and weaknesses of military officers as formulators and implementers of policy. Discipline and organizational capacity should never be confused with the ability to direct the development process; although military officers may be able to run their own affairs efficiently—or so it is usually assumed—that is no guarantee that they can formulate and coordinate broader government policies quite so successfully.

One important shortcoming of military officers is that they frequently lack the bargaining skills necessary to reach the political compromises essential to governing complex, pluralistic societies. Thus, when South Korean officers were surveyed in the early 1980s, they scored well in terms of honor, justice, responsibility, and anticommunism, but they scored less well on management capability, flexibility, and adaptability.[17] Whatever its ideological pretentions, no military can govern entirely on its own—if for no other reason than that it lacks sufficient trained manpower to staff all bureaucratic posts—and an alliance between military officers, bureaucrats, and technical advisers is, of necessity, created when the military rules. Lacking the skills needed to communicate and work with civilian groups, military leaders have often found that they could not govern effectively.

It is important to view politics in the Third World as the interaction of elite groups, and to examine the political role of the security forces within this context. It has often been suggested that Third World armed forces act as the defender of upper-class interests (and, by definition, of the capitalist system). Various attempts have been made to link such behavior to the class background of military officers, but such attempts have not been very successful—in part because class background is but one factor influencing the behavior of members of the armed forces. In many Third World countries, the armed forces *do* frequently support civilians in their attempts to exclude the mass of the population from the political and economic decision-making process. One reason for this exclusionary stance is that military elites fear that increased participation by the poor would lead to alterations in existing political and economic structures that would be inimical to their own institutional interests.

It is important to recognize, however, that Third World elites seek not only to guard against the dissolution of a political and economic system that has enabled them to amass considerable personal wealth and power; they also seek to maintain their preeminent position within that system. There are upper-class (capitalist) elites, socialist elites, feudalist elites, and semi-feudalist elites. Each of these elite groups can be divided according to occupational differences, ethnic divisions, generational gaps, regional divisions, racial differences, and hierarchical disputes. These subgroups, in turn, often pursue policies that are disadvantageous to members of the same class—witness the disorder in Somalia since the fall of Siad Barre in 1991. There are many instances of civilians seeking military support in order to exclude other political and economic elites from positions of power, even when the groups involved all share similar class backgrounds and operate within essentially the same economic framework.

In a country such as Thailand, where cliques are the basic building blocks of all political activity, different military groups ally with different civilian groups, and each major coalition attempts to gain as much power and wealth as possible for itself—but all of this occurs within the same economic system. Since 1932, Thailand has experienced at least six successful coups d'états, many unsuccessful ones, and several elections of varying degrees of fairness. Yet none of this has produced any serious alteration in the composition of the Thai elite.[18]

In assessing the political role played by security forces, it is useful to ask who the security forces are protecting, and from whom these individuals and groups are being protected. The security forces are frequently given—or claim for themselves—the responsibility for preserving internal security in a society torn by conflicts arising from a diverse set of societal ills, including poverty and inequality, ethnic and religious differences, leftist insurgencies, and drug cartels. In combating these problems, however, the security forces generally do not seek to make all citizens equally secure, but rather to protect the interests of particular groups or elites. Indeed, military-devised security policies often exacerbate these conflicts, producing yet greater instability.[19]

Because governments in the developing world have tended to represent the interests of a very small segment of the population of a country, regimes may not be very stable, leading to a situation in which governments replace each other with great regularity. An extreme example is Bolivia, which has had seventy-seven governments since it became independent in 1824.[20] Even with a lower rate of government turnover, it is difficult to formulate and implement policies that will promote economic and political development. The losers in such situations have invariably been the poor and the powerless.

THE ECONOMIC IMPACT OF SECURITY FORCES

The development of political systems responsive to the needs of pluralistic societies has been a low priority for virtually all Third World governments, whether aligned with the East or the West. Rather, as we have seen, elite groups have vied with one another for control over the government, and support from the security apparatus—or portions of it—has often been instrumental in winning and maintaining power in the developing world. Not only has this process stunted the development of democratic institutions, but it has also helped to prevent the development of economic systems capable of a rational and equitable allocation of resources in many parts of the Third World. Even in an era of privatization, the proportion of national resources controlled by developing country governments can be substantial. By being in a position to determine or strongly influence the allocation of state resources, security forces can influence the way in which the economy develops as a whole.

The most direct route by which the security forces can influence economic development is through the security budget itself. In common with other forms of pubic expenditure, outlays in the security sector can both promote and hinder economic growth. Military outlays will tend to encourage economic growth if resources that were previously idle are employed for this purpose, or if the balance between resources consumed and resources invested is altered in favor of investment. To the extent that expenditure in the security sector contributes to inflation, reduces the rate of saving, causes the misallocation of resources, or increases a country's debt, it will hinder economic growth.

It is difficult to generalize about the relative weight that should be accorded these effects, because the situation varies both among countries and within individual countries over time. For example, while security expenditure might increase aggregate economic demand, the benefits are most likely to be felt where excess capacity exists. Increased demand from the security sector may not, however, enable that excess capacity to be employed since output may be restricted by factors unrelated to the level of demand, such as a lack of foreign exchange to purchase production inputs from abroad.

Similarly, the size of a country's security budget and the level of its military-related imports are not a sufficient guide, in and of themselves, to the magnitude of its military-related debt. Some countries, such as Saudi

Arabia, spend a considerable share of their national budget in the security sector and import a large quantity of weapons and related equipment, but have adequate supplies of foreign exchange to finance these purchases without significant borrowing. Others, such as India, have bartered domestically produced goods for weapons and arms-production technology, substantially reducing their outlays of foreign exchange. Still others, such as Israel and Cuba, have received large portions of their military-related procurement free-of-charge from their major power patrons, the United States and the Soviet Union.[21] To understand the effects of security expenditure on the economies of Third World countries thus requires considerable knowledge of each country's economy and the composition of its security expenditure.[22]

It is not sufficient to argue that an increase in investment in military industries will promote economic growth, as argued by some. Merely investing in the military-industrial sector does not guarantee that a viable arms industry will be created. Countries without a strong, integrated industrial base already in existence will not succeed in creating a viable arms industry of any size.[23] Many governments, for example that of the Shah of Iran during the 1970s, have misunderstood or ignored this necessary progression. They believed that by importing arms-production technology from the industrial countries they could jump start the modernization of their economies. But in Iran, as often occurs under these circumstances, the nascent military-industrial sector was poorly integrated into the economy, and almost all inputs for the new defense industries had to be imported. Not only did this reduce backward linkages ("spin-offs") to the civilian economy, but it also increased the foreign exchange costs of domestic production substantially.[24] The true beneficiaries of Iran's military industrialization program were foreign arms corporations.

Another avenue by which security forces affect developing economies is by influencing the allocation of national resources outside the security sector. In Chile, following the military coup that toppled the Allende government, public investment was cut back sharply, as responsibility for investment was shifted to the private sector. Outlays in the public housing and health sectors fell dramatically during the mid- to late 1970s, while expenditure in the security sector rose substantially.[25]

While armed forces in the developing world have exercised the most direct influence over budgetary allocations outside the security sector when they control the government, their influence can extend beyond the security sector, even when the government is nominally under civilian control. Hence, the promotion of domestic military industries increases the likelihood that the industrial sector will receive substantial outlays from the government, often at the expense of the agricultural sector. Such efforts also increase the likelihood that capital-intensive rather than labor-intensive industrial techniques will be promoted, doing little to generate employment in countries with high levels of unemployment and underemployment.

Finally, security forces in the developing world have participated directly in the economy, often buying and running major businesses. In many cases, they have assumed this economic role in order to find nongovernmental sources of revenue for the security budget. But the patronage and privileges that such a system provides to members of the armed forces has clear political attractions as well.

The Indonesian armed forces used its martial law powers to place Dutch enterprises under military control in late 1957. When these firms were subsequently nationalized, the armed forces continued to be involved in their management. In addition, the armed forces began to establish their own companies, often as joint ventures with Chinese businessmen. By the late 1970s, the Indonesian armed forces were at the center of an extensive network of private firms engaged in activities as diverse as oil production, shipping, forestry, fishing, tourism, banking, and air transport.[26] The income generated by these military-run enterprises has enabled the Suharto government to keep budgetary outlays for the armed forces at perhaps 50 percent of actual military expenditures. Bringing the income of these companies into the public coffers would be economically advantageous for Indonesia, but would undoubtedly prove to be politically counterproductive and thus is not likely to occur.

There are many reasons why a large proportion of Third World economies function poorly. The allocation of resources to the security sector and the misuse of resources by the military forces is often one of these reasons, but it may not be the only or the most important reason. Based on the history of the last forty years, however, it is fair to state that the countries that allocate a large share of their national resources to the security sector, and that allow the security forces to become actively involved in the economy, are less likely to wind up with economies that provide the entire population with the basic requirements of food, shelter, clothing, and social services.

THE CHALLENGE OF THE 1990s

The early and mid-1990s clearly constitutes an historical turning point. The potential for restructuring political relations within and among countries is greater than at any time since the end of World War II. Democratization, conflict resolution, nonaggression, collective security, and compromise have begun to replace authoritarianism, war, military alliances, unilateral intervention, and confrontation as internationally accepted modes of behavior. The challenge before us is whether we can—individually and collectively, industrial and developing countries alike—grasp the opportunity before us.

For the Third World, a number of the trends that emerged during the transition years 1989 to 1991 could, if continued into the later 1990s and beyond, contribute to a slowdown of militarization and provide the basis upon which to build sustainable economic and political development. First, the Third World's share of global military expenditure, which had exceeded 20 percent in the late 1970s and early 1980s, dropped to 14.5 percent in 1989 (the last year for which data are available). Second, in certain regions—especially South America—the number of governments directly controlled by the military declined significantly during the 1980s. Third, the process of democratization in Eastern Europe found echoes in countries as diverse as Malawi, Nigeria, Thailand, Zaire, and Zambia. Finally, a process of conflict resolution was inaugurated by the major powers in the late 1980s to resolve the conflicts in Afghanistan, Angola, Cambodia, El Salvador, and Namibia.

Clearly, fewer regional conflicts, fewer military governments, greater popular participation, and lower security budgets would mean fewer heavily militarized states. The chances that conflicts would be resolved peacefully by political means would be increased. The likelihood that the external powers would be drawn into regional conflicts would decline, thereby promoting not only local and regional stability but also a reduction of tensions at the international level. Under these conditions, the opportunities for economic and political development would expand.

But will this really happen? Will these trends be sustained throughout the 1990s, and form the basis for domestic and international relations in the twenty-first century? Or will "business as usual" continue to characterize North-South and South-South relations?

It is, unfortunately, extremely difficult to foresee the direction governments will take in these areas. The number of military governments in the developing world has waxed and waned throughout the postwar period. In Latin America, only four countries—Guyana, Mexico, Costa Rica, and Belize—have not been ruled directly by the armed forces at some point since 1945. In 1954, twelve of the twenty countries in the region were under direct military rule; by mid-1961, only one country had a military government. But seven coups occurred between 1962 and 1964, and, by 1975, the military again ruled in twelve countries. Ten years later, that number had fallen to three. The historical record, therefore, argues in favor of caution when evaluating how long political disengagement by Third World militaries will last. (See Chapter 3.)

The decline in the developing world's share of global military expenditure reflects the difficult economic conditions that Third World governments have faced during the mid- to late 1980s. Were economic conditions to improve in the 1990s, some Third World governments would undoubtedly choose to spend a larger share of their resources in the security sector. What is more, not all Third World regions experienced a decline in military spending during the 1980s: in South Asia, one of the poorest areas on the globe, military expenditure grew by nearly 65 percent between 1980 and 1989 (in constant U.S. dollars); it also rose by about 15 percent in Latin America and by 10 percent in East Asia.[27]

International efforts to settle regional conflicts peacefully have also not proceeded altogether smoothly. Despite the withdrawal of U.S. and Soviet assistance to the warring parties in Afghanistan, the conflict has continued into 1993 as different Muslim fundamentalist groups vie for power. And, as described earlier, the unwillingness of the Khmer Rouge to disarm may be placing the Cambodian peace accords in jeopardy. Apart from these specific regional conflicts, the possibility also exists that the larger powers in the Third World will increasingly seek to play a dominant role in their regions as the United States and Russia devote more and more attention to their own pressing domestic problems. If the emerging powers choose to assert their will militarily, increased interstate conflict could result.

The fragility of Third World political systems and the concentration of political and economic power in the hands of relatively few individuals have frequently created situations in which governments have had to rely on the armed forces to remain in power. One means of gaining or rewarding this support has been by purchasing sophisticated weapons and keeping the troops, particularly the officer corps, well paid. Many authoritarian governments also spend large sums on police and paramilitary gear for use by the security forces in quelling dissent. Thus, significant and enduring cuts in military budgets require the resolution of both external and internal conflicts.

Current efforts in the developing world to move toward multiparty political systems and to increase popular participation in the political process reflect the need to develop institutions capable of mediating between the competing needs of different societal groups domestically. The greater the domestic political power of the armed forces, the harder it will be to establish such institutions and to have compromise and cooperation replace confrontation as the cornerstone of domestic and regional relations. Civilian control over the armed forces is a crucial component of participatory government, and leaders in newly democratizing countries are acutely aware of the need to transform civil-military relations.

Although it is ultimately from within the developing world that changes in domestic and regional relations must emerge, the industrial countries and the multilateral community have an important supporting role to play. They, too, must take a hard look at their priorities and devise policies that will promote reduced tensions and increased development at all levels.

The post–Cold War international climate offers a significant opportunity to develop norms limiting the kinds of weapons governments can procure, to breathe new life into older norms enshrined in the United Nations Charter—particularly nonintervention and nonaggression—and to define an appropriate balance between military and nonmilitary expenditures. These norms must be applied to all countries. The greater the disparity between the actions that the industrial countries take and the behavior they expect from developing countries, the more difficult it will be to convince the developing countries to change their policies.

Many Third World governments feel strongly that it is impossible to apply one set of politico-military doctrines to the Third World and another to the industrial world. They argue that if industrial countries require certain categories of weapons (for example, ballistic missiles) to ensure their defense, the same weapons should be at the disposal of governments in the developing world. Arms-control agreements must, therefore, require the same behavior from all signatories. The preferred model should be the recently concluded Chemical Weapons Convention (CWC)—under which *all* adherents will destroy existing stocks of weapons—rather than the Nuclear Nonproliferation Treaty (NPT)—which created two categories of states, those that already had nuclear weapons and were allowed to retain them, and those that did not possess nuclear weapons and promised never to produce them.

Similarly, military budgets should be reduced in all countries allocating more than a modest share, say 10 percent, of their central government expenditure to the security sector. Peacemaking, peacekeeping, and conflict resolution are critical activities that must involve the entire international community. When military intervention is necessary, as it undoubtedly will be from time to time, it should be multilateral, not unilateral, in nature. Simply stated, urging military reform on the developing countries gains legitimacy when combined with military reform in the industrial countries.

The international lending community must work with the developing countries to convince them of the need to reorder military priorities and then to reward their steps toward change. Since 1989, when IMF managing director Michel Camdessus and then-World Bank president Barber Conable first broached the issue of excessive military spending, the members of the international lending community have been engaged in a debate on how best to integrate military issues into the development dialogue.

Considerable attention has been given, particularly in the public debate, to a single tool: "conditionality," or the provision of an economic benefit (such as a loan) only when its potential recipient agrees to undertake or abstain from specific actions (e.g., by reducing its military outlays). There is, however, a much wider variety of strategies that lenders can adopt to press for changes. Many of these approaches are less confrontational than conditionality and therefore may have a better chance of producing reform in certain situations.[28]

• *Persuasion*, through both public statements and private policy dialogue, has played a central role in recent efforts to introduce military policies and expenditures into the debates on development strategy. Policy dialogue can also be useful in helping to create a sense of ownership for the reform process within borrowing countries. Finally, it is a precondition for exerting pressure, since it is counterproductive under normal conditions to reduce aid without giving fair warning.

• *External support* can facilitate efforts by borrowers to implement reform. Financial assistance can help governments absorb extra costs associated with reform. Thus, many of the major lenders have helped to finance the reintegration of demobilized soldiers into the civilian economy in such countries as Angola, El Salvador, Nicaragua, and Uganda. Technical assistance can provide skilled manpower or equipment to carry out specific tasks required by reform.

• *Conflict resolution and mediation* may be required to create the necessary political conditions for significant reductions in military budgets in countries facing significant security threats. The major powers, which have participated either directly or indirectly in many external and internal conflicts in the developing world, have a special role to play in bringing their clients to the negotiating table and in fostering compromise. More use must be made of international and regional organizations in finding solutions to conflicts that protect the vital interests of the participants and at the same time promote stability and development.

• Finally, *pressure* can be exerted with or without conditions. By setting expenditure and performance targets in nonmilitary sectors, such as health, education, and deficit reduction, the World Bank and the International Monetary Fund are attempting to influence the level of military expenditure indirectly. Lenders are also experimenting with offering "carrots" instead of "sticks." The Japanese government, for example, plans to reward countries for "good behavior" in the military sector (for example, through reduced military spending and arms purchases) by increasing their aid—an approach it terms "positive linkage," in contrast to the "negative linkage" of conditionality.

In the final analysis, military reform in developing countries will occur only if governments and citizens in those countries accept the need for change. They must take a hard look at their priorities and devise polices that will promote reduced tensions and increase development. This will require compromises to be struck, both domestically and among states. The industrial countries can underline their commitment to the emerging norms by making them the cornerstone of their own policies. They can also help to instill new modes of behavior by conditioning relations with other countries on adherence to these norms. But it is ultimately the people and governments of developing countries who must seize the opportunities presented by recent changes in the international system to create a more equitable and prosperous future for themselves.

Notes

1. This chapter draws on a number of earlier works by the author, including *Security and Economy in the Third World* (Princeton, NJ: Princeton University Press, 1988); "The Military in Politics: Who Benefits and How," *World Development*, Vol. 9, no. 6 (1981), pp. 569–582; and *Pressing for Peace: Can Aid Induce Reform?*, Policy Essay no. 6 (Washington: Overseas Development Council, 1992).

2. See, for example, Robert S. McNamara, "The Post–Cold War World: Implications for Military Expenditures in the Developing Countries," in *Proceedings of the World Bank Annual Conference on Development Economics, 1991,* Supplement to the *World Bank Economic Review* and the *World Bank Research Observer* (Washington: The World Bank, March 1992), pp. 95–125.

3. Quoted in Hobart Rowen, "Conable Warns Poor Nations on Arms," *The Washington Post,* September 27, 1989. Lewis Preston, who took over the World Bank presidency from

Conable in September 1991, has continued in his predecessor's footsteps. See, for example, Paul Blustein, "World Bank, IMF to Press Defense Cuts: Institutions Hint at Withholding Loans," *The Washington Post,* October 19, 1991.

4. The data for 1955 were taken from the annual *Yearbook* of the Stockholm International Peace Research Institute (SIPRI); the data for 1989 are taken from U.S. Arms Control and Disarmament Agency (ACDA), *World Military Expenditures and Arms Transfers, 1990* (Washington: U.S. Government Printing Office, 1991). The ACDA figures, by and large, omit expenditure on police and paramilitary forces, while SIPRI makes an effort to include them. Although it is not advisable to mix sources, since definitions of military expenditure vary (as the issue of expenditure on police and paramilitary forces indicates), there are no ACDA figures available for the 1950s and SIPRI data for the late 1980s are incomplete.

A relatively few countries have accounted for a large share of Third World military expenditure. Until quite recently, China was consistently responsible for between one-quarter and one-half of all Third World military expenditure. After 1975 or so, the Middle East contributed another one-third, while East Asian countries have been responsible for another 10 to 15 percent during the 1980s. Within these regions, a number of countries can be singled out as major spenders; for example, North and South Korea in East Asia, or Peru and Argentina in South America.

5. ACDA, *World Military Expenditures, 1990,* p. 39.

6. See: Victor Mallet, "Spratly Spat Moves into Murkier Water," *Financial Times* (London), July 28, 1992.

7. ACDA, *World Military Expenditures, 1990,* p. 61.

8. See Barry Ames and Ed Goff, "Education and Defense Expenditures in Latin America: 1948–1958," in Craig Liske, William Loehr, and John McCamant, eds., *Comparative Public Policy: Issues, Theories and Methods,* (New York: Halstead Press/John Wiley, 1975), pp. 181–184; and Philippe C. Schmitter, "Foreign Military Assistance, National Military Spending and Military Rule in Latin America," in Philippe C. Schmitter, ed., *Military Rule in Latin America: Function, Consequences and Perspectives* (Beverly Hills, CA: Sage, 1983), pp. 159–163.

9. See Mark Webster, "Liberia Pays the Price for Change," *Financial Times* (London), 30 May 1980; "Les nouveaux dirigeants n'ont pas reussi a emporter l'adhesion de la population," *Le Monde* (Paris), September 4, 1980; and ACDA, *World Military Expenditures and Arms Transfers, 1985* (Washington: U.S. Government Printing Office, 1985), p. 71.

10. See, for example, Victor Mallet, "Thai Election Raises the Price of Corruption," *Financial Times* (London), March 11, 1992; Paul Handley, "Veterans on Parade," *Far Eastern Economic Review,* March 21, 1991, pp. 50–51; Steven Erlanger, "In Thailand's Coup, A Familiar Regional Variation on Democracy," *The New York Times,* March 3, 1991; M. R. Sukhumbhand Paribatra, "Troubled Waters," *Far Eastern Economic Review,* December 6, 1990, pp. 18–19; Henry Bienen and David Morell, "Transition from Military Rule: Thailand's Experience," in Catherine M. Kelleher, ed., *Political-Military Systems: Comparative Perspectives* (Beverly Hills, CA: Sage, 1978); J. Stephen Hoadley, "Thailand: Kings, Coups and Cliques," pp. 9–24, in J. Stephen Hoadley, ed., *The Military in the Politics of Southeast Asia: A Comparative Perspective* (Cambridge, MA: Schenkman, 1985); Harold Crouch, "Generals and Business in Indonesia," *Pacific Affairs,* Vol. 48 (Winter 1975–1976), pp. 519–520; and David Jenkins, "The Military in Business," *Far Eastern Economic Review,* January 13, 1978, p. 24.

11. The Indian government for many years had supplied Tamil rebels with weapons to use in their fight against the Sri Lankan government. In July 1987, the late Rajiv Gandhi's government sent some 45,000 troops to Sri Lanka to attempt to disarm the Tamil separatists after having forced the government in Colombo to sign an agreement "requesting" this intervention. Cuba's extraterritorial involvements were, of necessity, financed by the Soviet Union, but Cuban officials insisted that they in no way contradicted Cuban foreign policy goals. The Pakistanis have been primarily interested in earning foreign exchange, and Pakistani forces have been involved in the Middle East and Libya.

For a survey of postwar intervention, see Milton Leitenberg, "The Impact of the Worldwide Confrontation of the Great Powers: Aspects of Military Intervention and the Projection of Military Power," in G. Fischer, ed., *Armaments-Development-Human Rights-Disarmament* Brussels: Etablissement Bruylant, 1985).

12. There are numerous accounts of the conflicts in Indochina. A useful source is Richard Dean Burns and Milton Leitenberg, *The Wars in Vietnam, Cambodia and Laos, 1945–1982: A Bibliographic Guide,* War/Peace Bibliography Series no. 18 (Santa Barbara, CA: ABC-Clio,

1984), which lists over 6,000 works. This brief rendition has drawn upon: George McTurnan Kahin and John W. Lewis, *The United States in Vietnam: An Analysis in Depth of the History of America's Involvement in Vietnam,* rev. ed. (New York: Dell, 1969); The Committee of Concerned Asian Scholars, *The Indochina Story* (New York: Pantheon, 1970); and William Shawcross, *Sideshow: Kissinger, Nixon and the Destruction of Cambodia* (New York: Pocket Books, 1979).

13. On efforts to implement the 1991 Cambodian peace accords, see John Mackinlay, "UN Monitors in Cambodia Have a Big Task Ahead," *Christian Science Monitor,* October 28, 1991; Alexander Nicoli, "Pressure Grows for UN to Halt Clashes in Phnom Penh," *Financial Times* (London), December 24, 1991; "GIST: Cambodia Settlement Agreement," *U.S. Department of State Dispatch,* June 9, 1992, p. 455; and "Cambodia's Cause for Concern," *The Economist,* June 20, 1992, pp. 31–32.

14. See, for example, Guy Pauker, "Southeast Asia as a Problem Area in the Next Decade," *World Politics,* Vol. 11 (April 1959), pp. 325–345.

15. By the late 1970s, the Soviet government began once again to stress the need to establish vanguard parties. See Charles C. Petersen, *Third World Military Elites in Soviet Perspective,* Professional Paper no. 262 (Alexandria, VA: Center for Naval Analyses, November 1979), esp. pp. 10, 20, 33. See also Francis Fukuyama, "Gorbachev and the Third World," *Foreign Affairs,* Vol. 64, no. 2 (Spring 1986), pp. 715–731.

16. See, for example, Ann Ruth Willner, "The Underdeveloped Study of Political Development," *World Politics,* Vol. 16 (April 1964); and Morris Janowitz, *The Military in the Political Development of New Nations* (Chicago and London: Phoenix Books, 1964). Another useful article is Ann Ruth Willner, "Perspectives on Military Elites as Rulers and Wielders of Power," *Journal of Comparative Administration,* Vol. 2 (November 1970), pp. 261–276.

17. See Jong-chun Baek, "The Role of the Republic of Korea Armed Forces in National Development: Past and Future," *Journal of East Asian Affairs,* Vol. 3, no. 2 (Fall/Winter 1983); and Do Young Chang, "The Republic of Korea Army and its Role in National Development," paper prepared for the Biennial International Conference of the Inter-University Seminar on Armed Forces and Society, Chicago, October 18–20, 1985 (mimeo), p. 9.

18. See David A. Wilson, "The Military in Thai Politics," pp. 253–254 in John J. Johnson, ed., *The Role of the Military in Underdeveloped Countries* (Princeton, NJ: Princeton University Press, 1962); David Elliott, *Thailand: Origins of Military Rule* (London: Zed Press, 1978); and Hoadley, "Thailand: Kings, Coups and Cliques" (note 10). An interesting exposition of this point as it relates to Ghana is found in Eboe Hutchful, "A Tale of Two Regimes: Imperialism, the Military and Class in Ghana," *Review of African Political Economy,* No. 14 (January-April 1979), pp. 36–55.

19. During the 1960s, militaries in Latin America and parts of Asia developed national security doctrines that equated national security both with the maintenance of territorial integrity against external threats and with the implementation of successful development programs. These doctrines assumed the existence of strong governments, efficient planning apparatuses, social control, and respect for hierarchical authority. In contrast to democratic political systems, pluralism and participation were considered a source of division within society. These doctrines were used to justify military rule during the 1960s, 1970s, and 1980s in countries such as Argentina, Brazil, Burma, Chile, Indonesia, and Peru. Similarly, the *dwi fungsi* (dual function) doctrine developed by the Indonesian armed forces, which has held power in Djakarta since 1966, gave the army the permanent right to intervene in the "ideological, political, social, economic, cultural and religious" aspects of Indonesian life.

For further reading on the doctrine of national security in its various forms, see Alfred Stepan, *The Military in Politics: Changing Patterns in Brazil* (Princeton, NJ: Princeton University Press, 1971), pp. 172–183; Stepan, "The New Professionalism of Internal Warfare and Military Role Expansion," in Stefan, ed., *Authoritarian Brazil* (New Haven: Yale University Press, 1973), pp. 47–53; Moshe Lissak, "Military Roles in Modernization: Thailand and Burma," in Amos Perlmutter and Valerie Plave Bennett, eds., *The Political Influence of the Military: A Comparative Reader* (New Haven: Yale University Press, 1980), pp. 455–462; and Crouch, "Generals and Business in Indonesia" (note 10).

20. Nathaniel C. Nash, "Army Unrest Stirs Bolivia, the Land of Coups," *The New York Times,* June 3, 1992.

21. The U.S. Government continues to supply Israel with over $3 billion in security assistance per year in the post–Cold War period ($1.8 billion military grants and $1.2 billion

Economic Support Fund grants). Russia, as the successor state to the Soviet Union, terminated all economic assistance to Cuba in 1991. On Cuba, see Spencer Reiss with Peter Katel, "Autumn of the Patriarch," *Newsweek* (August 10, 1992), p. 42.

22. Disaggregated security expenditure is difficult to come by. Most sources that regularly report Third World security expenditure provide only one aggregated figure. Some data are available in Ball, *Security and Economy*, Appendix 2, pp. 396–402, and in Ball, *Third-World Security Expenditure: A Statistical Compendium*. For information not included in either of these publications, researchers are advised to consult national budget documents, which are available at the Joint World Bank-International Monetary Fund Library in Washington, D.C., and produce their own breakdown of expenditure.

23. See Michael Brzoska and Thomas Ohlson, eds., *Arms Production in the Third World* (London and Philadelphia: Taylor & Francis, 1986), esp. pp. 281–282, and Ball, *Security and Economy*, pp. 335–385.

24. See Ann Tibbitts Schulz, *Buying Security: Iran Under the Monarchy* (Boulder, CO: Westview Press, 1989), pp. 101–115. The Military Industries Organization was the largest single purchaser of machine tools in Iran; three-quarters of the metallurgical and metalworking machinery sold in Iran during the 1970s was imported. Military demand for plastics had to be met by imports as well because the domestic plastic industry manufactured primarily consumer goods.

25. Carlos Portales and Augusto Varas, "The Role of Military Expenditure in the Development Process—Chile 1952–1983 and 1983–1980: Two Contrasting Cases," *Ibero Americana*, Vol. 12, nos. 1–2 (1983), pp. 48–49.

26. See, for example, David Jenkins, "The Military's Secret Cache," *Far Eastern Economic Review*, (February 8, 1980), pp. 70–72; Jenkins, "The Military in Business" (note 10); Crouch, "Generals and Business in Indonesia" (note 10); and Alexis Rieffel and Aninda S. Wirjasuputra, "Military Enterprises," *Bulletin of Indonesian Economic Studies* (July 1972), p. 106.

27. ACDA, *World Military Expenditures, 1990*, pp. 48, 50, 68. ACDA's figures for East Asia include Japan; the growth rates cited here exclude Japan. In contrast, military expenditure in Africa stagnated in real terms, and declined by around 15 percent in the Middle East.

28. These strategies are discussed in more detail in Ball, *Pressing for Peace* (note 1), and Ball, "Levers for Ploughshares: Using Aid to Encourage Military Reform," *Arms Control Today*, November 1992, pp. 11–17.

12 / International Human Rights after the Cold War

JACK DONNELLY

Government officials typically present human rights and national security as radically different, even antagonistic, foreign policy concerns. International human rights violations, however, can help to create national security problems. For example, long-standing U.S. support of repressive regimes in Iran and Nicaragua contributed significantly to U.S. foreign policy problems with the new revolutionary governments in these countries in the late 1970s and early 1980s. And the long-run *world* security implications of persistent human rights violations may be especially important. The particular form of the violence now raging in the former Yugoslavia, and the less violent but still ominous struggles between competing nationalities in many parts of the former Soviet Union, is in part the result of decades of totalitarian repression. Likewise, the senseless devastation of the Somali famine reflects, in part, the aftermath of the repressive Siad Barre regime. In addition, civil strife caused by human rights violations may spill over to neighboring countries.

In recent years, we have also seen renewed interest in the old Kantian idea that democracies are less inclined to fight wars (at least with one another) than authoritarian regimes. Some critics of conventional ways of thinking about human rights and security have even challenged the very notion of a conception of "security" that does not include protection of internationally recognized human rights. What kind of security does not include protection of the rights to life, liberty, and security of the person? Can one really be secure without rights to food and health care?

Still another reason for considering human rights in a volume devoted to world security is the fact that one of the characteristic features of the global political changes of the 1980s and early 1990s has been the demise of repressive regimes and ideologies. Beginning with liberalizations and democratizations in South America, reaching a dramatic climax in the collapse of the Soviet empire in 1989 and the demise of the Soviet Union itself in 1991, and continuing with rapidly accelerating liberalizations in Africa in the 1990s, we have seen dramatic human rights improvements in literally dozens of countries. Such changes, along with no less striking changes in the global balance of military and economic power, have led to much talk of a new world order in which internationally recognized human rights have a greatly elevated status.

There is a certain element of truth to each of these claims, as well as to the argument that human rights and national security often conflict. The old

Cold War order certainly has gone. As a result, at least some characteristic forms of human rights violations have been dramatically reduced. I will argue, however, that even the dramatic political changes of the last few years are likely to lead to only modest changes in *international* human rights policy. The world is likely to remain a somewhat better place, from a human rights perspective, but continued progress is by no means assured, and the positive human rights impact of international forces is likely to be modest.

The first two-thirds of this chapter reviews international human rights policies during the Cold War era and offers a preliminary assessment of the direct impact of the end of the Cold War. This is followed by briefer discussions of the problematic course of recent liberalizations and democratizations and of new human rights problems characteristic of the post–Cold War era, especially nationalism and markets. The final section addresses some of the special problems faced in consolidating, or even maintaining, recent human rights progress in an environment of economic crisis, which is unfortunately more the norm than the exception in liberalizing and newly democratic countries.

INTERNATIONAL HUMAN RIGHTS: THE COLD WAR BASELINE

The Cold War was an international human rights paradox. An era of pervasive antihumanitarian interventions by both superpowers, it was also the period in which human rights first became an established subject of international relations.

Before World War II, human rights practices were generally considered an internationally protected prerogative of sovereign states. The European great powers and the United States did occasionally intervene in the Ottoman and Chinese Empires, and in Latin America and the Caribbean, to rescue nationals caught in situations of civil strife or to establish or protect special rights and privileges for Christians, Europeans, or Americans. Rarely, if ever, though, did they intervene to protect foreign nationals from their own government. Likewise, the "humanitarian law" of war, expressed in documents such as the 1907 Hague Conventions, limited only what a state could do to foreign nationals, not the ways a state treated its own nationals (or subject peoples over whom it exercised colonial rule). Even slavery, which was a subject of multilateral diplomacy as early as the Congress of Vienna in 1815, was not outlawed by international treaty until 1926.

In the interwar period, the International Labor Organization (ILO), created in 1919, dealt with some limited workers' rights issues. The League of Nations' Minorities System was established to protect the rights of ethnic minorities in areas where boundaries had been altered following the war. But except for these marginal exceptions, when World War II broke out human rights simply was not a topic of international relations. The Covenant of the League of Nations did not even mention human rights.

The catalyst that made human rights an issue in world politics was the Holocaust, which shocked the conscience of the international community (at least after the obsession with victory was overcome) but was not clearly prohibited by international law. At the Nuremberg War Crimes Trials of 1945–46, leading Nazis were prosecuted under the novel charge of crimes against humanity. It was in the newly created United Nations, however, that human rights emerged as a standard subject of international relations.

The Preamble of the UN Charter includes a determination "to reaffirm faith in fundamental human rights." "Encouraging respect for human rights and for fundamental freedoms for all" is listed as one of the UN's major purposes in Article 1. Article 55 explicitly includes human rights among the responsibilities of the Economic and Social Council (ECOSOC), which created a Commission on Human Rights in 1946. And the United Nations proceeded to elaborate a strong set of international human rights standards.

In 1948, the UN General Assembly adopted the Universal Declaration of Human Rights without dissenting votes. This document, which provides a relatively short but comprehensive list of human rights, is widely recognized as an authoritative statement of international human rights norms. The International Human Rights Covenants, which further developed and sought to give binding legal force to the rights in the Universal Declaration, were opened for signature and ratification in 1966, and entered into force in 1976.

The Universal Declaration of Human Rights treats civil and political rights and economic, social, and cultural rights in a single document without categorical distinctions. The "interdependence and indivisibility" of all human rights was, and remains, a much-repeated theme in international discussions. Nonetheless, the Cold War both revealed and helped to create profound fissures beneath this verbal consensus. The United States criticized violations of civil and political rights in Soviet bloc countries while condoning, or even encouraging, violations of the same rights in "friendly" countries. Conversely, the Soviet Union emphasized the denial of economic, social, and cultural rights in the West, but systematically denigrated civil and political rights (except racial discrimination in the United States).

The universality of internationally recognized human rights was also challenged by theoretical arguments that there were "three worlds" of human rights—three distinctive and valid conceptions of international human rights norms.[1] The First World conception, it was argued, stressed civil and political rights and the right to property.[2] The Second World conception treated economic, social, and cultural rights as an overriding priority and a prerequisite to the effective enjoyment of civil and political rights. The Third World conception also emphasized economic, social, and cultural rights, along with the right to self-determination and the overriding priority of the struggle for development.

Although most states continued to insist that all human rights were "interdependent and indivisible" and valid across cultural and political divisions, this (broad but shallow) verbal consensus had little or no discernible policy impact in the 1950s and 1960s. Altering the terms of debate, though, did mark a first step toward altering practice. It also provided human rights activists with a powerful starting point for their arguments.

The United Nations, however, made no headway during this period in implementing these human rights norms. States agreed that they ought to follow international human rights standards. They did not, however, agree to let the United Nations (or anyone else) implement or enforce these norms. In fact, there was not even any regular discussion of human rights conditions in particular countries until the late 1960s, when human rights violations in southern Africa and in the territories occupied by Israel after the 1967 war became a fixture on UN agendas.

In the 1970s, however, the UN Commission on Human Rights was authorized to conduct confidential investigations of systematic human rights violations. In the past two decades, nearly forty countries have been subjects of such reviews. In the 1980s, the commission began regular public discussions of human rights practices in a growing number of countries. It also developed largely depoliticized "thematic" monitoring programs on disappearances, torture, and arbitrary and summary executions.[3] Outside the Commission on Human Rights, several human rights treaties require parties to submit periodic reports to independent monitoring committees. The Human Rights Committee, an eighteen-member expert committee, began to review periodic reports submitted under the International Covenant on Civil and Political Rights. And a new Committee on Economic, Social, and Cultural Rights was created in 1986 to improve reporting and monitoring in this important area.[4]

The strongest "enforcement" power available to any of these bodies, however, is public condemnation in a critical resolution or report. These are monitoring—not enforcement—procedures, which aim to bring informed international public opinion to bear on repressive states. This does not mean that they have no impact. International public opinion may influence the practice of repressive states, not only directly but also indirectly, through its impact on the policies of other states and the activities of nongovernmental organizations. Such possibilities for influence should neither be ignored nor confused with international enforcement.

The regional record is more varied.[5] At one end of the spectrum stands the regional enforcement regime covering the twenty-three (primarily Western European) members of the Council of Europe. The European Commission of Human Rights investigates complaints from individuals and states, and the European Court of Human Rights can, and does, issue binding legal judgments, with which states almost invariably comply. At the other end of the spectrum, there are still no intergovernmental regional human rights

organizations in Asia and the Middle East. The Americas and Africa lie between these extremes.

The Inter-American Commission of Human Rights, an organ of the
Organization of American States, has significant investigatory powers, and
its reports receive considerable regional and international publicity. For
example, its reports on Chile and Argentina were major sources of information for international efforts in the 1970s and 1980s against the military
regimes in these countries. The Inter-American Commission, however, has no
real enforcement powers. The Inter-American Court of Human Rights may
issue legally binding judgments, but to date it has handed down decisions on
only three cases (dealing with a disappearance in Honduras, military violence against two journalists in Peru, and military violence in Suriname).

The African regional regime is significantly weaker. The African Commission on Human and Peoples' Rights has only very modest investigatory
powers and no enforcement powers of any sort. In addition, there is no
regional human rights court in Africa.

A significant quasi-regional human rights regime was developed in the
1970s among the thirty-five (now fifty-four) European and North American
countries involved in the "Helsinki process" of the Conference on Security
and Cooperation in Europe (CSCE). During the last fifteen years of the Cold
War, CSCE review conferences provided prominent international forums in
which Soviet bloc regimes were pressured to improve their human rights
practices. The significance of the Helsinki process is attested to by the desire
of the more progressive of the new governments of Central and Eastern
Europe to deepen what is now called the human dimension of the CSCE.
New investigation and conciliation procedures were established at the 1989
Vienna review meeting, and important new statements of principles were
issued in Copenhagen and Paris in 1990. Nonetheless, the CSCE still lacks
enforcement powers.

During the last two decades of the Cold War, human rights also became
a significant issue in bilateral foreign policy. In 1973, the U.S. Congress
called for, and in 1975 legislatively mandated, a link between human rights
and foreign aid. In 1979, the Netherlands explicitly incorporated human
rights into its foreign policy. In the 1980s, many other countries followed
suit. Although even today one can point to few cases in which any state has
been willing to bear a significant foreign policy cost in pursuit of human
rights objectives,[6] even talk, backed by an occasional halt in foreign aid,
represents a major change from prior practices.

Another important development during the Cold War was the rise to
prominence of human rights nongovernmental organizations (NGOs). Amnesty International, which was founded in 1961 and received the Nobel
Peace Prize in 1977, is the best known such organization. In the United
States, Human Rights Watch and the Lawyers Committee for International
Human Rights have been especially active lobbyists for international human
rights. These two organizations regularly issue reports that document and

seek to publicize human rights violations, testify before congressional committees and lobby legislators and staff members working on human rights issues, do extensive work with the media, and issue an annual critique of the State Department country reports on human rights. Other human rights NGOs engage in similar efforts to influence policy through acquiring and disseminating information and organizing public pressure. Again, though, such activities provide only international monitoring, not implementation or enforcement, of human rights.

In summary, a fairly extensive system of formal and informal international human rights monitoring, through international and regional organizations, NGOs, and bilateral diplomacy, was established during the Cold War. International action, however, was modest in scope and impact. Except in Europe, no procedures were established to provide real international enforcement of internationally recognized human rights.

THE IMPACT OF THE END OF THE COLD WAR

In recent years, the bipolarity and ideological struggle that defined the Cold War international order have largely disappeared. We should not underestimate either the reality of the progress that this implies or its limits.

Ideology and Intervention

We need only say "Guatemala, 1954" or "Czechoslovakia, 1968" to recall the major role of the superpowers in reversing progress toward more rights-protective regimes in their Cold War spheres of influence. Marcos in the Philippines, Duvalier in Haiti, Park in South Korea, the Shah in Iran, Pinochet in Chile, Stroessner in Paraguay, and Mobutu in Zaire are only some of the more prominent dictators who benefited from U.S. support. The Soviet record was comparably appalling. In addition to forcibly imposing rights-abusive communist regimes in Central and Eastern Europe, the Soviets were the principal backers of the Mengistu regime in Ethiopia, one of the most barbaric Third World regimes of the past two decades, as well as Afghanistan's vicious Karmal and Najibullah governments.

Economic decline and internal political change have largely eliminated Soviet (now Russian) incentives and capabilities for such behavior. The United States still retains the capability to project immense conventional power at a great distance, as the Persian Gulf war vividly illustrates. The end of the Cold War, however, has removed this justification for supporting repressive regimes.

Whatever the root causes of U.S. foreign policy, much U.S. support for rights-abusive regimes in the Cold War had a substantial element of anticommunism. (Anticommunism certainly was essential to selling such policies to Congress and the public.) During the Cold War, unsavory dictators often obtained, or at least maintained, American support by playing on anti-communism. This is no longer possible. The post–Cold War international environment for human rights thus should be significantly improved.

U.S. intervention in the Third World, of course, existed before, and will continue after, the Cold War. Strategic and economic interests will not disappear from U.S. foreign policy. For example, the low level of official U.S. concern with human rights violations in Indonesia (including, but by no means limited to, East Timor) owes much to Indonesia's strategic location and oil. "Elections," "free markets," and "the war on drugs" may even be emerging as new ideological bases for policies destructive of human rights. But without the overarching appeal to anticommunism, American administrations will find it much more difficult to muster domestic support for repressive foreign regimes. Relatively few countries are of real strategic significance, a point that is becoming clearer as anticommunist paranoia subsides. And economic interests, other than oil, have played a minor role in U.S. foreign policy toward the Third World since the mid-1970s.

Although we should not underestimate the remaining problem, the current situation represents genuine progress attributable to the demise of the Cold War. For example, the armed forces in both Guatemala and El Salvador, no longer able to play the anticommunist card with much impact, have been forced to eliminate, or severely curb, many of their worst human rights violations. They have even been forced to accept negotiations with the guerrillas, which in El Salvador, at least, seems to have ended a decade of civil war. Elected civilian leaders do not fully control the military. The human rights situation in Guatemala in particular remains far from good. Nonetheless, the end of the Cold War has brought considerable human rights progress in these countries.

Reducing support for repressive regimes, however, does not necessarily translate into new positive international human rights policies. Although the United States and Russia are less regularly acting to harm human rights, there is little or no evidence of an increased commitment to provide substantial positive assistance. Neither the Bush administration nor the Congress was willing to expend substantial political or financial capital on behalf of international human rights. In fact, Bush spent considerable political capital to reopen relations with China, one of the world's few remaining Stalinist-style totalitarian dictatorships. And the occasional references to human rights by Clinton during the campaign provide no reason to expect a dramatic reversal of U.S. policy.

Complex Interdependence and the End of Bipolarity

If we turn from Cold War ideological rivalry to the underlying international balance of power, we see a similar picture of limited progress. Numerous observers have emphasized the relative decline of the old superpowers, the reduced relative importance of the "high politics" of national security, and the growing disjunction between military, economic, and political power. "Power" is no longer a simple, undifferentiated capacity, even as a first approximation. Military power remains largely bipolar, but economic power is tripolar (Europe, Japan, and the United States), and it is difficult to characterize the current distribution of international political power. Today's "great powers" are "powers" in very different senses of the term. And some states, such as Saudi Arabia, are significant powers on some international issues, but negligible actors in most others.[7]

As a result, international political processes and outcomes vary dramatically from issue to issue. While the end of U.S. (and Soviet) hegemonic leadership may create new opportunities for progressive international action, it also means that we cannot automatically generalize from one issue area to another. In particular, we must not jump from changes in international economic relations to a prediction of comparable changes in international human rights policies.

Some developed states are, indeed, increasingly willing to relinquish significant elements of economic sovereignty. We see this not only in the increasing globalization of production, but also in formal multilateral organizations (most notably in the European Community) and in less formal modes of international cooperation, such as the annual economic summits. In addition, Third World states are increasingly relinquishing economic sovereignty through IMF-imposed structural adjustment packages—although often out of dire necessity, rather than genuine desire. More complex and less state-centric patterns of order and cooperation, based on relatively deep conceptions of international interdependence, are also emerging in some noneconomic issue areas, such as the international regulation of ozone depleting chemicals.

In security relations, however, perceived interdependence has not penetrated very far, especially in U.S. policy. For example, President Bush stressed that the new world order "does not mean surrendering our national sovereignty."[8] A state-centric, sovereignty-based conception of international order also remains the norm for international human rights.

For all the talk of a new world order, most states today still jealously guard their sovereign prerogatives in the field of human rights. Consider, for example, the relative weakness of the multilateral human rights procedures discussed above in contrast to, say, GATT and IMF. Even in Europe, the relatively strong regional human rights system pales in comparison to the restrictions on state sovereignty achieved through regional economic institutions. And nowhere are states advancing new proposals to enhance significantly the power of existing human rights bodies (except perhaps the CSCE) or to create new bodies with strong powers.

In fact, recent events at the United Nations suggest that simply maintaining current (very modest) levels of activity is the best that can be hoped for. For example, in 1990 the UN Commission on Human Rights refused to adopt an embarrassingly mild draft resolution on human rights in China that did not even explicitly condemn the Tiananmen massacre. Japan was the only Asian country, Swaziland the only African country, and Panama the only Latin American country to vote for the resolution. A draft resolution on Iraq met a similar fate. Furthermore, the Group of 77, the caucusing group for the Third World, tried to replace the independent rapporteurs and working groups on disappearances, torture, and arbitrary executions with "geographically balanced" working groups made up of professional diplomats—that is, to repoliticize the commission's human rights monitoring. They also tried to impose restrictions on the activities of human rights NGOs, because of their independence from political control. Although these efforts ultimately failed, they suggest that new regimes in the post–Cold War world can be as reluctant to allow strong international monitoring of national human rights practices as their authoritarian predecessors. In fact, the enlargement of the commission to fifty-three members will make it even more difficult for it to function as a working body, while the addition of four African, three Asian, and three Latin American and Caribbean members shifts the balance of power in a way that is likely to prevent any significant enhancement of the commission's powers.

The one unambiguous sign of qualitative human rights progress in the United Nations is the observer group in El Salvador, which has unprecedented authority to engage in extensive on-site monitoring of human rights practices. El Salvador, however, voluntarily accepted such UN involvement. There is no reason to imagine that many other states will choose to allow similar interventions. Furthermore, it is only a temporary measure, agreed to as part of a broader political settlement, intended to help smooth the transition to a new government. Although important, it should not be confused with human rights monitoring in more settled situations.

This distinction between "normal" and transitional, or other extraordinary situations, also helps to account for the aggressive efforts to provide humanitarian assistance in Somalia, which have had, at most, the grudging consent of those in (or, rather, with) power. The Somali state had completely disintegrated. This intervention thus has few implications for more settled situations.

Much the same is true of recent interventions in Iraq and Bosnia. In each case, the international community has treated the conflict as an interstate conflict, despite the assertions to the contrary by Iraq and Serbia. The UN security zone in northern Iraq is the result of a cease-fire agreement. It has the consequence of protecting the human rights of Iraqi Kurds. But it provides absolutely no precedent for multilateral military protection of endangered minorities in more normal circumstances. Likewise, the Bosnian intervention has been conceived of as assistance against aggression, rather than human rights intervention, even if the result is to protect the lives of many

Bosnians from a force that claims to be their government (but whose claim is rejected by the international community).

Somalia also reminds us of the distinction between humanitarian assistance and international human rights policies. Emergency aid to victims of natural or man-made disasters is a noble and important activity. But we have no reason to expect a spillover into international human rights activities, as they have been conventionally understood—namely, to aid foreign nationals whose internationally recognized human rights are being actively violated by their own government. Even during the Cold War, massive famine usually provoked an international response that largely transcended politics. The Reagan administration's assistance to Ethiopia, one of the world's most reprehensible Marxist-Leninist regimes, is perhaps the most striking example. But there has been a huge gulf between disaster relief and providing even food aid once the immediate crisis is over, let alone international human rights intervention. We have no reason to expect fundamental change in such perceptions or behavior in the so-called new world order.

I do not want to belittle the importance of these recent humanitarian interventions. Lives have been saved in ways that just a few years ago would not have seemed possible to most observers. Nonetheless, these cases have few implications for international intervention to protect foreign nationals whose human rights are being violated by their own government.

The regional picture is, again, more varied. The Council of Europe's new program of human rights assistance for the countries of Central and Eastern Europe is clear evidence of a desire to begin to prepare the former Soviet bloc states for entry into the European human rights regime. Because good human rights practices are a major condition of acceptance into "Europe," with the associated symbolic and material benefits, the efforts of the Council of Europe are likely to have a significant impact, at least in the more progressive states of Central Europe. But the Europeans have not acted aggressively in either Croatia or Bosnia.

In the Americas, the overall human rights environment has improved dramatically: elected (although not necessarily democratic) governments held office in all the mainland countries of the hemisphere throughout 1991. In addition, the OAS General Assembly, which in the early 1980s refused to even discuss the practices of gross and persistent human rights violators such as Chile and Argentina, has recently acted quickly, and relatively forcefully, on behalf of human rights. The embargo against the military government in Haiti represents relatively aggressive regional human rights action. The rapid criticism of the suspension of parliamentary government in Peru is also a promising sign.

Regional human rights procedures in Africa, Asia, and the Middle East, however, remain weak or nonexistent. As is often the case in the field of human rights, where conditions are relatively good they get better (because the governments in question are committed to human rights progress). Progress remains slow in places where human rights conditions are worse.

Sovereignty, Interdependence, and Human Rights in the Post–Cold War World

The inherent sensitivity of human rights issues helps to explain the persisting strength of the commitment to sovereignty. Even relatively rare or isolated human rights violations can be of sufficient political sensitivity to deter some states from accepting strong international procedures. The limited nature of international cooperation in human rights, however, also reflects the particular character of states' interests in international human rights.

International human rights policies rest largely on a perceived moral interdependence, in contrast to the material interdependence that underlies most (noncoercive) economic, environmental, and military/security cooperation. A country that values the protection of human rights in other countries can enjoy that good only with the cooperation of the governments of those other countries. There is genuine interdependence in such situations. Nonetheless, political processes based on moral interdependence are likely to operate very differently from those based on material interdependence.

Moral interdependence is largely intangible. The harm caused by a foreign state violating the human rights of its own nationals is a moral harm, a sense of disgust or discomfort, rather than a loss of income, a deterioration in one's quality of life, or a reduction in perceived security. For better or worse, though, most states, like many individuals, are unwilling to pay very much to act on or assuage their moral sensibilities. This does not mean that they do not see themselves as morally interdependent, any more than the refusal of many individuals to incur significant economic costs in order to act morally toward strangers means that private morality does not exist. It does, however, suggest that we should not expect human rights to have a high place on foreign policy agendas of states.

Even if states do choose to give higher priority to international human rights, there are unusually high hurdles to implementing international human rights policies. In a typical instance of economic interdependence, each side controls relatively comparable (i.e., monetary) values. Each side thus has fairly direct (if not necessarily equal) unilateral power to prevent the enjoyment of the benefits of cooperation. Therefore, in case of noncompliance, self-help retaliation is likely to be both relatively readily available and relatively effective. This reduces the likelihood of escaping punishment for violations of international norms, which in turn reduces the risks and increases the likelihood of international cooperation.

In the case of human rights, however, retaliatory enforcement of international human rights norms is inherently problematic. Moral suasion, which responds directly to the nature of the international offense, is notoriously weak. Any other type of retaliation, however, must be imported from another issue-area, increasing both the cost of responding and the risk of escalating the dispute. Furthermore, because the means are not clearly and directly tied to the violation, their legitimacy may appear questionable.

A fundamental asymmetry in the ability of outside actors to help and to harm human rights further impedes effective international action. The eventual failure of foreign military intervention in Vietnam, Afghanistan, and Eastern Europe may suggest that even massive outside military force cannot ultimately maintain repressive rule. But these cases also provide striking examples of the capacities of foreign powers to tip the political balance of power in favor of forces of repression in the short and medium run. To remain in power, repressive regimes need only mobilize relatively small numbers of well-placed supporters, and assure that the mass of the population remains passive. They do not require active mass support, as democratic regimes usually do. In addition, foreign financial and political support can be relatively easily put to effective use by repressive forces that already have considerable control over, or access to, politics, the economy, or the military.

Foreign intervention, however, has rarely been central in establishing a strong and stable rights-protective regime. Rights-protective regimes are almost always established by domestic, not international, political forces. Even Japan and Germany, in some ways exceptions, confirm the rule: change came only after total defeat in a devastating war that completely discredited the prior regime.

Taken together, these observations on the character of power and interdependence in the post–Cold War world suggest that progress in international human rights remains constrained by deep structural forces. As opposed to the end of Cold War ideological rivalry, the end of bipolarity is likely to have few significant short or medium run implications for international human rights. International human rights norms have indeed been internationalized. But even in the 1990s, the implementation of those norms remains largely in the hands of national political authorities who only rarely are subject to substantial coercive pressures from foreign states or multilateral organizations.

The fate of human rights in the post–Cold War world therefore is primarily a matter of national, not international, politics. Foreign policy initiatives must focus on responding constructively to national political processes, to which we must now briefly turn our attention.

LIBERALIZATION, DEMOCRATIZATION, AND RIGHTS-PROTECTIVE REGIMES

The collapse of authoritarian and totalitarian regimes over the past decade is an element of the "new world order" rhetoric that has direct relevance to human rights. Political changes have indeed been extensive and relatively deep in Latin America and Central and Eastern Europe, and somewhat more uneven in Asia. More recently, long-entrenched authoritarian regimes in Africa have collapsed or been forced to liberalize, as in the dramatic electoral defeat in November 1991 of Kenneth Kaunda, Zambia's president for its first quarter century of independence.

Such changes, in addition to their immediate local impact, have helped to deepen the relatively shallow Cold War normative consensus on the interdependence and indivisibility of all human rights. In Central and Eastern Europe, the so-called socialist conception of human rights lies in shambles, revealed to be largely a cover for the systematic violation of human rights. In many Third World countries, we see a similar rejection of old arguments that equated human rights with the struggle for self-determination and development. Despite exceptions such as Cuba and China, radical cultural-relativist arguments have little persuasive power today, either internally or internationally. The terms of debate have changed. The universality of the Universal Declaration of Human Rights and the International Human Rights Covenants is now the starting point for discussion.

We must be careful, however, not to overestimate the extent to which international human rights ideas have penetrated national human rights practices. In particular, we must not confuse decreased tolerance for old forms of repressive rule with support for, let alone institutionalization of, rights-protective regimes.

Very roughly, we can distinguish three levels of political progress toward respect for internationally recognized human rights. "Liberalization" decreases human rights violations and opens political space for at least some previously excluded groups. "Democratization" is a process of establishing a regime characterized by universal suffrage, responsible government, and relatively free and open political participation.[9] As we shall see, though, democratic regimes, thus understood, may not protect all internationally recognized human rights. That requires what I call a "rights-protective regime," a political system that makes the protection of internationally recognized human rights a central element of its mission and justification, and that through extensive, intense, and sustained effort has had considerable success in realizing this aspiration.

Many recent liberalizations have led to only modest human rights progress. For example, in Bulgaria and Romania in 1990 the most notorious of the old guard were purged and a few new faces brought in. Generally, though, last year's communists were elected as this year's noncommunists. In Russia, the conservatives who control the legislature were actually elected during the era of communist rule.

In many countries, semidemocratic liberalizations have become frozen, rather than proceeding toward full democratization. Even where all parts of the state apparatus are under the control of freely and fairly elected civilian governments, human rights are not necessarily secure. Democracy assures only popular control over the makeup and direction of government. Even genuinely democratic governments may use their power in ways that systematically violate, threaten, or fail to defend internationally recognized human rights.

Consider the former Czechoslovakia, and especially the newly created Czech Republic, where substantial progress has been made toward establishing a rights-protective regime. As part of the process of coming to grips with the legacy of the communist past, a parliamentary commission has been charged with exposing as many as 150,000 informants for the old secret police. The commission, however, operates without even the appearance of due process. The accused often are not even allowed to see the "evidence" against them. This is the old system of denunciations and the presumption of guilt, in an updated (and somewhat less devastating) form.

There may be a certain "poetic justice" in treating informers to a bit of their own medicine, or denying people public opportunities on the basis of political associations that once brought them special advantage. The desire for vengeance and the fear of communist resurgence are understandable. Nonetheless, these are still serious and troubling violations of human rights. Rights are being denied to people on the basis of past immoral—but not illegal—acts, or merely for having worked in or for core institutions of the old repressive regime.

Even opportunists and morally repugnant individuals are citizens, and should have the same public opportunities as other citizens. The Czechoslovak investigatory procedure remains profoundly unjust, even if not a single innocent person were to be wrongly "exposed" as an informer. All human beings, including the guilty, have the same human rights, which they are entitled to enjoy equally.[10] In fact, the way that the guilty and despised are treated provides one of the best indications of the extent to which human rights ideas and practices have penetrated society and the political system.

It is (relatively) easy to seek redress for victims of injustice or to accept the burden of respecting the rights of those who appear to be innocent. To be solicitous of the rights of the apparently guilty, the immoral, or the corrupt is a more difficult, sometimes even distasteful, task. Human rights, however, are the rights of *all* human beings, not just good persons or members of favored groups. The enjoyment of human rights is precarious until the rights of even the "guilty" and despised are secure, and the state intervenes to protect, rather than restrict or infringe, the rights of the unpopular and the immoral. Few new democracies have come to appreciate, let alone institutionalize, this point. Without it, however, the road to establishing a true rights-protective regime is precarious.

Establishing a rights-protective regime requires developing an appreciation of the profound limits on government posed by individual human rights. Human rights can, and often do, impede the realization of other legitimate governmental aims. For example, investigatory procedures with procedural safeguards are slow and cumbersome. Their purpose, however, is to protect the rights of all individuals against abuses of state power, not to maximize the number of the guilty that are caught. As a result, human rights are often "inefficient." But in a democratic society they are of greatest importance precisely when considerations of efficiency would set aside individual rights and dignity to pursue some other social goal.

In fact, "democracy," free popular participation in politics, can easily lead to violations of human rights. Many people, both individually and in groups, want to use their political power to harm their enemies or to unfairly advantage themselves. Proto-fascist demagoguery is one natural outgrowth of populist politics in times of crisis. Consider, for example, Croatia's revival of the symbols of the wartime Nazi regime that massacred half a million Serbs, and the citizenship restrictions imposed on ethnic minorities.

Because they are concerned with each, rather than all, human rights are fundamentally nonmajoritarian. Human rights aim to protect every person, not just most, against majorities no less than minorities. In democratic societies, where the majority is relatively well-positioned to care for its own rights and interests, one of the most important functions of human rights is precisely to constrain the majority. Until such new ways of rights-protective thinking deeply penetrate both society and the government, the enjoyment of human rights will remain insecure.

NEW HUMAN RIGHTS THREATS IN THE POST–COLD WAR WORLD

So far we have covered some of the positive elements of the new post–Cold War order, arguing that they represent real, but limited, international human rights progress. In this new order, however, we are seeing the emergence (or reemergence) of serious new threats to human rights, especially those posed by nationalism and markets.

Nationalism and International Human Rights

Internationally recognized human rights rest on the idea that all individuals, simply because they are human beings, have certain basic rights, and that all human beings have (and ought to enjoy) these rights equally. Aggressive, exclusive nationalism often challenges this central premise of radical political equality.

Although asserting national identity has often been an important element in struggles against outside domination, self-determination hardly guarantees the implementation or protection of internationally recognized human rights. The dreary decades following decolonization in sub-Saharan Africa remind us that self-determination may simply substitute local despots for foreign ones.

In Central and Eastern Europe, communist rule typically suppressed ethnic rivalry by establishing the political hegemony of one ethnic group— most dramatically, of ethnic Russians in the Soviet Union. As a result, in recent years nationalism has often appeared to be not only a force with which to oppose oppressive ethnic domination, but a guarantee of liberty and respect for human rights. This is simply false. Furthermore, Yugoslavia tragically demonstrates the risk associated with a transformation of a sense of national difference into a sense of national superiority or ethnic privilege. And throughout the region, ethnic differences are being politicized, often at the cost of human rights.

Some previously dominant groups, such as Serbs in Yugoslavia, have become even more aggressively overbearing. Others, such as Russians in the other Soviet republics, now fear nationalist retribution. Some previously subordinate groups, such as the Slovak nationalist who joined former communists in forcing the dissolution of Czechoslovakia, have been as concerned with addressing old ethnic grievances as with establishing a new democratic order. Many other previously subordinate groups continue to find their interests ignored (e.g., ethnic Hungarians in Czechoslovakia) or actively under attack (e.g., ethnic Turks in Bulgaria). Still other minorities, such as Ossetians in Moldova and Georgia, have simply seen new ethnic oppressors replace the old.

Rapid economic growth might allow such grievances to be addressed by directing a greater share of new resources to disadvantaged groups. In times of scarcity, however, especially in poor countries, politics tends to turn into a zero-sum contest for shares of an inadequate pie. Where an expanding supply of goods and services cannot be used to help defuse intergroup rivalries, there is a relatively high chance that communal competition will lead to ethnic conflict, and in some cases violence. Given the continent-wide decline in per capita income over the past decade, we should expect particularly severe problems in Africa in the coming years.

Separatism has been a solution of sorts in parts of the former Soviet Union and Yugoslavia. The Baltic republics—Croatia, Slovenia, and Slovakia—all represent potential "success" stories. But their small size also raises serious questions. Balkanization is a real economic, political, and human rights problem, even when it does not lead to nationalist violence. There were good (although perhaps not sufficient) reasons for trying to create a multiethnic Yugoslavia or a binational Czechoslovakia. The likely costs of fragmentation are especially great in Africa, where the problems of political transition and economic development are severe enough without opening up the possibility of years, even decades, of tumults that may lead to nothing more than nationalist repression or the creation of new, and even more feeble, states.

Nonetheless, separatist demands for self-determination must be taken seriously even where dominant nationalities are not oppressive, let alone when they are. Both internally and internationally, there is a genuine dilemma. All international human rights issues are inherently problematic in a world structured around sovereign states. Questions of self-determination are perhaps the most problematic of all, because they are about defining the very units that are entitled to participate in international relations. Morally as well, claims of self-determination raise the question of defining the community within which human rights are to be pursued and protected. It is unclear whether foreign actors have a right to do anything at all beyond encouraging the peaceful resolution of disputes and attempting to moderate the severity of conflicts that lead to violence.

Markets and Economic and Social Human Rights

Market-oriented economic reforms present a further set of old human rights problems that are (re-)emerging in the post–Cold War world. The failure of command economies obviously played a major part in the fall of the Soviet empire. In much of the Third World as well, developmental dictatorships have been delegitimized by economic failure (in addition to the pressures from Western lenders and Western-dominated international financial institutions). The faults of command economies, however, should not blind us to the human rights problems of markets. In fact, much of the state economic intervention now under attack was provoked by the dismal failure of traditional growth-oriented, "trickle down" modernization strategies.

Markets may be economically efficient: with a given quantity of resources, market systems of allocation and distribution usually will produce a higher total quantity of goods and services. But a market system also distributes that production to those with "market power" (income, wealth, and information), rather than on the basis of human needs. As a result, although markets may produce more overall, they need not produce more for all. In fact, free markets typically produce gross inequalities in income, wealth, and living conditions. This, in turn, often leads to infringements of internationally recognized economic, social, and cultural rights, such as rights to food, health care, work, and education, especially (but not only) in poorer countries.

Economic and social human rights are concerned with distributing certain basic goods, services, and opportunities to every person. The arguments for markets stress instead increased aggregate production, largely ignoring the issue of how that new production is distributed. Even if we grant the claim of efficiency—and many markets in the Second and Third Worlds are not, and in the short run cannot be, efficient—the resulting system may systematically violate the economic and social rights of many, or even most, individuals. We have here a different version of the conflict between a human rights perspective's focus on each and an alternative, essentially utilitarian, focus on all. Even if, on average, individuals are better off, this need not mean that the median individual, let alone those at the bottom of the social order, are better off.

In Central and Eastern Europe, we are already beginning to see some of the negative human rights consequences of markets. Consider unemployment. The communist alternative of systematic underemployment may not have been very attractive, but to many it is beginning to seem preferable, even in eastern Germany, where an excellent social security system is in place. Or consider health care. Soviet bloc consumers for many years had to provide gifts, gratuities, and simple bribes to doctors and other health-care workers. Market-based health-care systems, however, will lead to price rationing that will exclude many who previously had at least minimal access. The United States presents a dismal picture of the consequences of a free market in medicine, even in an extremely wealthy society.

In the Third World, market-oriented "structural adjustment" programs usually cut social services from already inadequate levels. Even if the costs of structural adjustment are primarily short run, as their defenders usually assert, these costs are heavy, and weigh most heavily on women, the poor, the elderly, and the disadvantaged. Even when the transition to a market-oriented economy has been successfully completed, there is no guarantee that large numbers of people will not be left behind. And, of course, there is no guarantee that reforms will be successful, that there will be any real social payoff for the massive sacrifices being forced on the poor and disadvantaged in the name of efficiency.

In conditions of absolute scarcity, the efficiency of markets may be essential to creating enough to go around relatively quickly. There may be no realistic alternative. But market reforms are also likely to foster social discontent that strengthens the appeal of demagogues, would-be dictators, and supporters of the old regime. The rise of neo-Nazi violence in Germany, which ominously links ethnic conflict and economic dislocation, is a particularly troubling example.[11] And when market reforms take place in an environment of economic crisis and failure, the threat to human rights is likely to be especially severe.

ECONOMIC CRISIS, INTERNATIONAL ASSISTANCE, AND THE FATE OF HUMAN RIGHTS

Whatever the human rights consequences of markets, most recently liberalized and newly democratic regimes face the problem of maintaining, and preferably deepening, recent human rights progress in an environment of economic difficulty, turmoil, and even crisis. The threat to human rights that this poses is hard to overestimate.

Economic failure tends to weaken whatever government is in power. In the 1980s this worked in favor of human rights, for it helped to undermine numerous repressive regimes. Today, however, it threatens many newly liberalized and democratic regimes, and the human rights progress that they represent. Consider, for example, the nostalgia for the good old days that some Russians are beginning to express publicly. These dangers are particularly great because in numerous countries the underlying economic problems that contributed to the collapse of the old regime persist. In fact, many of the problems are beyond the control of any government.

Restoring—or, in some countries, initially instituting—civil and political rights may yield enough legitimacy to help a new government ride out even severe economic problems. If a government can create a sense that it is acting decisively and with some prospect of success, it may also increase its perceived legitimacy. Nonetheless, with virtually all new democracies and recently liberalized regimes today facing severe economic problems, it would be dangerous to underestimate their vulnerability.

This would seem to be one area in which external assistance could have a significant positive impact. Although foreign actors can usually play only a supporting role in establishing rights-protective regimes, at crucial turning points, and in the stage of democratic consolidation, the right kind of external support can indeed make a difference. For example, foreign technical and financial assistance may make a real contribution, not only through its direct impact on economic and social rights but also by generally strengthening new governments, whose legitimacy is likely to be enhanced by demonstrated economic efficacy. Such assistance is also attractive because it is likely to avoid charges of intervention.

Real support, however, will require more than just words of encouragement and a reprogramming of already appropriated aid. It will require a willingness to pay for further international human rights achievements. No state, and certainly not the United States, has thus far proved willing to make the sizable financial investment required.[12] Even forgiving past debt, let alone providing substantial new resources, seems more than most countries are willing to do. Simply retaining U.S. foreign aid at its already pitifully low levels will require substantial work.

Opposing systematic human rights violations is no longer enough. As we have already seen, ending old forms of abuse is only a first step. Without additional measures, human rights remain at risk. Unfortunately, there is little evidence that these new needs and opportunities are being seriously explored, let alone exploited.

Notes

1. Perhaps the best expression of this view is Adamantia Pollis, "Liberal, Socialist, and Third World Perspectives of Human Rights," in Peter Schwab and Adamantia Pollis, eds., *Toward a Human Rights Framework* (New York: Praeger, 1982).

2. In fact, this was hardly an accurate description of European human rights ideas or practices. It did have a certain plausibility for the United States, especially in the 1950s and 1980s. The United States, however, has been and remains an embarrassing anomaly, rather than a exemplar, of the Western approach to economic, social, and cultural rights.

3. For an excellent review of the activities of the Commission on Human Rights over its first forty years, see Howard Tolley, Jr., *The U.N. Commission on Human Rights* (Boulder, CO: Westview Press, 1987).

4. For an overview of this global human rights regime, see Jack Donnelly, *Universal Human Rights in Theory and Practice* (Ithaca: Cornell University Press, 1989), chapter 11, or

David P. Forsythe, *Internationalizing Human Rights* (Lexington, MA: Lexington Books, 1991), chapter 3.

5. For comparative overviews of regional human rights regimes, see Donnelly, loc. cit. and Burns H. Weston, Robin Ann Lukes, and Kelly M. Hnatt, "Regional Human Rights Regimes: A Comparison and Appraisal," in Claude and Weston, *Human Rights in the World Community* (Philadelphia: University of Pennsylvania Press, 1989).

6. Sanctions against South Africa may come close to being an exception (although only for Britain and the frontline states of Africa did they involve significant costs). Even this isolated instance, however, required more than a quarter of a century of intense national and international political action before the sanctions campaign showed any real success.

7. In the mid-1970s, Robert O. Keohane and Joseph S. Nye, *Power and Interdependence: World Politics in Transition* (Boston: Little Brown, 1977) usefully characterized this emerging international system as one of complex interdependence. These changes in the character of power long predate the end of the Cold War. They are, however, being intensified by the demise of bipolarity.

8. *Vital Speeches of the Day,* Vol. 57, no. 15, May 15, 1991, pp. 450–452.

9. This is a fairly common definition of formal or institutional democracy. It should not be confused with what might be called substantive democracy (which has been variously characterized as involving an egalitarian distribution of power, opportunities, or goods), and is much closer to what I call a rights-protective regime.

10. The principal widely accepted exception is the incarceration of convicted criminals. My point is that the guilty have the same rights to due process, and these rights must be respected, even if it results in some guilty people evading legal punishment for their crimes.

11. The official German response has also been troubling. After initially ignoring the violence against foreigners, the first responses of the central government (other than unsupported statements of regret) focused more on getting rid of the victims and potential victims than on protecting them or prosecuting their attackers. Even after finally deciding to act against this new wave of violence, the official German response has given inordinate emphasis to outlawing fringe political organizations, thus violating the rights of free speech and association of members of these groups. We have yet to see aggressive efforts to protect the rights of victims by enforcing ordinary laws against violence and intimidation.

12. Only in the former German Democratic Republic has there been a massive influx of money, an "exception" that, in fact, strongly confirms the rule of no major increase in *foreign* assistance.

13 / Global Violence against Women: The Challenge to Human Rights and Development

CHARLOTTE BUNCH AND ROXANNA CARRILLO[1]

Significant numbers of the world's population are routinely subject to torture, starvation, terrorism, humiliation, mutilation, and even murder, simply because they are female. Crimes such as these against any group other than women would be recognized as a civil and political emergency, as well as a gross violation of the victim's humanity. Yet, despite a clear record of deaths and demonstrable abuse, women's rights are not commonly classified as human rights. Similarly, despite mounting evidence that violence against women has a profoundly negative impact on the prospects for social and economic progress in the less-developed countries, the advancement of women's rights is not normally seen as a fundamental task of development. This disregard of women's rights is problematic both theoretically and practically, because it has grave consequences for the way society views and treats the fundamental issues of women's lives. This chapter questions why women's rights and human rights are viewed as distinct, looks at the policy implications of this schism, and discusses different approaches to changing it.

Women's human rights are violated in a variety of ways. Of course, women sometimes suffer abuses, such as political repression, in ways that are similar to abuses suffered by men. In these situations, female victims are often invisible because the dominant image of the political actor in our world is male. However, many violations of women's human rights are distinctly connected to being female—that is, women are discriminated against and abused on the basis of gender. Women also experience sexual abuse in situations where their other human rights are being violated, for example, as political prisoners or members of persecuted ethnic groups. In this chapter, we address those abuses in which gender is a primary or related factor, because gender-related abuse has been most neglected and offers the greatest challenge to the fields of human rights and development today.

The concept of human rights is one of the few moral visions ascribed to internationally. Although its scope is not universally agreed upon, it strikes deep chords of response among many. The promotion of human rights is a widely accepted goal and thus provides a useful framework for seeking redress of gender abuse. Furthermore, it is one of the few concepts that speaks to the need for transnational activism and concern about the lives of people globally. The Universal Declaration of Human Rights,[2] adopted in 1948, symbolizes this world vision and defines human rights broadly. While not much is said about women, Article 2 does entitle all to "the rights and freedoms set forth in this Declaration, without distinction of any kind, such as race, color, sex, language, religion, political or other opinion, national or social origin, property, birth or other status." Eleanor Roosevelt and the Latin American women who fought for the inclusion of sex in the declaration and for its passage clearly intended that it would address the problems of women's subordination.[3]

Since 1948, the world community has continuously debated varying interpretations of human rights in response to global developments. Little of this discussion, however, has addressed questions of gender, and only recently have significant challenges been made to a vision of human rights that excludes much of women's experiences. The concept of human rights, like all vibrant visions, is not static or the property of any one group; rather, its meaning expands as people reconceive their needs and hopes in relation to it. In this spirit, feminists redefine human rights abuses to include the degradation and violation of women. The specific experiences of women must be added to traditional approaches to human rights in order to make women more visible, and to transform the concept and practice of human rights in our culture so that it takes better account of women's lives.

By the same token, the degradation of women must be seen as a significant obstacle to development. The United Nations Decade for Women (1975–85) helped bring attention to the critical importance of women's activities to economic and social development. However, after fifteen years of efforts to integrate women into development, women are still only marginal beneficiaries of development programs and policy goals. Various studies show that women remain in a disadvantaged position in employment, education, health, and government. There is no major field of activity and no country in which women have obtained equality with men.[4]

In spite of the slow process of change, issues critical to women that had not traditionally been understood as central to the development process have been identified over the past decade. One such area is gender violence. Violence against women has previously been seen, if at all, as a private matter, a cultural and family issue, or, at best, pertinent to social welfare policies. Among those concerned with the general position of women, gender violence has been addressed within the framework of promoting peace, and increasingly, as part of the human rights agenda; these approaches underscore the multiple aspects of such violence, but they in no way exhaust our understanding of the problem. In particular, there are still large gaps in our knowledge concerning the dimensions and effects of gender violence on the development process itself—but what we do know suggests that its impact is severe. It is critical, therefore, that we seek to understand how violence as a form of control affects women's participation in the development process.

GENDER VIOLENCE: A GLOBAL EPIDEMIC

The most insidious myth about women's rights is that they are trivial or secondary to the concerns of life and death. Nothing could be farther from the truth; sexism kills. There is increasing documentation of the many ways in which being female is life-threatening. The following are a few examples:

• Before birth: Amniocentesis is used for sex selection leading to the abortion of more female than male fetuses at rates as high as 99 percent in Bombay; in China, the most populous nation, more males are born than females, even though natural birth ratios would produce more females.[5]

• During childhood: The World Health Organization (WHO) reports that in many countries, girls are fed less, breast fed for shorter periods of time, taken to doctors less frequently, and die or are physically and mentally maimed by malnutrition at higher rates than boys.[6]

• In adulthood: The denial of women's rights to control their bodies in reproduction threatens women's lives, especially where this is combined with poverty and poor health services. In Latin America, complications from illegal abortions are the leading cause of death for women between the ages of fifteen and thirty-nine.[7]

Sex discrimination kills women daily. When combined with race, class, and other forms of oppression, it constitutes a deadly denial of women's rights to life and liberty on a large scale throughout the world. The most pervasive violation of females is gender violence with its many manifestations from wife battery, incest, and rape, to dowry deaths,[8] genital mutilation,[9] and female sexual slavery. These abuses occur in every country and are found in the home and in the workplace, on streets, campuses, and in prisons and refugee camps. They cross class, race, age, and national lines; and, at the same time, the forms this violence takes often reinforce other oppressions, such as racism, "able-bodyism," and imperialism.

Even a short review of random statistics reveals that the extent of violence against women globally is staggering. Official statistics and survey data in the United States, for example, dramatically convey the endemic nature of gender violence. A rape occurs somewhere in the United States every six minutes, and domestic battery is the single most-significant cause of injury to women—more than car accidents, rapes, and muggings combined.[10] Yet, a 1985 FBI report estimates that wife assault is underreported by a factor of at least ten to one. Researchers produce chilling numbers: Strauss, Gelles, and Steinmetz reveal that one in eight couples admitted there had been an act of violence between them that could cause serious injury; in a study at a Connecticut hospital, Stark and Flitchcraft report that battery accounted for 25 percent of suicide attempts by women.[11]

Statistics from other industrialized countries are equally disconcerting. Reports from France indicate that 95 percent of all victims of violence are women, 51 percent of these at the hands of their husbands. In Denmark, 25 percent of women cite violence as the reason for divorce, and a 1984 study of urban victimization in seven major Canadian cities found that 90 percent of victims were women. One in four women in Canada can expect to be sexually assaulted at some point in their lives, one-half of these before the age of seventeen.[12]

While there are fewer studies in the Third World, the pattern of gender violence there bears a remarkable similarity to that of advanced industrialized societies. Its manifestations may be culturally specific, but gender-specific violence cuts across national boundaries, ideologies, classes, races, and ethnic groups. A Mexican organization estimates that domestic violence is present in at least 70 percent of Mexican families, but most cases go unreported. The Mexican Federation of Women's Trade Unions reports that 95 percent of women workers are victims of sexual harassment, and complains that the impunity of these crimes limits women's participation in the work force.[13]

A national survey on domestic violence undertaken by the Papua New Guinea Law Reform Commission showed that, in some areas of the country, as many as 67 percent of wives had experienced marital violence and that 61 percent of people killed in 1981 were women, the majority by their spouses.[14] Over two-thirds of Korean women are beaten regularly by their husbands,[15] while in Nicaragua 44 percent of men admit to having beaten their wives or girlfriends regularly.[16]

Another study published by the Indian government shows that crimes against women are "an increasing trend in the last decade," while the rate of conviction has declined. Meanwhile, the female suicide rate in that country doubled during the period from 1987 to 1988. A newspaper survey in Pakistan revealed that 99 percent of housewives and 77 percent of working women were beaten by their husbands and listed the following types of violence committed against women: murdered over land disputes, blinded by husbands frustrated on some issue, kicked to death, burnt in anger, abducted, sold, sexually harassed, raped.[17] Other reports cited in a United Nations document also found a high incidence of family violence in countries as different as Bangladesh, Colombia, Kenya, Kuwait, Nigeria, Vanuatu, and Uganda.[18]

Violence against women not only maims and debilitates; femicide kills women on a large scale from pre-birth throughout life. Amartya Sen has pointed out the deadly cost of social and economic inequalities between men and women by analyzing the sex ratio (of females to males) in the less-developed countries (LDCs). Whereas there are 106 women per 100 men in Europe and North America, there are only 97 women per 100 men in the LDCs as a whole. In some areas, especially India and China, an examination of sex-ratio data yields chilling results: given the number of men in those two countries, a sex ratio like that found in Africa (1.02) would suggest that there should be about 30 million more women in India and 38 million more in China. These missing females disappeared through gender violence ranging from female feticide to selective malnourishment and starvation of girls, neglect of health problems, dowry deaths, and various other forms of violence.[19]

GENDER VIOLENCE AND HUMAN RIGHTS

These statistics do not reflect the full extent of the problem of violence against women, much of which remains hidden. Yet, rather than receiving recognition as a major world conflict, this violence is accepted as normal, or even dismissed as an individual or cultural matter. Few governments exhibit more than token commitment to women's equality as a basic human right in domestic or foreign policy. No government determines its policies toward other countries on the basis of their treatment of women, even when some aid and trade decisions are said to be based on a country's human rights record. Among nongovernmental organizations (NGOs), women are rarely a priority, and Human Rights Day programs on December 10th of each year seldom include discussion of issues such as violence against women or reproductive rights.

When it is suggested that governments and human rights organizations should respond to women's rights as concerns that deserve such attention, a number of excuses are offered for why this cannot be done. The responses tend to follow one or more of these lines: (1) sex discrimination is too trivial, or not as important, or will be addressed only after larger issues of survival have been dealt with; (2) abuse of women, while regrettable, is a cultural, private, or individual issue and not a political matter requiring state action; (3) while appropriate for other action, women's rights are not human rights per se; or (4) when the abuse of women is recognized, it is called inevitable or so pervasive that consideration of it is futile or will overwhelm other human rights questions. It is essential to challenge these stock responses.

The narrow definition of human rights, recognized by many in the West as solely a matter of state violation of civil and political liberties, impedes consideration of women's rights. In the United States, the concept has been further limited by some who have used it as a weapon in the Cold War, almost exclusively to challenge human rights abuses perpetrated in communist countries. Even then, many abuses that affected women, such as forced pregnancy in Romania, were largely ignored.

Some important aspects of women's rights do fit into a civil liberties framework, but much of the abuse of women is part of a larger socioeconomic web that entraps women, making them vulnerable to abuses that cannot be delineated as exclusively political or solely caused by states. The inclusion of socioeconomic human rights to food, shelter, and work—which are clearly delineated as part of the Universal Declaration of Human Rights—is vital to addressing women's concerns fully. Furthermore, the assumption that states are not responsible for most violations of women's rights ignores the fact that abuses, although committed perhaps by private citizens, are often condoned or sanctioned by the state.

Violence against women is a touchstone that illustrates the limited concept of human rights and highlights the political nature of the abuse of women. As Lori Heise states: "this is not random violence . . . the risk factor is being female."[20] Victims are chosen because of their gender. The message is domination: stay in your place, or be afraid. Contrary to the argument that such violence is only personal or cultural, it is profoundly political. It results from the structural relationships of power, domination, and privilege between men and women in society. Violence against women is central to maintaining those political relations at home, at work, and in all public spheres.

Failure to see the oppression of women as political also results in the exclusion of sex discrimination and violence against women from the human rights agenda. Female subordination runs so deep that it is still viewed as inevitable or natural, rather than seen as a politically constructed reality maintained by patriarchal interests, ideology, and institutions. But we do not believe that male violation of women is inevitable or natural. Such a belief requires a narrow and pessimistic view of men. If violence and domination are understood as a politically constructed reality, it is possible to imagine deconstructing that system and building more just interactions between the sexes.

The physical territory of this political struggle over what constitutes women's human rights is women's bodies. The importance of control over women can be seen in the intensity of resistance to laws and social changes that put control of women's bodies in women's hands: reproductive rights, freedom of sexuality whether heterosexual or lesbian, laws that criminalize rape in marriage, and so on. Denial of reproductive rights and homophobia are also political means of maintaining control over women and of perpetuating sex roles and power, which have human rights implications. The physical abuse of women is a reminder of this territorial domination and is sometimes accompanied by other forms of human rights abuse, such as slavery (forced prostitution), sexual terrorism (rape), imprisonment (confinement to the home), or torture (systematic battery). Some cases are extreme, such as the women in Thailand who died in a brothel fire because they were chained to their beds. Most situations are more ordinary, such as denying women decent education or jobs, which leaves them prey to abusive marriages, exploitative work, and prostitution.

This raises, once again, the question of the state's responsibility for protecting women's human rights. Feminists have shown how the distinction between private and public abuse is a dichotomy often used to justify female subordination in the home. Governments regulate many matters in the family and individual spheres. For example, human rights activists pressure states to prevent slavery or racial discrimination and segregation, even when these are conducted by nongovernmental forces in private, or proclaimed as cultural traditions, as they have been in both the southern United States and in South Africa. The real questions are: (1) who decides what are legitimate human rights, and (2) when should the state become involved and for what purposes. Riane Eisler argues that:

> the issue is what types of private acts are and are not protected by the right to privacy and/or the principle of family autonomy. Even more specifically, the issue is whether violations of human rights within the family such as genital mutilation, wife beating, and other forms of violence designed to maintain patriarchal control should be within the purview of human rights theory and action. . . . The underlying problem for human rights theory, as for most other fields of theory, is that the yardstick that has been developed for defining and measuring human rights has been based on the male as norm.[21]

The human rights community must move beyond its male-defined norms in order to respond to the brutal and systematic violation of women globally. This does not mean that every human rights group must alter the focus of its work. However, it does require examining patriarchal biases and acknowledging the rights of women as human rights. Governments must seek to end the politically and culturally constructed war on women, rather than continue to perpetuate it. Every state has the responsibility to intervene in the abuse of women's rights within its borders and to end its collusion with the forces that perpetrate such violations in other countries.

GENDER VIOLENCE AND DEVELOPMENT

The emergence of violence as a crucial issue for Third World women's development has occurred organically, arising from grass-roots women's endeavors, and has not been dictated by outside authorities or international agencies. For example, projects funded by the United Nations Development Fund for Women (UNIFEM) in various regions of the world increasingly identify violence as a priority concern, and/or as a problem that limits women's participation in—or capacity to benefit from—development projects. Women have taken leadership in making violence against women visible, and in addressing its causes, manifestations, and remedies. From the Uganda Association of Women Lawyers, to the Trinidad Rape Crisis Centre and the Fiji Women's Rights Movement, women's leadership in the developing world is struggling to include issues of violence against women on national agendas, and to demonstrate the ways in which violence blocks development. In Latin America, ISIS International has identified 156 women's projects dealing with various aspects of violence against women.[22]

Within the context of the United Nations Decade for Women, many have begun to recognize the problem of violence against women. At all three World Conferences on Women—Mexico City (1975), Copenhagen (1980), and Nairobi (1985)—and at the parallel nongovernmental forums, women's advocates raised the issue of gender violence and demanded special attention to the constraints it places on women's full participation in society. The official documents produced at these events are powerful indictments of the discrimination that women face in all countries, regions, and cultures, and provide a useful foundation for a different understanding of sex-related violence. They establish the concerns of the international community, and acknowledge the responsibility of governments and all members of society for its eradication. They constitute the building blocks for framing new strategies and policies to address these issues.

One of the most significant UN documents addressing gender violence in relation to development is the "Forward Looking Strategies" paper produced at the 1985 Nairobi World Conference to Review and Appraise the Achievements of the UN Decade for Women. It includes Resolution 258, which calls for the elaboration of preventive policies and the institutionalization of assistance to women victims of the various forms of violence experienced in everyday life in all societies. It acknowledges that "women are beaten, mutilated, burned, sexually abused and raped," and that such violence is "a major obstacle to the achievement of the objectives of the Decade and should be given special attention."[23]

Another important UN document for addressing this issue is the *Human Development Report* (HDR) that was adopted by the United Nations Development Program (UNDP) in 1990. Reassessing the different approaches that marked the three previous UN Development Decades, this document questions the ability of statistical indicators, such as growth and national income, to measure development adequately. Rather, it suggests the need to focus on other aspects of development that provide more accurate and realistic indicators of human development: nutrition and health services, access to knowledge, secure livelihoods, decent working conditions, security against crime and physical violence, and participation in the economic, cultural, and political activities of their communities. From this perspective, the goal of development is to create an environment that enables people to enjoy long, healthy, and creative lives.

Despite three decades of significant progress toward human development in the Third World, particularly in relation to life expectancy, education, and health, one has to examine cautiously the results from a cross-cultural gender perspective. Nowhere do females enjoy the same standards as males, and in some areas gaps have widened so considerably that one must question whether development attempts are intrinsically gendered to the disadvantage of females. As the HDR states: "In most societies, women fare less well than men. As children they have less access to education and sometimes to food and health care. As adults they receive less education and training, work longer hours for lower incomes and have few property rights or none."[24]

Discrimination against females extends to every aspect of life. If women are fed less, have poorer health and less education than males, and their contribution to society's production and reproduction is underestimated, it is no wonder that wide gender gaps between males and females persist in human development indicators. Looking at development from a human-centered gender perspective requires that development studies focus on women as a demographic category, and that development indicators be recorded according to gender.

In order for women to benefit from the development process, a fundamental emphasis must be placed on increasing women's self-confidence, as well as their ability to participate in all aspects of society. Violence against women is in direct contradiction to securing human-centered development goals. It disrupts women's lives and denies them options. It erodes women's confidence and sense of self-esteem at every level, physically and psychologically. It destroys women's health, denies their human rights, and hinders their full participation in society. Where domestic violence keeps a woman from participating in a development project, or fear of sexual assault prevents her from taking a job, or force is used to deprive her of earnings, development does not occur.

Women experience violence as a form of control that limits their ability to pursue options in almost every area of life: in the home, schools, workplaces, and most public spaces. Violence is used to control women's labor in both productive and reproductive capacities. For example, case studies of victims of domestic violence in Peru and of garment workers in the Mexican maquilas showed men beating their wives frequently to demand the income women had earned.[25] Indonesian female workers returning to their villages complain of their helplessness in the face of harassment and sexual abuse; quite often their wages are withheld for months, preventing the possibility of escape or resistance. In the Philippines, women workers in export-oriented industries claim that male managers give female employees the choice of "lay down or lay off."[26]

The socially constructed dependency of women on men is key to understanding women's vulnerability to violence. This dependency is frequently economic, and results from various layers of sexist discrimination. First, much of women's work is unpaid labor at home and in the fields, which is not valued by society nor calculated as part of the gross national product—the productive work of a nation. Second, even in paid jobs, women work longer hours for lower pay, with fewer benefits and less security than men.

Female dependency extends to other areas, as well. Women are trained to believe that their value is attached to the men in their lives—fathers, brothers, husbands, and sons. They are often socially ostracized if they displease or disobey these men. Women are socialized to associate their self-worth with the satisfaction of the needs and desires of others, and thus are encouraged to blame themselves as inadequate or bad if men beat them. This socialization process is reinforced by cultures in which a woman is constantly diminished, her sexuality commodified, her work and characteristics devalued, and her identity shaped by an environment that reduces her to her most biological functions.

Women's socioeconomic and psychological dependency makes it difficult for them to leave situations of domestic violence or sexual harassment. In rural settings it is often physically impossible; women literally have no place to go or the means to get away, and there are no services available to them. But even in large urban settings, where it may be easier for women to leave abusive relationships, there is often nowhere to go, as illustrated by the links between domestic violence and homelessness. A shelter for homeless women in Boston reports that about 90 percent of its occupants are victims of domestic violence,[27] and New York City shelter workers note a similar trend. Australian sociologist Robert Connell sees the lack of alternative housing as one of the reasons women stay in, or return to, violent marriages.[28]

Violence against women also affects the development and well-being of children. It seems increasingly clear that the best way to reduce infant mortality is through the education of women.[29] The UNDP *Human Development Report* underlines the high social dividend that comes with female literacy, as demonstrated by lower infant mortality rates, better family nutrition, reduced fertility, and lower population growth. Other studies show a connection between women's self-confidence and child mortality. Since the health and psychological well-being of children is connected to the future development of a country, the gender violence implicit in disproportionate female illiteracy is clearly contrary to development. Improving women's self-confidence and education is, therefore, a crucial investment that may have long-lasting effects on children and the future of a nation.

THE COSTS TO SOCIETY

Violence against women deprives society of the full participation of women in all aspects of development. Many work hours are lost as a result of violence, not to speak of the costs of providing services to victims. To this we should add the work time lost by the victim herself, plus the work time of police, and others in the legal, medical, mental health, and social services professions. It is almost impossible to quantify the total costs of the problem given the limited information available on the extent of such violence.

Beyond such calculable costs lie the costs in human suffering, which are vast. The most significant long-term effect and ultimate cost of gender violence, however, is the perpetuation of the societal structure that keeps women inferior and subordinate to men politically, economically, and socially—thus impeding the vast developmental benefits of women's full participation in society.[30]

Violence against women is often a direct obstacle to women's participation in development projects. For example, in a Mexican project funded by UNIFEM, instances of wife battering increased with women's sense of empowerment through their participation in the project. Observers found that men perceived the growing empowerment of women as a threat to their control, and the beatings could be explained as an attempt to reverse the process of empowerment the women experienced, in order to drive them away from the project.[31] Similarly, a revolving-fund project of the Working Women's Forum in Madras almost collapsed when the most articulate and energetic participants stopped participating because they experienced increased incidents of domestic violence after they had joined.[32] Faced with the same problems, the Association for the Development and Integration of Women (ADIM) in Lima succeeded in its work by initiating programs that combined income-generating schemes with legal aid to battered wives and women abandoned by their partners.[33]

Another long-term effect of gender violence (and of the cultural atmosphere that demeans women by condoning such violence) is that it denies developing countries the full talents of their female citizens. Family control and violence encourage some of the best-educated women to leave their countries, contributing to the "brain drain" in the Third World and to the loss of highly skilled women who could be contributing to the development process. Women who stay often must comply with the subordinate role that society assigns them, and may be reluctant to be promoted to more visible and productive positions for fear of upsetting their husbands.

Health is usually recognized as an important development issue, and one of the clearest facts about gender violence is that it is detrimental to women's physical and mental health, including women's very survival. A 1989 report by the surgeon general of the United States, C. Everett Koop, affirms that battered women are four to five times more likely than non-battered women to require psychiatric treatment, and more likely to commit suicide. He reports that, each year, some one million women in the United States are sufficiently injured to seek medical assistance at emergency rooms from injuries sustained through battering. These injuries include bruises, concussions, broken noses and teeth, broken ribs and limbs, throat injuries, lacerations and stab wounds, burns, and bites. In view of the extensive evidence, Koop calls it "an overwhelming moral, economic, and public health burden that our society can no longer bear."[34]

The AIDS crisis has cast unequal gender relations in a new light. In Africa, a continent where the AIDS epidemic has reached staggering proportions, women are experiencing the effects of male control in multiple and deadly ways. A report of the Health Ministry of Uganda reveals that there are twice as many cases of AIDS among girls between fifteen and nineteen years old as among boys of the same age group. These numbers reflect a common belief among sexually active adult men that they will have less possibilities of being exposed to the AIDS virus if they engage in sexual intercourse with younger women.[35]

In some areas where the control of women is reflected in traditional practices like female circumcision and infibulation of the clitoris, the risks of acquiring the disease have multiplied. Deeply entrenched attitudes and traditions around the world justify men's easy access to women's bodies, and result in the transmission of the virus via rape, incest, and other forms of coerced sex. Thus, although hard data proving the connection between AIDS and violence against women are not yet available, this is a research area that would greatly expand our understanding of the deadly impact of AIDS on women.

DIRECTIONS FOR POLICY

The way that societies characterize human rights and development concerns is more than just a semantics problem, because it has practical policy consequences. In virtually every country, human rights (narrowly defined) and economic development are still considered to be more important than women's rights. The distinction perpetuates the idea that the rights of women are of a lesser order than the "rights of man," and, as Riane Eisler describes it, "serves to justify practices that do not accord women full and equal status."[36] And, as we have seen, the failure to address gender violence as part of the developmental process has contributed to the continuing subordination and exploitation of women—at great cost to the goals of development itself.

If we are to advance the cause of women's rights and to enhance the well-being of all human beings, it is essential that we eliminate the false distinction between human rights and women's rights, and make the eradication of gender violence a fundamental goal of long-term development—whether in the industrialized countries or in the Third World.

To begin this process, we offer four basic approaches to linking women's rights to human rights. These approaches are presented separately in order to identify each much more clearly. In practice, these approaches often overlap, and while each raises questions about the others, they are complementary. These approaches can be applied to many issues, but we will illustrate them primarily in terms of how they address violence against women in order to show the implications of their differences on a concrete issue.

Women's Rights as Political and Civil Rights

Taking women's specific needs into consideration as part of the already recognized "first generation" human rights of political and civil liberties is the first approach. This involves both raising the visibility of women who suffer general human rights violations, as well as calling attention to particular abuses women encounter because they are female. Thus, issues of violence against women are raised when they connect to other forms of violation, such as the sexual torture of women political prisoners in South America.[37] Groups such as the Women's Task Force of Amnesty International have taken this approach in pushing for Amnesty to launch a campaign on behalf of women political prisoners that would address the sexual abuse and rape of women in custody, their lack of maternal care in detention, and the resulting human rights abuse of their children.

Documenting the problems of women refugees and developing responsive policies are other illustrations of this approach. Women and children make up more than 80 percent of those in refugee camps, yet few refugee policies are specifically shaped to meet the needs of these vulnerable populations who face considerable sexual abuse. For example, in one camp where men were allocated the community's rations, some gave food to women and their children in exchange for sex. Revealing this abuse led to new policies that allocated food directly to the women.[38]

The political and civil rights approach is a useful starting point for many human rights groups; by considering women's experiences, these groups can expand their efforts in areas where they are already working. This approach also raises contradictions that reveal the limits of a narrow civil liberties view. One contradiction is to define rape as a human rights abuse only when it occurs in state custody, but not on the streets or in the home. Another is to say that a violation of the right to free speech occurs when someone is jailed for defending gay rights, but not when someone is jailed, or even tortured and killed, for homosexuality. Thus, while this approach of taking women and stirring them into existing first generation human rights categories is useful, it is not enough by itself.

Women's Rights as Socioeconomic Rights

The second approach includes the particular plight of women with regard to "second generation" human rights, such as the rights to food, shelter, health care, and employment. This is an approach favored by those who see the dominant Western human rights tradition and international law as too individualistic, and who identify women's oppression as primarily economic in origin.

This tendency has its origins among socialists and labor activists who have long argued that political human rights are meaningless to many without economic rights as well. It focuses on the primacy of the need to end women's economic subordination as the key to other issues, including women's vulnerability to violence. This particular focus has led to work on issues such as women's right to organize as workers and opposition to violence in the workplace, especially in settings like the free-trade zones that have targeted women as cheap, nonorganized labor. Another focus of this approach has been highlighting the feminization of poverty, or what might better be called the increasing impoverishment of females. Poverty has not become strictly female, but females now comprise a higher percentage of the poor.

Looking at women's rights in the context of socioeconomic development is another example of this approach. Third World peoples have called for an understanding of socioeconomic development as a human rights issue.

Among those working on women in development, there is growing interest in violence against women as both a health and development issue. If violence is seen as having negative consequences for social productivity, it may get more attention. This type of narrow economic measure should not, however, determine whether such violence is seen as a human rights concern. Violence as a development issue is linked to the need to understand development not just as an economic issue but also as a question of empowerment and human growth.

Women's Rights and the Law

The creation of new legal mechanisms to counter sex discrimination characterizes the third approach to women's rights as human rights. These efforts seek to make existing legal and political institutions work for women, and to expand the state's responsibility for the protection of women's human rights. National and local laws that address sex discrimination and violence against women are examples of this approach. These measures allow women to fight for their rights within the legal system.

The primary international illustration of this approach is the Convention on the Elimination of All Forms of Discrimination Against Women.[39] The convention has been described as "essentially an international Bill of Rights for women and a framework for women's participation in the development process . . . [which] spells out internationally accepted principles and standards for achieving equality between women and men."[40] Adopted by the UN General Assembly in 1979, the convention has been ratified or acceded to by 104 countries as of January 1990. In theory, these countries are obligated to pursue policies in accordance with it and to report on their compliance to the Committee on the Elimination of Discrimination Against Women (CEDAW).

While the convention addresses many issues of sex discrimination, one of its shortcomings is failure to directly address the question of violence against women. The CEDAW committee passed a resolution at its eighth session in Vienna in 1989, expressing concern that this issue be on its agenda and instructing states, in their periodic reports to the committee, to include information about statistics, legislation, and support services in this area.[41]

The convention outlines a clear human rights agenda for women that, if accepted by governments, would mark an enormous step forward. It also carries the limitations of all such international documents, in that there is little power to demand its implementation. Within the United Nations, it is not generally regarded as a convention with teeth, as illustrated by the difficulty that CEDAW has had in getting countries to report on compliance with its provisions. Furthermore, it is still treated by governments and most nongovernmental organizations as a document dealing with women's (read "secondary") rights, not human rights. Nevertheless, it is a useful statement of principles, endorsed by the United Nations, around which women can organize to achieve legal and political change in their regions.

Feminist Transformation of Human Rights

Transforming the human rights concept from a feminist perspective, so that it will take greater account of women's lives, is the fourth approach. This approach raises the question of how women's rights relate to human rights, by first looking at the violations of women's lives and then asking how the human rights concept can change to be more responsive to women. For example, the Gabriella women's coalition in the Philippines simply stated that "Women's Rights are Human Rights" in launching a campaign last year. As Ninotchka Rosca explained, coalition members saw that "human rights are not reducible to a question of legal and due process. . . . In the case of women, human rights are affected by the entire society's traditional perception of what is proper or not proper for women."[42] While work in the three previous approaches is often done from a feminist perspective, this last view is the most distinctly feminist, with its woman-centered stance and refusal to wait for permission from some authority to determine what is, or is not, a human rights issue.

This transformative approach can be taken toward any issue, but those working from this approach have tended to focus most on abuses that arise specifically out of gender, such as reproductive rights, female sexual slavery, violence against women, and "family crimes" such as forced marriage, compulsory heterosexuality, and female mutilation. These are also the issues most often dismissed as not really human rights questions. This is, therefore, the most hotly contested area, and one that requires that barriers be broken down between public and private, and governmental and nongovernmental, responsibilities.

Those working to transform the human rights vision from this perspective can draw on the work of others who have expanded the understanding of human rights previously. For example, two decades ago there was no concept of "disappearances" as a human rights abuse. However, the women of the Plaza de Mayo in Buenos Aires did not wait for an official declaration, but stood up to demand state accountability for these crimes. In so doing, they helped to create a context for expanding the concept of responsibility for deaths at the hands of paramilitary or right-wing death squads, which, even if not carried out by the state, were allowed by it to happen. Another example is the developing concept that civil rights violations include "hate crimes," violence that is racially motivated or directed against homosexuals, Jews, or other minority groups. Many accept that states have an obligation to work to prevent such human rights abuses, and identifying violence against women as a hate crime is being pursued by some.

Many strategies for change involve elements of more than one of these approaches, and all of them contain aspects of what is necessary to achieve women's rights. At a time when dualist ways of thinking are in question, the creative task is to look for ways to connect these approaches and to see how we can go beyond exclusive views of what people need in their lives. In the words of one early feminist group, we need bread and roses, too. Women want food and liberty, and the possibility of living lives of dignity free from domination and violence. In this struggle, the recognition of women's rights as human rights can play an important role.

Beyond this, we must find sustainable ways of deterring global violence against women. On a very direct level, grass-roots projects can experiment with techniques or interventions that focus on, or deal with, gender violence. With respect to deterrence, projects that test one or more education campaigns that seek to make violence unacceptable within a society can serve as models that demonstrate the possibilities and benefits of such approaches. In a similar way, projects dealing with the consequences of violence—rape crisis centers, training programs for police, magistrates, hospital personnel, and so forth—should be supported, especially when they have some possibility of testing a new approach, or of influencing the government to initiate services and expand on tested approaches to addressing gender violence.

The international development community, and particularly women's agencies within that community, can also undertake new initiatives in this area. This would involve making gender violence visible as a development issue in relation to many other developmental themes. By disseminating data and reports on violence against women—and on successful efforts to raise this issue at the community level—women's advocates within the development community can highlight the impact of violence on program activity.

Overall, development agencies and organizations addressing women in development must conduct their program and project work with an increased sensitivity to the issue of violence, and the ways in which development itself brings forth new forms of gendered violence. It is important to address gender violence as an aspect of many other development initiatives, such as income-generating schemes or housing plans, and not just those specifically focused on violence against women. International development agencies, such as the UN Development Program, UNIFEM, WHO, and the International Labor Organization, which are concerned with the issue of women in development, need to use their leverage and prestige as international agencies to expand the legitimacy and give voice to the groups working on these areas at the national or community level.

Attempts to promote international human rights and to integrate women into development are doomed to failure if they do not address the issue of global violence against women. This chapter has attempted to build the case for the inclusion of efforts to combat gender violence as a major goal of international human rights and development efforts. Likewise, it maintains that projects that deal with violence toward women are building blocks for a more comprehensive, empowering, and therefore sustainable effort, which will tap women's full participation in social and economic development, to the benefit of all.

Notes

1. This chapter is based on the essays by Bunch and Carrillo in their *Gender Violence: A Development and Human Rights Issue* (New Brunswick, NJ: Center for Women's Global Leadership, Douglass College, Rutgers University, 1991). Portions of the essay first appeared in *Human Rights Quarterly,* Vol. 12, no. 4 (November 1990).

2. Universal Declaration of Human Rights, adopted December 10, 1948, G.A. Res. 217A(III), Doc. A/810 (1948).

3. See Blanche Wiesen Cook, "Eleanor Roosevelt and Human Rights: The Battle for Peace and Planetary Decency," in Edward P. Crapol, ed., *Women and American Foreign Policy: Lobbyists, Critics, and Insiders* (New York: Greenwood Press, 1987), pp. 98–118; and Georgina Ashworth, "Of Violence and Violation: Women and Human Rights," *Change Thinkbook II* (London, 1986).

4. R. L. Sivard, *Women . . . A World Survey* (Washington: World Priorities, 1985), p. 5.

5. Vibhuti Patel, *In Search of Our Bodies: A Feminist Look at Women, Health and Reproduction in India* (Bombay: Shakti, 1987); Lori Heise, "International Dimensions of Violence Against Women," *Response,* Vol. 12, no. 1 (1989), p. 3.

6. Sundari Ravindran, *Health Implications of Sex Discrimination in Childhood* (Geneva: World Health Organization, 1986). These problems and proposed social programs to counter them in India are discussed in detail in "Gender Violence: Gender Discrimination between Boy and Girl in Parental Family," paper published by CHETNA (Child Health Education Training and Nutrition Awareness), Ahmedabad, 1989.

7. Debbie Taylor, ed., *Women: A World Report, A New Internationalist Book* (Oxford: University Press, 1985), p. 10. See Joni Seager and Ann Olson, eds., *Women in the World: An International Atlas* (London: Pluto Press, 1986) for more statistics on the effects of sex discrimination.

8. Frequently, a husband will disguise the death of a bride as suicide or an accident in order to collect the marriage settlement paid to him by the bride's parents. Although dowry is now illegal in many countries, official records for 1987 showed 1,786 dowry deaths in India alone. See Heise, "International Dimensions of Violence Against Women," p. 5.

9. For an in-depth examination of the practice of female circumcision, see Alison T. Slack, "Female Circumcision: A Critical Appraisal," *Human Rights Quarterly,* Vol. 10 (1988), p. 439.

10. National Center on Women and Family Law, Information Package on Battered Women (no. 47), 1988.

11. N. A. Straus, R. Gelles, and S. K. Steinmetz, *Behind Closed Doors: Violence in the American Family* (New York: Doubleday, 1981); E. Stark and A. Flitchcraft, "Domestic Violence and Female Suicide Attempts," paper presented at the 107th annual meeting of the American Public Health Association, New York, November 1979.

12. L. MacLeod, *Women and Environment,* Vol. 12, no. 1 (Fall 1989-Winter 1990), p. 12.

13. Instituto Latinamericano de Estudios Transnacionales (ILET), no. 97 (November 1989), no. 100 (February-March 1990), no. 104 (June 1990), also special issue on "Contra-violencia" (December 1988).

14. C. Bradley, "Wife-Beating in PNG—Is it a Problem?" *Papua New Guinea Medical Journal,* September 1988.

15. Asian Women's Research and Action Network (AWRAN), Report, Philippines, 1985.

16. ILET, June 1990 (see note 13).

17. AWRAN Report, 1985 (see note 15).

18. J. F. Connors, *Violence Against Women in the Family* (New York: United Nations, Center for Social Development and Humanitarian Affairs, Division for the Advancement of Women, 1989), p. 20.

19. Amartya Sen, "Gender and Cooperative Conflicts," in Irene Tinker, ed., *Persistent Inequalities: Women and World Development* (New York and Oxford: Oxford University Press, 1989), pp. 123–149.

20. Heise, "International Dimensions of Violence Against Women," p. 3.

21. Riane Eisler, "Human Rights: Toward an Integrated Theory for Action," *Human Rights Quarterly*, Vol. 9 (1987), p. 297. See also Alida Brill, *Nobody's Business: The Paradoxes of Privacy* (New York: Addison-Wesley, 1990).

22. ISIS International, *Violencia en Contra de la Mujer en America Latina y el Caribe*, Proyecto RLA/88/W01, UNIFEM (Santiago, Chile: ISIS International, 1990).

23. United Nations, *The Nairobi Forward Looking Strategies for Women*, Nairobi, July 15–26, 1985 (UN Pub. E.85.IV.10).

24. United Nations Development Program, *Human Development Report 1990* (New York and Oxford: Oxford University Press, 1990), p. 31.

25. R. Vasquez and G. Tamayo, *Violencia y Legalidad* (Lima: Concytec, 1989); J. Bruce and Dwyer, *A Home Divided* (Stanford: Stanford University Press, 1990).

26. AWRAN Report, 1985 (see note 15).

27. *The New York Times*, August 26, 1990.

28. Robert W. Connell, *Gender and Power* (Stanford: Stanford University Press, 1987), p. 11.

29. See Report of the White House Task Force on Infant Mortality, cited in *The New York Times*, August 12, 1990; M. Buvinic and S. W. Yudelman, *Women, Poverty, and Progress in the Third World* (New York: Foreign Policy Association, 1989).

30. Connors, *Violence Against Women in the Family*, p. 24.

31. Unpublished UNIFEM report, 1990.

32. H. Noponen, "Grassroots Women's Worker Organizations—Rhetoric and Reality," unpublished essay, 1989.

33. Buvinic and Yudelman, *Women, Poverty, and Progress*, p. 44.

34. C. E. Koop, "Violence Against Women: A Global Problem," address at a seminar of the Pan American Health Organization, Washington, D.C., May 22, 1989, pp. 5–6.

35. *The New York Times*, October 28, 1990.

36. Eisler, "Human Rights," p. 29.

37. Ximena Bunster describes this in Chile and Argentina in "The Torture of Women Political Prisoners: A Case Study in Female Sexual Slavery," Kathleen Barry, Charlotte Bunch, and Shirley Castley, eds., *International Feminism: Networking Against Female Sexual Slavery* (New York: IWTC, 1984).

38. Report given by Margaret Groarke at Women's Panel, Amnesty International New York Regional Meeting, February 24, 1990.

39. Convention on the Elimination of All Forms of Discrimination Against Women, G.A. Res. 34/180, U.N. Doc. A/Res/34/180 (1980).

40. "The Convention on the Elimination of All Forms of Discrimination Against Women," Summary of CEDAW prepared by the International Women's Rights Action Watch, Humphrey Institute of Public Affairs, Minneapolis, 1988.

41. CEDAW Newsletter, 3rd Issue, 13 April, 1989.

42. Speech given by Ninotchka Rosca at Amnesty International New York Regional Conference, 24 February, 1990, p. 2.

14 / The Environment and International Security

JESSICA TUCHMAN MATHEWS

The 1990s will demand a redefinition of what constitutes national security. In the 1970s the concept was expanded to include international economics as it became clear that the U.S. economy was no longer the independent force it had once been, but was powerfully affected by economic policies in dozens of other countries. Global developments now suggest the need for another analogous, broadening definition of national security to include resource, environmental, and demographic issues.

The assumptions and institutions that have governed international relations in the postwar era are a poor fit with these new realities. Environmental strains that transcend national borders are already beginning to break down the sacred boundaries of national sovereignty, previously rendered porous by the information and communication revolutions and the instantaneous global movement of financial capital. The once sharp dividing line between foreign and domestic policy is blurred, forcing governments to grapple in international forums with issues that were contentious enough in the domestic arena.

Despite recent headlines—the disappearing ozone layer, the climatic extremes, the accelerating deforestation and flooding that plague the planet—human society has not arrived at the brink of some absolute limit to its growth. The planet may ultimately be able to accommodate the additional five or six billion people projected to be living here by the year 2100. But it seems unlikely that the world will be able to do so unless the means of production change dramatically. Global economic output has quadrupled since 1950 and it must continue to grow rapidly simply to meet basic human needs, to say nothing of the challenge of lifting billions from poverty. But economic growth as we currently know it requires more energy use, more emissions and wastes, more land converted from its natural state, and more need for the products of natural systems. Whether the planet can accommodate all of these demands remains an open question.

Individuals and governments alike are beginning to feel the cost of substituting for (or doing without) the goods and services once freely provided by healthy ecosystems. Nature's bill is presented in many different forms: the cost of commercial fertilizer needed to replenish once naturally fertile soils; the expense of dredging rivers that flood their banks because of soil erosion hundreds of miles upstream; the loss in crop failures due to the indiscriminate use of pesticides that inadvertently kill insect pollinators; or the price of worsening pollution, once filtered from the air by vegetation.

Whatever the immediate cause for concern, the value and absolute necessity for human life of functioning ecosystems is finally becoming apparent.

Moreover, for the first time in its history, humankind is rapidly—if inadvertently—altering the basic physiology of the planet. Global changes currently taking place in the chemical composition of the atmosphere, in the genetic diversity of species inhabiting the planet, and in the cycling of vital chemicals through the oceans, atmosphere, biosphere, and geosphere are unprecedented in both their pace and scale. If left unchecked, the consequences will be profound and, unlike familiar types of local damage, irreversible.

EFFECTS OF RESOURCE DEGRADATION

Population growth lies at the core of most environmental trends. It took 130 years for world population to grow from one billion to two billion: it will take just a decade to climb from today's five billion to six billion. More than 90 percent of the added billion will live in the developing world, with the result that by the end of the 1990s the developed countries will be home to only 20 percent of the world's people, compared to almost 40 percent at the end of World War II (see Figure 14.1). Sheer numbers do not translate into political power, especially when most of the added billion will be living in poverty. But the demographic shift will thrust the welfare of developing nations further toward the center of international affairs.

The relationship linking population levels and the resource base is complex. Policies, technologies, and institutions determine the impact of population growth. These factors can spell the difference between a highly stressed, degraded environment and one that can provide for many more

Figure 14.1 / World Population Growth, 1750–2100

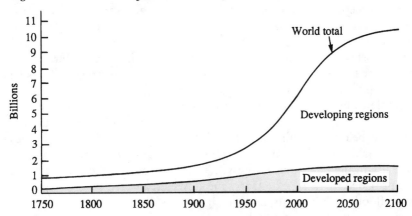

Sources: Thomas W. Merrick et al., "World Population in Transition, *Population Bulletin*, Vol. 42, No. 2 (1986), Figure 1, p. 4, and *World Resources Report 1988–1989*, World Resources Institute, p. 16.

people. At any given level of investment and knowledge, absolute population numbers can be crucial. For example, traditional systems of shifting agriculture—in which land is left fallow for a few years to recover from human use—can sustain people for centuries, only to crumble in a short time when population densities exceed a certain threshold. More important, though, is the *rate* of growth. A government that is fully capable of providing food, housing, jobs, and health care for a population growing at 1 percent per year (therefore doubling its population in seventy-two years), might be completely overwhelmed by an annual growth rate of 3 percent, which would double the population in twenty-four years.

Today the United States is growing at just under 1 percent annually, and Europe is growing only half that fast. But Africa's population is expanding by almost 3 percent per year, Latin America's by nearly 2 percent, and Asia's by somewhat less. By 2025, the working-age population in developing countries alone will be larger than the world's current total population. This growth comes at a time when technological advance requires higher levels of education and displaces more labor than ever before. For many developing countries, continued growth at current rates means that available capital is swallowed up in meeting the daily needs of people, rather than invested in resource conservation and job creation. Such policies inescapably lay the foundations of a bleak future.

An important paradox to bear in mind when examining natural resource trends is that so-called nonrenewable resources—such as coal, oil, and minerals—are in fact inexhaustible, while so-called renewable resources can be finite. As a nonrenewable resource becomes scarce and more expensive, demand falls, and substitutes and alternative technologies appear. For that reason we will never pump the last barrel of oil or anything close to it. On the other hand, a fishery fished beyond a certain point will not recover, a species driven to extinction will not reappear, and eroded topsoil cannot be replaced (except over geological time). There are, thus, threshold effects for renewable resources that belie the name given them, with unfortunate consequences for policy.

The most serious form of renewable resource decline is the deforestation taking place throughout the tropics. An area the size of Austria is deforested each year (see Table 14.1). Tropical forests are fragile ecosystems, extremely vulnerable to human disruption. Once disturbed, the entire ecosystem can unravel. The loss of the trees causes the interruption of nutrient cycling above and below the soil: the soil loses fertility; plant and animal species lose their habitats and become extinct; and acute fuelwood shortages appear (especially in the dry tropical forests). The soil erodes without the ground cover provided by trees and plants, and downstream rivers suffer siltation, causing floods and droughts, and damaging expensive irrigation and hydroelectric systems. Traced through its effects on agriculture, energy supply, and water resources, tropical deforestation impoverishes about a billion people.[1] This pattern is endemic throughout Central America, much of Asia, sub-Saharan Africa, and South America.

Table 14.1 / Annual Rates of Tropical Deforestation, 1976–1980 *(millions of hectares per annum)*

	Closed forests				Open woodlands[a]	
	ALL TROPICAL		MOIST TROPICAL			
	Area	Percent of total	Area	Percent of total	Area	Percent of total
Africa	1.33	0.61	1.20	0.59	2.34	0.48
Asia-Pacific	1.82	0.59	1.61	0.61	0.19	0.61
Latin America	4.12	0.61	3.30	0.54	1.27	0.59
Total	7.27	0.61	6.11	0.57	3.8	0.52

[a]Projections for 1981–85.
Sources: For all tropical closed forests and open woodlands, see Jean Paul Lanly, Tropical Forest Resources, *FAO Forestry Paper No. 30* (United Nations Food and Agriculture Organization, Rome, 1982), Table 6d, p. 80 and Table 6e, p. 84. For tropical moist forests, see Alan Grainger, "Quantifying Changes in Forest Cover in the Humid Tropics: Overcoming Current Limitations," *Journal of World Forest Resource Management*, Vol. 1 (1984), Table 8, p. 21. Original table from *World Resources Report 1988–1989*, World Resources Institute, p. 71.

The planet's evolutionary heritage—its genetic diversity—is heavily concentrated in these same forests. It is therefore disappearing today on a scale not seen since the age of the dinosaurs, and at an unprecedented pace. Biologists estimate that species are being lost in the tropical forests 1,000 to 10,000 times faster than the natural rate of extinction.[2] As many as 20 percent of all the species now living may be gone by the year 2000. The loss will be felt aesthetically, scientifically, and, above all, economically. These genetic resources are an important source of food, materials for energy and construction, chemicals for pharmaceuticals and industry, natural pest controls, and dozens of other uses.

The only reason that species loss is not a front-page issue is that the majority of species have not yet been discovered, much less studied, so that none but a few conservation biologists can even guess at the number and kinds of species that are vanishing. The bitter irony is that genetic diversity is disappearing on a grand scale at the very moment when biotechnology makes it possible to exploit fully this resource for the first time.

Soil degradation is another major concern. Both a cause and a consequence of poverty, desertification (as it is generally called) is causing declining agricultural productivity on nearly two billion hectares, 15 percent of the earth's land area. The causes are overcultivation, overgrazing, erosion, and salinization and waterlogging due to poorly managed irrigation. In countries as diverse as Haiti, Guatemala, Turkey, and India, soil erosion has sharply curtailed agricultural production and potential, sometimes destroying it completely. Though the data are uncertain, it is estimated that the amount of land permanently removed from cultivation due to salinization and waterlogging is equal to the amount of land newly irrigated at great expense each year.[3]

Finally, patterns of land tenure, though not strictly an environmental condition, have an immense environmental impact. In 1975, 7 percent of landowners in Latin America possessed 93 percent of all the arable land in this vast region. In Guatemala, a typical case, 2 percent of the population in 1980 owned 80 percent of the land, while 83 percent of farmers lived on plots too small to support a household. At the same time, even in Costa Rica, with its national concern for social equity, 3 percent of landowners held 54 percent of the land.[4] These large holdings generally include the most desirable land and are often inefficiently used or not used at all. The great mass of the rural population is pushed onto the most damage-prone land, usually dry or highly erodible slopes, and into the forests. Some of this land is so environmentally fragile that it should not be used at all. Some of it could be sustainably farmed, but, lacking ownership, these farmers have no reason to undertake the hard labor necessary to ensure the soil's long-term productivity. Land reform is among the most difficult of all political undertakings, but without it many countries will be unable to create a healthy agricultural sector to fuel economic growth.

Environmental decline occasionally leads directly to conflict, especially when scarce water resources must be shared. Generally, however, its impact on nations' security is felt in the downward pull on economic performance and, therefore, on political stability. The underlying cause of turmoil is often ignored; instead governments address the poverty and instability that are its results.

In the Philippines, for example, the government regularly granted logging concessions of less than ten years. Since it takes thirty to thirty-five years for a second-growth forest to mature, loggers had no incentive to replant. Compounding the error, flat royalties encouraged the loggers to remove only the most valuable species. A horrendous 40 percent of the harvestable lumber never left the forests but, having been damaged in the logging, rotted or was burned in place. The unsurprising result of these and related policies is that out of 17 million hectares (1 hectare = 2.47 acres) of closed forests that flourished early in the century, only 1.2 million remain today. Moreover, the Philippine government received a fraction of the revenues it could have collected if it had followed sound resource management policies that would have also preserved the forest capital. This is biological deficit financing writ large.[5]

Similarly, investments in high-technology fishing equipment led to larger harvests but simultaneously depleted the stock. Today, ten of fifty major Philippine fishing grounds are believed to be overfished; the net result of heavy investment is that the availability of fish per capita has actually dropped. These and other self-destructive environmental policies, combined with rapid population growth, played a significant role in the economic decline that led to the downfall of the Marcos regime. So far, the government of Corazon Aquino has made few changes in the forestry, fishery, and other environmental policies it inherited.[6]

Conditions in sub-Saharan Africa, to take another case, have reached catastrophic dimensions. In the first half of the 1980s, export earnings fell by almost one-third, foreign debt soared to 58 percent of GNP, food imports grew rapidly while consumption dropped, and per capita GNP fell by more than 3 percent. A large share of those woes can be traced to Africa's dependence on a fragile, mismanaged, and overstressed natural resource base (see Table 14.2).

Exports of mineral and agricultural commodities alone account for a quarter of the region's GNP, and nearly three-quarters of the population makes its living off the land, which also supplies, as fuelwood, 80 percent of the energy consumed. The land's capacity to produce is ebbing away under the pressure of rapidly growing numbers of people who do not have the wherewithal to put back into the land what they take from it. A vicious cycle of human and resource impoverishment sets in. As the vegetative cover—

Table 14.2 / Sub-Saharan Africa Today

Indicator	Africa	All developing countries
Only region with declining per capita GNP, 1980–86	−3.05	—
Highest foreign debt as percent of GNP, 1986	58%	37%[a]
Highest annual rate of population growth, 1980–86	3.1	2.0
Highest infant mortality (infant deaths per 1,000 live births), 1986	113	67
Lowest life expectancy, 1986	49 years	57.3 years
Only region with declining per capita agricultural production	✔	—
Only region with declining per capita food consumption	✔	—
Highest percentage of population severely malnourished (less than 80% of FAO/WHO caloric requirement, 1980)	25	16
Highest proportion of soils with fertility limitations	81	—
Highest percentage of productive drylands desertified	84	61
Heaviest reliance on fuelwood as energy source	80	—
Lowest percentage of arable land potentially irrigable	5	—

[a]Average for 109 developing countries
Source: J. T. Mathews, *Africa: Continent in Crisis,* World Resources Institute, 1988.

trees, shrubs, and grass—shrinks from deforestation and overgrazing, soil loses its capacity to retain moisture and nourish crops. The decline accelerates as farmers burn dung and crop residues in place of fuelwood, rather than using them to sustain the soil. Agricultural yields then fall further, and the land becomes steadily more vulnerable to the naturally variable rainfall that is the hallmark of arid and semiarid regions, turning dry spells into droughts and periods of food shortage into famines. Ethiopia is only the most familiar case. The sequence is repeated throughout the region—with similarly tragic results.[7]

When such resource and population trends are not addressed, as they are not in so much of the world today, the resulting economic decline leads to frustration, resentment, domestic unrest, or even civil war. Human suffering and turmoil make countries ripe for authoritarian government or external subversion. Environmental refugees spread the disruption across national borders. Haiti, a classic example, was once so forested and fertile that it was known as the "Pearl of the Antilles." Now deforested, soil erosion in Haiti is so rapid that some farmers believe stones grow in their fields, while bulldozers are needed to clear the streets of Port-au-Prince of topsoil that flows down from the mountains in the rainy season. While many of the boat people who fled to the United States left because of the brutality of the Duvalier regimes, there is no question that—and this is not widely recognized—many Haitians were forced into the boats by the impossible task of farming bare rock. Until Haiti is reforested, it will never be politically stable.

Haitians are by no means the world's only environmental refugees. In Indonesia, Central America, and sub-Saharan Africa, millions have been forced to leave their homes in part because the loss of tree cover, the disappearance of soil, and other environmental ills have made it impossible to grow food. Sudan, despite its civil war, has taken in more than a million refugees from Ethiopia, Uganda, and Chad. Immigrants from the spreading Sahel make up one-fifth of the total population in the Ivory Coast.[8] Wherever refugees settle, they flood the labor market, add to the local demand for food, and put new burdens on the land, thus spreading the environmental stress that originally forced them from their homes. Resource mismanagement is not the only cause of these mass movements, of course. Religious and ethnic conflicts, political repression, and other forces are at work. But the environmental causes are an essential factor. (See Chapter 15.)

GLOBAL CHANGE

A different kind of environmental concern has arisen from humankind's new ability to alter the environment on a planetary scale. The earth's physiology is shaped by the characteristics of four elements (carbon, nitrogen, phosphorous, and sulfur); by its living inhabitants (the biosphere); and by the interactions of the atmosphere and the oceans, which produce our climate.

Humankind is altering both the carbon and nitrogen cycles, having increased the natural carbon dioxide concentration in the atmosphere by 25 percent. This has occurred largely in the last three decades through fossil-fuel use and deforestation. The production of commercial fertilizer has doubled the amount of nitrogen nature makes available to living things. The use of a single, minor class of chemicals, chlorofluorocarbons, has punched a continent-sized "hole" in the ozone layer at the top of the stratosphere over Antarctica, and caused a smaller, but growing loss of ozone all around the planet. Species loss is destroying the work of three billion years of evolution. Together these changes could drastically alter the conditions in which life on earth has evolved.

The greenhouse effect results from the fact that the planet's atmosphere is largely transparent to incoming radiation from the sun, but absorbs much of the lower energy radiation reemitted by the earth. This natural phenomenon makes the earth warm enough to support life. But as emissions of greenhouse gases increase, the planet is warmed *un*naturally. Carbon dioxide produced from the combustion of fossil fuels and by deforestation is responsible for about half of the greenhouse effect. A number of other gases, notably methane (natural gas), nitrous oxide, ozone (in the lower atmosphere, as distinguished from the protective ozone layer in the stratosphere), and the synthetic chlorofluorocarbons are responsible for the other half (see Figure 14.2).

Figure 14.2 / Past and Future Warming Contribution for Primary Greenhouse Gases (Warming per Decade)[a]

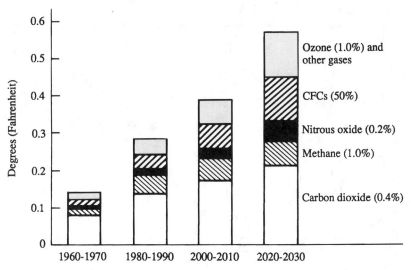

[a] Figures in parentheses indicate annual rate of increase of each gas as of 1986.
Sources: World Resources Institute, based on radiative forcing estimates in V. Ramanathan et al., 1985. *Journal of Geophysical Research* 90: 5547–5566. Annual rates of increase in atmospheric concentration from U.S. EPA, D. A. Lashof, and D. Tirsak, eds., *Policy Options for Stabilizing Global Climate* (1989).

Despite important uncertainties about aspects of the greenhouse warming, a virtually unanimous scientific consensus exists on its central features. If present emission trends continue, and unless some as yet undocumented phenomenon (possibly increased cloudiness) causes an offsetting cooling, the planet will, on average, get hotter because of the accumulation of these gases. Exactly how large the warming will be, and how fast it will occur, are uncertain. Existing models place the date of commitment to an average global warming of 1.5° to 4.5°C (3° to 8°F) in the early 2030s. The earth has not been this hot for two million years, long before human society, and indeed even Homo sapiens, existed (see Figure 14.3).

Hotter temperatures will be only one result of the continuing greenhouse warming. At some point, perhaps quite soon, precipitation patterns are likely to shift, possibly causing dustbowl-like conditions in the U.S. grain belt. Ocean currents are expected to do the same, dramatically altering the climates of many regions. A diversion of the Gulf Stream, for example, would transform Western Europe's climate, making it far colder than it is today. The sea level will rise due to the expansion of water when it is warmed and to the melting of land-based ice. The oceans are presently rising by one-half inch per decade, enough to cause serious erosion along much of the U.S. coast. The projected rise is one to four feet by the year 2050. Such a

Figure 14.3 / Average Global Temperatures

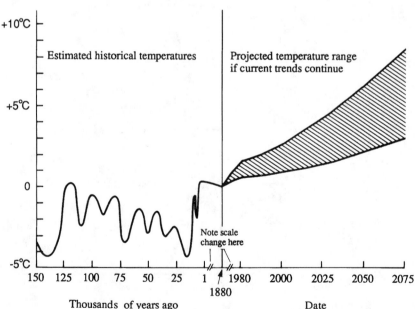

Sources: *Ozone Depletion, the Greenhouse Effect, and Climate Change.* Hearings before the Subcommittee on Environmental Pollution of the Committee on Environment and Public Works, U.S. Senate. June 10–11, 1986, p. 94; and the World Resources Institute.

large rise in the sea level would inundate vast coastal regions, erode shore-lines, destroy coastal marshes and swamps (areas of very high biological productivity), pollute water supplies through the intrusion of salt water, and put at high risk the vastly disproportionate share of the world's economic wealth that is packed along coastlines. The great river deltas, from the Mississippi to the Ganges, would be flooded. Estimates are that a half-meter rise in Egypt would displace 16 percent of the population, while a two-meter rise in Bangladesh would claim 28 percent of the land where 30 million people live today and where more than 59 million are projected to live by 2030.[9]

Positive consequences would be likely as well. Some plants would grow more quickly, fertilized by the additional carbon dioxide. (Many of them, however, will be weeds.) Rainfall might rise in what are now arid but potentially fertile regions, such as parts of sub-Saharan Africa. Conditions for agriculture would also improve in those northern areas that have both adequate soils and water supplies. Nonetheless, as the 1988 drought in the United States vividly demonstrated, human societies, industrial no less than rural, depend on the normal, predictable functioning of the climate system. Climate undergoing rapid change not only will be less predictable because it is different, but may be inherently more variable. Many climatologists believe that as accumulating greenhouse gases force the climate out of equilibrium, climate extremes—such as hurricanes, droughts, cold snaps, and typhoons—will become more frequent and perhaps more intense.[10]

Since climate change will be felt in every economic sector, adapting to its impact will be extremely expensive. Developing countries, with their small reserves of capital, shortages of scientists and engineers, and weak central governments, will be the least able to adapt, and the gap between the developed and developing worlds will almost certainly widen. Many of the adaptations needed will be prohibitively costly, and many impacts, notably the effects on wildlife and ecosystems, will be beyond the reach of human correction. A global strategy that relies on future adaption almost certainly means greater economic and human costs, and vastly larger biological losses, than would a strategy that attempts to control the extent and speed of the warming.[11]

Greenhouse change is closely linked to stratospheric ozone depletion, which is also caused by chlorofluorocarbons. The increased ultraviolet radiation resulting from losses in that protective layer will cause an increase in skin cancers and eye damage. It will have many still uncertain impacts on plant and animal life, and may suppress the immune systems of many species.

Serious enough in itself, ozone depletion illustrates a worrisome feature of humans' newfound ability to cause global change. It is almost impossible to predict accurately the long-term impact of new chemicals or processes on the environment. Chlorofluorocarbons were thoroughly tested when first introduced, and found to be benign. Their effect on the remote stratosphere was never considered.

Not only is it difficult to anticipate all the possible consequences in a highly interdependent, complex system, but also the system itself is poorly understood. When British scientists announced the appearance of a continent-sized "hole" in the ozone layer over Antarctica in 1985, the discovery sent shock waves through the scientific community. Although stratospheric ozone depletion had been the subject of intense study and debate for more than a decade, no one had predicted the Antarctic hole and no theory could account for it.

The lesson is this: current knowledge of planetary mechanisms is so scanty that the possibility of surprise, perhaps quite nasty surprise, must be rated rather high. The greatest risk may well come from a completely un-anticipated direction. We lack both crucial knowledge and early warning systems.

THE ROAD FORWARD

Absent profound change in our relationship to the environment, the future does not look bright. Consider the planet without such change in the year 2050. Economic growth is projected to have quintupled by then. Energy use could also quintuple; or, if post-1973 trends continue, it may grow more slowly, perhaps only doubling or tripling. The human species already con-sumes or destroys 40 percent of all the energy produced by terrestrial photo-synthesis, that is, 40 percent of the food energy potentially available to living things on land.[12] While that fraction may be sustainable, it is doubtful that it could keep pace with the expected doubling of the world's population. Human use of 80 percent of the planet's potential productivity does not seem compatible with the continued functioning of the biosphere as we know it. The expected rate of species loss would have risen from perhaps a few each day to several hundred a day. The pollution and toxic waste bur-den would likely prove unmanageable. Tropical forests would have largely disappeared, and arable land, a vital resource in a world of ten billion peo-ple, would be rapidly decreasing due to soil degradation. In short, sweeping change in economic production systems is not a choice but a necessity.

Fortunately, this grim sketch of conditions in 2050 is not a prediction, but a projection, based on current trends. Like all projections, it says more about the present and the recent past than it does about the future. The planet is not destined to a slow and painful decline into environmental chaos. There are technical, scientific, and economical solutions that are suit-able to many current trends, and enough is known about promising new approaches to be confident that the right kinds of research will produce huge payoffs. Embedded in current practices are vast costs in lost opportu-nities and waste, which, if corrected, would bring massive benefits. Some such steps will require only a reallocation of money, while others will re-quire sizable capital investments. None of the needed steps, however, requires globally unaffordable sums of money. What they do demand is a sizable shift in priorities.

For example, family-planning services cost about $10 per user, a tiny fraction of the cost of the basic human needs that would otherwise have to be met.[13] Already identified opportunities for raising the efficiency of energy use in the United States cost one-half to one-seventh the cost of new energy supply. Comparable savings are available in most other countries.[14] Agroforestry techniques, in which carefully selected combinations of trees and shrubs are planted together with crops, can not only replace the need for purchased fertilizer, but also improve soil quality, make more water available to crops, hold down weeds, and provide fuelwood and higher agricultural yields all at the same time.[15]

But if the technological opportunities are boundless, the social, political, and institutional barriers are huge. Subsidies, pricing policies, and economic discount rates encourage resource depletion in the name of economic growth, while delivering only the illusion of sustainable growth. Population control remains a controversial subject in much of the world. The traditional prerogatives of nation-states are poorly matched with the needs for regional cooperation and global decision-making. And ignorance of the biological underpinning of human society blocks a clear view of where the long-term threats to global security lie.

Overcoming these economic and political barriers will require social and institutional inventions comparable in scale and vision to the new arrangements conceived in the decade following World War II. Without the sharp political turning point of a major war, and with threats that are diffuse and long term, the task will be more difficult. But if we are to avoid irreversible damage to the planet and a heavy toll in human suffering, nothing less is likely to suffice. A partial list of the specific changes necessary suggests how demanding a task it will be.

Achieving sustainable economic growth will require the remodeling of agriculture, energy use, and industrial production after nature's example—their reinvention, in fact. These economic systems must become circular rather than linear. Industry and manufacturing will need processes that use materials and energy with high efficiency, recycle by-products, and produce little waste.[16] Energy demand will have to be met with the highest efficiency consistent with full economic growth. Agriculture will have to rely heavily upon free ecosystem services instead of nearly exclusive reliance on synthetic substitutes. And all systems will have to price goods and services to reflect the environmental costs of their provision.

A vital first step, one that can and should be taken in the very near term, would be to reinvent the national income accounts by which gross national product is measured. GNP is the foundation on which national economic policies are built, yet its calculation does not take into account resource depletion. A country can consume its forests, wildlife, and fisheries, its minerals, its clean water, and its topsoil, without seeing a reflection of the loss in its GNP. Nor are ecosystem services—sustaining soil fertility, moderating and storing rainfall, filtering air, and regulating the climate—valued, though their loss may entail great expense. The result is that economic policymakers are profoundly misled by their chief guide.[17]

A second step would be to invent a set of indicators by which global environmental health could be measured. Economic planning would be adrift without GNP, unemployment rates, and the like, and social planning without demographic indicators—fertility rates, infant mortality, literacy, life expectancy—would be impossible. Yet environmental policymaking must proceed today without comparable indicators.

Development assistance also requires new tools. Bilateral and multilateral donors have found that project success rates climb when nongovernmental organizations distribute funds and direct programs. This is especially true in agriculture, forestry, and conservation projects. The reasons are not mysterious. Such projects are more decentralized, more attuned to local needs and desires, and have a much higher degree of local participation in project planning. They are usually quite small in scale, however, and not capable of handling very large amounts of development funding. Often, too, their independent status threatens the national government. Finding ways to make far greater use of the strengths of such groups without weakening national governments is another priority for institutional innovation.[18]

More broadly, bilateral and multilateral aid donors must be convinced to view environmental considerations as an essential, constructive element of successful development lending, rather than a hurdle to be surmounted before a loan agreement can be signed. Though evidence supporting this truism is pouring in from the donors' own analysts—from hydroelectric projects that lose their capacity in years instead of decades due to deforestation, to African livestock projects with a 100 percent failure rate—the needed transformation in understanding is proceeding slowly, and unevenly.

Better ways must also be found to turn the scientific and engineering strengths of the industrialized world to the solution of the developing world's problems. The challenges include learning enough about local constraints and conditions to ask the right questions, making such research professionally rewarding to the individual scientist, and transferring technology more effectively. The international centers for agricultural research, a jointly managed network of thirteen institutions launched in the 1960s, is a successful model that might be improved upon and applied in other areas, such as energy, forestry, and soil management.

On the political front, the need for a new diplomacy and for new institutions and regulatory regimes to cope with the world's growing environmental interdependence is even more compelling. Put bluntly, our accepted definition of the limits of national sovereignty as coinciding with national borders is obsolete. The government of Bangladesh, no matter how hard it tries, cannot prevent tragic floods, such as it suffered in 1988. Preventing them requires active cooperation from Nepal and India. The government of

Canada cannot protect its water resources from acid rain without collaboration with the United States. Eighteen diverse nations share the heavily polluted Mediterranean Sea. Even the Caribbean Islands, as physically isolated as they are, find themselves affected by others' resource management policies, as locusts, inadvertently bred through generations of exposure to pesticides and now strong enough to fly all the way from Africa, infest their shores.

The majority of environmental problems demand regional solutions that encroach upon what we now think of as the prerogatives of national governments. This is because the phenomena themselves are defined by the limits of watershed, ecosystem, or atmospheric transport, not by national borders. Indeed, the costs and benefits of alternative policies cannot often be accurately judged without considering the region rather than the nation.

The developing countries especially will need to pool their efforts in the search for solutions. Three-quarters of the countries in sub-Saharan Africa, for example, have fewer people than live in New York City. National scientific and research capabilities cannot be built on such a small population base. Regional cooperation is required.

Dealing with global change will be more difficult. No one nation or even group of nations can meet these challenges, and no nation can protect itself from the actions—or inaction—of others. The United States, in particular, will have to assign a far greater prominence than it has heretofore to the practice of multilateral diplomacy. This would mean changes that range from the organization of the State Department and the language proficiency of the Foreign Service, to the definition of an international role that allows leadership without primacy, both in the slogging work of negotiation and in adherence to final outcomes. Above all, ways must soon be found to step around the deeply entrenched North-South cleavage and to replace it with a planetary sense of shared destiny. Perhaps the successes of the UN specialized agencies can be built upon for this purpose. But certainly the task of forging a global energy policy in order to control the greenhouse effect, for example, is a very long way from eradicating smallpox or sharing weather information.

The proposal by the former Soviet Union to turn the UN Trusteeship Council, which has outlived the colonies it was created to oversee, into a trusteeship for managing the global commons (the oceans, the atmosphere, biological diversity, and planetary climate) deserves close scrutiny. If a newly defined council could sidestep the UN's political fault lines, and incorporate, rather than supplant, the existing strengths of the United Nations Environment Program, it might provide a useful forum for reaching global environmental decisions at a far higher political level than anything that exists now.

Today's negotiating models—the Law of the Sea Treaty, the Nuclear Nonproliferation Treaty (NPT), even the promising Convention to Protect the Ozone Layer—are inadequate. Typically, such agreements take about fifteen years to negotiate and enter into force, and perhaps another ten years before substantial changes in behavior are actually achieved. (The NPT, which required only seven years to complete these steps, is a notable exception.) Far better approaches will be needed.

Among these new approaches, perhaps the most difficult to achieve will be ways to negotiate successfully in the presence of substantial scientific uncertainty. The present model is static: years of negotiation leading to a final product. The new model will have to be fluid, allowing a rolling process of intermediate or self-adjusting agreements that respond quickly to growing scientific understanding. The recent Montreal agreement on the ozone layer supplies a useful precedent by providing that one-third of the parties can reconvene a scientific experts group to consider new evidence as it becomes available. The new model will also require new economic methods for assessing risk, especially where the possible outcomes are irreversible. It will depend on a more active political role for biologists and chemists than they have been accustomed to, and far greater technical competence in the natural and planetary sciences among policymakers. Finally, the new model may need to forge a more involved and constructive role for the private sector. Relegating the affected industries to a heel-dragging, adversarial, outsiders role almost guarantees a slow process. The ozone agreement, to cite again this recent example, would not have been reached as quickly, and perhaps not at all, had it not been for the cooperation of the chlorofluorocarbon producers.

International law, broadly speaking, has declined in influence in recent years.[19] With leadership and commitment from the major powers, it might regain its lost status. But that will not be sufficient. To be effective, future arrangements will require provisions for monitoring, enforcement, and compensation, even when damage cannot be assigned a precise monetary value. These are all areas where international law has traditionally been weak.

This is only a partial agenda for the needed decade of invention. Meanwhile, much can and must be done with existing means. Four steps are most important: prompt revision of the Montreal Treaty, to eliminate completely the production of chlorofluorocarbons no later than the year 2000; full support for and implementation of the global Tropical Forestry Action Plan developed by the World Bank, the UN's Development Programme, the Food and Agricultural Organization, and the World Resources Institute; sufficient support for family-planning programs to ensure that all who want contraceptives have affordable access to them at least by the end of the decade; and, for the United States, a ten-year energy policy with the goal of increasing the energy productivity of our economy (i.e., reducing the amount of energy required to produce a dollar of GNP) by about 3 percent each year. While choosing four priorities from dozens of needed initiatives is highly arbitrary, these four stand out as ambitious yet achievable goals on which a broad consensus could be developed, and whose success would bring multiple, long-term global benefits touching every major international environmental concern.

Reflecting on the discovery of atomic energy, Albert Einstein noted "everything changed." And indeed, nuclear fission became the dominant force—military, geopolitical, and even psychological and social—of the ensuing decades. In the same sense, the driving force of the coming decades may well be environmental change. Humans are still utterly dependent on the natural world but now have for the first time the ability to alter it, rapidly and on a global scale. Because of that difference, Einstein's verdict that "we shall require a substantially new manner of thinking if mankind is to survive" still seems apt.

Notes

1. FAO, WRI, The World Bank and the United Nations Development Programme, "The Tropical Forestry Action Plan," FAO, Rome, June 1987, p. 5.

2. E. O. Wilson, ed., *Biodiversity*, National Academy Press, Washington, D.C., 1988, pp. 3–18.

3. World Resources Institute and International Institute for Environment and Development, *World Resources Report 1986*, Basic Books, New York, 1986, Chapters 4 and 8. Also, see M. W. Holdgate, et al., *The World Environment 1972–1982*, United Nations Environment Programme, Dublin, 1982, p. 267.

4. A. Maguire and J.W. Brown, eds., *Bordering on Trouble: Resources and Politics in Latin America*, Adler & Adler, Bethesda, 1986, p. 397.

5. E.L. Boado, in R. Repetto and M. Gillis, eds., *Public Policies and the Misuse of Forest Resources*, Cambridge University Press, Cambridge, 1988.

6. G. Porter and D.J. Ganapin, Jr., *Resources, Population and the Philippines' Future*, World Resources Institute, Washington, D.C. 1988, pp. 35–44 and 45–53.

7. J.T. Mathews, "Africa: Continent in Crisis," White Paper prepared for International Foundation for the Survival and Development of Humanity, World Resources Institute, August 1988.

8. N. Myers, *Not Far Afield: U.S. Interest and the Global Environment*, World Resources Institute, Washington, D.C., 1987, pp. 29–30.

9. United Nations Environment Programme (UNEP), "The Changing Atmosphere," UNEP Environment Brief No. 1, UNEP, Nairobi, undated.

10. G. Titus, ed., *Effects of Changes in Stratospheric Ozone and Global Change*, Vol. 1, *Overview*, U.S. Environmental Protection Agency, Washington, D.C., 1986.

11. J.T. Mathews, "Global Climate Change: Toward a Greenhouse Policy," *Issues in Science and Technology*, Spring 1987, pp. 57–68.

12. P.M. Vitousek, et al., "Human Appropriation of the Products of Photosynthesis," *BioScience*, Vol. 36, No. 6, 1986, pp. 368–73.

13. N. Sadik, "The State of World Population 1989," United Nations Population Fund (UNFPA), 1989, p. 19.

14. A.H. Rosenfeld, "Conservation, Competition and National Security," testimony on the Role of Conservation in the National Energy Picture, Subcommittee on Energy and Power, Committee on Energy and Commerce, U.S. House of Representatives, Nov. 4, 1987. Also, W.U. Chandler, et al., "Energy Efficiency: A New Agenda," American Council for Energy Efficient Economy, Washington, D.C., 1988. Also, W. Keepin and G. Kats, "Greenhouse Warming: Comparative Analysis of Nuclear and Efficiency Abatement Strategies," *Energy Policy*, Vol. 16, No. 6, 1988, pp. 538–61.

15. R. Winterbottom and P.T. Hazlewood, "Agroforestry and Sustainable Development: Making the Connection," *Ambio*, Vol. 16, No. 2–3, 1987.

16. G. Speth, "The Greening of Technology," *The Washington Post*, Nov. 20, 1988.

17. R. Repetto, et al., *Wasting Assets: Natural Resources in the National Income Accounts*, World Resources Institute, Washington, D.C., 1989.

18. P. Harrison, *The Greening of Africa: Breaking through in the Battle for Land and Food*, Penguin Books, New York, 1987, pp. 278–318.

19. W.P. Bundy, "The 1950s Versus the 1990s," in E.K. Hamilton, ed., *America's Global Interests: A New Agenda*, W. W. Norton & Co., New York, 1989, pp. 33–81.

15 / Environmental Scarcity and Intergroup Conflict

THOMAS HOMER-DIXON[1]

By the year 2025, the planet's human population will soar from 1992's 5.3 billion to a figure probably over eight billion. Global economic output—the total production of goods and services traded in markets around the planet—will also skyrocket from around $20 trillion to perhaps $60 trillion in current dollars. Largely as a result of these two global trends, environmental change will occur much faster, and be much more widespread and severe. Around the planet, human beings will face a steady decline in the total area of high-quality agricultural land. Much of the planet's remaining virgin forests will vanish along with the wealth of species they shelter. We will also see the exhaustion and pollution of many rivers, aquifers, and other water resources; the collapse of key fisheries; further ozone depletion in the stratosphere; and maybe significant climate change due to global warming.

We can think of these environmental changes as "scarcities" of vital renewable resources such as soil, water, forests, fish, the stratospheric ozone layer, and an equable climate.[2] Although people have long speculated that such scarcity could contribute to intergroup conflict, little clear evidence was available. But in the last three years, various researchers have gathered enough information to reach a disturbing conclusion: scarcities of renewable resources (or "environmental scarcities," as I call them here) are already contributing to very violent conflicts in many parts of the developing world. Moreover, these conflicts may be the early signs of an upsurge of violence in the coming decades—especially in poor countries—that is caused or aggravated by environmental change.[3]

Experts have proposed numerous possible links between environmental change and conflict. Some have suggested that environmental change may shift the balance of power between states either regionally or globally, causing instabilities that could lead to war.[4] Another possibility is that global environmental damage might increase the gap between rich and poor societies, with the poor then violently confronting the rich for a fairer share of the world's wealth.[5] Severe conflict may also arise from frustration with countries that do not go along with agreements to protect the global environment, or that "free-ride" by letting other countries absorb the costs of environmental protection. Warmer temperatures could lead to contention over more easily harvested resources in the Antarctic. Bulging populations and land stress may produce waves of environmental refugees, spilling across borders and disrupting relations among ethnic groups. Countries might fight among themselves because of dwindling supplies of water and the effects of upstream pollution.[6] A sharp decline in food crop production and grazing land could lead to conflict between nomadic tribes and sedentary farmers.

Environmental change could in time cause a slow deepening of poverty in poor countries, which might open bitter divisions between classes and ethnic groups, corrode democratic institutions, and spawn revolutions and insurgencies.[7] In general, many experts have the sense that environmental problems will "ratchet up" the level of stress within states and the international community, increasing the likelihood of many different kinds of conflict—from war and rebellion to trade disputes—and undermining possibilities for cooperation.

Which of these scenarios are most plausible, and why? In the following pages, I discuss why environmental issues have become prominent in recent years, and provide a framework for understanding them. I then identify the likely links between environmental change and violent conflict, and illustrate these links with several case studies. The chapter concludes with a discussion of international environmental negotiations culminating in the 1992 United Nations conference in Rio de Janeiro, and with a series of recommendations for action by both rich and poor countries.

The case studies discussed in this chapter reflect the results of a three-year research project on "Environmental Change and Acute Conflict" jointly organized by the Peace and Conflict Studies Program at the University of Toronto and the American Academy of Arts and Sciences in Cambridge, Massachusetts. This project brought together a team of thirty researchers from four continents. We found that poor countries are likely to be affected sooner and more harshly by environmental scarcity than rich countries. This is because they usually do not have abundant financial, material, and intellectual resources, and because their economic and political institutions are often weak and inflexible. Poor societies, therefore, are less able to buffer themselves from environmental scarcity and the social crises it can cause.

Our research also suggests that violence arising from environmental change will generally not follow the age-old pattern of conflicts over scarce resources, where one group or nation tries to seize the water, oil, or minerals of another. This is partly because some environmental resources—such as the climate and the ozone layer—are held in common. It is also because the social effects of environmental scarcity are often insidious, such as slow population displacement and economic disruption, that can in turn lead to clashes between ethnic groups and to social rebellion. But, while these types of conflict may not be as conspicuous or dramatic as wars between countries over scarce resources, they may have critical implications for the security interests of rich and poor nations alike.

UNFORESEEN THRESHOLDS

Why are people suddenly paying attention to environmental issues? Clearly, the end of the Cold War has given the public and its leaders a chance to think about problems other than U.S.-Soviet hostility. But there is another factor at work: during the last decade there has been a genuine shift in experts' perceptions of global environmental problems. Experts used to perceive environmental systems as relatively stable and resilient, in spite of the fact that humans were harvesting resources and dumping wastes on a massive scale. They thought that these systems would change only slowly in response to human insults. But now scientists have discovered that these systems may exhibit sudden changes or "threshold" effects, which means that it may be much easier than was previously thought to push a system from one equilibrium state to a very different equilibrium state. Thus, in 1987, geochemist Wallace Broecker noted that recent polar ice-core and ocean-sediment data indicate that "Earth's climate does not respond to forcing in a smooth and gradual way. Rather, it responds in sharp jumps which involve large-scale reorganization of Earth's system. . . . We must consider the possibility that the main responses of the system to our provocation of the atmosphere will come in jumps whose timing and magnitude are unpredictable."[8]

A dramatic example of such a threshold effect in a complex environmental system was the discovery of the Antarctic ozone hole in the mid-1980s.[9] The scientific models of ozone depletion used to that point had, for the most part, assumed that ozone depletion would increase in steady, constant steps as chlorofluorocarbon (CFC) emissions increased. But it turns out that, if the conditions are right, massive depletion can occur at lightning speed, stripping the ozone from mile-thick layers of the stratosphere in a matter of days. The Antarctic ozone hole was startling evidence of the instability of environmental systems in response to human inputs, of the ability of humans to significantly affect the ecosystem on a global scale, and of our inability to predict exactly how the system will change.

This new perception of the nature of the environmental system has percolated out of the scientific community into the policymaking community. It may also be influencing the broader public's view of environmental problems. Scientists, political leaders, and the general public are beginning to interpret data about environmental change in a new light: constant, step-by-step degradation of environmental systems is not as tolerable as it was once considered to be. We do not know where and when we might cross a threshold and move to a radically different and perhaps very undesirable system.

KEY VARIABLES AND RELATIONSHIPS

The environmental problems facing humankind might seem overwhelming. They are large-scale, long-term, and poorly understood. They strike directly at our most intimate links to the biosphere, including our ability to get the food and water we need for survival and for the stability of our societies.[10] But we must avoid slipping into simpleminded "environmental determinism"; in other words, we must not assume that the environment surrounding us determines, inescapably and inevitably, our behavior and degree of happiness. Our societies are often very flexible; human beings can be very creative; and many factors often permit great variability and adaptability in human-environmental systems.

Some of these factors are identified in Figure 15.1. It shows that the total effect of human activity on the environment in a particular ecological region is a function of two main variables: first, the product of total population in the region and physical activity per capita; and, second, the vulnerability of the ecosystem in that region to those particular physical activities.[11] Activity per capita is a function of available physical resources in the region (including nonrenewable resources, such as minerals, and renewable resources, such as water, forests, and agricultural land) along with social and psychological factors (such as institutions, social relations, preferences, and beliefs). The figure also shows that environmental change, such as the degradation of agricultural land, might cause certain types of social effect, such as the large-scale migration of people out of the affected region. This could in turn lead to various kinds of conflict, especially ethnic conflict as newcomers of one group come in contact with local residents of a different group. There are important feedback loops from social effects and conflict to the social and psychological factors at the top of the figure, and then back to activity per capita and population. For example, migration could alter relationships among classes and ethnic groups in a society, which might in turn affect its economic activity.

The factors at the top of Figure 15.1 are particularly important. This social and psychological context is broad and complex. It includes the degree of inequality of land and wealth distribution in a society; the system of

Figure 15.1 / Main Variables and Causal Relations

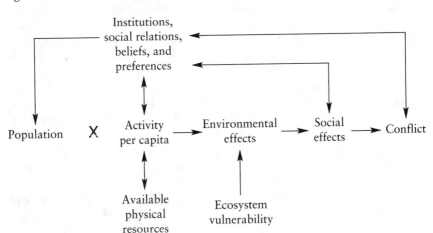

property rights and markets that encourages or discourages the production of goods and services within the economy; family and community structures; perceptions of the chances of long-run political stability within the society; historically rooted patterns of trade with other societies; the distribution of power among countries in the international system; and beliefs about the relationship between humans and nature.

Without a deep understanding of these factors we cannot begin to grasp the true nature of the relationships between human activity, environmental change, and its social effects, or the vulnerability, adaptability, and flexibility of societies when faced with environmental stress.[12]

ENVIRONMENTAL SCARCITY AND ITS SOCIAL EFFECTS

We have used the term "environmental scarcity" in our discussion to this point without a precise definition. There are three main sources of human-induced environmental scarcity. First, human activity can either reduce the quantity or degrade the quality of an environmental resource faster than the resource is renewed. Experts often refer to this process using terms similar to those we use for money in a bank, where we talk about "capital" and the "interest" or "income" it earns. The capital of a renewable resource is the resource stock (say, a forest) that generates a flow of income (the annual wood production through normal growth of the forest) that can be tapped for human consumption and well-being. A "sustainable" economy should not produce an average loss of the resource greater than this income.

The second main cause of environmental scarcity is population growth, which can reduce the amount of a renewable resource available per person. For example, a given flow of water or a given area of cropland might, over time, have to be divided among more and more people.

Third, a change in the way a resource is distributed in a society can concentrate the resource in the hands of a few people, thereby consigning the rest of the population to extreme scarcity. The property rights that affect resource distribution often change as a result of large-scale development projects or the introduction of new technologies that alter the relative values of resources.

These three sources of environmental scarcity can operate singly or in combination, and can have a variety of critical social effects, including declining food production, general economic stagnation or decline, displacement of population, and the disruption of institutions and traditional social relations among people and groups. These social effects, in turn, are often interlinked, and sometimes reinforce each other. For example, migration resulting from a drop in food output may further reduce food production by causing a shortage of farm labor. Or, economic decline may lead to the flight of people with wealth and education, which in turn weakens universities, courts, and institutions of economic management—all of which are crucial to a healthy economy.

Agricultural Production

Experts often suggest that constrained food output is the most worrisome possible result of environmental scarcity.[13] Around the world, agricultural land is decreasing in availability and quality. Currently, total global cropland amounts to about 1.5 billion hectares, which is roughly twice the area of the lower forty-eight states. Optimistic estimates of potential cropland on the planet range from 3.2 to 3.4 billion hectares, but nearly all of the best land has already been used. What is left is either less fertile, not sufficiently rain fed or easily irrigated, infested with pests, or harder to clear, plow, and plant. During the 1980s, cropland grew in the developing countries at just 0.26 percent a year, less than half the rate of the 1970s. More importantly, cropland per capita dropped by 1.9 percent a year.[14] Without a major increase in the amount of cropland in developing countries, experts expect that the world average of 0.28 hectares per capita will decline to 0.17 hectares by the year 2025, given the current rate of world population growth.[15] Moreover, large areas of land are being lost each year to a combination of problems, including encroachment by cities, erosion, depletion of nutrients, acidification, compacting, and salinization and waterlogging from over-irrigation.[16] For certain regions, the drop in the availability of good cropland may in time sharply limit food output, depending upon the ability of societies to increase the "intensity" of their agricultural practices (that is, to increase yields per hectare through mechanization, greater fertilization and irrigation, and the use of new seeds).

But there are many other factors besides land availability that may influence agricultural production, including deforestation, depletion of water supplies, greenhouse warming, and increased ultraviolet radiation from ozone depletion. The Philippines provides a good illustration of deforestation's impact on food output.[17] Across the archipelago, logging and land clearing have accelerated erosion, changed regional hydrological cycles (the cycles of water among the atmosphere, land, and plants), and decreased the land's ability to hold water during rainy periods. The resulting flash floods have damaged irrigation works while plugging reservoirs and irrigation channels with silt.

Greenhouse warming and climate change may also affect agricultural production, although this is a contentious issue.[18] Coastal croplands in countries such as Bangladesh, Egypt, and China are very vulnerable to storm surges. Such events could become more common and devastating, because global warming will cause sea levels to rise and could intensify storms. The greenhouse effect will also change rainfall patterns and soil moisture; while this may benefit some agricultural regions, others will suffer. Countries at special risk from climate change will be those—such as the nations of the

Sahel in sub-Saharan Africa—with an imbalance between population and food growing ability, and with little money to fund changes in their agricultural systems. As some areas become too dry to grow food, while others, formerly dry, suddenly have enough water, many poor countries will not be able to afford the new dams, wells, irrigation systems, roads, and storage silos that they need in order to adjust.

Many plants grow faster and larger in a warm environment rich in carbon dioxide, and they often use water more efficiently. Some scientists therefore conclude that greenhouse warming will increase global agricultural output. But optimistic estimates of increased crop yields have been based on laboratory experiments under ideal growing conditions, including ideal amounts of soil nutrients and water. In addition, these estimates have ignored the influence on yields of more frequent extreme climate events (especially droughts and heat waves), increased insect infestation, and the decreased nutritional quality of crops grown in a carbon-dioxide enriched atmosphere.[19]

In general, the magnitude of climate change is likely to be less of a problem for poor countries than the *rate* of change. Around the world, human beings and their agricultural systems have adapted to differences in temperature far greater than the maximum warming predicted for the next 100 years. But the rapid rate expected for this change will produce new pressures on human society at a time when they are already stressed by other population and resource problems. These changes may be too fast and complex for societies that have limited buffering capacities.

Economic Decline

A very important social effect of environmental scarcity is the further poverty it causes in already poor countries. A country's ability to produce wealth may be affected directly by environmental stress, or indirectly by lower food output and population movements caused by environmental problems. There are numerous possible mechanisms. For instance, the higher ultraviolet radiation caused by stratospheric ozone depletion is likely to raise the rate of disease in humans and livestock, which may cost poor societies dearly. Similarly, logging for export markets—as in Southeast Asia, West Africa, and Central America—may produce short-term economic gains for a country's elite, but the resulting deforestation can also greatly affect longer-term economic productivity. The increased water runoff caused by deforestation damages roads, bridges, and other valuable infrastructure; and extra siltation reduces the capacity of rivers to generate hydroelectric power, as well as their usefulness as transport routes for ships and barges. As forests are destroyed, moreover, wood becomes scarcer and more expensive, and it takes up more of the household budget of poor families using it for cooking and heating fuel.

Farming is the source of a large share of the wealth generated in poor societies. It is not uncommon for nearly 50 percent of a country's GNP to be generated by farming, and for 60 percent or more of its population to depend on agriculture for jobs. Food output has soared in many regions over the last decades because expanded irrigation, fertilizer use, and new agricultural technologies (such as high-yielding varieties of grain) have produced a "green revolution" that has more than compensated for the declining soil fertility and depth.

In many poor countries, the effects of land scarcity and degradation will probably become much clearer as the gains from green-revolution technologies are fully realized. But, despite the extravagant claims of some commentators, there is no new generation of agricultural technologies waiting in the wings to keep food productivity rising. Genetic engineering may in time help scientists develop salinity-resistant, drought-resistant, and nitrogen-fixing grains, but their wide use in poor countries is probably decades in the future.

Damage to the soil is already producing a harsh economic impact in some areas. Unfortunately, measuring the actual cost of land degradation is not easy. Current national income accounts—statements of GNP—do not include measures of resource depletion. The economist Robert Repetto comments: "A nation could exhaust its mineral reserves, cut down its forests, erode its soils, pollute its aquifers, and hunt its wildlife to extinction—all without affecting measured income."[20] Such weak measures of economic productivity reinforce the belief of government officials in poor countries that there is a direct trade-off between economic growth and environmental protection; this belief, in turn, encourages societies to generate present income at the expense of their potential for future income.

A more realistic assessment of the economic consequences of environmental damage would challenge these beliefs. Thus, after a careful analysis of soil types, cropping practices, logging, and erosion rates in upland areas of Java in Indonesia, Repetto concludes that the country's national income accounts "significantly overstate the growth of agricultural income in Indonesia's highlands." Taking lost future income into account, Repetto calculates the one year cost of erosion in Indonesia to be $481 million, which is about 40 percent of the annual value of upland cropland production. He also estimates that costs downstream from eroded hillsides, including the higher expense of clearing waterways and irrigation channels of silt, come to $30 to $100 million a year.[21]

A similar assessment emerges from recent research on China, in which Vaclav Smil has estimated the combined effect of environmental problems on current economic productivity. The main economic burdens he identifies are reduced crop yields caused by water, soil, and air pollution; more human sickness from air pollution; farmland loss because of construction and erosion; nutrient loss and flooding due to erosion and deforestation; and timber loss arising from poor harvesting practices. Smil calculates the current cost to be at least 15 percent of China's gross domestic product, and he is convinced that the economic toll will become much heavier during the coming decades.[22]

Population Displacement

Some commentators have claimed that environmental degradation may produce vast numbers of "environmental refugees."[23] For example, sea-level rise due to global warming may drive people back from coastal and delta areas in Egypt; soil degradation and desertification may empty countries in the African Sahel as their populations move south; and Filipino fishermen may leave their ruined fishing grounds for the cities. But the term "environmental refugee" is misleading, because it implies that environmental scarcity will be the direct and sole cause of refugee flows. Usually, it will be only one of a large number of interacting physical and social factors that *together* force people from their homelands. The term also does not distinguish between people who are genuine "refugees" from disaster and acute hardship, and those who are "migrants" for a variety of less urgent reasons. In general, migrants are motivated by a combination of "push" and "pull" factors, while refugees are motivated primarily by "push" factors.

The northeast region of the Indian subcontinent provides a good example of population displacement arising from environmental scarcity. Over the last three decades, land scarcity has been a key factor causing the large-scale movement of people from Bangladesh to the Indian state of Assam. In the future, people may be driven from Bangladesh by other environmental problems, including rising sea-levels combined with cyclones (made worse by climate change), and by terrible flooding due to deforestation in watersheds upstream on the Ganges and Brahmaputra rivers. Similarly, Vaclav Smil predicts that, over the coming decades, tens of millions of Chinese will try to move from the country's impoverished interior and northern regions, where water and fuelwood are desperately scarce and the land often badly damaged, to the booming cities along the coast. In all likelihood, bitter disputes will develop among these regions over water sharing and migration.

Disrupted Institutions and Social Relations

All societies are held together by a thick fabric of institutions, organizations, rules, customs, and habitual behavior. Environmental scarcity will tear this fabric, mainly as a result of the social effects described above. Falling agricultural output will weaken rural villages through malnutrition and disease, and by encouraging people to leave. Economic decline will corrode confidence in the national purpose, and undermine financial, legal, and political institutions. And mass migrations of people into a region will drive down wages, shift relations between workers, peasants, and land owners, and upset the long-standing balance of economic and political power among ethnic groups.

We must pay particular attention to how environmental scarcity affects the state in developing countries.[24] Environmental scarcity sharply raises financial and political demands on government by requiring huge spending on new infrastructure. It also drives up the number of "marginal" people who barely survive on the edges of society and who are desperate for government help. Simultaneously, the loss of renewable resources, from fish and fertile land to abundant forests, can reduce tax revenues to local and national governments. We have, then, the potential for a widening gap between demands on the state and its financial ability to meet these demands. Such a gap could in time boost frustration within a poor society, erode the state's legitimacy, and increase competition between cliques and factions within its elite as they struggle to protect their shares of the economic pie.

ENVIRONMENTAL SCARCITY AND VIOLENT CONFLICT

If food production stagnates, if developing societies slide further into poverty, if large numbers of people leave their homelands, and if institutions and social relations are disrupted, what kinds of conflict are likely to develop?

We do not have much data with which to answer this question. This may be partly because environmental and population pressures have not yet passed a critical threshold of severity in many poor countries. Also, until recently, there was little good research on the conflicts caused by environmental scarcity. But three types of conflict seem most likely: scarcity, group-identity, and deprivation conflicts.

Scarcity Conflicts

Scarcity conflicts are those we intuitively expect when countries calculate their self-interest in a world where the amount of resources is fixed. Such conflicts will probably arise over three types of resource in particular: river water, prime fisheries, and good cropland. These are likely to spark conflict because their scarcity is increasing swiftly in some regions, because they are often critical to human survival, and because they can be physically seized or controlled.

The current controversy over the Euphrates River illustrates how scarcity conflicts can arise. On January 13, 1990, Turkey began filling the giant reservoir behind the new Ataturk Dam in eastern Turkey. For one month, Turkey held back the main flow of the Euphrates River, which cut the downstream flow in Syria to about a quarter of its normal rate. By early in the next century, Turkey plans to build a huge complex of twenty dams and irrigation systems along the upper reaches of the Euphrates. This will reduce the annual average flow of the Euphrates within Syria by more than a third. Syria is already desperately short of water: almost all water for its towns, industries, and farms comes from the Euphrates, and the country has been chronically vulnerable to drought. Syria's population growth rate, at 3.6 percent per year, is one of the highest in the world, which gives a further push to the country's demand for water.

Turkey and Syria have exchanged angry threats over this situation. Syria gives sanctuary to guerrillas of the Kurdish Workers Party (the PKK), which has long been waging an insurgency against the Turkish government in the eastern part of the country. Turkey suspects that Syria might be using these separatists to gain leverage in bargaining over Euphrates water. Thus, in October 1989, then prime minister Turgut Ozal said that Turkey might cut off the river's water if Syria did not restrain the PKK. Although he later retracted the threat, the tensions have not been resolved, and there are currently no high-level talks on water sharing.

Clearly, the problem of Euphrates water is tangled up with issues of territorial integrity and relations between government and ethnic minorities in both Syria and Turkey. Although water scarcity is a source of serious tensions between Syria and Turkey, and may produce interstate violence in the future, this dispute is not a pure example of a scarcity conflict. Truly pure examples may be impossible to find.

Experts in international relations who address the security implications of environmental scarcity usually emphasize the potential for interstate scarcity conflicts.[25] Yet, our research shows that these conflicts will not be the most common to arise from environmental stress. Indeed, as discussed below, ethnic disputes and corrosive conflict within countries deserve greater attention from analysts.

Group-identity Conflicts

Group-identity conflicts are likely to arise from the large-scale movements of populations caused by environmental scarcity. As different ethnic and cultural groups are pushed together by these migrations, we should expect people in these groups to see themselves and their neighbors in terms of "we" and "they"; in other words, they will use the identity of their own group to judge the worth of other groups, often negatively.[26] Such attitudes can lead to violence. The situation in the Bangladesh-Assam region is a good example: Assam's ethnic strife over the last decade has apparently been catalyzed by in-migration from Bangladesh (see the case study on p. 302).[27]

As population and environmental stresses grow in poor countries, we can also expect surging immigration to the industrialized world. People will seek to move from Latin America to the United States and Canada, from North Africa and the Middle East to Europe, and from South and Southeast Asia to Australia. This migration has already shifted the ethnic balance in many cities and regions of the richer countries, where governments are struggling to contain a backlash against "foreigners." Such racial strife will undoubtedly become much worse.

Although it seems probable that environmental scarcity will cause people to move in large numbers, thereby producing conflict, several qualifications are needed. First, refugees tend to be weak, which limits their ability to organize and to make demands on the government of the receiving society. Rather than provoking overt violence, therefore, a common result will be silent misery and death, with little destabilizing effect. Second, displaced groups often need the backing of a state (either that of the receiving society or an external state) before they have sufficient power to cause conflict. And, finally, we must remember that migration does not always produce negative results. It can, for instance, ease labor shortages in the receiving society—as has been the case, for instance, in Malaysia. We only have to look to countries as diverse as Canada, Thailand, and Malawi to conclude that the capacity of societies to absorb migrants without conflict is often substantial.

Deprivation Conflicts

As poor societies produce less wealth because of environmental problems, their citizens will probably become increasingly angered by the widening gap between their actual standard of living and the standard they feel they deserve. The rate of change is key: the faster the economic deterioration, the greater the discontent. Lower-status groups will usually be more frustrated than others, because elites will use their power to maintain, as best they can, the same standard of living despite a shrinking economic pie. At some point, the frustration and anger of some groups may cross a critical threshold, and they will act violently against those groups perceived to be the agents of their economic misery, or those thought to be benefiting from an unfair distribution of economic rewards in the society.[28]

In general, experts on conflict within societies tell us that rebellion, revolution, and insurgency are likely when: (1) there are clearly defined and organized groups in a society; (2) some of these groups regard their level of economic achievement, and in turn the broader political and economic system, as wholly unfair; and (3) these same groups believe that all peaceful opportunities to achieve change are blocked, yet regard the balance of power within the society as unstable—in others words, they believe that there are opportunities for overthrowing authority in the society.[29]

Environmental scarcity helps produce both the second and third of these conditions. As we have seen, a key social effect of this scarcity in poor countries is the disruption of institutions, such as the state. Thus, environmental problems may not only increase the frustration and anger within poor societies (through increased deprivation); in addition, by weakening the state and other institutions, environmental problems may open up opportunities for angry groups to overthrow existing authority.

CASE STUDIES

We can now review several case studies of environmental conflict in today's world. Earlier, I identified three sources of environmental scarcity: degradation and depletion of renewable resources, population growth, and changes in resource distribution among groups. In this section, I will show how these three sources operate singly or in combination to produce the types of conflict just discussed. The case studies below, which deal in particular with shortages of good agricultural land, suggest that group-identity and deprivation conflicts will be especially common outcomes of environmental scarcity (see Figure 15.2).

Bangladesh-Assam

In some cases, population growth by itself will be a key source of social stress and conflict. Bangladesh, for instance, does not suffer from critical degradation or loss of agricultural land, because the normal floods of the Ganges and Brahmaputra rivers lay down a layer of silt every year that helps maintain the fertility of the country's vast plains. But the United Nations predicts that Bangladesh's current population of 115 million will grow to 235 million by the year 2025. Cropland is already desperately scarce at about 0.08 hectares per capita, but since all of the country's good agricultural land has already been exploited, population growth will cut this figure in half by 2025. Land scarcity and the brutal poverty and social turmoil it produces have been made worse by extreme floods and the susceptibility of the country to cyclones.

Over the last four decades, these stresses have caused millions of people to migrate from East Pakistan/Bangladesh to neighboring areas of India. Detailed data are scarce; the Bangladeshi government is reluctant to admit that there is significant out-migration, since the question has become a major source of friction with India. But Sanjoy Hazarika, an investigative journalist who reports for the *New York Times* from South Asia, has pieced together demographic information and experts' estimates. He concludes

Figure 15.2 / Some Sources and Consequences of Environmental Scarcity

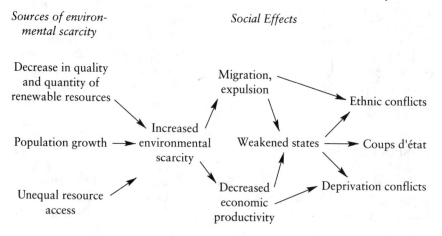

that migrants from Bangladesh and their descendants have increased the population of neighboring areas of India by fifteen million people, of which only one or two million can be attributed to migration caused by the 1971 war between India and Pakistan that resulted in the creation of Bangladesh. He estimates that the population of the Indian state of Assam has swelled by at least seven million people, of Tripura by one million, and of West Bengal by about seven million.[30]

This enormous movement of people has produced sweeping changes in the politics and economies of the receiving regions.[31] It has altered land distribution, economic relations, and the balance of political power between religious and ethnic groups, and it has triggered serious intergroup conflict in Assam. Members of the Lalung tribe, for instance, have long resented Muslim Bengali migrants, and they accuse the newcomers of stealing the area's richest farmland. In early 1983, violence finally exploded during a bitter election for federal offices in the state. In the village of Nellie, Lalung tribespeople used machetes, knives, and spears to hack to death nearly 1,700 Bengalis in one five-hour rampage.

In the neighboring Indian state of Tripura, the original Buddhist and Christian inhabitants now make up only 29 percent of the state's population, with the rest consisting of Hindu migrants from East Pakistan/Bangladesh. This shift in the ethnic balance precipitated a violent insurgency between 1980 and 1988 that was called off only after the government agreed to return land to dispossessed Tripuris and stop the influx. But as the migration has continued, this agreement is in jeopardy.

The Senegal River Basin

Elsewhere in the world, population growth and damage to renewable resources often encourage large-scale development projects that can alter access to resources. This, in turn, can produce dire environmental scarcity for poorer and less powerful groups whose claims to resources are opposed by elites, and this may lead to violence. A good example is the dispute that began in West Africa in 1989 between Mauritania and Senegal over the Senegal River basin that defines their common border.[32]

Senegal has fairly abundant agricultural land, but much of it suffers from high to severe wind and water erosion, loss of nutrients, salinization, and compaction caused by agriculture. The country has an overall population density of 380 people per square kilometer and a population growth rate of 2.7 percent, giving a doubling time of about twenty-five years. Except for the Senegal Valley along its southern border and a few oases, Mauritania is largely arid desert and semiarid grassland. Although its population density is very low at about twenty people per square kilometer, the growth rate is 2.8 percent. This combination of factors led the UN Food and Agriculture Organization (FAO), in a 1982 study, to include both Mauritania and Senegal in their list of "critical" countries whose croplands cannot support their current and projected populations without a large increase in agricultural inputs, such as fertilizer and irrigation.

The floodplains fringing the Senegal River are broad and fertile, and support a productive economy—farming, herding, and fishing—based on the river's annual floods. During the 1970s, a serious drought and the prospect of a chronic food shortfall in the region encouraged the region's governments to seek international financing for the high Manantali Dam on the Bafing River tributary in Mali and for the Diama salt-intrusion barrage near the mouth of the Senegal River between Senegal and Mauritania. These dams were designed to regulate the river's flow to produce hydropower, expand irrigated agriculture, and provide river transport from the Atlantic Ocean to landlocked Mali. But as anthropologist Michael Horowitz has found, anticipation of the new infrastructure sharply increased land values along the river where irrigation could be installed. This led the white Moor elite in Mauritania to rewrite legislation governing land ownership, effectively stripping black Africans of their rights to continue farming and herding along the Mauritanian bank of the river.

There has been a long history of racism by white Moors in Mauritania toward their non-Arab black compatriots. In the spring of 1989, tensions in the river basin triggered an explosion of black Senegalese hostility toward the Moors. Within a few weeks, almost all of the 17,000 shops owned by Moors in Senegal were pillaged or destroyed, several hundred people had been killed and thousands injured in ethnic violence in both countries, nearly 200,000 refugees fled in both directions across the border, and the two countries were nearly at war. The Mauritanian regime used this occasion to activate the new land legislation, declaring the black population along the Mauritanian portion of the river basin to be "Senegalese," stripping them of their citizenship, and seizing their properties and livestock. Many of these blacks were forcibly expelled to Senegal, and some launched cross-border raids to retrieve expropriated cattle.

We see here the interaction of the three sources of human-induced environmental scarcity I have identified. Agricultural shortfalls, caused in part by population pressures and degradation of the land resource, encouraged a large development scheme. These factors together raised land values in one of the few areas in either country offering the potential for a rapid move to high-intensity agriculture. The result was a change in property rights and resource distribution, a sudden increase in resource scarcity for an ethnic minority, expulsion of the minority, and ethnic violence.

The Philippines

In many parts of the world, we see a somewhat different process: unequal resource access combines with population growth to produce environmental damage. This can lead to economic deprivation that spurs insurgency and rebellion. In the Philippines, Spanish and American colonial policies left behind a grossly unfair distribution of land. Since the 1960s, the introduction of green-revolution technologies has permitted a dramatic increase in lowland production of grain for domestic consumption and of cash crops that has helped to pay off the country's massive external debt. This modernization has raised demand for agricultural labor. Unfortunately, though, the gain has been overwhelmed by a population growth rate of 2.5 to 3.0 percent. Combined with the maldistribution of good cropland and an economic crisis in the first half of the 1980s, this growth produced a surge in agricultural unemployment. With insufficient rural or urban industrialization to absorb excess labor, there has been unrelenting downward pressure on wages.

Economically desperate, millions of poor agricultural laborers and landless peasants have migrated to shantytowns in already overburdened cities, such as Manila; millions of others have moved to the least productive, and often most ecologically vulnerable territories, such as steep hillsides.[33] In these uplands, settlers use fire to clear forested or previously logged land. They bring with them little money or knowledge to protect their fragile ecosystems, and their small-scale logging, production of charcoal for the cities, and slash-and-burn farming often cause horrendous environmental damage—particularly water erosion, landslides, and changes in the hydrological cycle. This has set in motion a cycle of falling food production, the clearing of new plots, and further land degradation. Even marginally fertile land is becoming hard to find in many places, and economic conditions are often critical for the peasants (see Figure 15.3).[34]

The Philippines has suffered from serious internal strife for many decades. But Celso Roque, the former undersecretary of the environment of

Figure 15.3 / Some Sources and Consequences of Environmental Scarcity in the Philippines

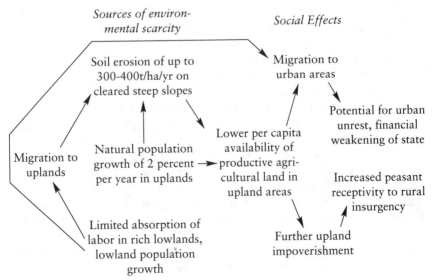

the Philippines, and his colleague Maria Garcia have concluded that resource stress appears to be an increasingly powerful force driving the present communist-led insurgency. Some senior Filipino politicians have reached the same conclusion. Daniel Lacson, the governor of the province of Negros Occidental under President Aquino, identifies two sources of poverty and injustice behind the insurgency: the accumulation of land in the hands of a few who have failed to deal with the problems of the poor; and land degradation that affects small farmers and is not alleviated by government action.

The upland insurgency is motivated by the economic deprivation of the landless agricultural laborers and poor farmers displaced into the hills, where they try to eke out a living from failing land; it exploits opportunities for rebellion in the country's peripheral regions, which are largely beyond the effective control of the central government; and it is helped by the creative leadership of the cadres of the insurgent New People's Army and the National Democratic Front. During the 1970s and 1980s, these groups found upland peasants very receptive to revolutionary ideology, especially where the repression of landlords and local governments left them little choice but to rebel or starve. The revolutionaries have built on local understandings and social structures to help the peasants define their situation and focus their discontent.[35]

THE LONG-TERM IMPLICATIONS FOR NATIONAL AND INTERNATIONAL SECURITY

In the coming decades, a poor country faced with severe environmental scarcity will follow one of four paths. Most optimistically, the country may be able to supply enough technical and social ingenuity to permit substitution of relatively plentiful resources for scarce resources, or to allow societal adaptation to scarcity. If this is not possible, the country might be able to "decouple" itself from dependency on its own environmental resources by making goods and services that can be traded on the international market for the environmental resources it needs (such as grain). The decoupling might, in fact, be achieved by rapidly exploiting the country's environmental resources, which allows it to accumulate enough money, industrial equipment, and education to permit a shift to other forms of production.

If the country is unable to do either of these things, the government's instruments to manage society—its financial, bureaucratic, and political machinery—may eventually be so damaged by environmentally induced social stress that chronic protest and violence arise. The country may then fragment, as peripheral regions come under the control of renegade authorities and "warlords." Such a weakening of government control over outer regions is already underway in the Philippines, and environmental scarcity may be a strong contributor to this process.

Finally, and most pessimistically, the state may avoid fragmentation by becoming a "hard" regime, that is, by resorting to authoritarian measures against internal opposition. A hard regime may also launch military attacks against neighboring countries to distract its people's attention from their rising grievances. External aggression may also result after a new government comes to power through civil violence: governments born of revolution, for example, are particularly adept at mobilizing their citizens and resources for war.[36]

Whether or not a given country will follow the third or fourth path above depends, in part, on the level of remaining resources and wealth in the country's economic system that can potentially be appropriated by the state for its own uses. This suggests that the countries with the highest probability of becoming "hard" regimes (and potential threats to their neighbors) in the face of environmental and economic stress are large, relatively wealthy developing countries that are dependent on a declining environmental base, such as Indonesia, Brazil, and perhaps Nigeria. In contrast, resource-poor countries, such as Bangladesh, Haiti, the Philippines, Ethiopia, and the Sudan, are more likely to fragment.

If many developing countries evolve in the direction of extremism, the military interests of rich countries may often be directly threatened. Of special concern here is the growing gap between rich and poor nations that may be widened by environmental scarcity. Some poor nations may be heavily armed, and may possess weapons of mass destruction; such regimes could be tempted to use nuclear blackmail to induce rich countries to transfer their wealth to the Third World. However, it is likely that environmental stress and the social disruption it produces will so weaken the economies of poor countries that they will be unable to build sizable armed forces. But the North would surely be unwise to rely on poverty and disorder in the South for its security.

WHAT CAN BE DONE?

The global environmental situation is critical, and is already causing social disruptions and intergroup conflict. But we are not powerless to alter these processes. We know a great deal about what we are doing to our environment, about which kinds of social systems damage the environment least, and about how we can best adapt to ecological stress.

Over the last few years, there have been some heartening moves in the right direction by national governments and international agencies. For example, countries and chemical companies have moved aggressively to limit and eventually stop the production of the CFCs that destroy the ozone layer. The international agreements to do this include novel ways of transfering funds from rich to poor countries to help them move to technologies that do not use CFCs. This may be a precedent for transfer mechanisms to help poor countries develop energy technologies that produce less carbon dioxide.

International financial agencies, like the World Bank, the Asia Development Bank, and the International Monetary Fund, have become much more aware of the intricate relationship between economic development and environmental scarcity. They are more cautious about funding large-scale, centralized development projects, such as hydroelectric dams, and they have begun to subject their financing to more careful environmental review. In addition, they will soon provide substantial funding for sustainable development projects around the world.

Without question, the most important recent event was the United Nations Conference on Environment and Development (UNCED) in Rio de Janeiro, Brazil, in June 1992. This was the largest and most inclusive international negotiation in history. In arduous meetings leading up to the conference, delegates from rich and poor nations tried to work out preliminary agreements to protect biodiversity, control carbon-dioxide emissions, and slow deforestation. Some environmentalists were disappointed by the final results of the conference: the United States refused to sign the biodiversity treaty; the carbon-dioxide agreement was significantly weakened (again, as a result of U.S. pressure); and some poor nations objected to the deforestation agreement. Nonetheless, the Rio conference was a milestone in humankind's efforts to meet the environmental challenge. It brought worldwide attention to the crisis, and it showed politicians and policymakers that good environmental policy can be a source of political authority and moral legitimacy.[37]

Our research project on "Environmental Change and Acute Conflict" has produced some recommendations for action in rich and poor countries to reduce the chances of environmentally induced conflict. Some of these recommendations are very general and will need elaboration by experts as well as continuing negotiation among governments; others are quite specific. Importantly, some recommendations do *not* require huge financial investments but may, nonetheless, make a great difference to the future well-being of our world.

While circumstances differ across the developing world, poor countries should in general act to control population growth, they should implement a fairer distribution of land and wealth within their societies, and they should encourage sustainable economic growth to provide employment for surplus labor. In the short-term, the leaders of many poor countries see a trade-off between economic growth and environmental protection, and this encourages overuse and the degradation of environmental resources. But the real trade-off is between short-term unsustainable prosperity and long-term growth potential. This is an answer to the common argument from poor countries that rich countries are using environmental issues to deny them the opportunity to grow: it is in the developing world's self-interest to prevent environmental decline. Policymakers in both rich and poor countries must, therefore, change their understanding of development to emphasize the true value of natural resources and the importance of efficiencies in production as a way of conserving resources. Scholars and researchers in universities, think tanks, and public agencies can play an important role in educating policymakers about these realities.

More thorough environmental impact assessments of resource-development projects, such as dams and irrigation systems, are needed. Principles of sound resource management should be incorporated into contracts between development agencies, financial institutions (such as development banks), and developing countries that receive resource-related aid. Unfortunately, many international development agencies do not yet have adequate internal capability for thorough assessments. Moreover, it is impossible to accurately and completely predict the effects of a given resource-development project; and, even if it were possible, a project's social costs and benefits often cannot be compared. Policymakers should therefore be humble about the potential gain from environmental impact assessments.

In general, environmental problems require regional or "ecosystem-wide" solutions, rather than policies based at the national level. This point also applies to the management of the social effects of environmental scarcity: for instance, large-scale migration caused by environmental change can be most effectively limited and managed through regional accords. Some successful solutions of regional environmental problems may be transferable from one region to another. A good example is the International Joint Commission between Canada and the United States that manages disputes over water. Another example is the 1960 Indus Water Treaty that apportions the waters of the Indus River basin between India and Pakistan.

Population stabilization is key to limiting environmental stress, and it clearly requires collaboration between rich and poor countries. Wealthy countries can usefully supply financial aid and technology to slow population growth, although ideological reasons have caused the United States to sharply curtail support for such programs since the mid-1980s (this may change under a Clinton administration). Unfortunately, poor countries may also resist family planning for political and ideological reasons; Islamic fundamentalists and the Roman Catholic Church, for example, are opposed to birth control. In addition, leaders of poor countries sometimes perceive that a large population will enhance military security.

Rich countries can additionally support land reform in developing countries, reduce the debt burden of these countries, and promote—through aid and transfers of appropriate technology—rural industrialization projects. Poor nations, under pressure from banks and international lending agencies to pay their foreign debts, often use their best lands to grow cash crops for export. As people are displaced from these lands, governments and development agencies can work to provide them with jobs. Ideally, land reform combined with labor-intensive rural industries will boost incomes and stem the flow of people into ecologically vulnerable areas and into cities that are increasingly unmanageable.

In addition, rich countries can help poor countries overcome their lack of expertise on environmental management. In the developing world, inequality in national expertise translates into inequality in national power. Countries with advantages in technical expertise can dominate their neighbors; they have the edge in negotiations over resource management, and this can lead to misperceptions, rivalry, and conflict. Charles Okidi, an international lawyer at Moi University in Kenya, notes that there are only three Ph.D.-level hydrologists in his country. The addition of four per country in East Africa would greatly improve prospects for regional water management. It is cost-effective for rich countries to provide funds for the training of environmental experts in the developing world, including hydrologists, soil and agricultural scientists, foresters, demographers, energy-systems engineers, and fisheries specialists. If research and teaching centers in poor countries are adequately equipped and staffed, the "brain drain" to rich countries could be stemmed. Moreover, networks of such centers established across national boundaries could start wider cooperation among a region's countries.

Beyond these policy recommendations, certain changes of attitude are needed. This was one of the main lessons of the recent United Nations conference in Rio. Rich countries must recognize that global environmental problems are, in important ways, problems of global fairness. Deep poverty in the developing world often causes activities and strengthens economic structures that harm the environment. Moreover, as poor countries industrialize, they will need massive financial and technological help to leapfrog over the environmentally damaging technologies and practices that were used by today's industrialized countries. Poor countries also argued at the Rio meeting that environmental degradation is often driven, not by large populations, but by the high consumption and waste production of wealthy countries. Poor countries are not the main causes of, yet may be most vulnerable to, the large-scale environmental problems getting most attention in the developed world, such as greenhouse warming and ozone depletion. For all these reasons, widespread environmental scarcity may force humankind at last to deal with the wrenching economic differences that plague our planet.

Notes

1. Portions of this article originally appeared in Thomas Homer-Dixon, "Environmental Scarcity and Global Security," *Headline Series* (New York: Foreign Policy Association, 1992); in Thomas Homer-Dixon, "On the Threshold: Environmental Changes As Causes of Acute Conflict," *International Security*, Vol. 16, no. 2 (Fall 1991) pp. 76–116; and in Thomas Homer-Dixon, Jeffrey Boutwell, and George Rathjens, "Environmental Change and Violent Conflict," *Scientific American* (February 1993). Permission for republication has been granted by MIT Press and the Foreign Policy Association.

2. A renewable resource has both a "stock" and a "flow." A stock is the quantity or quality of the resource that is available for consumption or that maintains a useful service; and a flow is the incremental addition to, or restoration of, the stock per unit of time. See David Pearce and Kerry Turner, *Economics of Natural Resources and the Environment* (Baltimore: Johns Hopkins University Press, 1990), pp. 52–53. A "nonrenewable" resource consists only

of a stock that is not replenished or restored over time; these include fossil fuels, metals, and minerals.

3. Although scarcities of nonrenewable resources may also contribute to conflict (for example, some people claim that the need for oil was a motivating factor behind the recent Persian Gulf war), I do not address this question in this chapter. For theory and historical analysis of nonrenewable resource conflicts, see Nazli Choucri and Robert North, *Nations in Conflict* (San Francisco: Freeman, 1975), and Ronnie Lipschutz, *When Nations Clash: Raw Materials, Ideology, and Foreign Policy* (Cambridge: Ballinger, 1989).

4. For example, see David Wirth, "Climate Chaos," *Foreign Policy*, Vol. 74 (Spring 1989), p. 10.

5. Robert Heilbroner, *An Inquiry into the Human Prospect* (New York: Norton, 1980), pp. 39 and 95; William Ophuls, *Ecology and the Politics of Scarcity: A Prologue to a Political Theory of the Steady State* (San Francisco: Freeman, 1977), pp. 214–217.

6. Peter Gleick, "Climate Change and International Politics: Problems Facing Developing Countries," *Ambio*, Vol. 18, no. 6 (1989), pp. 333–339; Gleick, "The Implications of Global Climatic Changes for International Security," *Climatic Change*, Vol. 15, no. 1/2 (October 1989), pp. 309–325; and Malin Falkenmark, "Fresh Waters as a Factor in Strategic Policy and Action," in Arthur Westing, ed., *Global Resources and International Conflict: Environmental Factors in Strategic Policy and Action* (New York: Oxford, 1986), pp. 85–113.

7. Ted Gurr, "On the Political Consequences of Scarcity and Economic Decline," *International Studies Quarterly*, Vol. 29, no. 1 (March 1985), pp. 51–75.

8. Wallace Broecker, "Unpleasant Surprises in the Greenhouse?" *Nature*, Vol. 328, no. 6126 (July 9, 1987), pp. 123–126.

9. J. C. Farman, B. G. Gardiner, and J. D. Shanklin, "Large Losses of Total Ozone in Antarctica Reveal Seasonal CO_2/NO_2 Interaction," *Nature*, Vol. 315, no. 6016 (May 16, 1985), pp. 207–210.

10. Readers interested in technical background on environmental issues should consult *World Resources 1992–93* (New York: Oxford University Press, 1992) and *World Resources 1990–91* (New York: Oxford University Press, 1990). This publication, produced biennially by the World Resources Institute (WRI) in collaboration with the United Nations Environment Programme and other organizations, is widely regarded as the most accessible, accurate, and comprehensive source for information on global change issues. The more popular *State of the World* report, published annually by the Worldwatch Institute, is useful but sometimes selective and tendentious.

11. In 1971, Ehrlich and Holdren introduced a product formulation similar to that in Figure 15.1. They proposed that $I = P \times F$, where I is the total negative impact on the environment, P is the population, and F is a function that measures per capita impact on the environment. See Paul Ehrlich and John Holdren, "Impact of Population Growth," *Science*, Vol. 171 (26 March, 1971), pp. 1212–1217.

12. Numerous writers, especially those considering the social impact of climate change, have generated diagrams similar to Figure 15.1. See, in particular, the excellent survey article by Richard Warrick and William Riebsame entitled "Societal Response to CO_2-Induced Climate Change: Opportunities for Research," *Climatic Change*, Vol. 3, no. 4 (1981), pp. 387–428.

13. See, for example, Lester Brown, "Reexamining the World Food Prospect," in *State of the World 1989* (New York: Norton, 1989), pp. 41–58.

14. Nafis Sadik, *The State of the World Population 1990* (New York: United Nations Population Fund, 1990), p. 8.

15. WRI, et al., *World Resources 1990–91*, p. 87.

16. See Vaclav Smil, *Energy, Food, Environment: Realities, Myths, Options* (Oxford: Oxford University Press, 1987), pp. 223 and 230.

17. For a thorough account of the Filipino environmental crisis, see World Bank, *Philippines: Environment and Natural Resource Management Study* (Washington: World Bank, 1989).

18. There is scientific debate about the likely magnitude, rate, and timing of greenhouse warming, and about its climatic, ecological, and social impacts. The current consensus is summarized in the reports prepared by Working Groups I and II of the Intergovernmental Panel on Climate Change under the auspices of the World Meteorological Organization and the United Nations Environment Program. The complete report of Working Group I has been

published as *Climate Change: The IPCC Scientific Assessment*, eds. J. T. Houghton, G. J. Jenkins, and J. J. Ephraums (Cambridge: Cambridge University Press, 1990). For a thorough assessment of climate change and agriculture, see M. L. Parry, T. R. Carter, and N. T. Konijn, eds., *The Impact of Climatic Variations on Agriculture, Volume 1: Assessments in Cool Temperate and Cold Regions; Volume 2: Assessments in Semi-arid Regions* (Dordrecht, Netherlands: Kluwer, 1989).

19. See R. A. Warrick, R. M. Gifford, and M. L. Parry, "CO_2, Climatic Change and Agriculture: Assessing the Response of Food Crops to the Direct Effects of Increased CO_2 and Climatic Change," in Bert Bolin, et al., eds., *The Greenhouse Effect, Climatic Change, and Ecosystems*, SCOPE 29 (New York: Wiley, 1986), pp. 393–474. See also Fakhri Bazzaz and Eric Fajer, "Plant Life in a CO_2-Rich World," *Scientific American*, Vol. 266, no. 1 (January 1992), pp. 68–74.

20. Robert Repetto, "Wasting Assets: The Need for National Resource Accounting," *Technology Review* (January 1990), p. 40.

21. Robert Repetto, "Balance-Sheet Erosion—How to Account for the Loss of Natural Resources," *International Environmental Affairs*, Vol. 1, no. 2 (Spring 1989), pp. 103–137.

22. Vaclav Smil, "Environmental Degradation as a Source of Conflict and Economic Losses in China," Occasional Paper of the American Academy of Arts and Sciences and the Peace and Conflict Studies Program of the University of Toronto, December 1993

23. Jodi Jacobson, *Environmental Refugees: A Yardstick of Habitability*, Worldwatch Paper 86 (Washington: Worldwatch Institute, 1988).

24. For an illuminating account of how population growth and resource shortages undermined state capacity in the past, see Jack Goldstone, *Revolution and Rebellion in the Early Modern World* (Berkeley: University of California Press, 1991).

25. One theory of war arising from resource scarcity is provided by Choucri and North in *Nations in Conflict* (San Francisco: Freeman, 1975).

26. Theoretical perspectives on group-identify conflict are provided by M. Sherif, *Group Conflict and Cooperation: Their Social Psychology* (London: Routledge & Kegan Paul, 1966); Henri Tajfel, *Human Groups and Social Categories: Studies in Social Psychology* (Cambridge: Cambridge University Press, 1981); and Donald Horowitz, *Ethnic Groups in Conflict* (Berkeley: University of California Press, 1985).

27. Myron Weiner, "The Political Demography of Assam's Anti-Immigrant Movement," *Population and Development Review*, Vol. 9, no. 2 (June 1983), pp. 279–292.

28. See John Dollard, et al., *Frustration and Aggression* (New Haven: Yale University Press, 1939); James Davies, "Toward a Theory of Revolution," *American Sociological Review*, Vol. 6, no. 1 (February 1962), pp. 5–19; and Ted Gurr, *Why Men Rebel* (Princeton: Princeton University Press, 1970). Gurr explicitly attempts to apply deprivation theories of civil strife to situations of environmental crisis in "On the Political Consequences of Scarcity and Economic Decline," *International Studies Quarterly*, Vol. 29, no. 1 (March 1985), pp. 51–75.

29. The importance of changes in the perceived "opportunity structure" facing challenger groups is emphasized by Doug McAdam, *Political Process and the Development of Black Insurgency, 1930–1970* (Chicago: University of Chicago Press, 1982); see also Charles Tilly, *From Mobilization to Revolution* (Reading, MA: Addison-Wesley, 1978).

30. Sanjoy Hazarika, "Bangladesh and Northeast India: Land Pressure, Migration, and Ethnic Conflict," Occasional Paper No. 3 of the Project on Environmental Change and Acute Conflict, February 1993.

31. Myron Weiner, "The Political Demography of Assam's Anti-Immigrant Movement," *Population and Development Review*, Vol. 9, no. 2 (June 1983), pp. 279–292.

32. For a full account, see Michael Horowitz, "Victims Upstream and Down," *Journal of Refugee Studies*, Vol. 4, no. 2 (1991), pp. 164–181.

33. A full account of these processes in the Philippines can be found in Maria Concepcion Cruz, et al., *Population Growth, Poverty, and Environmental Stress: Frontier Migration in the Philippines and Costa Rica* (Washington: World Resources Institute, 1992).

34. Gareth Porter and Delfin Ganapin, Jr., *Resources, Population, and the Philippines' Future: A Case Study*, WRI Paper No. 4 (Washington: World Resources Institute, 1988).

35. Gary Hawes, "Theories of Peasant Revolution: A Critique and Contribution from the Philippines," *World Politics*, Vol. 42, no. 1 (January 1990), pp. 261–298.

36. See Theda Skocpol, "Social Revolutions and Mass Military Mobilization," *World Politics*, Vol. 40, no. 2 (January 1988), pp. 147–168.

37. For further information on the Rio summit, see Peter Hass, Marc Levy, and Edward Parson, "Appraising the Earth Summit: How Should We Judge UNCED's Success?" *Environment,* Vol. 34, no. 8 (October 1992), pp. 7–11, 26–33. A summary of the treaties and documents produced by UNCED, including Agenda 21 (a plan for global sustainable development into the next century), is provided in Edward Parson, Peter Haas, and Marc Levy, "A Summary of the Major Documents Signed at the Earth Summit and the Global Forum," *Environment,* Vol 34, no. 8 (October 1992), pp. 12–15, 34–36. The concept of "sustainable development" was given wide currency by the final report of the World Commission on Environment and Development (popularly called the Brundtland Commission) in *Our Common Future* (Oxford: Oxford University Press, 1987).

16 / Demographic Change and Ecological Insecurity

DENNIS PIRAGES

Large-scale demographic changes are disruptive forces that generate both domestic and international insecurities. Rapid population growth is the demographic factor most commonly linked to civil disorder and to various kinds of tensions and conflicts among nations. But population movements, differential growth patterns, and even declining rates of population growth are also associated with political and economic insecurity, and will impact on the world security environment well into the next century.

The relationship between rapid population growth, economic dislocations, and political discontent in the less-industrialized countries is well understood. In these countries, large increases in numbers must be matched by very rapid economic growth if even existing living standards are to be maintained. Thus, in countries such as Uganda, Kenya, and Iraq—where annual population growth is 3.7 percent—large numbers of new jobs must be created for growing and restive populations where nearly half the population is under fifteen years old.[1]

There are also more subtle demographic forces at work that represent threats to individual, national, and world security. People in motion—whether moving from rural to urban areas within a country or from one country to another—are often perceived as threats to the established order in their new places of residence. Thus, migrants pouring into Germany from Central and Eastern Europe, into France from North Africa, and into the United States from the Caribbean and Latin America often meet with hostility, ranging from verbal attacks to physical injuries.

Paradoxically, even slow or negative population growth—brought on by declining birth rates in industrialized countries—is another type of demographic change leading to various kinds of economic and political insecurities. The United States, Japan, and most European countries are experiencing declining birthrates that, when combined with new, life-prolonging technologies, are creating "graying" societies and a related set of potentially divisive social issues that could lead to serious intergenerational conflict. The "birth dearth" in these countries threatens to pit old people against young people over major entitlement issues such as social security, since a dwindling work force will be faced with picking up the costs of these expensive programs that were established when labor forces were growing and the retired portion of the population was relatively small.[2]

Today, the world community can be characterized as a demographically divided one. On the less-industrialized side of the demographic divide, rapid population growth and the related urbanization create insecurities by overwhelming the capability of the environment and the existing political order to absorb growing numbers of people. But, on the industrialized side of the divide, graying populations confront problems of increasing sociopolitical arteriosclerosis. And people moving across the divide often provoke the wrath of those who see these migrants as a threat to the established economic order.

SOURCES OF ECOLOGICAL INSECURITY

In the 1950s and 1960s, security was defined largely in military terms, and the focus was on potential East-West conflict. In the 1970s and 1980s, however, successive oil crises and associated dislocations called attention to the economic aspects of security and to a North-South dimension of potential conflict. In the 1990s, ecological security—focusing largely on the capabilities of the global ecosystem to meet the needs of growing numbers of human beings—is becoming of primary concern.[3] (See Chapter 14.)

Ecological security is a multidimensional aspect of human well-being that is ensured by maintaining compatibility among the demands of Homo sapiens, those of other species, and the capabilities of nature. It includes not only safety from physical attacks from other human beings, but also safety from ecological and economic impediments to human well-being. These impediments can include assaults by other species and subspecies (ranging from locusts to viruses), retribution from nature (including floods, earthquakes, and droughts), and economic decline associated with ecosystem mismanagement.

Ecological insecurity can thus arise from human populations growing too rapidly and coming into conflict over natural resources, the human population collectively growing to exceed the carrying capacity of the earth, or from clashes with growing populations of other species. Growing human populations, for example, require additional resources in order to maintain living standards. If they cannot be obtained domestically, and if capabilities exist to get them elsewhere, lateral pressure to move across borders is likely to develop.[4] Insecurity can also come from the flourishing of competitor organisms. Plagues of locusts have competed with human populations for food since biblical times. A more contemporary example of such competitors is a migration of European Zebra Mussels, transported on the hulls of ships, which has invaded the American Great Lakes and caused hundreds of millions of dollars worth of damage to fisheries.[5] And, while viruses are not usually thought of as security threats, it should be kept in mind that the most deadly battle ever fought was the struggle between Homo sapiens and the influenza virus in 1919—it is estimated that 19 million people lost their lives worldwide during this struggle.[6]

The relationship between the growing total human population and its increasing resource demands is presently a major source of ecological insecurity. For most of its history, Homo sapiens has existed in relative harmony with nature. Numbers grew very slowly, and, while the local environmental impact of individual populations might have been considerable, the global impact was small.[7] During the early stages of the Industrial Revolution, however, the world's population began to expand rapidly. In 1650, there were only 500 million human beings on the earth. This number doubled to one billion in only 200 years. Only eighty years later, by 1930, the world's population had doubled once again. The next doubling, to four billion, took only forty years. Today, there are more than 5.6 billion people occupying an ever more densely populated world.

As these numbers have grown, ecological insecurity has increased apace, and the carrying capacity of the planet has been placed under ever greater stress. Today's densely populated world is experiencing increasing numbers of so-called natural disasters, as burgeoning human populations press into areas—for example, coastal lowlands and earthquake areas—that should not be occupied.[8] And the numbers of humans are likely to keep growing. The medium, and most likely UN population growth projection sees 10 billion human beings living in the world by the year 2050; a more pessimistic scenario projects 12.5 billion people by that time.[9]

A DEMOGRAPHICALLY DIVIDED WORLD

While the rapid rate of world population growth is clearly a primary threat to ecological security, today's demographically divided world is experiencing other kinds of population dislocations as well.[10] The industrial countries have generally passed through a period of demographic transition in which birth rates have fallen in response to rising affluence and related value changes. Some countries have even dropped below zero population growth. In the less-industrialized portion of the world, however, rapid population growth continues. The result is a kind of demographic fault line that separates the two groups. On the industrial, or "North," side of the fault, declining growth rates raise concerns about the future socioeconomic impact of "graying" populations, while on the other, "South," side of the divide, the Malthusian problems associated with rapid population growth remain to be resolved (see Table 16.1).

These disparities in population growth rates can be attributed to the dynamics of the demographic transition. According to demographic transition theory, which is based on the historical experience of the early industrializing countries, there are three demographic phases (related to industrialization) through which societies pass.[11] The first phase is charac-

Table 16.1 / The Demographic Divide

	Natural Increase (%)	Under 15 (%)	Over 65 (%)	Population 1992	Population 2025
Syria	3.8	49	4	13.7	38.7
Zambia	3.8	49	2	8.4	24.2
Iraq	3.7	45	3	18.2	51.9
Togo	3.7	49	2	3.8	11.3
Kenya	3.7	49	2	26.2	62.3
Uganda	3.7	49	2	17.5	49.6
Cote d'Ivoire	3.6	48	3	13.0	39.3
Malawi	3.5	48	3	8.7	23.1
Tanzania	3.5	48	3	27.4	77.9
All Less Developed	2.0	36	4	4196.0	7153.0
Hungary	−.2	20	14	10.3	10.4
Germany	−.1	15	15	80.6	73.7
Bulgaria	0.0	20	13	8.9	8.6
Denmark	.1	17	16	5.2	4.8
Latvia	.1	21	12	2.7	3.0
Austria	.1	17	15	7.9	8.2
Romania	.1	23	11	23.2	24.4
Ukraine	.1	22	12	2.7	3.0
Greece	.1	19	14	10.3	10.0
All Developed	.5	21	12	1224.0	1392.0

Source: *World Development Report 1992*, Table 26. Population data in millions.

terized by both high birth and death rates, and thus by population equilibrium. In the second phase, death rates plummet while birth rates remain high, resulting in rapid population growth. In the third phase, birth rates drop to match the lower death rates, and population equilibrium is reestablished.

Preindustrial societies, of which there are now very few, are in the first, pretransformation phase of the demographic transition. People living in these societies have historically experienced high infant mortality, and the pronatalist norms and values governing reproduction that have evolved reflect this experience. Couples feel that they are doing the "right" thing by having eight to ten children, since experience shows that a large percentage of children will never reach adulthood.

Most of the countries on the South side of the demographic divide are working their way through the second stage of the demographic transition. Having received the benefits from a surge of technology transfer—including substantial medical knowledge—these countries have experienced a substantial drop in infant mortality rates and an increase in average life expectancy. These changes are the result of better diets and the introduction of life-prolonging medical technologies, which work together to reduce infant mortality and to increase life expectancy. But birth rates remain high because the old norms and values (which encourage large numbers of children) tend to lag well behind new realities due to the time needed for social learning. Thus, in countries like Tanzania and Haiti, birth rates are now well above death rates because people continue to behave reproductively as if they were living in the world of their parents or grandparents.

Countries moving through the second stage of the demographic transition face an additional problem of "demographic momentum" inherent in the youthfulness of these rapidly growing populations. Most of the population in these countries is in the prereproductive years. Thus, in Kenya, Togo, Uganda, and Zambia, nearly one-half of the population is under fifteen and only 2 percent is over sixty-five. This means that if, by some demographic miracle, couples were to cut back to a two-child family immediately, there would still be considerable population growth because the pent-up momentum in such youthful societies would reverberate as population "surges" through succeeding generations.

On the North side of the demographic divide, most of the industrialized countries have already worked their way well into the third phase of the demographic transition. In this phase, industrialization, urbanization, and secularization combine to produce a shift toward much smaller families. Thus, demographic data for Denmark in 1950 indicate that the statistically average woman produced 2.58 children during her lifetime. By 1985, this had dropped to 1.45. The similar figure for West Germany in 1950 was 2.10, and it dropped to 1.29 by 1985.[12] For the industrialized world as a whole, there is now an average of fourteen births per 1,000 people and nine deaths, yielding a population growth rate of 0.5 percent annually. But on the less-industrial side of the divide there are still twenty-nine births per 1,000 and only nine deaths, yielding a population growth rate of 2.0 percent.[13]

A smooth progression by the less-industrialized countries through these phases, similar to that experienced by the early industrializers, cannot be assumed. It is not clear that many of the less-industrialized countries can avoid a "demographic trap" set in the second stage of the transition, and thus move on to the third stage. Many of these countries appear to be economically bogged down and unable to move forward rapidly enough to avoid ecological and economic deterioration brought about by persisting high birth rates.[14]

It is also unclear that the demographic transition is limited to only three phases. There appears to be a fourth phase now evolving in Europe. This transition—to negative population growth—seems to be based on desires by individuals for self-fulfillment apart from parenthood, and could well result in other, unforeseen types of demographic dislocations.[15]

Related to the growing numbers on the one side of the demographic divide, and the potential for a birth dearth on the other, are problems of population migration. The pressures of rural population growth in less-industrialized countries, combined with perceived economic opportunities in urban areas, leads to large-scale population movement into cities. Worldwide, in 1965, 36 percent of the world's population lived in cities; by 1990, the portion living in cities had increased to 50 percent. In the "low-income" countries, however, the percentage living in cities more than doubled, growing from 18 to 38 percent. In China, the percentage increased from 18 to 56 percent, and in Tanzania it jumped from 5 to 33 percent.[16]

Rapid urbanization is creating a parallel problem of growing "megacities." By projecting current urbanization trends forward to the year 2034, we find that Mexico City and Shanghai could have populations of 39 million, Beijing 35 million, Sao Paulo 32 million, and Bombay 31 million.[17] Providing adequate housing, sanitation, transportation, jobs, security, and other amenities for such rapidly growing numbers of urbanites will be a staggering undertaking. So will the task of maintaining order among the restless army of unemployed in these crowded and polluted megacities.

Large numbers of people are also moving, legally and illegally, across the demographic divide. The combined pressures of population growth, declining economic opportunity, and political instability are pushing growing numbers of migrants toward the perceived opportunities on the other side. This is manifest in a crush of migrants moving into the United States from Asia, the Caribbean, and Latin America at a rate in excess of 600,000 annually. Western Europe is being pressured from several directions: estimates suggest that between 1991 and 2000, as many as 4 million Eastern Europeans, 3.5 million citizens of the former USSR, 2.5 million North Africans, 2 million sub-Saharan Africans, and one million Asians could arrive in Western Europe seeking jobs.[18] As the number of immigrants becomes significant, resistance to them grows apace. Hence, neo-Nazis in Germany have repeatedly harassed non-German immigrants, while right-wing politicians in France have called for the deportation of foreigners. Among the economically advanced countries, only Japan, with very strict immigration policies, seems untouched by the discontents caused by people in motion.

People migrate for a variety of reasons. Historically, the largest share of migrants has moved in search of better economic conditions. But contemporary migration is also being fueled by military conflict, ethnic violence, and the collapse of nations. It is very difficult to estimate the numbers and types of migrants and refugees in the world today. The largest share of them remain in their countries of origin; the next largest portion of them cross boundaries only within the less-industrialized world; and the smallest share cross the demographic divide into the industrialized nations. Millions of migrants cross borders legally each year, and there are several million contract laborers living abroad at any given time.

It is illegal migrants, asylum-seekers, and refugees that attract most attention. By definition, illegal migrants are very difficult to count. It is roughly estimated that between 100,000 and 300,000 people slip into the

United States illegally each year.[19] And all industrialized countries, except Japan, have recently seen a large increase in people seeking political asylum. In most of these countries the wheels of justice turn very slowly, permitting those seeking asylum to stay for long periods or to slip quietly out of sight.[20]

The most troublesome political and moral dilemmas are associated with refugees. The United Nations estimates that there are about 17 million refugees that have crossed national borders. There is probably a similar number of refugees within countries.[21] Thus, protracted conflicts, civil wars, ethnic "cleansings," and a variety of similar human tragedies have created a large population of semipermanent refugees, most of whom live dreary and hopeless lives under primitive conditions in refugee camps. Currently, Pakistan tops the list of countries housing refugees, with 3.6 million of them (almost all of whom are from Afghanistan). Iran follows closely behind, with nearly three million Afghan refugees. Other countries with large refugee populations include Jordan (900,000), Malawi (720,000), Ethiopia (700,000), and Sudan (690,000).[22]

POPULATION GROWTH, RESOURCE LIMITS, AND INSECURITY

There are many aspects of ecological insecurity that arise from growing populations in the less-industrial world competing for a static or shrinking resource base.[23] Thus, growing populations are stressing the environment in most of the countries on the southern side of the demographic divide. It is estimated that 60 percent of the less-industrialized world's poorest people live in ecologically vulnerable areas.[24] Trees that can be used for firewood, for example, are disappearing before the demands of growing populations, and the related deforestation increases soil erosion and the danger of flooding.

Water is another limiting factor in many rapidly growing areas of the world, representing a threat to both personal and national security. Rapidly growing populations in the Middle East are competing for very limited water supplies. Israel and the Palestinians are at odds over a dwindling water supply, and Jordan and Syria are accusing each other of stealing water from a river located between the two countries. Similarly, Syria, Turkey, and Jordan are feuding over the use of water from the Tigris and Euphrates rivers.[25]

Starvation and malnutrition are also closely related to the growing pressure on land and water. While growth in worldwide food production has slightly exceeded world population growth over the last decade, this has not been the case in many countries on the southern side of the divide. When data from 1979–81 is compared with 1988–90, food production per capita actually declined in fifty-eight low- and middle-income countries. (See Chapter 18.)

There is also a widening gap in global economic opportunity that parallels the demographic divide. The richest one-fifth of the world's population produces 83 percent of the gross world product, while the poorest one-fifth produces only about 1 percent. And the income gap seems to be widening: between 1960 and 1989, the per capita income difference between the average person in the top 20 percent of the world's population and the bottom 20 percent grew from $1,864 to $15,149.[26] Between 1965 and 1990, there was a decline in per capita GNP in at least twenty-four countries on the southern side of the demographic divide.[27]

Economic stagnation and decline is related, in turn, to political turmoil and insecurity. There is a well-established relationship among rapid population growth, poverty, social violence, political instability, and authoritarian forms of government.[28] When politics involves the allocation of deprivations it is very difficult for democratic regimes to survive. In Haiti, for example, the birth and death rates are by far the highest in the Western Hemisphere, and authoritarian regimes and political violence have been commonplace. Similarly, authoritarian governments and violence have been commonplace in African countries such as Angola, Ethiopia, Liberia, Somalia, Sudan, and Uganda.

URBANIZATION

Aside from the problems created directly by growing numbers in the less-industrialized world, human settlement patterns there can also give rise to various kinds of ecological insecurity. This is particularly true of the rapidly growing cities of the South. Populations are exploding in these cities both because of a high rate of natural population increase and because of a wave of migrants from rural areas. The number of people living in urban areas in less-industrialized countries is expected to grow from 966 million in 1980 to 1.9 billion by the year 2000. Many of the migrants to urban areas become squatters, having no chance to own land or a home of their own. More than two million of Calcutta's population, for instance, live in slums and squatter settlements, as do more than one million of the population of Rio de Janeiro, Jakarta, Manila, Bogota, Lima, Casablanca, and Istanbul.[29] It is estimated that by the year 2000, 90 percent of the absolute poor in Latin America and the Caribbean, 40 percent of the poorest in Africa, and 45 percent of the poorest in Asia will live in cities.[30]

In Rio de Janeiro, as in many other large and growing cities, urban crowding, combined with the lack of (legitimate) economic opportunities, is leading to the breakdown of social order. On one recent weekend, there were fifty-seven murders in the metropolitan region. Holdups along Rio's beaches are so common that diplomats refer to them as "tourist taxes." Kidnappings of wealthy children for ransom have become commonplace. A Brazilian psychiatrist describes the situation as "living in an era where each call for social responsibility is made fun of, as a moralizing fable or the kind of prayer an orphan might make on Christmas Eve."[31]

Cities in the less-industrialized countries are also giant "resource sinks," since they are highly dependent on the surrounding countryside for needed resources. Large quantities of resources are needed to sustain ever-increasing numbers of people who produce little food and often cannot find work. In addition, urban sprawl often destroys much of the fertile agricultural land surrounding cities. It is estimated that 1.4 billion hectares (1 hectare = 2.47 acres) of arable land will be removed from agricultural use between 1980 and 2000 because of the growth of cities.[32] But growing cities also need tremendous amounts of water for drinking and sewage treatment—water that is often not available. In Dhaka, Bangladesh, for example, only one-fifth of the population is served by a sewage system. And in Bangkok, Thailand, demand is depleting the groundwater in much of the city, and parts of it are sinking at a rate of between five and ten centimeters per year.[33]

Mexico City is expected to be the largest of the world's cities by the middle of the next century, and is already experiencing many of the destructive environmental problems associated with rapid urbanization. Located in a basin at an altitude of 7,300 feet, Mexico City lacks a sufficient supply of fresh air to meet the competing needs of people, automobiles, and industry. Ozone levels were so high in 1992 that the government was forced to expand a one-day-per-week ban on automobile use to two days per week, thus keeping 40 percent of the region's automobiles off the streets on any given weekday. The health ministry has advised against outdoor exercise, and the education minister has banned all outdoor exercise in schools. But, even in the face of such a dire situation, the population continues to grow, and is expected to increase from its present 20 million to 26 million by the year 2000.[34]

POPULATION, POVERTY, AND PESTILENCE

Over the last few decades there has been remarkable progress in fighting the many diseases that afflict human beings. But there are now indications that the rapid increase in human numbers, increasing density of human populations, poverty, and ecological changes are making human populations much more vulnerable to disease-bearing microorganisms. The World Health Organization has reported that 1.3 billion people (roughly 20 percent of the world's population) confront a major health crisis of disease or malnutrition. Tropical diseases now infect nearly 500 million people. In the less-industrialized countries, 2.8 million people die annually from vaccine-preventable diseases, 4 million die of diarrhea, 4 million die of respiratory infections, and 3 million die of tuberculosis.[35]

Concern with the impact of traditional diseases and emerging viruses is not limited to the less-industrialized countries. In the United States, a drug-resistant strain of tuberculosis seems to be spreading. And the AIDS virus, which is estimated to have infected more than one million people in North America, has infected between 10 and 13 million people worldwide. These numbers are expected to grow to 17.5 million by 1995; two-thirds of the cases are expected to be in sub-Saharan Africa.[36]

Most of the bacteria and viruses that pose future threats are not new. They have coexisted with Homo sapiens in various parts of the world for a long time. It is changes in human behavior, population growth, patterns of residence, poverty, and rapidity of transport that have altered the people-microbe balance. In the words of Nobel Laureate Joshua Lederberg, "Some people think that I am being hysterical, but there are catastrophes ahead. We live in evolutionary competition with microbes—bacteria and viruses. There is no guarantee that we will be the survivors."[37] Thus, the greatest future threat to global security may not come from large missiles with powerful thermonuclear warheads, but from microorganisms too small to be seen by the human eye.

GRAYING AND SOCIAL INSECURITY

Most industrial countries are now well into the third stage of the demographic transition and have reached, or are approaching, zero population growth (ZPG). As this shift takes place, the portion of the population under fifteen shrinks, and the portion beyond retirement age—benefiting from longer life expectancy—continues to grow. In Denmark, for instance, 16 percent of the population is now over sixty-five and only 17 percent is under fifteen. This movement to and beyond ZPG has been called the second demographic transition. The first was "dominated by concerns for family and offspring, but the second emphasizes the rights and self-fulfillment of individuals."[38] Whatever the motivation might be for the transition now under way in the North, the result is population "graying," which presents its own peculiar set of challenges to established values and institutions.

The economic, political, and social implications of graying have been inadequately investigated both because the deepest impacts of this demographic trend still lie ahead and because of the politically explosive nature of the associated issues. Graying in all of the industrial countries could lead to intergenerational warfare as unfunded liabilities growing out of entitlement programs that were nurtured during a period of rapid population and economic growth must be paid for during a period of zero population growth and limited economic opportunity. An expanding gray population will expect to receive extensive pension and medical benefits at a time when a shrinking working-age population will be hard-pressed to pay the bills.[39]

The Organization for Economic Co-operation and Development (OECD) has examined some of the longer-term social policy implications of graying within its member countries. It estimates that, by the year 2030, 27 percent of the population of Switzerland and 26 percent of the population of Germany will be over sixty-five; in the United States and Japan, 20 percent will be over sixty-five.[40]

This graying will alter dramatically future "aged-dependency ratios" in the industrial countries. An aged-dependency ratio is found by taking the number of those over sixty-five compared to those of working age (fifteen to sixty-five) and multiplying by 100. In the United States, in 1990, the ratio stood at 18.5, meaning that one elderly person could theoretically be supported by about five people in the labor force, if all eligible people (fifteen to sixty-five) were gainfully employed. By the year 2030 this ratio nearly doubles to 31.7, meaning that each person over sixty-five would be supported by only three active workers. In Switzerland the ratio rises from 20.8 to 47.2, and in Germany from 22.3 to 43.6.[41] In both of these countries, in the year 2030, there will be only about two active workers for each retiree. These figures conjure up visions of a new proletariat toiling long hours to pay taxes necessary to keep politically organized retirees in the style to which they've become accustomed. Assuming that all people of working age are employed in these countries—a dubious assumption at best—each retiree would be supported by only two or three productive workers, clearly an impossible situation.

These trends are already manifest in increasing real social expenditure in OECD countries. Between 1965 and 1985, for example, social expenditures climbed nearly twice as fast as gross domestic product, leading many OECD countries to run significant deficits.[42] In the United States, nearly one-half of the $1.5 trillion 1992 federal budget was mandated to meet entitlements and debt servicing. It is estimated that U.S. social security expenditures will grow from $275 billion in 1992 to $500 billion by 2000.[43]

The insecurities and potential conflicts associated with aging are not limited to the industrially advanced nations. In China, a vigorous family planning policy stressing one-child families has created more rapid graying than is taking place in many other countries. Estimates indicate that by the year 2040, fully 35 percent of the population could be over the age of sixty. This is five times the present ratio.[44] The dilemma facing Chinese leaders is that the one-child policy, made necessary by ecological limitations, is creating the potential for significant future social expenditures before substantial economic growth provides the capital to accommodate them.

Similar long-term problems will be faced by the former socialist countries of Central Europe (i.e., Hungary and Poland), where a demographic transition has been completed under conditions of relative economic austerity. Unless significant growth takes place over the next two decades, the social welfare burden for these countries could easily overwhelm the economic capabilities of dealing with it.

When future burdens associated with graying are added together, it is likely that the generous systems of social protection that evolved in an expansionist era are going to be increasingly under attack. Unfunded and underfunded pension systems and growing medical-care costs for the aged will place greater demands on smaller work forces in more slowly growing economies. In this atmosphere, highly charged for intergenerational conflict, one of the first casualties may well be education and other programs for the dwindling number of young people. It is ironic that on the southern side of the demographic divide it is a large and growing number of young people that pose a threat to social and economic security, while on the northern side it is a growing number of retired persons that could well lead to similar security threats.

THE HAZARDS OF DIFFERENTIAL GROWTH

While rapid population growth can lead to insecurity, different patterns of demographic change among populations located in close proximity to each other can be a more direct precipitant of insecurity and conflict. Population pressures tend to force people outward from "high pressure" rapid-growth areas to "low pressure" areas of slow population growth. These pressures naturally produce anxiety among the slower growing or ZPG populations.

Among nations, those with slow population growth rates often perceive themselves to be potential targets of rapidly growing neighbors. Israel, with an annual rate of natural population increase of 1.5 percent, feels threatened by Arab neighbors with populations growing at between 3 and 4 percent. Israel has compensated for this perceived imbalance by encouraging large-scale immigration, particularly from the former Soviet Union. This, in turn, increases insecurity among Palestinians in the West Bank and Gaza areas who fear that the influx will increase pressure on their lands. As former Israeli Prime Minister Shamir put it succinctly in 1990, "A big immigration needs a big Israel."[45]

One of the biggest sources of potential future instability is the rapid growth of Islamic populations compared to their non-Islamic neighbors. There are now forty countries in the world in which more than 50 percent of the population is Islamic, and another seven in which Moslems are a very significant minority (25–49 percent). In recent years, these forty-seven countries had a population growth rate of 2.8 percent annually, while their non–Islamic counterparts in the less-industrialized world were growing at only 2.3 percent.[46] Given a worldwide increase in Islamic fundamentalism, neighbors of Islamic countries feel increasingly insecure in the face of these burgeoning populations.

The demographic divide that stretches the length of the Mediterranean is one of the arenas in which rapidly expanding Islamic populations, in this case in North Africa, confront more stable non-Islamic populations. On the European side of this demographic fault line almost all countries have reached or are approaching zero population growth; the Islamic countries of

North Africa, by contrast, are growing at about 2.6 percent annually. The total population of North Africa, 147 million in 1992, is expected to nearly double to 274 million by 2025, while the European countries are expected to grow hardly at all.[47] The primary reason for these differences is that the original demographic transition has been essentially completed in affluent European countries, while only limited progress has been made in economically stagnant North Africa. In France and Italy, the average number of children per married female in the 1980s was below replacement rate, at about 1.8; in Northern Africa, by contrast, large families are still the rule. In Algeria, the average was 4.2 children, and in Morocco it was about 4.5.[48]

Given its historical ties to North Africa, France has been the country most directly affected by a surge of migrants. Afflicted by recent diminishing rates of economic growth, the French response to these demographic pressures has been largely negative. Migrants have become a significant issue in French politics, and the National Front—the right-wing political party headed by Jean-Marie Le Pen—has been able to garner as much as 10 percent of the vote, while suggesting that all immigrants be returned to their countries of origin. Germany has also been affected by large-scale immigration from the south and the east. Discontent with immigration laws and an influx of foreigners was manifest in violence against foreigners in several parts of Germany in 1992.

Even within the United States, differential population growth rates will be an important force in reshaping the political map over the next few decades. The perquisites of the "WASP" (White Anglo-Saxon Protestant) population that has traditionally been in political control are increasingly under attack from African-American, Hispanic, and Asian minorities that collectively are on the way to becoming a new majority. The traditionally dominant white portion of the population is near zero population growth, while the minority populations are growing much more rapidly. This demographic shift is obviously of great interest to both major political parties because their traditional bases of support are eroding and changing. Although there is a link between differential growth rates and the violence that has recently rocked U.S. cities, future tensions arising from differential growth are just as likely to be manifest in the political arena as on the streets.

Differential population growth rates will be a source of significant change on a global scale. The collective population of the stabilized North is close to ZPG, while that in the South is rapidly growing. Thus, by the year 2025, there will be almost six people living south of the divide for every person in the industrialized North.[49] The less-industrially developed countries will have a young, growing, and potentially restive population, while the industrialized world will be older and more likely to be conservative in outlook. New challenges to global security are likely to come from radical doctrines and revolutionary movements arising from within large pockets of poverty in the South, and they are unlikely to be sympathetically received by the aging, conservative political leaders of the North.

CHANNELING THE DEMOGRAPHIC CURRENTS

Understanding and channeling the demographic currents of change is a long-term process that is essential to the task of creating a more sustainable and less conflictual way of life on a planetary scale. Preserving ecological security means developing and promoting global policies that are designed to maintain an equilibrium between nature and the human population. This implies a continuous process of adjustment of values, institutions, and reproductive patterns to changing ecological realities. And this ongoing process of managing demographic currents requires anticipatory thinking in order to avoid the harsher long-term consequences of current human behavior.

Unfortunately, there are no "magic bullets" or wonder cures for the various population problems caused by the shifting demographic currents because they lie at the center of a bundle of complex moral, social, economic, and political dilemmas. On one hand, unchecked population growth can often lead to environmental decay, starvation, malnutrition, economic stagnation, and political instability. But, on the other hand, zero population growth and longer lifespans create another set of deep issues involving ethical questions of entitlement and intergenerational equity.

Attempts to regulate population growth through public policy are anathema to most politicians because such policies often run contrary to deeply held religious values that were originally shaped during a period of human history when the future well-being of Homo sapiens was ensured through vigorous reproduction. As John Weeks suggests, "It must be remembered that all nations that have survived to the present day did so by overcoming high levels of mortality."[50]

One of the biggest barriers to resolute action on population growth is a very tight linkage between reproductive patterns and traditional religious values. The dogma and practices of some of the world's leading religions present formidable obstacles to change. Hence, the position taken by the leadership of the Roman Catholic Church—banning all forms of artificial birth control—has certainly been an obstacle to family planning, although there is evidence that official church policies are often ignored at the local level, particularly in Latin America.[51] And while there are apparently no special Islamic prohibitions against birth control practices, in male-dominated Islamic societies it is very difficult to change traditional attitudes related to optimal family size.[52]

Another roadblock to resolute action is persistent quibbling among population scholars over the depth and causes of these problems. While there is a preponderance of scholarly opinion that the world's population is growing too large, many academic hairs have been split over its optimum level.[53] Pronatalists, such as economist Julian Simon, muddy the waters when they declare that the human population is the "ultimate resource" and that "population growth, along with the lengthening of human life, is a moral and material triumph."[54] The issue ignored by these population "optimists" when discussing how many people the earth can support is the suffering that must be endured by the growing numbers of starving and malnourished in the less-affluent neighborhoods on the disadvantaged side of the demographic divide.

The domestic and international politics of family planning also hinder efforts to shape coherent policies to deal with population growth. A political split between North and South first became apparent in 1974 at the World Population Conference in Bucharest, Romania. The industrial countries, led by the United States, sought the adoption of a World Population Plan of Action that would have made family planning a central part of economic development efforts. But many of the leaders of southern countries resented this as an intrusion into their internal affairs, and argued that economic development must take priority since it is the "best contraceptive." This split persisted over the next decade and surfaced again at the 1984 International Population Conference in Mexico City. And, at the Rio de Janeiro "Earth Summit" of June 1992, the population issue was very much ignored because of pressure from religious institutions, various womens' groups, and leaders of southern countries who blamed the bulk of the world's environmental ills on the industrial world.

Discontinuities in U.S. policy are also part of the problem. Historically, the United States has been at the forefront in global family planning activity. Throughout the 1940s, noted demographers such as Dudley Kirk, Frank Notestein, and Kingsley Davis called attention to the impact of colonialism on population growth. These insights influenced U.S. policy, and every secretary of state from Dean Rusk to George Shultz strongly supported family planning. The United States began to encourage population limitation as part of development policy during under the Kennedy administration, and this emphasis persisted through the Carter administration.[55] Beginning in the mid-1980s, however, this support was held hostage to domestic politics. In 1984, the United States astonished family planning advocates when Secretary of State James Baker, addressing the World Population Conference in Mexico City, declared that steady population growth was a natural phenomenon that neither advanced nor hindered economic growth.[56] The Reagan administration subsequently withheld funding from the United Nations Population Fund (UNFPA), the largest multilateral agency providing family planning services and, for many years, the recipient of considerable U.S. aid. When George Bush became president in 1989, there was hope that the U.S. contribution to UNFPA would be restored. Bush had been an outspoken advocate of family planning in the 1960s and 1970s, and even advocated making contraceptives available worldwide on a "massive scale."[57] But family-planning assistance under Bush got snarled in political infighting between Congress and the president, and the cuts were not restored. No doubt the Clinton administration will take a more vigorous approach to family planning, but much time was lost during many years of inaction under Reagan and Bush.

In 1989, seventy-nine countries, including the United States, met in Amsterdam and drew up a plan to stabilize population growth and to extend the availability of contraceptives to 75 percent of the world's women. The Amsterdam Declaration called for worldwide family-planning assistance to increase to $10.5 billion by 1991, a target that was never reached. This amounted to 4 percent of the total foreign assistance given by industrial countries. Only Norway devotes this percentage to family planning. Moving rapidly to reach the goals set forth in the Amsterdam Declaration would certainly be a major step forward in slowing global population growth.

Addressing the problem of rapid population growth requires a continuing dedicated effort, as the crux of the problem is to modify human behavior on a massive scale at a time when political leaders in many countries lack public trust. People in rapidly growing countries must be convinced that their outmoded pronatalist values are at the roots of numerous problems in the contemporary world. And, once convinced, they must have regular access to family-planning information and technologies. Although significant strides have been made in various parts of the world in reducing rates of population growth, changing reproductive behavior is an extremely difficult proposition, and both wise and responsible political leadership, as well as tens of billions of dollars annually, will be required.[58]

Stemming the influx of people into the cities of the less-industrialized countries is also difficult because it requires local action and, for the most part, has not been a priority in many countries. The problem could be somewhat ameliorated by successful family-planning efforts. But future sustainable development requires creative alternatives to keep people from migrating to already overcrowded and polluted cities. Such alternatives might include attempts to direct economic growth to smaller cities, as well as economic incentives in rural areas to keep more people in agricultural occupations.

Dealing with the future impact of graying in industrial countries is a much more insidious problem. Graying may already be having a negative impact on global economic growth. The economic stagnation and policy confusion of the early 1990s may be an early warning of more severe dislocations to follow as the industrial countries attempt to control social welfare expenditures in the face of new economic difficulties. As the countries on the northern side of the demographic divide grapple with significant budget deficits, they are much less likely to provide the types of family planning and economic assistance necessary to help the less-industrial countries out of their demographic traps. Coping with these emerging and linked demographic uncertainties will require anticipatory thinking on an unprecedented scale, as well as a new approach to future policymaking, stressing global security, the human interest, and the welfare of future generations.

Notes

1. Unless otherwise noted, population data come from *1992 World Population Data Sheet* (Washington: Population Reference Bureau, 1992).

2. See Ben Wattenberg, *The Birth Dearth* (New York: Pharos Books, 1989).

3. See chapter 14 in this volume.

4. See Nazli Choucri and Robert North, *Nations in Conflict* (San Francisco: W. H. Freeman, 1975); and Nazli Choucri, *Population Dynamics and International Violence* (Lexington, MA: D. C. Heath, 1974).

5. "Zebra Mussel Invasion Threatens U.S. Waters," *Science* (September 21, 1990).

6. See Alfred Crosby, *America's Forgotten Pandemic: The Influenza Epidemic of 1918* (Cambridge: Cambridge University Press, 1990).

7. See J. Donald Hughes, *Ecology in Ancient Civilizations* (Albuquerque: University of New Mexico Press, 1975).

8. See Anders Wijkman and Lloyd Timberlake, *Natural Disasters: Acts of God or Acts of Man* (London: Earthscan, 1984).

9. *World Population Prospects 1990* (New York: United Nations, 1991).

10. See Lester Brown and Jodi Jacobson, *Our Demographically Divided World* (Washington: Worldwatch Institute, 1986).

11. The term demographic transition was coined by demographer Frank Notestein in 1945 to refer to Western European demographic experiences.

12. Dirk J. van de Kaa, "Europe's Second Demographic Transition," *Population Bulletin* (March 1987), p. 19.

13. Figures from *1993 World Population Data Sheet*.

14. Brown and Jacobsen, *Our Demographically Divided World*, pp. 32–34.

15. van de Kaa, "Europe's Second Demographic Transition," p. 5.

16. Data from The World Bank, *World Development Report 1992* (New York: Oxford University Press, 1992), Table 31.

17. Leon Bouvier, "Planet Earth 1984–2034," *Population Bulletin* (February 1984).

18. "The Floodgates are Bursting," *Business Week* (September 9, 1991).

19. Susan Kalish, "Immigration: IRCA Tops Out," *Population Today* (November 1992).

20. See Doris Meissner, "Managing Migrations," *Foreign Policy* (Spring 1992).

21. Ibid., p. 68.

22. Don Podesta, "Europe's Migrants Swell Refugee Wave," *The Washington Post* (October 6, 1989).

23. Brown and Jacobsen, *Our Demographically Divided World*, p. 35.

24. *World Resources 1992–93* (New York: Oxford University Press, 1992), p. 30.

25. Jonathan Randal, "A Dwindling Natural Resource," *The Washington Post* (May 13, 1992).

26. United Nations Development Program, *Human Development Report 1992* (New York: Oxford University Press, 1992), p. 35.

27. Data from *World Development Report 1992*, Table 1. Data for many poor countries are not available.

28. See Dennis Pirages, "Political Stability and Conflict Management," in Ted Gurr, ed., *Handbook of Political Conflict* (New York: The Free Press, 1980), pp. 432–441.

29. Figures from *World Resources 1988–89* (New York: Basic Books, 1988), pp. 36–37.

30. *World Resources 1988–89*, p. 37.

31. Eugene Robinson, "Crime is Choking Rio," *The Washington Post* (October 4, 1990).

32. United Nations Center for Human Settlements, *Global Report on Human Settlements, 1986* (New York: Oxford University Press, 1987), p. 130.

33. *World Resources 1988–89*, p. 45.

34. Edward Cody, "Mexico City Choked by Pollution Emergency," *The Washington Post* (March 26, 1992).

35. Susan Okie, "Health Crisis Confronts 1.3 Billion," *The Washington Post* (September 25, 1989); World Health Organization, "Global Estimates for Health Situation Assessment and Projections 1990," (Geneva: 1990).

36. See "The Sobering Geography of AIDS," *Science* (April 19, 1991); and Jonathan Mann, ed., *AIDS in the World* (Cambridge: Harvard University Press, 1992).

37. "Emerging Viruses, Emerging Threat," *Science* (January 19, 1990).

38. van de Kaa, *Europe's Second Demographic Transition*, p. 5.

39. Jared Bernstein and Lawrence Mishel, *The State of Working America* (Washington: Economic Policy Institute, 1992).

40. *Ageing Populations: The Social Policy Implications* (Paris: OECD, 1988), p. 22.

41. *Ageing Populations: The Social Policy Implications,* p. 32. The German figures are for West Germany.

42. *The Future of Social Protection* (Paris, OECD, 1988), p. 13.

43. "Debt Poses Politicians Staggering Challenges."

44. Jean-Claude Chesnais and Wang Shuxin, "Population Aging, Retirement Policy and Living Conditions of the Elderly in China," *Population* (Volume 2), p. 7. See also, H. Yuan Tien et al., "China's Demographic Dilemmas," *Population Bulletin* (June 1992).

45. Jackson Diehl, "Exodus of Soviet Jews May Alter Israel's Fate," *The Washington Post* (June 10, 1990).

46. John Weeks, "The Demography of Islamic Nations," *Population Bulletin* (December, 1989), p. 13.

47. Figures are from *1992 World Population Data Sheet.*

48. Ecole Nationale D'Administration, "Defense, Securite, Strategie et Disequilibre Demographique," in *La Population de la France* (Paris, 1989), p. 41.

49. *1992 World Population Data Sheet.*

50. Weeks, "The Demography of Islamic Nations," p. 18.

51. Thomas Merrick, "Population Pressures in Latin America," *Population Bulletin* (July 1986), p. 41.

52. See Weeks, "The Demography of Islamic Nations," pp. 18–21.

53. See Paul Ehrlich and Anne Ehrlich, *The Population Explosion* (New York: Simon and Schuster, 1990); William Catton, *Overshoot: The Ecological Basis for Revolutionary Change* (Urbana: University of Illinois Press, 1980); S. Fred Singer, ed., *Is There an Optimum Level of Population?* (New York: McGraw-Hill, 1991); Robert Goodland, "The Case that the World has Reached Limits," *Population and Environment* (Spring 1992).

54. Julian Simon, *The Ultimate Resource* (Princeton: Princeton University Press, 1981), p. 9.

55. See Peter Donaldson, "On the Origins of the United States Government's International Population Policy," *Population Studies* (November 1990).

56. See Chet Atkins, "International Family Planning: Where's the Leadership?" *Washington Post* (August 27, 1991).

57. See Jessica Mathews, "World Population: As the President Turns," *The Washington Post* (November 1, 1990).

58. See Thomas Merrick, "World Population in Transition," *Population Bulletin* (April 1986), pp. 30–37.

17 / Global Debt and Third World Development

VINCENT FERRARO AND MELISSA ROSSER

In 1919, writing about a massive debt imposed upon Germany by the Allied Powers as reparations for a catastrophic war, John Maynard Keynes expressed contempt for the wisdom of the policy:

> The policy of reducing Germany to servitude for a generation, of degrading the lives of millions of human beings, and of depriving a whole nation of happiness should be abhorrent and detestable—abhorrent and detestable, even if it were possible, even if it enriched ourselves, even if it did not sow the decay of the whole civilised life of Europe. Some preach it in the name of Justice. In the great events of man's history, in the unwinding of the complex fates of nations Justice is not so simple. And if it were, nations are not authorised, by religion or by natural morals, to visit on the children of their enemies the misdoings of parents or of rulers.[1]

Twenty years later, the debt, partially responsible for the rise of the Nazis, had been repudiated and Keynes's views had been confirmed.

Seventy-four years later, the world confronts another massive debt, although not one imposed by a treaty of peace. Indeed, this debt, totaling $1.362 trillion in 1991, has no identifiable demons: One cannot point to the vindictiveness of a Clemenceau, or the opportunism of a Lloyd George, or the naive idealism of a Wilson. Nonetheless, this debt has had the effect of plunging millions of people into conditions of economic despair and desperation. Most tragically, this debt will jeopardize the chances for the happiness of millions of children who will have committed no crime other than that of being born into a poor society. Ultimately, this debt, like the German debt, will not be repaid in full.

This chapter will examine the causes and consequences of the global debt crisis. It begins by first defining the crisis and then develops an explanation for the crisis from two perspectives: first, a general explanation based upon the desperate economic conditions that characterize developing countries; and second, an explanation of the more specific reasons why poorer countries expanded their debt burdens so dramatically in the 1970s. The chapter then examines the costs of the debt crisis to both developing and developed countries, and pays some close attention to the possibility of an international banking collapse in the early 1980s. Finally, the chapter reviews some general solutions to the debt crisis and offers suggestions for future responses.

WHAT IS THE "DEBT CRISIS?"

To be fully accurate, one should refer to the multiple debt crises that exist in the world today. For our purposes, however, the "debt crisis" will refer to the external debt, both private and public, of developing countries, which has been growing enormously since the early 1970s. Our focus should not obscure, however, the other debt crises that trouble much of the global economy: the budget deficits of the United States government, its balance of trade deficits, and the insolvency of many of its savings and loans institutions. These crises are highly interconnected, particularly as they relate to the issues of interest rates, export values, and confidence in the international banking system. The "debt crisis," then, is a global phenomenon, and any attempt to understand it fully needs a global perspective.

However, the greatest suffering thus far in the crisis is found within developing countries, and therein lies the justification for our focus. But even within the developing world, our attention can be directed toward a variety of problems depending on how one chooses to think about debt. One can focus on the integrity of the international financial system, in which case one's emphasis is on the countries with the largest debts, such as Mexico or Brazil. Alternatively, a primary concern can be on the desperate human costs of the debt, which would direct attention to sub-Saharan Africa, for example. Yet another perspective, the strategic dimensions of the problem, would concentrate on debtors such as Turkey or South Korea.

We will pay primary attention to what have been termed the most heavily indebted nations within the developing countries. This focus is not neutral, since it generally refers to those nations with the largest debts and whose threat of default represents a serious concern to lending agencies.[2] The bias of the focus, however, should not divert attention from the smaller countries, particularly those in Africa, whose debts are crushingly large to their people, even though the banks and international lending agencies consider them less important or less threatening.[3]

The accelerating magnitude of debt for the most heavily indebted nations is staggering. In 1970, the fifteen heavily indebted nations (using the World Bank classification of 1989—see note 2) had an external public debt of $17.923 billion—which amounted to 9.8 percent of their GNP. By 1987, these same nations owed $402.171 billion, or 47.5 percent of their GNP. Interest payments owed by these countries went from $2.789 billion in 1970 to $36.251 billion in 1987. Debt service, defined as the sum of actual repayments of principal and actual payments of interest made in foreign currencies, goods, or services on external public and publicly guaranteed debt, accounted for 1.5 percent of their GNP and 12.4 percent of their total exports of goods and services in 1970. In 1987, those figures had risen to 4.3 percent and 24.9 percent, respectively.[4] Table 17.1 gives the statistics, using the World Bank's 1992 classification of heavily indebted countries.

Table 17.1 / Selected Debt Statistics of the Fifteen Most Severely Indebted
Developing Nations

	Total External Debt (Millions of $US)	Total External Debt (as a % of GNP)	Debt Service (as a % of Exports)	
	1990	1980	1980	1990
Algeria	26,806	47.1	27.1	59.4
Argentina	61,144	48.4	37.3	34.1
Bolivia	4,276	93.3	35.0	34.1
Brazil	116,173	31.2	63.1	20.8
Bulgaria	10,927	1.1	0.3	56.9
Congo	5,118	98.0	10.8	20.7
Cote d'Ivoire	17,956	58.8	28.3	38.6
Ecuador	12,105	53.8	33.9	33.2
Mexico	96,810	30.5	49.5	27.8
Morocco	23,524	53.3	32.7	23.4
Nicaragua	10,497	112.1	22.3	4.1
Peru	21,105	51.0	46.5	11.0
Poland	49,386	16.3	17.9	4.9
Syria	16,446	27.1	11.4	26.9
Venezuela	33,305	42.1	27.2	20.7

Source: World Bank, World Development Report, 1992 (Washington, D.C.: The World Bank, 1992) Tables 21 and 24, pp. 258–259, 264–265.

For the developing world as a whole, in 1991, the total external debt was $1.362 trillion, which was 126.5 percent of its total exports of goods and services in that year, and the ratio of debt servicing to the gross domestic product of the developing world reached 32.4 percent.[5]

THE CAUSES OF THE DEBT CRISIS: (1) POVERTY AS A GENERAL MOTIVE FOR BORROWING

The economic debts of the developing world will not be fully repaid, quite simply because the people who live in the developing world cannot afford to repay them. The harsh reality of poverty in poorer countries was an initial stimulus for the loans. As we shall see below, economic conditions suggested that borrowing money was a reasonable course of action in the 1970s, particularly for poor countries, which perceived few, if any, alternative ways to address the economic plight of their citizens. Those who live in the rich countries of the developed world can readily observe profound poverty: all who live in the wealthy, industrialized nations do not have equal access to education, health care, good nutrition, and housing. The fact that these deprivations exist alongside great wealth is shocking, but they pale when compared to the scale of global poverty. The hunger, homelessness, illness, and suffering of the poor in the developed countries must be multiplied a thousand times, in some respects a million times, to begin to reflect the scope of poverty in the world's poorest nations. In 1987, the average per capita income for people living in the poor countries in the South was only 6 percent of the income in the developed countries of the North. In Africa, one-fifth of the population lives in poverty, with those in sub-Saharan Africa bearing the heaviest burden.[6] A child in the developing world suffers a risk of death four to ten times greater than that of a child in Western Europe or North America. A pregnant woman in the developing world is 50 to 100 times more likely to die in childbirth than women in the wealthy, developed nations.[7]

Despite the overwhelming number of statistics and indicators, global poverty is as hard to measure as it is to conceptualize. Although it is simple to characterize abstractly the living conditions of the world's impoverished population, there is no widely accepted, standard method of identifying the poor, and, therefore, of measuring the exact extent of global poverty. Economists, social scientists, politicians, and agencies for international aid each advocate their own particular definition of poverty depending upon the interests, whether noble or self-serving, which they are protecting or pursuing. Nonetheless, whatever the bias of the analyst or the method used to estimate the number of global poor, the statistics are appallingly high, almost beyond comprehension. Consider, for example, these estimates taken from the September 1990 UN *Chronicle* (p. 46):

- 1 billion people live in absolute poverty
- 100 million persons are completely homeless
- 800 million persons go hungry every day
- 1.75 billion people are without access to safe drinking water
- 1.5 billion persons are without access to primary health care

The central debate concerning the definition of poverty centers around the two most prominent types of measurements: income analysis and basic needs analysis. Income analysis, the most common measure of poverty, assumes that poverty is a direct function of income and individual purchasing power within nations. It argues that citizens with a higher income should have greater access to goods and services that will satisfy their basic needs. The countries with a higher GNP and GNP per capita presumably will have a proportionally higher standard of living for all their citizens. Consequently, the income analysis approach uses a cross-national comparison of GNP, GNP per capita, and GDP (gross domestic product) statistics to define poverty. In 1990, the World Bank's definition of poverty was all of the world's population living on less than $370 a year; a figure derived from the average of the poverty lines of the poorest nations in the world. By this criteria, over 20 percent of the world's population live in poverty.

The relative ease with which GNP and related economic indicators can be calculated, and the ability to set an actual "poverty line" based upon these "hard" figures, are attractive features of the income analysis method. However, the method has many hidden weaknesses. First, despite the seemingly accurate nature of the income definition of poverty, it is, in fact, based upon averages. For instance, the GNP per capita indicator measures the average income of each person in a nation by dividing the total gross national product by the total population. It is a highly inaccurate measurement because it does not consider the unequal distribution of wealth within the country. Many people in developing nations do not live within the organized market economy, and, in many countries, a rigid class and social structure prevents the integration of the poor into the economic activity of the country as a whole. Most of the very poor meet their needs through subsistence methods, such as farming, hunting, and bartering. The national income has no direct, or even indirect, effect on their existence, and a money income definition of poverty will not reflect their standard of living whatsoever.

The basic needs approach to the definition of poverty conceptualizes poverty differently. It is not a lack of money that causes people to live impoverished lives, it is a lack of food, shelter, education, sanitation, safe drinking water, and health care. Basic needs analysis sets a minimum standard for each of these life-sustaining variables and classifies as poor those who have access to less than a minimum allowance. The picture of the impoverished, according to the basic needs analysis, is one who is malnourished, illiterate, short-lived, sickly, and lacking proper shelter and sanitation. The poorest nations, as ranked by a basic needs index, are those who do not provide for the basic needs of their people. Significantly, they are not always the nations with the lowest GNP. For example, Sri Lanka is ranked 120th in the world by per capita GNP, but is listed as 75th in the United Nation's 1990 Human Development Report (which ranks countries by the HDI or Human Development Index), well above the United Arab Emirates, whose real GDP per capita is six times that of Sri Lanka.[8]

Although the basic needs analysis illustrates the living conditions of the world's poorest people better than a simple income definition, it, too, has its drawbacks as a method for measuring the extent of poverty in the world. The data for basic needs analysis is extremely difficult to collect. An accurate study is a time-consuming, expensive, and meticulous undertaking. Consequently, basic needs analysis often relies upon rough estimates and averages and even some income-related data. In addition, the categories of basic need and their importance relative to one another are somewhat subjective.

Creating a definitive way of calculating global poverty is much more than merely a matter of precision or exactitude. The way one defines poverty has a decisive impact on the kinds of policies that are chosen to combat it. Those who use income analysis regard economic growth as the answer to world poverty. This method of analysis depends on the theory of "trickle-down economics," that is, any increase in the productivity and relative wealth of a nation will eventually trickle down to benefit every sector of a country's economy and, consequently, each family unit and individual. The World Bank, for instance, implements economic recovery programs and internal structural readjustments to help poor nations increase the rate of growth in their GNPs, and ostensibly raise the standards of living in their society. Those who favor the basic needs analysis do not think that national economic growth is enough to eradicate world poverty, and, rather, emphasize questions of how that growth is distributed. They cite evidence that few of the benefits of increased productivity ever reach the most disadvantaged in low-income countries, and, therefore, advocate programs that directly target the poor and their suffering by subsidizing and redistributing basic needs and services. Such programs include vaccination and health outreach services, nutritional supplements, campaigns against illiteracy, infant and maternal mortality, and the problems of sanitation and clean water resources.

Regardless of the method of calculation, it is clear that many people in the world are suffering needlessly and living lives of wretched deprivation. This is especially true for women and children in the developing world. Women and children are the most vulnerable members of any society, but they are the principal victims of poverty. Females as a group, in poor regions, regardless of age, receive less education, less health care, and less food than men or male children. The female literacy rate in the developing world is three-quarters that of the male literacy rate. Women work, on average, twice as many hours, including the unpaid labor of subsistence farming, gathering, and caring for the young, the old, and the ill.[9] Due to poorer nutrition, hard labor, lack of professional health care, and unsanitary living conditions, women in the developing world account for 99 percent of maternal deaths worldwide.[10] The health of children is even more threatened. Every six seconds, a child dies and another is disabled by a disease for which there is already an effective immunization. Each year seventeen million children die from the combined effects of poor nutrition, diarrhea, malaria, pneumonia, measles, whooping cough, and tetanus, diseases that are rarely fatal in the developed countries. One in twenty of these impoverished children dies before reaching the age of five.[11]

These are the conditions that cause nations to borrow. There were, however, specific economic conditions in the 1970s that led to a massive explosion of the debt burden of developing countries. The tragedy of the debt crisis is that this borrowing only made the suffering significantly worse.

THE CAUSES OF THE DEBT CRISIS:
(2) THE SPECIFIC ECONOMIC CONDITIONS
OF THE 1970s

The conventional explanation is that the debt crisis of the 1980s was due to a number of highly contingent circumstances that were essentially unpredictable at the time many of these loans were made. For example, William R.

Cline of the Institute for International Economics summarized the causes as follows:

> The external debt crisis that emerged in many developing countries in 1982 can be traced to higher oil prices in 1973–74 and 1979–80, high interest rates in 1980–82, declining export prices and volume associated with global recession in 1981–82, problems of domestic economic management, and an adverse psychological shift in the credit markets.[12]

The story actually begins earlier than 1973 because debt has been solidly entrenched in the finances of developing countries for many years. The United States was a heavily indebted country in the nineteenth century, and poorer countries have always needed outside infusions of investment capital in order to develop their resources. The logic of indebtedness is commonplace and not especially arcane: one incurs a debt in hopes of making an investment that will produce enough money both to pay off the debt and to generate economic growth that is self-sustaining. An important characteristic of developing-country debt prior to 1973 was that it was largely financed through public agencies, both bilateral and multilateral. These agencies, such as the World Bank, presumably guided the investments toward projects that held out genuine promise of economic viability and success.

After the oil crisis of 1973–74, however, many commercial banks found themselves awash with "petrodollars" from some oil-producing states, and these private banks were eager to put this windfall capital to productive use. The banks assumed that sovereign debt was a good risk since there was a prevalent belief that countries would not default.[13] Many developing countries, reeling from oil price increases, were eager to receive these loans. These countries assumed that loans were an intelligent way to ease the trauma of the oil price increases, particularly given the very high inflation rates at the time. Other developing countries, the oil-exporting ones (Colombia, Ecuador, Mexico, Nigeria, and Venezuela, for example), saw the loans as a way to capitalize on their much-improved financial status, and they assumed that oil prices would remain high in real terms for an extended period of time.

In retrospect, it is easy to point out that these actions did not conform to the typical logic of indebtedness. These loans were being used to pay for current consumption, not for productive investments. The money was not being used to mobilize underutilized resources, but rather to maintain a current, albeit desperate, standard of living. Moreover, these loans were being made in an unstable economic environment: since the unraveling of the Bretton Woods Agreement in 1971 (precipitated by the U.S. termination of the gold standard), global economic relationships had been steadily worsening. The developing countries began to experience a long-term, secular decline in demand for their products as the developed countries tightened their economic belts in order to pay for oil and as they initiated tariffs and quotas to reduce their balance of payments deficits.

The proof of the wrongheadedness of the lending in the 1970s became dramatically apparent in 1981. Interest rates shot up, and global demand for exports from developing countries plummeted. The very deep global recession of 1981–82 made it impossible for developing countries to generate sufficient income to pay back their loans on schedule. According to the United Nations Conference on Trade and Development (UNCTAD), commodity prices (for essentially foodstuffs, fuels, minerals, and metals) dropped 28 percent in 1981–82, and between 1980 and 1982 interest payments on loans increased by 50 percent in nominal terms and 75 percent in real terms.[14] In 1982, Mexico came to the brink of what everyone had thought impossible just two years earlier—a default.[15] This critical situation marked the beginning of what is conventionally termed "the debt crisis." Private banks abruptly disengaged from further lending because the risks were too great. In order to prevent a panic, which might have had the effect of unraveling the entire international financial system, a number of governmental and intergovernmental agencies, led by the United States, stepped in to assure the continued repayment of the Mexican loans.

At this same time, the International Monetary Fund (IMF) emerged as the guarantor of the creditworthiness of developing countries. The IMF had performed this role in the past, but primarily with regard to its "own" money—that is, money lent by the IMF to assist countries in addressing balance of payments problems. This new emphasis on creating conditions primarily to assure payments to private institutions, while in theory not a new undertaking, was different in character and content from what the IMF had done in the past, largely because of the enormous amount of money involved. Unfortunately, the IMF, in spite of the unprecedented situation, did not perceive that its responsibilities had changed in any significant way, and gave its seal of approval for additional loans only to those countries that accepted its traditional policies, which are generally referred to as stabilization programs of "structural adjustment."

Programs of structural adjustment are designed to address balance of payments problems that are largely internally generated by high inflation rates, large budget deficits, or structural impediments to the efficient allocation of resources, such as tariffs or subsidies. The IMF structural adjustment programs highlight "productive capacity as critical to economic performance" and emphasize "measures to raise the economy's output potential and to increase the flexibility of factor and goods markets."[16] A fundamental assumption in a structural adjustment program is that current consumption must be suppressed so that capital can be diverted into more productive domestic investments. A further assumption of an IMF stabilization program is that exposure to international competition in investment and trade can enhance the efficiency of local production. In practice, these programs involve reduced food and transportation subsidies, public sector layoffs, curbs on government spending, and higher interest and tax rates.[17] These actions typically affect the poorer members of society disproportionately hard.[18]

When one is dealing with a particularly inefficient economic system, structural adjustment is perhaps acceptable medicine; and there were many examples of gross inefficiency, not to mention outright corruption, in many of the countries that were soliciting IMF assistance. In this respect, the IMF programs were probably regarded as the correct approach by the public and private agencies that were being asked to reschedule or roll over loans. But the critical difference between the traditional IMF role and its new role as guarantor of creditworthiness is that the suppression of demand, previously designed to free capital for domestic investment, simply freed capital to leave the country.

Moreover, the approach assumes that it was primarily inefficient economic management in the developing countries that led to the debt crisis. From this point of view, the developing countries had gorged themselves on easy money in the 1970s, with the debt crisis being the rough equivalent of a fiscal hangover. Indeed, according to Stephen Haggard, the IMF believed that a large majority of the failures of adjustment programs were due to "political constraints" or "weak administrative systems," as opposed to external constraints that were largely beyond the control of the developing countries, for example, high interest rates.[19]

It is extraordinarily difficult to determine the validity of this perspective. Clearly, some loans have been used in inappropriate ways.[20] Nonetheless, developing countries cannot be accused of fiscal irresponsibility in such matters as the increase in interest rates or the global recession in 1981–82. The assessment of culpability is in some respects crucial and in other respects irrelevant: crucial, because one would like to understand the crisis so that a repetition of a similar crisis can be avoided in the future; irrelevant, because the current situation is so desperate that solutions must be found no matter where the blame for the crisis actually lies. In the final analysis, blame rests on a system of finance that allowed developing countries and banks to engage in transactions reasonable only in the context of wildly optimistic scenarios of economic growth. Additionally, much blame rests on policies of the United States government that were undertaken with insufficient regard for their international financial implications.

William Cline attempted to distinguish between the internal and external causes of the debt crisis by looking at figures for the effects of oil price and interest rate increases in order to determine the degree to which each were responsible for the crisis. His figures, reproduced in Table 17.2, should be treated as only suggestive because there is a high degree of "double counting" (loans were taken out in some cases to cover earlier loans) in many of these figures. Nonetheless, as a rough approximation, the data suggest that external factors were significantly more important than the internal causes of inefficiency and corruption.

The IMF stabilization programs, with their nearly exclusive emphasis on the internal economic policies of heavily indebted countries and relative disregard for the factors that Cline identifies, have failed to encourage the

Table 17.2 / Impact of Exogenous Shocks on External Debt of Nonoil
Developing Countries (Billion $US)

Effect	Amount
Oil Price Increase in Excess of US Inflation (1974–82 cumulative)	260
Real Interest Rate in Excess of 1961–80 Average: 1981 and 1982	41
Terms of Trade Loss, 1981–82	79
Export Volume Loss Caused by World Recession, 1981–82	21
Total	401
Total Debt Increase, 1973–82	482

Source: William R. Cline, *International Debt: Systemic Risk and Policy and Policy Response*
(Washington, D.C.: Institute for International Economics, 1984), p. 13.

very type of economic growth that might have helped the developing
countries to grow out of their indebtedness. In fact, these programs have had
exactly the opposite effect: they have further impoverished many of the
heavily indebted countries to a point where their future economic growth
must be seriously doubted. Many observers have come to share Jeffrey
Sachs's assessment of structural adjustment programs: "The sobering point
is that programs of this sort have been adopted repeatedly, and have failed
repeatedly."[21]

This failure of traditional techniques to alleviate the debt problem suggests that perhaps the conventional interpretation of the debt crisis is
incomplete or misleading. Indeed, much evidence suggests this inference.
Perhaps the most compelling evidence is the fact that periodic debt crises
seem to be endemic to the modern international system. There have been
cycles of debt and default in the past, and some of the same debtors have
experienced similar crises in almost regular cycles.[22] Thus, the debt crisis of
the 1980s cannot be ascribed solely to the contingent circumstances of oil
prices and U.S. monetary and fiscal policy, at least as the conventional perspective portrays these factors. This explanation must be supplemented by
factors that are more structural and deep-seated.

There are at least two issues relatively unexplored by the conventional
explanation of the debt crisis that deserve greater attention, and they both
relate to the vulnerability of the developing countries to changes in the
world economy over which they have little direct control: their sensitivity to
monetary changes in the advanced industrialized countries, and their dependence on primary commodities as sources of their export earnings. The
first consideration is perhaps the more dramatic.

It is no mere coincidence that the United States experienced its own very
serious debt crisis in the same year that panic arose over the external debt
of developing countries.[23] The massive government debt of the United
States and its related balance of trade deficit precipitated a deliberate strategy of economic contraction that had global effects. Interest rates in the
United States had achieved very high levels in 1979, but the inflation rates

at the time were also very high. After the deep economic recession of 1981–82, the inflation rate declined markedly, but the interest rates remained high.[24] Interest rates remained high because they were necessary to attract foreign investments to finance the extraordinary U.S. budget deficits created by the tax reductions pushed by the Reagan administration and passed by the Congress. In turn, the high interest rates inflated the value of the dollar, reducing U.S. demand for developing-country exports and further diminishing the ability of the indebted countries to repay their loans.

The United States, however, did not experience a debt "crisis" because it was able to reassure its creditors that its promises to pay were plausible. But the high real interest rates forced upon the developing countries as their loans were turned over created a situation where no similar guarantees could be offered. As it became obvious that the debtor countries could not meet the increased payments, the private banks tried to pull back, bringing about the very crisis they wished to avoid. Only very persistent efforts by official governmental agencies managed to stabilize the situation enough to avoid a precipitous default. In a very real sense, however, it was the actions of the United States that created the immediate crisis, and not some event or pattern of events in the developing world itself.

Similarly, this debt crisis aggravated an already bad situation with respect to the ability of the developing countries to pay back their loans. Many of the developing countries were extremely poor prior to the crisis, which was one reason why they took out such massive debts in the first place. There was no evidence, before 1973, that this condition of relative poverty was changing in any but a few of the developing countries, such as the newly industrializing countries of South Korea, Singapore, and Taiwan. In fact, most of the traditional measures of economic development suggest that most developing countries were falling farther behind the advanced industrialized countries at an increasingly faster rate.

The developing countries will always be relatively poorer than the advanced industrialized countries as long as they rely heavily on primary commodities, such as copper and rubber, for export earnings. Trade may be a stimulus to growth, but trade is not an effective way to overcome relative poverty if the values for primary commodities fail to keep pace with the value of manufactured products. This relationship between the values of manufactured exports and the values of primary commodities exports (the terms of trade) has been carefully examined by many economists, and some of them, such as Prebisch, have argued that the international division of labor is systematically biased against the interests of countries that rely heavily on the export of primary products. This debate, which has been extended into what has been termed a theory of dependency, is a difficult one to resolve with clear empirical evidence. Some recent evidence, however, suggests that raw materials producers have indeed suffered relative economic losses in the twentieth century. Enzo R. Grilli and Maw Cheng Yang analyzed the terms of trade between primary commodities and manufactured goods since 1900 and found that "the prices of all primary commodities (including fuels) relative to those of traded manufactures declined by about 36 percent over the 1900–86 period, at an average annual rate of 0.5 percent."[25]

Thus, the developing countries are at a structural disadvantage compared to the advanced industrialized countries. The newly industrializing countries of East Asia are the exceptions that prove this rule. Because they have been able to expand manufactured exports, they have improved their relative economic situation tremendously in recent years. Other countries have been less successful, and the recent resurgence of protectionist measures against manufactured products from the developing world will make this type of transition only more difficult. Ultimately, the solution to the debt crisis, and the underlying poverty that spawned it, must address this terms of trade issue. This imperative will be discussed in further detail below. Clearly, however, the solutions to the debt crisis will require a perspective that looks at the problem as more than a temporary aberration precipitated by bad luck and incompetence.

WHAT ARE THE COSTS OF THE DEBT CRISIS?

This explosion of debt has had numerous consequences for the developing countries, but this section will focus on only three consequences: the decline in the quality of life within debtor countries, the political violence associated with that decline, and the effects of the decline on the developed world. The next section of this chapter will explore separately the most publicized cost of the debt crisis, the possibility that it might have instigated a global banking crisis.

The first, and most devastating, effect of the debt crisis was, and continues to be, the significant outflows of capital to finance the debt. According to the World Bank: "Before 1982 the highly indebted countries received about 2 percent of GNP a year in resources from abroad; since then they have transferred roughly 3 percent of GNP a year in the opposite direction."[26] In 1988, the poorer countries of the world sent about $50 billion to the rich countries, and the cumulative total of these transfers since 1984 is nearly $120 billion.[27] The problem became so pervasive that even agencies whose ostensible purposes included aiding the indebted countries were draining capital: in 1987 "the IMF received about $8.6 billion more in loan repayments and interest charges than it lent out."[28] The IMF has since reversed the flow of money in a more appropriate direction, aided principally by the global decline in interest rates, as well as by some success in renegotiating some of the loan agreements.

This capital hemorrhage has severely limited prospects for economic growth in the developing world and seriously skewed the patterns of economic development within it. The implications for growth are summarized by Table 17.3.

The decline in average growth, from 6.3 percent a year to 1.7 percent a year, is even worse than it seems. Given the rate of population increase in these countries, a 1.7 percent increase in GDP translates into a net decline in per capita GDP. In other words, the populations of these countries were significantly worse off economically during the period of the debt crisis; and this decline further jeopardizes opportunities for future economic growth given its implications for domestic demand and productive investment. The terms of trade statistics, which reflect the relative movement of export prices to import prices, are similarly grim: developing countries are getting much less in return for their exported products when compared to their costs for imported items. In short, these countries must export even more of their products in order to maintain current levels of imports. The total effects for the quality of life in the highly indebted countries were summarized by the United Nations Conference on Trade and Development:

> Per capita consumption in the highly-indebted countries in 1987, as measured by national accounts statistics, was no higher than in the late 1970s; if terms of trade losses are taken into account, there was a decline. Per capita investment has also fallen drastically, by about 40 percent between 1980 and 1987. It declined steeply during 1982–83, but far from recovering subsequently, it has continued to fall.[29]

Table 17.3 / Effects of External Debt on Economic Growth and Trade

	Gross Domestic Product (Average Yearly Growth)		Terms of Trade (1987=100)	
	1965–80	1980–90	1985	1990
Algeria	**	3.1	174	99
Argentina	3.4	−0.4	110	112
Bolivia	4.4	−0.1	167	97
Brazil	9.0	2.7	92	123
Bulgaria	**	2.6	**	**
Congo	6.2	3.6	145	99
Cote d'Ivoire	6.8	0.5	110	80
Ecuador	8.8	2.0	153	109
Mexico	6.5	1.0	133	110
Morocco	5.7	4.0	88	86
Nicaragua	2.5	−2.2	111	110
Peru	3.9	−0.3	111	78
Poland	**	1.8	94	103
Syria	9.1	2.1	125	87
Venezuela	3.7	1.0	174	164
Averages	6.3	1.7	118	101

Source: The World Bank, *World Development Report, 1992* (Washington, D.C.: The World Bank, 1992), Tables 2 and 14, pp. 220–221 and 244–245.

Jeffrey Sachs portrays the situation in even starker terms:

> As for the debtor countries, many have fallen into the deepest economic crisis in their histories. Between 1981 and 1988 real per capita income declined in absolute terms in almost every country in South America. Many countries' living standards have fallen to levels of the 1950s and 1960s. Real wages in Mexico declined by about 50 percent between 1980 and 1988. A decade of development has been wiped out throughout the debtor world.[30]

Sachs is not overstating the case. Before the debt crisis, global poverty had reached staggering proportions, as described above. One can document the extent of poverty in the world by pointing out statistics on gross national product, per capita income, or the number of telephones per thousand in a particular country. But these statistics obscure too much in their sterility. In 1988, one billion people were considered chronically underfed. Millions of babies die every year from complications from diarrhea, a phenomenon that typically causes mild discomfort in the advanced industrialized countries. Millions of people have no access to clean water, cannot read or write their own names, and have no adequate shelter.

And this misery will only continue to spread. The debt crisis has a self-reinforcing dynamic. Money that could have been used to build schools or hospitals in developing countries is now going to the advanced industrialized countries. As a consequence, fewer babies will survive their first year; those that do will have fewer opportunities to reach their intellectual potential. To raise foreign exchange, developing countries are forced to sell more of their resources at reduced rates, thereby depleting nonrenewable resources for use by future generations. Capital that could have been used to build factories and provide jobs is now sent abroad; as a result, the problems of unemployment and underemployment will only get worse in poor countries.

A second effect of the decline in living standards in the heavily indebted countries concerns the increased potential for political violence. There have been over twenty violent protests in recent years specifically against the austerity measures imposed by the IMF, with over 3,000 people killed in those protests.[31] The most recent outburst occurred in Venezuela, where about 300 people were killed. Harold Lever posed the problem well in 1984:

> Will it be politically feasible, on a sustained basis, for the governments of the debtor countries to enforce the measures that would be required to achieve even the payment of interest? To say, as some do, that there is no need for the capital to be repaid is no comfort because that would mean paying interest on the debt for all eternity. Can it be seriously expected that hundreds of millions of the world's poorest populations would be content to toil away in order to transfer resources to their rich rentier creditors?[32]

Political violence will only continue in the future, but its implications are hard to predict. Political instability may make it more difficult for democratic regimes to survive, particularly in Latin America, and may lead to the establishment of authoritarian regimes. Similarly, popular pressures may lead to regimes radically hostile to market economies, thus setting the stage for dramatic confrontations between debtor countries and the external agencies that set the terms for debt rescheduling or relief. Finally, political violence can spill over into international security issues. One can only imagine what sustained political conflict in Mexico would do to the already troubling issues of drug smuggling and immigration between Mexico and the United States. Debt-related issues complicated political relations between the United States and the Philippines over the military bases, and the extraordinary impoverishment in Peru (a decline in real GNP of between 15 to 25 percent from September 1988 to September 1989) has certainly led to an increase in the drug-related activities of the Shining Path.[33]

Debtor governments will find themselves forced to demand certain concessions on debt repayment in order to maintain their legitimacy, and these concessions will invariably be cast at least in terms of lower and more extended payments, if not reduction or outright debt forgiveness. If the debt crisis is not resolved in terms that address the inevitable political consequences of declining living standards, then the prognosis for recovery is dim, even if debtor governments, banks, and the international lending agencies agree upon acceptable financial terms. The political dynamics of the debt crisis must be considered an integral part of the solution: to ignore the violence and protest as less important than the renegotiated interest rates will produce agreements that have little hope of success.

A final cost of the debt crisis has been one experienced by the developed countries themselves, in particular by the United States. Increasing poverty in the developing countries leads to a reduction of economic growth in the developed countries. The debtor countries have been forced to undergo a dramatic decline in imports in order to increase the foreign exchange earnings needed to pay back their debts. The decline in the average annual growth rate for imports of the seventeen most heavily indebted countries is dramatic: the average annual growth rate for these countries in 1965–80 was 6.3 percent; in 1980–87, that figure had fallen to minus 6 percent, for a total shift of minus 12.3 percent.[34] One estimate is that the seventeen most heavily indebted nations decreased their imports from the developed world by $72 billion from 1981 to 1986.[35]

The United States has been profoundly affected by this decline in imports because most of its exports to the developing world have, historically, gone to the Latin American states most seriously affected by the debt crisis. The United Nations Conference on Trade and Development suggests that this decline in U.S. exports is a more important explanation for U.S. trade difficulties than for the deficits of other countries:

> Because of this import compression by the highly-indebted developing countries, United States exports to them actually declined by about $10 billion between 1980 and 1986. . . . As a result, the United States recorded a negative swing in its trade balance of about $12 billion between 1980 and 1986; the corresponding

negative swings for the other developed market economy countries were much smaller: about $3 billion for Japan, $2.4 billion for the Federal Republic of Germany and $1.6 billion for the other EEC countries.[36]

These declines seriously aggravated an already bad trade situation for the United States. The absolute declines were quite large; and if one extrapolates losses from an expected increase for export growth based on recent history, the declines are quite significant. Richard Feinberg translated the export loss to the United States in terms of lost jobs when he testified before the Senate: ". . . roughly 930,000 jobs would have been created if the growth trend [of U.S. exports to the Third World] of the 1970s had continued after 1980. In sum, nearly 1.6 million U.S. jobs have been lost due to recession in the Third World."[37]

This final point deserves more sustained attention than it has yet received: it is also in the interests of the advanced industrial nations to seek an equitable solution to the debt crisis. No one's long-term interests are served by the increasing impoverishment of millions of people. The financial health and stability of the richer countries depends crucially on debt-resolution terms that allow and foster the economic growth and development of the poorer countries.

HOW REAL WAS THE THREAT OF AN INTERNATIONAL BANKING COLLAPSE?

The global cost most talked about in lending circles was that of a massive default by the debtor countries, which might have had the effect of unraveling the international financial system. The point at which the debt crisis actually made it to the front pages of newspapers in the advanced industrial countries was in 1982, when it became clear that Mexico was unable to meet its financial commitments. The size of the Mexican debt, coupled with the overexposure (lending in excess of capital assets) of the private banks that had provided loans to Mexico, raised the possibility of a widespread banking collapse, reminiscent of the bank failures in the 1930s. Table 17.4 gives some idea of the extent of overexposure in 1982.

The threat of a banking collapse was perhaps overstated at the time since these types of measures only imperfectly reflect the vulnerability of banks to a profound crisis of confidence. Nonetheless, it was clear that some of the most important banks in the United States stood to lose a great deal of money if one of the major debtor nations defaulted on its loans. Under even normal conditions, a banking collapse is always possible since banks rarely have enough capital to cover their commitments. Indeed, it is generally considered inefficient to maintain this much available capital. Banks generally have nothing to fear from their overcommitment of resources since it is almost never the case that people wish to question the financial integrity of banks. In 1982, however, it became clear that psychological confidence in

Table 17.4 / Exposure as a Percentage of Capital, Major Banks, end of 1982

	Argentina	Brazil	Mexico	Venezuela	Chile	Total
Citibank	18.2	73.5	54.6	18.2	10.0	174.5
Bank of America	10.2	47.9	52.1	41.7	6.3	158.2
Chase Manhattan	21.3	56.9	40.0	24.0	11.8	154.0
Morgan Guaranty	24.4	54.3	34.8	17.5	9.7	140.7
Manufacturers Hanover	47.5	77.7	66.7	42.4	28.4	262.8
Chemical	14.9	52.0	60.0	28.0	14.8	169.7

Source: William R. Cline, *International Debt: Systemic Risk and Policy Response* (Washington, D.C.: Institute for International Economics, 1984), p. 24.

the banking system had lost some important underpinnings, and only the rapid intervention of governmental institutions averted events that might have completely undermined public confidence. Since that time, most private banks have stopped lending money to developing countries and have increased their reserve holdings to offset any potential losses from a major loan default. At the end of 1982, the nine major U.S. banks had lent out over 287 percent of their capital to the developing countries; by the end of 1988, that percentage had dropped to 108 percent.[38]

In addition, the major private lenders have increased their reserve holdings to cover possible losses on their loan accounts. Citicorp first announced that it was enlarging its loss reserve in 1987, and the other major banks quickly followed suit.[39]

The net effect of these two actions—the sharp reduction in loan exposure and the creation of reserves against potential losses—has insulated the major banks from any threat of a banking collapse precipitated by a widespread default on loans by developing countries. Indeed, these actions have been partially responsible for the revival of the stock prices of these banks, signaling renewed investor confidence in the banks, as well as supplying new capital to offset the equity losses generated by the creation of the reserve holdings. The strengthened position of the major banks led William Seidman, chairman of the Federal Deposit Insurance Corporation, to assert in 1989 that the banks would remain solvent even if they were forced to "write-off 100 percent of their outstanding loans" to the six largest debtor countries.[40] Indeed, talk of the "debt crisis" was rarely heard in the developed world in the early 1990s, even though the total amount of debt owed by developing countries steadily increased.

The newly protected position of the banks alleviates the threat of a collapse, but leaves the developing countries with fewer sources of external assistance. Banks are not apt to enter into any new or extensive commitments to developing countries now that they do not necessarily need to protect the loans already made. If there were a serious downturn in global economic activity that would further imperil the ability of the developing countries to raise the money to pay back their debts, the only alternative for the debtors would be public assistance, either bilateral or multilateral. In short, while the gains from debt repayment will still be private, the costs will be shifted onto the public sector.

This shift now appears to be the strategy of the major banks. In response to new proposals for debt reduction, the banks, represented by an organization called the Institute for International Finance, have demanded certain conditions for accepting these proposals. In the words of Walter S. Mossberg of *The Wall Street Journal*, "the banks indicated they would be willing to make major debt reductions and new loans only if they receive new loan guarantees, tax breaks, and other financial sweeteners from the U.S., other countries, the World Bank and the International Monetary Fund."[41] The institute also asserted that "any government effort to force debt forgiveness 'would be contested in the courts' as 'an unconstitutional taking of property' unless the government pays the banks compensation."[42] The truculent tone of this position confirms that the banks no longer fear an imminent collapse of the international financial system.

SOLUTIONS

One fact is undeniable: Someone is going to have to pay for past debts. It could be the people in debtor countries, or the banks, or the people in advanced industrial countries. Most likely it will be some combination of these three groups. In the last ten years, there have been a variety of proposals which, unfortunately, usually reflect only the special interests of the groups proposing them. Generally speaking, these solutions fall into three categories: repudiation, minor adjustments in repayments, or reduction.

Debt repudiation, in the sense of a unilateral cessation of repayment, occurred in a number of countries: Bolivia, Brazil, Costa Rica, Dominican Republic, Ecuador, Honduras, Nicaragua, Panama, and Peru.[43] With the exception of the Peruvian cessation, however, most of these actions have been taken with assurances that the stoppages were only temporary. Peru announced that it was unilaterally limiting its debt repayments to a percentage of its export earnings; and since Peru took this action, other nations have indicated that they will act similarly. There have been no serious proposals for a widespread and coordinated repudiation of global debt.

The economist Jeffrey Sachs offers several reasons for this absence of a general repudiation.[44] First, debt repudiation is a dramatic and abrupt act. Most nations would prefer to defer such decisions as long as there are advantages to muddling through, and growth prospects are sufficiently ambiguous to make this muddling a viable course. Second, debtor countries fear retaliation from commercial banks. If the banks were to cut off nondebt related activities, such as trade credits, the situation could be made even worse. Third, the debtor countries fear retaliation from creditor governments and multilateral lending agencies. Grants from development banks could be affected, and trade relations would probably be seriously disrupted. Finally, the leaders of most of the debtor countries have interests in maintaining good relations with the richer countries, and repudiation would jeopardize these interests.

Repudiation would also seriously disrupt global economic relations, probably far beyond the immediate losses of the debts themselves. Retaliations would follow, because it would be politically impossible for lenders not to react, and because there would be a conscious effort to warn other potential defaulters against similar action. The escalation of economic warfare would have the effect of sharply reducing international economic interactions in trade, investment, and exchange. Such an outcome is in no one's interest.

The vast bulk of activity since 1982 has involved adjusting the timing and method of repayment. The number of specific proposals is bewildering.[45] One can read about debt-equity swaps, in which businesses or properties in the debtor country are purchased at a discount by the banks as partial repayment; debt-for-debt swaps, where bonds are offered as discounted repayments; exit bonds, which are long-term bonds tendered essentially as take-it-or-leave-it offers to creditors who have no interest in investing any further and wish to cut their losses; or cash buy-backs, where the debtor country simply buys back its loan at a deep discount.[46] Some of these proposals, notably the debt-for-nature swaps, where the debtor country promises to protect the environment in return for purchases of the debt by outside groups, are creative and could have important effects.

This array of proposals is referred to as a "menu" approach to debt repayment, and its logic is superficially sound. It was the logic of the plan offered by Secretary of the Treasury James Baker in 1985. By providing a number of different options, repayments can be tailored to the specific circumstances of a country, thereby easing the burden. Critical to the success of the menu approach is the assumption that countries will "grow out of" their debt. Yet, the evidence suggests that this assumption is not entirely sound. This approach further assumes the repayment of debts on terms that are essentially dictated by the creditors. No lender is obligated to accept any one of these possibilities. Moreover, the opportunities for swaps and buy backs are limited: there are, after all, a relatively small number of investment opportunities in poorer countries, and the debt crisis itself has further limited those possibilities. Finally, some of these swaps can actually increase the drain on the capital of a country, particularly if profit remittances on successful investments turn out to be very high.

The final proposals have to do with debt reduction, and these only became a real possibility in the spring of 1989 with the announcement of a new plan, dubbed the Brady Plan, after U.S. Secretary of the Treasury Nicholas Brady. The plan originally called for a total reduction of about 20 percent of global debt, with the IMF and the World Bank offering guarantees for the repayment of the other 80 percent of the debt.[47] Since 1989, Argentina, Brazil, Costa Rica, Mexico, Morocco, the Philippines, and Venezuela have reached agreements concerning their debts under the auspices of the Brady proposal.[48] This approach recognizes that many of the menu approaches were, in fact, schemes for debt reduction on a case-by-case basis. This formal recognition of the need for systematic debt reduction is a hopeful sign, but the plan clearly does not go far enough.[49] In market terms, developing-country debt is already selling on the secondary market at about thirty-five cents to the dollar.[50] In other words, debt reduction has already occurred in the marketplace, and any plan that incorporates reductions must take this into account.

There are some serious problems with debt reduction. Debt reduction could reduce the incentive for debtor nations to make economic changes that could lead to greater efficiency. Or, it could set a precedent that would have the effect of reducing, or even eliminating, the possibility for any future bank lending for economic development projects. Finally, debt reduction could have the effect of saddling public lending agencies, like the World Bank, with enormous burdens, thereby vitiating their future effectiveness.

These concerns are genuine. Counterposed to these possibilities, however, is the stark reality of hundreds of millions of people living in desperate conditions with no hope of relief in the near- or medium-term future. Any plan for easing the debt burden, therefore, must try to incorporate a number of legitimate, but competing, concerns of varying importance. First, the repayment of the debt itself has ceased to be the central concern. Private banks obviously have an interest in the repayment of the debt and, to the extent possible, these interests must be accommodated. But the security of the international banking system is no longer at risk, and that, as a legitimate public concern, can no longer dictate possible necessary actions. The central concerns now are the reestablishment of economic growth in the heavily indebted countries, the effective and meaningful distribution of that growth into all sectors of their societies, and their reintegration into the international economic system. Only after sustained economic growth returns to the heavily indebted countries can the international community even begin to determine manageable rates and methods of debt repayment.

Second, the International Monetary Fund must fundamentally reassess its policies. Programs of structural adjustment may be appropriate for the original purpose of the IMF—to assist nations having temporary difficulties in maintaining currency values because of transient balance-of-payments difficulties. But these programs are profoundly counterproductive in current circumstances and, indeed, are guided by a wildly inappropriate perspective. The inflows of capital to the IMF from the heavily indebted countries were more than a gross embarrassment; they were conclusive evidence of the IMF's misunderstanding of the causes of the debt crisis. The IMF should shift its perspective to more creative or appropriate ways of stabilizing or depressing interest rates rather than raising them, or ways to prevent capital flight from developing countries, or any number of issues that concern the specific conditions of economic growth. The mechanical application of a "model" of economic growth is wrongheaded.[51]

Third, the resolution of the debt crisis depends upon a clear recognition that much of the debt, as formally constituted, will not, because it cannot, be repaid. Some countries, such as those in sub-Saharan Africa, ought not to repay their debts. Other countries, particularly the heavily indebted ones, can pay something on their debts, and perhaps the appropriate percentage is about half. Viewed in this light, the real question becomes one of allocating the costs of this nonpayment of debts. The current emphasis of forcing the poor to pay with broken lives and broken spirits is demeaning to both rich and poor, and ill-serves the long-term interests of rich as well as poor.

Finally, there are genuine issues of responsibility that deserve to be made explicit. The debt "crisis" is only a symptom of an international economic system that tolerates growing and abysmal poverty as a normal condition. This need not, and should not, be the case. The developed countries have a responsibility to create conditions whereby the poorer countries can interact more productively in international economic activities: their single most important contribution to this end might be in the area of reducing trade restrictions on the products of poorer countries. Similarly, the developing countries have a responsibility to see that money is more effectively utilized within their own borders. The obscene personal profits accumulated by such leaders as Marcos of the Philippines and Mobutu of Zaire should not be fostered by the strategic interests of other countries. The banks should also face up to the fact that their single-minded pursuit of profits almost led them to the brink of bankruptcy. The lesson to be learned from this experience is that for economic growth to be sustained, close attention must be paid to the mutual interests of all parties involved.

Notes

We wish to thank Stephen Ellenburg, Anthony Lake, Tammy Sapowsky, Daniel Thomas, Sharon Worcester, and Diane C. Yelinek for all their assistance in the writing of this chapter.

1. John Maynard Keynes, *The Economic Consequences of the Peace* (London: Macmillan and Co., Ltd., 1919, reprinted in 1924), pp. 209–210.

2. There are a myriad of classifications used to describe "the most severely indebted countries." The original classification was used in the context of the initiative of U.S. Secretary of the Treasury James Baker, which identified the following nations: Argentina, Bolivia, Brazil, Chile, Colombia, Cote d'Ivoire, Ecuador, Mexico, Morocco, Nigeria, Peru, Philippines, Uruguay, Venezuela, and Yugoslavia. This classification is still used by the International Monetary Fund. The World Bank, however, added Costa Rica and Jamaica in 1989. The World Bank, in its 1992 *World Development Report,* lists the following countries as "severely indebted middle-income countries": Algeria, Argentina, Bolivia, Brazil, Bulgaria, Congo, Cote d'Ivoire, Ecuador, Mexico, Morocco, Nicaragua, Peru, Poland, Syrian Arab Republic, and Venezuela. The different lists make comparisons over time of the status of heavily indebted countries very difficult.

3. For an analysis of the economic catastrophe faced by many African nations, see Richard J. Barnet, "But What About Africa?: On the Global Economy's Lost Continent," *Harper's*, Vol. 280, no. 1680 (May 1990), pp. 43–51.

4. The World Bank, *World Development Report, 1989* (Washington: The World Bank, 1989), Table 24, p. 211.

5. International Monetary Fund, *World Economic Outlook,* October 1992 (Washington: International Monetary Fund, 1992), Tables A46 and A48, pp. 157 and 162–163.

6. "Poverty," United Nations *Chronicle,* Vol. 27, no. 3 (September 1990), p. 46.

7. Beverly Winikoff, "Women's Health in Developing Countries," in *Health Care of Women and Children in the Developing World,* edited by Helen Wallace and Kanti Giri (Oakland, CA: Third Party Publishing Co., 1990), p. 170.

8. United Nations Children's Emergency Fund, *State of the World's Children* (New York: Oxford University Press, 1992); United Nations Development Programme, *Human Development Report* (New York: Oxford University Press, 1990), p. 128.

9. UNICEF, *State of the World's Children,* op. cit., p. 57.

10. Beverly Winikoff, "Women's Health in Developing Countries," op. cit., p. 170.

11. Helen Wallace, "Health Care of Children in Developing Countries," in *Health Care of Women and Children in the Developing World,* op. cit., p. 7

12. William R. Cline, *International Debt and the Stability of the World Economy,* Policy Analyses in International Economics, No. 4 (Washington: Institute for International Economics, September 1983), p. 31.

13. Jeffrey Sachs cites Citicorp chairman Walter Wriston as justifying the heavy bank activity with the observation that "countries never go bankrupt." Jeffrey D. Sachs, "Introduction," in *Developing Country Debt and the World Economy,* edited by Jeffrey D. Sachs, a National Bureau of Economic Research Project Report (Chicago: The University of Chicago Press, 1989), p. 8. Sachs also points out Wriston's self-interest in this belief, as international operations accounted for 72 per cent of Citicorp's overall earnings in 1976.

14. United Nations Conference on Trade and Development, *Trade and Development Report, 1988,* UNCTAD/TDR/8 (New York: United Nations, 1988), pp. 92–93.

15. For an excellent analysis of the Mexican debt crisis, see Adhip Chaudhuri, "The Mexican Debt Crisis, 1982," Pew Program in Case Teaching and Writing in International Affairs, Case #204 (Pittsburgh, PA: University of Pittsburgh, 1988).

16. International Monetary Fund, *Annual Report, 1989* (Washington: International Monetary Fund, 1989), p. 17.

17. Cheryl Payer, *The Debt Trap: The International Monetary Fund and the Third World* (New York: Monthly Review Press, 1974), p. 33.

18. See, for example, Kathy McAfee, "Why the Third World Goes Hungry: Selling Cheap and Buying Dear," *Commonweal,* Vol. 117, no. 12 (15 June 1990), pp. 380–385.

19. Stephen Haggard, "The Politics of Adjustment: Lessons from the IMF's Extended Fund Facility," *International Organization,* Vol. 39, no. 3 (Summer 1985), p. 506, citing Tony Killick, et al., *The Quest for Economic Stabilization: The IMF and the Third World* (New York: St. Martin's Press, 1984), p. 261.

20. The Philippines was one such example. See Penelope Walker, "Political Crisis and Debt Negotiations: The Case of the Philippines, 1983–86," Pew Program in Case Teaching and Writing in International Affairs, Case #133 (Pittsburgh: University of Pittsburgh, 1988). See also Tyler Bridges, "How Our Loan Money Went South," *Washington Post,* 19 March 1989, p. C2. One should not make too much out of such examples without also remembering that political corruption, such as the savings and loan scandals in the United States, afflicts the rich as well as the poor.

21. Jeffrey Sachs, "Introduction," op. cit., p. 29.

22. See Peter H. Lindert and Peter J. Morton, "How Sovereign Debt Has Worked," in *Developing Country Debt and the World Economy,* edited by Jeffrey D. Sachs, a National Bureau of Economic Research Project Report (Chicago: University of Chicago Press, 1989), pp. 225–237; Albert Fishlow, "Lessons from the Past: Capital Markets During the 19th Century and the Interwar Period," *International Organization,* Vol. 39, no. 3 (Summer 1985), pp. 383–440; and Tim Congdon, *The Debt Trap: The Dangers of High Interest Real Interest Rates for the World Economy* (Oxford: Basil Blackwell, 1988), pp. 109–110.

23. The following discussion relies heavily on the explanations offered by Jan Joost Teunissen, "The International Monetary Crunch: Crisis or Scandal?" *Alternatives,* Vol. 11, no. 3 (July 1987), pp. 359–396; and Gerald Epstein, "The Triple Debt Crisis," *World Policy Journal,* Vol. 2, no. 4 (Fall 1985), pp. 625–658.

24. "Real interest rates charged to less developed countries (LDCs) jumped from 1% in 1980 to between 6.73 and 8.50% in 1981–84 . . ." James R. Barth, Michael D. Bradley, and Paul C. Panayotacos, "Understanding International Debt Crisis," *Case Western Reserve Journal of International Law,* Vol. 19, no. 1 (Winter 1987), pp. 31–52, footnote 4, as quoted in *Current Readings on Money, Banking, and Financial Markets,* 1990 Edition, edited by James A. Wilcox and Frederic S. Mishkin (Glenview, IL: Scott, Foresman/Little, Brown Higher Education, 1990), p. 306.

25. Enzo R. Grilli and Maw Cheng Yang, "Primary Commodity Prices, Manufactured Goods Prices, and the Terms of Trade of Developing Countries: What the Long Run Shows," *The World Bank Economic Review,* Vol. 2, no. 1 (1988), p. 34.

26. World Bank, *World Development Report, 1989,* op. cit., p. 17.

27. *New York Times,* 18 September 1989, p. D1.

28. *New York Times,* 11 February 1988, p. D1.

29. United Nations Conference on Trade and Development, *Trade and Development Report, 1988,* UNCTAD/TDR/8 (New York: United Nations, 1988), p. 101.

30. Jeffrey Sachs, "Making the Brady Plan Work," *Foreign Affairs,* Vol. 68, no. 3 (Summer 1989), p. 91.

31. Susan George, "The Debt Crisis: Global Economic Disorder in the 1990s," Speech given at Smith College, Northampton, MA, 10 April 1989.

32. Harold Lever, "The Debt Won't Be Paid," *New York Review of Books,* Vol. 31, no. 11 (28 June 1984), p. 3. Emphasis in the original.

33. The statistic on the decline in the Peruvian GNP comes from Jeffrey D. Sachs, "A Strategy for Efficient Debt Reduction," *Journal of Economic Perspectives,* Vol. 4, no. 1 (Winter 1990), p. 20.

34. World Bank, *World Development Report, 1989,* op. cit., Table 14, p. 191.

35. James D. Robinson 3d, "It's Time to Plan a Third World Revival," *New York Times,* 28 August 1988, p. F3.

36. UNCTAD, *Trade and Development Report,* op. cit., p. 66.

37. Statement by Richard E. Feinberg, vice president, Overseas Development Council, before the Subcommittee on International Debt of the Committee on Finance, United States Senate, Washington, D.C., 9 March 1987, mimeo, pp. 6–7.

38. Jeffrey Sachs, "Making the Brady Plan Work," op. cit., p. 89.

39. Sarah Bartlett, "The Third World Debt Crisis Reshapes American Banks," *New York Times,* 24 September 1989.

40. As quoted in Jeffrey Sachs, "A Strategy for Efficient Debt Reduction," op. cit., p. 21. For statistics on how the values of bank stocks increased dramatically at this time, see Mark Fadiman, "Bad News is Good News for Big Bank Stocks," *Investor's Daily,* 27 September 1989.

41. Walter S. Mossberg, "Major Banks Vow to Fight Any Effort to Force Third World Debt Forgiveness," *The Wall Street Journal,* 12 January 1989, p. A16.

42. Idem.

43. Jeffrey Sachs, "Introduction," op. cit., p. 26.

44. His arguments are summarized from his "Introduction," op. cit., pp. 26–27.

45. For a comprehensive analysis of many of the proposals, see *Analytical Issues in Debt,* edited by Jacob A. Frenkel, Michael P. Dooley, and Peter Wickham (Washington: International Monetary Fund, 1989).

46. Peter T. Kilbourn, "Debt Reduction: Ways to Do It," *New York Times,* 6 April 1989, p. D1; see also International Monetary Fund, *Annual Report, 1989* (Washington: International Monetary Fund, 1989), pp. 26–27.

47. Peter T. Kilbourn, "Greenspan Backs Shift on Debt," *New York Times,* 17 March 1989, p. D1.

48. Jonathan Fuerbringer, "Brazil and Banks Reach Agreement on Reducing Debt," *New York Times,* 10 July 1992, p. A1.

49. There have been debt reductions brought about in Mexico, Brazil, and Argentina (among other countries) under the terms of the Brady Plan. Nonetheless, while the economic outlook in 1992 seemed hopeful, there is still doubt about the actual effects of the Brady Plan. See Jorge C. Castaneda, "Mexico's Dismal Debt Deal," *New York Times,* 25 February 1990, p. F13; Nathaniel C. Nash, "Latin Debt Load Keeps Climbing Despite Accords," *New York*

Times, 1 August 1992, p. A1; and Thomas Kamm, "Brazilian Accord Puts End to Debt Crisis in Region, but Not to Economic Troubles," *Wall Street Journal,* 10 July 1992.

50. Jeffrey Sachs, "Making the Brady Plan Work," *Foreign Affairs,* Vol. 68, no. 3 (Summer 1989), p. 90. The range of discounts is quite wide. In July 1989, Peru's debts were discounted by 97 percent; Chile's by a little more than 35 percent. See Peter B. Kenen, "Organizing Debt Relief: The Need for a New Institution," *Journal of Economic Perspectives,* Vol. 4, no. 1 (Winter 1990), p. 9.

51. The International Monetary Fund denies that it applies a uniform "model" of structural adjustment, and, in a strict sense, this is certainly true: there is a great degree of variation in the plans agreed upon by the IMF and different countries. But, in a larger sense, the plans all stress similar *objectives,* which by and large conform to a general pattern of demand reduction and reduced government spending. See *IMF Conditionality, 1980–91,* a white paper researched and prepared by the staff of the IMF Assessment Project (Arlington, VA: Alexis de Tocqueville Institution, 1992); Karim Nashashibi, et al., *The Fiscal Dimensions of Adjustment in Low-Income Countries,* Occasional Paper No. 95 (Washington: International Monetary Fund, April 1992); and Francois Bourguignon and Christian Morrisson, *Adjustment and Equity in Developing Countries: A New Approach* (Paris: Organisation for Economic Co-Operation and Development, 1992).

18 / World Hunger: A Scarcity of Food or a Scarcity of Democracy?

JOSEPH COLLINS

In 1974, Henry Kissinger, then U.S. secretary of state, proclaimed in an address to the United Nations World Food Conference that "in ten years not one child shall go to bed hungry." Nevertheless, in 1984, more children went hungry than a decade before, with malnutrition being invariably the crucial factor in the deaths that year of more than fifteen million children under five years of age.[1] And, throughout the 1980s, the number of hungry people increased five times faster than in the previous decade.[2] Although statistics about hunger are admittedly imprecise, since the data are scarce and at times suppressed by embarrassed governments, they consistently point to an increase in the numbers of the hungry. According to a World Bank calculation, by 1988 at least one billion human beings were chronically underfed.[3] The United Nations Food and Agriculture Organization (FAO) placed the number of hungry people in the Third World in 1988–90 at about 786 million.[4] World Bank estimates are considerably larger, in part because it characterizes as hungry all those who lack sufficient energy (calories) to sustain an active working life, and not just those lacking a diet adequate to prevent stunted growth and serious health risks.

Quantifying the numbers of hungry people is very difficult.[5] Nevertheless, even the most circumspect estimates of those who suffer from undernutrition to a greater or lesser degree, and from associated diseases, are truly alarming. They also underscore the pervasive apathy with which the world community has dealt with the scandal of pervasive human hunger at the end of the twentieth century. In the words of one respected scholar of world hunger, "The exact number of people suffering from hunger is unimportant, it is enough to know that the number is huge."[6]

THE PRODUCTION "SOLUTION"

Since at least as far back as the late 1940s, the conventional wisdom in government and scholarly circles (amplified by the mass media) has been that increased food production, particularly through new technologies, constitutes the appropriate response to chronic world hunger. Hence, the "war against hunger" has been repeatedly defined as a war to boost food production in a race against population growth. This "war" has been waged with considerable financial and political backing by the United States and other governments, by foundations such as Rockefeller and Ford, and by international financial institutions led by the World Bank.[7]

Approaches to greater food production that center on the introduction of varieties of seeds that yield more in response to increased inputs—especially synthetic fertilizers and regulated watering through irrigation—have been widely celebrated as successful. In journalistic jargon, such technologies have been hailed as the "green revolution."[8] By the late 1970s, the results of this narrow technical focus, at least in the short-term, were clear: significantly more food per person was being produced. The world's output in grains alone was two pounds a day—more than 3,000 calories and ample protein—for every man, woman, and child on earth.[9] And that calorie estimate, enough for even working adults, does not include the many other nutritious foods that people eat: beans, nuts, fruits, vegetables, root crops, seafoods, and grass-fed meats.

On a global basis, it has become an indisputable fact of our time that hunger can no longer be blamed on a shortage of food.[10] Nevertheless, the fact is that in the early 1980s the number of hungry people was growing precisely at a time when global food stocks were building up to record levels.[11] The additional food required by the world's hungry to close their dietary gap is small. Based on 1987 calculations by the FAO,[12] as well as estimates by the International Food Policy Research Institute, only fifteen to twenty million tons of cereal grains annually (out of a total production at that time of some 1,660 million tons) would be sufficient to raise the diets of the world's undernourished people[13] to adequate levels.[14]

Production of food grains has increased significantly, not only in the industrial countries but also in many nations in the Third World. By the mid-1980s, "green revolution" seeds were being sown on roughly half of the total rice and wheat acreage in the Third World.[15] The production of these key grains, together with other food staples in the Third World during the 1960s and 1970s, followed, for a variety of reasons, a clearly upward trend, with an average annual growth rate of 2.6 percent.[16] Over this period, the growth of food production was slightly faster than the unprecedented rise in population.[17]

Even in countries where chronic hunger is widespread, by the 1970s there was enough food available to wipe out hunger. One hypothetical question highlights how misleading it is to think that absolute food shortages, even in Third World countries, are the root cause of hunger: how much of the food now available within Third World countries would it take to make up for the food now lacking in the diets of each nation's chronically hungry people? According to the World Bank, the answer for country after country with widespread hunger is a very small percentage.[18] In India, home to over one-third of the world's hungry people,[19] a mere 5.6 percent of the country's food supply, if eaten by the hungry, would make an active life possible for everyone.[20] For Indonesia, with the second greatest number of undernourished people in the world, [21] only 2 percent of the country's food supply would make the difference.[22] For the Philippines, where 70 percent of the children are thought to be undernourished, only 1.9 percent of the total food supply would make up the entire deficit in the diets of all the hungry.[23] In Brazil, the world's second-largest food exporter (after the United States), a redistribution of only 1.6 percent of the total food supply would meet all the needs of the eighty-six million Brazilians estimated in 1984 to be undernourished.[24] Nowhere does an absolute shortage of food explain chronic hunger.

AFRICA'S "FOOD CRISIS" AND THE REALITIES OF HUNGER

The 1980s witnessed a worldwide explosion of awareness of the hunger and starvation in Africa. A flood of commentaries, in official, scholarly, and media circles, argued that the drought of the mid-1980s had exacerbated a preexisting general decline in African food production. It was repeatedly stated that in sub-Saharan Africa—in contrast to virtually everywhere else— food production per person was lagging behind population growth. Typically, the 1983 FAO *World Food Report* stated that "Africa south of the Sahara is losing the race to keep food production ahead of population growth."[25] Moreover, the fact that tropical Africa, starting in the 1970s, became a significant net importer of basic foods, notably cereal grains, was "readily understood" by many prominent analysts of world hunger as flowing from lagging local food production.[26]

In fact, evidence for stagnation in per capita food production in much of Africa is both very thin and subject to significant bias.[27] The reasons for this conclusion are instructive.

Given the self-assurance of the claims about African food production, one might assume that the data upon which these conclusions were based were reasonably well-founded and accurate. But as analyst Philip Raikes has convincingly argued, "Nothing could be further from the truth."[28] There are few countries in sub-Saharan Africa where the level of food production is known within any reasonable parameters.[29] For instance, in Tanzania— by no means the African country with the least effective agricultural ministry—government production estimates for important food crops vary by a factor of up to three for the same year.[30] FAO production estimates for staple food production in Tanzania also vary considerably. The 1982 FAO *Production Yearbook* shows Tanzanian corn production in 1982 to have been 0.8 million tons. Yet, the 1984 edition of the *Yearbook* puts the figure for Tanzanian corn production in 1982 at 1.55 million tons. In 1985, the FAO expert most qualified to estimate corn production in Tanzania was of the opinion that total corn production was well over 2 million tons and had been for some years.[31]

Such messy data for Tanzania are hardly exceptional. Raikes compared estimates of corn production for 1982 in the 1982 and 1984 FAO *Production Yearbooks* for the twenty largest sub-Saharan countries and found that only five remain unaltered. Eight are revised between 1 and 10 percent, another five between 11 and 50 percent, and two by over 50 percent. As Raikes notes, "While this gives some idea of the degree of uncertainty, there is no reason to suppose that because figures have not been revised, they must necessarily be accurate."[32]

Part of the problem of obtaining reliable agricultural statistics, especially in Africa, is that most staple food production comes from a large number of marginal, small peasant farms—the vast majority of which are covered by no system of registration or crop reporting. It is nearly impossible to produce even reasonably accurate estimates of the area cultivated, much less of actual harvests. Many peasant farm families consume part, even much, of the food they produce, making it even more unlikely that such unmarketed production will be officially counted. Where marketing is not government-controlled, the many small- to medium-size traders in food crops are likely to underreport their sales in an effort to minimize taxation; where the government theoretically monopolizes marketing, much (and perhaps most) of the crop will be illegally marketed in private and, thus, is even more likely to go unreported. Officials, whose greatest interest might well be in knowing what food the government has at its disposal, often tend to estimate food production from that portion of it that is marketed through government channels, or to allow this figure to shape their estimations.

For all these reasons, when considering whether food shortages are at the root of the chronic hunger in Africa, it is essential to remember that there is a high probability of a significant downward bias in official reporting on local food production.[23]

Government policymakers—in Africa and elsewhere in the Third World—as well as international agency officials, strongly prefer that chronic hunger be diagnosed in terms of inadequate and declining food production. Raikes argues that such a diagnosis "points to conclusions which most policymakers would like to draw in the first place: that more food needs to be imported and that rapid technical change is needed to increase aggregate production." Moreover, "there is some reason to suspect dramatization and exaggeration of 'food gaps' by governments anxious to increase or maintain levels of food aid."[34]

None of this is to underplay the difficulties that confront food producers in Africa. The point is that, even in sub-Saharan Africa, where official statistics might at first suggest otherwise, chronic hunger cannot be blamed on an absolute scarcity of food.[35] (Here we have to distinguish persistent, *chronic* famine from temporary famines and bouts of starvation occurring relatively suddenly due to climatic anomalies or armed conflict. In the 1980s and early 1990s, a number of major famines resulted from acute food shortages due to such conflicts, especially where food blockades and "scorched earth" policies were used as weapons of war.[36]) Ground-breaking historical research carried out in the 1970s and 1980s revealed that there have on occasion been major famines in which millions of people died, while local food output and availability remained high and undiminished.[37] Indeed, some famines, such as the Bangladesh famine of 1974, have occurred in periods of peak food availability.[38] Famines have been caused not by scarcity of food but by large numbers of people being unable to acquire it.

THE ROOTS OF HUNGER

What can be learned from the pursuit, in numerous countries around the world, of the single-minded "production solution" to hunger? Most fundamentally, more and more people can—and do—go hungry *no matter how high the aggregate levels of food production*, not only on a global basis but in the very countries in which they live.

Large numbers of people go hungry most of the time, or on a seasonal basis, without any local shortage of food. This is because people eat only when they have access to the resources to produce (and keep) enough food to feed themselves, or enjoy a livelihood that gives them enough money to purchase the food they need; failing both, they go hungry unless they have the political power to lay claim to subsidized or free food. The chronically hungry are those who are deprived of enough land and other food-producing resources, those who cannot find regular employment at adequate wages, those who cannot keep enough of what they produce due to excessive rents or taxes, and those who get paid too little for their produce or handicrafts.

It is not that production is unimportant—a patently absurd position. Clearly, food production will eventually have to increase if populations continue to grow. However, what is most crucial for the survival prospects of the hungry is how democratic or how tightly concentrated is the distribution of economic power, especially in terms of access to food-producing and/or income-generating resources. Hunger is a problem not of supply but of *distribution*—specifically, the inequitable distribution of economic power.

Inequalities in economic power operate on every level—from the household, to the village, to the nation, and to the realm of international commerce and finance. Inequitable control is often most strikingly manifest at the village level in people's access to agricultural land; few aspects of economic life more directly affect the food well-being of so many hundreds of millions of human beings. A 1975 study by the World Bank cited a survey of eighty-three Third World countries in which it was found that, typically, only 3 percent of all landowners control a staggering 79 percent of all farmland, preventing most rural families from owning any land at all.[39] Land-deprived families working in agriculture often cannot grow enough food for themselves (or retain enough of it after paying steep rents to landlords), or earn enough money to purchase their food necessities. The fact that, in many countries, the portion of families who are land-deprived has grown faster than population growth since the early 1960s goes a long way toward explaining widening worldwide poverty and, thus, growing hunger.

When a new production technology—such as hybrid seeds that yield more in response to irrigation, fertilizers, and pesticides (the so-called green revolution)—is introduced into a social system riddled with inequalities, it can be assumed that the beneficiaries will be those who already possess some combination of land, money, creditworthiness, and political influence.[40] By the mid-1970s, abundant documentation from around the world[41] confirmed that development strategies that avoid the social-political issues of who controls land and other productive assets, and that attempt instead simply to get more food produced, set into motion processes that actually worsen the plight of the poor majority. Enhancing the productive capacity of the land (invariably, irrigated largely at public expense) attracts a new class of "farmers"—moneylenders, merchants, bureaucrats, military officers, speculators, and multinational agribusiness companies—who rush in and take control of the land. Land values usually soar—in India, for instance, they rose three- to five-fold in only a few years in the green revolution areas. As land values rise, so do rents, thus driving tenant farmers into the ranks of the landless. Seeing new profit possibilities, landlords evict tenants and cultivate the land themselves with new machinery and seasonal farm workers.[42]

In northwest Mexico, the birthplace of green revolution technologies, the average farm size jumped over a twenty-year period from 200 to 2,000 acres, with over three-quarters of those working in agriculture deprived of owning, or even renting, any land at all.[43] In India, the portion of the rural work force that is landless doubled in the two decades following the introduction of high-response seeds.[44] And while more rural people become landless through the expansion of larger operators, they must compete—due to mechanization—for fewer jobs and, therefore, are likely to earn lower real wages. Thus, in the very areas of northwest Mexico where agricultural production has boomed, the average number of days of employment for a farm worker has shrunk from 190 to 100.[45]

Narrow production strategies have produced more food in many countries, but hunger has only widened and deepened. A series of major studies conducted in the mid-1970s for the International Labor Organization found that in seven South Asian countries—Pakistan, Bangladesh, India, Sri Lanka, Malaysia, the Philippines, and Indonesia—where the focus has simply been on getting more food produced (and where food output per person has in fact risen), the rural poor were worse off than before. The study concludes that "the increase in poverty has been associated not with a fall but with a rise in cereal production per head, the main component of the diet of the poor."[46] In-depth investigations by the United Nations Research Institute for Social Development (UNRISD) of the impact of green revolution technologies in twenty-four different Third World countries have confirmed this consistent pattern—a decline in well-being, including nutritional status, for much of the rural majority, even as agricultural production increases.[47]

Increasing food production while ignoring the critical issue of *who is in control* of that production is not even a neutral strategy. It does not even "buy time"—that is, feed more people until the difficult questions of control can be addressed. In fact, it tends to marginalize larger numbers of people from control over productive resources and, therefore, from consumption, while further enriching the minority and making them more able than ever to resist the democratization of economic power.

In the 1990s, it is widely assumed, we will witness a second "revolution" in agricultural production—this one based on developments in biotechnology, through which the molecular constitutions of living organisms are manipulated for some sought-after end. It is claimed that bioengineered crops will produce higher yields per acre and, therefore, alleviate the hunger problem. However, even leaving aside the other concerns about biotechnology (and they are many and varied[48]), it cannot responsibly be argued that increased food production will end hunger so long as problems of control are left unattended.

The tightening of control over productive resources generates a concentration in income, and, as a consequence, a limited internal market for what is produced from those resources. Even the vital needs of millions of neighboring human beings will not count: through no fault of their own, they cannot translate their needs into money, the only language an increasingly globalized market understands. Those who monopolize productive resources—far from advocating redistributive reforms—see their future in terms of catering to the upscale tastes of already well-fed high-income consumers at home and in the industrial countries.

Particularly indicative of this tendency of large producers to bypass the vital needs of hundreds of millions of hungry people has been the continuing orientation of agricultural production to animal feeds so as to meet the burgeoning demand for more grain-fed meat, poultry, eggs, and milk in the diets of the world's better-off people.[49] Indeed, despite widespread hunger and increased numbers of undernourished people, the 1970s witnessed, in most of the Third World, an explosion in the demand for livestock feed; on average, the demand for feed in the Third World grew 75 percent faster than the demand for food.[50] During this period, the fastest growth in the use of food for animal feed was in Central America, a region known for widespread malnutrition; feed production more than doubled during the decade.[51] Rapid growth of feed use occurred also in Western Asia, Northern Africa, and East and Southeast Asia.[52] Worldwide, by the 1980s, more than 40 percent of all grain went to livestock, up from 33 percent a decade earlier.[53]

In Mexico, where two-thirds of the people are economically marginalized and, therefore, chronically undernourished,[54] the impact of market pressures is especially visible. The area planted in the foods most consumed by the poor majority—corn and beans—did not expand in the 1960s and 1970s, despite the enormous growth in population.[55] Over the same period, the percentage of Mexico's grain production fed to livestock increased as much as *eight times*, to virtually half the total output. Not only does a very small fraction of the nutrients fed to livestock return to humans, but at least twenty-five million Mexicans are too poor to eat beef, and even poultry and dairy foods are largely beyond their reach.[56]

THE 1980s

The 1980s witnessed a further decline in the power of the poor majority of many countries, especially in Latin America and Africa, to obtain adequate food. In addition, measures taken by governments to pay off enormous debts to foreign creditors became a major new factor in the hunger equation.

In the 1970s, Third World governments found it easy to borrow hundreds of billions of dollars. The borrowing was totally undemocratic: the vast majority had no say in the process, nor did the loans support broad-based development. Much of the borrowed money was squandered on "showcase" projects—conference centers, high-tech hospitals, and administrative buildings—with little hope of generating enough foreign exchange to pay off the loans and interest.[57] Some of the borrowed money went to import consumer goods, invariably for the better-off. The Stockholm International Peace Research Institute (SIPRI) has estimated that 20 percent of Third World debt (OPEC nations excluded) can be attributed directly to arms purchases.[58] And, of course, healthy chunks simply disappeared due to graft and corruption.

The money lent by banks that were encumbered with huge deposits (especially those made by the newly rich oil-exporting countries) seemed reasonably cheap; during much of the 1970s, interest rates were actually below the rate of inflation.[59] But the interest rates were, in most cases, adjustable, meaning that the cost of using the borrowed money could change over time. And it did. In the Reagan era, as the United States stepped up military spending and lowered rates of taxation on the wealthy, heavy borrowing by the deficit-strapped U.S. government fueled higher interest rates worldwide. The billions of dollars in increased interest payments for Third World borrowers came on top of a sharp run-up in the prices of imported oil, making it necessary for many Third World countries to borrow additional billions of dollars on top of their already snowballing loans.

By 1982, many governments could no longer afford to service their debts. Unable to obtain even short-term credits for imports, they turned to the lender of last resort, the International Monetary Fund (IMF). But the IMF lends money only when the borrowing government agrees to reorganize its economy according to IMF guidelines so that the banks can be repaid. This reorganization is formally called "structural adjustment."

Instead of penalizing the wealthy and the military, the burden of structural adjustment has fallen squarely on the poor and the middle class. The IMF prescription to Third World governments to spend less ("demand management") means drastically cutting consumption; for the poor, who already live on the edge, consumption cuts mean increased malnutrition, illness, and higher mortality rates. Government subsidies for transportation, water, electricity, and cooking fuel are dramatically curtailed and in some cases totally eliminated; government spending on health and other social services is slashed. In countries that tried to keep basic food affordable for the poor, consumer subsidies for basic staples have been removed. Sweeping devaluation of the local currency makes vital imports far more expensive. Imported basic foods, medicines, spare parts, and essential farm inputs become impossible luxuries, out of reach of the majority of urban poor and small farmers. Bank credit is tightened and made so expensive that local businesses fail, thereby driving up unemployment. (See Chapter 17.)

Structural adjustment also mandates governments to step up dollar earnings through the further orientation of their economies for export production. For most countries, this means devoting more topsoil, water, and labor to the production of raw or semiprocessed agricultural goods. With the IMF *simultaneously* directing dozens of countries to step up such exports, world markets are flooded and so prices plummet. By the late 1980s, commodity prices sank to their lowest levels in years, while the price of many of the manufactured goods and chemicals imported from industrial countries to produce those agricultural goods increased. Low prices on world markets drive countries to export even more, just to try to keep revenues from falling. This vicious, debt-induced cycle creates pressures for increased export-crop production at the expense of crops for local consumption and at the expense of the environment.

Governmental pressures on peasant households to grow cash crops for export diverts labor—especially women's labor—away from food production for the family. Moreover, women seldom have a say over the disposal of money from cash-crop sales. Especially in African societies, this is the man's domain, and men tend to spend the money on things other than food. When women are obliged to labor long hours on cash crops, child care and cooking suffer as well.[60] Poor women and children—invariably the least powerful members of society—are the most harmed.

Between 1982 and 1990, IMF-dictated measures resulted in Third World countries transferring to the banks of the developed world a total of $418 billion more in interest and principal payments than they received in new loans, grants, trade credits, and direct private investment.[61] The result, predictably, was a significant widening of world hunger.

In Latin America, structural adjustment greatly worsened the already widespread unemployment. The International Labor Organization (ILO) reported that official unemployment in Latin America rose by 40 percent between 1980 and 1984.[62] Huge numbers of people desperately seeking work drive down wages for everyone. Hence, the purchasing power of those farm workers in Latin America who *did* find work fell sharply throughout the 1980s, to levels significantly below those of two decades earlier. A survey carried out in greater Mexico City in 1984 estimated that 40 percent of the population was undernourished, and that those with nutritional deficiencies ate mostly corn tortillas, bread, beans, and rehydrated milk, all of which were, at the time, subsidized. In 1986, these subsidies were eliminated as part of the IMF-required cutbacks.[63] While official statistics have not been made available, no one doubts that, in the 1980s, an even greater percentage of Mexicans fell into undernutrition as the country stepped up its export of food and other agricultural products to higher-bidding foreigners in an effort to pay off the interest on Mexico's huge foreign debt.

In Peru, the buying power of those workers who could find work fell precipitously in the early 1980s as debt-repayment austerity measures were applied. A Peruvian worker earning the minimum wage in 1980 had to work seventeen minutes in order to buy a kilo of rice; just four years later, it took two hours and five minutes of work. A can of powdered milk cost seventeen minutes of labor in 1980, but eighty-three minutes in 1984.[64] It is hardly surprising then that a former governor of Peru's Central Bank declared in 1979 that the IMF adjustment policies mean "the death of some 500,000 children."[65]

The military dictatorship in Brazil contracted the Third World's largest debt, over $100 billion by 1982—with a great part of the loans going for military ends. In the 1980s, Brazil paid dearly for the junta's excess, falling behind in meeting even the gargantuan interest payments. As previously noted, Brazil has become the world's second-largest exporter of food—yet, in 1985, the government estimated that two out of three Brazilians were underfed, double the percentage arrived at by a respected household survey carried out in 1961.[66]

In mineral-rich Zaire, where the public debt and the private fortune held outside the country by dictator Mobutu are both estimated to be $6 billion, hunger has been on the rise since 1983. By the mid-1980s, reportedly half of the children in some areas were dying before reaching the age of five. One survey found that in the two largest cities, the average daily calorie consumption had fallen to starvation levels.[67] Throughout sub-Saharan Africa, policies mandated for debt-burdened countries caused economies to contract, shrinking the employment and purchasing power of millions of Africans.

THE 1990s

The 1990s opened without any sign of a letup in the pressures driving ever-larger numbers of people into the ranks of the persistently hungry. The food riots triggered by debt-driven austerity programs in numerous countries in the 1980s threaten to become more frequent, as the victims of these programs grow ever more numerous. Long before the decade's end, these victims may well decide that they will not quietly watch themselves and their children starve.

Many Third World countries, especially in sub-Saharan Africa, became significantly more dependent in the 1980s on imported food. To a great extent, this was a result of governments being told that they could export their way out of the debt crisis while, at the same time, opening their doors to the importation of "cheap" grains.[68] Zimbabwe is only one case in point. In 1991, the World Bank strongly pressured the government of Zimbabwe to export a major part of its million-ton grain surplus. At the same time, the United States and the World Bank conditioned aid to Zimbabwe on cuts in prices offered to local farmers for corn in order to discourage surplus production in the future. And it worked: in the 1991–92 season, farmers switched to export crops and, as a consequence, planted only 60 percent of the area previously allocated to corn. The timing could not have been worse: the most severe drought in years struck Zimbabwe—which, stripped of reserves, had to import grain from the United States, Canada, Australia, and Argentina at roughly three times the prices received from its sale of surplus grain the year before.[69]

Another factor in this increased dependence on imports is chronic food "aid," which has, in many cases, undermined local food producers, and—as intended by many donors—helped to create demand in recipient countries for products that they cannot reasonably grow themselves (for example, wheat in tropical countries). In Mozambique, which desperately needs to promote economic development and food security after years of internal warfare, U.S. strategy is to create a market for American corn. Thus, the United States has conditioned food aid and economic assistance on moves by the government to increase the price of locally produced corn (the principal staple food) so that it is as costly as corn imported from the United States.[70]

Any further softening of world markets for exports from Third World countries—the result of competition among the numerous producers of the same commodities, as well as from a protracted worldwide recession—would widen and deepen world hunger. Major U.S. commitments to sell grain to Russia, and other bilateral agreements of this sort, will significantly diminish the supplies from which smaller and poorer countries must purchase needed food. Under these conditions, any future climatic or commercial shock, such as a sharp rise in prices for petroleum (which would directly affect fertilizer and fuel costs), could send prices on these "residual" markets skyward (in no small measure thanks, also, to commodity speculators), thereby creating even greater hardship for needy purchasers.[71]

The forceful promotion of trade liberalization by the industrialized nations of the Organization for Economic Cooperation and Development (OECD), even to the point of undermining the local production of food staples, serves not only the commercial but also the political interests of the dominant nations. As noted by John Block, secretary of agriculture during the Reagan administration, "Food is a weapon, but the way to use it is to tie countries to us. That way they'll be far more reluctant to upset us."[72] For many nations, the price will be sustained, even increased, hunger.

The reintroduction of dogmatic "free-market" policies into societies that had previously taken food-producing resources and employment/job security out of the marketplace began in the 1980s and continued in the early 1990s. The market, by definition, responds to economic power and not to need. The more widely purchasing power is dispersed within a society, the more the market will, in fact, respond to human needs and preferences. But the market, left to its own devices, will concentrate wealth and purchasing power, and every gain in power over resources sets the stage for further gains. Concentrating land into ever fewer hands, ignoring the vital needs of those who cannot pay, increasing exports in the face of growing hunger—all are normal marketplace behavior. Unless ground rules are established and enforced to counteract the tendency toward excessive concentration, countries that have reintroduced free-market policies are likely to experience the negative consequences, including chronic hunger. China, without different ground rules, is likely to become more like India—a country of widespread chronic hunger in spite of considerable food production.

Some of the ground rules that are needed if a market society is to eliminate hunger are land tenure policies to keep ownership from becoming concentrated, plus tax and credit policies geared to the needs of smaller farmers. Also needed are tax, credit, and social welfare policies that actively disperse buying power.[73] The dogmatic imposition of free-market policies without reform of such ground rules will widen the grip of poverty and hunger in the 1990s, not only in the Third World but also in the United States and the other OECD nations.

POPULATION AND POWERLESSNESS

A population "explosion" is frequently advanced as the fundamental cause of hunger. This Malthusian paradigm dominates the popular understanding of the hunger problem in the United States. The world's population has indeed "exploded," more than doubling since 1950 (with 85 percent of that growth occurring in the Third World). Some analysts have argued that rapid population growth is not a problem, claiming that the historical record shows that it should stimulate higher technological development and, thereby, in the long-term, promote economic development and higher standards of living.[74] But population growth *is* a major problem. If populations continue to grow at rates similar to those of the recent past, and if the resource depletion inherent in elite-driven agricultural production systems and prevailing consumer life-styles in the "developed" world persist, the world's environment will be utterly devastated. Just as obviously, increased population in the Third World, without democratization of control over productive resources and techniques, will spell greater poverty, and, therefore, greater worldwide hunger.

Nevertheless, to suggest that there is little use in doing anything to confront the problem of hunger until population growth is curbed is tragically wrongheaded. In a world of huge unmarketable surpluses of food, *sheer numbers of people* are not the real cause of hunger and chronic malnutrition. Diminishing population growth would have no effect on the proportion of hungry people, because the number of people is not the primary cause of food poverty. As we have seen, the primary cause of hunger is not a scarcity of food but rather the inequitable control of economic resources, depriving some people of the means to produce or purchase food.

Rapid population growth is rooted in economic insecurity generated and perpetuated by antidemocratic power structures.[75] Indeed, rapid population growth can perhaps best be understood as a consequence of efforts by the poor to survive in the face of the concentrated economic power of the elite. Thus, for rural families deprived of land assets, children from a remarkably early age can enhance the survival income of the family by laboring on other people's land, and through other economic activities. Hunger and rapid population growth often occur together, *not* because one is caused by the other but because both have a common cause.

Studies of the societies that have lowered their fertility rates[76] indicate that this is largely the product of democratizing shifts in power relations in key and interrelated aspects of family, community, and national life—shifts that have made lowered fertility rates both *desirable* to many families as well as *possible* for them. In this context, the most significant democratizing shifts are those that have led to the enhanced power of the poor—and especially of poor women—through the provision of resources for literacy, education, employment, health, and old-age security. Also critical are programs that have enhanced the power of peasants to provide food and income for themselves through broadened access to land, credit, markets, and other economic resources.

The right to eat is not the same as the right to charity, whether private or public. Fundamentally, the right to eat is the right to share in control over a society's economic resources, and, therefore, to be able to produce or purchase at least enough food for one's needs. Wherever political rights for all citizens truly flourish, people will see it to it that, in due course, they share in control over economic resources vital to their survival. Lasting food security thus requires real and sustained democracy.

Notes

1. Estimate by UNICEF. See *The State of the World's Children, 1989* (New York: Oxford University Press, 1989), p. 87.

2. Estimate by World Food Council, *President's Report to the Fifteenth Ministerial Session* (Rome: World Food Council, 1989), p. 3.

3. Based on extrapolations from World Bank studies. See *Poverty and Hunger: Issues and Options for Food Security in Developing Countries* (Washington: World Bank, 1986); and Shlomo Reutlinger and Marcelo Selowsky, *Malnutrition and Poverty: Magnitude and Policy*

Options, World Bank Staff Occasional Paper No. 23 (Baltimore: Johns Hopkins University Press, 1976).

4. UN Food and Agriculture Organization (FAO) and World Health Organization, *Nutrition and Development: A Global Assessment, 1992* (Rome: FAO, 1992), chap. 1.

5. For a discussion of some of the methodological problems, see Amartya Sen, *Hunger and Entitlements* (Helsinki: World Institute for Development and Economic Research), p. 6; and Thomas T. Poleman, "Quantifying the Nutrition Situation in Developing Countries," *Food Research Institute Studies*, Vol. 18, no. 1, (1981) . Efforts to estimate the number of hungry persons may underappreciate the extent to which poor people manage by one way or another to acquire food.

6. Keith Griffin, *World Hunger and the World Economy* (London: Macmillan, 1987).

7. See Andrew Pearse, *Seeds of Plenty, Seeds of Want* (Oxford: Clarendon Press, 1980), esp. chap. 2.

8. For a critical discussion of the range of issues associated with the "green revolution," see Frances Moore Lappe and Joseph Collins, *World Hunger: Twelve Myths* (New York: Grove Press, 1986), chap. 5; and Lappe and Collins, *Food First: Beyond the Myth of Scarcity* (New York: Ballantine Books, 1978), part IV.

9. For calculations, see Lappe and Collins, *Food First*, p. 13.

10. World Food Council, *President's Report to the Fifteenth Ministerial Session*, p. 3.

11. World Food Council, *The Cyprus Initiative Against Hunger in the World* (Rome: World Food Council, 1989), pp. 10 ff. In fact, the other OECD governments, as well as the U.S. government in the 1980s, have been pursuing policies intended to reduce food "surpluses." A 1983 U.S. government acreage restriction program reduced grain harvests by over 100 million tons (approximately by 30 percent).

12. UN Food and Agriculture Organization, *Fifth World Food Survey, 1987* (Rome: FAO, 1988).

13. Throughout this chapter, *undernourished* and *hungry* are used interchangeably. Most often, the literature cited employs these terms to refer to those who regularly consume below 90 percent of the energy standard developed jointly by the Food and Agriculture Organization and the World Health Organization. The standard is based on the caloric intake required to replace energy expenditure and to provide for growth in childhood. Standards were set on an individual country basis by accounting for observed demographic patterns in body weights, age, and sex structure. The world average is 2,350 calories per person per day.

14. World Food Council, *The Cyprus Initiative*, p. 10.

15. Lappe and Collins, *World Hunger*, p. 47.

16. Leonardo Paulino and John Mellor, "The Food Situation in Developing Countries," *Food Policy*, Vol. 9, no. 4 (November 1984), p. 292.

17. Ibid.

18. World Bank, *Poverty and Hunger*, pp. 19 ff. Based on the calculation of the aggregate caloric deficit in the diets of the hungry as a percentage of the total caloric value of all the food produced.

19. The FAO, using its minimal standard, estimated, in the early 1980s, that of the 435 million hungry in the Third World, 201 million were in India. See FAO, *Dimensions of Needs* (Rome: FAO, 1982). Other studies estimate the number of chronically hungry people in India to be closer to 300 million. See, for instance, U.S. Department of Agriculture, *Agricultural Outlook* (December, 1985).

20. World Bank, *Poverty and Hunger*, p. 20.

21. FAO, *Dimensions of Needs*, part III.

22. World Bank, *Poverty and Hunger*, p. 20.

23. Ibid.

24. See World Bank, *Poverty and Hunger*, p. 20, for percentage. For Brazil's rank as a food exporter, see *FAO Production Yearbook, 1988*.

25. UN Food and Agricultural Organization, *FAO World Food Report, 1983* (Rome: FAO, 1983), p. 9.

26. See, for example, Paulino and Mellor, "The Food Situation," p. 298.

27. Philip Raikes, *Modernizing Hunger* (London: James Currey, and Portsmouth, NH: Heinemann, 1988), chap. 2.

28. Ibid., p. 17.

29. Ibid., p. 18.

30. FAO estimates also vary considerably.

31. See Raikes, *Modernizing Hunger*, p. 18.

32. Ibid., p. 18.

33. See also Sara S. Berry, "The Food Crisis and Agrarian Change in Africa: A Review Essay," *African Studies Review*, Vol. 27, no. 2 (June 1984).

34. Raikes, *Modernizing Hunger*, p. 20.

35. See Lappe and Collins, *World Hunger*, p. 13.

36. The United Nations World Food Program estimated that, in 1987, almost three-quarters of the seventy-nine emergency food operations were under way in response to war situations. Angola, Mozambique, Ethiopia, Eritrea, and the Sudan were particularly affected by war-created famine, when food denial was used as a weapon of war. In the early 1990s, the armed conflicts and consequent threat of mass starvation, especially in the Horn of Africa, only worsened. See John Prendergast, *Peace, Development, and People of the Horn of Africa* (Washington: Institute on Hunger and Development, 1992).

37. See Amartya Sen, *Food, Economics and Entitlements* (Helsinki: World Institute for Development Economic Research, 1986).

38. M. Alamgir, *Famine in South Asia: Political Economy of Mass Starvation in Bangladesh* (Boston: Oelgeschlager, 1987).

39. World Bank, *Assault on World Poverty* (Washington: World Bank, 1975), p. 244. See also Milton J. Esman, *Landlessness and Near Landlessness in Developing Countries* (Ithaca: Cornell University, Center for International Studies, 1978).

40. Andrew Pearse dubs this marked phenomenon the "talents-effect" after the well-known parable in Matthew, Chap. 25. See Chapters 15 and 16 in Lappe and Collins, *Food First*.

41. United Nations Research Institute for Social Development (UNRISD), multivolume study, *The Social and Economic Implications of the Large-Scale Introduction of New Varieties of Food Grains* (Geneva: UNRISD, 1975); see also the excellent overview of this study authored by Andrew Pearse. See also Keith Griffin and A. R. Khan, *Landlessness and Poverty in Rural Asia*, prepared for the International Labor Organization, Geneva, Switzerland.

42. Lappe and Collins, *Food First*, pp. 136 ff.

43. Cynthia Hewitt de Alcantara, *Modernizing Mexican Agriculture* (Geneva: UNRISD, 1976), p. 30.

44. For an explanation of the author's preference for the term "high-response seeds," rather than the much more frequently used "high-yield seeds," see Lappe and Collins, *Food First*, p. 129ff.

45. Hewitt de Alcantara, op. cit., p. 318. Between 1973 and 1983, the number of tractors throughout the Third World doubled in the face of surging numbers of landless agricultural laborers. Calculated from the *FAO Production Yearbook* for 1975 and 1984.

46. See Griffin and Khan, *Poverty and Landlessness*.

47. See UNRISD, op. cit., and Pearse, *Seeds of Plenty*.

48. Biotechnology for Third World agriculture will reinforce trends associated with the green revolution, especially exacerbated inequalities, further impoverishment of poorly capitalized producers with severely restricted access to credit to purchase commercial inputs, and dramatically heightened dependence on factors outside national control. Alarmingly, even more than green-revolution technologies (which were developed in quasi-public international research centers) biotechnologies will be in the hands of private corporations seeking monopolistic profits for patented genetic material and processes. See Frederick H. Buttel, Martin Kenney, and Jack Kloppenburg, Jr., "From Green Revolution to Biorevolution: Some Observations on the Changing Technological Bases of Economic Transformation in the Third World," *Economic Development and Cultural Change*, Vol. 34, no. 1 (October 1985), pp. 31-35; Frederick H. Buttel and Jill Belsky, "Biotechnology, Plant Breeding, and Intellectual Property: Social and Ethical Dimensions," *Science, Technology, and Human Values*, Vol. 12, no. 1 (Winter 1987), pp. 31-49; Henk Hobbelink, *Biotechnology and the Future of World Agriculture* (London: Zed Press, 1991); and Robert Walgate, *Miracle or Menace? Biotechnology and the Third World* (Budapest, London, Paris, Washington: The Panos Institute, 1990).

49. For a critical discussion of the "meat mystique," see Frances Moore Lappe, *Diet for a Small Planet* (New York: Ballantine Books, revised 1982), part II.

50. Pan A. Yotopoulos, "Competition for Cereals: The Food-Feed Connection," *Ceres*, Vol. 17 (September-October 1984), p. 23.

51. Paulino and Mellor, "The Food Situation," p. 295.

52. Ibid., p. 295.

53. Lappe and Collins, *World Hunger*, p. 58; based on calculations in *FAO Food Balance Sheets*. See also David Barkin, Rosemary L. Batt and Billie R. DeWalt, *Food Crops vs. Feed Crops* (Boulder and London: Lynne Rienner, 1990).

54. According to the National Nutrition Institute of Mexico, 66 percent of the Mexican population suffer from nutritional deficiencies. Reported in *La Jornada* (Mexico City), June 16, 1985.

55. Steven Sanderson, *The Transformation of Mexican Agriculture* (Princeton: Princeton University Press, 1986), Tables 4.7 and 4.8.

56. Billie R. DeWalt, "Mexico's Second Green Revolution," *Mexican Studies*, Vol. 1, no. 1 (Winter 1985), p. 49.

57. See, for example, Kathie L. Krumm, *The External Debt of Sub-Saharan Africa* (Washington: World Bank, 1985), p. 11.

58. Cited by Susan George, *A Fate Worse than Debt* (New York: Grove Press, 1988), p. 22.

59. George, *A Fate Worse than Debt*, p. 28.

60. J. Hanger and J. Morris, "Women and the Household Economy," in Robert Chambers and J. Morris, eds., *Mwea: An Irrigated Rice Settlement in Kenya*, Afrika-Studien No. 83, IFO, Munich.

61. Susan George, *The Debt Boomerang: How Third World Debt Harms Us All* (London: Pluto Press, 1992), p. xv.

62. George, *A Fate Worse Than Debt*, p. 121.

63. Ibid., p. 139.

64. Ibid., p. 136.

65. Quoted in ibid., p. 135.

66. Ibid., p. 137.

67. Ibid., p. 108.

68. U.S. farm policy in the 1980s continued to make the United States a major "dumper" of grain on the world market, selling way below production costs, with U.S. taxpayers covering the difference. In 1988, for instance, the United States was selling corn overseas at about $1.10 a bushel when U.S. production costs were running between $2 and $3.50 a bushel. Farmers in Third World countries, with ever less government assistance due to "structural-adjustment" and "free-market" policies, are often unable to compete.

69. Bill Rau, "Drought in Southern Africa," *Washington Notes on Africa* (Summer 1992), p. 4. Published by the Washington (D.C.) Office on Africa.

70. Ibid.

71. Susan George, "On the Need for a Broader Approach," *Food Policy* (February 1985), p. 78.

72. U.S. Senate, Committee on Agriculture, Nomination of John Block, *Hearings*, 1981.

73. Sweden, a developed democratic nation, gives some example here. Even though overall wealth in Sweden is still tightly concentrated, some time ago Swedes decided that farming and food were too important to be left to the market alone. In Sweden, therefore, only working farmers are permitted to own farmland, and sales of farmland are closely monitored by county boards to ensure that prices paid are not so high as to eliminate young farmers from the competition. See Mark B. Lapping and V. Dale Forster, "Farmland and Agricultural Policy in Sweden: An Integrated Approach," *International Regional Science Review*, Vol. 7, no. 3 (1982), pp. 297, 299. Moreover, wholesale food prices are not allowed to fluctuate with the market, wreaking havoc on the family farm; instead, they are periodically set when farm representatives, government officials, agribusiness executives, and consumer food cooperative officers sit down at the negotiating table. See Lappe and Collins, *World Hunger* p. 83.

74. Julian Simon is a prime exponent of this view. See Julian Simon, "Resources, Population, and Environment: An Oversupply of False Bad News," *Science*, Vol. 208 (June 27, 1980), p. 1434; and *The Ultimate Resource* (Princeton: Princeton University Press, 1981).

75. For a fuller development of the "power-structure" paradigm, see Frances Moore Lappe and Rachel Schurman, *Taking Population Seriously: The Missing Piece in the Population Puzzle* (San Francisco: Food First Books, 1989).

76. China, Sri Lanka, Colombia, Chile, and Cuba, as well as the state of Kerala in India, are among those most often cited in this regard.

19 / Building World Security: The Need for Strengthened International Institutions

ROBERT C. JOHANSEN

OVERCOMING INTELLECTUAL AND INSTITUTIONAL INERTIA

As we stand amidst the extraordinary fluidity of vast political, economic, and environmental changes in the international system and attempt to lay plans for enhancing U.S. and global security, we would do well to heed the historians who have warned that generals (and others) tend to overlook inconvenient realities and to prepare defenses that are more appropriate for the last war than for the next one, or that respond more to wishful thinking than to real security problems.

One might expect that mental inertia would not be a problem during a time of major change, such as the sudden disappearance of the Cold War, because obvious transformations can hardly be ignored. But in the post–Cold War era, few if any governments have laid plans to take advantage of the opportunities that are now present and that civilizations only rarely encounter for achieving fundamental, positive change. Few governments have paid heed to the need and opportunity to institutionalize a new code of international conduct that is more peaceful, just, and environmentally sound. Yet we probably face not merely the most important systemic opportunity of the decade, or even of our lifetime, but of several centuries. It will be a tragedy of unimaginable proportions if we let the opportunity slip through our fingers.

Policymakers in many capitals seem snared in perhaps the oldest and most widely honored maxim of international relations: "If you want peace, prepare for war." This is not the place to debate whether preparations for war throughout history have more often lead to war than to peace.[1] But it seems increasingly clear to people—at least to those not closely wedded to the vested interests of traditional policies—that *if we want peace we must prepare for peace*. This can be done by strengthening international norms and institutions *against* war, not by reorganizing institutions and arsenals for the conduct of war. To replace the East-West conflict with North-South conflict or intercivilizational conflict (e.g., Orthodox Serbs against Muslim Bosnians) without aiming in the long run to replace the balance of military power with a legally constituted balance of political power will do little to reduce the likelihood or costliness of violence. Nor will the maintenance of the present international system be an effective bulwark against new challenges to security that are likely to arise in the future. The way to make international relations more peaceful in the long run is to *institutionalize* a more peaceful code of conduct. This requires new global institutions to prevent backsliding once gains have been made and to provide services and incentives to engage reluctant governments in a more pacific code of conduct.

What policies and institutions could truly come to grips with the security challenges that press upon people throughout the entire world community? In the preceding chapters the authors have recommended a variety of specific initiatives to enhance security. Here I will try to integrate these recommendations and move beyond them, and to chart the long-range direction that policy must follow if the people of the United States and the world are to survive with dignity for themselves and respect for each other. My intention is to develop guidelines that can inform the policies of *all* nations, and also to show how the United States in particular can change its own direction to chart a fundamentally new path.

At the heart of a new security concept must be a transformation of views on the role of military power. This transformation was anticipated, even before the end of the Cold War, in the envisaging of "common security" by such leaders as Willy Brandt of Germany and Olaf Palme of Sweden, and reflected in reports of the four well-known international commissions that they, and later Gro Harlem Brundtland of Norway and Julius Nyerere of Tanzania, headed.[2]

The four international commissions suggested many measures, most of which have not been integrated into any major government's policies, to strengthen international institutions and to revamp the customary code of international conduct, in order to equip them with sufficiently attractive national representation and accountability at the global level to manage the pressing economic, military, and environmental problems that no national government can handle separately.

Although U.S. policy now includes more sensitivity to multilateral diplomacy than in the 1980s, it still relies more on the continued development of sophisticated weapons and traditional bilateral diplomacy than on a multilateral diplomatic program to demilitarize the global system. Policies seem blind to the possibility that even the large U.S. arsenals of the future, although unequaled elsewhere, may still be outflanked by desperate societies with crude weapons of mass destruction, or by nonmilitary security threats such as environmental decay, economic decline, and migratory pressures that simply cannot be managed by military might.

Despite some reductions in U.S. and world military expenditures, the cuts are a far cry from a new orientation that would attempt to encompass the security of all nations and reduce the role of military power in international affairs generally. Most national security managers do not acknowledge that people's security in the future will rest on finding alternatives to the military postures that have characterized the nation-state system up to now, rather than on modernizing those postures. Symptomatically, more attention in Washington has been devoted to identifying vague alternatives to the former communist security threat than to finding an alternative to the international security system, based almost exclusively on nation-states, that has produced recurring threats throughout its existence since the Peace of Westphalia in 1648. This system never has prevented war permanently and presumably never will. Yet, permanent prevention of major war must be the aim of any serious security policy today.

UNDERSTANDING THE FUTURE OF WORLD SECURITY

To avoid remaining enmeshed in a traditional worldview, it is essential that we develop basic guidelines to orient citizens' actions, to inform political leaders, and to hold them accountable to what the commonweal needs and the new realities require. The preceding chapters make clear that a useful security concept in the postmodern age must emphasize both *common* security and *comprehensive* security.

Common Security

As the Independent Commission on Disarmament and Security (the Palme Commission) concluded in 1989, the destructiveness of modern war, even so-called conventional war, has become so horrendous that "war is losing its meaning as an instrument of national policy, becoming instead an engine of senseless destruction that leaves the root causes of conflict unresolved." Once humanity has become proficient in building weapons of mass destruction, the commission noted, nations "can no longer hope to protect their citizens through unilateral military measures." Rather than traditional security thinking, *common security* policies are needed. Such policies are rooted in the recognition that "all states, even the most powerful, are dependent in the end upon the good sense and restraint of other nations."[3]

Clearly, an adequate understanding of security in the current era must encompass not only one's own nation and its allies, but, surprisingly, one's adversaries and neutral bystanders as well. In an environmentally fragile age endowed with nuclear and nonnuclear weapons of mass destruction, either we hold security in common with all other nations or we simply cannot achieve it. If the United States seeks to enhance its security by building new weapons that increase the threat, even inadvertently, to an adversary, the latter will usually try to develop more weapons to increase the threat to the United States. If the adversary possesses advanced industrial and technological capacities, as did the former Soviet Union, the weapons deployed will be similar to those built by Washington; if the adversary lacks an equivalent industrial base, it will resort to less sophisticated, or perhaps unorthodox, weapons and methods of attack on U.S. interests. Whether the security threat resembles the nuclear arsenal of the former Soviet Union or the danger of nuclear proliferation in Iraq, no country can, in the long run, increase its own security while ignoring or increasing the insecurity of other societies.

Insecurity for one's adversaries eventually rebounds into insecurity for oneself. Even if continually advancing U.S. technologies of destruction remain beyond the capabilities of U.S. adversaries, in the absence of security policies designed to reduce reliance on the threat-system of international relations, one adversary or another in the future will be able to bring catastrophe home to U.S. citizens by launching nuclear weapons, delivering suitcase bombs, or engaging in chemical, radiological, biological, environmental, or economic warfare. The world's societies are so intertwined and easily despoiled that more armaments do not lead to more security. On the contrary, arms buildups impede the growth of security by siphoning off resources and attention from the new security requirements to enhance the common security of all countries, and to address nonmilitary security threats (to which we now turn).

Comprehensive Security

To be successful, new security policies must be far more comprehensive in addressing nonmilitary problems than such policies have been in the past. If the first duty of government is to provide safety for its people, this duty must include protection against whatever dangers may kill people, shorten their lives, or disrupt a society—be they environmental jeopardy, economic deprivation, or the threat of invasion by foreign armies. Human activity that thins the layer of ozone in the stratosphere or that thickens the density of carbon dioxide in the atmosphere probably constitutes a more clear and present danger to national security than the unlikely possibility of a major nuclear attack.

The entrance of environmental concerns into the security equation places security beyond the reach of even enlightened traditional diplomacy. As Jessica Tuchman Mathews points out in Chapter 14, traditional diplomacy is too slow, cumbersome, and simplistic to meet pressing environmental problems. Moreover, the environmental security threat cannot be encompassed by traditional security thinking and political "Realism," which have been based on ideas about sovereignty that make a spatial, territorial distinction between friend and foe. The persons who thin the ozone and intensify atmospheric carbon dioxide do not live on the other side of our borders and wear the uniforms of another country; the most irresponsible consumers in our own society do that. Since a simple territorial distinction between friend and enemy no longer applies, we must change our ideas about what constitutes a true security community.

Similarly, the bleeding of the U.S. economy caused by the Reagan and Bush administrations' enormous deficit spending on unnecessary military hardware harmed the well-being of U.S. people far more than the compensations of "standing tall" before the fading military threats of the 1980s. U.S. policies continue to provide further confirmation of Paul Kennedy's finding that mature great powers over the last five centuries have declined because they spent so much on military purposes that they destroyed the economic health on which their power depended.[4] In times of challenge, leaders have repeatedly made the *wrong* decisions for their own good.[5]

For security policy to encompass the subjects that are essential if it is to be truly effective, it must extend even beyond economic and environmental threats, and attend to human rights, and to psychological and spiritual dimensions of peoples' security. The political, economic, and psychological changes required to build a safe world are of such a large order of magnitude that people with personal insecurities, even if these insecurities are well-hidden, will be unable to provide reliable political help. High levels of personal security facilitate openness to new ways of thinking and to new forms of identity that transcend national, racial, class, gender, and generational boundaries. These boundary-crossing forms of identify are essential to sustaining a prudent security policy in the future.

INSTITUTIONALIZING A PRINCIPLED WORLD POLICY

To interrupt the inertial tendency to remain unresponsive to changing security needs, it is essential to develop a *principled world policy*, designed to implement and institutionalize clearly desirable values that serve, not one or several national interests, but what might be called the "human interest."[6]

To embrace key principles for the conduct of nations can produce several positive results. First, awareness of central principles gives constancy to policy and reduces the damage arising from partisan politics when elected officials and candidates—in the interest of obtaining votes—fan the flames of adversarial nationalism, reinforce exaggerated fears of foreigners and unfamiliar ideologies, and suggest that jingoism, militarism, economic protectionism, or the stifling of dissent are congruent with patriotism.

Moreover, just as a principled policy may reduce the disruption of narrow-minded nationalism and domestic political partisanship, so the establishment of a principled policy can alleviate the conflict-generating tendency in international relations to believe that one's own nation may legitimately give higher priority to its *interests* than to other peoples' *rights*. This tendency is one manifestation of what could be called "national partisanship" in an age of global interdependence. In a world where the entire species becomes an important constituency in decision making, any national perspective, however bipartisan it may be from the standpoint of domestic politics, is partisan from a global perspective.

Finally, by articulating and honoring an explicitly principled code of conduct, U.S. and other policymakers can more readily encourage all governments to follow suit and to institutionalize diplomatic progress. To have a peaceful and just world order, people and governments must increasingly move away from an us-versus-them mentality toward common standards of conduct and fair play for all. The expansion of human identities that this implies need not be seen as an unwise sacrifice of legitimate national interests; as in domestic society, one person can willingly give up his or her "right" to act in disregard for the law in return for other persons' compliance with it. Washington can advance legitimate U.S. rights most effectively amidst the claims of other governments when all operate within a global political structure that requires disputes to be settled in a principled manner through political and legal means.

Five basic principles, each suggesting innovations in international institutions, are useful in defining the human interest and shaping policies that will enhance security for people in the United States and all other nations: *reciprocity, equity, environmental sustainability, democratization,* and *demilitarization.*

RECIPROCITY

Reciprocity, the first and most fundamental principle, simply means that a government willingly evaluates its own actions by the same standards that it holds for other nations' behavior. A national government that respects the principle of reciprocity does not insist on a right for itself that it does not willingly grant to others, nor does it specify a duty for others that it does not accept for itself.[7] This principle is almost universally endorsed by people regardless of nationality, religion, or ideology; in practice, however, it is violated frequently, in part because the world lacks institutional frameworks to encourage respect for it. In any case, its universal endorsement provides a basis for attempting to hold governments accountable to a fundamental ordering principle that transcends cultural differences.

If rigorously implemented, this principle could by itself eliminate most wars. Since no nation wants to be the target of aggression, no nation can legitimately act aggressively itself. In addition, any government that contends that its adversaries have no right to promote external armed insurrection, or to finance clandestine movement of arms or military forces across borders, must not claim that "right" for itself, as the United States did in trying to overthrow the Nicaraguan government in the 1980s. To carry the argument further, if the United States claims the right to develop new weapons of mass destruction, can it find persuasive grounds on which to deny that "right" to others? If Washington seeks to limit the spread of nuclear weapons, it should implement such a policy by submitting itself to equitable constraints and by establishing international monitors and enforcement to uphold the principle of nonproliferation for all.

A rigorous respect for reciprocity is also an effective antidote to one of the most serious dangers associated with a principled foreign policy: namely, that its proponents may assume a moralistic attitude, based on the assumption that their policies are more virtuous than the policies of other governments. They may insist on their own way, evangelize for the "correct" point of view, and use military threats to implement their policies. To nullify this common, yet poisonous, tendency, reciprocal rights and obligations should be authoritatively interpreted wherever possible by multilateral institutions representing the human interest rather than a single national or ethnic interest.

Representative Institutions

The most reliable path for implementing reciprocity in world affairs is to move toward a more just representation of all people in increasingly effective international institutions. Progress in building international institutions would enable or require societies to be less narrowly focused on unfair, selfish interests, and to share responsibility for deciding global issues such as how to limit arms, avert global warming, or wisely use scarce global resources. Every country's legitimate national interests can be served by more effective multilateral institutions in peacekeeping, because, as Joseph Nye has pointed out, such institutions help share the burdens of global policing, increase the legitimacy of such policing, constrain negative behavior, and motivate positive policies by other countries.[8]

Most people also have a strong (though seldom acknowledged) self-interest in securing balanced representative procedures in international organizations and courts, where reciprocity can be impartially defined, because such procedures are virtually the only way to increase all peoples' claim to freedom in an increasingly interdependent world in which one person's freedom can easily encroach on another's. Indeed, representation is so strongly related to freedom that Thomas Paine, one of the revered leaders of the American Revolution, wrote that "representative government is freedom."[9] Rejection of more representative international institutions to adjudicate disputes and enforce settlements will lead frequently to violence or gross injustice as the strong or ruthless dictate to the weak or fair-minded.

From now on, societies must employ international institutions to accept transnational, collective responsibility for major decisions regarding military security, environmental protection, economic well-being, and human rights. Such institutions cannot be effective unless they represent fairly the people affected by their decisions, because societies will not commit themselves to implementing their decisions unless they have been well represented in the decision-making process.[10]

In addition to gradually expanding the representation of those people who are now underrepresented in existing international organizations such as the UN Security Council and the World Bank, the world community should create several new agencies to meet specific needs, widen the use of other relatively impartial international political institutions such as the World Court and regional courts, and broaden the authority of multilateral forums for negotiating the settlement of disputes. These will be discussed below in the context of the remaining four principles.

EQUITY

The second principle, to advance equity throughout global society, arises from a moral desire for more justice and equal opportunity, from an economic need for more economic rationality and global productivity, and from a political imperative for more international cooperation and willingness to sacrifice for the good of all. This principle aims to expand economic opportunity, to meet basic human needs, and to achieve a fairer distribution of political influence and economic resources throughout the world.

The world economy now functions so inefficiently that its deficiencies harm all nations, rich and poor alike. Today's economic structures leave approximately one billion people living in poverty, facing serious shortages of food, and often leading unproductive lives. In part because the world community has not eliminated glaring inequities, the North's industrial capacity remains underutilized while the South urgently needs goods that the North could produce. In addition, poverty adds pressures on limited food resources, tillable land, and timber supplies; overfishing, overgrazing, desertification, and loss of topsoil cause a declining standard of living, eventually, for the species everywhere.[11] Poverty also stimulates unwanted population growth that would be reduced if more equitable, higher standards of living were attained throughout the world.

From the standpoint of enlightened pragmatic politics, poverty needs to be abolished because the worldwide cooperation needed to build a durable security system cannot be achieved with this planet divided, economically half slave and half free. Poverty also leads to the degradation of the biosphere, because poor governments often feel forced to cut development costs by accepting low environmental standards to attract capital, or by destroying rain forests to earn cash. As a result, to abolish poverty would serve the security interests of the rich even if they have little moral concern for justice or the well-being of the poor.

Institutions to Abolish Poverty

To achieve greater equity will require several institutional innovations. First, a systematically replenished development fund is needed to divert financial resources from wasteful or unnecessary spending into the reduction of poverty. States should cooperate in establishing and contributing to a global development fund that would be financed through what would amount to an element of "universal taxation" based on a country's ability to pay.[12] The purpose of the fund would be nothing less than to implement a serious program to abolish extreme poverty worldwide within the next twenty-five years. Without some form of legally binding replenishment of a capital fund for investment, debt and poverty will afflict large segments of the human race, and poverty-stricken people increasingly will be forced to exert environmentally threatening leverage over future generations and the rich.

Second, a World Economic Council, representing the economic ministries of two or three dozen of the world's most influential economies, should be established to set up the proposed fund and to coordinate exchange, trade, and development policies affecting the world political economy. If the UN's existing Economic and Social Council (ECOSOC) could be restructured, it could perform the needed proposed functions, integrate and oversee the UN's diverse economic programs, and report to all the countries of the world through the General Assembly. This body needs to focus on two goals: first, the elimination of gross poverty, and second, the establishment of sustainable economies. It could help build consensus on the optimal means for addressing global economic and social problems, and for organizing joint action to carry out the steps agreed upon.

Third, the International Monetary Fund (IMF), the World Bank, and the General Agreement on Tariffs and Trade (GATT) must be reformed to increase the portion of their aid that focuses on reducing poverty (as opposed to projects that do not meet basic needs). International lending banks should aim to achieve more equitable burden-sharing by establishing stable exchange rates, adjusting balance of payments deficits, expanding international liquidity, and dealing with the debt that keeps many societies buried in poverty.[13] Decision-making procedures need to expand representation both of poor countries' governments and of citizen's groups engaged in some of the world's most effective development programs that are people-centered and sensitive both to equity and environmental protection.

With a serious international program to share and conserve resources, hunger and poverty could be abolished within two decades by using only a portion of total world military expenditures or a modest fraction of the likely increase in income of the richest one-third of the world's population. Moreover, because present environmental decline is in part a consequence of poverty, advances in equity, which seem a prerequisite to increasing worldwide sensitivity to environmental protection, will directly meet future security needs. Greater equity also would encourage the world's people, many of whom are now alienated from prevailing political and economic institutions, to support what would become a politically more stable and fair international system.

SUSTAINABILITY

The third principle, environmental sustainability, emphasizes that a deeper respect for nature is essential to maintaining a healthy biosphere, without which lives of human dignity will be impossible. Environmental issues pose planet-enveloping dangers with the prospect of such irretrievable damage that they constitute the most serious long-range security problem in the world today. As country after country declared during the World Conference on Environment and Development in Rio de Janeiro in 1992, life-support systems for the human species face severe danger from pollution, resource depletion, and population pressure.[14] These dangers obviously cannot be addressed through the traditional security instruments of military strength, nor even through enlightened diplomacy within the old structures of the international system. Only more effective international institutions, with legally binding powers, and the transfer of massive financial resources and brainpower from military to environmental purposes will enable the species to enhance its security.

The idea of global sustainability suggests that the current flurry of fragmented international activity should be orchestrated within an integrated global program to set permissible levels for emission of pollutants, to apply money and technology throughout the world at the points where they are most likely to produce substantial benefits (regardless of the host society's ability to pay), and to enforce agreed upon standards and financial obligations. The goal is to achieve a sustainable world society that "satisfies its needs without jeopardizing the prospects of future generations." From now on, each generation must take responsibility for ensuring "that the next one inherits an undiminished natural and economic endowment."[15] This third principle dovetails with the second, because the goal of sustainability takes root in the desire to achieve intergenerational *equity*.

Institutions for Sustainable Societies

If the human species is to face security challenges squarely, it needs, first of all, to establish a new Environmental Council within the United Nations system to unify presently scattered efforts to avert climate change and ozone depletion and to manage all other major intercontinental environmental problems. A new agency is required to speed the treaty-making process (so that a new forum does not need to be created every time another treaty is to be negotiated), to build world political consensus, to implement treaties and ensure compliance with the ozone convention and the more than 170 other existing environmental treaties (most of which have completely inadequate monitoring and enforcement provisions), to help settle disputes over the implementation of treaty provisions, and to provide incentives (primarily financial) to encourage reluctant states to join a unified environmental effort. Such a unified agency could have much higher visibility than a haphazard collection of diverse organizations focused on only a single aspect of the environmental crisis.

The council might be made up of representatives from the environmental ministries of a score of national governments, and, building upon the example set by representation in the International Labor Organization, representatives from business management, labor, and citizens' environmental organizations such as Friends of the Earth, Greenpeace, or EarthAction. (Citizens' groups need to be represented in the council's proceedings because they help enormously in monitoring compliance with global norms, in carrying grievances to governments at all levels, and in building public support for needed environmental measures.) The proposed council should report to the UN General Assembly.

With the proper representation and authority, the council could set global emission standards for a strictly limited number of pollutants, such as chlorofluorocarbons and carbon dioxide, which pose the most severe threats to human security. Acting as a truly representative global body, it could help equalize the burden of such standards so that all countries will receive fair treatment and that existing undesirable incentives for free riders to abuse the environment in order to gain competitive advantages will be eliminated. The benefits of experience from the existing United Nations Environment Program (UNEP) could be utilized by restructuring UNEP, which has no authority to enforce compliance with treaties, to make it an environmental secretariat for the proposed Environmental Council.[16]

If, in the future, a government were to violate community decisions, its case could be handled in an environmental mediation service established by the council or referred to the World Court. In such cases, the Court should have compulsory jurisdiction and binding authority. Although the implementation of these suggestions would constitute a significant departure from past state practice, precisely such a departure is necessary. It would not threaten the legitimate interests of any society. Significantly, more than thirty countries have expressed support for proposals such as these in the Hague Declaration, which called for a council empowered to render legally binding decisions on vital issues affecting the biosphere through veto-free voting procedures.[17]

Second, security enhancement also requires the world community to consider measures now, before sovereign claims in space intensify, to govern all uses of space. An agency jointly established by and reporting to the Security Council and the proposed Environmental Council is needed to ensure fair and orderly uses of space, to protect the atmosphere from excessive pollution, to ban weapons from being deployed in space, to manage space debris, and to establish fees—payable to the U.N. system—for using outer space (such as a "parking fee" for placing a space vehicle in geosynchronous orbit).

Third, more substantial funding must be raised to encourage sustainability. Probably the best mechanism for this is to establish a tax on all atmospheric releases of carbon dioxide. This step would begin to pay for a small portion of the enormous environmental damage that fossil-fuel consumption has caused, but for which consumers have not reimbursed the injured world community or future generations. An existing institution that holds some promise of financial aid is the Global Environmental Facility, established by the World Bank in 1990. Based on voluntary contributions and jointly administered by the World Bank and UNEP, this fund should be expanded, made responsive to a newly established UN Commission on Sustainable Development and to the proposed Environmental Council (if and when it is established), and encouraged to provide funds conditionally in a manner that will enforce desirable international standards.

Successful environmental management could nurture networks of cooperation across existing adversarial boundaries, suggest models of representation and veto-free deliberations in strengthened international institutions (that might be applicable to other issues as well), and establish exemplary instruments of community-wide adjudication and enforcement. These could facilitate parallel cooperation in the even more sensitive field of military security (discussed below).

DEMOCRATIZATION

Democratization, the fourth principle, aims to increase every government's accountability to the people who are affected by its major decisions, regardless of whether those people live inside or outside of that country's territory. Ensuring that all governments become and remain accountable to the people who are affected by their decisions is not merely a desirable moral value. Immediate steps in that direction are essential for pragmatic security policies in the future. Without governmental accountability, major decisions— whether made at national, regional, or global levels—will lack sufficient legitimacy and support to avoid unacceptable risks, costs, and disruptions of international life. To enhance global security through deepening democracy requires progress in both "horizontal" and "vertical" accountability.

Horizontal and Vertical Accountability

"Horizontal accountability" refers to a government's responsibility for activities that extend across national borders. Traditionally, scholars and politicians alike have not recognized a need for any horizontal accountability beyond what could occur through normal diplomatic representation. But increasingly, more reliable representative institutions are needed to enable citizens to influence the decisions that directly affect them yet may be made in another country.

As interdependence increases, the number of decisions that affect U.S. citizens and yet occur outside the United States also increases. The economic security of the U.S. public depends on decisions made in Tokyo or Brussels as well as on Wall Street; to erect a tariff wall of economic protection or engage in Japan-bashing will not eliminate this reality. Similarly, the security of U.S. citizens depends on military decisions in Moscow or Tel Aviv, in Berlin or Baghdad, as well as in Washington. If the political, economic, and environmental decisions that affect U.S. people increasingly occur outside the United States, while U.S. (and global) political institutions remain constant, then the element of democracy in U.S. political life declines, even though fair elections, a free press, and competing political parties remain operational within the United States as they have in the past.

If people in other lands pollute the atmosphere, then U.S. citizens suffer environmental degradation without representation. Alternatively, if U.S. economic policies cause worldwide inflation, then people in other lands suffer inflationary "taxation" without representation. To take yet another example, those who plan, build, and operate nuclear plants, such as the one at Chernobyl, might reasonably be held accountable to standards established by all those who are likely to be affected by their operations or possible breakdown, whether they live in Sweden, Italy, Ukraine, Russia, or elsewhere. For a forward-looking security policy at century's end, democratic accountability must be transnational, as well as national and local.

As military force becomes less applicable to problem solving and less widely accepted as legitimate, and as economic power becomes more widely diffused throughout the world, the United States will want to ensure that its voice is heard in international institutions that are reliable and democratic and that guarantee rights for global minorities as well as majorities. The society relevant to our lives now is global as well as national and local, so supporters of democracy must reconstruct sovereignty and transform the profoundly inadequate institutions—in terms of their representativeness, authority, and power—at the global level.

A healthy concern for cross-border government accountability also entails concern for accountability within national and local contexts—or "vertical accountability"—since global representation and decisions cannot implement the democratic principle unless the structure beneath them facilitates fair representation. As Nicole Ball has demonstrated in Chapter 11, authoritarian governments are less likely to serve the interests of their people—including security, in the broadest sense—than are more popular, responsive governments. The growth of internal democracy also aids the growth of peace, because democratic societies have related more peacefully to each other than they have to authoritarian societies or than authoritarian societies have to each other.[18]

The Institutional Nurture of Democracy

As a modest step in encouraging democracy, the world community needs, first of all, to institutionalize within the United Nations an electoral monitoring agency to help administer elections, when invited to do so, and to certify whether election results have been fair. Such services, provided on an ad hoc basis in the past, already have contributed both to achieving peace and to deterring violations of electoral procedures in Nicaragua, El Salvador, Namibia, and Haiti.[19] To perform electoral monitoring expeditiously and with an indisputable reputation for impartiality can contribute enormously to the prevention of violence and the growth of democracy, especially in a world where more and more conflict stems from interethnic disputes within a single country. It puts pressure, through a concrete and unambiguous procedural test, on authoritarian leaders to rise to international electoral standards. To make international observers readily available to verify that an election has not been stolen also removes a common justification for external military intervention.

Second, democracy can be aided over the long run by implementing existing human rights treaties and upgrading human rights institutions. Specifically, the position of UN High Commissioner for Human Rights needs to be established with powers to hear reports from Amnesty International and other reputable human rights groups, as well as governments. By using widely agreed upon norms contained in the Universal Declaration of Human Rights, the Covenant on Civil and Political Rights, and the Covenant on Economic, Social, and Cultural Rights, the office of high commissioner should prepare an annual UN report on human rights and designate a special rapporteur to investigate gross violations of human rights.[20] To encourage all states to ratify and implement the covenants, those governments with the best human rights records should be placed near the top of the list of potential recipients for economic aid and debt relief.

Third, a UN Human Rights Court should be established. It could be patterned after the European Human Rights Court, which enables citizens to bring human rights claims from within their own societies into a multinational judicial process, thereby helping to establish minimum human rights standards throughout Europe. The proposed UN court could provide the legal basis for justifying fair international penalties or sanctions against those who violate fundamental international prohibitions of arbitrary imprisonment, torture, and execution.

Protecting People's Rights

The United Nations needs to discuss standards and institutional procedures under which it may be entitled to intervene within a country to create safe havens for people when gross violations of human rights—such as genocide or ethnic cleansing—victimize an entire people. In recent years, a growing segment of the international community has come to accept the idea that certain domestic policies, such as apartheid, genocide, and massive human rights violations, "should not be tolerated by the community of civilized nations."[21] The creation of safe havens for Kurds in Iraq added an important precedent that could have far-reaching consequences for traditional notions of state sovereignty. French officials recently have said that international law recognizes a "'duty to intervene' in cases where a government's actions are creating a humanitarian catastrophe."[22]

The idea that the United Nations might, in carefully defined circumstances, have the right to intervene in what has formerly been held to be the sacrosanct domain of domestic jurisdiction is, of course, highly controversial. Yet the gradual development of international law in the field of human rights has led an increasing number of governments to endorse the notion that the UN should intervene to protect people against ethnic cleansing, such as occurred in Bosnia in 1992–93, or to avert mass starvation resulting from civil war, as occurred in Somalia and Sudan in the early 1990s.[23]

Three issues need to be resolved in an international convention or UN action: What kind of emergency warrants collective intervention? What form of collective authorization is required to justify intervention? What interventionary actions are permissible? Clearly, any intervention should be attempted only with wide international support, conducted with caution, and informed by a desire to avoid loss of life. None of these issues had been resolved when the Security Council faced the need to authorize intervention against Saddam Hussein's genocidal repression of the Kurds in northern Iraq in 1991–92. Despite overwhelming opposition to Hussein's aggression against Kuwait, many countries in the UN coalition were reluctant to intervene on the Kurdish question because they viewed this matter as more fully within Iraq's internal affairs. Nevertheless, a UN force was deployed to provide protection to UN humanitarian workers. Following this precedent, the three questions posed above might be resolved by justifying intervention only when gross violations of rights occur, only when the Security Council (or Security Council plus General Assembly) authorizes it, and only to provide protection for relief workers or to create safe havens for those fleeing immediate threats to their lives.

Centuries of political experience demonstrate the need to maintain strong protection for minorities, regardless of whether dictators or majorities rule. Reinforcing such protection at every opportunity will not only encourage minorities to accept and support majoritarian procedures associated with democracy, but also prevent the deepening of fears and hostilities among ethnically diverse populations, such as occurred with tragic consequences in Yugoslavia, the former Soviet Union, parts of Africa, and elsewhere in the early 1990s. To prevent a spiral of negative reactions that descend into genocidal violence, it will be necessary to establish effectively functioning regional or global institutions, such as the proposed UN High Commissioner and a Human Rights Court, to monitor human rights and to ask the UN Security Council to enforce court decisions or cease-fires on warring parties where genocide threatens. Such institutions should be established as quickly as possible, so that their durability and fairness can soon be established.

Expressing the Human Interest

Finally, the principle of democratization suggests the need in the long run to find ways to represent local people directly on the global level. Existing representational schemes give primary, almost exclusive, representation to national governments. Yet, these do not always express people's interests well. Nor is it true that national governments acting to serve their national interests will find the best way to serve the human interest.

To give more accurate voice to the human interest, people should insist on the establishment of an Independent Commission on World Governance (as the Stockholm Initiative of 1991 recommended[24]) to study, among other topics, the best means for establishing a World Assembly to represent people directly in a chamber parallel to the General Assembly. Representatives to such an assembly could be selected by national legislatures or, preferably, elected directly by voting constituencies throughout the world. In addition, it would be useful to establish a world council of citizens' organizations, where representatives of grass-roots movements would meet to offer ideas, technical assistance, and advice to intergovernmental organizations in a systematic way, while attempting to build consensus, both globally and locally, for preferred policy directions in crafting a just and peaceful world society.

DEMILITARIZATION

The fifth principle, global demilitarization, is inspired by the desire to reduce the role of military power in international relations generally, not merely to reduce arms of one sort or another. To be sure, one way of constraining the use of military force is to reduce and eliminate weapons that exacerbate insecurities, so demilitarization includes gradual reduction of arms; however, it goes far beyond arms control to aim at the gradual elimination of all countries' offensive military capabilities. In addition, demilitarization includes steps to demilitarize national economies, the habits of political and educational institutions, and the social and psychological patterns that sustain collective violence as well. Demilitarization aims at dismantling national and international military culture and replacing it with a culture of legal obligation and nonlethal forms of dispute settlement.

Demilitarization is necessary because, even in the post–Cold War world, nations are unlikely to achieve a lasting, just peace within a balance of power system that is endowed with national armed forces that may be unilaterally employed at any time, with the continued development of new military technology, and with the prospect of yet unimagined weapons of mass destruction and environmental vulnerabilities always close at hand. In addition, demilitarization is required because military institutions, regardless of ethnic or ideological setting, organize and train people, as well as shape economic and political institutions, in ways that are antithetical to democratic processes and the other four principles discussed above.[25]

To reduce the role of military power in world affairs and simultaneously to address people's legitimate fears of adversaries will, of course, require further revisions in the international code of conduct and the strengthening of world security institutions. These changes must eventually enable national governments to create a world without war, although it will not be a world without conflict. Existing UN security institutions need sufficient reforms over the next two decades to provide reliable assurances that arms reductions can be enforced and that security eventually can be maintained by dependable UN or other global institutions, acting in concert with regional, national, and popular public efforts to create and maintain a less violent code of international conduct.

Decreasing the Role of Military Power

Because of its influence, resources, and relatively unthreatened security position, the United States could be a path breaker in permanently reducing the role of military force. A carefully orchestrated diplomatic program should focus on these goals: to reorient all existing military power toward nonoffensive defenses; to establish clear standards against the spread of weapons of mass destruction to additional countries, and against the testing, manufacture, or deployment of any more such weapons in countries now possessing them; to reduce gradually all national armed forces; and to develop international peacemaking, monitoring, and enforcing institutions in order to establish and enforce norms of permissible military conduct.

In recognition of the need to implement common security policies in today's interdependent world, the United States and other like-minded governments could ask all countries to confine themselves more strictly to defense by halting the development and deployment of weapons that by their speed, stealth, destructive power, or range are extremely threatening to other countries. One of the most important ways of making military postures less offensive is to end the proliferation of all weapons of mass destruction, beginning with nuclear arms. The United States could independently announce that it will halt all further nuclear weapons tests as long as other countries do the same; after arranging adequate verification measures with the other major powers and adherents to the Nuclear Nonproliferation Treaty, they could invite any remaining countries to reciprocate. Together, the constraining countries could exert enormous influence on any countries dragging their feet and thereby bring about a complete worldwide ban on nuclear weapons tests, thus eliminating one of the foremost security threats in the world today.

Furthermore, to underscore that a strengthened nuclear nonproliferation regime will not be inequitable, with the nuclear "haves" enjoying privileges denied to the "have nots," the nuclear weapons countries need to reduce their arsenals further and downgrade the importance they assign to nuclear arms. During the transition toward abolition of nuclear arsenals, a small number of nuclear arms, for retaliatory deterrence purposes only, might be retained by nuclear weapons powers under joint control with United Nations monitors.

Yet, arms reductions in themselves will not make people secure. In addition to implementing a worldwide campaign to constrict offensive capabilities and to reduce the armed forces of national governments, an effective security policy needs to upgrade and institutionalize robust peacemaking, monitoring, and enforcement instruments so as to bridle the potential misuse of the military option.

Developing Reliable Peacemaking and Monitoring Institutions

To be an effective peacemaker, the world community needs to be better prepared to reduce tensions before they explode, to monitor closely governments' compliance with rules leading toward a less militarized code of international conduct, and to conduct peacekeeping and enforcement operations when violations of that code occur.

First, the UN Security Council must be far more serious about becoming the world's crisis management center. Toward that end, the Security Council and the secretary-general need more timely information, communication, and negotiation capabilities. The secretary-general now lacks an extensive early warning system and secure communication lines. The Security Council should authorize the secretary-general to employ more roving ambassadors to observe conflicts, report back to the UN Secretariat, and mediate disputes. In addition, the council and secretary-general should establish standing conflict-resolution committees in each region of the world. These committees could provide secure, instant, two-way communication for the United Nations to make and implement recommendations for dampening conflicts before they get out of hand.

Second, an international monitoring agency under UN auspices is needed to integrate diverse monitoring functions and to bring the weight of the entire world community behind the effort to ensure compliance with arms control agreements, regional military restraints, environmental standards, and other rules as these are established. Such an agency could utilize surveillance by high-altitude aircraft, satellites, and other means. Data could be gathered from the UN's own craft, or by leasing satellite capability from Landsat or former Soviet systems that have need of income. National governments could also supplement UN efforts by making relevant intelligence available to the United Nations.

In addition to monitoring arms agreements, such an agency could: help deter clandestine tests of missiles or warheads anywhere on earth; observe cease-fire lines in the Middle East; discourage illegal technology shipments and infiltration of arms across borders in Central America, Africa, or elsewhere; hamper covert operations to manipulate political events in small countries; and, in general, help resolve questions of fact that national intelligence services by themselves are incapable of resolving to each other's satisfaction. Such an agency is also needed to monitor the UN arms trade registry to be established in 1993, to assist UN peacekeeping missions, to stop covert operations aimed at manipulating elections or other political events in countries where the UN is operating, and to allow UN decisions to be made without relying on secondhand intelligence reports from member governments whose findings are usually viewed by adversaries as deceitful.

Strengthening Peacekeeping and Enforcement

Even improved capabilities for surveillance and negotiation will not be enough, of course, to deter those who might pose a threat to the peace. The UN's deterring strength can be enhanced by preparing several instruments to be available for immediate use.

First, the Security Council should give the secretary-general blanket authority, in advance of any particular crisis, to dispatch unarmed UN observers at any time within a ten-kilometer corridor along borders anywhere in the world. After the world community grows accustomed to this practice, the council might extend similar advance authority for the secretary-general to send UN observers not only to borders, but also to any place where he or she determines that their presence is needed to contribute to peace. Still later, armed UN personnel might be similarly authorized.

Second, the more sophisticated UN enforcement needed in the future can be aided enormously by the creation of a permanent UN peacekeeping force. As the Iraqi invasion of Kuwait in 1990 demonstrated, the United Nations has been handicapped in its reliance on ad hoc UN peacekeeping forces because the secretary-general cannot dispatch a force to a trouble spot immediately. If a standing UN force had existed in July 1990, it could have been moved to the Kuwaiti border before the Iraqis invaded. Faced with UN peacekeepers on his border, Hussein would have been more acutely aware that any attack against Kuwait would provoke a severe international response; at the very least, a preventive deployment of UN forces could have bought more time for diplomacy to work. Even in its infancy, such a force could help, as have ad hoc UN peacekeeping forces, to deter border violations and small-scale aggression by militarily adventurous states.

A standing UN force would enable the concept of "UN-protected countries" to become a realistic possibility. Small countries could feel some reassurance if UN forces were always ready to come to their aid in time of need. By having an opportunity to draw upon UN peacekeepers, small UN-protected countries, which are unable to protect themselves militarily against larger, determined aggressors anyway, would be able to relieve themselves of the financial burden of maintaining their own armed forces. They would also be freed of the danger that their own military may threaten democracy, or the prospects for it, at home. As the UN role in maintaining security for small states increased, the temptation for external military powers to intervene would decline; incentives for international arms sales, foreign bases, and the projection of military power abroad would also decrease.

What is proposed here would differ from past UN peacekeeping not only in being permanent, but also in consisting of individually recruited persons instead of contingents from various national military forces. Direct recruitment by the UN from among volunteers of all countries would enable personnel burdens to be shared more equitably than at present, without raising fears that any government's national military units would play a partisan role underneath the UN flag. To have personnel of many nationalities working side by side, regardless of their homelands' former or current animosities, would powerfully symbolize the prospects for enforcing norms on behalf of the world community without prejudice to any nationality. Such a force, even though quite small, would help set the institutional stage for educating publics and governments about the possibilities for gradually and reliably curtailing national uses of military power by impartially enforcing key rules against armament and aggression.[26]

Until such a permanent UN force is established, *standby* UN forces made up of national units contributed by member states should be readied, so that they can respond quickly if a preventive deployment should be needed. In his "Agenda for Peace," Secretary-General Boutros Boutros-Ghali has called for as many countries as possible to train and prepare earmarked units of their armed forces to be on call for UN service within twenty-four hours.[27] President Francois Mitterrand committed France to offer such forces, and Canada, the Nordic countries, and several other states already train troops for UN duty.[28]

Supportive governments can institutionalize peacekeeping further by responding favorably to Boutros-Ghali's request that governments fulfill the provision in Article 43 of the Charter, calling upon all members to conclude special agreements to "make available to the Security Council" armed forces and assistance to help in maintaining peace and security. It is now time to conclude these agreements so as to provide troops, training centers, equipment, logistical support, food, supplies, and even bases for prepositioned supplies in various points throughout the world.

Making the Security Council More Representative and Effective

With the Security Council frequently rendering critical decisions for the first time in its nearly five-decade history, it is important to change its membership to reflect current political and economic realities more accurately. It needs to be expanded by five or six members to include influential countries and regions that were not well represented at the founding of the organization.

The Japanese, for example, are not permanently seated in the Security Council. Yet they provide the largest source of investment capital in the world and operate the world's second largest economy; they also contribute the second largest amount of money to the UN budget and donate more overseas development aid than any other country.[29] For Japan not to be a permanent member is politically unfair, economically unwise, and morally unjustifiable. It is dangerous to argue that the present permanent members sit on the Security Council because they are nuclear powers, or even because they can contribute more conventional arms to enforcement; such argumentation provides incentives for other states to procure weapons as the admission ticket to the council. Instead, countries such as Japan, with strong economies and reservations about projecting military power, should be invited to become permanent members without flexing any military muscles. If the world is to demilitarize, it is wise to represent fully those who are themselves less militarized.

Equity also requires broader representation from less-industrialized segments of world society. Michael Renner has suggested criteria for Security Council membership to ensure that the permanent members together would include at least half of the world's population, economic productivity, military strength, and contributions to the UN budget.[30]

As the Security Council increases its enforcement roles, it should establish guidelines for employing economic sanctions and for using peacekeeping forces. Such guidelines would help prevent abuses of power by national officials pursuing their own goals within a UN operation. In addition, wise guidelines would ensure the broad political support required not only for an initial UN decision to use peacekeepers, but also for their continuing successful operation.

The development of such guidelines for Security Council approval could be begun by the now moribund Military Staff Committee. This Security Council Committee, which is made up of the chiefs of staff (or their representatives) of the five permanent members, was established by the UN Charter, but has never functioned as intended. During the Cold War, the permanent members could never agree, and since then the United States has been reluctant to empower this committee lest the UN gain such legitimacy and effectiveness that it would constrain U.S. freedom to act unilaterally. On the other hand, nonpermanent members eye the committee dubiously because of the special privileges given to the permanent five and the failure of the Security Council to give adequate representation to regionally powerful countries, such as Germany, Japan, Brazil, India, Egypt, and Nigeria.

Despite these problems, the Military Staff Committee should be revived with a new membership and mandate. One of the virtues of the Charter provisions for this committee is that they contain sufficient flexibility to overcome many of the objections raised against it. The Charter allows for any UN members to be invited to Military Staff Committee deliberations when the "efficient discharge" of the committee's responsibilities requires it.[31] This would enable other great powers, such as Germany, Japan, and India, which are not yet permanent members of the Security Council, to be well represented in important matters of enforcement, if only the Security Council would invite them to sit permanently, with reasonable powers, on this committee. By using the Military Staff Committee in a serious manner and increasing its representativeness of the world community, it could provide a practical bridge between the present Security Council, whose membership is now outdated, and a future Security Council with membership formally changed as a result of Charter revision.

The Military Staff Committee is also needed to carry out another Charter-mandated function that it has never exercised: to make recommendations for "the regulation of armaments, and possible disarmament."[32] If the Military Staff Committee and Security Council would take this duty seriously, they could specify prohibitions against the spread of weapons of mass destruction. The Security Council has already declared that nuclear proliferation is a "threat to peace and security," thereby giving itself power to take actions to address any breach of nonproliferation guidelines.[33] The Security Council thus can exercise existing authority to protect peace and security by drawing upon Military Staff Committee expertise to make these prohibitions technologically sophisticated, legally binding, and subject to enforcement. For the Military Staff Committee to plan a serious, worldwide arms control program that no nation on earth would be allowed to violate could focus national professional military attention on how to enhance security through intelligent international constraints on military power.

The purpose in strengthening UN enforcement capabilities is not to endorse the deployment of a large UN army. Instead it is to enable future UN peacekeeping and enforcement operations—which are likely to be similar to, yet move beyond, past ad hoc peacekeeping operations—to be carried out with more respect for human life, with more careful advance planning (and thereby enhanced deterring qualities), with more effectiveness, and with the benefit of the broader political support that is required to enable the UN to obtain financial backing and to command high moral ground in any conflict.

Peacebuilding

The world community also needs to extend into the international domain the use of those instruments that are most widely accepted in the domestic domain for solving disputes between individuals and groups: processes of impartial adjudication and legal settlement. Security Council members should remind themselves and other states of their Charter obligation to settle disputes "in conformity with the principles of justice and international law." Although many disputes are characterized as political rather than legal, any conflict can be amenable to legal analysis based on equity and customary international law if the parties are willing to be bound by adjudication. In order to institutionalize a larger role for the International Court of Justice, all countries should be pressed to accept before the year 2000 the general jurisdiction of the Court under Article 36 of its Statute, without any reservation.

If the Security Council were willing to do so, it is already authorized to declare that a state's refusal to submit a dispute to the World Court may constitute a threat to the peace. The Charter authorizes the Security Council to require adversaries to bring their disputes to the Court or to accept a binding determination made by the Security Council for resolution of a dispute. The Security Council is also authorized to use its enforcement powers to ensure compliance with a Court decision if war threatens because the dispute cannot be settled through legal means.[34]

Financing Demilitarization

National governments are calling upon the United Nations to undertake more extensive and varied forms of peacekeeping and enforcement, but in case after case members have refused to authorize sufficient financial support for the United Nations to mount an optimal effort. When the United Nations is insolvent, yet has been harnessed to carry new responsibilities, those countries that do not pay their dues (yet have the ability to do so) scarcely conceal their own moral bankruptcy. The United States, the biggest offender, and Russia together account for 75 percent of the unpaid regular and peacekeeping dues. These unpaid debts starkly reveal the world's national priorities: for every dollar that national governments contributed to UN peacekeeping since 1948, they have spent $3,000 for national military purposes.[35]

To institutionalize more fiscal responsibility, the United Nations should establish a single peacekeeping fund to pay all peacekeeping and enforcement costs. This fund should be replenished through regular UN assessments, which are legally binding on members, with all defaulting countries being deprived of their votes in all UN proceedings. In addition, the United Nations could follow the Brandt Commission's recommendation that an international tax be levied on national military spending, on profits of arms manufacturers, or on international arms transfers to help offset the costs of peacekeeping.

EMPHASIZING SPECIES SECURITY: THE KEY TO REAL SECURITY

The contributors to this volume have demonstrated that a fundamental transformation of policies and world security institutions must occur to bring real safety to people in the postmodern world. To chart a purposeful course toward common security and comprehensive security, we need a clear vision of the values—reciprocity, equity, sustainability, democratization, and demilitarization—to inspire a principled world policy. These ends must be clear, not only to develop the most useful means for their attainment, but also to motivate and shape the forces necessary for change. Focusing on explicit goals—the benefits of which should flow equitably to all people—can help us recast our understanding of how to relate to other people and to the planet. If we honor these principles in our personal and national political lives, we will demonstrate what world politics and security can be.

One of the severe weaknesses of U.S. foreign policy in recent years has been that no leadership has articulated a positive vision of the U.S. role in the world. Yet a clear call to positive action for serving the human interest and species security, based on principles such as the five proposed here, could be heard above the din of "politics as usual" in Washington. Because the state system persists is not in itself reason to persist with traditional military conduct. To do so betrays the prospect of finding better ways for countries to relate to each other and of changing the state system in the long run.

A truly effective world policy, which can be distilled from the preceding chapters, not only must set new policy directions and create new institutions—it must also draw upon moral inspiration to guide its direction and to enhance its political strength. To serve the human interest in justice and in peace does not compromise national prudence; it is prudence of the long run. In our era, as never before in history, what is ethically desirable to do in relating to one's neighbor converges with what is politically prudent for oneself. That is the full meaning of the preceding chapters' emphasis on the mutuality and comprehensiveness of security. A truly realistic security policy recognizes that species security provides the firmest foundation for national security. Such a policy can be pursued effectively through legal, political, economic, environmental, psychological, and educational means, but not, as in the past, through chronic preparations for war.

Notes

1. Although one nation or another may benefit for a limited time from high levels of military preparedness, international society as a whole suffers in the long run from chronic preparations for war. For elaboration, see Robert C. Johansen, "Do Preparations for War Increase International Peace and Security?" in Charles W. Kegley, ed., *The Long Postwar Peace* (Glenview, IL: Scott, Foresman, 1990), pp. 224–244.

2. See Independent Commission on International Development Issues, Willy Brandt, chairman, *North-South: A Programme for Survival* (Cambridge, MA: MIT Press, 1980); Independent Commission on Disarmament and Security Issues, Olaf Palme, chairman, *Common Security: A Blueprint for Survival* (New York: Simon and Schuster, 1982); World Commission on Environment and Development, Gro Harlem Brundtland, chairman, *Our Common Future* (New York: Oxford University Press, 1987); and South Commission, Julius Nyerere, chairman, *The Challenge to the South* (Oxford: Oxford University Press, 1990).

3. The Palme Commission on Disarmament and Security Issues, *A World At Peace: Common Security in the Twenty-first Century* (Stockholm: The Palme Commission, 1989), pp. 6–7.

4. For extensive historical evidence, see Kennedy, *The Rise and Fall of the Great Powers: Economic Change and Military Conflict from 1500 to 2000* (New York: Vintage, 1987).

5. Indeed, officials of great powers throughout history have seemed surprisingly driven to embrace self-defeating policies. The best our present knowledge can do to explain this chronic self-destructive tendency is to view it as derived in part from psychologically compulsive behavior. The insistence of U.S. decision-makers on high levels of military spending in an era when there are few, if any, military threats to U.S. security, and the chronic inattention

to building an effective system of world law and security institutions, reveals patterns of thought deeply ingrained and rooted in well-disguised fears that resemble addictive patterns of behavior. Such leadership denies its own faults by projecting them onto various enemies and focusing mainly on the adversaries' flaws, rather than by trying to better understand their own motivation. See Ralph White, *Fearful Warriors: A Psychological Profile of U.S.-Soviet Relations* (New York: Free Press, 1984), pp. 109–188.

6. These ideas build upon the concept of the human interest developed in Robert C. Johansen, *The National Interest and the Human Interest: An Analysis of U.S. Foreign Policy* (Princeton: Princeton University Press, 1980), pp. 3–37.

7. This principle represents a modest international expression of Immanuel Kant's categorical imperative, in which each person should behave in ways that, if everyone else behaved in the same way, would result in his or her own happiness.

8. Joseph Nye, "What New World Order?" *Foreign Affairs,* Vol. 71 (Spring 1992), pp. 83–96.

9. Quoted by Louis Henkin, *The Rights of Man Today* (Boulder: Westview, 1978), p. 20, from Thomas Paine, *The Rights of Man,* edited by Henry Collins (Harmondsworth: Penguin, 1969), p. 223.

10. Indeed, the need for building more effective international institutions is so pressing that an international commission of widely respected leaders from throughout the world declared in a far-reaching but largely ignored statement, known as the Stockholm Initiative, that "a World Summit on Global Governance" should be called, "similar to the meetings in San Francisco and at Bretton Woods in the 1940s," and that "an independent International Commission on Global Governance" should be established immediately. The Stockholm Initiative on Global Security and Governance, *Common Responsibility in the 1990s* (Stockholm: Prime Minister's Office, 1991), p. 45.

11. For the negative impact of poverty on the environment, see Alan B. Durning, *Poverty and the Environment: Reversing the Downward Spiral* (Washington: Worldwatch, 1989).

12. Independent Commission on International Development Issues, Willy Brandt, chairman, *North-South: A Programme for Survival,* p. 274.

13. For a promising set of suggestions, see Walter Russell Mead, *The United States and the World Economy* (New York: *World Policy Journal* Reprint, 1989), especially pp. 425–468.

14. See Gareth Porter with Inji Islam, *The Road From Rio: An Agenda for U.S. Follow-up to the Earth Summit* (Washington: Environmental and Energy Study Institute, 1992).

15. Lester R. Brown, Christopher Flavin, and Sandra Postel, "Picturing a Sustainable Society," in Lester R. Brown, ed., *State of the World 1990* (New York: Norton, 1990), pp. 173–190.

16. The decision at the Rio summit to create a UN Commission on Sustainable Development is a positive step because it can encourage governments to focus resources on environmentally sound development policies. But it is far too limited in purpose to cover the functions that the above proposals embody. It either could report to an Environmental Council, once created, or be transformed into an organization along the lines recommended here.

17. The group included Australia, Brazil, Canada, Egypt, Germany, France, Hungary, Ivory Coast, India, Indonesia, Italy, Japan, Jordan, Kenya, Malta, New Zealand, Netherlands, Norway, Senegal, Spain, Sweden, Tunisia, Venezuela, and Zimbabwe. Those at the Hague meetings have solicited additional signatures since the meeting. The original twenty-four nations have been joined by Austria, Belgium, Czechoslovakia, Denmark, Ireland, Luxembourg, Pakistan, Portugal, and Switzerland. China, the United States, and the Soviet Union were not invited because they were unlikely to endorse the declaration. See Hilary F. French, "An Environmental Security Council?" *World Watch,* Vol. 2 (September-October 1989), p. 7.

18. See Bruce Russett, "Toward a More Democratic and Therefore More Peaceful World," in Burns Weston, ed., *Alternative Security* (Boulder: Westview, 1990); and Michael Doyle, "Liberalism and World Politics," *American Political Science Review,* Vol. 80 (1986), pp. 1151–1161.

19. Indeed, ten UN missions since 1988 have assisted in some way the resolution of domestic conflicts and the transition to more democratic political systems.

20. See B. G. Ramcharan, "Strategies for the International Protection of Human Rights in the 1990s," *Human Rights Quarterly,* Vol. 13 (May 1991), pp. 1160–1161.

21. Edward C. Luck and Toby Trister Gati, "Whose Collective Security?" *The Washington Quarterly* (Spring 1992), p. 53.

22. Quoted by Luck and Gati, "Whose Collective Security?" p. 53.

23. Indar Jit Rikhye approvingly notes that "the balance of opinion in the Security Council seems to be swinging toward greater preparedness to intervene in domestic conflicts, especially when they threaten the stability of neighboring states or involve gross human rights violations." Indar Jit Rikhye, *Strengthening UN Peacekeeping: New Challenges and Proposals* (Washington: U.S. Institute for Peace, 1992), p. 12.

24. Stockholm Initiative on Global Security and Governance, *Common Responsibility in the 1990s,* (1991), pp. 36–42.

25. These points are elaborated in Robert C. Johansen, "Military Policies and the State System as Impediments to Democracy," *Political Studies,* Vol. 40 (1992), pp. 99–115.

26. For elaboration of this point, see Robert C. Johansen, "The Reagan Administration and the U.N.: The Costs of Unilateralism," *World Policy Journal,* Vol. 3 (Fall 1986), pp. 601–641.

27. Boutros Boutros-Ghali, "An Agenda for Peace: Preventive Diplomacy, Peacemaking, and Peace-keeping," A/47/277; S/24111, (New York: United Nations, 1992), pp. 20–21.

28. Russell M. Dallen, "Summit Stresses Global Cooperation," *The Interdependent,* Vol. 18 (Spring 1992), p. 2.

29. Jeffrey Laurenti, *The Common Defense* (New York: United Nations Association of the United States of America, 1992), p. 49.

30. Michael Renner, "Preparing for Peace," *State of the World 1993* (New York: Norton, 1993), p. 157.

31. Article 47 (2).

32. Article 47.

33. Thomas R. Pickering, "The Post-Cold War Security Council: Forging an International Consensus," *Arms Control Today,* Vol. 22 (June 1992), p. 9.

34. In Article 94 (2), the Security Council is empowered to "decide upon measures to be taken to give effect to the [Court's] judgment."

35. Michael G. Renner, "A Force For Peace," *World Watch,* Vol. 5 (July-August 1992), p. 39.

Index

About the Contributors

Nicole Ball is director of the Program on Enhancing Security and Development at the Overseas Development Council in Washington, D.C. She is the author of *Security and Economy in the Third World* (1988) and *Pressing for Peace: Can Aid Induce Reform?* (1992).

Seyom Brown is Wien Professor of International Cooperation and chair of the department of politics at Brandeis University, and associate at the Center for International Affairs at Harvard University. His published works include: *International Relations in a Changing International System; The Causes and Prevention of War;* and *New Forces, Old Forces, and the Future of World Politics.*

Charlotte Bunch is the director of the Center for Women's Global Leadership at Douglass College and a member of the faculty of the School of Planning and Public Policy of Rutgers University. She has edited seven feminist anthologies and is the author of *Passionate Politics: Feminist Theory in Action* (1987).

Roxanna Carrillo is the executive assistant to the director of UNIFEM, the United Nations Development Fund for Women. A Peruvian activist in the international women's movement for many years, she was one of the founders of Centro de la Mujer Peruana Flora Tristan in Lima.

Joseph Collins is a cofounder of the Institute for Food and Development Policy in San Francisco and a visiting professor at the University of California at Santa Cruz. He is the author of *Food First* (1977), *Aid as an Obstacle* (1980), *World Hunger: Twelve Myths* (1986), and *The Chile Model: Free-Market Economics on Trial* (1993).

Zachary S. Davis is an analyst in international nuclear policy in the Environment and Natural Resources Policy Division of the Congressional Research Service of the Library of Congress. He is the guest editor of a special Spring-Summer 1993 issue of the journal *Security Affairs* on international relations theory and nuclear proliferation.

Jack Donnelly is the Andrew Mellon Professor of International Studies at the Graduate School of International Studies at the University of Denver. He is the author of *Universal Human Rights in Theory and Practice* (1989) and *International Human Rights* (1993).

Vincent Ferraro is the chair of the International Relations Program at Mount Holyoke College in South Hadley, Massachusetts. He is the author of many articles on strategic doctrine and the international political economy.

Thomas Homer-Dixon is coordinator of the Peace and Conflict Studies Program at the University of Toronto, and assistant professor in the department of political science. He is also codirector of an international research project on environmental change and acute conflict jointly organized by his program and the American Academy of Arts and Sciences in Cambridge, Massachusetts. His most recent publication is "On the Threshold: Environmental Changes as Causes of Acute Conflict," *International Security* (Fall 1991).

Donald L. Horowitz is the Charles L. Murphy Professor of Law and a professor of political science at the Duke University School of Law. He is the author of *Ethnic Groups in Conflict* (1985) and other works.

Robert C. Johansen is the director of graduate studies at the Kroc Institute for International Peace Studies and a professor of government at the University of Notre Dame. He is the author of numerous articles on world affairs and *The National Interest and the Human Interest* (1981).

Terry Lynn Karl is associate professor of political science and director of the Center for Latin American Studies at Stanford University. She has published widely on the comparative politics of Latin America, with special emphasis on democratization, the politics of oil-exporting countries, and U.S. policy toward Central America.

Margaret P. Karns is director of the Center for International Studies and a professor of political science at the University of Dayton. She is the coauthor, with Karen Mingst, of *The United States and Multilateral Institutions* (1990).

Michael T. Klare is the Five College Professor of Peace and World Security Studies (a joint appointment at Amherst, Hampshire, Mount Holyoke, and Smith Colleges and the University of Massachusetts at Amherst) and director of the Five College Program in Peace and World Security Studies (PAWSS). He is the author of *American Arms Supermarket* (1985) and coeditor of *Low-Intensity Warfare* (1988).

Allan S. Krass is professor of physics and science policy at Hampshire College in Amherst, Massachusetts. He is the author of *Verification: How Much Is Enough?* (1985) and *The Verification Revolution* (1989).

Louis Kriesberg is director of the Program on the Analysis and Resolution of Conflicts and a professor of sociology at the Maxwell School of Citizenship and Public Affairs of Syracuse University. He is the author of *Social Conflicts* (1981) and *International Conflict Resolution* (1992), and coeditor of *Timing the De-escalation of International Conflicts* (1991).

Jessica Tuchman Mathews is vice president of the World Resources Institute in Washington, D.C. and a regular contributor to *The Washington Post*. She served on the National Security Council from 1977 to 1979 as director of the Office of Global Issues.

Michael McFaul is a research associate at the Center for International Security and Arms Control of Stanford University and codirector of its Program on Military Conversion and Privatization in Russia. He is the author of *Post-Communist Politics: Democratic Prospects in Russia and Eastern Europe* (1993) and coauthor of *The Troubled Birth of Russian Democracy* (1993).

Karen A. Mingst is a professor of political science at the University of Kentucky. She is the author of *Politics and the African Development Bank* (1990) and, with Margaret Karns, the coauthor of *The United States and Multilateral Institutions* (1990).

Daniel N. Nelson is director of the Graduate Program in International Studies at Old Dominion University in Norfolk, Virginia. In 1991, he served as the senior foreign policy adviser to House Majority Leader Richard A. Gephardt. He is the author and editor of many books, including *The Balkan Imbroglio* (1991) and *Security after Hegemony* (1993).

Dennis Pirages is a professor of government and politics and director of the Harrison Program on the Future Global Agenda at the University of Maryland. He is the author or editor of eight books, including *Global Ecopolitics: A New Framework for International Relations* (1978) and *Global Technopolitics: The International Politics of Technology and Resources* (1989).

Melissa Rosser is a graduate of Mount Holyoke College and is currently doing graduate work at the University of Dakar in Senegal.

Philippe C. Schmitter is professor of political science and director of the Center for European Studies at Stanford University. Formerly, he taught at the University of Chicago and the European University Institute in Florence, Italy. His research focuses on interest politics, regional integration, and democratization in Europe and Latin America.

Daniel C. Thomas is a Ph.D. candidate in government at Cornell University and an International Institutions Fellow at the Center for International Affairs at Harvard University. He is the coeditor, with Michael Klare, of the fifth edition of *Peace and World Order Studies: A Curriculum Guide* (1989).